Hannah Arendt
Karl Jaspers
Correspondence

BOOKS BY HANNAH ARENDT

*Antisemitism**
Betweeen Past and Future
Crises of the Republic
Eichmann in Jerusalem
Essays in Understanding
The Human Condition
*Imperialism**
*The Life of the Mind**
*Men in Dark Times**
On Revolution
*On Violence**
*The Origins of Totalitarianism**
*Rahel Varnhagen: The Life of a Jewish Woman**
*Totalitarianism**

BOOKS BY KARL JASPERS

Existentialism and Humanism
The Future of Mankind
The Great Philosophers (3 volumes)
The Idea of the University
*Kant**
Man in the Modern Age
The Origin and Goal of History
*Plato and Augustine**
The Question of German Guilt
Reason and Anti-Reason in Our Time
*Socrates, Buddha, Confucius, Jesus**
Truth and Symbol
The Way to Wisdom

*Available in Harvest paperback editions from Harcourt Brace & Company

Hannah Arendt
Karl Jaspers
Correspondence
1926–1969

EDITED BY

LOTTE KOHLER AND HANS SANER

TRANSLATED FROM THE GERMAN BY

ROBERT AND RITA KIMBER

A HARVEST BOOK

HARCOURT BRACE & COMPANY

SAN DIEGO   NEW YORK   LONDON

The photos in this book were furnished by Lotte Kohler (1, 5),
Hans Saner (2, 3, 4, 6, 8) and the Photo Archive of the
Süddeutscher Verlag (7).

This is a translation of
Hannah Arendt Karl Jaspers
Briefwechsel 1926–1969.

Library of Congress Cataloging-in-Publication Data
Arendt, Hannah.
[Hannah Arendt Karl Jaspers. English]
Hannah Arendt Karl Jaspers : correspondence, 1926–1969 / edited by
Lotte Kohler and Hans Saner : translated from the German by Robert
and Rita Kimber.—1st U.S. ed.
p.   cm.
Includes bibliographical references and indexes.
ISBN 0-15-107887-4
ISBN 0-15-622599-9 (pbk.)
1. Arendt, Hannah—Correspondence.   2. Jaspers, Karl 1893–1969—
Correspondence.   3. Political Scientists—Germany—Correspondence.
4. Philosophers—Germany—Correspondence.   I. Jaspers, Karl,
1883–1969.   II. Kohler, Lotte.   III. Saner, Hans, 1934–   .
IV. Title.
JC263.A7413 1992
320.5'092-dc20   91-34000

Designed by Trina Stahl

Printed in the United States of America
First Harvest edition 1993
A B C D E

Contents

Introduction

Hannah Arendt, who came to the United States as a refugee from Hitler's Germany, became well known as a political scientist and philosopher. Among her books are *The Origins of Totalitarianism* (1951), *Eichmann in Jerusalem* (1963), and *The Life of the Mind* (1978). Karl Jaspers was one of the two main representatives of existentialist philosophy, which originated in Germany in the 1920s. (The other was Martin Heidegger.) In the history of thought, the correspondence between Hannah Arendt and Karl Jaspers is the first extensive one between two philosophers of the opposite gender.

It began in 1926, when the twenty-year-old Arendt was studying philosophy under Jaspers at Heidelberg University. It was interrupted by Arendt's emigration and Jaspers' "inner emigration," and was resumed in the fall of 1945, when members of the United States occupation army helped reestablish the link between the two. In the latter period, the teacher-student relationship developed into a close friendship, in which Jaspers' wife, Gertrud, was soon included, and then, increasingly, Arendt's husband, Heinrich Blücher. After Arendt and Blücher's first joint visit to Basel, in 1961, all four began to use the familiar, "Du," form of address. The friendship lasted until Jaspers' death in 1969.

Apart from a few letters before 1933, the significant part of the correspondence falls in the postwar period. It reflects not only the way both writers lived, thought, and worked, but also the way they experienced the history of the postwar years. Because neither, probably, ever thought this correspondence would be published, and because they had absolute trust in each other, there is hardly a trace of self-censorship in these letters. They reveal themselves in a more personal, spontaneous, warmer, and, at the same time, more ruthless way than they do in their works. For Arendt, this correspondence is the first published document from her private life. For Jaspers, it is certainly an unusual one: the "North German block of ice," as he once called himself (Letter 159), displays tones of irony, tenderness, and human warmth, which some readers find lacking in his autobiographical writings.

The relationship took on another dimension as a result of Arendt's thirteen visits to Basel after 1949. These visits included days and often weeks of intensive discussion. These conversations should not be pictured as altogether idyllic, however, since both loved to argue and sometimes did so with abandon. That they were able to say anything and everything to each other without screening their thoughts or filing the rough edges and that they always felt an affinity in their mode of thought, despite their disagreements about details, are what formed the basis of their trust. There are no other witnesses to these conversations, but the intellectual climate surrounding them is evident in the spontaneity of the letters.

When they reestablished contact in 1945, both had the sense of having survived the deluge. Until 1951, Arendt led "the infinitely complex red-tape existence of stateless persons" (L. 34). Although she had made something of a name for herself as a writer, she had not "become respectable in any way" (L. 34). From her "perspective of frequent emigration and exposure to so-called world history" (L. 154), she rejected any integration into society. "I'm more than ever of the opinion that a decent human existence is possible today only on the fringes of society" (L. 34). But even on the fringes there was still a center: "Monsieur," her husband—"we're the only people we know who speak the same language" (L. 43). Otherwise, feelings of being alien, homeless, and alone characterized her existence. Jaspers shared these feelings completely, but he saw in them, as did Arendt, the possibility of a new beginning. After years of official banishment, he had suddenly become "respectable" again, indeed, almost a paragon of respectability for the nation. He had a profound mistrust of this "stale fame" (L. 32) that brought him "a life of irreality . . . ruled by haste" (L. 35). For him, too, there was only one place where he felt absolute trust: with his wife, who, as a Jew, had suffered immeasurably in the recent past. Yet the "gates of hell are wide open" (L. 35), he wrote, and it was important to live in the consciousness that the deluge had "to remain our point of orientation" (L. 60), to remember that "everything that constitutes our world can be wiped out in a month" (L. 107).

Thus a question subliminally present throughout this correspondence was: On what can one depend in this time of threatening deluge, a deluge we have survived once but that threatens to break over us again at any time—on what nations, what ideas, what people? The question is one of politics, of philosophy, and of the endurance of human nature.

This correspondence focuses on three countries in particular: Germany, Israel, and the United States. At no time did Arendt have an uncritical view of any of them. Jaspers was subject to great vacillation. Before the Nazis came to power, he shrouded Germany in the mystery of the "German essence"; later, he made a radical break with this view. He almost beatified Israel in the 1950s, then yielded to serious doubts about it. After the liberation of Germany, he idealized the United States, but felt doubts later, although he never quite abandoned that earlier picture. Arendt and Blücher played a major role in bringing about all these changes. They provided the facts that forced on him a different, more concrete understanding whenever he was given to turning his imagination loose in larger dimensions.

Disagreement over the "German essence" began before the Nazi period and continued for a few years after the war. In 1932, Jaspers published, with a nationalistic publisher in his home city, a study of Max Weber that bore the subtitle *Deutsches Wesen im politischen Denken, im Forschen und Philosophieren* ("The German Essence in Political Thought, in Scholarship, and in Philosophy"). The study was, as he said at the time, an "attempt, hopeless perhaps, to give it [the word "German"] ethical content through the figure of Max Weber" (L. 23). He sent a copy of the book to Arendt. She did not thank him for a very long time; when she did, she expressed her views with great candor. She objected to Jaspers' equating the "German essence" in Max Weber with " 'rationality and humanity originating in passion' " (L. 22). As a Jew, she could say neither yes nor no to that. "For me, Germany means my mother tongue, philosophy, and literature" (L. 22). Jaspers could agree with that in part, but it was not concrete enough, not historical enough, for him. "All you need add," he wrote back, "is historical-political destiny, and there is no difference left at all" (L. 23). He ran against a brick wall. She could not "simply add a German historical and political destiny." This was, she said, "because I do not have in myself, so to speak, an attestation of 'German character' " (L. 24). "Germany," she added, "in its old glory is your past" (L. 24). She did not criticize other foolish statements that had even more serious ramifications. Her experience of anti-Semitism had made her politically more perceptive than he was. When Jaspers, after the catastrophe of the war and troubled by "what my being a German means" (L. 60), again asked her whether she was a Jew or a German (L. 46), she replied in a rather offhand way: "To be perfectly honest, it doesn't matter to me in the least on a personal and individual level" (L. 50), but: "Politically, I will always speak only in the name of the Jews whenever circumstances force me to give my nationality" (L. 50). That meant of course that she would never speak as a German. Jaspers agreed with her that of the German character "only the language" (L. 52) remained, that the nation had become a matter of little consequence and nationalism a disaster. But he still harbored the hope of someday publishing "my Germany dream" (L. 107).

Fifteen years passed before he realized that dream, a period of increasing disappointment. While in Heidelberg, Jaspers, "still 'naïve' " (L. 383), had hoped for a political reversal. When the Federal Republic of Germany was founded, he put his faith in Konrad Adenauer, a leader whose foreign policy he admired for a long time. He hated *Der Spiegel*, finding it a "corrupt" (L. 316) and "nihilistic" (L. 319) publication, and was willing to risk everything to save Berlin. Yet at the same time, he was inwardly separating himself almost completely from the Federal Republic. As early as 1949 he wrote that he did not belong among "*those* Germans" (L. 83), and in 1952 he said that in a political sense he was "not a German . . . even though I am a German according to my passport, but that gives me no pleasure" (L. 138). Later, he fought with determination against "the pretense of freedom" (L. 300), against the illusion of reunification; and in 1961, he confessed, "I would vote SPD, but I am not allowed to . . ." (L. 296). Adenauer had become, in his eyes, "a rather insignificant [figure] as far as real substance is concerned" (L. 300), and the entire republic could become a "locus of corrupt party oligarchy" (L. 316). Along with some brash suggestions, such as giving up Berlin, he ended with the quite "convincing rejection of the basic view of Germany on which the Federal Republic rests" (L. 376). This was the time during which he published his "Germany dream," *Wohin treibt die Bundesrepublik?* By then the dream had become a nightmare.

How great the influence of Arendt and Blücher, the antinationalist par excellence, was in bringing this transformation about can only be guessed. Arendt had said early in the correspondence that during the war all she cared to remember about Germany was her time as a student with Jaspers. Perhaps there was, however, along with reluctance ever to set foot on German soil again, something like a hope that "the first nation that, as a nation, has gone to ruin" could open a new dimension in European politics. Her visits to Germany during the 1950s apparently dashed that hope. She reported to Jaspers that the people were "profoundly unhappy . . . malicious, secretly hoping that everything will fall apart . . . full of resentment against everybody and everything" (L. 254). As early as 1952, Jaspers complained to Blücher that she showed "greater detachment toward Germany. I haven't progressed as far" (L. 129), and as late as 1959 her detachment pained him "somewhat" (L. 253). At the beginning of the 1960s, she gave up all hope. "This so-called republic is really like the last one" (L. 311); Adenauer "can tolerate only yes-men" (L. 318). She advocated "neutrality for West Germany" (L. 263), considered Berlin lost (Ls. 243, 297), and felt that the Federal Republic's "decline is written all over its face" (L. 377). "Things operate there on automatic pilot, without interest—I hope!" (L. 408). Automatic decline seemed less dangerous to her than collapse brought about by the corrupt machinations of politicians. Thus, Arendt and Jaspers both came to the same, final, decision: Withdraw completely from German politics.

Before reaching this conclusion, both had given attention to the only thing that could possibly speak for the rehabilitation of Germany's honor: the German resistance. Arendt's brief description and tough-minded judgment of the principles and motives of the resistance fighters in her book on Eichmann occasioned this discussion. Jaspers wrote about this often in letters; he had studied the sources thoroughly at the time and had worked on a short history of the German resistance. On basic issues, Arendt and Jaspers were in agreement: The only people who should be regarded as resistance fighters were, as Jaspers wrote, those who "worked *actively* to bring about the fall of the Hitler regime" (L. 332), and in such a way that resistance to the regime itself became a principle. Arendt felt that no individual in the movement fit this description. In "word and deed," they were all "infected by the plague" (L. 333) of acceptance of the regime. Carl Goerdeler, for instance, the "so-called intellectual leader" (L. 369), was "stupid and ridiculous" in his plans for the period after the coup. "But any other plans besides stupid and ridiculous ones didn't exist, and that seems crucial to me" (L. 369). Jaspers' judgment was not so sweeping. He honored Julius Leber and Hans and Sophie Scholl and recognized, within limits, the sincerity of a few others. Arendt was intent on demythologizing the entire movement; Jaspers, on singling out the few great and pure figures. But they reached a similar judgment on the glorification of the movement that was gradually spreading throughout Germany. In Jaspers' words it arose from "a lie that German life has not been willing to do without" (L. 334) and that "stands in the nationalistic tradition and perpetuates it" (L. 376). It was simply not possible to rescue Germany's honor, certainly not by way of the army, but also not by shifting the responsibility onto genetic abnormalities in the Führer. Jaspers, citing the conclusion of a Swiss psychiatrist, wrote: "It was not Hitler who was 'guilty'; it was the German people who followed him" (L. 384).

For Jaspers, the question of what it meant to be a Jew was almost as pressing as the question of what it meant to be a German. His interest in this was generated not only by the Jewish heritage of Arendt and of his wife, but also by the fate of the Jews under the Nazis and, most important, by the significance of Judaism for Western culture since the "axial period." He saw this significance in three things: the religion of both the Old and New Testaments; the monotheistic concept of a god not represented by a graven image; and the idea of a covenant between a people and their infinitely distant transcendence. The greatness of Judaism was linked to the fact that the Jewish people, without a nationality and scattered among many nations, stood firm in the face of all their sufferings. Jews could and should, he thought, assimilate themselves politically in whatever nations they found themselves, yet remain Jews in the religious-metaphysical sense.

Jaspers tried to learn from Arendt how she had appropriated her heritage, and he often asked her about this. She said that in this regard she was "by virtue of my background . . . simply naïve. I found the so-called Jewish question boring" (L. 135). From the perspective of her naïve assimilation, she made the Jewish experience her own "with no little difficulty" (L. 135), and her appropriation of it remained limited to the historical and political dimensions. She oriented herself by "a Zionist critique of assimilation" (L. 135) and with complete religious independence from Judaism (L. 61), which, like all religion, held "nothing whatsoever" (L. 109) for her any longer. She worked her way into this critique first in literary form, with her book on Rahel Varnhagen; then politically, through her work with various Zionist organizations in her émigré years. What evolved from that experience was a position diametrically opposed to Jaspers' view. For him, the religion of the Jewish people meant everything; for her, it meant nothing. He thought political assimilation of the Jews in the Diaspora desirable; she thought it "politically and socially impossible" (L. 160). He feared that autonomic politicizing of the Jewish people in Palestine and Israel could mean "great potential danger for the essence of Jewish existence" (L. 60) in the leveling process of forming a nation; she affirmed the founding of a Jewish state, although she did not approve of how that founding had taken place.

Once the state existed, Jaspers reacted as he often did in his life. He put his reservations aside and saw the reality as identical with a better possibility. Israel *was* the state of the Jews, not just the nation of the Israelis. During the Suez crisis, he admired its level-headedness and courage and saw in it "a moral-political force such as appears in the founding periods of states that have content and permanence" (L. 205). Israel was "becoming the touchstone of the Western world" (L. 203), which would suffer the same fate as Hitler's Germany if it let the new state die. His feeling was that "the destruction of Israel would mean the end of humankind" (L. 205).

In her political astuteness, Arendt thought that view vastly exaggerated and did not find it "justified . . . even as a feeling" (L. 206). Israel was neither humankind nor the Western world nor the Jewish people, but merely one nation among nations, and a nation with its share of questionable political figures who would not shrink from lies and political mass murders if such tactics served their purposes. Over the years she kept supplying evidence for this view, and in 1958 she must have told Jaspers in a conversation that he was "blind concerning Israel" (L. 234). The Eichmann trial provided the first effective correction of his vision. For Jaspers, it became a test of Israel's real character, and for Arendt, it confirmed her worst fears.

In April 1961, she traveled to Jerusalem to report on the Eichmann trial for *The New Yorker*. Before the trial began, she had written to Jaspers about its political and legal premises and consequences; and she wrote him detailed reports from Jerusalem. He had developed a vision of how Israel could "prove true to the Jewish tradition" (L. 278) in this trial. It should, he thought, conduct no more than a "process of examination and clarification" (L. 273), show to the world the facts of the Nazi genocide, place those facts legally under the heading crimes against humanity, but not pass sentence, because for such crimes national courts are not the appropriate authorities. Of all this, probably the only thing that interested Arendt was the category of "crimes against humanity." Apart from that, her attention was focused on another point: the "banality of evil," as represented by Eichmann, an evil that should in no way be dignified by ascribing it to demonic or mysterious forces. Neither Jaspers nor Arendt doubted the fairness of the trial. But for Jaspers it was, to the extent that it was a national trial moving to judgment, "wrongly conceived at its very root" (L. 273). For Arendt, the demonizing of Eichmann made it too theatrical, and the neglect of the question of Jewish collaboration made it too unfaithful to the facts. That showed her "how rotten this state is" (L. 277).

The publication of her book *Eichmann in Jerusalem* unleashed a storm of outrage. The book's tone hurt some readers, but it was something else that evoked a "deep-seated sense of having been struck a mortal blow" (L. 338): No one had ever pointed out with such clarity—and then proceeded to document—how the Jewish Councils had collaborated with the Nazis. "I dragged out a part of the Jewish past that has not been laid to rest" (L. 331), she wrote to Jaspers. This exposure of a national lie led to a campaign of defamation that lasted about two years in the United States, Israel, and Germany, a campaign conducted "on the lowest level" (L. 331), she wrote, and constituting a "classic case of character assassination" (L. 336). (In Germany, the focus was primarily on her interpretation of the German resistance.) She described for Jaspers in full detail the tactics used against her in this campaign. It was one of the most shattering experiences of her life.

Jaspers declared himself in total solidarity with her and wanted to take her side publicly after the book came out in Germany. After reading it, he wrote her that he found it "marvelous in its subject matter. It bears witness, in its intent, to your uncompromising desire for truth. In its mind-set, I find it profound and full of despair" (L. 341). A shadow fell, for him, on everyone who took part in the campaign against her, and there were some of his friends among them; but perhaps the darkest shadow of all fell on Israel. It represented from this point on only the "Jewish total assimilation into modern nationalism" (L. 272), a collection of disparate elements without an informing political or metaphysical idea. He no longer knew what to make of this state, whereas Arendt, after the passage of some years, found ways of reconciliation with it.

In his disappointment over the increasing nationalization of the world, Jaspers felt that "for political order and freedom, America is the only hope" (L. 83). For the rest of his life, he remained grateful to the United States, and to England, which he saw embodied in Churchill, for liberating Europe. He saw the United States as a model for a united Europe. He said early in this correspondence that the only thing he would like to be if he were not a German (L. 35) is an American. And he could still write in the late 1950s that "we all feel in some sense like potential fellow citizens of America, no matter how far away from it we may be" (L. 205). In this mixture of gratitude and admiration and in his fear of the spreading of totalitarianism, he almost uncritically applauded U.S. policies for a long time. Only when he, like so many prominent Europeans, discovered during the Joseph McCarthy era that members of the international Congress for Cultural Freedom had been misused and deceived by the U.S. government did he resign from that organization. But the trust he had placed in the United States remained the basis of his judgments on world politics.

Arendt felt "eternally grateful" that she was "washed ashore" (L. 113) in the United States, where "nationality and state are not identical" (L. 59) and where "a republic at least still has a chance" (L. 428). The leftist influence of both her husbands—the first was Günther Stern (Anders)—and her central philosophical interest in recognizing "totalitarian elements springing from the womb of society, of mass society itself, without any 'movement' or clear ideology" (L. 160), made her seismographically sensitive to everything of this kind that occurred in the United States. As a result, she was often worried about the country: "We have no great desire to watch another republic go to the dogs" (L. 423).

For twenty-five years she instructed Jaspers in all the ills of the country to make clear to him that, as she wrote in 1953, "it is no longer possible . . . to stand up for America without any reservations, as we both did" (Ls. 142, 415). She analyzed the "informant system" (L. 142) of the McCarthy era; the persecution of leftist intellectuals; the Eisenhower administration, governed "by big business" based on a "society of jobholders" (L. 142); the background of the racial problem (which in her opinion was behind Kennedy's assassination); the disintegration and "bizarre conditions" in the major cities (L. 369); the collapse of public services and schools; the "national disaster" of [Faubus] juvenile delinquency (L. 369), and the "crazy, filthy, and pointless war" in Vietnam (L. 389). She rejected almost every politician in a top position; she thought that Eisenhower suffered from "native stupidity" (L. 268), and Nixon was "a hypocrite and a liar" (L. 268). She mistrusted Kennedy, who, she feared, was "really a seriously ill man" (L. 289). Johnson was "provincial," a clever political tactician "without any understanding of anything" (L. 343). "I've taken potshots at the whole mob" (L. 142), she wrote in 1953. Although she wasn't always after them with that degree of ferocity, she remained true to the principle of always speaking out for the free republic but never for a government project. Her dominant impression was "how this country has gone to the dogs if you measure it by nothing but its own standards" (L. 235). It was these standards that her book on the American Revolution was meant to call back to mind.

Apart from a few temporary phases reflecting reestablishment of the republic, such as the overcoming of McCarthyism and the defeats of Goldwater and Nixon, she found the 1960s student unrest in Berkeley of great interest and a hopeful sign. At no point did she see the students as a mass, a mob. They were a self-constituting force operating by democratic principles. The student movement gave rise to her essay "Reflections on Violence." Among the French students, she liked Danny "le rouge" Cohn-Bendit, a son of close friends, and she put her hopes, temporarily, in the rebellion of the German students, saying, "the German professors must really be on the verge of panic at this point" (L. 369). "It seems to me that children in the next century will learn about the year 1968 the way we learned about the year 1848" (L. 428). This was perhaps one of her illusions nourished by personal experience. After the persecution she suffered from the Jewish establishment, she felt the universities—primarily the students—had been her salvation. Jaspers was sympathetic to her point of view. He had always preferred rebels to the obedient herd.

As for the perspective on the political world that these letters offer, almost every crucial event is discussed: the rebellion in East Berlin, the Hungarian revolution, the Korean and Vietnam wars, the separation of parts of North Africa from Europe, the Bay of Pigs and the Cuban crisis, the building of the Berlin Wall, Khrushchev's fall, Kennedy's assassination, the gradual rise of China, and the unreliable Pax Russo-Americana in the light of the threat that the H-bomb could become available to "chauvinistic" nations (L. 204). On all of this, neither Jaspers nor Arendt was reluctant to offer hypotheses, and some of them may sound odd today. Their intent was not to prophesy, but to try to understand what was happening in the world and to submit their interpretations to the corrective of the other's thinking. For Jaspers, this brought the world into the realm of reason. For Arendt, it brought reason into the world.

The answer to the central underlying question throughout this correspondence—on what can one depend in the politics of an era that is under the constant threat of the deluge?—based on the facts of the period, has to be: on almost nothing—not on nations, not on ideologies, not on the apparently firm structures of society, and not on military security, which harbors the apocalypse within itself. For Jaspers, there remained the *possibility* of a reversal; for Arendt, the possibilities of revolution and of council democracy. Revolution and council democracy had been achieved in history, and so were not empty dreams, but realities to be reclaimed. Reclaiming them, however, would have to be preceded by expansion of thought, expansion that, for Jaspers, had to take place in the broadest reaches of a philosophy rooted in communication; for Arendt, in political theory thoroughly grounded in history.

In her studies with Heidegger and Jaspers, Arendt experienced German existential philosophy *in statu nascendi*; and she was drawn to existential thought's penchant for the existentially concrete. A natural consequence of this was her extended study of the assimilated Jew Rahel Varnhagen, a project that made her aware that she was not politically assimilated herself. Through Anders and, primarily, Blücher, she became familiar with the social philosophers of the revolutionary and Hegelian tradition. It was these philosophers who opened another field of the concrete to her: the study of history and politics. So, immediately after the war, she came to see herself as "something between a historian and a political journalist" (L. 31), who would gradually, in her own eyes, evolve into a political theorist. Although she always maintained a close affinity for philosophical thought, she twice took leave of philosophy in its stricter sense: during the early years of her emigration, when she took up practical Zionist social work, and when she consciously set out into the field of "political theory."

In the early years of his career, when he was still a psychiatrist, Jaspers' work was characterized by a will to strict scientific discipline. When Arendt first got to know him, he had become, by way of psychology intent on illuminating existence, a philosopher of "existential illumination." It was his belief that philosophy could never be an exact science, and for that reason had to find its way to purity *sui generis*. The essential tool for doing this, he thought, was a methodological consciousness that made clear to the philosopher what it was possible to think about and, in each individual process of thought, how he could know what he had thought. That constituted the quite different rigor of his thinking, to which he always remained true. But Nazi rule shook him awake, and right after the war, he wrote, "It becomes meaningless to speak as I have been speaking . . . in view of present conditions" (L. 52). "Philosophy has to be concrete and practical, without forgetting its origins for a minute" (L. 44). Its origins were in the mutually informing relationship of existence and of a reason that was open to everything and drew everything together. Philosophy's concrete and practical field was concern for the world. It had no use for "philosophy as international convention" (L. 92) and an "esoteric affair" (L. 352). Its task—never clearly outlined by Jaspers, however—was "world philosophy." In this development, he said farewell twice himself—but to politics. In his youth, he was willing to discuss the overall intellectual and political situation but refused to comment on concrete political issues and events. In his old age, after considerable experience as a "political writer," in which, he admitted, he had perhaps taken on too much and quite consciously put his reputation as a philosopher at risk, he called "it quits for good with politics" (L. 398). He found writing about politics "so much easier than philosophy" and felt that it "lowers the level of one's inner being" (L. 398). He did not mean to include in that judgment Arendt's political theory, only his own political writings.

From their different proximity to philosophy the two nonetheless developed a similar perspective. They agreed that all philosophy has political consequences and is to that extent one of the premises on which politics is based. They agreed, too, that philosophy is rooted in the realities of political life, and from that perspective they saw it as the social task of philosophy to purify the symbol world and, by doing so, to destroy all ideologies and forms of magic, which, whatever their natures might be, reduce the chances of conducting rational politics; and at the same time, in the world of actual politics, to combat all conditions that interfere with the free development of thought. "The dream of political freedom" (L. 328) linked with the dream of justice set their agenda. Whether the focus was philosophy or political theory, both disciplines should, in independence of thought, fulfill these requirements, and, in terms of that agenda, understand history and tradition, subject the present to criticism, and lay a foundation for the future.

The personal experiences that underlay concrete judgments were different. Jaspers' one and only central political experience was of totalitarian rule in the Third Reich. Arendt had constantly before her the "fundamental contradiction" in the United States of the "coexistence of political freedom and social oppression" (L. 34). This often led to significant differences in their historical and political judgments. This is especially evident in their letters about Marx, whom Arendt valued for a long time because "a passion for justice had seized him by the scruff of the neck" (L. 106). Jaspers, by contrast, had all his life seen Marx as a philosophical and political disaster, and not much more. In historical disagreements of this kind, Arendt almost always eventually came around to Jaspers' point of view, not for the sake of peace, but because Jaspers had a more exact and at the same time broader knowledge. His just assessment of Engels and his later love for Rosa Luxemburg show, incidentally, that his critique of Marx was not merely that of someone in the opposite ideological camp.

Among contemporary philosophers, Jaspers and Arendt found few major figures. Since her time in Paris, Arendt had valued Camus highly, Sartre less so, because he was too much the litterateur. She despised Adorno, whom she accused of a failed attempt to ingratiate himself with the Nazis, but she harbored friendly feelings all her life for Walter Benjamin. Jaspers had broken with all his major contemporaries in the world of philosophy—or they had broken with him. In later years, he read them but did not study any of them, with the exception of Heidegger. For both correspondents, Heidegger evoked painful memories. This is reflected in some extremely harsh judgments in the letters. Immediately after the war, it was Jaspers who sought to moderate these judgments; later, it was Arendt. She found her way to reconciliation; Jaspers never did.

They were, in a sense, contemporary philosophy for each other, and each demonstrated that indirectly, in studying, praising, and criticizing the other's work.

Jaspers read almost everything Arendt wrote. He thought her powers as a writer to be "like Lessing's" (L. 332), the boldness of her ideas often visionary, and her courage in pursuit of the unvarnished truth exemplary. He found *The Origins of Totalitarianism* a truly great work, pointing the way for its time. In his view, perhaps only her book *On Revolution* surpassed it "in the profundity of its political outlook and the masterly quality of its execution. . . . Your insight into the nature of political freedom and your courage in loving the dignity of man in this arena are wonderful" (L. 327). But above any of her works, he loved her independence, her freedom from any ideology or any political power. In that he saw her quality as a philosopher. He therefore considered it a "joke" (L. 363) that she did not want to be a philosopher, but it was a joke that gave him pause in relation to some of the characteristics of her work.

As early as her dissertation, he had, often like a somewhat pedantic schoolmaster, reproached her for lack of attention to scholarly details. After the war he sometimes urged her to present things "in a historically more correct and less visionary way," to translate her vision "more into demonstrable terms" (L. 41). "You lean toward Hegelian thinking" (L. 41), he wrote. "If something of the old 'total' underlying view of history should remain in your text," it always invests history with a "false grandeur" (L. 100). He felt that she did not see "the greatness of the 'Enlightenment' " (L. 134). In regard to *The Origins*, he was concerned that "you perhaps border on the dogmatic here and there" (L. 217). Behind this was a reminder to reflect on method; therefore, the repeated advice to study Max Weber. Despite all the praise Jaspers heaped on her, he probably never thought she would be completely free from the danger "that in the light of the highest standards a shadow will fall on you" (L. 134): the shadow of horses that had run away with her. In the book about her he was planning, Jaspers would no doubt have pursued that shadow with the implacable tenacity characteristic of him. She knew that, and she felt herself let off the hook when he gave up this project, the thought of which made her "blush with the honor of it and turn pale with fear" (L. 356).

Apart from Arendt's reservations about the ethical fulfillment of the "German essence," these letters contain no fundamental criticism of Jaspers' philosophy, provided he was not included when she wrote of Western philosophy's guilt in having dealt with the "fact of plurality tangentially" (L. 109). But there are occasional individual criticisms; that of *Die Schuldfrage* is one deserving of attention. In regard to his work, she consciously assumed a different role, at any rate in the later years. She was almost always the person who was the quickest to see the central idea and to lift it out of all the narrow constraints in which the professional philosophers would bury it. When she read the first volume of Jaspers' *Logik* (*Von der Wahrheit*), this "de-provincializing of Western philosophy," she immediately fell into "speculation as to whether this isn't perhaps the last book of Western philosophy, its last word, so to speak, and at the same time the first book of a world philosophy, its first word, so to speak" (L. 105). At that time and for decades to come, no one really saw that, although it is precisely what Jaspers' intention had been. Almost twenty years later, he was still complaining about the general lack of understanding of his fundamental insight, "this key" (L. 374), that he had been applying everywhere ever since. Only she had understood: "This is the greatest of your books and a very, very great book indeed" (L. 105). In the philosophy of the "axial period," she instantly recognized the "element of reconciliation" and the new chance "to be a citizen of the world again" (L. 71). She felt "the overall atmosphere" in *The Great Philosophers* to be "one of wonderful freedom" and loved Jaspers' courage in making judgments, which was so "wonderfully refreshing compared with fake Alexandrine respect" (L. 209). She saw in *Freiheit und Wiedervereinigung* the "heaviest blow that has yet been struck against German nationalism" (L. 263). In his book on the Federal Republic, she instantly saw to the heart of the matter: "What doesn't suit [the Germans] is that you think concretely. . . . And in that sense [your book] is a very 'un-German' book" (L. 397). She had praised the clarity of his writing earlier: "This is philosophy without magic . . . and compared with what you have written here all conceptual language is a kind of magic" (L. 373).

Jaspers was flattered by her ability to read him well, an ability that grew out of their long dialogue. But that was not the most important thing about her for him, nor were her works. He ultimately thought "this writing of books" no more than "an enjoyable business" (L. 163) that was "very secondary" (L. 85) in the context of a human relationship. People were more important to him than books. And Arendt was in full agreement with him about that.

Both had a strong need for communication, but because of their different constitutions (Jaspers was ill all his life), their opportunities to satisfy that need were different. Also, because their temperaments were different, their capacities to satisfy it differed.

Jaspers often kept his distance for a long time in personal relationships. He was very reserved and interested only in objective discussion. Anyone who did not understand that this was also a technique for encouraging independence could think Jaspers was cold. But if he was certain of a person's independence, then he was open and cheerful and concerned about personal matters. He had that kind of relationship with few people, and had to rely on the impulse coming from them. He never sought anyone's friendship as spontaneously as he did Heinrich Blücher's, "a remarkably kindred spirit" (L. 178). His wife occupied a special place in his life. She was the only person he loved unconditionally and totally. Compared with him, she seemed an extravagant sort, very open, although easily wounded, without frivolity and without a lightness of reflection, but with a warm, profound humanity. He no doubt interpreted his relationship with her as a symbol of metaphysical love.

Arendt had, in contrast, a large circle of friends. It started growing in her youth and continued to grow in her later years. A number of major writers and scholars belonged to it, but so did many people who appeared seldom or not at all in the public arena of the intellectual world. Subject to the emotionality of a great temperament, she quickly dropped her reserve when she encountered people who were free of ideology and sentimentality but were bright and human. This correspondence does not reveal how close to her and her husband their friends were or of what nature their sometimes stormy relationships were, including ones that were revived after breaches. "Never in my life have I loved any nation or collective. . . . I love only my friends," she said in her Gaus interview. But she loved them with a loyalty and reliability that lasted over decades and repeatedly found expression in concrete, practical aid. In this rich field of relationships, Blücher was the dependable rock and at the same time the intellectual confidant in the background. A self-educated man, he was appointed to a professorship at Bard College and lectured for years at the renowned New School for Social Research. Because of his keenness of mind, his originality, and his firm refusal ever to publish anything, his friends called him "an identical twin of Socrates" (L. 340).

Everything that Arendt did for Jaspers over the years would no doubt have become burdensome to him if she had not done it in her matter-of-fact way. In the early postwar years, until Jaspers and his wife moved to Basel, she essentially fed them, with the three food packages she sent each month, and, he said, "in such grand style that we are living as in peacetime" (L. 46). She interpreted this as hospitality rendered from afar, and she did it (and not for him alone) because in her years as a refugee she had become used "to maintaining a little solidarity," without which "every last one of us would simply have gone under at some point or another" (L. 154). She also placed his postwar essays with prominent magazines in the United States and created a name for him there. She kept an eye on all the translations of his works, advised him on all his contracts, and personally took charge of the translation of *The Great Philosophers*. What meant more to him than "all this success I could easily dispense with," however, were her repeated public acknowledgments that she was "of one mind"

(L. 60) with him. The first book she published in Germany after the war she dedicated to him, from one Noah to another, as it were. Later, her book *On Revolution* was dedicated to him and Gertrud Jaspers; and in 1958 she gave the eulogy when he received the peace prize of the German Book Trade, the awarding of which had been fiercely debated in Germany. Moreover, she undertook numerous trips to visit him after the war.

In comparison, he did little for her. He recommended her for fellowships early in her career, tried to help her get restitution from the Federal Republic for the habilitation for which she was qualified but which the Nazi takeover prevented her from completing (restitution she finally did receive years after Jaspers' death). He wrote a foreword to the German edition of *The Origins of Totalitarianism*, but he never dedicated a book to her, and there is no indication that he ever thought of doing so. Because he kept taking on new projects all the time, he never completed his literary monument to her, though he worked on it for years. He knew that he was in her debt. But she never felt that to be so. What he was for her meant more to her than what he did for her.

Arendt lost her father early in life. As she often wrote to Jaspers, she found in him in her youth, and through her entire life, the "only [teacher] I have ever been able to recognize" (L. 140), the man whose composure held "the possibility of magically charming" her and others "into a lifelong allegiance to reason" (L. 64). Psychologists may see Jaspers as a surrogate father, especially in view of the fact that Arendt occasionally speaks of her "schoolgirl fear of you" (L. 36) and of her "child's wish not to disappoint you" (L. 69). That wish came from Jaspers' Socratic demand that she never be his "student," that she prove herself to him in her independence from him. By virtue of his personal integrity, that "fusion of freedom, reason, and communication" he exemplified, she said at his memorial service, he remained her model. When, after the war, a friendship developed out of their acquaintanceship, it made possible her "return to Germany" (L. 173). In Basel, she found her "home in Europe" (L. 169), where her friendship with Jaspers gave her "the guarantee for the continuity" of her life (L. 216). The "always fresh joy" of visiting him was "being able to speak without reservation" (L. 99); it was also the "immediate communication" in the " 'bright rooms,' " and the "reliable purity of the air" (L. 182). Finding that "such talk existed," she told Gaus, was her "most powerful experience in the postwar years."

Arendt did not set a standard for Jaspers, either through her work or through her ethos. She was one of the "great gifts" (L. 198) of his life. Among the people close to him after the war, she was surely the most important and the only one who brought "shared memories of a lost past" (L. 168), and thus a little continuity into his life as well. A greater gift she brought was concrete knowledge of the world, which he was able to acquire for himself only to a small extent. Best of all was "a human reality" (L. 168) he perceived through her: her "enthusiasms" (L. 54) and "wonderful high spirits" (L. 153), rooted in unimpeachable seriousness (L. 46); her metaphysical happiness (L. 109) coupled with her "insight into the way things work," an insight that was "basically so pessimistic" (L. 387); her love for the world and for life, "full of courage" (L. 66) along with a "vulnerable softness" (L. 198) and persistent feeling of being an alien. All these things, plus her beauty, were "irreplaceable" (L. 107) for him and even transformed her "precarious vacillation" and her "tendency to let [her] passions run away with [her]" into "the informing forces" (L. 198) of her life. She was, as it were, a guarantee "that all is not lost with humankind" (L. 188), the person who dispelled "the specters of scorn for humankind" (L. 100).

In reply to the question On what can one depend in this time of deluge? perhaps both Arendt and Jaspers would have put at the top of the list: friendship and talk grounded in reason.

LOTTE KOHLER, HANS SANER

Notes on the U.S. Edition

All of the correspondence between Hannah Arendt and Karl Jaspers that has been preserved—a few letters must have been lost—is presented here except for two passages of a purely repetitive nature and a few comments omitted out of consideration for living persons or on legal advice. These omissions have been indicated by ellipses within brackets. Much thought was given to cutting some letters and to leaving some out entirely; the conclusion was that doing so might do damage to the whole or raise needless questions. Indeed, the letters have been supplemented by a few from Gertrud Jaspers and Heinrich Blücher, when these lead to understanding better the letters of the principals. The original letters are in the Archives for German Literature in Marbach/Neckar. Arendt's originals are, with few exceptions, typewritten. Jaspers' are mostly written by hand.

Orthography and punctuation were made to conform to current practice, provided deviations in the originals were not expressions of personal style. Words obviously left out are supplied in brackets. Other occasional errors, such as repetitions of phrases or references to wrong antecedents in long sentences, have been corrected in the text.

Personal names are identified, briefly, only once in the notes, usually on their first occurrence. The page with the identification is in boldface type in the index. In most cases, no identification is given for well-known figures or where adequate identification is provided in a letter. Historical events and situations alluded to are explained only to make the letters understandable. Bibliographical details for books and articles mentioned in the letters are provided once in the notes, and that reference is given in boldface in the indexes of works by Arendt and by Jaspers. For other authors, reference is made to the page in the notes where full bibliographical information is given, unless it occurs closely following.

Dr. Lotte Kohler, a friend of Hannah Arendt for many years and, with Mary McCarthy, executor of her literary estate, was responsible for editing Hannah Arendt's letters; Dr. Hans Saner, for editing Karl Jaspers' letters, which he did on commission from the Karl Jaspers Foundation in Basel. He is grateful to Dr. Marc Hänggi and Frau Liselotte Müller for their help with this. Both editors wish to express their thanks to the Archives for German Literature in Marbach for permission to print the letters and for the courteous, friendly assistance the Archives provided throughout this project.

The Karl Jaspers Foundation is also grateful to the following institutions for their financial support of the editorial work: the Fritz Thyssen Foundation (Cologne), the Swiss National Fund for the Encouragement of Scholarly Research (Bern), the Max Geldner Foundation (Basel), the Fund for Teaching and Research (Basel), the Department of the Interior, and the firms Ciba-Geigy, Hoffman–La Roche, and Sandoz, all in Basel.

Letters

1   *Hannah Arendt to Karl Jaspers*

Heidelberg, July 15, 1926

Dear Professor Jaspers,

I hope you will permit me to make use of your offer to accept written questions. Some of the final points you made in our last seminar meeting[1] concerning the possible philosophical interpretation of history continue to puzzle me.

I can understand history only from the perspective which I myself occupy. My absolute consciousness attempts to enter into communication with the absolute consciousness that lies behind, as it were, the works that have been passed down to us. That would mean that I try to *interpret*[2] history, try to understand what is expressed in it, from the perspective I have gained through my own experience. What I am able to understand in this way I make my own; what I cannot understand I reject. If I have understood your view correctly, then I have to ask:

How is it possible, on the basis of this view of the interpretation of history, *to learn something new from history*? Doesn't it make history simply a *sequence of illustrations* for what I want to say and for what I already know without benefit of history? To submerge oneself in history would thus mean no more than finding an abundant source of appropriate examples.[3]

Respectfully yours,
Hannah Arendt

2   *Hannah Arendt to Karl Jaspers*

Heidelberg, October 10, 1928

Dear Professor Jaspers,

Because I am afraid I left you with the impression yesterday afternoon that I am not fully conscious of my violations of scholarly rigor and objectivity, please allow me to assure you once again that I will, of course, check through my work as carefully as I possibly can, no matter how long it may take me.[1]

Sincerely yours,
Hannah Arendt

Berlin, Fasanenstr. 57 III
January 28, 1929

Dear Professor Jaspers,

It is very embarrassing for me to have to ask you for a reference before my dissertation is even in print. Frau Täubler's[1] efforts on my behalf were, unfortunately, not successful. But in the meantime I have met a man here who knows one of the major financial backers of the Jewish Academy[2] well and who will recommend me to this man and urge him in turn to support my application to the academy. Because the people at the academy are overwhelmed with requests of this kind, this acquaintance of mine feels I urgently need not only proof of previous scholarly achievement but also confirmation that the project I have in mind will be a significant contribution to scholarship.[3] On the basis of the existing relevant literature, which I have looked through, I personally feel that one can make that claim with good conscience.

I hope you will understand, Professor Jaspers, that I would not annoy you with such matters if circumstances did not force me to do so. Please send the letter of reference to Herr Justizrat Pink, Potsdam, Markgrafenstr. 12.

With many thanks and my best regards to you and your wife, I am,

Yours sincerely,
Hannah Arendt

4   Hannah Arendt to Karl Jaspers

February 24, 1929

Dear Professor Jaspers:

Please forgive my delay in thanking you for your generous help. I had hoped to be able to tell you right away what the response to my application was. But unfortunately I still have not received word.

I hope to be done with my work on St. Augustine by early April. I have been reading a number of relevant books I had not read before, the Genesis interpretations in particular.[1] That has slowed me down more than I had anticipated.

With gratitude and respect,
Your
Hannah Arendt

Neubabelsberg, June 13, 1929

Dear Professor Jaspers,

Please forgive me for sending you the second, revised version of my dissertation only now, contrary to all my earlier expectations. Benno von Wiese[1] has no doubt told you the most important reason for the delay. I was married four weeks ago. I hope you will understand why I did not let you know earlier myself, but the completion of my work weighed on me, and I did not want to write to you with personal news before I had fulfilled my scholarly obligations. I hope I have met them to your satisfaction. I made major changes on pages 36–65, 99–110, and 119–121. The point of the first change was to do a close study of the *memoria*, which I mentioned in my first text but the basic significance of which I had not spelled out. I've provided supporting documentation for the passages about *facere* and the fundamentally alien state of human beings in the world (p. 52f.) and also clarified these passages further. I rewrote the third section—aside from a few pages I've retained—but did not make it longer, as I had originally planned. I have followed your advice and put the historical digressions, which interrupted the text too much, into appendices to the individual sections. I have once again checked all the notes and quotations against the Migne edition[2] and against as much of the Vienna edition[3] as has appeared to date. In doubtful cases I followed the Vienna edition (with the one exception of Part II, footnote 116). The placement of the notes after the text in the copy I am sending you does not mean that they will appear there in the book. Instead, they will come on each page under the appropriate text. The separation of the notes here was done for the printer's benefit.

Unfortunately, the Jewish Academy turned down my application because it (1) is short of funds and (2) feels it would be more appropriate for the Notgemeinschaft[4] to support my Rahel study.[5] If I decide to apply to the Notgemeinschaft, I would be most grateful to you if I could again use the recommendation you wrote for the Jewish Academy.

I am very pleased that you have news of me from no other than Benno von Wiese because the danger of acquiring information by way of town gossip is greater in Heidelberg than elsewhere. Because B. v. Wiese is a friend I am still in touch with, you have had the news from someone close to me. No one else knows and understands my situation as well as he.

With gratitude and respect,

Sincerely yours,
Hannah Arendt-Stern

P.S. I hope B. v. Wiese also told you that because of our present circumstances G. Stern[6] and I have not yet been able to legalize our marriage. Both his parents and mine recognize the necessity for this provisional state of affairs.

6 Karl Jaspers to Hannah Arendt

Heidelberg, June 16, 1929

Dear Frau Arendt:

Many thanks for your letter. I wish you all the very best!

Your dissertation has not arrived yet. When I do have it, you'll have to allow me some time now that I'm in the middle of the semester.

Please do use my letter for the Notgemeinschaft. But please *wait* a while yet. If I can, I would like to get recommendations for you from Heidegger[1] and Dibelius.[2] The Notgemeinschaft has turned down so many excellent applications that we must do all we possibly can.

With warm regards,
Your K. Jaspers

7 Hannah Arendt to Karl Jaspers

Neubabelsberg, June 23, 1929

Dear Professor Jaspers,

Thank you very much for your prompt note. It was particularly soothing to my nerves because I have no other copy of my dissertation *with the changes included*. Thank you, too, for your permission to use your letter of recommendation for a possible application to the Notgemeinschaft and for speaking to Professor Heidegger on my behalf. At the moment, I am not planning to submit an application because I don't have a copy of my dissertation to present to the Notgemeinschaft.

Please thank your wife for me once again for putting me in touch with the Jewish Academy.

Most sincerely,
Your
Hannah Arendt

8 *Hannah Arendt to Karl Jaspers*

Neubabelsberg, July 24, 1929

Dear Professor Jaspers,

I hope I may come to you with still another request. Not long ago an acquaintance of mine told me about the Abraham Lincoln Foundation. When I inquired at the foundation, I was directed to a Dr. H. Simons, with whom I had an interview today and who informed me about the foundation's specific goals. It is a private institution that provides support for intellectuals whose work does not fall within the ready purview of existing academic and economic institutions. Dr. Simons urged me to present as many recommendations as possible so that the foundation's committee could form a picture of me and my work. Is it all right with you if I use for this purpose the recommendation you originally wrote for the Jewish Academy and also made available to me for a possible application to the Notgemeinschaft? You kindly offered a while ago to obtain a recommendation from Professor Heidegger, too, and I would be most grateful if you would ask him for one now.

Please do not take it amiss that I come to you so often for help with my affairs.

With gratitude and respect,

Your devoted
Hannah Arendt

9 *Karl Jaspers to Hannah Arendt*

Heidelberg, August 2, 1929

Dear Frau Arendt,

Of course you can use my recommendation for the Lincoln Foundation, too.

Enclosed are recommendations from *Heidegger* and *Dibelius*.

7

I already had Heidegger's letter in hand. It was originally intended for the Notgemeinschaft and addressed to it. I asked for and received Heidegger's permission for you to use it for the Lincoln Foundation. Dibelius's letter you may use for both applications, if that seems advisable to you.

Now that the semester is coming to an end I will soon be able to read your work and report back to you.

For now, I wish you all success with the Lincoln Foundation.

With warm regards
Your Karl Jaspers

10   Karl Jaspers to Hannah Arendt

Heidelberg, August 4, 1929

Dear Frau Arendt,

I have sent your manuscript to Springer.[1] I hope no difficulties will arise there. The manuscript is messy and not in very good shape for the printer. I have not, however, read the whole text again. It will be easier to check it over when it's in galleys. For now I will rely on you. I checked only a few pages (pp. 102ff.) and corrected a number of *spelling* errors there.

In preparing your work for print, please note the following: You will have to read the proofs *slowly* and always *twice*: once for meaning and once visually, watching for printing errors in letters and syllabification. Reading proofs is *very* strenuous, and it has to be done thoroughly. *Duden*'s dictionary contains the *proofreader's marks* you will need for making corrections.

You will receive two sets of proofs: first the "galleys," later the "page proofs." The actual corrections are made on the galleys. But the page proofs have to be read through once again *completely* because whole lines can be either omitted or out of order.

Any changes cost Springer a lot of money. You may correct *only mistakes*. Stylistic improvements that should have been made in the manuscript are no longer possible.

Springer correctly assumes that in publishing these monographs he is doing scholarship a service. They cost him money rather than bringing him profit. So please keep that in mind and be polite when you correspond with him.

At publication time it's good to know *which journals you want to receive review copies.* For your dissertation, some theological ones are possibilities, too. Please compile a list and add to it as ideas occur to you so that it will be ready, and you can send it to Springer for his advertising department.

Well, you must be thinking that you've had quite enough instructions by now. And I—I've played the schoolmaster once again. — Please let me know if you have any questions.

With all best regards,
Your Karl Jaspers

11   Hannah Arendt to Karl Jaspers

August 9, 1929

Dear Professor Jaspers,

First let me thank you very much for getting the recommendations for me, especially the letter from Professor Dibelius, which I was not expecting. They have all been sent on. I'll have a final decision in early October. I'll let you know right away what the outcome is.

I'm delighted that my manuscript is at Springer's now. I'll be conscientious about all the proofreading details you so kindly called to my attention. All the quotations will be checked against the originals once more, by me and probably by a classicist I know who is familiar with the material.

Now that the printing of my dissertation marks the end of my schooling, externally anyhow, I want to thank you once again for all the help you have given me during these last years.

Your most devoted,
Hannah Arendt

12   Hannah Arendt to Karl Jaspers

Heidelberg, October 8, 1929

Dear Professor Jaspers,

After having got married in Berlin, my husband and I are now in Heidelberg. I would very much like to stop by to see you if you would let me know a time when my visit would be convenient for you.

Your most devoted,
Hannah Stern-Arendt

13   Karl Jaspers to Hannah Arendt

[Postmark] Oldenburg, October 10, 1929

Dear Frau Stern,

Unfortunately we're not in Heidelberg. We'll be back on October 20. If you are still in Heidelberg then, please come see me whenever it suits you.

With warmest regards,
Your Karl Jaspers

14   Karl Jaspers to Hannah Arendt

Heidelberg, March 30, 1930

Dear Frau Stern,

Many thanks for your lecture.[1] I read it with great interest. And now, having read it, I wish we could have a talk together so I could ask my questions and get a clearer idea in the give and take of our conversation of what you mean. For merely to write you a few pronouncements seems to me an inadequate response when I can see that, despite the deliberate objectivity of your presentation, something else is going on here. But as I have no other choice I will write a few remarks, however open to misunderstanding they may be.

You objectify "Jewish existence" existentially—and in doing so perhaps cut existential thinking off at the roots. The concept of being-thrown-back-on-oneself can no longer be taken altogether seriously if it is *grounded* in terms of the fate of the Jews instead of being rooted in itself. Philosophically, the contrast between floating free and being rooted strikes me as very shaky indeed.

The passages from the letters, which you have chosen so well, suggest something quite different to me: "Jewishness" is a *façon de parler* or a manifestation of a selfhood orginally negative in its outlook and not comprehensible from the historical situation. It is a fate that did not experience liberation from the enchanted castle.

But these are not "objections."

Needless to say I'm pleased with the content of your work, and I'm glad that you're continuing to work on Rahel.

The first two pages and some formulations later on strike me as somewhat mannered. Your philosophical argument there is thetic and dogmatic, or so it seems to me at any rate, and it strikes me as weak. But *very* seldom.

The best of luck as you go ahead with this project!

With warm regards,

Your Karl Jaspers

Like most other people you probably won't be able to read my handwriting. So you'll have to come visit us again when you can.

Please send me your *new address*. I don't want to take the chance of your manuscript going astray in the mail. So I won't send it until I'm sure of your address.

15   *Hannah Arendt to Karl Jaspers*

Frankfurt/Main, March 24, 1930

Dear Professor Jaspers,

Thank you so much for your letter. I'm sure you know how pleased I would have been if I could have answered you immediately person to person. I will come to see you as soon as possible and whenever it is agreeable to you. That probably won't be until early or mid-April because we have so much to do setting up our new apartment.

But for now I'd like to make some altogether tentative responses to your comments. I was not trying to "ground" Rahel's existence in terms of Jewishness—or at least I was not conscious of doing so. This lecture is only a *preliminary* work meant to show that on the foundation of being Jewish a certain possibility of existence *can* arise that I have tentatively and for the time being called fatefulness. This fatefulness arises from the very fact of "foundationlessness" and can occur *only* in a separation from Judaism. I did not intend at all to provide an actual interpretation of this having-a-fate. And for such an interpretation the fact of Judaism would be of no importance anyhow.

An objectification is in fact there in a certain sense, but not an objectification of Jewish existence (as a gestalt, for example) but of the historical conditions of a life which can, I think, mean something (though not an objective idea or anything like that). It seems as if certain people are so exposed in their own lives (and only in their lives, not as persons!) that they become, as it were, junction points and concrete objectifications of "life." Underlying my objectification of Rahel is a self-objectification that is not a reflective or retrospective one but, rather, from the very outset a mode of "experiencing," of learning, appropriate to her. What this all really adds up to—fate, being exposed, what life means—I can't really say in the abstract (and I realize that in trying to write about it here). Perhaps all I can try to do is illustrate it with examples. And that is precisely why I want to write a biography. In this case, interpretation has to take the path of repetition.

I don't like the first two pages either. I wrote them only in deference to the setting in which I gave the talk.

I am most grateful to you for your comments, and I remain with the warmest greetings,

Your
Hannah Stern

My new address as of *Jan. 4*: Schwanthalerstr. 73. Until then, as before: Oederweg 128, 2.

About two weeks ago I sent my application in to the Notgemeinschaft.

16   *Hannah Arendt to Karl Jaspers*

Frankfurt/Main, May 1, 1930

Dear Professor Jaspers,

I've just received word that my application to the Notgemeinschaft has been approved. I expect to be in Heidelberg on May 7 and 8 and will take the liberty of calling you immediately.

With warmest greetings

Your devoted
Hannah Stern

17   *Karl Jaspers to Hannah Arendt*

Heidelberg, May 4, 1930

Dear Frau Stern!

Congratulations.

And thank you for letting me know that you are coming. I am always happy to see you, but I'm sorry to say that neither the 7th nor the 8th is possible for me. On the 7th I have office hours and a seminar; on the 8th my parents are coming. The 10th would be best for me—

though even then I can spare only an hour. But please don't change your plans on my account. We'll surely have a chance to get together some other time.

With warm regards
Your Karl Jaspers

18 *Karl Jaspers to Hannah Arendt*

Heidelberg, December 23, 1930

Dear Frau Stern!

Either Thursday or Saturday is fine with me. If it's convenient for you, 12–1 and 6–7 are the best times for me. Send me a card so I'll know when to expect you.

I am not inviting you for a meal this time because we have house guests who will not interest you.

I hope all is going well for you.

With best regards,
Your K. Jaspers

19 *Hannah Arendt to Karl Jaspers*

Berlin-Halensee, November 2, 1931

Dear Professor Jaspers,

I was delighted to receive your book,[1] and I hope you won't be angry with me for taking so long to thank you for sending it to me. I wanted to be far enough into it so that I would have something substantial to say about it. I'm enclosing my remarks here.[2] I have commented only on those things with which I was not in full agreement. Everything in my remarks should be perfectly clear, and especially that this book makes me realize once again how profoundly indebted I am to you.

You will perhaps have heard in the meantime that we have left Frankfurt and have moved to Berlin. Because of problems with the faculty my husband's habilitation would have had to drag on for some indeterminate length of time. That in itself would not have been disastrous, because his examiners, with one exception, had all responded positively after a preliminary reading of his work. But in the course of our stay and of negotiations about the habilitation, Herr Tillich[3] proved to be so obviously unreliable and subject to passing influences that if waiting any longer was to have any point at all, then it would be only if my husband kept Tillich under constant pressure and made concessions to his weaknesses. And on top of that the situation became totally untenable, that is, humiliating for all concerned, because one conference with Tillich ended with a display of contrition and a confession of sins (*voluptas contritionis*) that were more than embarrassing. In view of all this, we preferred to leave Frankfurt and for the time being to try to make a living outside academe.

My work on Rahel proceeds by fits and starts because I have been writing a number of short pieces recently, in part to earn some money. If I may, I would like to send you an essay on Hofmannsthal[4] as soon as it appears.

I don't need to tell you how pleased I am that your *Philosophie* is about to be published. I await it eagerly. —It is very sad that I no longer have the opportunity to visit you now and then.

With warmest regards and all good wishes, as always—

Your Hannah Stern

20   Karl Jaspers to Hannah Arendt

Heidelberg, November 16, 1931

Dear Frau Stern!

Thank you very much for your letter and your comments. Your letter was the first word I had that you had left Frankfurt, and I am sorry to hear it. I sense an antiacademic tone in your report, understandably. I hope your husband has some other opportunities and plans. I regret that all this has stood in the way of your Rahel project, of which I expect great things. I look forward to your Hofmannsthal essay. It would be nice if we could talk again despite the distance. Perhaps I'll have to come to Berlin for that. If I do, I'll let you know ahead.

Your critical comments were valuable to me.[1] I think the understanding of Herder's view of history that you hold up against mine is correct. Incorporating it would expand my schematic representation in a major way. What you have to say as a consequence of this idea, especially about the role of nothingness, frightens me. Because I believe what you say, I want to speak with you in give and take, not in a doctrinaire-sounding written reply. I don't accept what you say at the end about the masses and the historical meaning of the proletariat, and I would hope to be able to convince you of my view on these things.

I hope that my *Philosophie* will appear in two or three weeks. If I have the publisher send you a copy, please don't regard that as an obligation to read the book. I'll be satisfied to know that it's in your hands and that you can look into it when you want to.

With best regards
Your Karl Jaspers

21 *Hannah Arendt to Karl Jaspers*

Berlin, January 26, 1932

Dear Professor Jaspers,

You will be very surprised to be hearing from me so late. I was hoping it would not take me long to reach the point when I could say something substantial about your great book at the same time that I thanked you for it.[1] But I can see now that that will have to wait much longer because I am still totally absorbed in the *Metaphysik*.[2] So for now let me simply thank you for your book and your letter.

I am finding it painful time and again, and particularly right now, that I am not able to visit you.

I've been fortunate enough to receive a Jewish fellowship—for a short time only but with prospects for an extension. Once I have that firmly in hand, I'll be able to drop all the less important work. But even now I'm spending more time with my Rahel project.

Please believe me when I say that neither I nor my husband harbor any resentment toward academe. I must have expressed myself poorly. What happened in Frankfurt was altogether untypical of academe.

With the warmest of greetings and wishes and in gratitude and respect,

Your
Hannah Stern

22 *Hannah Arendt to Karl Jaspers*

Berlin, January 1, 1933

Dear Professor Jaspers,

Thank you very much for the Max Weber,[1] which I am delighted to have. There is a good reason, however, why I am writing only now to thank you for it: The title and introduction made it difficult for me from the start to comment on the book. It does not bother me that you portray Max Weber as the great German but, rather, that you find the "German essence" in him and identify that essence with "rationality and humanity originating in passion."[2] I have the same difficulty with that as I do with Max Weber's imposing patriotism itself. You will understand that I as a Jew can say neither yes nor no and that my agreement on this would be as inappropriate as an argument against it. I do not have to keep my distance as long as you are talking about the "meaning of the German world power" and its mission for the "culture of the future."[3] I can identify with this German mission, though I do not feel myself unquestioningly identical with it. For me, Germany means my mother tongue, philosophy, and literature. I can and must stand by all that. But I am obliged to keep my distance, I can neither be for nor against when I read Max Weber's wonderful sentence where he says that to put Germany back on her feet he would form an alliance with the devil himself. And it is this sentence which seems to me to reveal the critical point here.

I wanted to convey this reservation to you, although it faded as I read further. I still feel there is a contradiction between the main body of the text and the introduction, a text in which it is stressed that freedom is not to be identified with Germanness and an introduction in which you make "rationality and humanity" out to be something like basic qualities of the German character.

I hardly need tell you that this book prompts the reader to read Weber himself and though it does not require any previous knowledge of Weber's work, it vividly conveys his intellectual power. I did feel, however, that the second section[4] of your presentation was a little too short and so left the final paragraphs somewhat schematic and abstract.

Since this summer we have been in our own apartment. I would be pleased no end if you could see for yourself that its charms (and my pride in it) derive from the fact that it does not in any way look like students' quarters. Despite household chores I am getting a lot of work done. Rahel is for the most part complete. I often try to imagine what you will say about the finished book.—I'm taking the liberty of enclosing an essay[5] that the editors cut rather heavily. By way of compensation, though, they made my name twice as long.

I've seen Afra Geiger[6] a few times. But we didn't connect very well for reasons that are not clear to me.

With all good wishes for the New Year,

With respect and gratitude

Your

Hannah Stern

23 Karl Jaspers to Hannah Arendt

Heidelberg, January 3, 1933

Dear Frau Stern!

How tricky this business with the German character is! I find it odd that you as a Jew want to set yourself apart from what is German. But instead of focusing on that I'd like to try to interpret the meaning of my sentences for you in the hope that, if not now, then in a later conversation, I'll win your assent.

I do not isolate the German character as a type, thus setting it apart from other types. It is not a general concept to which other concepts may be subsumed; rather, an indeterminate and emerging historical totality. When I say that the German character is rationality, etc., I am not saying that rationality is exclusively German. That is why I quite consciously balance, without contradicting myself, the introductory sentence with the later one that says rationality etc. is not to be construed as Germanness.[1]

My reason for choosing this somewhat odd formulation has to do with my pedagogical impulse. Our nationalistic youth have so much goodwill and genuine élan tangled up in their confused and wrongheaded jabbering that I wanted to make them aware of the demands on themselves that are inherent in being German while at the same time acknowledging their need to feel pride in being German. That is why I felt a nationalistic publisher[2] was appropriate for reaching the readers who are in need of this educational impulse and who perhaps even yearn for it themselves. Not in one single sentence did I make any compromises. The subtitle is a compromise I agreed to because the publisher asked for it, claiming that Max Weber was unknown. The compromise does not lie in the content of the subtitle, however, but in the fact that I added a subtitle at all. The word "German" is so much misused that one can hardly use it at all anymore. I made the attempt, hopeless perhaps, to give it ethical content through the figure of Max Weber. That attempt, however, would have proved successful only if you, too, could say: That's the way it is. I want to be a German. When you speak of mother tongue, philosophy, and literature, all you need add is historical-political destiny, and there is no difference left at all. This destiny *today* is that Germany can exist only in a unified Europe, that her revival in her old glory can come about only through the unification of Europe, that the devil with whom we will inevitably have to make our pact is the egoistic, bourgeois anxiety of the French; for the empire of what is German, an empire that would have to reach from Holland to Austria, from Scandinavia to Switzerland is an impossibility and would still be too small in today's world anyhow. Well, those are all subjects that had no place in the Max Weber book, although they seem to me to grow naturally from it. The point of the book was simply to call attention to the premises inherent in this line of thought.

With warm regards, also to your husband,

Your Karl Jaspers

24   *Hannah Arendt to Karl Jaspers*

Berlin, January 6, 1933

Dear Professor Jaspers,

Many thanks! I too hope eagerly for a meeting, but for the time being I want to make some altogether tentative responses.

What troubled me first of all of course is the term "German character." You say yourself how misused it is. For me it is almost identical with misuse. But that is unimportant. Even if I were just to hear the term, as if you were to speak of it for the first time, I would still balk at it. Perhaps I have not understood what you meant by an emerging historical totality. I took it to mean that this character manifests itself from time to time in history. It would remain, then, despite its basic indeterminateness, something absolute, something untouched by history and Germany's destiny. I cannot identify with that, because I do not have in myself, so to speak, an attestation of "German character."

Despite that, I am of course a German in the sense that I wrote of before. But I can't simply add a German historical and political destiny to that. I know only too well how late and how fragmentary the Jews' participation in that destiny has been, how much by chance they entered into what was then a foreign history. And even if we were to summon the last hundred and fifty years as crown witnesses against this view, we would still be left with this fact: When we speak of Jews, we cannot really mean the few families that have been in Germany for generations now, but only the immigrant stream from the east for whom the process of assimilation keeps going on. Germany in its old glory is your past. What my Germany is can hardly be expressed in one phrase, for any oversimplification—whether it is that of the Zionists, the assimilationists, or the anti-Semites—only serves to obscure the true problem of the situation.

You speak of the unification of Europe. I hope for that, too, but with a difference. You want it at any price, for Germany's sake. I can't want it in the only form in which it seems possible today, that is, under the hegemony of France, of the one country that is relatively secure and undevastated. In this form, unification would be the most dreadful thing imaginable, and Germany's revival could in no way compensate me for that.

With warm regards and with best wishes from my husband

Always your,
Hannah Stern

25 *Karl Jaspers to Hannah Arendt*

Heidelberg, January 10, 1933

Dear Frau Stern!

I've had a chance to read your essay,[1] and I thank you very much for it. I find it excellent because of its forceful train of thought and the importance of its theme. Your second letter indicates that you have drawn conclusions from your interpretation that I cannot go along with. But that is material for a conversation, which I would open with the question of what it is you are really after. We cannot live solely from negations, problems, and ambiguities. All these things need to be informed by something positive. How that is to be accomplished in the totality of human society without the devil is the question I would ask you, or with what other devil would you prefer to make your pact.

I am looking forward to your Rahel book with the greatest interest. You will find an eager reader in me. And so I hope for you, but also

19

on my own behalf, that your work will proceed apace and soon be completed.

I would like very much to see your totally unstudentlike apartment. That you are "proud" of it could be a subtle sign of that positive attitude I am looking for.

With warm greetings from one house to another,

Your K. Jaspers

Have you seen Karl Hillebrand's essay on Rahel in *Zeiten, Völker und Menschen*, vol. 2 (*Wälsches und Deutsches*)?[2]

26   *Karl Jaspers to Hannah Arendt*

Heidelberg, April 12, 1933

Dear Frau Stern!

I'd love to see you. I'll be at home at the end of April and all the time before. The closer the semester comes, the more pressed I am. So if it is convenient for you, the earlier our meeting can take place, the better it will be for me, perhaps right after Easter. My wife is in Berlin, will be back on Friday.

All best regards

Your K. Jaspers

27   *Hannah Arendt to Karl Jaspers*

Paris, March 27, 1936

Dear Herr Jaspers,

I haven't heard anything from you for so dreadfully long and not let you hear anything from me that I hardly know any more how I should begin to write to you.

Would you let me know whenever you happen to take a trip? I get around in the world quite a bit, and I'd like to at least avoid being near you without even knowing it.

As always,

Your

Hannah Stern

Geneva, August 8, 1936

Dear Herr Jaspers,

Don't be angry about my belated thanks.[1] I'm here on vacation. My husband went to America a few weeks ago. But for the time being I'll stay in Europe.

This will reach you during the holidays, which I hope will be pleasant for you.

Warmest greetings to you and your wife,

Your
Hannah Stern

29   *Karl Jaspers to Hannah Arendt*

September 1938, Colpach,[1] Redange s/Attert,
Gd. Duché de Luxembourg

Dear Frau Hannah!

Much distressed that things have not worked out![2] Viénot,[3] who surely knows his way around in these matters, thinks it impossible that the Präfektur, on such short notice, will issue a paper that will do. You mustn't under any circumstances endanger yourself. I should have initiated the process long ago but didn't dare risk it because I didn't know Frau Mayrisch[4] at all at that point and so did nothing but accept her suggestions. Here, in view of her kindness and the situation, I finally made my wish known. I hope we'll be able to get together another time. —Pollnow[5] will report to you what went on here.

Warmest greetings
Your K. J.

30   *Karl Jaspers to Hannah Arendt*

Heidelberg, October 28, 1945

Dear Hannah Arendt!

Dr. Lasky[1] is here right now but, unfortunately, has to leave again immediately. He is just here on a visit. What things he has brought us from you! And for the second time. I thank you very much, as

21

does my wife, who is speaking with Dr. Lasky now. We have become friends.

To hear of you, to read your essays,[2] with which I could agree wholeheartedly—that was a delight. Often over the past years we worried about your fate and for a long time now did not have much hope that you were still alive. And now not only do we have your reappearance but also a lively, intellectual presence from the wide world! You have, it seems to me, unerringly retained your inner core, whether you have been in Königsberg, Heidelberg or America or Paris. Anyone who is a real human being has to be able to do that. I have been spared *that* trial by fire. Here we have to see now what we can rebuild out of chaos. I am optimistic, provided world history does not just roll over us and destroy us. We still have young people eager to learn, few of them—but then, the masses have always been obtuse and tied to the clichés of their times.

The books, which, thanks to you, have been lying next to me for the last ten minutes, regard me with promising glances. You can imagine how hungry we are for everything that has been thought and done outside Germany. Jonas[3] passed through a short while ago, on his way to Palestine as a soldier of the English army's Jewish brigade. He was happy to have word of you.

If luck is good to me, I will be able to send you—I hope—what at the moment is still in my desk drawer in manuscript form, the work of eight years of "retirement" and of not being allowed to publish.[4]

Dr. Lasky tells me you expressed interest in a talk I gave here in August.[5] I am enclosing it and would of course be *delighted* to see it translated. If we should be able to lecture at the university again[6]—I still have to keep quiet for the moment; we can't either publish or speak; but that will surely change very soon now—I'll lecture for one hour per week on the intellectual situation in Germany.[7] I can tell from your essays that you have inklings. But you can't really know how things are here now.

Warmest greetings
Your Karl Jaspers[8]

November 18, 1945

Dear, dear Karl Jaspers,

Ever since I've known that you both came through the whole hellish mess unharmed, I have felt somewhat more at home in this world again. I needn't tell you that I worried about you all those years—although I lived for a long time in the comforting illusion that you were in Zurich.[1] Some stupid rumor. But what I want to tell you after not being able to write for more than twelve years now is this. I may have thought or done some things in those years that will put you off, but there is hardly anything I've done that I didn't do without thinking how I would tell you about it or justify it to you. And when I read again in your *Philosophie* now or the few quotations from your speech[2] that have appeared in the newspapers, you are as present to me as in the years of my youth.

I am glad that you feel optimistic. Everything does depend on a few, but the few mustn't become too few. We have all seen in these years how the few constantly became fewer still. That was essentially as true among emigrants as it was in Germany. There are many routes to accommodation with the powers that be. The only people who will count are those who refuse to identify themselves with either an ideology or a power.

We are waiting impatiently here for you to publish. The editors of *Partisan Review*[3] (Lasky will tell you what that is) were very enthusiastic when I told them you would lecture on the intellectual situation.[4] Unfortunately, Lasky had forgotten to enclose your speech. I would also very much like to have your reply to Sigrid Undset.[5] When will *Die Wandlung*[6] start appearing? If Dolf Sternberger[7] wants to publish something here and you think it's good, he too should simply send it to *PR* by way of Lasky. I've told them who Sternberger is.

I am of course pleased that you agree with my articles—although I don't know what you have read. I haven't sent anything myself but will as soon as there is regular postal service again. And then I will have to ask for your indulgence, which is to say, ask you not to forget that I'm writing in a foreign language (and that is *the* problem of emigration) and that for twelve years the peace necessary to do intellectual work has been something I've known only from hearsay. Since I've been in America—that is, since 1941—I've become a kind of freelance writer, something between a historian and a political journalist.

In the latter capacity I've focused primarily on questions of Jewish politics. I've written about the German question[8] only when growing hatred toward Germany and increasing idiocy about it made it impossible to remain silent, especially if one is a Jew. Along with this activity I am also presently working on a research project for a Jewish organization,[9] which means in reality that I am in charge of it. That is typical in this land of research. And then this winter I will probably be teaching a course about dictatorships—that for returning soldiers at a local college.[10]

I have to add (I find it hard to comprehend that I haven't seen you for so many years) that I've been married again, for nine years, to a German.[11] That is probably a "punishment" for my foolishness right after 1933, when, as a consequence of the compromises with the regime that I saw almost all of my non-Jewish friends making (the Jewish ones compromised with Stalin or Daladier[12] or whoever only later), I slid into an automatic distrust of non-Jews, though making exceptions, as Jonas does. From whom I had a few nice lines in which he too told me about his visit with you.

"That is all and is not enough
   but it shows you perhaps that I'm still there . . ."
I could say in the words of Brecht's Emigration Song.[13]

But that is not all, because I want to know if you need medicines and which ones. Penicillin? Sulfa? Other or more specialized drugs? Please let me know through Lasky. I know lots of doctors here.

Furthermore, dear Gertrud Jaspers, don't rely on my not very highly developed housewifely instincts but write me what you'd like to have. In the last packages, I put in a kosher wurst; you have to be very careful with pork here because of trichinosis. If I should send bacon (I've forgotten the German word for it, the hell with it), please always fry it just this way: Put the slices in a moderately hot pan and fry them over a low flame. Keep pouring the fat off until the slices are crisp. Then nothing can go wrong with either the fat or the bacon. What about vitamins? Do you want fruit juice or dried fruit? Maybe concentrated lemon juice? Do you drink coffee? I seem to recall that your husband drinks tea and milk and therefore went lightly with coffee. Do you need cigarettes for any of your friends? Please just give Lasky or anyone else a list.

Warmest wishes   Your
Hannah Arendt

December 2, 1945

Dear Hannah Arendt!

Your first letter arrived today. We both thank you very much. I sense in your words not only your personal loyalty but also the spirit of a natural humanity that is infinitely comforting. Tears came to my eyes while I was reading your letter because I felt how rare that spirit is—and because just yesterday I was disappointed by others who are searching together for new directions to follow. Yes, the few mustn't be "too few"! For a long time my wife and I had almost no one except my sister.[1] There are others, many of them. But one doesn't meet them. The very few suffice to give one hope. They keep alive in us the awareness of a truth that is not tangible, a bright room that opens to us. It is there in what the tradition has handed down to us, and it is present when the kind words of a friend reach us.

I have read your essays, your reviews in *Politics*,[2] which Lasky lent us this summer, and now your essay on German guilt in the anthology[3] you sent me. A wonderful essay—and something like that can be published in America! Lucky America, in spite of everything.

I'm finding that I can't write because I want to write too much. It will have to wait. Perhaps it will be possible to print something after all. One of the works I would like to send you, "Von der Wahrheit"[4]—1,400 typewritten pages—would, I hope, express something of the quality that can link people together without "compromises" (compromises you see on *all* sides and with the same horror as I do). I also have a *Psychopathologie*[5] done, a completely new book in what would be its fourth edition. The publication of such things is still technically impossible here.

But here I go again with these essentially trivial matters. I'd rather hear more about you. Tell me about your husband. I don't even know what your last name is. In what kind of circumstances are you living? You are obviously a literary presence. What I have read by you shows that. But what is your personal life like? The last image of you that got through to us was of you in Paris, moving on constantly from one room to another and so careless about your papers that the trip to Luxembourg came to naught.[6]

How bemused you would be if you came into our apartment here: the same rooms, as if nothing had happened. You could sit in the chair at my desk again the way you used to as a doctoral candidate. And yet everything is different, only a ghostly continuation of externals from the past into this transformed world. I've been lecturing again for two weeks now, but under the auspices of the theological faculty,[7] because the university itself is still not open. I'm lecturing in the old hall (to students of theology and medicine), on "Proofs of God's Existence."[8]

The first issue of *Die Wandlung* was ready yesterday. I'm enclosing a copy. Would you like to write an essay for us? You can see that the length has to be limited, to about 12 pages of print. What you write about is up to you. Perhaps you could write something on what truly unites us across all the barriers between us—and by us I mean Americans and Europeans, including Germans? Or maybe you would prefer a concrete subject—the kind of thing we are eager for here—information about American philosophical thought at the moment? If this issue of the magazine would prompt you to speak a word, how welcome it would be! —The fee (25 marks per printed page) will be of no help to you at all. Even here you can't buy anything with that unless you have the necessary stamps or coupons, too. —Please forgive this prose. Everything is jumbled together in one's head in this world, which is just starting on its way back, or perhaps is on its way back, to some kind of order in which it is possible to live for tasks worthy of human beings.

December 10

You wrote: "I may have thought or done some things in those years that will put you off. . . ." I thank you for trusting me. When one has become so indifferent to what "people" say when they appear only as a manifestation of mass and time, when one experiences, as I have, these amazing reversals: ignored and avoided for years, now overwhelmed with 20 and more letters a day and stale fame—then one becomes all the more sensitive and feels a greater need to hear from the few. That is why your loyalty inspires me. How happy I would be to hear these "things that will put me off," to be together with you and respond to them. —I know in advance that they would make me reexamine my views and—whatever else they may be—would deepen my respect for you.

I read English only with some difficulty and have to use the dictionary sometimes. I can't speak a word. But I like to read it. I was particularly delighted with your essays on the German problem (in

Partisan Review[9]) and on German guilt.[10] I felt as if I were breathing the air I so yearn for: openness and justice and a hidden love that scarcely allows itself expression in language. Only in that way can we talk about these things. When Lasky lent us *Partisan Review* this summer we were elated—as if a world was opening up in which people can talk with each other and discuss things—and there was nothing of those conceptual clichés that are so tiresome in American newspapers. I particularly liked an article by Dwight Macdonald,[11] also on the question of guilt.

Whether it will be necessary to distance oneself from Thomas Mann's[12] ethical and political views is a question that troubles me. I value him so highly as a writer and novelist that I would be reluctant to say anything against him. But if the confusion he is causing here is not cleared up, we will have to find some response to his attacks and behavior—because he is a German and is speaking as a German. If the response is to be meaningful, it has to be thorough. One would have to go back as far as his essay of 1915 on Frederick the Great[13] (which pained me as much at the time as his present effusions do now).[14] But one should also be familiar with his radio talks.[15] If these talks have been *collected*—as I have heard here—and if you could get hold of a copy (I understand they were published in Sweden)—could I, after all the riches you have heaped upon us, ask for this book, too? It is by no means essential, and I'm still not at all sure whether I would write anything or not. I love his son Golo Mann.[16] I would be reluctant to pain him. By the way: when Werfel[17] died recently, Golo spoke movingly on Radio Luxembourg. His father followed shortly thereafter with a vapid, very conventional, and embarrassingly subjective talk from America.

I must apologize for my handwriting!

With warmest wishes
Your Karl Jaspers

33 *Hannah Arendt to Karl Jaspers*

New York, December 6, 1945

Dear Herr Jaspers,

Hasso von Seebach[1] is a very close friend of ours. He left Germany as a young man ten years ago because he could not stand the Nazi regime and the impossibility of doing anything effective against it.

Now that the regime has collapsed, he has seized the first opportunity to return to Germany. It would be nice if you could see him and speak with him.

As always—
Your
Hannah Arendt

34   Hannah Arendt to Karl Jaspers

January 29, 1946

Dear Karl Jaspers—

Thank you so much for your warm letter. You speak of trust. Do you remember our last talks together in Berlin, in 1933? I did not find some of your arguments convincing, but on a human and personal level you were so utterly convincing that for many years I was, so to speak, more sure of you than I was of myself. I didn't write after that because I was afraid of endangering you. The Luxembourg trip[1] didn't fall through just because of my bungling. How could I explain to you on the telephone or even in the context of a letter the infinitely complex red-tape existence of stateless persons?

You ask questions, and your questions are truly "like an outstretched hand." But I don't know where to start or where to stop. I have a vague recollection that your birthday falls sometime in February, so let me begin by wishing you all the best and telling you how grateful I am that you were born. I read your response to Sigrid Undset[2] in the *Staatszeitung*.[3] (I know about the original attack only by hearsay. I don't read much of this "literature" because I'm a bit afraid of the revulsion it evokes in me.) What you wrote does indeed create that "bright room" in which things once again fall into their proper place. The sad thing is that yours is almost the only voice so far to speak this way. *Die Wandlung*, for which I thank you very much and which is making the rounds here now, though I was reluctant to let it out of my hands, is a good beginning. Your introduction[4] is wonderful, and I hope that Dwight Macdonald will publish it along with your speech.[5] I wasn't able to give the speech to *Partisan Review*, because they had already printed their January issue and I did not want to wait until April or May. I gave the typed manuscript to Leo Baeck,[6] who took it along with him to London. He was so eager to have it, and because I already had a printed copy, I couldn't refuse the manuscript to the old man, who has become truly impressive in his absolute fearlessness and self-assurance.

I think about your study, which has always been that "bright room" for me—with the chair at the desk and the armchair across from it where you tied your legs in marvelous knots and then untied them again. I can well imagine how your own apartment strikes you as ghostly, but I'm very glad it is still there, and I hope someday to sit once again on that aforementioned chair.

If I were sitting on that chair, I would probably tell you more than I can here. My husband's name is Heinrich Blücher—written description impossible. During the war his knowledge of military history and affairs enabled him to do some work here for the army, some for universities, and some as a broadcaster. When the war ended, he left all these more or less official jobs, and now he is doing economic research for private companies. He comes from a working-class family in Berlin, studied history with Delbrück[7] in Berlin, then was an editor for a news service, and was involved in various political activities. I continue to use my old name. That's quite common here in America when a woman works, and I have gladly adopted this custom out of conservatism (and also because I wanted my name to identify me as a Jew).

By now you must be saying that I'm avoiding telling you what you really want to know. You no doubt want to know how I have fared in this life. That's hard to answer. I'm still a stateless person, and your picture of me living in furnished rooms is to some degree still accurate. We live, with my mother,[8] in a furnished apartment. I was, thank God, able to get her to France in time after the November pogroms[9] and then to bring her over here. As you see, I haven't become respectable in any way. I'm more than ever of the opinion that a decent human existence is possible today only on the fringes of society, where one then runs the risk of starving or being stoned to death. In these circumstances, a sense of humor is a great help. I'm fairly well known here, and in certain matters I have a little authority with some people; that is, they trust me. But that is partly because they know I'm not about to turn my convictions or "talents" into a career.

Perhaps some examples will clarify what I mean. If I had wanted to become respectable, I would either have had to give up my interest in Jewish affairs or not marry a non-Jewish man, either option equally inhuman and in a sense crazy. This all sounds idiotically pathetic somehow, and I don't mean it that way. For you are quite right to say "lucky America"—where, because of a basically sound political structure, so-called society has still not become so powerful that it cannot tolerate exceptions to the rules.

There is much I could say about America. There really is such a thing as freedom here and a strong feeling among many people that one cannot live without freedom. The republic is not a vapid illusion, and the fact that there is no national state and no truly national tradition creates an atmosphere of freedom or at least one not pervaded by fanaticism. (Because of the strong need the various immigrant groups feel to maintain their identity, the melting pot is in large part not even an ideal, much less a reality.) Then, too, people here feel themselves responsible for public life to an extent I have never seen in any European country. For example, when all Americans of Japanese descent were locked up willy-nilly in concentration camps at the beginning of the war, a genuine storm of protest that can still be felt today went through the country. I was visiting with an American family in New England at the time. They were thoroughly average people—what would have been called "petty bourgeoisie" in Germany—and they had, I'm sure, never laid eyes on a Japanese in their lives. As I later learned, they and many of their friends wrote immediately and *spontaneously* to their congressmen, insisted on the constitutional rights of all Americans regardless of national background, and declared that if something like that could happen, they no longer felt safe themselves (these people were of Anglo-Saxon background, and their families had been in this country for generations), etc.

The high degree of practical political understanding, the passion to straighten things out, not to tolerate unnecessary misery, to see that in the midst of often cutthroat competition the individual is guaranteed a fair chance—all this has a flip side, however, which is that nobody worries about what cannot be changed. The attitude of this country toward death will never cease to shock us Europeans. The basic response when someone dies or when something goes irrevocably wrong is: Forget about it. That is, of course, only another expression of this country's fundamental anti-intellectualism, which, for certain special reasons, is at its worst in the universities. (Chicago University and a few other universities are not exactly glowing exceptions to this rule, but they are exceptions nonetheless.) Every intellectual here is a member of the opposition simply because he is an intellectual. The reasons for that are the all-pervasive social conformity, the necessity to rebel against the god of success, etc. Among themselves, however, these intellectuals maintain a remarkable solidarity, and in their discussions and debates they are unfanatical and open-minded to an astonishing degree. From your acquaintance with Lasky you will have a good idea of what these people are like.

The fundamental contradiction in this country is the coexistence of political freedom and social oppression. The latter is, as I've already indicated, not total; but it is dangerous because the society organizes and orients itself along "racial lines." And that holds true without exception at all social levels, from the bourgeoisie on down to the working class. This racial issue has to do with a person's country of origin, but it is greatly aggravated by the Negro question; that is, America has a real "race" problem and not just a racial ideology. You doubtless know that social anti-Semitism is taken completely for granted here and that antipathy toward Jews is, so to speak, a consensus omnium. The Jews maintain an almost equally radical isolation and are, of course, also protected by that isolation. A young Jewish woman, a friend of mine born in this country, had in our home what I believe to be her first social meeting with non-Jewish Americans. This doesn't mean that people would not stand up for the Jews politically, but socially both sides want to "keep to themselves."

My literary existence, as opposed to my existence as a member of society, has two major roots: First, thanks to my husband, I have learned to think politically and see historically; and, second, I have refused to abandon the Jewish question as the focal point of my historical and political thinking. And this brings me to your question about *Die Wandlung*. Need I tell you how much your request that I contribute pleased me? And how happy I would be if I could simply write something and send it.

I know you will not misunderstand me when I say that it is not an easy thing for me to contribute to a German journal. At the same time, I am unhappy about the desperate resolve of the Jews to leave Europe (you are probably aware of the mood in all the refugee camps both in and outside Germany; and that mood cannot be ignored). I am also more anxious than I care to say about the frightening possibility of further catastrophes, particularly in Palestine, given the behavior of other governments and our own suicidal tendencies in politics. Yet one thing seems clear to me: If the Jews are to be able to stay in Europe, then they cannot stay as Germans or Frenchmen, etc., as if nothing had happened. It seems to me that none of us can return (and writing is surely a form of return) merely because people again seem prepared to recognize Jews as Germans or something else. We can return only if we are welcome as Jews. That would mean that I would gladly write something if I can write as a Jew on some aspect of the Jewish question. And quite apart from other problems—objections you might raise to my text, for instance—I don't know if you would be able to print something of that nature under the present difficult circumstances.

The Thomas Mann book—the radio talks and a *Neue Rundschau* with another essay on this subject (a particularly unpleasant one, it seems to me)—is in the mail. It really is absurd to take him seriously politically, important as he is as a novelist—except that he does exert a certain vague influence. The correspondence between him and Walter von Molo[10] of all people borders almost on the comic. I've sent along a few magazines with the Mann items, and I'll send some others soon which you may find of interest. You'll find in them a few articles of mine—not that I feel you're obliged to read them and struggle with the English. I'm sending them to clear my conscience, that is, because they are things that may "put you off," and because I would feel, now that it is possible to mail things, that I was hiding something if I didn't send them.

I'm very glad that you like "Organized Guilt"[11] (that was the original title). I wrote it when I had just learned from Tillich that you were not in Switzerland, and I thought of you often then. The astonishing thing isn't so much that something like it can be published in America but, rather, that a Jewish newspaper, after years of stupid propaganda, accepted it with glee and obvious relief and, by including it as the only statement about Germany in its anthology, put its official seal of approval on it once again. I'm sending you the original German text. Because it is really yours anyhow. If you like, you can of course use it in *Die Wandlung*.[12] (As a counterweight, as it were—ironically speaking—to the Morgenthau Plan.)[13]

I await your books with great impatience. That you were able to work like that despite the hell and loneliness you were living in is marvelous and reason to rejoice. That you are lecturing again brings a touch of order into this world out of joint. Have I ever told you how wonderful your Nietzsche book is?[14]

I've just seen here that you'd like a report on American philosophy for *Die Wandlung*. I couldn't do that because I don't know enough about it. But I know someone I could ask, an American and an editor at *Partisan Review*, William Barrett. He's an intelligent and pleasant young man. —I've just recalled, too, that Kristeller[15] asked me to send you his regards. And others have, too. (Do you remember him, a classical philologist . . . ? He's teaching Italian at Columbia University.) He'd like to know what became of his former teacher Hoffmann.[16]

I hope this letter isn't too long. If I don't stop now, there'll be no end to it.

Stay healthy (as the Jews say, with good reason), and please accept warmest greetings from

Your
Hannah Arendt

35 Karl Jaspers to Hannah Arendt

Heidelberg, March 12, 1946

Dear Hannah Arendt!

What a pleasure your letter of January 29 was! I've read it over and over again and reassured myself beyond all doubt of the solidarity we share. What a comfort that is! —Thank you for the gift of your manuscript.[1] The German text speaks to me more directly of course than the English one did earlier. With it in hand, I've been able to correct two quotes I translated from it for a talk I gave in January. The corrections are just in time to make it into the galleys. When the talk appears in print, I'll send you a copy ("Vom lebendigen Geist der Universität"[2]—the title comes from Gundolf's[3] inscription,[4] which was removed in 1933 and has been replaced now). I would of course like to print your manuscript in *Die Wandlung*. We don't often get anything as important and serious as this. Sternberger agrees. I can't know with any certainty if there will be further hurdles to clear. The publisher has veto power over all submissions. But I'll do what I can to push this one through. It would be a source of pride for the magazine to publish your work. —I am touched that you were thinking of me, of our situation in Germany, when you wrote this.

You didn't write much about your husband—and how could you! It is obviously impossible—but you've said enough for me to sense that he has intellectual energy and is a clever politician and your good companion. Give him my regards—I know I will like him.

You write incisively about America and your situation there. It is after all the most desirable of countries today, in spite of everything.

And if I were not a German I would not want to be anything but an American.

I fully understand what you had to say about the question of "returning" to Europe. My wife's experiences made all that clear to me a long time ago.

We would be delighted if William Barrett would write a short essay on American philosophy for us. Unhappily, we can't pay honoraria outside of Germany. So his essay would be an outright gift to our *Wandlung*.

It cheered me to know that you like my Nietzsche book. It appeared just as I became an "outlaw," and so it was ignored in the Nazi press. And there were some unfriendly reactions to it from abroad. —Now it's impossible to buy any of my books anymore.

It is not easy to describe things here. It is a life of irreality. I'm eaten up by day-to-day chores. Reflection withers. I find myself slipping into a modern life ruled by haste. Things can't go on this way. There seems to be no place at all for real thought. But we know that life goes on in spite of it all, even in famine, which has not touched us at all yet. Every day I say to myself: Patience, just be patient. Don't be discouraged, no matter what. If we do what we can, the rewarding moments are bound to return.

I have a number of students in my seminar[5] who are studying the *Kritik der Urteilskraft* with great intensity and with real understanding as well. There are lively and meaningful discussions. Compared with my lectures,[6] which are peopled by a large, dull mass, the seminar is like a dream, evidence of irrepressible German youth, however small their numbers.

Now, before I close, thank you for your wealth of gifts. I find the magazines and journals extremely stimulating. Unfortunately, though, *your* published essays were *not* included. Or will I still find something tucked away in *Politics*, of which there was a whole bundle? Along with them were three numbers of the *Deutsche Blätter*, a surprise and pleasure for us both. —The *Neue Rundschau* with Thomas Mann's talk on Germany, Thomas Mann's radio talks (thank you for fulfilling this wish of mine!). [. . .] But, alas, alas, *your* works are missing. Thank God that at least the manuscript was there. —My wife sends her thanks for the three packages and the package of medicines, even though I am the one who benefits most from them!

Please give my regards to Kristeller. I remember him well. Hoffmann was pleased to hear from him by way of me. Hoffmann is lecturing again, though not much. He is intellectually very alert but has a heart condition that slows him down. Like us, he's still living in his old apartment, which remains undamaged. He recently gave a nice lecture on the Brethren of the Common Life (which produced Thomas a Kempis, Nicolaus Cusanus, Erasmus).

3/17/46

Lasky is here right now. He'll take this letter with him. I'll quickly add a few lines—I really wanted to write another, less weary letter.

Your essay will appear in our *Wandlung*. I don't really see what could possibly prevent it now. A short note will convey, as you so rightly request it should, that your point of view is entirely that of a Jew. We are happy with that. The German reader will show how he reacts. For *us*, however, this is not a "political" or "tactical" move. The point has to be made with absolute clarity and as a matter of course.

My wife shares your worry about Palestine. She thinks about it all the time. Your comment has made her worry all the more. But where is there no worry these days? The gates of hell are wide open. We can only live braced for the next lethal eruption. There is still nothing on the horizon that even begins to resemble a Pax Romana.

In one's private life, there are in addition trivial worries about seeing one's manuscripts published. It would mean a lot to me to see my work "Von der Wahrheit" printed and thus saved for a future we cannot yet envisage. But despite the willingness of publishers, the material means simply aren't available. All our industry remains crippled. There's no paper for such large books that aren't absolutely necessary. My *Psychopathologie* is being set. The book will be ready in September at the earliest. A few short items will appear soon. I'll send them to you if it's possible.

I'm just writing down odds and ends—there's so much I want to talk about with you. —That will have to wait.

Warmest greetings from my wife
and Your Karl Jaspers

April 22, 1946

Dear Karl Jaspers—

I'm writing just a short note today so that you won't feel any obligation to reply. I'm somewhat disturbed because Joe Maier[1] wrote me about your bronchial hemorrhages, and I was even more troubled by the sentence in your letter about wanting "to see my work 'Von der Wahrheit' printed." I don't want to pester you with such questions.

I've been wanting to write for a long time, but I was waiting for the enclosed letter[2] and then I had to take an unexpected trip, something I've come to hate after all my involuntary world travels. Now to the letter: It is from William Phillips, one of the editors at *Partisan Review*, who is also an advisory editor for a large publishing house here, the Dial Press. He is writing on behalf of this house. Lasky wrote me that you had given *Geistige Situation der Zeit* as lectures again, and I thought you might have something of this kind available. Politically, this would be quite a significant publication, for the reasons that Phillips enumerates. The business end of it would presumably be handled as it is with every American author; that is, the publisher would have to pay an advance, between \$500 and \$1,000, and then the customary royalties. How this will be done under the present circumstances, suspended as we are between war and peace—and this state of suspension seems inclined to go on forever—remains a mystery to me.

My second urgent concern is this: Are you still intending to respond to Thomas Mann? If so, I feel I have to tell you what you may already know through Golo Mann, which is that Thomas Mann is very ill, apparently with a lung tumor, and will be operated on any day now. I learned this by chance through friends of the family.

I'm very glad that you want to print "Organisierte Schuld." Your approval is for me the most gratifying, indeed the only possible, confirmation of continuity with the past. And that I can (and may) write to you again is a wonderful proof that we can master time and space if only we will.

Two articles about you have appeared here in recent months, one by James Collins[3] in *Thought* and the other in a Jesuit journal. Löwith[4] called my attention to them—I read hardly any magazines; I don't have the time. I'll send them to you soon. Write me what else you want. Santayana has a new book out, *The Idea of Christ in the Gospels*,[5] and there is Dewey's[6] *Problems of Men* and a lecture on "Physics and Experience" by Russell.[7]

Something must have gone wrong with my articles. It's possible that I forgot to include them in the package. I'll send them to Lasky in one of the April packages. Or perhaps Lasky forgot to deliver them to you. Most likely is that I suffered some schoolgirl fear of you because of the philosophy article in *Partisan Review*.[8] In the meantime I've sent you a copy of it in printed form and in the German manuscript.

Will you have some peace now? Before the summer semester begins? Though I can't quite imagine how anyone can have any peace there now. "The gates of hell are still wide open"[9]—and from what I hear and read about Italy and France—not just in Germany. I would gladly send you French magazines (or perhaps you're getting them already), but at the moment it's not possible to buy them here, and I'm forced to borrow them.

Good-bye for now. Try to stay healthy, and let me know if I can do anything to help you with that.

With regards and affection

Your
Hannah Arendt

37 *Hannah Arendt to Gertrud Jaspers*

April 22, 1946

Dear Gertrud Jaspers,

Thank you for your kind letter.[1] Yesterday I got a long letter from Joe Maier, who told me about his visit with you. He is a good-hearted boy whom I've come to know primarily through our interest in the Jewish question. And there he has shown that when he has understood something, he knows how to defend it. That counts for a great deal in our time and his generation. —Lasky writes now and again about the lectures of the "Professor," as he likes to call him. I'm always very touched by that.

Joe wrote about Marianne Weber.[2] I'll send a package to him[3] next week, marked "from Hannah Blücher," so you can tell the difference. I vaguely remember Karl Löwenstein,[4] don't know, though, where I could find him now. The best solution seems to me to be this: *Politics* sends packages to intellectuals in every European country, but can't send any to Germany except through roundabout channels like me. The last packages to you were, so to speak, the honorarium for your husband's article[5] (or however you want to look at it). I'll send packages to Dolf Sternberger, too ("from Heinrich Blücher," and that by no means exhausts our possibilities; my mother is still here, too). Neither Sternberger nor Marianne Weber will have any direct contact with *Politics*—if they don't want to. Dwight Macdonald and his circle feel a total solidarity with European antifascists and also feel, if you will, responsible for their fate. They aren't looking for anyone to "thank" them at all. On the contrary, they are grateful for any opportunities given them. On top of that, they get from their readers a great many donations that are explicitly meant for Germans who were not Nazis but that they can't use because of the many difficulties involved. I don't belong to this group politically at all; but morally they are, as people say here, all right.

Now for our bookkeeping: I was a little upset because there were rumors going around here that sending packages would become more difficult and because some soldiers had asked that none be sent anymore. In the meantime that has, thank God, proved to be nonsense or exaggerated. In March, I sent one package to Joe Maier (which he has already received) and one to Lasky, which was sent at the same time and so ought to be there, too. In (early) April I sent two packages to Lasky, a week apart for safety's sake, and day before yesterday one to Joe Maier. From now on I'll send three packages a month, because I gather the food situation has gotten worse. Please, please, *write me if that isn't enough*. And write too if you need any medicines and which ones. Just to be safe for future reference: All the packages for you will be marked "from H. A." I'll be sure to send one package a month for Marianne Weber and for Sternberger, too. (That is, of course, too little for Sternberger if he isn't getting anything from his brother-in-law.) Let me know what Marianne Weber would most like to have.

With warmest wishes
Your
Hannah Arendt

And please forgive this "business letter."

I want to get it in the mail, and I'm too tired to write a proper letter.

May 8, 1946

Dear Hannah Arendt!

Your solicitude is unprecedented and effective. Thank you. My wife will write in more detail. I'm distressed at the burden it is for you, but not only does it add to our physical strength; it also warms our hearts. That an "honorarium" could have a part in it borders on the fantastic. If a later honorarium could wind up in your hands, I'd be delighted. Unfortunately I can't fulfill the wish of your publisher friend[1] right now. I was extremely pleased and encouraged by this wish, or, rather, this commission, and I wish *very* much that I could send a manuscript that would fill the bill. But I won't be writing about Germany until the winter semester. My essay on the question of guilt,[2] preceded by my opening lecture for the winter semester, is hardly the right thing for him (it's about 25 to 30,000 words). Once it's published I'll try to send you a copy.

You're concerned about my health? —I'm touched that that is possible. But your worries are groundless. I've had well over 100 hemorrhages over the last thirty years. They were the worst in 1918. The blood gurgled in my throat, and I had to stay in bed a few weeks. Because you can never know with light bleeding how bad it can become, you have to be careful. That's why it was impossible for me to speak with J. Maier.

Your wonderful essay[3] has appeared here now. Sternberger has written to you. I hope that a copy will reach you. It has made a deep impression on some people here. The responses I've heard have been out of the ordinary. Our American officer responsible for the university called it "the most impressive and outstanding essay he had ever read on the question of guilt." My excellent assistant, Dr. Rossmann,[4] was deeply moved. Your essay set the tone for the issue. I'm glad that there are still people here who sit up and take notice of ideas like yours. Sternberger has written about the honorarium. It will stay in an account here until you can make use of it. It isn't worth much. There's quite a bit of money in Germany.

I'd given up the idea of responding to Thomas Mann. Your own words convinced me. It is inappropriate. The man is too substantial as a writer to pain him unnecessarily. His own suffering as an emigrant deserves respect, and he isn't doing us any harm. In the meantime, we've heard here that his operation was a success, and that he's already gone home.

I'm looking forward to your philosophy article in *Partisan Review*.[5]

I don't have any wishes, but how nice it is that I may have them! I'll write if I want something.

My wife is reading *Menorah*[6] with great interest. I haven't had time yet.

Warmest greetings and thanks

Your Karl Jaspers

Forgive my great weariness—in the evening! But given my circumstances I'm quite healthy.

I'll give William Phillips's letter some further thought. For the time being, please give him my thanks. I hope that he'll still be interested in something from me next winter.

I hope "Vom lebendingen Geist der Universität" has reached you. I wrote it for the occasion of the restoration of the Gundolf inscription that was removed from the lecture hall in 1933. (Unfortunately the Americans are still occupying the building for their purposes.)

39 Hannah Arendt to Gertrud Jaspers

May 30, 1946

Dear Gertrud Jaspers,

Our letters[1] crossed. I haven't written for so long because I was trying to catch by the tail a minutely small possibility of coming to Germany, and this process made me too unsettled and impatient to write. In the meantime my possibility has tucked in its tail and only wags it encouragingly every now and then. From now on, however, I've decided to remain unmoved by this.

I didn't know about Pollnow's[2] death, only about his father's. Because he was from Königsberg, I knew him well, and I talked with him at length back then when he had come from visiting you. He was relying on his French passport and settled somewhere in the country in France. Yes, that's the way it was. One false move, one miscalculation, and you were lost. Or perhaps he was just tired and didn't want to move on again, didn't want to face a totally alien world, a totally alien language, and the inevitable poverty, which so often, particularly at first, comes wretchedly close to utter destitution. This exhaustion, which often went along with a reluctance to make a big fuss, to summon so much concentration just for the sake of this little bit of life, that was surely the greatest danger we all faced. And it was the death of our best friend in Paris, Walter Benjamin,[3] who committed suicide in October 1940 on the Spanish border with an American visa in his pocket. This atmosphere of sauve qui peut at the time was dreadful, and suicide was the only noble gesture, if you even cared enough to want to perish nobly. In our time you have to hate murder a lot to escape the seductive power of suicide.

What you wrote about "our" problem[4] moved me very much. Of course we're not fit for polite society—praise, glory, and hallelujah be to God for that. Here all the news about Jews is "front-page news," especially in New York, of course. But that doesn't make things significantly better, although it does make them somewhat better. I was very glad that you rejected your husband's "I am Germany."[5] (I hope he won't take my saying that amiss. For me, who didn't care to recall anything in Germany except him, I mean nothing truly alive, the temptation to see him as Germany was and is very real and very easy to yield to.) He is not Germany, it seems to me, if for no other reason than that it is much more to be a human being. Germany is no single person. It is either the German people, whatever their qualities may be, or it is a geographical-historical concept. And we certainly don't want to consign him to history yet. Those who come after us will have time and opportunity enough for that. But I don't know either how one can stand to live there as a Jew in a society that doesn't even deign to speak about "our" problem—and today that means our dead. Except that I know it would be good if one could.

I'm glad that the package business is working. Unfortunately I still don't have Joe Maier's new address, and I want it badly. Because I don't have it, I've sent all three of your packages for this month to Lasky. I don't like to send too much to the same address. Perhaps you have a soldier acquaintance nearby; that would be safer. We are very upset here about the constantly deteriorating food situation. I hope you will write and tell me whether I'm sending the right things or whether you need different ones now. I'll send packages again next week for Marianne Weber and Sternberger. Maier dutifully sends me all the letters he gets from Heidelberg. Perhaps you could ask Marianne Weber too to send me a list of what she would most like to have. I'm writing to Lasky and Maier by this same mail to tell them I need request letters for all three return addresses. Our post office is making things difficult for us.

I'm pleased every time I can get hold of Die Wandlung. Gurian[6] sent me the second issue. Now I'm waiting for the book about guilt, although I'm waiting even more for the one on truth. Has word of Broch's[7] *Tod des Vergil* reached you there? It is a great work, the greatest in German, I think, since Kafka's death. Broch has succeeded in uniting speculation so closely with his literary material that the speculation itself becomes plot, that is, a suspenseful plot, which is what it basically always is. I'm very fond of the book because, among other virtues, it has an inner affinity with the "Professor's" philosophy. And then, too, because it has restored my faith in the magnificence of the German language and in its vital possibilities for growth. Broch is a Jew—like Kafka, like Proust. We can no longer be struck out of the great, productive development of modern Western culture, not by murdering us and not even by the tawdry journalism we continue to spew out in excess, now as before. Broch told me that *Vergil* will be published in Switzerland. That no doubt means that you will have it soon in Germany—important for *Die Wandlung*, too. If you can't get it, I'll send it to you.

Need I tell you that I worry about your husband's health? And that I would be very grateful to you for a report on it? I hope life has become somewhat more peaceful. The busywork must be very painful—although it is never pure busywork and something of value remains, even when we hardly expect it to. This letter is, of course, meant for you both. I've addressed it only to you so that you don't both feel obliged to reply. (My God, how much I would like to come. We have the two little wings, made famous in song.[8] The only thing we're lacking is the necessary papers.)

Don't write if you don't have time. Or only very briefly.

With warmest wishes   Your

Hannah Arendt

40 *Karl Jaspers to Hannah Arendt*

Heidelberg, June 9, 1946

Dear Hannah Arendt!

Our kindly and worthy Josef Maier will take a letter along for you. I don't want to let the chance to send you a quick word slip by. I'll repeat in part what I've already written:

1) First and always, thank you! You can't know what encouragement your handclasp gives me—now in the form of this clear, true, and serious essay on existential philosophy.[1] When we opened your pack-

age, the first of two, and I found the *Partisan Review*, I ran right off to read it and left my wife alone. When I came back all fired up, she handed me the German text.[2]

The facts in the note on Heidegger[3] are not exactly correct. In regard to Husserl,[4] I *assume* that you're referring to the letter that every rector had to write to those excluded by the government. Heidegger's offer to continue teaching was *probably* not made with direct reference to "reeducation." But then, I don't really *know* how all that was. What you report is of course in substance true. However, the description of the actual process strikes me as not quite exact.

Thank you for your other writings: "Privileged Jews,"[5] "Imperialism, Nationalism, Chauvinism,"[6] for the "Andere Deutschland,"[7] and the essay by Fedotov[8] (all these are lying next to me and are as yet unread).

2) The commission for a book—as I wrote to you—pleases me immensely. Whether I can do it I can't promise with certainty; perhaps it won't be done until winter.

Die Schuldfrage will appear in two weeks. I hope I will be able to get a copy to you quickly then. If *this* book strikes you as worth translating, either whole or in part—I can't imagine it; it is directed too much at my German readers—then I'm giving you the translation rights here and now. No further inquiry is necessary. You are free to make whatever publishing arrangements you like. Any income deriving from this project is, of course, yours. This "just in case."

3) I'm giving Mr. Maier another copy of "Vom lebendigen Geist" —a lecture I gave in January when all I had was the English version of your "Organisierte Schuld" (for the printed version I was able at the last minute to correct my bad translation with the help of your original text, which had arrived in the meantime). When I was delivering this talk, a tear no one noticed came to my eye when I spoke of you, though without mentioning you by name. That is now a long, long time ago.

Mr. Maier is also taking along a copy of *Die Idee der Universität*.[9] This was written in April/May *1945*. The Americans were here. I hadn't been reactivated, but I was eager to see the university revived. This work strikes me now as almost old-fashioned. It calls up only the past, on which we stand. The manuscript lay idle for a year, and now it is appearing too late—the licenses and bureaucratic problems! With this too, you are free to have a section translated, just as outlined above. But in this case it will surely be out of the question.

4) The printing of *Allgemeine Psychopathologie* will soon be done (unfortunately about 800 big pages!)—Piper Verlag will have "Von der Wahrheit" in production soon.

Well, I've written only about myself! This is no letter. Mr. Maier is waiting in the next room.

Warmest greetings
Your Karl Jaspers

41   Karl Jaspers to Hannah Arendt

Heidelberg, June 27, 1946

Dear Hannah Arendt!

Yesterday your package arrived via friend Lasky—for the last time, because he is leaving—(one package, the two others will no doubt follow), the precious journals, among them your essays, and your letter to my wife. Thank you! My wife will write herself. I'll jump right to the main thing on my mind.

Both your manuscripts, which Sternberger received, were of great interest to us. "Imperialismus"[1] will appear in our eighth issue. We're having some problems with the other essay.[2] I'll write you what I said to Sternberger about it. My first reaction: We have to publish something like this. Why? To express in as clear a way as possible the *seriousness* of anti-Semitism. Finding that you feel this way is profoundly satisfying to me. We are not dealing with any trivial matter here. It is not a question of taste, not one of only secondary importance. "Let's put the Jewish question aside. . . ." "Let's not talk about the Jews all the time. . . ." "Let's not keep dwelling on these breaches of good taste. . . ." That's the kind of thing one heard all the time in 1933, and then the conversation moved on to what was really quite good about National Socialism, and so forth. Even Jews talked that way then. And, incomprehensible as it may seem, things are no different now. That this question is inextricably linked with the history of humankind, that clarity is essential here not only for its own sake but also for decision-making on all important political issues—all that you see and are able to express forcefully. But now for my reservations: You "exaggerate"—and even as I use this word I find it wrong, because you *don't* exaggerate in your overall picture but, for instance, in regard

44

to the *Protocols of the Wise Men*[3] as a source for Nazi policy, or so it seems to me. The authors of this bogus document are, of course, from the same mold as the fascists. The way you've stated your point, the reader who does not already agree with you will say: Nazi propaganda in reverse. He will quickly calm himself—with false arguments that you make easy for him—and we don't accomplish our purpose: conviction based on real insight. There are many brilliant, persuasive formulations and observations in your essay—quite apart from the passion, which is central to it. I don't know what to suggest to you. Would it be possible to articulate the connections more cautiously and therefore more powerfully—that is, to present them in a historically more correct and less visionary way? The vision, the genuine one, should perhaps be translated more into demonstrable terms. —The anti-Semitism of the past 2,000 years wasn't always fascistic. The *new* attitude to emerge should perhaps be that we do not instantly assume that today's anti-Semites all over the world are also fascists. We have to help these anti-Semites to understand themselves and to show them the danger that they would want to avoid themselves if they were aware of it. You know all this better than I, and you have stated it, but not clearly enough. You don't offer a bridge of understanding to the stupid and the narrow-minded. —I daresay the international aspect of anti-Semitism was not initially what it has become now. What was it in the Wars of Liberation? The international element in it was the appeal to Christianity. —I accept your vision. But what you are seeing is an altogether modern phenomenon, and as such it ought to be accurately delineated and its origins made clear. —Then, too, instead of the *Protocols*, one could take Dostoevski's *Demons*[4] and other things that Hitler learned from. He probably didn't *learn* from anything, but it lies in the nature of the matter that when something like this begins, the consequences follow automatically: —in the structure of the *Protocols*—in Dostoevski's imagination—in the reality of Hitler. — Wonderful: Disraeli[5] as the first who, out of Romanticism and vanity, thought in terms of racial theory and of Jewish secret societies, —and then the Jews' failure to take advantage of political opportunities! — But for all that I still have trouble with one thing: "the Jews"—*no* statement applies to them all, except in external matters. Some limits have to be put on thinking in collectives, and that applies to us, too. —"Germany's sacrifice to the fascistic international"—in this vision, too, there is much that is correct, but at the same time it is a vast "exaggeration." You lean toward Hegelian thinking. Your principle of interpretation is a "stratagem of reason"—or, rather, of the devil. —Valera[6] and Salazar[7]: new to me, truly astonishing. I don't understand. But are you right? It *still* strikes me as fantastic. —Brilliant and true: the transposition of lies into reality! —These are just a few notes. I'm afraid that you won't want to attempt something that may not work out.

In the Nazi years I occasionally said to my wife, "I am Germany," to help us both hang onto our common ground. A statement like that is meaningful only in its context. Taken out of that context or even passed on to someone else, it becomes intolerably arrogant. You are, of course, absolutely right. It is meaningless politically. My wife and I were in agreement even when she rejected the statement. I am not German in any crucially different way from the way she is German. We mustn't let Hitler suggest anything to us. Now that Germany is destroyed—in a sense and to a degree and in a finality that hardly anyone here has really grasped—I feel at ease as a German for the first time (when I gave my Max Weber book the subtitle "The German Character . . ."[8] I had to overcome internal resistance, and did it in the situation of that time). In what sense we are Germans—and it is in no absolute sense—I would like to be able to articulate. That is the book[9] I will send you for America, if I can manage to write it.

Die Schuldfrage will come out next week. I hope I'll soon be able to find a way to send it to you. A translation is supposed to appear in England with either Drummond or Gollancz. My representative, Mr. Schimansky, told me that the translation rights apply only to England and don't affect what happens in America at all. I hope very much that he is right. If not, then I will have to annul the arrangements. I haven't signed a contract yet. The same problem will come up in the future. Mr. Schimansky wants to publish philosophical books of mine with Bless (or something like that) in London. What *you* can or want to do for me, however, has absolute precedence.

6/29 Lasky has just brought me a letter from Mr. Phillips. I am writing to him that you—Hannah Arendt—have legal power over *all* my work. The first copies of my *Schuldfrage* arrived today. I'll try to get copies to you and Mr. Phillips right away through Lasky.

I beg your pardon for this weary and wandering letter. But I guess it is still better than no letter at all.

A visit from you—it would be like a fairy tale—one of these days it will happen! The thought makes me happy but sad as well. How very disappointed you will be!—"Aus der Jugendzeit . . ." Rückert's poem[10] is so true.

Warmest greetings
Your Karl Jaspers

42   Hannah Arendt to Karl Jaspers

July 9, 1946

Lieber Verehrtester [Dear esteemed one]—

On the very evening before I left on vacation Joe Maier visited us —and brought your good letter and the two brochures (about which soon) and the two pictures of your wife, which, although they evoked the past so strongly for me, I gave back to him because they were meant for her nieces. And there were three completely wobbly little snapshots of you, in which—despite all wobbliness—you are fully present. And then of course he told us all the news in his naïve, innocent way, and we celebrated the event properly with whiskey and wine, in which I, very conveniently, could drown my sorrow and anger over the fact that it was he and not I who had been in Heidelberg.

First, to your letter. I was so relieved by what you said about the *PR* article.[1] For a variety of reasons but also—apropos of your "not having pupils"—because, even today and after all these years, our students' fear of being a "pupil" is still so much in my bones or, more accurately, in my memory that I'm reluctant to give you anything to read that ultimately and in its subject matter derives from you. We were thoroughly convinced in those days that you would say of any "pupil" that he hadn't understood anything at all.

Regarding the Heidegger note, your assumption about the Husserl letter is completely correct. I knew that this letter was a circular, and I know that many people have excused it for that reason. It always seemed to me that at the moment Heidegger was obliged to put his name to this document, he should have resigned. However foolish he may have been, he was capable of understanding that. We can hold him responsible for his actions to that extent. He knew very well that that letter would have left Husserl more or less indifferent if someone else had signed it. Now you might say that this happened in the rush of business. And I would probably reply that the truly irreparable things often—and deceptively—happen almost like accidents, that sometimes from an insignificant line that we step across easily, feeling certain that it is of no consequence anymore, that wall rises up that truly divides people. In other words, although I never had any professional or personal attachment to old Husserl, I mean to maintain solidarity with him in this one case. And because I know that this letter and this signature almost killed him, I can't but regard Heidegger as a potential murderer. I shouldn't have written that business about the "reeducation," although I learned it here on good authority. Sartre[2] told me later that four weeks (or six weeks) after Germany's defeat, Heidegger wrote to a professor at the Sorbonne (I've forgotten his name), talked about a "misunderstanding" between Germany and France, and offered his hand in German-French "reconciliation." He received no reply, of course. Then, later, he wrote to Sartre. You'll be familiar with the various interviews he gave after that. Nothing but inane lies with what I think is a clearly pathological streak. But that's an old story.

Forgive me for dwelling so long on this dismal and upsetting story. What I really wanted to get to right away was *Die Idee der Universität* and *Vom lebendigen Geist*. I read them both twice right away and was delighted with them. The first chapters of the *Universität* should be published here no matter what. The writing in them is particularly beautiful and powerful. And on top of that, there is a kind of "scholarly crisis" among intellectuals here, and since they don't know anything but Dewey, they don't know where to turn next. Heavy of heart, because I'm reluctant to let it out of my hands, I'll send my copy to Eric Bentley at *The Kenyon Review* (an excellent university publication). He also has connections at Reynal and Hitchcock and will be able to tell me if there's any chance of publishing the whole thing. And while I'm on this subject: Thanks very much for the "translation rights." But I'm nervous about them. I'm out of the question as a translator. Bentley is a possibility. He is an Englishman, is married to a German Jew, knows German very well and is used to translating; and, most important of all, he has the requisite background and education (a very rare thing here). May I make a suggestion? It might be helpful if you would indicate in your dealings with publishers that they should show me the translation manuscript the way one ordinarily would show it to the author. The reason why I can't do the translations myself is that one can really translate only into one's native language and shouldn't attempt it with others. Writing English is linguistically much easier than translating. Dial Press, which is very interested in the Schuld manuscript, should have written to you by way of Lasky. I hope the letter reached Lasky before he left.

There are a few practical points in the *Universität* book on which I don't quite agree with you. Because none of them are crucial, I'll just list them here: I'm afraid, from a political point of view, that the freedom to express one's opinion is the basis for freedom in teaching today. That could only not be so if one held a dogmatic concept of the truth. Although truth may well be the exact opposite of opinion, truth is nonetheless obliged politically, in every democracy, to go about in the guise of opinion. In other words, the body politic cannot and ought not decide what truth is, and the only way it has to protect the freedom to speak the truth is to protect the freedom to speak one's opinion. That brings me to the relationship between the state and the university. Because somebody has to pay for the whole show, the state clearly remains the best donor of money. It would be good, though no doubt difficult to bring about in Germany, if the professors would not, despite this, see themselves as civil servants. A dictatorial regime will "bring the universities into line" anyhow, whether they are financed by the state or not. There is no way to insure against that, because there is no such thing as unpolitical insurance against politics. To be perfectly honest, your suggestion of supplementary foundations makes me wary, and it is my experience in this country that makes me so. Unfortunately the Maecenas, who really isn't a Maecenas anymore, is not satisfied with honors alone. I wouldn't fret over the honorary doctorate. In this country at least, the donors to universities want to control them so that their sons and grandsons and great-grandsons will get the kind of education they think proper for them. And whatever you may, in theory, imagine the "ideas" of a cigarette manufacturer to be, he'll manage to outdo your wildest imaginings. The resistance of the professors, who are badly paid to begin with (and intentionally so, to show them what their place is), against the terror of the trustees and the president is not exactly overwhelming, to put it mildly. Then it seems to me, too, that on the practical level the question of fellowships will be the crucial one in present-day Germany, not because I think that too few people are able to find the money they need for university studies, but because I'm afraid that lack of money may be preventing the right people from studying. The Scholarship Foundation[3] was an excellent institution. I don't know how much of the university budget the students' tuition covers. You'll recall that at the Ecole Normale[4] no one *is permitted* to pay, neither tuition nor, if he lives in the dormitory, room and board. Because of that, scholarships do not have the onus of charity attached to them. The same applies, I think, to the question of support for privatdocents. It's much better to give them all a modest living (and by that I don't mean starvation wages), even those who don't need it, than to put up with the stigma of charity and everything that goes along with it, like proof of need, inquiry into family finances, etc. That just poisons the atmosphere and takes the starch out of people. It's wonderful how aware you are of the failings everywhere. They are indeed immensely important.

It is almost a struggle for me to write about your lecture.[5] Your thoughts had a powerful effect on me and at the same time made me so happy that it seems to me I have no business adding anything. But if I then go ahead and say something anyhow—[I admire] this wonderful balance between pure flight and a firm grasp on reality. Everything in the area of the real and practical in *Universitätsidee* that struck me as questionable is as if blown away. Then there's the assimilation of technology—my God, how right you are about that. What it all comes down to is that we're trying for the first time and in all seriousness to turn the universum into the mundus, if I may go back to old Augustine once again. Whether this lecture can find a publisher here I can't say. For Germany, it is surely more important than *Die Idee der Universität*, for the moment anyhow. But the crucial general points are also in *Die Idee der Universität* and in more detailed form there, and the lecture will not be readily understood here where people are still living in an undamaged body politic. They won't understand why the university, of all institutions, is supposedly so important— and you are absolutely right: It is the only thing Germany has left. It is even a political factor today.

That is the very reason why it is so bad that the universities "lost their dignity"[6] in 1933. I don't know how one should go about rehabilitating their reputation, for they made themselves ridiculous. Denazification, important as it may be, is, after all, only a word, because the institution itself—worse yet the standing of the scholar—has become ridiculous. The key point here isn't that professors didn't become heroes. It's their humorlessness, their obsequiousness, their fear of missing the boat. I always think of what I hope is an apocryphal story about Regenbogen[7] translating the Horst Wessel[8] song into Greek. Now I know that many of them, probably even the majority, were never Nazis in earnest. But one begins to wonder even about that when one sees what, for example, the Freiburg historian Gerhard Ritter[9] has to say on the subject. He had an article in *Die Gegenwart* that was, unfortunately, reprinted here.

I'm very much looking forward to the enlarged version of your *Psychopathologie*. It is really amazing how productive these years were for you.

This letter has grown unreasonably long. I want to add quickly, though, that I've taken a job with Schocken publishers. I took the other job only with hopes of getting a quick trip to Europe out of it. This new job could, under the right circumstances, turn out to be a lot of fun, that is, if I can manage to get along with the very imperious boss,[10] Bismarck personified, so to speak.

I hope this letter will not find you at home. Joe Maier mentioned a trip to Switzerland. I wish you the very best for it, above all, a good rest. Good-bye for now, be well, and accept my warmest regards

As always, your,

Hannah Arendt

P.S. The packages: I received the new address at the very last minute. The June packages still went to Lasky. July: as always, three for you and one for Marianne Weber. And in addition a CARE package by regular mail. There was some Normacol in a June package. I'll send more in August. Dear Gertrud Jaspers, if this letter had not grown so dreadfully long, I would try to write something to you about the Palestine situation so that you wouldn't be downcast by my articles, which have a specific political meaning for a specific moment in our political situation. I save that for another time. With warmest greetings

H. A.

---

43   *Hannah Arendt to Karl Jaspers*

August 17, 1946

Lieber Verehrtester—

Let me begin with business matters: Two copies of the *Schuld* brochure have arrived, and Phillips has received a copy too, which he immediately handed over to Dial Press. After my return, I went to Dial Press and talked with Sidney Phillips there. The upshot was as follows: Dial is very much interested in the book, although it does not anticipate a very large printing. The problem is that the publishing of books printed in Germany comes under the law against business dealings with hostile countries, and Dial needs approval from the State Department to print the book. Dial has applied for it but hasn't received a reply. Such an approval hasn't yet been granted in a single case (the reason is bureaucratic red tape and inertia; it's easier to say no than to initiate an inquiry). But Dial thinks it will get permission in your case because it can support its application with an American license number. A much more difficult problem is this: All income from the book will automatically go to the administrator of enemy property, i.e., the U.S. Treasury Department. I've talked to a lawyer about this, and I assume that Dial will also consult with its legal adviser. I suggested writing into the contract that the publisher will begin making payments only after, say, one or two years. Then we can at least go on the hope that these regulations will be lifted in that time. Another possibility might be for you to give away your rights. The recipient would then have to apply for a license in order to accept the gift. Presumably a license would be granted to your relatives living here. I assume that it's not important to you to have the money paid out to you in Germany. It's not totally impossible that we could obtain a license for such a transfer. It would be good perhaps for further negotiations, which will take place once the State Department has given permission for printing, if you could tell me how you've solved these problems in England. That your English representative has the rights for England only is correct—unless you have explicitly granted him American rights as well. —During my talk with Dial Press it became clear that Dial is extremely interested in your *Psychopathologie*. But, to my annoyance, not at all in pure philosophy. In concluding this discussion I have to stress that I really have no business head at all (and that is an understatement). You probably know that well enough. William Phillips and Clement Greenberg, both good friends of mine and both more or less officially involved with Dial, swear up and down that a publisher of that size simply can't afford to deceive you or me.

I haven't written for so long because I've been turning your *Schuldfrage* over and over again in my mind and having repeated detailed discussions of it with Monsieur [Heinrich Blücher]. What follows should therefore be written in the first person plural, though it somehow goes against my grain. Well, then, "we" are very much in agreement with you in all the major points and very thankful not only for the clarification but also for the implicit explanation of a psychological situation that is very difficult to picture to oneself from a distance. In agreement, but with limitations and additions. Monsieur, even more

52

than I, insists that assuming responsibility has to consist of more than an acceptance of defeat and of the consequences following on that. He has been saying for a long time now that such an assumption of responsibility, which is a precondition for the continuing existence of the German people (not of the nation), has to be accompanied by a positive political statement of intentions addressed to the victims. That obviously does not mean that anyone should attempt to make good what cannot be made good, but, rather, that one could say to displaced persons,[1] for example: We understand very well that you want to leave here and go to Palestine, but, quite apart from that, you should know that you have every right of citizenship here, that you can count on our total support. Mindful of what Germans have inflicted on the Jewish people, we will, in a future German republic, constitutionally renounce anti-Semitism, stipulating, for example, that any Jew, regardless of where he is born, can become a citizen of this republic, enjoying all rights of citizenship, solely on the basis of his Jewish nationality and without ceasing to be a Jew. (That it would be almost impossible to translate such ideas into reality in Germany today is clear.) I read with horror the Stuttgart Länderrat's suggestions for reparations, which are considerably less liberal than comparable suggestions made by most other European countries. Poverty can't be used to excuse this. The spirit in which this document was written becomes utterly clear in the paragraphs dealing with state support for the education of children whose fathers died in concentration camps. This act of simple justice is based on the argument that one can reasonably expect that these children will have inherited strong character and the strength of their convictions. In other words: The Nazi division between German superhumans and Jewish less-than-humans has made inhuman monsters out of both. We Germans won't escape from this inhuman situation until we try to help you escape yours. The most important practical step in this direction would be to close down all the camps. I'd like to note here that for us Jews the closing down of the concentration camps (or internment camps) is the most important political demand of all. It's clear that it is a question of basic existence. It would not be insignificant for us if the Germans would make some kind of declaration of goodwill, for the simple reason that everything that's happening now—that is, the migration from German DP camps to the Palestinian Atlit Camp[2] and to the concentration camps on Cyprus[3]—is possible only because the whole world sees it as "humane" in comparison to Auschwitz. Apart from all the speeches and declarations, one consequence of the death camps is that Jews are regarded a priori, so to speak, as potential inhabitants of concentration camps.

Now, for myself, I have these additional things to say: Your definition of Nazi policy as a crime ("criminal guilt"[4]) strikes me as questionable. The Nazi crimes, it seems to me, explode the limits of the law; and that is precisely what constitutes their monstrousness. For these crimes, no punishment is severe enough. It may well be essential to hang Göring, but it is totally inadequate. That is, this guilt, in contrast to all criminal guilt, oversteps and shatters any and all legal systems. That is the reason why the Nazis in Nuremberg are so smug.[5] They know that, of course. And just as inhuman as their guilt is the innocence of the victims. Human beings simply can't be as innocent as they all were in the face of the gas chambers (the most repulsive usurer was as innocent as the newborn child because no crime deserves such a punishment). We are simply not equipped to deal, on a human, political level, with a guilt that is beyond crime and an innocence that is beyond goodness or virtue. This is the abyss that opened up before us as early as 1933 (much earlier, actually, with the onset of imperialistic politics) and into which we have finally stumbled. I don't know how we will ever get out of it, for the Germans are burdened now with thousands or tens of thousands or hundreds of thousands of people who cannot be adequately punished within the legal system; and we Jews are burdened with millions of innocents, by reason of which every Jew alive today can see himself as innocence personified. On the other hand, it seems to me that what you call metaphysical guilt[6] encompasses not only the "absolute," where indeed no earthly judge can be recognized anymore, but also that solidarity which is the political basis of the republic (and which Clemenceau expressed in the words, "L'Affaire d'un seul est l'affaire de tous").

You realize that these are all only marginalia, so to speak. I was especially taken with your view of the Nuremberg trial. I was so pleased by it, because it always seemed to me that particularly in the Germany of today these things are bound to be nearly incomprehensible.

I've received two copies of Number 5/6 of *Die Wandlung* but none of the previous issues, except the first. This issue is excellent and very lively. First of all your "Thesen über politische Freiheit"[7]—absolutely wonderful. I'd like to publish them here as an introduction to *Die Schuldfrage* to save them from being scattered and lost in a magazine. Truly fine. I'm very pleased with the report on and evaluation of the 20th of July.[8] I'm in complete agreement too with your notes on biblical religion.[9] Paul Herzog's report[10] was very useful—the best thing I've read on this subject to date. I'm trying right now to convince Dwight Macdonald to print it. Always a bit difficult, because he doesn't read a word of German.

Now to your letter about my exaggerations. It's the nicest letter I've ever had from you, and it made me simply ecstatic. Of course I feel altogether like the farmer with the biggest potatoes, because it was really stupid of me to send you the piece at all. You're absolutely right: as it stands now, you cannot and should not print it. Something like that should only appear in a larger context anyhow. Here I could print it because, first, it appeared in a Jewish journal and because, second, I wrote it right after the German surrender as a warning, so to speak. I'll save anti-Semitism for another time. I distinguish in modern times between two kinds of anti-Semitism. First comes anti-Semitism in the nation-state (beginning with the Wars of Liberation in Germany, ending with the Dreyfus affair[11] in France), which came about because the Jews emerged as a group particularly useful to the state and receiving special protection from it. As a consequence of that, every group in the population that came into conflict with the state became anti-Semitic. Then comes the anti-Semitism of the imperial age (which began in the 1880s). This latter form was, from the outset, international in its organization. As far as the two-thousand-year-old history of hatred for the Jews is concerned, it rests primarily on the claim of the Jewish people to be the chosen people. This history—like all Jewish history—has unfortunately been so falsified, with a few major exceptions, being presented by the Jewish side as the history of an eternally persecuted people and by the anti-Semitic side as the history of the devil, that we somehow have to revise everything in it. In view of all that, it makes no sense just to revise the article. For *Die Wandlung* it should be completely rewritten and made longer and better. As soon as I have a little time, I'll do it.

I hardly need explain why your letter was such a great delight to me. Intellectually I live here only with Monsieur; that is, we're the only people we know who speak the same language. (He didn't know, N.B., that I had sent the article, and he was incensed by such vast stupidity.) But now, when you debate me like this, coming from outside, as it were, it seems as if I had solid ground under my feet, as if I were back in the world again.

I hope this letter will reach you before your trip to Switzerland.[12] I hope you'll get some rest. I hope you'll have a good time. Sartre speaks German well; Camus[13] is fluent. Jean Wahl,[14] who wrote me that he is going to Geneva, too, speaks and understands less well than one thinks he does. Camus is probably not as talented as Sartre but much more important, because he is much more serious and honest. Jean Wahl is a nice person but a bit dumb. You probably know that Waelhens[15] is writing a book about you. With the next packages I'll send a Mexican journal with an essay by Waelhens about you[16]—written in French.

I'm not altogether happy about the reactions to my guilt article. I'm getting letters from Germany—these people all feel so well "understood," and none seem to have picked up my bias against the "philistine." On top of that, the wretched *Hessische Nachrichten* has declared that I am "Germany in the finest sense." All I can say to that is "And what the fates can do to you / Is all too clear to see."

Your remark "Now that Germany is destroyed I feel at ease as a German for the first time" I found devastating. In part because my husband said the same thing in almost exactly the same words a year ago.

Good-bye, be well, get some rest, take good care of yourself, and accept the warmest greetings from

Your
Hannah Arendt

44 Karl Jaspers to Hannah Arendt

Zurich, September 18 1946

Dear Hannah Arendt!

You are constantly with us in spirit as one of our orientation points in this chaotic world, but that sounds false, for it is you yourself, your existence that is such a blessing. I felt that all the more strongly in Geneva, where I, along with others in a gathering of Europeans, gave a talk[1] and took part in discussions. It was like a dream to be in bodily contact with the intellectual world again. Our time there was a great joy for us, for my wife and me, for her brother, Ernst Mayer,[2] and Paul Gottschalk.[3] They all came to see us again. Intellectually the whole business was, unfortunately, rather questionable and, when you get right down to it, conventional. A few young men from the French resistance movement made a profound impression on me: direct, thoughtful, serious, modest. You could believe them. I was told that they are not typical, but the exceptions. What struck me about them was their simplicity: their humanity, their willingness to risk their lives for it—and their independence. Stephen Spender[4] was there from England, a youth like Gundolf, only more realistic and of course without a master and without dogma.[5] I think I established the beginnings of a relationship with him. The theme was the European spirit. And some of the speakers developed something resembling a European nationalism. But all the reasonable people had the world in mind. Bernanos[6] produced an accusatory litany worthy of Abraham a Sancta Clara.[7] J. Benda[8] was the eternal rationalist, a clever and naïve descendant of the nineteenth century. I received applause amounting to an ovation, but I doubt that anyone understood what I'd said. In spite of everything, I felt as if I'd been set back fifty years into a world that, oddly enough, knows about the catastrophes of the recent wars and is talking about them. My wife and I could not resist the temptation to enjoy the beauty of Geneva, the city and the landscape, to see Mont Blanc with the eyes of the eighteenth century, the big fountain near the harbor, the lovely parks and opulent buildings. The palace of the League of Nations, immense and dead. —Jean Wahl was there. I met him for the first time. He said very little. A likable, well-meaning man. —I spoke only German. A newspaper remarked that through me the German language had regained its place in the world. —But enough of all this. You can imagine what this entrée into the world meant for us after ten years. It would be ungrateful of me to be dissatisfied.[9]

So you're working at Schocken now. Please do tell me about it—and how you manage to get along with the "imperious boss."

A few practical matters:

In granting translation rights to you I did *not* mean to suggest that I expected you to do any translating; *only* that you should have the power to arrange for translations. The reason: I hope they will generate some occasional income to compensate you for the valuable packages. I am not permitted to make any contracts at all myself—and if I did, then all the money would wind up in the reparations till. That's why you alone, as present owner of the translation rights, have to receive the fees.

I wanted to publish in *Die Wandlung* the essay on existential philosophy that you wrote for *Partisan Review*,[10] the German original of which you sent to me. The entire editorial staff and the publisher were against it: too difficult for our readership! (Please keep this to yourself.) But L. Schneider,[11] a first-rate publisher, wanted to publish your essay as a separate brochure for the German reading public interested in philosophy. He was going to write you about this. This was all several months ago. I haven't heard anything further, and I'm not doing anything more about it myself, but I wanted you to know about it. —Your excellent essay on imperialism will appear in the next issue.[12] Sternberger is justifiably saddened about the increased impediments to postal traffic with you in America. Your essays, which he and we were hoping to receive, will not reach us for the time being. I presume that a long letter—as difficult to read as this one—about your second essay, the one on the Jewish people, never reached you?[13] It was written several months ago.

I always have to beg your pardon, and not only because of my poor handwriting. I am in rather poor shape physically. My heart is weak and often affects my general state of health adversely, so that I spend most of my time lying down. But on days when I have to lecture, my façade is so good for that one hour that everybody thinks I'm a robust fellow.

On Sunday, September 22, we hope to return to Heidelberg by car. I want to continue my lectures on Germany.[14] In the spring, the lack of trust I felt from my audiences robbed me of my courage, and so in the summer I limited myself to a purely philosophical lecture on timeless subjects.[15] But I wasn't satisfied with that either. I have to try again. Philosophy has to be concrete and practical, without forgetting its origins for a minute. Yet my intellectual possibilities are so limited, my knowledge so lacking. I tell myself it's always better to do what you can than to do nothing at all. I have to become more indifferent to the masses. In any case, whatever of importance comes out of Germany now can originate only with individuals and small groups. Chaos grows.

It is difficult for me to speak when I see hostile faces. I need from my audience, as a minimum, a willing suspension of distrust. Never before 1937 did I experience so little of a kindly attitude toward me in the auditorium as I do now. Publicly I'm left in peace. But behind my back people slander me: the Communists call me a forward guard of National Socialism; the sullen losers, a traitor to my country. When this kind of thing has been said to my face, I've been able to put out the fires so far with a mild and persuasive response. This is what happened when I received a long "open letter" from a newspaper editor. He wanted to publish this letter right away with a response from me. When he received my reply, he gave up the project "in the interest of our shared cause." You would be amazed if you could read such an exchange of letters. We live in an atmosphere of slander. If a weak point is in fact found, then you are lost. That too is part of the current state of affairs in which, in spite of everything, I hope something vital can flourish. When I go to my seminar,[16] I can still believe in that positive possibility. We recently heard a superb report on the "idea" in Plato and in Hegel, totally abstract, followed by a discussion that was as alive and intense as if we were dealing with the most current of problems. These few excellent young people have no interest at all in politics, only scorn and mistrust; but despite that they are extremely well informed, as you find out when you talk with them.

I hold you in the warmest regard and join my wife in sending greetings

Your Karl Jaspers

45 *Hannah Arendt to Gertrud Jaspers*

New York, October 5, 46

Dear Gertrud Jaspers—

I hope your trip home was pleasant and that you are well. I met your niece[1] here, so I know that the trip was indeed a good one. Then too, *Time* magazine[2] reported the conference and quoted Jaspers. Did any real communication take place? I saw that Bernanos was there. He is an important person—no great writer but a very great journalist. Do you know *Les grandes cimetières sous la lune?*[3] About Spanish fascism. Certainly the most impressive book I know on this subject. He often runs off at the mouth but has a very big and genuine personality. He's really an orator. His *Lettre aux Anglais*,[4] written during the war, is important too. A lot of political instinct without a precise grasp of things. I mention this only in case you have some time and interest in a good book, and if you read French easily.

My main reason for writing today is to get clear on our package accounting. I'm assuming that the three packages you mentioned in your August letter[5] were the July packages. Four packages were sent in August (one with the medicine in it; I've forgotten the name momentarily); then three packages in September and, yesterday, three packages for October, too. In addition, I ordered two CARE packages, which should also arrive at some point. I sent Marianne Weber one package in July in care of you and one in September, with flour in it, directly to her. I assume she's getting packages now from other people, too. If that's not the case, let me know.

I've just read through your letter again. I can't recall for the life of me anymore what it was I called "suicidal." I hope it wasn't important and didn't cause any serious dismay.

I'm sorry to say I still haven't any word from Dial Press, because the reply from the State Department hasn't come yet. In the meantime, magazines too have, senselessly, become afraid of printing things without a permit. When will we ever have "normal" conditions again? It is even more annoying now, because there's really no good reason for it.

I *never* get *Die Wandlung*. That is, of course, another exaggeration. I have the first issue and Number 5/6. Joe Maier has Number 8 and will lend it to me. I haven't even read the prepublication excerpt from the book yet, but will get it one of these days now.

Your niece is charming. She passed on the lobster secret to me. You see, if I don't get the information I need directly, I get it the roundabout way.

The publishing job is both a lot of work and a lot of fun. At the moment, I'm working much less than I did last winter, and I'm enjoying a little laziness.

I hope the trip to Switzerland brought a little rest and relaxation. For you, it must have. I can well imagine what it must mean not to have to think about food for a few weeks. How nice that things worked out with your brother. And how, just how did the world look to you?

With warmest greetings to you both

Your

Hannah Arendt

46 Karl Jaspers to Hannah Arendt

Heidelberg, October 19, 1946

Dear Hannah Arendt!

I have so very much to write to you. I'd like to talk with you for hours, for days on end. Your letters, your essays lift my spirits to a degree that you can hardly imagine. We are all so lonely, deliver our monologues, are "successful," and everything sinks, like stones that are tossed into the mud. In you I finally hear someone speaking whose seriousness is beyond any doubt, someone who, I feel, values the same things I do. The only difference is that you strike me as braver than I am.

I want to deal with practical matters before I speak further. Your letter of October 5 to my wife just arrived. The four August packages have arrived; the September packages will probably come soon (the August packages came at the end of September). The two CARE packages have not yet arrived. But according to the newspaper reports, there is no problem with them. We will have to be patient. My wife will write you. I thank you. We receive quite a few other packages, but only regularly from you, and in such grand style that we are living as in peacetime and are much healthier than we were a year ago.

I wrote to you from Geneva in mid-September.[1] My gift of the translation rights, the intention of which I explained in that letter (I had never meant that you should do any translating yourself; that is of course impossible), you will find repeated on the enclosed sheet of paper.

10/23. At this point I was interrupted by a visit from my sister from Oldenburg, the first after three and a half years. Now I'll pick up where I left off. In the meantime, my lectures have begun; today I had office hours. But even if nothing reasonable comes of this, I want at least to have written to you. —I am pleased that Lambert Schneider wants to publish a book of your essays,[2] both the ones that have and have not appeared in *Die Wandlung*. That will make an essay volume of real stature in the intellectually thin, though already massive, German literary production. —My *Psychopathologie*[3] has been published—750 pages—the publisher (Springer) and I own the translation rights 50-50. If the possibility of translation should really loom, the publisher will, unfortunately, have to be consulted. Now I'll have to see whether and how I can get a copy to you. The book is not stylistically polished. I have, as it were, retrogressed to my youth and written again with the naïveté and lack of inhibition, also with the tediousness, of a medical man. —Hoops[4] (the English literature man here, whom you no doubt recall) came to me today and told me about an American professor who would like to translate my *Idee der Universität*. He was here when I was in Switzerland. I asked Hoops to refer him to you. You decide what you think best. This presumes that you are willing to accept the gift of the translation rights. Hoops will write to this professor that you have full authority over the rights. He is Dean Dr. Earl James McGrath, 108 Schaeffer Hall, University of

Iowa, Iowa City, Iowa. —You needn't do anything but wait and see if he writes to you. Arrangements like this always strike me as vague and insubstantial. —I've told Sternberger repeatedly that you haven't received most of the issues of *Die Wandlung*. The mailings were returned. We have to try some other way.

Your critical remarks have deeply influenced my thinking, especially your demand for a positive, political declaration of intentions directed to the victims.[5] The fact that I agree with you *completely* makes me all the more uneasy, for at the same time I sense the impossibility of this in Germany today, and I therefore feel disconsolate about the future of the Germans if we can't even expect agreement to a declaration of this kind. The possible moments for such a declaration have not all been passed by yet. Your idea is implanted in me; I won't forget it.

I'm not in such strong agreement with you on the two other critical remarks you made about *Die Schuldfrage*. You say that what the Nazis did cannot be comprehended as "crime"—I'm not altogether comfortable with your view, because a guilt that goes beyond all criminal guilt inevitably takes on a streak of "greatness"—of satanic greatness—which is, for me, as inappropriate for the Nazis as all the talk about the "demonic" element in Hitler and so forth. It seems to me that we have to see these things in their total banality,[6] in their prosaic triviality, because that's what truly characterizes them. Bacteria can cause epidemics that wipe out nations, but they remain merely bacteria. I regard any hint of myth and legend with horror, and everything unspecific is just such a hint. My more sober outlook is hardly widespread in Germany. Many people make a great thing of it that Göring managed to escape the gallows, when nothing but the sheer incompetence of the prison staff was responsible. Your view is appealing—especially as contrasted with what I see as the false inhuman innocence of the victims. But all this would have to be expressed differently (how, I don't know yet). The way you do express it, you've almost taken the path of poetry. And a Shakespeare would never be able to give adequate form to this material—his instinctive aesthetic sense would lead to falsification of it—and that's why he couldn't attempt it. There is no idea and no essence here. Nazi crime is properly a subject for psychology and sociology, for psychopathology and jurisprudence only.

Then there's "solidarity." What you mean presumably has nothing to do with the subject of metaphysical guilt. The demand of political solidarity can be valid only where one can depend on the cooperation

62

of a majority of the population. It showed up often in Italy under fascism. In Germany it simply doesn't exist and cannot be directly called upon. It evolves only out of the sum of lives lived together.

I find all your critical comments on my *Idee der Universität*[7] correct.

I share your judgment of Heidegger[8]—alas. My earlier remarks[9] referred only to the correctness of the facts as you presented them. —

Something I forgot: Final arrangements for the translation of my *Schuldfrage* in England have not been made yet. Because I haven't heard anything for a long time, I'm expecting difficulties of the kind you've encountered. Gollancz,[10] who is going to publish the volume, may visit me. Then I'll learn the details. Until now, I've spoken only with a Mr. Schimansky, who has acted as a representative so far. I'll let you know as soon as I hear anything. I've given the translation rights for *Die Schuldfrage* in England to my brother-in-law Gustav Mayer.[11]

When I think that you will have to read my almost illegible hand and will feel frustrated to the point of anger with it, then I send my letters off with some reluctance.

Would you give your husband my regards? I am grateful to him for the part he took in your criticism.

Aren't you, too, as Heine was, according to your characterization,[12] both a Jew *and* a German? For me you are, unavoidably, but whether you want to be is another question. Or whether you deny it, as my wife does?

I haven't told you anything about Switzerland today. It was immensely important for us: seeing our relatives—the realization of a dream—experiencing the world—being spoken to. Many people understood German. I had an interpreter [Jeanne Hersch] who beautifully translated everything I said into French. I was "a success," the only German there. At the end of my lecture I received the next thing to an ovation—but I still felt at a distance. We, too, are not at home anywhere today.

With warmest greetings
Your Karl Jaspers

(Enclosure)   Heidelberg, October 25, 1946
Dear Hannah Arendt!

Because you are a former student of mine who earned her doctorate with me twenty years ago in Heidelberg and who has remained a loyal friend to me through all these years, I hereby give to you as the person nearest to me the translation rights to all my works for the English language in America, to the extent that I possess said rights. I do this in the hope of expressing my thanks to you in a symbol both intellectual and material. This gift is valid for your lifetime.

With warmest greetings as always
Your Karl Jaspers

47 *Hannah Arendt to Karl Jaspers*

November 11, 1946

Lieber Verehrtester—

Your letter from Zurich sounded so lively, and then I heard you were sick again.[1] (Please allow me to worry a little. I have worried for many years anyhow, that is, without your permission; actually, ever since you told me about your illness[2] I don't know how many years ago.) I'm troubled too by what you write about your lecture and even, in another way, by your positive remarks about your seminar. The enmity of the masses—we hear that over and over again in all the letters we get from Germany. And I don't honestly believe that this animosity toward reason can be explained solely by hunger and poverty. What frightens me about your gratifying seminar students is that they, like us in our time—of unblessed memory—are not interested in politics.[3] This lack of interest is part of an overall picture. It is also a false elitism, and behind it lurks impenitence, even if in a more complicated form. What I mean to come to with all this is simply a question—one I've been holding back for a long time—and that is: whether you wouldn't be better off going to Switzerland. Lasky wrote me something about a call. And then I'm just plain afraid for you.

What you had to say about the French of the Resistance made me very happy. Yes, I know, there are still some genuine human beings around; they represent a pitifully small minority, of course, but they are there, and the important thing is that they're still ready to fight and risk their lives. We are, unfortunately, only used to our enemies being ready to risk their lives. And they do so not out of heroism but because a certain modern type will gladly run the risk of being murdered as long as he gets a chance to be a murderer himself. It isn't any great feat to be a "hero" if you hate life.

I don't know Stephen Spender and have read only a little of him. I want to catch up on him now. Bernanos's great eloquence can't help us anymore; he has a great gift for saying in an accusatory way what is. I don't like Benda at all. I don't believe in his "naïveté." I read an article in *Die Weltwoche*[4] about you. There was a nice photo too, but I like the one your wife sent me better. *Time* magazine[5] had a short report on the conference that said how much in the center of things you were. That was both somewhat funny (because *Time* is what it is) and nice.

Dial Press has learned from the State Department that the proscription against German books will be lifted in a few weeks. Now they have asked me to ask both you and the publisher of *Die Schuldfrage* to give them or me the rights or your agreement. All I have from you is passages in letters, and they want a separate letter for their files and presumably for the authorities as well. Then, too, *Commentary* has presumably already written to you to ask for the speech you gave in Geneva. That is a new Jewish journal that is very lively and widely read and to which John Dewey, among others, contributes. Things all work quite differently here than in Europe. (Please don't worry about the cost of the packages. For the time being we're quite prosperous.) Please write if you need books.

For now, I'm enjoying working at Schocken a lot. So far, I've got on well with the old man.[6] He has a well-developed sense of humor and hasn't tried to tyrannize me yet. He is intelligent and has a passionate, almost worshipful respect for intellectual and scholarly accomplishment and intellectual people. Since, as we all know, it is easier for a camel to go through the eye of a needle than for a rich man to enter the kingdom of God, much will depend on whether he can manage to become a camel. Altogether possible.

Seriously, though, things are such that I no longer have a place in Jewish politics anyhow, and I think nothing more of any significance can be done within the official world of the organizations and of the Zionist movement, at least not at the moment. And so I have no other choice but to content myself with a modest cultural-political opportunity—and that of course is what a Jewish publishing house like Schocken is. On top of that, almost all my colleagues are pleasant, particularly the American ones, some of whom were hired on my recommendation. In short, it is not the harsh reality of the workaday world, and it's not writing (which can become a very unpleasant activity if you have to earn money with it), and it's fun.

Don't think I've given up my plans for a visit. I just don't know how I can manage it. And don't think that I'm homesick, for Heidelberg or any other place. (If I were ever to feel homesick, it would be for Paris.) And I'm not homesick for my youth either. I don't really want to do anything else but come to see you and visit you. And I've been wanting to do that since 1933, and that hasn't changed a whit. Wasn't Nietzsche perhaps right with his "Happy the man who has no homeland"?[7] I, at any rate, am quite content with Monsieur as my portable homeland (which isn't a substitute for anything at all).

It's too bad that Sartre wasn't in Geneva. I'm even sorrier that you didn't get to meet Camus. He is one of those young men from the Resistance of whom you wrote. He is absolutely honest and has great political insight. Now, all of a sudden, there is a new type of person cropping up in all the European countries, a type that is simply European without any "European nationalism." I knew an Italian like that. And Camus belongs to that type too. They are at home everywhere. They don't even have to know the language very well. Sartre is, by contrast, much too typically a Frenchman, much too literary, in a way too talented, too ambitious. This is something new for me. Before this war I hardly ever saw people like this. It's as if the common experience of fascism, if people really had it, instantly brought about something in them that had previously been only an idealistic program without any reality to it. Compared with these people, the earlier "good Europeans" look like high-minded drudges.

I'm eagerly awaiting your Geneva speech, which your wife said was on the way from Paris. The few quotes I've read here and there have pleased me and whetted my appetite.

Good-bye; take good care of yourself; and accept the warmest greetings from

Your
Hannah

48   *Karl Jaspers to Hannah Arendt*

Heidelberg, November 17, 1946

Dear Hannah!

I wrote the enclosed letter[1] to the Information Control Division,[2] and I'm sending you this carbon copy. I received an inquiry about it by way of Berlin. I hope that my having given this gift twice doesn't cause any problems.

I'm writing this in haste. But I have to thank you once more. My wife and I are in excellent health again. I am back up to 150 pounds, my wife to 101. We both look well nourished and feel correspondingly good.

Warmest greetings,
Your Karl Jaspers

Marianne Weber is also very well cared for. It makes one's own good fortune all the better if others do not have to suffer.

Also, we have an adequate fuel supply for this winter.

If you were to visit us, you would find tranquil, well-provisioned people in the old quarters so familiar to you. Teaching is fully underway.

49 *Karl Jaspers to Hannah Arendt*

Heidelberg, November 30, 1946

Dear Hannah!

I enclose still another declaration,[1] which I hope will accomplish its purpose. I sent another to you weeks ago,[2] but it was a general one applying to all my writings for which I retain the translation rights. I also sent you a copy of my letter to the local ICD,[3] and I am enclosing another copy of that here.[4]

I'm sorry to say that I had to pass *Commentary*'s[5] inquiry on to the publisher De la Baconnière in Neuchâtel[6] because that house—and not I—owns the translation rights to my Geneva speech and will also, unfortunately, own the profits from it. I had to accept these terms as a concession to the Geneva committee. The only right I retained was to a one-time publication in German, and this will soon appear with Piper.[7] The talk isn't particularly good anyhow. I hope that it's at least respectable. Your letters to my wife and to me have given us both profound pleasure. Our hearts harbor the warmest of feelings for you. But for now all I can do is deal hastily with this inquiry. I'll send you a decent reply during the Christmas holidays. There's a great deal to do.

How nice that you are content at Schocken Books and are enjoying the respect that is your due. It gives me great pleasure to think of you there.

My health is fine. Better yet, the American food has made me far stronger than I was at this same time last year.

I own only half of the translation rights to my *Psychopathologie*.

With warmest thanks
Your Karl Jaspers

50 *Hannah Arendt to Karl Jaspers*

New York, December 17, 1946

Lieber Verehrtester—

This letter is not a letter, but deals only with "business." Everything has arrived: *Psychopathologie*, the gift of translation rights to me and of the rights to *Die Schuldfrage* to Dial Press. These last letters I forwarded immediately to Dial but have no reply yet. They will have to negotiate further now with the American authorities. *Psychopathologie* is a marvelous book, inspiring in its analytical sobriety. I gave it to Dial Press even before I'd really finished reading it, because I didn't want to lose any time, and I told them that this book, together with your *Psychologie der Weltanschauungen*,[1] makes a truly remarkable "psychology," in which everything is contained that can be said on this subject today. No reply so far, but there are other publishers interested. Hermann Broch, much insulted that I didn't lend him the book right away, suggested Princeton University Press if Dial doesn't take it. (I felt obliged to offer it to Dial first.) Another possibility is Houghton Mifflin in Boston, one of the oldest publishing houses in the country and with whom I have just signed a contract for my imperialism book.

I've received your letter from Geneva,[2] and you, I hope, my reply. —

I'm very pleased about Lambert Schneider. But I have a request which I hope you will not find embarrassing. You surely know, without my having to mention it, that this book belongs to you and that I didn't write one of those essays without thinking of you. I would like to acknowledge this publicly, preferably in the form of a preface, which could be a letter to you. If you don't want that, then I could simply dedicate the book to you. If you don't want that either—and believe me, you should feel free to say no—then I'll do nothing, and this can remain between us. I'll have to write a preface in any case, it seems to me, and I'll do that at the end of this month or the beginning of next. Then the stupid problem comes up again that this is really illegal. It's quite legal to print the essays, because they will all be reprints. An original contribution is something else again—I was told here that I had the right to give away anything I liked. But can the publisher do that? Please don't you trouble yourself with this. Sternberger will take care of it all. I wouldn't have even mentioned it if I hadn't had to ask you about the dedication.

Professor McGrath from Iowa: He hasn't got in touch with me. He has a good reputation here. Perhaps I'll write to him to find out where he would like to publish the *Idee der Universität*.

What you write about the impossibility of a positive political declaration of intention didn't surprise me. I didn't mean it as a criticism. Right after the end of the war, Monsieur attempted something like that, as best he could as an emigrant, and he couldn't manage to collect the necessary non-Jewish signatures. The only German who was one hundred percent behind this project then was a former friend of the Trotts, Hasso von Seebach, who is returning to Germany this month and may turn up in Heidelberg sometime. He studied with Adam von Trott[3] and was a close personal friend of his even though he and von Trott parted ways politically in the period right before and during the war. —I found what you say about my thoughts on "beyond crime and innocence" in what the Nazis did half convincing; that is, I realize completely that in the way I've expressed this up to now I come dangerously close to that "satanic greatness" that I, like you, totally reject. But still, there is a difference between a man who sets out to murder his old aunt and people who without considering the economic usefulness of their actions at all (the deportations were very damaging to the war effort) built factories to produce corpses. One thing is certain: We have to combat all impulses to mythologize the horrible, and to the extent that I can't avoid such formulations, I haven't understood what actually went on. Perhaps what is behind it all is only that individual human beings did not kill other individual human beings for human reasons, but that an organized attempt was made to eradicate the concept of the human being.

Your handwriting: I read it with ease! I say this because you keep mentioning it in every letter.

Please excuse this letter. I'm just plain tired, and I know I'd have to put off writing it for several days if I didn't write it quickly now. I didn't want to do that.

I have so much to write and even more to say. But have to stop. In January everything will get better, or that's what I keep telling myself every day at any rate. At least there'll be a break from teaching,[4] which I've again found very enjoyable despite all. And things are organized enough at Schocken that we can begin to rely on established routine.

With warmest regards,

Your Hannah

I just noticed your question again about whether I'm a German or a Jew. To be perfectly honest, it doesn't matter to me in the least on a personal and individual level. Unfortunately, Heine's solution doesn't work anymore. It was after all the solution of a ruler over a dream world. But then, despite all external evidence to the contrary, it's not such an important issue anymore. I'd put it this way: Politically, I will always speak only in the name of the Jews whenever circumstances force me to give my nationality. That is easier for me than for your wife, because I'm at a further remove from this whole question and because I never felt myself, either spontaneously or at my own insistence, to "be a German." What remains is the language, and how important that is one learns only when, more nolens than volens, one speaks and writes other languages. Isn't that enough?

51   Karl Jaspers to Hannah Arendt

Heidelberg, December 28, 1946

Dear Hannah!

An office of the American military government (Investigation and Enforcement Section) has notified me that according to Law No. 53 I have to have a permit in order to give translation rights to my works to anyone in a foreign country. To my regret I therefore have to take back the gift I made to you of the translation rights to my writings on the question of guilt.

Practically, there is hardly anything I can do. I would have great difficulty filling out the application form that was given to me, because the questions have no bearing on my particular case. And I understand that a response to such an application is likely to take six months and will probably be negative.

The only possibility now is for you or the Dial Press to apply for permission to print the translation of my work. To the extent that I am consulted and have any decision to make, I will agree to everything. Because the translation rights belong exclusively to me and not to the publisher, I am free to dispose of them as I choose, provided I am allowed to. But for me to do what I may do, the initiative will have to come from over there. Unfortunately, the matter is out of my hands.

I'll write soon. The Christmas holidays have just begun.

With warm regards
Karl Jaspers

52 *Karl Jaspers to Hannah Arendt*

Heidelberg, January 1, 1947

Dear Hannah!

You can hardly imagine what pleasure it gave me that you want to address the preface to your book to me. In this bizarre world, where it becomes eminently clear to one that one is, in a positive and negative sense, a doll that is hauled out or tossed back into the toy chest according to others' whims and that one's true self is of no consequence, the judgments of the world necessarily become increasingly a matter of indifference to one—and I say that without arrogance—and so the acclaim of those few whose judgment one respects is all the more precious, and the friendship of those individuals whose recognition makes one's own self-respect possible becomes more precious still. And because we are so few and live in a small circle whose public includes potential unknown friends, a public expression of affection is particularly gratifying if it is rendered by someone in possession of his true self. I am therefore most pleased by your plan, and I thank you very much. I don't know what you intend to write, but I am certain that I will be delighted with every sentence.

I have to write you the enclosed business letter.[1] It appears I have unknowingly broken the law and have to take back my gift for the time being. I hope that you will be able to so arrange things at your end that I may make this gift to you. Intellectual exchange will doubtless soon be in full flow again. The main thing for me is, of course, that a translation be made.

The "German essence"—it is indeed the language and only the language. I quite agree with you. But that is no small thing, and it would be wonderful if German were still spoken and written somewhere in the world in future centuries. That is no longer a sure thing. And that will depend on whether the principle of freedom will ultimately emerge victorious or whether we have not a world order but a world empire established through a dictatorship. How meaningless the "nations" have become today, and yet their shrieking dominates the foreground of visible political activity.

I'm lecturing on Germany again this semester, for the last time, I think. Next semester I want to lecture on ancient philosophy (in China, India, and Greece), an altogether presumptuous enterprise, considering my need to rely on translations in the Asian world.[2] I want to incorporate into my teaching now the things that during the Nazi period were such a great aid to me in reflecting on the very basic elements of human life. China has become—if I may speak in such an exaggerated and foolish way—almost a second homeland for me.

Things are well with us. But that is an almost abnormal situation here. Now that the cold weather is here, it appears that the supply of coal is insufficient. The rivers are frozen; the locomotives break down and can be repaired less and less often. No new ones are being built. Industries close down suddenly for lack of coal. No work has been done at Lambert Schneider for the last three days. Half the copies of the twelfth issue[3] are done; all at once everything has to stop. It looks as if the cold could hang on for a long time. We still have some coal left over from past years, because we were sparing of it back in the Hitler period and sat wrapped in blankets. So now the temperature inside is 11 degrees Celsius with minus 6 outside. Those who have nothing have to endure the worst, and there are many in that situation.

Our questions and concerns become insignificant in light of the misery most people are experiencing. It becomes meaningless to speak as I have been speaking—not ultimately, but in view of present conditions. When basic needs are paramount, that's all anyone will care about. One finds little response if one says: The defeated could have been dealt with far more harshly. The response is: It's just a matter of method. The way things are going now, half of the population will perish, and the rest can then eke out a minimal existence on the land. The overall direction will become clear in March when, at the negotiations in Moscow,[4] the Russians reveal what they want and don't want. Gollancz made an extraordinary impression on many people here.[5] His eight demands[6] are simple and reasonable and humane. But even actions such as his are quickly forgotten in view of what is actually being done in the British Zone. All in all, the situation is by no means extreme; worrying about future ills exaggerates their gravity; and present misery forgets that this cold spell will be over in a few weeks.

This is not the letter I meant to write. I can't manage it. I hope I can some other time.

Warmest greetings
Your Karl Jaspers

Please give my regards to Monsieur. I sense his presence when you write, but I still don't know how to write to him.

53 Hannah Arendt to Karl Jaspers

March 1, 1947

Lieber Verehrtester:

First of all, "business": Enclosed is a letter from December from the military government to Dial Press,[1] according to which everything was already in the best of order back then. The translation of *Die Schuldfrage* is almost done, and I'll have the manuscript to go over next week. Since the Enemy Trading Act[2] will be rescinded as of March 4, I'll get in touch with Sidney Phillips at Dial Press and discuss with him what we can do now to straighten out the question of the fees.

In the meantime, the German edition of *Die Schuldfrage*, published by Artemis Verlag in Switzerland, is available on the market here, and the magazine *Notre Dame Lawyer* has already published an excerpt from it.

Day before yesterday, I had a letter from Hermann Weyl[3] at the Institute for Advanced Study at Princeton inquiring whether *Universitätsidee* and *Schuldfrage* were available for translation. I told him about Dial Press and also about the Iowa professor, McGrath (or something like that), from whom, by the by, I haven't heard anything further at all. Princeton University Press is a very good publisher, and it would be good if Professor Weyl were able to bring out *Universitätsidee* with *Lebendiger Geist* and your Geneva speech. That, at any rate, is what I suggested to him, and I hope that is all right with you. He would like to have his wife [Anna Dick Weyl] do the translations. I hope she is competent. It is hard to find really good translators; and the Germans who have been here in this country for a few years or even for more than ten assume, usually without any reason at all, that they have mastered the language. There are a few exceptions, but not very many.

I wanted to write to you at length about your Geneva speech, which I've been able to see only briefly and which, I think, I like almost best of everything political you have said since 1945. I was particularly happy with what you said about the tradition and the transcending of the purely European framework. It's wonderful that you'll be lecturing about China and India. I don't know the first thing about them, and for years now they have always been rather exotic entities to me, but you're absolutely right, and I'm glad that you'll be doing this. I like the Chinese; I knew a lot of them in Paris; they are very much like us. Now to the tradition and your remoteness from it. The important thing is that a few people have seen that the tradition as such is of no help anymore, in no way, and that that citing of it in which someone like Hofmannsthal was a master and which is offered up in excess now on a lower level in most German magazines gradually begins to look like a magic trick by which one hopes to evoke reality by calling up the past. I've had Broch's *Tod des Vergil* sent to you, if you should have some spare time. He has, as a writer, described this "standing at the door and knocking." Perhaps that will speak to you. He calls it "not yet and yet already."

I'm enclosing a copy of the dedicatory preface.[4] I've sent the original to Sternberger. Please change whatever and wherever you like. You see, one of the times when you encouraged me some twenty years ago, I became "ambitious" for the first and last time in my life, that is, I had the ambition not to "disappoint" you. And now you have permitted me to dedicate this little book to you. That those youthful dreams should have come to fruition despite world conflagration is possible only because the dreams have taken on new meaning. All in all, it's like a miracle.

Monsieur sends his warm regards. I'm no great describer, and he is even less a writer.

Let me thank you, too, for your great kindness to Hasso Seebach. He was overwhelmed by it.

Always your
Hannah

Heidelberg, March 19, 1947

Dear Hannah!

I've received your kind letter and your, for me, very moving preface. Sternberger had the manuscript quite a while and then passed it on directly to the printer, so that I'm reading it now for the first time. We share a similarity of outlook, or so it seems to me, to a remarkable degree. Even though I'm a little embarrassed by your praise, I suppose I may put false modesty aside and be as genuinely pleased as I am that you have publicly confirmed for me what no academy or state can. What you have said to me reflects the idea by which I live, even though in reality I am far from attaining it. But what a justification for my office it is that this idea could become manifest and stay alive with you over decades—and even though I know very well that the major factor here is your generous intellectual eye, which, aided by your affectionate fantasy, magnifies what in reality is quite modest.

If we were sitting down together, I would perhaps urge you to make minor stylistic and organizational changes in your preface, but none in its substance. The language is somewhat complex, and some German readers will either not understand it or will understand just the reverse of what you mean.

Stylistically, because of the phrase "without suspicion," the transition seems to me to lead almost by association to the question: "Which of us [did you] . . . murder?"[1] Although this point is central to what you are saying, the form makes it appear almost parenthetical and therefore perhaps unintentionally provocative, because your sentence, which contains an undeniable symbolic truth, would have to be answered this way in reality: Most Germans, 99.9%, did not commit such murders, not even in their thoughts. However, as we sometimes experience here, the fact that so many of the remaining 0.1% are still among us can lead us, when we are physically face to face with an unfamiliar person, to ask that hidden question. Almost always the question is unjustified, but once, as I personally experienced, it was justified. And that is enough. Well, I've digressed: Some readers will be put off by that sentence, perceiving it as an injustice toward them because they do not understand its symbolic meaning and because, forgetting that they are Germans who lived under the regime, they find it monstrous for such suspicion to be directed at them personally.

"The basis of facts"—"not assumed that they had to be that way, necessarily and for all time."[2]—Excellent! Once again I worry that

75

this is not simple enough for our normal reader, because he is not used to such writing. Your thoughts are interwoven—for *me* straightforward and clear.

Who here will sense that in this passage you are "justifying" yourself in the face of unsympathetic forums! —Well, it won't do anybody any harm. But I feel a little sad on our account because the reality of our present reading public becomes very clear to me when I imagine the effect your preface may have. Perhaps I am mistaken. I hope so! And then, of course, your book is not written just for the moment. It is a document that is not tied to the audience of 1947.

I like the Noahs.[3] Yes, that's the way things are, but saying so will be perceived as arrogant. The world always stands in opposition to the Noahs. They are "individualists," "aristocrats," "reactionaries," "unsocial elements," depending on the point of view. On that, both East and West agree with the Nazis. And the more some people insist on this view of the Noahs, the truer your point is, and we live in accordance with it, and this is the outlook that *will* carry the future.

Hasso von Seebach was a real event for us. Not a Jew and yet all that suffering. A superior being and yet not of steady nerve. I can't deny that I worry about him. We haven't heard anything from him since he left for Hesse and Hamburg. When I spoke to him openly about realities here, he said at one point: "I feel as if in a trap"; but at no time did this destroy his confidence or keep him from looking bravely into the future and at his own possibilities. We asked him all manner of questions about you. The results were meager. Yet I can still picture you and Monsieur in your "establishment," your enthusiasms, your gaiety; and I heard, with pride, how you have made your way in the USA but also, despite initial problems with your finances, that you live without any capital reserves and solely from your current income, which fluctuates constantly; heard about your mother, whom you rescued (I don't like to think what would have happened if you had not succeeded in that!); heard of your contact with a varied intellectual world, although I cannot picture that world clearly. He can't relate, can't develop a subject. To every question I asked I got only a vague and general answer. Even his own life remained completely in the dark. There's nothing for it: You've got to come yourself!

Unfortunately, I do *not* own the translation rights to the Geneva speech. De la Baconnière in Neuchâtel has to grant permission for every publication of it. The generous fee I received for the "Rencontres," all consumed in Switzerland, made it difficult for me to request a contract different from that of all the other speakers. Also, as a German, I felt I should not press for special terms. Now I'm annoyed that I went along, and I hope that De la Baconnière will grant the rights free or for only a nominal fee. I won't get any money in any case, which doesn't trouble me in the least, because I earn more money than I care to and I have to give almost all of it back in taxes anyhow (95% in the highest bracket, which I have reached).

And so this letter ends with the crassest of business concerns.

We're breathing easier. Spring is here. We don't have to sit around in blankets anymore; we can move about and enjoy the sun in a Heidelberg that is still beautiful and magical, that I still love as if I were just arriving here as a youth. Three steps out of the house, and one's spirits are lifted by the visual joys of the place.

Today, just as I was finishing this letter, a fantastic package arrived—my wife will write about that. I'm afraid that we're living better than you are. For over a year never hungry, always spoiled, and now well nourished.

The project Deutsche Selbstbesinnung[4] will require a great deal of work. Every sentence has to be thought through, felt through, with an eye toward its nuance. *If* this project is to have any value at all, the German reader has to feel both awakened and encouraged by it.
—Is it plagiarism if I use your suggestion (a law by which any Jew can apply for citizenship in Germany and immediately be granted it while still remaining a Jew)[5] without naming you as the source? The reasoning will be my own—does this meet with your approval?

With warmest greetings
Your Karl Jaspers

55 *Hannah Arendt to Gertrud and Karl Jaspers*

March 23, 1947

Dear Friends—

I'm writing in haste and therefore to you both at once. I'm enclosing the Dial Press contract[1], signed by me, which has now become possible with the rescinding of the "trading with the enemy" law. I'm also enclosing an inquiry I received from Secker & Warburg in England.[2] Dial Press has answered it, saying they would be glad to send Secker & Warburg the galleys of the translation once it is finished and has been printed. It would be good if the same translation appears in all the English-speaking countries.

I'm also sending here a letter from Professor Weyl[3] in Princeton as well as his lecture characterizing the German university. I think he is right and that it would be better to publish *Universitätsidee* with this lecture as an introduction. As to the lecture itself, it should be revised a bit so that the spoken quality of it is not so pronounced (that is easy to do and not terribly important). But I feel that it also needs to be changed slightly to lessen the much too one-sided praise of the German university and to let the excellent description stand by itself. This applies particularly to the final pages (from p. 22 on). Otherwise, the lecture could create the impression of propaganda for the German university and against the American one. That has to be avoided if we want this publication to have the proper effect and be incorporated in a rational way into the ongoing discussion here on the role of the university. I'll send these suggestions to Weyl, making clear, however, that this is my personal opinion, that I have sent his lecture to you, and that the final decision will have to be yours.[4]

Now I would like to ask a big favor of you. A friend and colleague of mine, Helene Wieruszowski, asked me to ask you for advice. She is toying with the idea of returning to Germany if there were any prospects of a university position for her. Her field is medieval history. She took her doctorate in Bonn and wanted to habilitate there in about 1932, but that didn't work out, because she was a Jew, and the faculty did not want to habilitate Jews anymore. She worked there for several years as a librarian. Her situation in America is very insecure. She has never been able to get a permanent post. She teaches at Brooklyn College but always only on a part-time basis. She's no longer young (about 50, I think) and is therefore very worried. She isn't versatile enough to work in any other field. She left Germany in 1933 and was in Spain at first. She's a baptized Jew, a niece of the jurist Ernst Landsberg[5] from Bonn and a cousin of Paul Landsberg[6], whom you may have known. She is a nice and decent person, no genius, but has good, solid knowledge of her field. She is, of course, afraid of Germany, primarily of anti-Semitism. And I should add, she is without inner defenses, very easily hurt, not very stable. Her difficulties here are hard to describe without also describing the overall atmosphere. She is very typically German. She knows a little too much or perhaps shows it too clearly. She is too honest and in a way too provincial to be pushy on her own behalf. She didn't get any elbows when they were handed out, and that's what makes her such a nice person. All she would like from you is some general advice, nothing detailed or specific. Just how you judge the situation in general for returnees like her.

Lieber Verehrtester, don't read any further. What comes next is package accounting. I received your letter of the 23rd[7] and the one about Hasso[8] at the same time. According to my tally, only one of the September packages didn't arrive. One from December seems lost—one of them contained medicines, which you confirmed receiving. The Swiss packages come directly to you and should be easy to distinguish from the others. I could put in a claim for that one December package, but I would have to know beforehand if that was all right with Lefebre.[9] The insurance company might make inquiry. You can't make a claim before six months have gone by anyhow. In March, as I've already written to you, I sent two packages as usual and one by way of Denmark to see if that is really quicker, as the ad promised it was.

March 25

All my haste didn't help after all. I was interrupted and will try now to bring this helter-skelter letter to some kind of conclusion. I'm glad that Hasso told you a little something. I should fill you in on my mother, but that will be very hard, because I don't think you know all of the very complicated background. I'm an only child and grew up fatherless. (My father[10] died when I was six and was ill before that, paralysis. My mother and I were lucky and remained healthy. Because my mother loved him very much, she didn't want to put him in an institution.) She married again later, and my stepfather[11] had two daughters from a previous marriage. One of them,[12] with whom I was friendly, committed suicide a few years before Hitler; the other[13] is living in England now. I'm not in touch with her at all. My stepfather, who was, thank God, never persecuted, remained in Königsberg and died there sometime during the war. After the November pogroms,[14] I took my mother to France and was lucky enough to get a visa to America for her, too. It is hard to transplant older people who don't have a completely independent intellectual existence, and I wouldn't have done it if I hadn't had to. It was easier for her in France, because she speaks French well—she studied for three years in Paris when she was young—and because she had more friends there, too. Here she's quite isolated, I'm afraid. We have very little time, and the only time we really see each other is at our evening meal together. But she is lively and healthy and physically capable of doing quite a bit (despite a serious injury, a femur fracture, that she had a few years ago and that—one of those American miracles—healed completely). She runs the household for us and up until a few months ago worked in a knitting factory (not because she had to, but simply because she wanted to and because all her friends of her age here were doing something like that). At present she feels unemployed and can't quite understand why I find that funny. I owe her a lot, most of all an upbringing without prejudices and with all possibilities open to me. Does that at least begin to answer your kind questions?

We're very much looking forward to your *Logik*. What is the little book you're working on now? I'm always so happy to see how much and how productively you're able to work, despite all the demands on your time.

I've just looked through your letter again: The report about the 5,000 returnees to Palestine[15] was incorrect. The Jewish Agency[16] claimed there were only 50. So there were probably about 500.

Best wishes and warmest greetings
Your
Hannah

56 *Karl Jaspers to Hannah Arendt*

Heidelberg, April 19, 1947

Dear Hannah!

It's evening again—despite the "semester break" I've been kept mindlessly busy with university administration—and if I'm going to write you at all, I have to write despite this weariness. So please forgive me if this letter is dull and deals only with business matters.

First of all, thank you for your communications about *Die Schuldfrage* and Professor Weyl. I'm pleased. But it is best if I send you a copy of the letter in which I was forbidden to grant translation rights. The cases that fall in the period before the letter are unaffected by it. But I can't make any agreements after it as long as I don't have a permit. And according to the information I was given at the Reichsbank when I inquired again a few days ago, it's unlikely I can get a license. Weyl's lecture has not reached me yet. Whatever *you* decide about that will be fine with me. We don't need to correspond about such matters any more at all.

Broch's book, *Tod des Vergil*, arrived a few days ago. Many thanks! My wife is reading it already. I haven't got to it yet.

For a number of reasons I've accepted an invitation to give some guest lectures in Basel[1] in the last two weeks of the semester. So I have to try to think up something new. I'm considering the subject of "philosophical faith"—or does that sound impossible on the face of it?

Now for Frau Wieruszowski: How wonderful it would be if she came here! When I mentioned her to my colleague for medieval history, Professor Ernst[2] (whose lecture[3] appears with my "Lebendiger Geist der Universität"), he was immediately enthusiastic. He does not know her personally, but he is familiar with her publications and told me about them. I am enclosing a letter from him to Frau Wieruszowski. Here are our thoughts: *If* Frau Wieruszowski should decide to come to Germany and to Heidelberg, she should write and let us know. Only *then* will we apply to the Department of Education, and we never know whether our requests will be approved. Only if the government approves would a trip make sense, for Frau Wieruszowski would then find firm footing here. But this has to be said too: This is *not* a tenured position. The government *can* always fire someone, though it has not usually done so up to now. But we don't know what will happen if the present fiscal shenanigans should end after the currency reform and we are forced to cut back mercilessly. In Germany there is no such thing as security.

Frau Wieruszowski would like my advice. I don't dare to give it. I can only describe how things look here. You in the States are better informed about the world situation and Germany's future than we are: *between* the major powers, this is a battleground for both of them, a garbage heap where all those people are tossed whom nobody wants anywhere else. The outlook from here: Heidelberg is magical; every day in the spring sunshine and in these streets between the hills can seduce you into finding the world infinitely beautiful and life wonderful. But overcrowded beyond belief. Two people to a room is normal. A married couple gets *one* room. Students may not live alone, only in pairs (things are different for single blue-collar and white-collar workers, for the so-called work force). The shortage of food is staggering. Without packages from abroad life is impossible (except in hunger, weakness, and inability to work). Dealing with the authorities—"the insolence of office"—wearying and exhausting, until you finally just give up (the reasons why my wife and I have it so good and enjoy some privileges in the way of work space are that we already had our apartment and furnishings, "the state of my health, my position in the scholarly world, and in view of the political persecution of my wife"). How much longer these conditions will last no one knows.

Oddly enough, I can't give any reliable answers to questions about anti-Semitism. That I never hear anything anti-Semitic myself comes as no surprise. But I am told that habitual anti-Semitism—thoughtless and ignorant—is still prevalent in the population. I have never thought "the people" to be really anti-Semitic. A spontaneous pogrom never took place, however much the Nazis may have wished for one and tried in vain to provoke it. If one is sensitive, one will witness some absurd things, not in deeds but in speech. And the atmosphere that you capture in your question "which of us [did you] murder?" is ineradicably present for people like my wife, although she is so warm and helpful toward any German she meets face to face once a few words have been exchanged.

There are hardly any German Jews left, except those in "mixed marriages." There are, however, many East European Jews, of vastly varied backgrounds, by and large not advantageous to the general view of the Jews—because they are sometimes demoralized (understandably after all those years) and almost always alien—except that every now and then one encounters those rare soulful, almost incomprehensibly human Jews among them. But they are not typical.

If Frau Wieruszowski can keep a retreat to America open, I would not hesitate to recommend that she try it here for a year and have a look around. The way things are, unpredictable, the decision will involve risk. It could be that she would feel "in a trap," as H. v. Seebach put it, if she came here. The one positive factor is that there are young people, minority though they are, who are eager to learn, indomitable, grateful, hungry for the life of the mind. Anyone who has a passion for teaching can have some wonderful experiences.

As far as the university is concerned, almost everything and everybody in Germany is against it: parties, state governments, unions, municipal administrations, etc.—a great deal of resentment of the university. But we've made it through so far. We have books in Heidelberg. The university is overloaded with students, over 4,000. Classrooms are available but cramped. The new classroom building is still occupied by the American army. For the soldiers: "Information and Education," also classrooms for the American children, who are brought here on buses from a large area around Heidelberg.

Well, I could go on for a long time yet. Frau Wieruszowski should feel free to ask questions if she would like to.

As soon as she should decide to come to Heidelberg and lets us know, we'll make application for her. Then she will have to wait in America to see what the response will be. I expect it will be good because the governments tend to be cooperative in such cases, for political reasons.

Please give my regards to Professor Weyl. I was very pleased by his friendly comments on my *Idee der Universität*.

Warmest greetings and, as always, thank you!
Your Karl Jaspers

57 Hannah Arendt to Karl Jaspers

May 3, 1947

Lieber Verehrtester—

You will find enclosed the pages of the dedicatory preface[1] on which I have made changes. I hope our good Lambert Schneider isn't growing impatient. You were absolutely right, and I was afterward, but really only afterward, amazed and annoyed that we here were unable to hear and see the provocative note. Precisely because this preface is a justification, I wrote it more and much too much with an eye toward the people around me here; and somehow, clearly, I wrote under that pressure. That the piece still remains a "justification" cannot be denied, and it saddens me that it saddens you, for that I cannot change. Not to explain would, it seems to me, be arrogant, and every explanation carries the germ of justification in it. So it seemed better to me to write a "justification," clearly and openly. Furthermore, I truly believe (and please say so if I am wrong) that a justification is needed for Germany, too, and not just for my Jewish friends. As far as I can tell, Jews in Germany up to now have published only with the tacit assumption that they are antifascist Germans. That is, they have acted as if nothing had changed since 1932. On the other hand, as far as I can judge, people in Germany are most anxious to avoid discussing the Jewish question, for which there are surely reasons. In other words and mutatis mutandis, I cannot but suspect that Germans in general do not have a fundamentally different attitude toward such a publication in Germany, and by a Jew, than the majority of the Jews do. I have intentionally expressed this very brutally.

On your remarks about the "murderers": You say 0.1% at the most. Perhaps I am completely mistaken, but that strikes me as a very small percentage and would correspond to about 70,000 people. What seems more important to me is this: Regardless of how many were directly involved, this in any case small percentage was no longer limited, as it was until 1942, to the convinced Nazis and carefully selected SS troops. Regular troop units, which represented a cross section of the people, could be and were employed for these purposes. That is a crucial point in terms of the world's reaction, and it was therefore a carefully calculated move. Then, too, it is said over and over again today, now that the entire population knows all the facts (and it is said not only by newspaper correspondents or propagandists but by many people, indeed by everyone who returns from Germany), that the percentage of those who even today would, let us say, cheer Hitler has if anything grown larger than it was in 1943. This seems to me almost to go without saying, and it is altogether in keeping with the expectations of the Nazis themselves. On the other hand, that can only mean that all these people, who are estimated by Ernst Wiechert,[2] for example, to make up 60–70% of the population, would consciously tolerate murder, which in no way makes them born murderers. They would probably do so even if their own lives were no longer safe.

All these problems essentially have nothing whatever or very little to do with Germany. Germany is the first nation that, as a nation, has gone to ruin. These things are not so blatantly obvious in other countries in part because external circumstances are better and in part because certain Western traditions, which would be no deterrent in a crunch either, still have some inhibiting influence. Today these questions are reflected in the influence they are having on German attitudes toward the Jewish people, and we are obliged to take these reflections seriously in all their awful reality. And it seems to me that in taking them seriously, despite all the traps one can fall into (and you have just saved me from falling into one of them), we have a chance to explain something that could perhaps be of general significance.

Now let me come to the question of the preface itself. It would perhaps be better to do away with the form of an open letter, to rewrite the piece simply as a preface, and then to dedicate the book to you— or not, whatever you think best. I would of course be unhappy if this will not work out as I had originally pictured it to myself, but in no way do I want to make your already difficult position there more difficult still. That alone should be the deciding factor. If the present version strikes you as at all troublesome or simply as inopportune, let me know right away, perhaps through Lefebre, and I'll send you a new one right away that is not in the form of a letter. It doesn't really matter that this will delay publication.

Hasso von Seebach: I was amazed by the accuracy of your description. As you probably know, Werner v. Trott[3] has in the meantime found him a post in Wiesbaden. Hasso is an honest and decent person, who at the very moment that he thought he was having good luck was in fact having bad, namely, when he met Frau Braun-Vogelstein, a very well-educated and gifted art historian with whom he has lived for many years now and who without quite realizing it herself has relieved him of all responsibilities and forced him into a cultural circle in which he was bound to be unhappy, because he was not productive in it. Monsieur tried to fix that and suggested that Hasso study radio technology, which he then did very well and with great enthusiasm, because he was finally doing something in which he could excel. After that he could not be moved to look for a job, simply because he didn't need the money. It's a long, complicated story, but I hope everything will turn out well after all. He has certain political gifts of a moral nature.

Come to Germany—my God, of course I'd like to come. It's very difficult to get a permit for Germany if one a) has nothing to do with the government, b) doesn't have any family left there, and c) isn't traveling on behalf of American business. Thank God there are no problems with getting a passport. I could, for example, get the necessary papers at any time for every other European country. But it all takes a long time and is also quite expensive.

Deutsche Selbstbesinnung: Princeton might be interested when you finish it. *Commentary* bought the rights for your Geneva speech for $150, which, together with the translation costs, amounts to about what they normally pay for a longer article. I haven't had any word from Princeton. They have *Die Idee der Universität*, *Vom lebendigen Geist*, the Geneva speech, and *Psychopathologie*.

That you think you can make some use of the suggestion about Jews in Germany pleases me very much. Of course without naming the source (N.B. that it comes from Monsieur). It is meaningful only if it comes from a German in Germany.

I laughed a lot about our lack of "capital reserves." I wasn't bragging. We do make a good living, even by American standards; and we have few needs because most of the things that cost money are boring and take up too much time. Getting my mother out of Germany and then all of us out of France cost us the little bit of money we still had tucked away here and there. When we arrived here, we had, if I remember right, about $50 in our pockets.

Lieber Verehrtester: Just one more word about the preface. All of us who studied with you always knew what I have written there, even if we weren't able to express it. That's why that comment, presumably Mannheim's,[4] to the effect that you had no disciples has always rather amused me as well as irritated me because in reality you have had a greater influence than all the others put together.

With warmest regards
Your
Hannah

May 4, 1947[5]

Just a few quick lines about the packages and to thank you for your letter of March 24, which, by the way, took even longer than usual to get here. I got a letter from Lefebre, too, that arrived at almost the same time as yours, of April 24. From now on we'll number the packages. I'm glad that the Danish package was so good. It wasn't expensive, on the contrary, and I've already ordered another. From now on you'll get one Danish package per month and two regular ones with milk, chocolate, etc., etc. I'll mail the two May packages next week. I didn't get to it yesterday on my usual package Saturday.

Kogon[6]: I read galleys of it here and tried to convince old Schocken to publish it here in English. Nothing doing, for no good reasons at all. It still makes me furious whenever I think about it. If you could get the book for me, I would be very grateful, because I need it very much for my own work.[7] I think that Bermann-Fischer will reissue it in German.

Benno v. Wiese: That's another one of those stories. In April or May 1933 he published an article[8] suggesting a plan of action for the German universities by which they would "of course" be purged of all alien elements. It was that simple. At that time there was no pressure on him to do that. And by writing that article he demonstrated in the clearest way possible his disinterest in the fate of the Jews, to put it mildly. And when he was so courageous as to call at Plöck Street,[9] wasn't Germany's imminent defeat perfectly clear? After all, he wasn't stupid, nor was he a convinced Nazi either. But none of that makes the story any better. He had a very nice mother; I wonder what happened to her.

Back to the packages: The only one I could and perhaps will put in a claim for is the December package. You've confirmed receiving the January and February packages. By now you must have received two for March and the three for April.

With all best wishes and much love

Your

Hannah

58   Karl Jaspers to Hannah Arendt

Heidelberg, May 16, 1947

Dear Hannah!

Your new version of the preface that means so much to me meets with my full approval. Thank you for taking this extra trouble with it.

I was not "saddened" on your account but because of the situation that makes such justifications necessary. There is indeed nothing you can do about that. It may be that for me the consciousness of being a German and the fact that from childhood on I have taken for granted that German Jews are Germans—both these things together have become a question to which I have a final answer on an emotional level, but it is not one I can formulate in words. About 1932 (I'm not sure of the year anymore) you and I became aware of a difference[1] between us that I did not perceive as a personal one even then, a difference that is not absolute in itself but is by no means trivial either. That it exists at all (it's the same between my wife and me, and we discuss it again every so often) is only a sign that we are working toward a state of the world in which such problems will cease to matter. I will never subscribe to a concept of Germanness by which my Jewish friends cannot be Germans or by which the Swiss and the Dutch, Erasmus and Spinoza and Rembrandt and Burckhardt are not Germans. I affirmed with Max Weber the idea of a German political greatness, and at the same time regarded Switzerland and Holland as German entities that fortunately lay beyond political risk and kept German qualities viable that were threatened in the German Reich (as in 1914). That

87

this German Reich has not only failed but has also by its criminal actions brought about the demise of what is best in Germany does not destroy that other possibility, which retains its place among our noble memories (from Freiherr vom Stein[2] to Max Weber). Our only failing has been to grossly overestimate that possibility. I did not realize until the National Socialist period that this moral evil had its origins as early as the 1860s, and our frightened eyes were opened to the true appearance of many a figure we had previously held in high esteem. Even farther back it was the same, when in the thirteenth century and later the revolt of the plebeians took a nationalistic turn. But I am digressing too far afield—some way for us to get our feet on the ground again will have to open. For now and for always, the ground under our feet is where the "Noahs" meet. That's why our friendship gives me such profound pleasure.

Because of my silence under Nazism I have to accept as understandable that you speak of the possibility of the preface being "troublesome" and "inopportune," but I hope I can also assume that your remark isn't altogether serious now that there is no Gestapo at the door and the threat of one is remote. Perhaps related to your fears are pleas from my brothers-in-law (particularly the Dutch one [Ernst Mayer]) that I keep quiet. This is all a remnant of that "suspicion" from which I certainly don't deserve to be excluded. But I can't quite believe you're serious about it.

I think you're right in what you say about the percentage of "murderers," and probably about the mass of the population, too. In spite of all that, I don't know what "the Germans" really are today. The mass of the people everywhere, in their visible appearance and in their mode of speech, is only a manifestation of "habits" determined by situation and upbringing. They don't know themselves and say what others say.

I found Weyl's lecture on the German universities excellent.

I won't answer every point in your letter. All I can do is thank you for it.

I'm finally finishing this letter on the 18th. I am in a foolish rush. In July I'll probably be going to Basel to give guest lectures there; here in Heidelberg I'm preparing an entirely new lecture.[3] Sometimes my head feels as if it will explode. And then, in addition, there is too much of what you call "nonsense." Things can't go on like this much longer, for contemplation and "laziness" are the sources of all good ideas. The way I'm living now, the "machinery" is a real danger to me.

Today I've been reading the Chinese Mo Ti[4] (5th century B.C.): a fanatical rationalist, utilitarian, monotheist, and believer in a planned economy (he'd be called a socialist today). Brotherly love is his basic principle, but he is without brotherly love, a violently ascetic political manipulator, who would introduce brotherly love by force. The old familiar story. I'm fascinated by the intellectual battles in China during those creative centuries. Not Mo Ti, but the truly great figures of that period were a great comfort to me after 1937. <u>Humanity does grow from a *single* root</u>. The purest, most natural humanity existed back then in China. Then at the end of the third century along came Tsin Shi Huang Ti,[5] the Hitler of China (if that isn't all too great an insult to this, in some respects, great Chinese). A speech by one of this despot's ministers, translated into French from a Chinese historian of about A.D. 100, sounds just like Goebbels. And that marked the end, for the time being, of the great creative thinkers. What followed were unoriginal scholars who served the state's purposes and some skeptics.[6]—Such are my preparations for my lecture.

In my seminar: Kant.[7] Two *excellent* papers already. Young people, some of them passionately clearheaded, with the energy for studying Kant. The two who gave the papers were a chemist and a mathematician.

Warmest greetings

Always your K. Jaspers

Shall I send you your doctoral dissertation?[8] I came across two copies and thought you might not have any left.

I'm sending you a volume of poetry by Haushofer[9] (son of the "geopolitician" and National Socialist Haushofer.[10] I found the book moving.

59 Hannah Arendt to Karl Jaspers

June 30, 1947

Lieber Verehrtester—

What a dreadful misunderstanding. Letter writing really is such a stupid, dangerous business. (You see, I'm exaggerating again.) No, I didn't mean anything at all with my "inopportune at the moment," except, first and foremost, that I'm genuinely anxious, that I can't judge the situation in Germany, and all I really know is that people who like to respond to arguments with revolvers have by no means died out. And, second, that I believe very much in the opportune and inopportune in politics, and you do, too; and that has nothing whatever to do with opportunism.

On your silence: I always respected it, even in 1933 when I still thought, during some months of delusion, that you could accomplish something if you spoke out. Perhaps you'll recall. You were in Berlin in April '33, and I asked you a direct question, and you gave me a direct answer. Please believe me: there are no "remnants" and no "suspicions," not for your brothers-in-law either. They are clearly just plain afraid, too. We just happen to be a fearful people. If you could tell me now that you're a terrific shot, as good as the sheriffs in America who can shoot through their pants pockets, lightning fast, then everything would be just fine.

Many thanks for the Haushofer book, which I too found very moving. It would be wonderful if you could send me the copies of my dissertation. I have only one copy left, and that one, anticipating further travels by water, fell into the bathtub in Paris and still looks waterlogged. Also, university libraries have occasionally asked me for copies.

But let me come back to the Jewish question. I recall our disagreement very well. In the course of it, you once said (or wrote) to me that we were all in the same boat. I can't remember now whether I answered you or only thought to myself that with Hitler as captain (this was before '33) we Jews would not be in the same boat. That was wrong, too, because under the circumstances you weren't in the boat much longer either or, if you were, then only as a prisoner. In conditions of freedom every individual should be able to decide what he would like to be, German or Jew or whatever. In an a-national republic like the United States, in which nationality and state are not identical, this becomes more or less a question with only social and cultural meaning but no political meaning. (For example, so-called anti-Semitism here is purely social, and the same people who wouldn't dream of sharing the same hotel with Jews would be astonished and outraged if their fellow citizens who happened to be Jews were disenfranchised. That may change, but for now that's the way things are.) In the European system of nation-states it is all much more complicated. But, my God, if a German says that he would rather be an Italian or vice versa and acts on that, why not?

If the German Jews don't want to be Germans anymore, that certainly can't be held against us, but it does of course look a little funny. What they really want to say by that gesture is that they have no intention of assuming any share of political responsibility for Germany; and in that they are right again. And that alone is the key point. For me and many others today it has become a matter of course that the first thing we do when we open a newspaper is to see what's going on in Palestine, even though I don't intend ever to go there and am almost totally convinced that things will not work out there.

What I would like to see and what cannot be achieved today would be such a change in circumstances that everyone could freely choose where he would like to exercise his political rights and responsibilities and in which cultural tradition he feels most comfortable. So that there will finally be an end to genealogical investigations both here and in Europe.

What seems most important to me at the moment is not to exaggerate the significance of all these questions, for we will otherwise continue to forget that this probably is the flood and we would do best not to settle down too permanently anywhere, not really to depend on any nation, for it can change overnight into a mob and a blind instrument of ruin.

Monsieur and I talk about the Jewish question every once in a while too, and if I let him go his way undisturbed, he always lands again on what I call his assimilatory feet. And so in the purely private sphere I readily admit that it's difficult to see why Mr. and Mrs. So-and-So aren't German when it's perfectly obvious that they are.

Helene Wieruszowski has written to you herself, after a long, long evening with me. You have made her very happy with your good letter. I was very happy, too, because regardless of what decision she makes, a letter like that was as essential to her as bread itself. She will never adapt to this country and will never feel really good here. In spite of that, going back is somehow more difficult for her because she had identified with Germany much more in the past and her reaction to what happened there is much stronger, in large part, too, because she is politically quite naïve.

How nice that you're in Basel,[1] and how nice that you can accomplish so much, though I hope too that you will manage to extract yourself from the administrative mill. Will you publish your Basel lectures?[2] The Geneva speech has been set at *Commentary*. I hope they'll publish it in the fall so that it will appear at the same time as *Die Schuldfrage*.

Things are lovely here, holidays. I really needed them this time.

With all my warmest wishes. And cross out those "suspicions." Please?

As always
Your Hannah

60   *Karl Jaspers to Hannah Arendt*

Crans in the Rhone valley, July 20, 1947

Dear Hannah!

Your letter reached us in Switzerland. What great pleasure in your holiday is evident in it! It has made clear to me for the first time what great claims your day-by-day work makes on you. And how much I wish—and wish I could demand—that someone as gifted as you are should have time and freedom for reflection and your creative work; for you truly have something to say and often have something like genuine visions. Now you have at least a few weeks. I hope that with this freedom, in pleasant surroundings, and sharing happy times with Monsieur, you will make progress with the work that matters most to you.

With my guest lectures here in Basel I've been a great "success." Because the papers from Berlin were delayed, I arrived here a week later than the appointed date. The semester was nearly over; the students were already leaving. The rector and the spokesman for the foundation that had invited me suggested I come in October; they would be hard pressed to fill a lecture hall now. They would pay for our vacation[1] now; the postponed lectures could then be successfully held in October. I was impertinent enough to insist on giving the lectures *now*. The semester in Heidelberg would prevent me from returning in October (because I couldn't take a second leave). A hall was found, and I satisfied myself that I could be seated there while I lectured. But on the very first day, the lecture had to be moved to the central auditorium. I was worried, because I hadn't seen what the seating possibilities were for me there. Five hundred attended. Every day more came. Toward the end the only way I could reach my seat was through the back door and the standees who were there, too. As you can see, this pleased me (otherwise I probably wouldn't be telling you about it), but the pleasure soon goes flat. It's all only a show, in which one is a puppet oneself and can perform only if one takes the business seriously for the moment. And that's why it goes flat afterward. But then I think about Hannah Arendt and that there are a few "Noahs" in the world, and I feel that what is more important to me than all this success I could easily dispense with is if you are of one mind with me.

My subject was "philosophical faith." Perhaps I'll have the six lectures printed and will then send them to you. I'm told that the theologians were "horrified." To think something like that is bad; to say it, much worse. (This kind of thing is even worse in Germany now. The Nazi set of mind has spread to the churches. I recently received a notice for the election of representatives of the Protestant congregation. To be eligible to vote, one had to submit a new written confession of faith in Christ, not in God!) The "existentialists" consider me a kind of old-fashioned theologian. There was a gathering at the end for discussion. Few people spoke. My "colleague" Heinrich Barth[2] (brother of the theologian[3] and himself full professor of philosophy in Basel) asked me where I felt most at home in the history of philosophy, and compared me to Fichte! I responded, I think, extremely tactfully, but characterized Fichte as he deserves to be characterized, despite his genius. After three other people spoke and I replied, silence set in. My attempts to encourage them with questions of my own were of no avail. I had the unhappy feeling that I had "talked them to death." Afterward I received a letter from a privatdocent who was present and who sent me a copy of his recently published book.[4] He expressed his thanks to me, as a "student" of mine—25 years ago— and said: Transcendence held no meaning at all for him. Existence is freedom, etc., precisely because it is *without* transcendence. He did *not* speak, because he felt it would have been obtrusive. So no real discussion took place. I was pleased by the positive response of a few people whom I respect; otherwise it was just a show. Another invitation for April!—we are much delighted by that prospect.

We are living in paradise here. My wife is already cutting back at table for fear of putting on weight. A delightful landscape, 1,500 meters above the Rhone valley, the high mountains all around. A constant play of clouds, not a day without sun. One lives in touch with the earth at every hour. We have a room with a view over the entire countryside, and with a balcony, so we are in the fresh air all the time. And we are truly alone for once. A magic spell that seems unreal and yet is a full and present reality! My wife is exploring the walking paths, and the ones I can manage we walk together. I have edited my lectures and made them more or less ready for print. They are on the whole rather abstract. For April, I've tentatively announced a more concrete topic: a view of world history as a whole.

Now at last to your very kind letter. I didn't really take your "suspicions" fully seriously. Thank you—they are crossed out. This is a point of oversensitivity with me. My *Schuldfrage* really does have important personal roots, all the more so because I know that I would act again just as I did in the past. I have good reason to be very modest. I am aware that you and my brothers-in-law are just plain "afraid" for me. I'm afraid myself. One has to be opportunistic in politics, of course—but I am never engaged in politics in this sense and would have no talent for it. I continue to learn how inept I am, even within the narrow limits of university politics, where every conniver has the advantage over me and uses me—not intentionally but instinctively.

I think I share all your views on the subject of the "nation" and on the freedom to choose political responsibility and therefore a state. There is, however, something that one cannot choose but has to "accept." The best and most just of world orders would not change that. And that does not seem a flaw to me but, rather, a good, though sometimes a painful good. If someone says: You are a German Jew —I am a German—those are of course just words, and everything depends on their interpretation. I think constantly now, with my heart, about what my being a German means. Until 1933 that was never problematic for me. But now one at least has to contend with a fact I perceive more strongly in Switzerland than I do at home in Heidelberg: The whole world shrieks at one, so to speak: You are a German. I hope to give my response to that sometime.

What a Jew is seems clearer to me than what a German is. Biblical religion and the idea of God and the idea of the Covenant are crucial to the Jew. Without them, it seems to me, a Jew ceases to be a Jew. But with them he is something that makes him independent of all politics and of Palestine as well. Palestine seems to me a transitory problem in the age of national thinking, uncommonly important for the question of Jewish existence. As a reality, however, it is not only politically uncertain (and what, after all, is not politically uncertain), but also a great potential danger for the essence of Jewish existence, that is, it threatens to reduce the Jewish people to the level of "nations" and so make them unimportant for the spiritual development of things.

"Assimilation" does not strike me as a fundamental issue. However, in the private sphere, there should be no prohibitions against it. You yourself and my wife have settled that through your actions. It would be equally pointless to *demand* assimilation. But I think it does make sense to fear assimilation, because something priceless would be lost if there were no more Jews, aware of themselves as Jews, in the world. Yet to do or plan anything in this regard or moralize about it strikes me as impossible.

One question is whether the whole Palestine business isn't a total assimilation in a spiritual and intellectual sense. The Jews will remain, but merely as one nation among many and as a very small and unimportant one at that. Will then every last trace of sublimation, of the "chosen people," disappear? That would amount to the loss of Judaism in the husks of people who are still nominally Jews. But that, too, is only a fear. No demands should be made here.

Yes, how right that you keep referring back to the flood. That has to remain our point of orientation. But something arises out of the flood. Life goes on. And we ought at least to find the star that leads us on: something like an idea for a world order, but one that remains influenced by transcendence and does not lead to the flatness of an organization, a rational law for each and every case, to the a-historicity of a presumed paradise. Without the Jews I can't imagine traveling this path, which is a historical one and therefore one bound to history. Hence my worry that the Jewish people could lose their soul in Palestine. Perhaps the solution is to desire Palestine but *not* go there, because the task is to live among *all* the peoples of the world, with them and against them as long as they are content to remain peoples and nothing more. This would be a new form of that influence "from afar" which has perhaps always been characteristic of biblical religion. And from that comes the tension and the excitement and the truly infinite nature of the task.

Oh, if only you were sitting here so we could talk! And yet I would have to disappoint you again, because I'm good for only an hour and then have to lie down; I get tired. The day before yesterday Vercors[5] was here with the business manager of his publishing house. He would like Edition de Minuit to do translations of as much of my work as possible, possibly all of it. It still can't be done. Vercors and his manager think they can obtain a license from Berlin for me because they have connections with the highest authorities in their country. I have my doubts. But of course I am eager for translations of my work. We have provisionally arranged everything. In the process, I got to know Vercors, and I instantly developed a great liking for him: smart, humane, a soulful eye. That goodness, clarity, unconditional commitment that one sometimes finds in the French, and then in such beautiful combination.

When you write to me in Germany, it is better *not* to mention translations and such matters. *Every* letter is opened. Even being questioned would be unpleasant for me because I never know when I have violated one of these devilishly devised laws. In case of an interrogation, matters between us look like this: I made you the gift of translation rights. Then came the American police. I made a long report and retracted the gift. This retraction came too late: you had already made use of the rights; and, furthermore, you refuse to accept the retraction. —The police wrote me—I sent you a copy of this letter— that they will *not take any further steps* regarding any *earlier* actions of mine. Therefore, I am not worried about *Die Schuldfrage* or about anything that is done without my explicit approval. —If you have anything of a business nature to discuss, we will have to hold that until April. I hope to be here again then, though only for ten days to two weeks. I'll write you ahead from Heidelberg to let you know the exact dates.

If you feel like it, please let me know what you are writing now. —Things are going slowly at Lambert Schneider. Constant technical problems. It's almost impossible to get repairs made on the machinery. The print shop is much too small for its work load. And the shortage of paper is catastrophic.

I'm writing with a fountain pen, which makes my handwriting still worse and more difficult to read. I hope deciphering this has not been too irritating.

Warmest regards
Your Karl Jaspers

61   *Hannah Arendt to Karl Jaspers*

September 4, 1947

Lieber Verehrtester—

Your nice long letter from Switzerland sounded so cheerful and touched on so many things that I'm eager to discuss with you (yet can approach only very cautiously), that I put it aside for the moment. I've just read it again and felt your presence as strongly as if you were sitting here in this room. I was very happy to hear about your success in Basel (I received the newspaper report, which was, by the way, very decently written; merci). Things like this are still a good thing, even if they are just shows. Some of your listeners always come away with something; and precisely because you can't know with whom you've connected or how or in what transmuted ways, the show becomes a kind of lottery in which the results will not be announced until much later. Indeed, the drawing day itself is a matter of chance, too; but despite all this you can somehow still be absolutely certain of pulling the winning number. You really can be absolutely certain. Yes, Switzerland is beautiful, although I have always felt a slight and no doubt unjustified antipathy for its inhabitants. I believe it was more than ten years ago that I was last in German Switzerland. I was struck then by the fact that people on the streets were speaking German. (That wouldn't surprise me anymore now. A lot of German is spoken on Broadway and on our delightful Hudson promenade.) I spent most of my time there in French Switzerland, Geneva, where a friend of my mother's,[1] who has since died, was living. Geneva was hideous then, the international gathering place of every possible superstition, of theosophy, Christian Science, metempsychosis, healing through prayer, whatever you wanted.

Will your lectures be printed? I didn't understand a few of your remarks about Christianity, and that troubled me. And what has become of "Logik"?[2] I should interject at this point that I have a confession to make: A Dr. Frise from Hamburg asked me to write an article about you for a collection of essays about great Europeans,[3] and I felt I could not agree. (That is N.B. the reason, I think, that I have put off writing to you for so long. I was ashamed.) It's a question of time and a genuine fear I have about getting into philosophy now. Besides my job at Schocken I have a contract for my imperialism book, and of course I'm already way behind with that. But that is not important. What is important is, first of all, that I haven't read "Logik" at all and am surely unfamiliar with much else; that I have inklings but don't really know what you mean by "philosophical faith"; and that if I attempted even the most modest of presentations, I would also get into philosophizing and thus onto a level of generality that is essentially relevant to me alone and from which perspective one cannot very well make a historical presentation.

And that brings me to your question about what I'm writing. I don't have a title, so I can give you only a rough idea. The first part, which is finished, is a political and social history of the Jews since the mid-eighteenth century. The point of view is limited exclusively to their propensity to be crystallizers for crucial political ideologies of the twentieth century. The second part, which I'm working on right now, analyzes the link between imperialism (i.e., in my terminology, the policy of pure expansion that begins in the 1880s) and the collapse of the nation-state. If all goes well, I should be done with that by the end of the year. The third and concluding part will be devoted to the structures of totalitarian states. I have to rewrite this completely because I've only recently become aware of some important things here, especially in regard to Russia.

About the Jews: Historically, you are correct in everything you say. But the fact remains that many Jews such as myself are religiously completely independent of Judaism yet are still Jews nonetheless. That may lead to the disappearance of the Jewish people; there's nothing anyone can do about that. All we can do is try to bring about political circumstances that do not make their continuing existence impossible. Then we can just quietly sit back and see what happens. As far as Palestine is concerned, you are absolutely right. It represents the only logically consistent effort at assimilation that has ever been attempted. By comparison, everything else of this kind, to the extent that it was not just an absorption of European culture but was carried out according to a plan, was a mere game and not even a serious one at that. The Zionists are the only people that can be taken seriously in this regard. They—and not the proponents of assimilation—are the only ones who no longer believe in the idea of the chosen people. What has been done in Palestine itself is extraordinary: not merely colonization but a serious attempt at a new social order, from which even the utopian elements of Tolstoyan provenance have recently been disappearing more and more. As far as the Jews as a people are concerned, an alteration of such great significance has taken place in them in recent years that we can speak of a genuine change in the so-called national character. (Whether it is permanent I can't say.) Most important of all is that large segments of the people, not only in Palestine and not only Zionists, reject survival as the goal of the total national life and are prepared to die. That is completely new. Secondly, however, there is a distaste, which is difficult to describe, for the idea of the chosen people. We might say the Jews are sick of it. This isn't an ideology, as Zionism is, but a mood of the people. But hand in hand with that—and this is truly dangerous—goes a basic mistrust of all other nations, a mistrust that is being taken for granted more and more and that is affecting ever larger segments of the population. The attitude toward Germany is in no way limited to Germany (which would not be so terrible) but has brought about a much more general rejection. This is nothing new either, but today it is found in all social groups, even in the Jewish socialists, for example. It is extremely dangerous and destructive because there is no semblance of an idea behind it (except for some vague notion like "we really are better people, but let's try to become worse"), no faith at all in God or in anything else. One could, of course, say that this is a transient episode of mass hysteria. I don't know. For all that, there are many positive things as well: Palestine, which, as you put it so well, holds the nation together "from afar"; the evolution of American Jewry, which is free and confident, also somewhat more barbaric than we are used to. The republic here, which gives nationalities freedom and yet includes every citizen, indeed, treats even an immigrant as a future citizen.

I've been back in the office since the beginning of August, and I'm trying as hard as I can to appear as dignified and solemn at meetings as the others do. But I'll never bring it off. If I have to take myself completely seriously, life isn't fun anymore. Old Schocken (Jewish Bismarck) with his two completely oppressed sons—it's a pity that I can't write humor. For all that, the job is an excellent arrangement. I'm able to accomplish a little something, now and then; and besides that, I'm treated very generously in terms of my time. —My mother, whom we shipped off to the country for the unbearable New York summer, is coming back tomorrow.

I assume that your wife isn't back yet, so I'll just do a quick package tally here. (Don't be vexed. Don't read it. Just save it for her.) I didn't send anything in June or July. You haven't confirmed receiving a package of sugar from May and (I'm not so sure about this) one Lef.[4] package. August: 1 CARE, 1 Standard from Holland or Denmark, and 1 Lef. Confiserie International, unnumbered. September: 1 milk package and 1 double package to Lef.

           With warmest greetings Your   Hannah
Thanks very much for the *Augustins*,[5] which just arrived.

New York, January 25, 1948

Dear Friends—

By the time you get this letter, you'll no doubt already have one foot in Basel.[1] How wonderful! I'm beside myself with joy, because Switzerland seems to me to be a midpoint between Germany, France, and Italy and because it's beyond all doubt that you belong there, difficult as it will be to take leave of Heidelberg. But, unless world history should suddenly upset all our calculations, you should finally, after all these years, have some peace, your peace, which you had to give up (that had its good side, too) and which you will need again now. I inquired about visa arrangements right away and learned that I can get a visa for Switzerland in just three days. That sounds very encouraging. France, with its usual administrative chicanery, is, of course, more difficult, but in no way impossible, and ship passage can be had, too. In short, all the conditions for at least fantasizing a trip to Europe are given. The harsh realities in my way are that my publisher is putting pressure on me and that, in view of the near impossibility of getting a visa for Germany, I haven't felt out my Schockens yet (they appear only in the plural; it's very funny) to see how they would feel about my taking a long vacation in the summer. And then there is Monsieur, who has declared categorically that he has had enough of traveling for now and all time, whom I can't tempt with anything, and who can happily use two months' rest from me. As you can see, I'm playing this for all it's worth; and play is, it seems to me, just as serious a preparation for a trip as getting scared is before giving a lecture.

The Goethe lecture[2] is very beautiful and very true. Thank you for the offprint, which I lent right away to American friends for whom it is very difficult to gain a perspective on Goethe, even if they know German. The *Logik* hasn't arrived yet, and I'm not even certain that it has been published. Helen Wolff (Kurt Wolff's[3] wife and a remarkable woman) is devouring the *Psychopathologie* at the moment. She is terribly excited by this "great book," the first edition[4] of which she read while still half a child, just as I did myself—she is about my age—and we are having wonderful long talks about it.

There isn't much to report about myself. I'm rather overworked. This writing along with my job is strenuous and often annoying. In February I'll take one or two weeks' vacation. I'm already looking forward to sleeping late.

I haven't sent any packages this year. The only ones still outstanding are a 22-pound package from Confiserie (from November), a Luso package from December, and a certificate for a Safe package. I won't send anymore for the time being, but I can't quite feel at ease about that.

I've been forgetting to tell you that I think *Die Wandlung* is getting better all the time. By far the best of all the magazines that come my way here.

With best wishes for the New Year in general and for your special one, which begins in February.[5]

With warmest wishes as always

Your

Hannah

P.S. Lefebre called once when I wasn't home. Nothing more from him since. A great shame. I should have written something about Palestine here, but all I have to do is think about it and, like Henriette Mendelssohn[6] of blessed memory, I feel "fed up with tout le monde."

63   Karl Jaspers to Hannah Arendt

Heidelberg, January 30, 1948

Dear Hannah!

I've just received your letter of January 25. My wife is in Basel. Permit me to dictate a few lines to you in my haste. I'm always inspired when I read a letter from you. And now you are already imagining our reunion! Wonderful! How easy it seems. But it's a pity that Monsieur does not want to come along. A great pity! Our situation has been made extremely difficult by the fact that I don't know whether the Americans will allow me to leave. It could actually happen that I will be forced to stay here. I would have thought such a thing impossible, but I'm told that my departure is very undesirable. I'm counting on it being more undesirable still for the Americans to curtail my freedom of movement. Now we may have to wait in suspense for weeks. All other arrangements for Basel are in the best of order. The university will provide us with a charming little house[1] in which you'll be able to visit us in comfort, with oil heat. When I received my first call to Basel in 1941—an offer meant solely to rescue us, for there wasn't a chair free—the Ministry of Education and the Security Service refused to let me leave.[2] Now I have a second call; a chair is available;

they want me there for professional reasons. But people in Germany, here in Heidelberg, want me too, with a determination that weighs on my heart. In a way I have never experienced before, they let me know how much they value me. Faculty, Senate, and even the City Council and the mayor. If I stay here, I'll have to make a public statement, just as I will if I leave. The contents will be the same in both cases. My love for Heidelberg is as great as my desire for European Basel and the peacefulness of a life there with friends who can visit us all the time. My departure signifies neither judgment nor confession. If I stay, I want to prevent nationalistic hearts from beating and applauding me for a deed of national heroism. My position in Heidelberg would surely suffer a great deal from that. The initial joy would ultimately result in a clear position, but one that puts me in deep shadow. A colleague's wife who is favorably disposed toward me recently told a friend of mine who passed the remark on to me: He has to stay here. The university needs him. He represents it to the rest of the world. My friend's response was: Yes, perhaps, but in Basel they want his philosophy. That of course does not preclude the fact that a great number of my colleagues truly and profoundly desire my presence here, including my philosophy. And what pains me most is a few young students who stand before me like children with big, frightened eyes and feel themselves abandoned. But they are very few.

How pleased I was to know that you approve of my Goethe lecture and that your friend Helen Wolff likes my *Psychopathologie* so much. It sometimes feels to me almost like my favorite book, because it's the book of my youth and because it is completely philosophical in its outlook, though not in its content.

It's dreadful that your job makes such heavy demands on you. In the summer the happiness of holiday ease sounded in one of your letters, and now the thought of two weeks' vacation is again a great joy for you simply because you'll be able to sleep late. What a hard life! And through it all you keep your head above water and are so cheerful and so alive with what really matters that I feel your spirit radiating over here to me through your letters and warming my soul.

You don't write about Palestine because you don't want to. My wife is very unhappy about the situation there. Her brothers[3] in Palestine continue to write full of courage and confidence.

The page proofs of my *Logik* were sent to you some time ago. If you have the proofs bound, you could perhaps read in it now and then. But considering how overworked you are I don't expect that of you at all. It suffices me to know that you have it. It was impossible to send the bound volume because of the weight—over 2 kg is forbidden. As soon as I have copies, I'll see that a proper copy gets to you by way of friends. The book has not been published yet.

My wife will write about the packages you have been so kind as to send. As best I can recall, the heavy package from the Confiserie and the certificate have arrived. I don't remember the Luso package. But my wife can give you an exact report. She usually writes right away to acknowledge receiving every package.

With warmest greetings,
Your
Karl Jaspers

64 *Hannah Arendt to Karl Jaspers*

March 18, 1948

Lieber Verehrtester—

I've been putting this letter off from one day to the next, hoping to hear something definitive from you about Basel. The first part of *Logik* still has not arrived. So here I am with only the second part, a much too precious symbol of the absurd circumstances under which we live. I still haven't been able to bring myself to read it from back to front, like a book in Hebrew. My holding out on that point is, as it were, a symbol of my determination not to make my peace with the absurdity of external circumstances. But as you know, one finally gives in after all.

Please excuse the jocular tone. You are surely very saddened by this, as I am, too. One cannot know how something like this sounds at such a great distance.

Your letter was a real ray of light. Yes, you will surely do everything you can to prevent "nationalistic hearts from beating," and you will do it the way you do everything, with that calm, natural composure that always has in it the possibility of magically charming into a lifelong allegiance to reason those few who are still able to hear that call.

Again, it's wonderful that you are eager to go to Basel. Don't let that strong desire fade. Things will work out somehow. I simply cannot imagine that they can risk holding you against your will.

I had a few lines from Rossman, not at all important but still indicating how much you will be missed. That did my heart good. Can't you arrange fellowships somehow for those few students you wrote about, the ones with the frightened eyes, so that you can take them out of Germany with you and into Europe? (As people in East Prussia used to say: Once the nose is in, the rest will follow.)

In the next few days I'll send you a longish essay about concentration camps,[1] a possible submission for *Die Wandlung*. But I would rather not send it to Sternberger before you have seen it. If you find it suitable, just pass it on. If not, don't.

Good-bye, stay healthy.

As always
Your
Hannah

65 *Karl Jaspers to Hannah Arendt*

Basel, March 22, 1948
Austrasse 126

Dear Hannah!

Just a few lines to tell you that we are in Basel with our things and our books and our maid.[1] We came here last night in a car supplied by the Basel municipal government; the moving van came today.[2] My wife is stuck in the chaos of our things in the house (which I still haven't seen); I'm sitting in a lovely hotel room and looking out on an enchanting spring landscape. —It's all like a fairy tale!—though not for my wife as long as she has to cope with her domestic wasteland. —Once we have overcome our weariness, the fresh impetus we feel already, despite our exhaustion, will, I hope, take full hold of us. — Is this an arrogant venture for people of our age? I don't want to believe it is. It seems to both of us strangely right and natural in some uncanny way.

And now we will see you again!

Warmest greetings,
Your Karl Jaspers

Basel, April 10, 1948

Dear Hannah!

Today I want to thank you right away for your kind telegram (arrived yesterday),[1] your letter, and your essay.[2] All of them gave me profound pleasure.

Your telegram cheered and encouraged us—your closeness and warmth a comfort to us when sometimes the soul feels cut off from air in the crush of other people—your letters full of concern but also full of courage—and your essay. I found it deeply moving, as if it were the first truly serious thing written about these concentration camps. Yes, the fear in which you live, not fear for yourself but for humankind, gives you great clarity of perception. And you recognize the danger of people not wanting to accept these facts, pushing them aside, not comprehending them, not believing they exist in the real world. You think the logical consequences through to the end. And what you reveal can truly make one's blood run cold. Yes, you ought to alert people—only by way of this knowledge can we prevent such things "from ever happening again." On the same day I received your letter, I had one from a student in the early stages of mental illness: that something like that actually happens, slipping helplessly into dissolution, fully conscious and in terror—it's something that has always been present to me from youth on—the fact that such things happen, happen every day. What you have learned, what you know and say, is analogous: the individual human's fear for what humanity can become. But that is *only* an analogy. For only the passive soul is resigned and says: après nous le déluge. —But you are determined that this shall not happen, and so you write and take the path of possible salvation.

I passed your essay on to Sternberger right away. The notes pose technical problems because *Die Wandlung* doesn't print notes. Perhaps you should write Sternberger as to whether he should omit the notes or whether you want to work some of that material into the text (perhaps in parentheses). The latter solution is awkward and threatens to destroy the powerful, concise structure of your essay.

In Basel, no one has any inklings of such "mental illness." I'm curious and not a little anxious about how I will be received here. At the moment, my name is creating something of a stir—why? I hope I won't fail. I'm going to lecture on "Problems of a World History of Philosophy," starting with a world historical overview. But it's

105

difficult to say much about this project in a few words. The central theme is: What do we do with history? —And: A totality from China right through to the Occident: the common root of humanity. That's biting off an awful lot.[3] If I don't make a good job of it, it will be nonsense. There's no in-between.

We were happy about your initial successes with the Zionists. Is it really too late for any help? The letters we get from Gertrud's brothers in Palestine are very serious but determined nonetheless. Unfortunately, her brothers are not "political" in the way you are. A rigidity prevails there, a mad will to fight. Your view: *no* territorial division, then wait and see, is clear and good. But how can it be realized now? It seems that any course taken now calls for violence. Is that the pattern being set everywhere in the world?

With warmest greetings,

Your Karl Jaspers

The Beacon Press, 25 Beacon Street, Boston 8, Mass., wrote to me about translating the *Universitätsidee*. They offered 10% and an advance of $100. The translation rights belong to you. I'm referring Beacon Press to you and to Frau Weyl,[4] who has, I believe, been instrumental in promoting this translation. Now, at last, I can write openly about these matters. In Germany, the Americans forbid me to make any gift whatsoever of translation rights. At the moment, because we are making a fresh start, even $100 would be welcome. —I am enclosing the letter and my reply to it.

The publisher is sending you a copy of my book[5] printed on a wood-fiber paper that is lighter. But *please*: Read it at your leisure and when the mood strikes you to dip into it. It's *impossible* to read straight through a book like that the minute it arrives. It would pain me to think the book was a burden for you.

67 Hannah Arendt to Karl Jaspers

April 18, 1948

Lieber Verehrtester—

How wonderful to be able to send this letter to a new address and one that is now firm. In the meantime I saw your parting words[1] (in good old *Aufbau*,[2] with which I so often squabble). I admired the sovereign assurance with which you reject everything that smacks in the least of humbug and with which you are always able to put your

106

finger on just what it is that deserves rejection. And with what skill you strike out amiably at both sides.

I'm glad too that I finally have some "business" news to report: There still aren't any statements from *Die Schuldfrage*,[3] except a very small one for $34. I'm afraid this little book has come out too late. And then, Dial Press didn't do much for it. Just as the book was coming out, the partner in the firm who had approached me was having such a terrible fight with the other partners that he was going to his lawyer and to court instead of to the office. As a consequence, the others gave hardly any attention to advertising the book, and I wasn't in a position to do much about it, because I had never dealt with any of them. Pantheon (Kurt Wolff)[4] would like to join forces with the English publisher to bring out a new edition of *Die Geistige Situation der Zeit*. That's a superb idea. As I once tried to indicate to you, Kurt Wolff would also like to have your *Psychopathologie*, but in an abridged edition aimed at an American audience. I assume he will write to you directly. He is about to leave for Europe anyhow, and he will surely come to see you.

I've written to Heidelberg repeatedly to say that only the second part of your *Logik* has arrived. It's so awful to begin a book like that in the middle. Monsieur has done so and is reading with great interest. I haven't been able to bring myself to that yet and hope that I can somehow take the book along with me for summer vacation. Perhaps there is a chance of getting the missing first part sent to me after all.

Sternberger has just written me that you took care of the contract for my essays with Lambert Schneider. I was very touched by that. I'm mentioning this, too, to tell you something I've been meaning to say for a long time, which is that you—because you are so adept at such things—probably can't even begin to imagine how catastrophically dim-witted I am with anything that has to do with money. It is therefore really much better that you speak with Kurt Wolff yourself, if at all possible, even though I know him quite well. He is very clever, doesn't have much money, but does have a good and respected publishing house. He is, if I really think about it, quite capable of taking advantage of me for as much as he can get away with unscathed. That is not meant at all as a judgment against him. He just happens to enjoy the game and I, I'm sorry to say, do not. As long as you were in Germany it didn't matter much. But now it fills me with genuine horror to think that I, with my financial frivolousness, am your representative here.

I wish I could write that I am coming this summer. But the political situation looks so bad that even we, who don't really believe a war is in the making, still sometimes feel a touch of fear. But no matter how I turn things over in my mind, I just don't see how I can manage a trip. My publisher here, who has received two-thirds of my imperialism book, is thoroughly satisfied but also firmly convinced that he will have the whole book by the end of this year at the latest. And he has every right to expect that; he has been very decent with me. I can't keep to that schedule unless I work right through the summer.

I've just reread your first lines from Basel. They sound wonderfully enterprising. You have doubtless moved out of your hotel room and into your house by now, and I hope your wife hasn't overworked herself. I'm eager to have first reports from both of you. It has always seemed to me that Basel is truly Europe, even more so than Zurich, located so beautifully as it is on the border of three countries.

With the very best of wishes
Your
Hannah

68   Karl Jaspers to Hannah Arendt

Basel, May 22, 1948

Dear Hannah!

I've been meaning to write for a long time, to thank you for your last letter—to tell you how sorry I am that you can't come this year (I understand completely; you *must* finish the book; the world situation is gloomy)—to report that K. Wolff still hasn't made me an offer, that I told him it was out of the question for you to abridge my *Psychopathologie*. Your time is totally taken up with your own extremely important work, and you are too good for such tasks.

But what has prompted me to write is a check for $100 from Beacon Press that came as a surprise to me, an advance for the *Universitäts-Idee*. Surely you are behind this. I'm still in the dark about it and am hoping that it relates to Frau Professor Weyl's translation and that *there is no conflicting arrangement. Could you please check on that?* I don't want to cash the check or reply to the press until I am sure on that point.

We are getting underway here. We had some bad luck, but it is all behind us now. All three of us had the flu. The maid was so sick she had to stay in bed. I had only a slight brush with it and taught despite a fever (something I haven't done for decades). I didn't want to give out any evil omens and let illness make a bad name for me right at the outset. I'm dreadfully proud that I pulled it off and that nobody noticed a thing. Now I'm rid of the fever but somewhat tired. —Then we ran into the difficulties a democracy has with its many agencies and commissions. I was worried about the pension for my wife in the event of my death (something that has preoccupied me all my life), but everything was in order on that score, indeed, in the best of order. State and foundation funds assured me a place in the state retirement system. And because of my advanced age I don't have to pay any further premiums![1] —Then they wanted to back down on renting me the house for life (and at a rent favorable to me), but after some negotiating back and forth we ended up with what had been promised me, and I cannot be turned out of the house during my lifetime (an important point in view of the housing shortage here). —The only drawback is that my wife will have to move out if she survives me.[2] But then, she wouldn't be able to pay the rent anyhow,[3] and the house would be larger than she would need.

So now I've related to you all these practical matters in which I've been investing my entire energy and my "diplomatic" skills, such as they are. Of course, in the back of one's mind lurks the question of when the Russians will wipe out this whole lovely edifice of security. But that question suggests another whole range of eventualities, for which one cannot plan and against which one can do nothing. In the context of the island we live on, this "security" has a comforting effect.

The milkman's truck at our door every morning is wonderful! A symbol for all of it.

My lectures and seminar[4] are underway and are, as things go here, very well attended. If this summer's lecture turns out well, I'll make a book out of it right away: "Ursprung und Einheit der Geschichte"[5]—no doubt a rather presumptuous project. Not a one of my books can be bought here. Philosophical texts for the seminar cannot be had—things were better in Heidelberg, where I got copies from Meiner for each of my students and bought up large stores for the department and stockpiled them for future classes (now my successor[6] will have the benefit of them).

I hope that a new copy of the *Logik*, sent by Piper, has reached you by now. But please don't read it—that can wait for *years!*

Now for the main thing: Your essays arrived from Lambert Schneider. I read your dedication again—and seldom have I felt such joy— these words from you, and that you stand by me publicly, mean more to me and honor me more than any Goethe Prize,[7] honorary doctorate,[8] or whatever. The things you say will last. I went on reading: a wonderful book! I'm curious to see what people in Germany will say about it. Perhaps nothing, as happens with almost all new publications.

Enough for now. With warmest gratitude,

Your Karl Jaspers

69   Hannah Arendt to Karl Jaspers

May 28, 1948

Lieber Verehrtester:

Your letters, the one from April and the one from May, which I received yesterday, both exude so much joie de vivre and so much faith and confidence that they warmed my heart and made me very happy. It's wonderful that you are embarking on your new life with such cheerful thoughts. I was touched by the fond mention you both made of the milk truck, but even more so by the feverish beginning of your lectures. What a wonderful subject. I'm eager to read everything you will write about it. And here a question straight off: The editor[1] of *Commentary* (which has already published parts of your Geneva speech) asked me a few days ago to tell you that he would very much like to have something else from you. I told him yesterday about "Ursprung und Einheit der Geschichte." Do you by chance have an introduction to that lecture series that could be published as a separate essay? He was very interested, an excellent man, as well educated in philosophy as professional philosophers here, and with wide reading and a lot of political and human insight. In addition to you, he has published Thomas Mann, Sartre, Dewey, etc. The magazine is regarded as very good by everyone and not just in Jewish circles. They pay about $150 for an article (more if it doesn't need to be translated).

And while we're on business matters: Please cash the Beacon Press check. Everything is in perfect order. The terms (10% royalties) are very good for a translated book. Publishers usually pay only 7–8% for the first 3 to 5,000 copies in such cases. And so I seized the opportunity right away. I wrote to Frau Weyl and advised her to get in touch with the people at Beacon directly herself. It is up to the publisher to select the translator, pay him, and so forth. I can't very well interfere there. It would not be good and not customary. Beacon Press has a good reputation, and they will do a good job. —I assume that Kurt Wolff has written to you in the meantime. He sent me your letter, which made me blush. Of course I will do the editorial work if that is agreeable to you. Unfortunately, an American psychiatrist will be needed, too, one that is not a psychoanalyst. Psychoanalysis has become a downright plague here or, more correctly, a madness. Wolff told me that he first has to get a general picture of how much the editing and translation will cost before he can propose terms to you. I'm glad that we have Beacon Press and one can cite their generosity as a precedent. —I'm not sending you the contract with Dial Press because I seem to recall having sent it to you before.[2] There aren't any statements yet, apart from the prepublication account. I have four copies of *German Guilt* left here. What shall I do with them? People here have come to want to hear almost as little about these things as they do in Germany. Russia overshadows everything else. Which leads people to the frivolous conclusion that fascism is dead. Meanwhile, it has won a victory in South Africa[3] that is depressingly similar to the Nazis' victory in 1929.[4] —Palestine: I'm so preoccupied by it at the moment that I simply can't write about it. Magnes[5] is here, the leader of the only group that is still willing to pursue an understanding with the Arabs; and without having much confidence in the whole business I've let my sense of duty drag me into quite a circus, complete with public speaking and secret memorandums. It will perhaps become clear next week whether there's any point to all this or whether it isn't wiser for me to pull back for the time being.

The complete *Logik* finally arrived a week ago. Many, many thanks. I'll take it with me on vacation. I have looked into it already of course, but only enough to see that you have gone beyond your earlier existential positions yet without giving them up. It is a great book, and wherever one happens to open it, it is written with the same bright, clear precision. (I've just read the section about Hamlet.)[6]

I'm looking forward to spending my holidays with the book. It's a bit as if I had been able to see you (no, not just a bit).

I'm much relieved that you agree with the concentration-camp article. It will be a chapter in my book, and though it is not necessarily central there at all, it is nevertheless clear that if the reader doesn't understand it, then he hasn't understood anything else. —If you still like the essay volume in its printed form, then all is surely well. (Even

though I myself know that "this is all there is, and it's not enough."[7])
Mixed in with my happiness at feeling a bond with you is the fulfillment
of a child's wish not to disappoint you. You are quite simply the
greatest educator of all time. Don't laugh; it's true; and only because
you are a philosopher.

As always—
Your Hannah

70   Karl Jaspers to Hannah Arendt

Basel, June 7, 1948

Dear Hannah!

Just a few lines on business matters, which you are handling so well
for me. I've cashed the check from Beacon Press and will write to
thank them for it.

On the essay for *Commentary*[1]: I'm enclosing a short section from
my manuscript. My wife copied it for me. But I doubt whether it is
suitable, whether it is understandable in itself, whether it isn't just too
"difficult" in its language. So I won't be disappointed if this essay is
not acceptable. You decide, and then the editors of the magazine.

How nice your letter was, how much it cheered me, as always!
Now you make me out to be "the greatest educator of all time"!—
funny, at this very moment I'm on a commission that has to fill the
teaching slot for pedagogy. My predecessor[2] taught pedagogy, a subject
I'm neither suited nor prepared for. A privatdocent will be hired to
teach it.

Warmest greetings
Your Karl Jaspers

71   Hannah Arendt to Karl Jaspers

Hanover, N.H., July 16, 1948

Lieber Verehrtester—

Every day when I open the newspaper I think about you and rejoice
that you are where you are. I'm writing to you from my vacation spot
but haven't much to tell about the vacation because I've just arrived.
I do, however, have two months this time, so I'm feeling very pleased.
I'll be leaving Schocken at the beginning of the winter, and because

of the war in Palestine[1] I've started to be politically active again. And that, of course, I can't shake off even on vacation. More on this another time.

I read *Der philosophische Glaube* right away and immediately passed on to Cohen your wonderful essay for *Commentary*. He will presumably write to you himself. You make your reader really want to be a citizen of the world again, or, to put it more correctly, you make that possible again. The essay is striking for its fresh and open naturalness, in which the entire Occident lights up and illuminates a landscape that it no longer circumscribes. Your relativizing of the Judeo-Christian faith, coming as it does from such a clear, unembittered, and profound understanding, provides a solid basis for the concept of humanity and reconciles in the best sense of that word. The key thing here, it seems to me, is this element of reconciliation, which you had not truly found before but which now informs everything you do.[2] I don't have *Wahrheit* here with me yet, because Monsieur is still reading it, but I will get it at the end of the month when he joins me here for two weeks. So I'll have more to say very soon.

Business: I'm still negotiating with Kurt Wolff. He wrote to Herbert Read at Routledge & Kegan Paul in London, because he felt he could take a chance on *Psychopathologie* only if he went in on it with an English publisher. He also asked me about *Der philosophische Glaube*, and I think his wife, who is in Europe right now, is reading it. Have you had *Wahrheit* and *Der philosophische Glaube* sent to Beacon Press too? If not, try to get your publisher to do that. Wolff always tries to get everything as cheaply as possible, and in a certain sense he has to because his is a young enterprise with practically no capital behind it. Beacon Press, on the other hand, is an old Boston publishing house that can afford to be liberal. I'm telling you this essentially because Kurt Wolff will always, for example, deduct the translation costs and any editorial costs from your author's honorarium, which Beacon Press does not do. I should note, however, that translation costs are, unfortunately, customarily handled this way, but not editorial costs.

It's good that you've gotten rid of pedagogy. My remark wasn't meant that way, of course. I was just trying to express myself in the American mode, half in jest, half in earnest. But it's true nonetheless, and what I like so much about your new books is that what made the most lasting impression on me in our earlier personal contact is now appearing, fully objectified (what a dreadful word!), in everything you write. But pedagogy as a discipline probably doesn't even really exist. It strikes me as similar to sociology, which is a substitute for history.

I'm assuming that classes are over and that you're sitting somewhere in the mountains on vacation. Or am I overly optimistic?

Sternberger asked me whether I wanted to take over the editorship of *Die Wandlung* during his absence. I turned him down—for reasons you'll have no trouble in guessing. And besides I probably—no, almost certainly—couldn't have left here for six months.

With warm regards to you both—

Your

Hannah

72 *Karl Jaspers to Hannah Arendt*

Basel, September 19, 1948

Dear Hannah!

It's been much too long since you heard from me last, and today I have a special reason for writing: a request for you to receive a brief visit from Dr. Jobst von der Groeben and his wife, [Alexandra,] who was born Countess Schwerin. Both of them were very close to us during the Nazi period. He is a psychiatrist but a man with broad learning. They are going to America—a move made possible because of special happy circumstances of their own making—because they simply can't stand it in Germany anymore: the "national" spirit and all the nastiness that goes along with it and that gets worse all the time. He feels that anyone who is "clean" is quietly pushed off to one side. So now these young people want to try to make a life for themselves in America. Thanks to their friend Yehudi Menuhin, they will not be dependent on their own earnings right away, but he would, of course, like to find some kind of psychiatric work as soon as possible. You can't help him find a job, but I had two thoughts: First, it will be an encouragement for von der Groeben to know that a person like you is living in America. And, second, it seemed possible to me that you might take pleasure in getting to know some young people like this from the coming generation. He is about thirty; she is twenty-one. We knew her as a schoolgirl through her mother [Gabriele, Countess von Schwerin], who, although she was Reichenau's[1] sister-in-law, was a wonderfully refreshing despiser of National Socialism and acted accordingly. The daughter was nonchalant in her behavior. She once

114

asked in school: Why can't we marry Jews if we can marry a Japanese? Her remarks finally brought the Gestapo down on her. Then the end of the war came along and saved her. Both of them are terribly disappointed with postwar Germany now and thoroughly weary of Germany. He was in Oxford for a few years as a student, hence his present possibilities. My wife and I are fond of these decent people.

How is your imperialism book coming? —Your vacation will be over by now. I read with some concern that you are giving up your job with Schocken. Did you find you couldn't put up any longer with old "Bismarck," as you once called the boss? —Now Sternberger will visit you. So he will get to see you again before I will. Well, I don't begrudge it to him. He's one of those people you can depend on. And all in all he's an excellent writer and editor, even though I sometimes find myself at odds with his intellectual and literary outlook and have to check myself to remain fair to him. He is a delight in Heidelberg because he is independent and open-minded and, as a citizen of the world, a man of goodwill. His cleverness, his caution, which will, however, boldly say what has to be said, has brought him through so far. I hope that continues to be so. Lambert Schneider made a convincing case to me that *Die Wandlung* would survive regardless of circumstances.

Of Basel all I can do is continue to say good things. We've been here for half a year now. During the holidays we got to know the city and its surroundings a bit. It is a little paradise. The landscape, the atmosphere in the city, buildings from the Middle Ages still undamaged—there was never a devastating war here. Basel was even spared in the Thirty Years' War. It's like a last island in the flood—when will the rising waters wash over it, too! There's still a brief reprieve.

During the holidays I put my summer lectures together into a book: "Vom Ursprung und Ziel der Geschichte"—presumptuous, as always, way beyond my powers. But one should do what gives one pleasure. Now, after a long pause, I'm reading a lot again and collecting material for my winter lectures "Einleitung in die Philosophie"—a heading under which one can read whatever one likes.

From the end of April on, we had visitors in the house. Now the rooms have been empty a few days for the first time. Next week Ernst Mayer is coming again for a week's stay; then we'll be without visitors for many weeks. In the winter we're expecting my sister-in-law from London,[2] in February, my sister from Oldenburg. Having visitors is wonderful. Sometime you will come too—if the world holds together a while longer.

Palestine remains a cause for worry. A few days ago Professor A. Fraenkel[3] from Jerusalem (a mathematician) spoke here. Very impressive in his matter-of-factness. Great accomplishments on the part of the Jews, also of the university. Remarkable, the optimism of this man. After hearing his lecture you could think: Everything will turn out fine. He trusts the Arabs: he thinks they could get on famously together. He had examples to illustrate that. The war, he said, was an English war against the Jews. Their military strength has increased the Jews' prestige in the world enormously (ultimately, all *anyone* pays any attention to in the end is the language of weapons, in spite of anything else they may say!). I feel very uneasy with all this sort of thing.

Warmest greetings
Your Karl Jaspers

73 Hannah Arendt to Karl Jaspers

October 31, 1948

Lieber Verehrtester:

Your good letter of September has gone unanswered for too long. Your friends haven't put in an appearance yet. I will of course be delighted to have them visit us.

Sternberger has been here and already left again. He was completely unchanged, though somewhat more cordial than before. We are both doubtless more open than we were in our youth. He has a good journalistic eye, thinks clearly, is perhaps a little too clever, understood a great deal about this country, an astonishing amount in such a short time. I'm afraid he would have stayed here most happily. I didn't really have time for him but did get him together with a few people. He drinks, as the Americans admiringly say, like a man from Tennessee.

I've also spoken at great length with Tillich and Helene Wieruszowski. There's no point in my recounting those conversations, but the upshot of them is nonetheless that I'm truly relieved that you are in Switzerland. Tillich, who, as you will no doubt have noticed, has not exactly changed, was quite befuddled and delighted by Germany. By and large out of sentimentality. Helene Wieruszowski was ecstatic about her visit with you. I am very grateful to you because you helped her so much to regain some self-confidence. Things are still hard for her here. There is some chance that a good friend of mine who thinks very highly of her will soon become chairman of the history department at Brooklyn College. Then perhaps she could finally get some real help.

Your article for *Commentary*[1] has been beautifully translated and will, I understand, appear this month. I read the proofs two weeks ago. Who is publishing "Ursprung und Ziel der Geschichte"? It's very important to have it appear here, and there's no doubt in my mind that you will be getting an inquiry about it. I wasn't able to talk with Wolff once my long vacation was over, because he was very ill. He's recovering slowly now. I hope *Commentary* has already sent you your payment. I've reminded them about it in any case.

I had two long months of vacation, during which my mother died. She had gone to England to see my stepsister and other relatives she hadn't seen for over ten years, and she had a heart attack on the ship.

I've been horribly busy since I came back. Magnes, the president of the Hebrew University in Jerusalem, had enlisted me, before I left for vacation, to act as a political adviser for his little American group. Through our correspondence this summer I developed a very close working relationship with Magnes himself, who was a magnificent sort. He died this week. I knew that he was very ill, and he did, too. That was one of my reasons for accepting his offer. What will happen now, I don't know. The man simply cannot be replaced. He was an unusual mix of typically American common sense and integrity along with a genuine, half-religious Jewish passion for justice. He exercised a personal influence on people and had a certain authority among both Jews and Arabs, not a real political influence but much more than none at all. His Palestinian group is always in danger of being sucked into the nationalistic wake, and he was the only person far and wide who always at the last minute kept them from that. I'm much afraid that they will now become more "realistic" and will consequently lose all their influence, representing nothing but pallid moderation, with one compromise after another, before they finally dissolve. I hope I'm being too pessimistic. There are real possibilities for getting somewhere with the Americans here, especially because we have *Commentary* and its editor, Elliot Cohen, on our side and because the group includes very rich lawyers and so forth who have good connections. With Magnes's help and total agreement, I was in the process of winning over intellectuals and socialists. But in the last analysis everything depends on the group in Palestine holding together, and over that I have not the slightest influence.

Please don't worry about Schocken. The job I have now[2] is better financially. Besides, we can always live, if only modestly, on what Monsieur makes. I'm making use of my concentration-camp essay right now to negotiate with a few organizations for a major project on the social, political, and psychological factors of concentration camps under totalitarian governments. This is, of course, like all such projects, in part pure humbug, humbug dressed up in scholarly clothing. But, for all that, I could make something good of it, and because all I would have to do would be to supply the lead ideas and direct a staff of people, I would have a lot of time for my work.

I've written a great deal. The book is three-fourths finished. I dread the last quarter and have to read lots more material, which I'm pulling together right now.

I've just reread your remarks on the situation in Palestine and that you felt "very uneasy" at the optimistic lecture. Of course the war is not England's war. It would look very different, Lord knows, if it were. The English have a great interest in keeping peace in the Near East (and they are constantly trying to influence the Arabs in that direction. They are not supplying any weapons, for example, while almost all the weapons shipments to the Jews come from the Soviet bloc). And they have an equally strong interest in not pursuing an anti-American policy there. American policy under Truman is for the time being determined by the fact that Truman wants to be elected president again and needs the Jewish vote and Jewish influence to win. That won't always be so; and he's really playing with fire. Apart from that, the Jews, who are prepared to make any sacrifice, are of course the better soldiers. Letters from Palestine all speak of this "inspiring time." How many more times do we have to go through this? Monsieur says, in his despair: "If the Jews insist on becoming a nation like every other nation, why for God's sake do they insist on becoming like the Germans?" There is, alas, some truth to that.

All my best to you both.

Your Hannah

Basel, November 6, 1948

Dear Hannah!

Your mother has died. I know next to nothing about her, only that you got her out of Germany and then later to America and that you lived with her. It is, of course, the way of nature that old people die. But a fundamental change takes place when a person's mother dies, and the pain is deep, if not devastating. I was 58 when my mother[1] died. The loss of one's mother is the loss of a refuge that has always been there for you, an unconditional affirmation.

Your book has made great progress—but is still not finished. I think you shouldn't hesitate too long and shouldn't read too much more. It would be better to write another book. The one you're working on has to be completed on the impetus that gave rise to it, and that will not last forever. After a certain period, the project loses interest for the writer. But I can't really say how that is for you. So this is all just pointless babbling!

I received $150 from *Commentary* this week. Fabulous! 640 francs here, a very considerable sum. Once again I owe thanks to you, who arranged it all. And I do thank you very much. And you write, as well, that the translation is excellent. Wonderful! But *you* wound up reading the proofs. Thank you for that, too.

Today I received an inquiry from the Philosophical Library in New York regarding translation of my *Philosophischer Glaube*. The letter asked about terms. I want to suggest among other things that the translation be submitted to you for *judgment* (you once told me you would be willing to take on things like this). All you should do is read sample passages and give your approval or disapproval, *not* make corrections. Is that all right with you? I'm going to make an attempt at the business arrangements, but here too I would like to refer the publisher to you. You can approve *any* terms if I have asked too much. The main thing is that the project be carried through. The Philosophical Library has put out a fourth edition of an excellent reference work, *The Dictionary of Philosophy*, edited by Dagobert Runes.[2]

I read what you had to say about Sternberger, Tillich, Palestine with great interest. Monsieur's view is my own, word for word. In the pleasure of our mutual agreement, I send him my warmest greetings.

And you, good friend, rejoice constantly that we are here in Switzerland. Yes, it is a remarkably benign fate. Our home ground is lost to us in any case. Here we are, as it were, on a perpetual trip, but a

119

pleasant trip, and we have some distance and can indulge in reflection. And on top of that the old ways—from the very beginning—of which the milk wagon is the symbol.

I'm also finding it quite a good thing that I'm starting out all over again here in my old age, as it were, especially because it's working out so well. I'm a "success." Last week the auditorium was full to overflowing for my inaugural lecture, "Philosophie und Wissenschaft."[3] People were standing in the aisles, and some couldn't get in at all. For Basel, quite a sensation. During it all, I had the feeling of being in a friendly small town. This city turned out in force, so to speak, to see what it had acquired for itself with this appointment. The people are reserved, even more so than in my homeland. People are chary with praise, reticent, perhaps even a bit poverty-stricken of soul. The dean, contrary to all local custom, came up to me afterward and said, "I was deeply moved." Well, I know you enjoy these little tales too. I take pleasure in such things and allow myself to enjoy them as innocently as a child would.

My book "Vom Ursprung und Ziel der Geschichte" is finished but still not at the printer's. I've been somewhat delinquent with the technical end. The book is going to appear in Munich, and also in Zurich, since there is no book trade with Germany yet.

With warmest greetings and, as always, my thanks,

Your

Karl Jaspers

Our young friends didn't visit you because they couldn't reach you by phone and they were no doubt too unpracticed in the ways of a new country. They had to leave again quickly and are now at Yehudi Menuhin's house in California. I hope you'll get to meet them at some later time.

75 *Karl Jaspers to Hannah Arendt*

Basel, November 9, 1948

Dear Hannah!

Today I'm sending you a carbon copy of my letter to the Philosophical Library. I hope it is all right with you if I trouble you again with what I beg you to make a minimum of "supervision." You musn't under any circumstances let yourself get dragged into this any further.

Don't, for example, read through the translation or, worse yet, read proofs.

Something occurs to me again that I've been repeatedly forgetting. In the April 1948 issue of *Jewish Frontier* Ben Halpern has a review of my book on the question of guilt.[1] He sent me the issue and an accompanying letter. I haven't responded. The essay is motivated by an a priori hatred and contains attacks on me, some of which are absurd. But as often happens, even hatred can sometimes provide incisive insights. And the points on which he is perhaps right deserve some reflection. He made me aware that in writing *Die Schuldfrage* I was in fact enjoying distinct intellectual pleasure. Isn't there then some real point to his reproach of my "arrogance"? —Are you at all familiar with the article? —At first I wanted to reply. If I had nothing else to do, then I would attempt it. But as it is, I've just kept my silence and let the thing be.

With warmest greetings
Your Karl Jaspers

76 *Hannah Arendt to Karl Jaspers*

November 19, 1948

Lieber Verehrtester—

Thank you for both your letters. The Philosophical Library, represented by the owner, Mr. Runes, called yesterday, and in the middle of next week I'll discuss all the details with him. I've already been in touch with his salesman, who is a former colleague of mine from Schocken, to find out what Runes is like to deal with. I know that he has the reputation of "a somewhat dubious honorable man."[1]

But for all that he is clearly a capable man and does something for his books. He won't dare to cheat you, first, because he just won't, and, second, because he knows that I'll be able, through his salesman, to keep track of the book's sales better than anyone else. It's very good that you inserted a clause about the translator in your contract draft, because Runes will of course try to save money on the translator. The contract draft is good in other respects, too, though it would not have been at all out of line to ask for an advance on the entire first edition (you might not have got it), which will be about 2,000 copies, perhaps more. I'll see if I can't still do something on that point. Also, there isn't any difference in America between bound and paperback copies, because there is always only one edition.

Thank you for what you had to say about my book. You're right, of course. The sad thing is that in my head this has always been one book; in reality, at least as far as the historical material is concerned, it is three books: anti-Semitism, imperialism, and totalitarianism. But to make three books of it would not have been good either, and not only because the Jews would have stoned me dead after the first one (a fate I've managed to postpone by my dawdling), but also because I couldn't have developed my political argument. Now the first two parts are done, finished, and the last is under way. Next month I'll start writing again. In the meantime, I've had to acquire a somewhat more thorough knowledge of the course of the Russian Revolution.

I'll write again as soon as I have more details from the Philosophical Library.

Until then, all my best to you both,

Your

Hannah

P.S. I just remembered: Ben Halpern. (I'd repressed that.) I know him well and had a horrendous fight with him about that really criminally stupid article. After I failed to bring him around, I decided not to reply to it because the whole thing struck me as just too idiotic. He has joined that dismal breed that thinks any non-Jew is per definitionem an anti-Semite. He explained this theory to Monsieur in great detail without noticing even for a second how absurd the situation was. We tried to explain to him that you were about the least likely person he could have chosen to illustrate the few things he said in that article that were right. He was hoping of course that I—or (better yet) you—would respond. I refused to give him your address and said I would respond only if the article drew a major reaction. He promised to send me everything that comes in about it. And because he's a very honest young fellow, I can trust him not to hold anything out on me. What did come in was an even crazier letter from Eugen Rosenstock[2] (remember him?), which neither Halpern nor I could understand. Whereupon I said to him: I told you so, and left for vacation with my mind at peace. Don't be angry that I never wrote you about this. Like so many things, I did that too out of mixed motives. First of all, I didn't want to bother you with what was, after all, a foolish business, especially when you had to cope with all the German attacks that followed your departure from Heidelberg.[3] And then, I was furious with myself for not having been able to bring Halpern around. Do you want to respond? Sometimes wading into something like this can be fun. *Jewish Frontier* would be delighted. Halpern is the managing editor; Greenberg, chief editor. People like controversies here because they enliven the scene a bit. Halpern got all riled up years ago about my "Organized Guilt,"[4] which Greenberg had commissioned and published.

77 Karl Jaspers to Hannah Arendt

Basel, November 23, 1948

Dear Hannah!

Just a quick business reply to your—as always—helpful letter.

My terms were accepted in a letter from Mrs. Morse. A check for $50 was enclosed. Another title was suggested, several in fact, all quite reasonable. The person who came up with them must have read my book and understood something of it. I've accepted the title *The Perennial Scope of Philosophy.*[1]

I take it that it is customary in America not to write a contract but to make do with an exchange of letters like this? Mrs. Rose Morse's signature on a sheet of the Philosophical Library's letterhead stationery doesn't strike me as a legally binding document by our standards. There ought to be two signatures and the designation *per procura*. But these are purely matters of form. Your reference to a "somewhat dubious honorable man," however, set me to thinking about such matters. —I'm delighted that you will judge the quality of the translation.

Commentary sent an unusually nice letter and $150. I think I mentioned that to you already.

I really don't feel like responding to Ben Halpern. In the summer I did, but I have too little time now. It seems to me, especially in light of what you have told me, that this isn't a substantive issue but more a personal matter—or that the substantive issue is so absurd that there's no point in talking about it.

Warmest greetings
Your Karl Jaspers

December 4, 1948

Dear Friends—

I'm enclosing a copy of my suggestion for the "somewhat dubious honorable man."[1] He acted astonished on the phone when I said a contract was required, but he asked me to send him a draft for one. I had already discussed with him the difference between an advance on 500 copies (which you suggested) and one for 1,000, which I consider more appropriate. The $50 he sent you is just a kind of option, which is customary here.

Apropos the "somewhat dubious honorable man": after my experience with the eminently decent but insufferably incompetent Schockens, I'm all for having a go with some shadier types. Kurt Wolff, for example, is not exactly an angel either.

More soon. I'm in a rush at the moment.

With all best wishes
Your
Hannah

79   *Hannah Arendt to Karl Jaspers*

New York, December 22, 1948

Lieber Verehrtester:

This is a New Year's letter in which I will include "business" matters. I'm sorry to say that Kurt Wolff got a negative response from England on the *Psychopathologie* and can't risk publishing the book in English on his own. That is a great pity, but Runes, from the Philosophical Library, told me that he is essentially interested in everything of yours and just wanted to begin with *Philosophischer Glaube*.

I received the contract from the Philosophical Library today, and I'm proud of myself for coaxing good terms out of Runes and getting them put down in written form. You'll be getting the contract in a few days and will see that he has agreed to pay higher royalties after the first printing of 2,500 copies and that he has doubled the advance. He didn't have to do either of these things, because you hadn't asked for them.

The painter and physician Alcopley[1] told us to our amazement that he had visited you. Dear friends, you will get photographs. Monsieur will overcome his Prussian-Protestant and I my Old Testament inhibitions, and we will betake ourselves to one of these ladies or gentlemen equipped with flash bulbs and other instruments of torture. Alcopley has told us that if we don't do it ourselves, he'll send a photographer to our apartment.

For the moment, though, I'm sending you a clipping from the *New York Times*,[2] which will also serve the purpose of letting you know what I've been up to lately. Now it's up to the directors to raise some money. I, at any rate, have done my part by helping to set up the foundation and by writing an introductory pamphlet about Jewish-Arab reconciliation. I'll send you a copy as soon as it is printed.

All is well with us. I'm working on my book in earnest again. The publisher has set a deadline—June 1. That is all to the good, because it puts some external pressure on me. At first I balked at deadlines, and the publisher was very considerate with me. At the moment I'm taking great pleasure in Christmas—or, as we call it—Weihnukkah[3] preparations. I'm buying all manner of truck for adopted nieces and nephews and giving considerable thought to the roasting of ducks.

All the warmest of wishes from our house to yours

As always, your
Hannah

80   Hannah Arendt to Karl Jaspers

New York, January 9, 1949

Lieber Verehrtester,

I still haven't heard anything from Italy,[1] and I've written to Dial that you are living in Switzerland now and can easily be reached. Perhaps you should send the publisher mentioned above[2] a copy of the German or Swiss edition.[3]

Apropos of Dial it just occurs to me: Have you received the royalty check that was due you according to the half-year statment Dial sent me?

Warmest greetings
Your
Hannah

Basel, January 13, 1949

Dear Hannah!

First of all I want to thank you for the picture from the newspaper—as a temporary substitute for a picture of you and Monsieur. We have looked at it, profoundly touched, again and again and are both attracted and taken aback. That's probably because you are not looking into the camera. We hardly recognized you! That's strange. Newspaper photos like this can—I know from experience—distort a great deal. But you áre not "distorted." You look so austere, spare, noble, and superior. If I didn't know you personally and your letters, I'd be a little afraid of you, but I'd be eager to speak with this person.

And then I want to thank you too for your adroitness in pushing through the contract with Runes. That's marvelous. I don't have it yet. But since you have it, it must be on its way to me. And these improvements of the terms beyond my suggestions! I used to think I was quite a good businessman. Now you have outdone me!

Forty dollars and a statement came from Dial Press quite a while ago. The sales were clearly poor. By the time the book[1] appeared, the issue was no longer of current interest.

I've written the Italian publisher in Florence that an Italian translation of my *Schuldfrage* already appeared, a year ago (in Naples).[2]

Did I tell you that my *Psychopathologie* has been translated into Spanish in Buenos Aires?[3] I recently received an advance of 1,700 francs, half of which I was unfortunately bound by contract to give to Springer. Only for my later books have I retained the translation rights for myself alone.

Your publisher seems to be a wise and good man in setting a deadline for you. We all need deadlines. You certainly need them more than most because you are always letting yourself be distracted by rendering aid to people such as me. That is, of course, very nice . . .

I'm eager to see your pamphlet on the Jews and Arabs. I find myself without arguments when well-meaning Jews say to me: The Arabs just don't want to cooperate. Magnes was a dreamer. He had hardly anyone behind him. I want to learn from you how I should respond. So far I have simply said: If the Arabs don't want to go along, then infinite patience will have to bring them to the point where they do want to, for the geographical context and the interests of today's major powers in that part of the world permit a long-term political existence for Israel only within the framework of the Arab world. Otherwise,

Israel will remain a purely defensive stronghold, maintained by American money; and, like all defensive strongholds, it will eventually be overrun.

England's ruthless interference is causing great consternation now. Holland's success[4] has presumably given them courage? It's almost as if the English wanted to prevent the agreements that are taking shape right now between the Jews, Abdullah,[5] and the Egyptians. Operating on the principle of *divide et impera*, the Jews have managed their power politics very cleverly and would no doubt have succeeded if it hadn't been for England?

I'm having a printed copy of my inaugural lecture in Basel sent to you (it's in *Die Wandlung*[6]). It's nothing special, trimmed to suit the occasion and the audience (innumerable colleagues and the city authorities).

Warmest greetings
Your Karl Jaspers

82 *Karl Jaspers to Hannah Arendt*

Basel, January 25, 1949

Dear Hannah!

Enclosed is a carbon copy of the letter I have sent to the Philosophical Library[1] along with the contract that arrived here yesterday.[2] Mr. Runes never put in an appearance himself. Mrs. Rose Morse must presumably have legal authority. As you will see, the contract too is signed only by her. I assume her signature is legally binding. It is customary here to have two signatures from publishing houses, one of which is the chief's. But I don't think we need insist on this. It can't, in any case, guarantee the main thing, which is that the translation be a decent one. Goodwill is the crucial thing. Mrs. Morse said in her accompanying letter that you had seen and approved this contract. That was enough for me. The minor emendation[3] contained in my letter mentioned above could, under some circumstances, be quite important.

For all this, once again my most heartfelt thanks!

Your Karl Jaspers

Basel, January 26, 1949

Dear Hannah!

From the enclosed letter you will see that Beacon Press wants to publish separately the section on tragic knowledge from my book *Von der Wahrheit*[1] . . . "so that the way will be prepared for publishing the entire work in the near future." The friendly feeling and good intentions expressed in that last clause are nice to hear, and the translation of this book section, which can stand very well alone, pleases me immensely. Once again you have brought all this about, and it is you I have to thank. Your care for my material well-being since 1945 has been fantastic.

Our life in Basel continues to be pleasant. I'm working harder on my lectures here than I did in Heidelberg. The fact is that I have to create a new footing for myself here. That doesn't bother me. But the thought that premature illness and aging might render me a financial loss to Basel does bother me. That still seems far from being the case. I'm keeping my chin up. That is the one thing that would have been different in Heidelberg: the rights that I had acquired through forty years of work. In other respects we remain delighted that we don't have to live there any longer. The news from Germany is not good. Here, at a distance, sympathy increases and anger subsides—but there is no denying that I do not belong among *those* Germans. That makes me all the more eager to write my Germany book, for there is something in the German character that I love above all else and that one perhaps loves best when one floats about homeless in the world. I often think of you in this connection, and the thought cheers and encourages me: to become a citizen of the world and a human being and not to be alone in doing so. For political order and freedom, America is the only hope. For philosophy, there is still at least *a* hope in the German character. I'm in agreement with Gundolf here: In the Western world, there are three peoples from whom individuals have peered into the depths—Jews, Greeks, Germans. But to put it that way is surely arrogant—let's at least conceal that arrogance!

With warmest greetings
Your Karl Jaspers

January 28, 1949

Lieber Verehrtester:

Just got your letter saying that the contract had arrived. I was surprised too that Mr. Runes stayed so much in the background. But it is customary here that contracts are signed by employees. I used to sign things at Schocken, too, without having any legal authority. And of course the contracts were actionable. My own contract with Houghton Mifflin is signed by the editor. Re translators: so far the Philosophical Library has been reasonable. They had chosen a translator, apparently a friend of Mr. Runes, and sent me sample pages that were impossible. They then went, without the slightest word of protest, to the same translator [Ralph Manheim] who did your article for *Commentary* and who has a good reputation here. Now we just have to wait and see. I don't know if he has accepted the offer. I know him well. He has translated for me occasionally; he's nearly bilingual.

We laughed a lot over your reaction to the newspaper photo. Yes, of course, it's distorted, but probably only to the extent that I distort myself on such occasions, a bit according to the principle: Oh, how good that no one knows my name is Rumpelstiltskin.

Your inaugural lecture on philosophy and science [*Wissenschaft*] is very good, also very well written and wonderful for students or, more correctly, for introducing young people to the field. I'd very much like to publish it here, because the debate for and against scholarship is in full swing. It is, of course, taking an exclusively pragmatic form that is characteristic of America. Sometimes I wonder which is more difficult: to instill an awareness of politics in the Germans or to convey to Americans even the slightest inkling of what philosophy is all about. I'll give this a little more thought and then let you know what I've done.

I was very pleased to hear about the translation of the *Psychopathologie* into Spanish. The Spanish as well as the Italians are extremely open-minded, and South America is culturally closer to Europe than the States are. Philosophical books are published in numerically respectable printings there, and somebody told me that you can buy Kant's *Critique of Pure Reason* at railroad-station newsstands in Brazil or Argentina. In New York it's a major accomplishment to turn up a copy in any language.

I have to tell you something else here that weighs on my soul: I haven't read *Von der Wahrheit* yet. I've looked into it, but every time I did I was overwhelmed by a fear that philosophy would gobble me up whole again for months on end. I can't take a chance on that as long as I'm still struggling with the last part of my book. I know you will understand that, and I don't mean it as an excuse but simply to tell you how things are. —*Philosophie*—the three volumes in one volume[1]—has arrived. Many, many thanks. My old copy is—or perhaps is no longer—in Paris. I stole for myself a copy of the *Psychologie der Weltanschauungen*. So pretty soon I'll have your works complete again. I managed to make off with somebody else's copy of *Nietzsche*, too; but then the lender took it back.

Please stop reading here. It's Frl. Dr. Lewin's[2] turn now, and this concerns your wife.

I'm afraid there's nothing I can do. Schocken is hardly worth considering. They would probably drag the business out so long that we'll all be dead first. The Jewish Publication Society[3] is a more likely prospect perhaps, but Täubler[4] or, better still, his wife[5] has connections there. Täubler is either completely unknown here or has ruined his reputation with all manner of stupid projects, playwriting among them. That is the literal truth. Not that I have anything against plays, but the ones he writes are not even worthy of a talented eighteen-year-old. The Americans, in whom respect for erudition is not very highly developed, seem to consider him some kind of pompous fool. A grant would be hard to get, but an advance would be a possibility and might do her just as much good. Of one thing I'm sure: No publisher is going to commit himself on the basis of a list of chapters. The best route to take is for Selma Stern-Täubler to write to the Jewish Publication Society and ask whether it would be worthwhile for Dr. Lewin to send sample chapters. Unfortunately, that all takes time. This all sounds so negative, and I understand so well how eager you are to be of help. But the only advice I can offer is simply to send several chapters in several copies.

I hope that by the time this letter reaches you you'll be alone again and can look forward to your sister-in-law's visit in peace. The older one gets, the more difficult it seems to be to live closely with people who are not rooted in precisely the same sphere as oneself. Then all of a sudden every word rubs you the wrong way, and there's nothing at all one can do about it, that is, about one's psychic nerves.

Good-bye for now. And may I say once again, for a change, how delighted I am that you are in Basel?

With warmest greetings always
Your
Hannah

Basel, February 3, 1949

Dear Hannah!

I'm guilty of a dire sin of omission. I didn't tell you that I had sent my inaugural lecture "Philosophie und Wissenschaft" to *Commentary* and that I'm waiting for their response (Mr. Warshow[1] wrote me months ago that they would be glad to publish me frequently in *Commentary*). Now you have made other inquiries—and I'm to blame for the confusion. I've heard from Sternberger in Heidelberg that *Partisan Review* has inquired about this essay—probably, as I presume from your letter today—prompted by you! I had to write back and ask *Partisan Review* to wait until I have heard from *Commentary*. I'm terribly annoyed with myself for this mess I've made.

Of course I understand perfectly that you are not reading my book *Von der Wahrheit* now—and I would understand too if you were never to read it. How awful if we should pain each other with our books; and since you "know all that anyway"—in a philosophical sense—tedious professorial rambling in overly fat books is at best a dubious enterprise. We ought to regard our books as very secondary products, even though we invest so much work in them and live in the unshakable faith that at some time they just could be important for someone. And in the course of time—who knows?—you may find one chapter or another useful to you.

Wera Lewin is a fine person. Your thoughts on the possibilities for her are clear. We'll talk with her and see if she wants to pursue the course you've suggested. I'm ready at any time to supply a very positive reference about her intellectual character. As a "nonexpert," I can't very well say much about her qualifications as a historian. She was educated in Germany, took her doctorate with Andreas,[2] and studied some with me back then (at the beginning of the Nazi period). The things of hers I have read are excellent.

Warmest greetings from your
Karl Jaspers

February 15, 1949

Lieber Verehrtester:

I was terribly pleased about the good news from Beacon Press. That is really wonderful and, for once, just the way things should go. You have probably heard from *Commentary* in the meantime. The essay appears to have been too purely philosophical for them. Warshow knew that *Partisan Review* was interested in it and has presumably let them know that the essay is now available for them. Even though it's possible that you will get a somewhat lower fee, I'm still essentially pleased that things have worked out this way because *Partisan Review*'s readership, primarily students and young intellectuals, is a more important one for this essay to reach.

Your remarks about Basel are so fresh and lively, and those about the rights you earned in Heidelberg I find touching. Hasn't it ever really occurred to you that you have these rights everywhere where your books are known or can be known? That is all utterly obvious and a matter of course, and the Baselers surely know that, too. And then there is Germany. We are no doubt in such complete agreement about it that there is little more one can say on the subject. The anger I leave to Monsieur (I have enough of that on my back with my Jews). As for the sympathy, I have trouble finding much of it sometimes. I'm waiting for your Germany book, for there is good reason for that arrogance you feel. In modern times, about the only thing that can measure up to German philosophy for profundity is English lyric poetry. Nietzsche clearly wasn't familiar with it, or he couldn't have said: "Mediocre mentalities of these upright Englishmen"[1] (he should have said "first-rate mentalities" anyway). And then, the validity of poems never comes through with the same intensity.

You have embarrassed me with what you wrote about my not having read your *Wahrheit* yet. Wherever I opened the book I was so caught up by it that I wasn't able to go back to my own very concrete material with any concentration again. And that's why I've had to put it aside for the moment.

The Philosophical Library has sent me the contract. It's not entirely clear to me whether that is proper or not. The publisher needs to retain the second copy, doesn't he? At any rate, I've tucked the contract safely away. —I didn't, by the way, have anything to do with the inquiry from Beacon Press.

I'm writing away diligently and keeping a visit with you in mind as my reward. The work is going very well, though not, on days like today, when the weather behaves in such a bizarre way that not even this continent can be admitted as a mitigating circumstance. We're having a sudden spell of summery warmth. I'm sitting by an open window with bare arms. It will probably end tomorrow in a snowstorm.

All my best to you both.
Your
Hannah

87   *Hannah Arendt to Karl Jaspers*

New York, March 11, 1949

Lieber Verehrtester:

A few business-related items are enclosed. As you can see, everything seems to be in order now regarding the translation of *Der philosophische Glaube*. The Philosophical Library wound up by choosing the same translator [Ralph Manheim] whom *Commentary* had and who has done some translating for me.

Two photos are enclosed that Monsieur says are characteristic of me. I had hoped to drag him along to the photographer, but some business of his interfered at the last minute. I have some old pictures from Paris, but I'd very much like to have new ones of him, and then I'll send them to you.

Now to important things, namely, your "Solon."[1] I was delighted with it. It is, it seems to me, the first purely political thing of yours that I've read, and in my concurrence with it, it became very clear to me again—even though I was completely unaware of it at the time— how well your philosophy prepared me for politics. Many, many years ago in the woods of Clamart, Monsieur instructed me on the nature of the statesman as exemplified by Solon, and I have always begun my courses on the history of European dictatorships with him.

Nothing new to report otherwise. Scholem,[2] more difficult than ever, is in America, and Hans Jonas is expected. Fanaticism has become a form of outright torture for me. But old friends are old friends, despite that. Reinhardt[3] wrote from Germany that he will be "exchanged" in Chicago. I love his books, the *Sophocles*,[4] and his new volume of essays,[5] too.

As always
Your
Hannah

Basel, March 15, 1949

Dear Hannah!

How happy we are to have your pictures! They are truly you, instantly recognizable. The same brilliant gleam of your eyes, but also etched in your face the sufferings of which your youth had no inkling. From your letters I have known for a long time now that you have come through undiminished. That was obviously not easy, and in these pictures I can see that it wasn't. You are a prodigal human being.

Thanks for all your communications. I hope checking the translation won't be too much trouble for you. Once again I am simply accepting your kindness. Mr. Manheim is doing me a great service—and obviously for primarily intellectual reasons. Tell him when you have the chance that I know what this kind of work means, that I am happy to have him as my translator, and that I am grateful to him.

Three copies of the Philosophical Library contract were prepared, one for the publisher, one for you, one for me.

The English publisher[1] will, I think, acquire this same translation. May that bring Mr. Manheim a higher fee!

I received an invitation to the Agentinian philosophers' congress[2] in November and declined at first—for reasons of health and reluctantly, because I would gladly have seen something of the world. Then came a request for a written contribution[3] to be read out loud. I've sent one—always with possible self-advertising in mind as well as the translation of my *Psychopathologie* in Buenos Aires. Professor Pareyson[4] from Turin visited me to act as liaison. I had good ties with him during the Nazi period. That's why I had no reservations about this arrangement, and I really don't have any now either, although these ostentatious refusals of American invitations are beginning to give me some second thoughts.

Will you come to Europe this year and visit us? My wife says: Hannah has priority over everything else. That is my feeling, too. Can Monsieur join you? He is there next to you as a palpable presence even though you almost never speak of him directly. I hope he really will deign to have his picture taken!

Warmest greetings

Your Karl Jaspers

I was happy about your concurrence on "Solon." Give my best to Monsieur!

April 18, 1949

Dear Friends,

I would have written long ago if I had known better what my plans would be. Now I see with a touch of horror that your good letter has gone unanswered for a month. The explanation is, of course, that I neither know whether I will be able to come nor when I can come. Both depend on negotiations for a job here. The prospects look good, and if everything turns out right, I would have to go to Europe in any case to work a few months in Paris. Then the thing to do would be for you just to tell me when a visit is convenient for you. One thing I can say for sure: I won't come before the end of the summer, at the earliest in August or September. That much is clear because I can't very well finish the book before that. In this last month other things have constantly got in the way—lectures with articles to put into shape afterward, things I couldn't very well refuse to do. Geneva would appeal to me a bit perhaps because I've lived away from all these things for so long, European things, I mean, that I'd really be curious. And I would very much like to hear you again and not just read you. (That "just" is there only for sentimental reasons.)

Gurian from *The Review of Politics* wrote that he would like to have the "Solon" but that he didn't know of a translator. Then, too, the *Review* doesn't pay anything. No scholarly journals pay here, but I don't think that's important in this case. I recommended Manheim to him but haven't heard anything back yet.

Buenos Aires: I sent the newspaper clipping only for your information, not because I thought the Americans were right. There is much more interest in philosophy there than there is here, and as long as they will print, under a dictatorship but not a totalitarian one!, what you have written in the way you have written it, then reservations seem to me superfluous. The only thing I find troublesome is something I didn't know before, namely, that America is being represented by two former Germans (both Jews, I believe), which is a bit grotesque but not really important. Helmut Kuhn[1] is one of them [. . .].

I'm reading right now in the third part of *Wahrheit*, the sections on falsity and lies.[2] I have immediate need of it for certain thoughts I'm developing in my work. The most important point for me is that truth is not possible without falsity, and then your masterly presentation of the philosophical implications of all possible modes of behavior. You say (apropos of Buenos Aires) you would like to get to know the world. That won't be easy for you, because you truly know it. And that strikes me as a miracle in the history of philosophy. It's as if the arrogance of philosophers had come to an end. That, it seems to me, was latent in all your books, but it wasn't until now so tangible or spelled out so completely. This is a marvelous book (if I may say so, as one politely adds here).

All best wishes. I'm dangling a bit between fear and hope as far as Europe and a visit are concerned. But there's not much I can do.

Your
Hannah

90 Hannah Arendt to Karl Jaspers

June 3, 1949

Lieber Verehrtester:

I'm very grateful to you for sending me the Curtius affair.[1] I've learned more about what is possible in Germany today from it than from all the reports in the world. What strikes me as characteristic is not so much the attack itself or the indeed unrivaled vulgarity of tone or even the way—really quite staggering for a scholar—in which quotations are misused. It is instead the profound dishonesty that informs every single line. He's coming to the Goethe celebration here.[2] There's probably nothing that can be done to prevent that. Then there's a story behind this lovely celebration, too; and, in some respects, a typically American story at that. Hutchins,[3] the president of Chicago University, is only the nominal organizer of this thing. The real power behind it is a German-American,[4] a real-estate dealer, who recently bought up a ghost town and then had the commercially brilliant idea of tying Goethe into his business. His sole motive is to exploit Goethe to make this town world famous, so he can then make a bundle of money from tourists. The whole thing is really quite marvelous. The second backer, however, is a less amusing figure: Do you remember Bergsträsser[5] from Heidelberg? After he had successfully accommodated himself to the regime, it was shown that he had a whole string of Jewish ancestors. He is the real moving force behind this program. I've spoken with my friends at *Commentary* and *Partisan Review*. Maybe they can do something with reporting.

At the moment, the general political atmosphere is dismal here, particularly at the universities and colleges (with the exception of the very eminent ones). The Red hunt[6] is going full steam, and American intellectuals, particularly those who have a radical past and who have become anti-Stalinists over the years, are to some degree falling into line with the State Department, partly because they are genuinely disappointed with Stalinist Russia and partly because they have grown older. That doesn't mean, of course, that American foreign policy isn't very often truly excellent. It means that these people are ready to put up with anything and are beginning to see in the FBI an instrument with which they can and may, for example, settle disagreements among the faculty. The consequence is that faculty colleagues don't speak openly with each other anymore, particularly at the small, state-supported colleges; and the general fear that at first held sway only in Washington among civil servants now lies like a poisonous cloud over the intellectual life of the whole country. Not only are people afraid to utter the name Marx, but every little idiot thinks he has the right and duty to look down on Marx now. And this all in a milieu in which a few years ago you had to be brave to say that Marx had not solved all the world's problems. At the universities themselves there is a battle between faculty and students going on under the surface, because the students naturally become all the more prone to Communism the more intolerantly and "properly" their teachers behave. There are, of course, other things going on, and what I've just said here should be taken very much cum grano salis. The repulsive aspect of it is that someone like Hook,[7] for example, if he's at odds with Sartre, whom he can't fit into the formula Stalinist versus anti-Stalinist, will then declare that Sartre is "a reluctant Stalinist." (I don't have much use for Sartre, but that's beside the point.)

I hope I haven't bored you with this. There were a few young professors here yesterday who were never Marxists or Stalinists or anything else and who were complaining bitterly.

I'm expecting Ralph Manheim's translation any day now but haven't heard anything from him personally.

Now some quick notes on the state of my plans: It seems almost certain that I'll come to Europe in September. I don't know yet when I'll begin my new job.[8] That depends only in part on me. I'll be finished with the book sometime around August 1. Then comes the technical stuff, checking the English, checking through, checking the notes, etc. The publisher writes me with amiable patience; he's obviously used to worse authors. I can't say for sure yet how my plans for Europe itself will fall out. It's very likely that I'll have to go to Germany and that this part of my trip, on behalf of a Jewish organization here, will have to suit their schedule. I would accept the assignment for financial reasons, too profitable to refuse. If that does not materialize, I'd be completely free.

As you have perhaps noticed, my plans are somewhat tentative. A friend of mine[9] is dying of lung cancer. She is fully informed and is completely in charge and holding up wonderfully. For the present she is still feeling all right and is still working. I'm afraid that her condition will deteriorate rapidly at the very moment when I can—have to? want to?—leave. The doctors refuse to make a definite prognosis. They can't operate. Voilà.

Please, please don't be upset about Curtius.

My best wishes to you both
Your
Hannah

91   Karl Jaspers to Hannah Arendt

St. Moritz,[1] August 4, 1949

Dear Hannah!

Your letter,[2] which touched both our hearts, just arrived. The pleasure you take in your new apartment and your own furniture[3]—how wonderful that is! It's like a game for you, and you don't complain about the privations you have had to bear for so long. You haven't lost your capacity for joy. Your mortally ill friend, of whom you write in such a way that one has to love her, is constitutionally blessed with that same capacity. She will still be able to participate in your joy. But you remain in fear of what this woman's body may yet make her endure.

Now you're preparing for your big trip, and we are hearing for the first time about your task. You'll be faced with problem upon problem. What new talents you will develop!

Whether we see each other a few months earlier or later is of no importance just as long as we do get together again. All you need do, as soon as that is possible for you, is name the time when you can come see us; and, as you must know, you are welcome in our guest room for as long as you want to stay. You can work at our house, too, if you care to. You know that I have limited energy for conversation during the semester. But we will always manage to fit in some time for talk.

Your book will soon be finished, a great event. I read your essay[4] in *Die Wandlung* a few days ago, surely a section from your book. Wonderful in its breadth of concept, clarity, and ease of comprehension. A masterpiece! If the whole book is like that, then it will be in a class by itself these days.

I was glad to have your approval of my publication.[5] I, like you, have often been outraged by that Goethe quote on order and injustice.[6] It contains a troublesome truth—and I have to confess to having similar feelings myself sometimes, especially when "justice" is not absolutely clear.

I'm disturbed by your judgment on Spinoza (or are you thinking only of that bad Spinozaism promoted in the world of German education): "the most dangerous kind of hocus-pocus against reality"?—we'll have to talk about that this winter. Do you know the "Theological-political Tract"?—and his last incomplete work, the "Political Tract"?—and his stand regarding Jan de Witt[7] among other things? Speculation that makes certain of God's existence is certainly not magic? —Spinoza, this pure soul, this great realist, the first human being to attempt to become a citizen of the world, a citizen of a kind that still hardly exists even today, this down-to-earth passion—I not only want to defend him against you but also sing his praises as one of the few human beings and thinkers whose existence is like a guarantee that there is something good in human beings after all. —Simmel[8] visited me in 1917 and said Spinoza was the only philosopher among the ones considered great whom he did *not* understand and considered completely absurd. He meant something quite different from what you do. Spinoza's inner equilibrium seems to me to be exemplary.[9] I love him with the respect one has for a man who, without self-deception, knew God—and here one can, on a rational level, put aside all his concepts and proofs as play, provided one has grasped their essence. —As late as 1936 I was able to lecture on Spinoza[10] in Heidelberg without interference and to the growing applause of my audience. Afterward, a student on holiday sent me a photograph of Spinoza's portrait in Wolfenbüttel, and I still have that photo hanging in my room. It was, at that time, a welcome sign to me of the outlook of some German students.

With warmest greetings
Your Karl Jaspers

139

Geneva, September 1, 1949

Dear Hannah!

Your good letter[1] with its enlivening effect for us has just arrived here in our hotel room. Thank you very much!

Your trip seems to be a sure thing now. But it will be winter by then! The authorities with their papers take so much time. Our friends who have already become English or American citizens have it better. The likes of us are tied down. They have a magic key in their pockets.

Thank you for checking the translation. I hope that you really limited yourself to sample passages in making your judgment. But I fear from what you say that you did more than that.

Spinoza—I value him above most philosophers. He, along with very few others, has a place in the adytum of philosophy. You express that with the word "magic." "What is alien to me is the immanence." And to me, too, as far as his formulations go, in some cases; but he has so succeeded with that "magic" that nothing but transcendence remains; he is, it seems to me, at the most profound level at one with Jeremiah. Hegel coined the term *Akosmismus*[2] [a-cosmism] to describe him because only God is real for him. A Jesuit—or was it Renan![3]—said: No one after Jesus has been nearer to God than Spinoza. What you circumscribe with the sentence "The philosopher does not want to be disturbed" is the actualization of this certainty of God, also a love of human beings that can become real only in purified reason. In this stillness, it seems to me, a single impetus emanates from Spinoza. Excellent, what you say about the contrast Spinoza—Hobbes. —Spinoza remains a riddle despite all this. You ask whether Spinoza was capable of laughter. I recall only one instance in which there is mention of his laughing. He put flies in a spider's web, then added two spiders so that they would fight. And he laughed out loud at that. Very strange and difficult to interpret. It struck a chord with me because I did the same thing as a boy. First flies, then little spiders, then larger spiders of about equal size. But I didn't laugh. I was anxious to see what would happen, to be horrified. And then once I had seen, I stopped doing it entirely. It was a confirmation of a basic reality (the Indians call it the "law of fishes"). Spinoza surely felt no empathy here. He gave his attention and his soul to the search for Being; he found it and achieved tranquillity, as Parmenides did, the first man who is reported to have reached this "tranquillity."

I've had some correspondence with Heidegger now and then.[4] I'll show you the letters when you visit us. He is completely absorbed in speculation about *Sein* (Being); he spells it *Seyn*. Two and a half years ago he was experimenting with "existence" and distorted everything thoroughly. Now he's experimenting more seriously, and, again, that doesn't leave me unconcerned. I hope he doesn't distort things again. But I have my doubts. Can someone with an impure soul—that is, a soul that is unaware of its own impurity and isn't constantly trying to expel it but continues to live thoughtlessly in filth—can someone living in that kind of dishonesty perceive what is purest? Or will he experience a revolution yet? —I'm more than doubtful but don't know. What is strange is that he has knowledge of something that hardly anyone notices these days, and that he impresses people with his inklings. The form is, to be sure, self-interpretation of *Sein und Zeit*, as if he had always wanted and done one and the same thing.

A great circus here in Geneva.[5] But interesting experiences for me that I should not go without. Everything is wide of the mark—and yet there's goodwill. Philosophy as international convention. The French spirit dominates.

Warmest greetings
Your Karl Jaspers

93 *Hannah Arendt to Karl Jaspers*

September 29, 1949

Lieber Verehrtester:

You will surely be back from Geneva by now. Your letter sounded so lively and cheerful. Last week we ran off quickly for an overdue fall holiday. Lovely, forested hill country with lots of wonderful walks. Next week we both have to be back in New York, but this is better than nothing. I'll have things easier now. The book is finished (almost 900 pages), and my job is pleasant and not strenuous. Baron,[1] who is my boss, so to speak—that is, president of the organization—would like me to leave in mid-November. I doubt that I can get the permit for Germany by then. Being without citizenship makes everything more difficult with the European authorities. Here it doesn't matter much, and the English gave me a visa immediately, too. The difference from European consulates is really striking.

Spinoza: I was very struck by the fly-spider anecdote. No, he certainly did not want to study something, as you did, and probably wasn't even in that way curious. It seems to me he wanted to conduct an experiment, not in a limited way—not just to see how two spiders behave with so and so many flies and that's that—but as if in a microcosm, as if he had created a microcosm. You see, I'm back with my magic again, despite everything that you said and that impressed me very much but that for me somehow still doesn't fit quite right for Spinoza. I feel mistrust, even toward the tranquillity, though not toward the formulations. I find them rather touching, and behind them is a genuine effort to state the truth in one sentence, an assumption that in the last analysis no more is needed, just one sentence.

Heidegger: because human beings are not consistent, not I at any rate, I was pleased. You are right a thousand times over in each of your sentences. What you call impurity I would call lack of character—but in the sense that he literally has none and certainly not a particularly bad one. At the same time, he lives in depths and with a passionateness that one can't easily forget. The distortion is intolerable, and the very fact that he is arranging everything now to look like an interpretation of *Sein und Zeit* suggests that it will all come out distorted again. I read his letter against humanism.[2] Also very questionable and often ambiguous but still the first thing of his that is up to his old standard. (I've read him here on Hölderlin and also his quite awful, babbling lectures on Nietzsche.[3]) This living in Todtnauberg,[4] grumbling about civilization and writing *Sein* with a "y," is really a kind of mouse hole he has crawled back into because he rightly assumes that the only people he'll have to see there are the pilgrims who come full of admiration for him. Nobody is likely to climb 1,200 meters to make a scene. And if somebody did do it, he would lie a blue streak and take for granted that nobody will call him a liar to his face. He probably thought he could buy himself loose from the world this way at the lowest possible price, fast-talk himself out of everything unpleasant, and do nothing but philosophize. And then, of course, this whole intricate and childish dishonesty has quickly crept into his philosophizing.

I was much saddened to hear from your wife about the death of your nephew.[5] Her brother Ernst wrote me so many nice notes when he forwarded things about you, newspaper clippings, that I feel as though this death touches someone I know.

All very best wishes to you both, and now we can almost start writing: See you soon!

Your
Hannah

November 22, 1949

Dear, dear Friends—

Everything is in order at last. I just got my Swiss visa. Many thanks, and my apologies for the dreadful telegraphic intrusion.

I fly day after tomorrow, will stay in Paris until the first, will then probably have to stay two full weeks in Germany because Baron is planning a directors' meeting here and wants a first report from me for that. So it is possible that instead of coming to Basel on the 10th or 11th as planned, I won't make it until the 17th or 18th. I'll know for sure in Germany after December 6. But perhaps it would be better if you figure on the later date. I'll telephone from Paris in any case.

I'm too excited to write.

Many, many thanks for your kind letter.[1]

With warmest wishes
Your
Hannah

Basel, December 28, 1949

Dear Mr. Blücher!

I hope you will permit me this salutation,[1] because you are in fact present here, an invisible companion to our dear visitor. Your Hannah is incredibly lively. In her work here, every door has opened so wide before her that she is finding her success a bit uncanny herself. She has told us not only about that but also about the bad years, the terrors, the miraculous strokes of luck, and how the two of you have made your way, firmly at home in the free realm of the mind, fully alive in the present, thinking and acting for the future. My wife and I are very happy. One takes courage oneself from someone like Hannah, in whom not only steadfastness and trust but also the exuberance of creative work is so evident. That kind of reality is the only reality there is today.

It would be nice if we could meet and talk together sometime. Will you make the next trip to Europe together? I know you now only as reflected through Hannah, who tells me little directly but all the more indirectly. I am drawn to you as a German, too. Germans are rare.

One keeps a lookout for them and is delighted at every single one one finds.

My wife and I send you our warmest greetings. And all best wishes for the New Year!

Your Karl Jaspers[2]

96 *Karl Jaspers to Hannah Arendt*

Basel, January 12, 1950

Dear Hannah!

Your visit has not faded away. You still inhabit this house, answering questions and spreading good cheer. But today I have a question the answer to which I do not have, and so I am writing to you:

Routledge (London) is making me a good offer for *Ursprung und Ziel der Geschichte* (7½% for the first 1,000, 10% up to 4,000, 15% above 4,000, and an advance of £50). However, he wants "worldwide English-language rights."

Max Pfeffer, a representative in New York, is offering similar financial prospects with Duell, Sloan & Pearce. Mr. Kennedy of that house will write to me. Everything there is still in the most preliminary of stages. The book is still being read. There's talk in rather grandiose tones of publishing all my other books in translation, but first they want to have copies to read.

There has been no mention of a translator, a specific person, at either house.

Routledge makes a very solid impression in every respect. They published a bad translation of my little Göschen volume years ago.[1] I can't pull translators out of thin air. Have to leave that to the publisher. My inclination: better any translation than none at all, particularly of the less philosophical, more concrete books.

What should I do? With Routledge, it seems to me, I've got something certain and respectable. I'd like to try granting them the rights they want except for the USA. If they say no, then I'd give them the world rights anyhow.

Perhaps the English book would be distributed in America like an American one?—it's certainly cheaper. As a large publisher, Routledge has, I think, not only an interest in such distribution but also the possibilities and capabilities for it.

Could you let me know your opinion quickly?

What haven't you experienced in the meantime! We're delighted with the prospect of seeing you again.

Warmest wishes
Your Karl Jaspers

Paris, January 15, 1950

Lieber Verehrtester—

Thoughts of you both have accompanied me everywhere. I haven't had a chance to write, that is, I didn't have the peace I need before I can even sit down at a desk. Now my friend[1] has just brought me your letter, and I will answer quickly and on my first impulse:

Almost every American publisher and almost every English publisher have established ties on the other side of the ocean. It seems to me that the people at Routledge want worldwide English-language rights primarily because (1) they would no longer be able, because of exchange rates, to buy the book from their American counterpart and because (2) they want the rights for Canada, too, which American publishers otherwise customarily keep for themselves. Duell, Sloan & Pearce is a very good big publisher. Once a house has published one important book by an author, there is a general and easily understandable tendency on its part to bring all the author's other books under its wing, which is very much in the author's best interest, too.

I would suggest that you inform England about the tentative offer from America. The most reasonable solution would be for this book to be printed in England and exported from there to America. That is very much cheaper, but it is sometimes a matter of prestige for the American publisher to do it otherwise, also sometimes better for him financially. You should probably also write to America at the same time and suggest this arrangement. What seems most important to me is that there not be two translations of the same text. The translation should be done jointly by the publishers, too. The costs used to be shared fifty-fifty, even if the translator was paid in dollars. Now the English can't pay so much and cover only 25% of the translation costs if they are paid in New York. In England, everything is incomparably cheaper and often better as well. (I have this from Secker & Warburg, with whom I spoke extensively in London.) I don't, of course, know

145

any English translators. Who else in England has translated you, I mean apart from the little Göschen book? The royalty terms are very good indeed.

In other words: It seems to me you would do better to try to bring Routledge and Duell, Sloan & Pearce together rather than secure the American rights. I don't foresee any problems—unless Routledge is bound by contract to another American publisher.

I still don't know exactly when I'll come. It will be either on February 4–5 or 11–12. For various reasons I can't enter the English Occupation Zone until after February 15. That could mean that I might not be able to go home until mid-March.

I'm leaving for Germany this evening. Address: Wiesbaden, Landesmuseum. Jewish Cultural Reconstruction. London was overwhelmingly beautiful and exciting. Paris, sad again, but this time minus the shock.

My visit in Basel is vividly present to me every minute and a treasure I can never lose.

All my warmest wishes to you both and regards to Erna,[2]

Your
Hannah

98 Karl Jaspers to Heinrich Blücher

Basel, February 5, 1950

Dear Mr. Blücher!

Hannah has copied out for me what you wrote to her about my philosophy.[1] Thank you very much. You have understood my intention at its deepest level, the great demand that I make of my work behind its apparent modesty. If, despite all its pitfalls, that work can be understood as you have understood it, then I am satisfied. And I feel an immediate bond with a man who understands that work as you have. For then it is a common undertaking. I provide only that which the other has already brought to it.

That you assent to the title "Systematik des vernünftigen Selbstbewusstseins" for my book[2] pleases me. The two volumes[3] that will follow will have to justify that title. Unfortunately, they are far from completion.

We will hold onto what we have begun, with Hannah's help, through this first exchange. And we hope to see the day when you make a trip to Europe with Hannah and set up your quarters in our house.

My wife shared my pleasure, and we both send our best regards.

Your Karl Jaspers

99 Hannah Arendt to Karl Jaspers

New York, April 10, 1950

Lieber Verehrtester!

The few weeks that I have been back have flown by. Much of that time has been spent, of course, in lengthy talks about Basel. With the trip in the immediate past, I realize more clearly now than I could during those hectic months how much it centered around my visit with you in Basel. That always fresh joy of being able to speak without reservation, a happiness that I otherwise know only at home and that has become a vital factor of my world because it is once again possible (outside one's own home, which one has, after all, constructed oneself).

But today I'm writing for "business" reasons. I'm enclosing a truly charming letter from Herbert Read,[1] which I didn't want to keep from you. Another and rather annoying item: Jean Wahl told me in Paris about an exchange of letters with Paeschke[2] that he wanted to show you, and I urged him to do so. If he has sent them to you, then you know the story: Wahl wanted to begin an article in *Merkur* about contemporary German philosophy with a few half political and really very moderate remarks, and Paeschke—instead of saying: We don't like that, or we don't dare to print it, or something like that—wrote back in what seems to me a typically dishonest way and said: We are aware of these facts. What Wahl said to me and what people in Germany seem incapable of understanding is that he can't afford—nor does he want—to publish in Germany again without a little introduction of this kind. As you know, I wanted to publish in *Merkur* myself, but now I'm not so sure. It becomes clearer all the time that *Die Wandlung*, which behaved so differently in such matters, should have been kept alive no matter what.[3] —Another thing: I was asked, also in Paris, whether you might accept an invitation this summer to Pontigny[4] (you know about that, don't you?), where the topic under discussion will be "Idée de la modernité." I said I didn't know (although it seemed pretty unlikely to me in what I thought would be the middle of your semester) because it seems to me that invitations never do any harm. —And last but not least, I've unofficially "offered" your humanism article[5] to *Commentary*, that is, I've urged them to publish it. If they do want it, they'll get in touch with you.

Well, that seems to be all for the moment. Have you got a good start on your work for the Easter holidays?

Warmly
Your
Hannah

Thanks very much for the Bultmann,[6] which arrived yesterday.

Monsieur sends his warmest regards.

100   Karl Jaspers to Hannah Arendt

Basel, April 20, 1950

Dear Hannah!

Many thanks for your first lines from your home. High spirits in every line—that's the way we should all be in this topsy-turvy world. And always these words of friendship, for which I am so grateful. Being in close touch with you dispels the specters of scorn for humankind and of heartless indifference. In my youth we were touched by the song "Man weiss nicht, was noch werden mag . . ." ["One can't know what may yet happen . . ."][1] and thought about our personal destinies. That remains so still, but those words have taken on a broader and deeper meaning. We are somehow young in the moment when they can touch us in that way.

I had a remarkable dream last night. We were together at Max Weber's. You, Hannah, arrived late, were warmly welcomed. The stairway led through a ravine. The apartment was Weber's old one. He had just returned from a world trip, had brought back political documents and artworks, particularly from the Far East. He gave us some of them, you the best ones because you understood more of politics than I.

I picture you now correcting proofs for your big book. Shouldn't you perhaps reread Max Weber on the archetype (and on other things too)? So that, if something of the old "total" underlying view of history should remain in your text, even this last trace will disappear? But perhaps that is unnecessary—despite the fact that all of us today are still inclined, in the intellectual atmosphere created by Hegel and Marx and still not abandoned by Spengler and Toynbee,[2] to nibble instinctively at the crumbs of the false grandeur that was loaded onto history once that grandeur was stolen from God.

Thanks for your notes on "business." The letter from H. Read reflects a wonderful character. I'm delighted with it, also because of my book. —Jean Wahl hasn't sent me anything yet. This business interests me a lot. Perhaps I'll ask Jean Wahl about it, mentioning your name. I'm *very* sorry about Paeschke. I thought he was better than that. It's no doubt difficult to maintain your integrity as a magazine editor in Germany. —I can't go to Pontigny, alas, as you knew. But it was nice of you *not* to say no right away.

You found your friend[3] still fully herself. What an awful time is coming! You will be a blessing to her. Illness and impending death tend to bring a dreadful isolation. People quietly break off communication. You will stay with her. For, as you tell it, this friend has something of Socrates' attitude about her. "You . . . will depart later, each at his own time. But me . . . fate calls now, and it is time that I repair to my bath . . . so that the women will be spared the trouble of washing my body."[4]

From this quote you can see that I want to lecture on Plato.[5] I'm reading him as though I were understanding him for the first time. Then too, the philologists have turned up some things worth knowing, just recently about the late "lecture" "On the Good."[6] The interpretation of this text, in which everything—despite lecture notes Aristotle made of it—comes to us through an intermediary, is extremely difficult, but it is clearly indispensable for a clearer view of Plato.

My warmest greetings to Monsieur, my secret German friend from the eighteenth century—

and for you I wish good progress with your book.

Your Karl Jaspers

101 Hannah Arendt to Karl Jaspers

June 25, 1950

Lieber Verehrtester—

Your kind letter with the dying Socrates—it was a comfort to me these past months and gave my friend pleasure, too. She died on June 6. Her death was in every sense more merciful than I feared it might be. She did not suffer much, did not have bad pain; and her physiognomy remained absolutely unchanged to her last day. Our relationship remained unbroken until the moment she lost consciousness. She was admirable, but I have to confess that I never really admired her. It was all so natural and matter-of-fact, and I was so grateful that up to the end she never forced me to lie to her. She had taken care of everything down to the last detail, always with an eye toward the lives of others. So there was no breach of communication, because she did not turn away from the living—and in a sense didn't have any need to turn away—and because the living did not turn away from her dying.

I've had a hard time getting used to the world again. Also, I'm just plain a bit tired. We're going away on vacation on July 6 (address: c/o Mrs. S. Franc, Manomet, Massachusetts, that will do it), and I hope I can stay away four or five weeks. This time I'm taking *Wahrheit* along (my own copy—have I even thanked you for it? It was so nice to find it here). Most of the rest of my time will be spent reading proofs. About 70% of the book has been printed, and now the publisher is in a great hurry (as always in this country, where everybody always dawdles until the last minute) because they want to have the book on the market by early November. I sent Paeschke a few chapters some weeks ago, but I've heard in the meantime that *Merkur* is going to stop publishing. Is that true?

Prompted by your dream I've read a lot of Max Weber. I felt so idiotically flattered by it that I was ashamed of myself. Weber's intellectual sobriety is impossible to match, at least for me. With me there's always something dogmatic left hanging around somewhere. (That's what you get when Jews start writing history.)

Are you still reading Plato? And what will you lecture on in Heidelberg?[1] That is, are you going to go there at all? That must be clear by now. And your wife? to Holland? And how is her heart?

The translation from England[2] hasn't arrived yet. It's probably still too early.

I'm enclosing the Churchill quotes[3] which, after I had despaired of ever finding them, finally emerged quietly from my heap of papers. I really don't understand it.

The city here has been talking about war since yesterday. We don't believe it, but world history being what it is, i.e., with world history running off the tracks anyhow, you can never know. Whenever somebody tells me again that Stalin certainly can't make war right now or doesn't have any interest in it, I always have to think of a Jewish joke: A Jew is afraid of a dog that is barking loudly. Someone says to placate him: You surely know that dogs that bark a lot don't bite. To which he replies: Yes, I know, but do I know that he knows that? And so I continue to be afraid, and of course more, and more concretely, than before my trip to Europe. Reality is indeed a strange thing.

Monsieur is fine and sends his best wishes.

All my best to you both.

Your
Hannah

102 *Karl Jaspers to Hannah Arendt*

Basel, June 29, 1950

Dear Hannah!

I talk with you a lot. Something you said comes to my mind again. After your visits, I have a more actual sense of your possibilities. A constant encouragement it is that you are there with your husband. Various things occur to me when I think about you. I should write you a long letter, but I can't now. Instead, I'm sending only a word of greeting so that I won't disappear entirely in silence.

I think I should be able to send you a bad book every now and then if I think the material might interest you or if its failure might stimulate your thinking. Bad books are sometimes useful. If not, throw it away. This one is Rüstow, *Zur Ortsbestimmung der Gegenwart*, Volume I,[1] and has not yet been followed by other volumes. Rüstow deals with imperialism here among other things. He presents his basic idea in a rather flat, black-and-white way. He works a not incorrect idea, indeed an important idea (although an old one), to death by expanding it wrongly. I knew the author[2] as a student (he is my age) in Göttingen in about 1903. In those days he was an adherent of the Fries school,[3] an ineradicable stigma of flatness. But he is very intelligent and has some excellent ideas. For many years he was secretary of an association for some branch of industry in Berlin. He knows a lot, has remained interested in philosophy, wrote an intelligent but essentially boring dissertation called *Der Lügner*[4] on the ingenious sophism of the ancient world. Now he's a full professor in Heidelberg, A. Weber's[5] successor. Is the printing of your book progressing well? Have you made arrangements for a German translation? The Verlagsanstalt would be a very good possibility. If you like, I can also ask Piper, who would surely be very much interested. I've heard a *rumor* that *Merkur* will fold. A pity despite all. Also, that the Verlagsgesellschaft is back in the hands of its original owners.

We plan to go to Heidelberg in two and a half weeks (around July 15). I'll be giving three guest lectures at the invitation of the student government. There will be some hostility. I didn't want to avoid the confrontation. I'll be going there with some uneasiness, a little curiosity, with great love for the city and landscape and the past, and with some eagerness for battle. I'll lecture on "reason."[6]

On August 20 we'll go to St. Moritz for a few weeks with our Erna, who will run the household in the house that our kind friends[7] are making available to us. It's like a fairy tale. An American car will take us there, as comfortable as can be. I wish you could be with us! We can take friends along. We're hoping Paul Gottschalk can come.

I sent a Nietzsche essay[8] to *Commentary*, just in case. (Nietzsche died fifty years ago this August. I wrote the thing at the request of the *Neue Rundschau* in Amsterdam. Nothing special.) It's probably too long, perhaps unsuitable for other reasons as well.

I hope you are both well and your spirits good. You have to continue to let your voice be heard in this world. That seems so important to me. We mustn't let disappear what you—and I, too, I hope—are living for.

With warmest greetings
Your Karl Jaspers

103 *Hannah Arendt to Gertrud and Karl Jaspers*

Manomet, Mass., July 11, 1950

Dear, dear Friends—

I don't know whether this letter will still reach you in Basel. Yours, which warmed my heart so much and really pulled me out of the hole of sadness, reached me just before we left for vacation. Where we have now arrived safe and sound. The sea, dunes, forest, a bit like the coast of Samland,[1] where I grew up. Very pretty, a lot of lakes. We're here with American friends, a young literary historian, very talented, of Russian Jewish background with the warmth and openness that go with that. His name, in case he should go to Europe sometime and have learned a little German by then, is Alfred Kazin.[2] He helped me a lot with the English of my book and is still helping now with the proofs.

I heard from the publisher that Rüstow's book was on the way, but it hasn't arrived yet. Mail from New York to here takes at least as long as from Europe to New York. Your description is simply wonderful. I suddenly saw you before me, in your room, completely present. Usually what I see when I think back (which I do often) is the stairway first and the three of us spread out on it. I'm at the top, then the two of you on the second floor or down below, and somehow talking together this way. That's what I dreamt recently anyhow. It was a superb conversation.

How are you liking Heidelberg, and how is it sitting with you? I'm very curious. —A lot of work here, of course, but also swimming and walks. Reading proofs is awful, that is, boring. I've taken a different epigraph from *Logik* from the one I mentioned to you before: "Give yourself up neither to the past nor to the future. The important thing is to remain wholly in the present."[3] That sentence struck me right in the heart, so I'm entitled to have it.

Paeschke has written that *Merkur* really is on the verge of folding, but it's still not certain. The Deutsche Verlagsanstalt has already taken an option from Harcourt, Brace, months ago apparently. I didn't hear anything about it. The divisions in large publishing houses here lead such separate existences that the one doesn't know what the other is doing. But that doesn't obligate me in any way. Does your saying "that the Verlagsgesellschaft is back in the hands of its original owners" mean that it is now being run by people with dirty hands? Should I retract and try with Piper instead? Give me your advice. Finding one's way around in Germany these days really requires major study if one has not been on hand to observe developments from close up.

I'm glad that things worked out with your brother and the trip to Holland, also that all this went off without hitches and that you're safely back in Basel.[4] What are people in Europe saying about the Korea business?[5] St. Moritz is wonderful. Perhaps we can work out something for next summer. It will all hang on money, the stuff of which my mother always said: It is of no importance to us; it is the least significant of things. —Monsieur sends his very best regards. I can hear him playing Ping-Pong right now, and I'm seeing for the first time something like ambition awakening in him. It's fun to watch him working so hard at it. He'll be lecturing at the New School[6] this winter. They asked him to teach after a few public lectures he gave this past winter drew considerable interest.

Good-bye for now, and "take good care of yourselves" [in English in original]. That means in German (or Jewish?): Be well. And accept my warmest greetings.

Your Hannah

104 Karl Jaspers to Hannah Arendt

Basel, August 19, 1950

Dear Hannah!

You would have every right to be displeased that I haven't written for so long, not even a word of greeting during your vacation. There's no excusing me, but perhaps I can invoke the unusually great pressure the Heidelberg lectures put on me (and which went to press a few days ago). I started writing them on July 13; then we went to Heidelberg. It was very rewarding. Old friends, the lovely city, colleagues cool toward me, students very warm. I never had the auditorium so full; there wasn't even any standing room left. Stamping on the floor was forbidden for fear the place would collapse. The door of the university was closed; hundreds of people were turned away. Then there were about twenty-five written queries for the colloquium afterward, some of them very serious. German students! There are so many good ones, even if they are a small minority, relatively speaking. Faces entirely different from three years ago: open, without masks or tension, bright, beautiful young people. I was moved. And yet for all that we were glad to return to Basel. I find cosmopolitan air much more enlivening. Our lack of native ground and alienation from our country strike me as right and natural. The students can come to Basel, too. There is foreign currency available now for German students. They can read me if they want to. I feel *no* guilt for leaving this Germany and for *not* yearning to go back. —A small detail: I'm a member of the Heidelberg academy. They happened to have a meeting while I was there. They *forgot* to invite me. A clear sign of how little I mean to those people. I less to them than they to me!

It was nice staying with the Waltzes. My wife kept meeting people on the street who were not merely delighted to see her but whose pleasure seemed almost boundless. Her spirits soared because she felt

154

how much she was loved by so many people who all stood by her in the Nazi period. The warmth of some, like the surgeon Bauer[1] and his wife[2] (I participated in the rebuilding of the university in 1945 with Bauer as rector), set them apart from the majority. With them we felt something of the old solidarity. Otherwise, the years 45 and 46 have been forgotten.

Now to your letters. The first (June 25) crossed with mine. The death of your friend: may we all die so quietly. Not to isolate oneself through untruth, even in the extremes of dying, shows a genuine bond with others. But the loss and the mystery remain. —Our dear, good friend Schwarber,[3] the director of the library, died here suddenly. He, too, fully conscious, taking leave of his family. I can see how much that has strengthened the bond of the survivors with him. My wife and I lost a great deal here with his death. Crucial matters in my appointment here I owe to him.

Thank you for the copies of the Churchill quotes from 1938. Apart from these, there must also be an open letter to Hitler that says roughly the same things.

Merkur is safe for another year. I don't know anything about the Verlagsanstalt during the Nazi period. I would have *no* reservations about publishing with them. I mentioned Piper *only* in case the Verlagsanstalt rejects your manuscript. But that is highly unlikely.

I haven't heard anything more about the translation of my history book in London. Seeing that nothing has been sent to you either yet, I'll have to inquire.

On the possibility of war: your story about the Jew and the barking dog hits the nail on the head. The course of the world depends at the moment on a few people in the Kremlin. No one knows whether, like Hitler, they want war no matter what—or whether they will content themselves with half the earth once their attempts at extortion and bluff have failed. The latter outcome is, in the light of all our historical experience, unfortunately not likely but still possible if the Kremlin decides that war entails excessive risk to itself and therefore keeps putting it off. I don't want to believe in the certainty of war coming. But like you I live with the uneasy feeling that it could come any day. In any case, the situation in Korea is good. If it sets off a world war, that would soon have happened anyhow without Korea. If not, then it will teach the Americans that a world order can't be attained with technology alone.

You've spent some happy weeks in a beautiful landscape with your husband and your friend Alfred Kazin, and now you're back in New York. I hope you've finished correcting proofs for your book. And so it will be out this winter. On the basis of the last chapter, what you have told me about it, and the earlier partial offprint, I'm expecting it to be a great success. One can never know, though, so I'm cautious out of superstition. But I'm already proud of you for having been able to write this book.

I'm terribly pleased that you are taking the epigraph for your book from my *Logik*. Every sign that shows I somehow belong together with you cheers me. The passage about the "dragon"[4] has a more direct bearing on your subject. The new one is philosophical and weightier.

We leave for St. Moritz in a few days; we're both looking forward to a good rest—I hope it won't be disturbed.

And we'll be thinking of you: that you will both come to Europe next year, if . . .

My wife's heart is significantly better, the episodes less frequent. Her overall condition is as good as it was a year ago. She feels so chipper that I have to slow her down and keep her from overdoing. She's packing our bags right now.

Warmest regards from us both, also to Monsieur

Your Karl Jaspers

105 *Hannah Arendt to Gertrud and Karl Jaspers*

October 4, 1950

Dear, dear Friends—

You've surely been back from St. Moritz long since, and the semester has presumably begun. This summer has slipped through my fingers so quickly after our wonderful vacation that it just struck me recently, when Helene Wieruszowski reappeared, how long it's been since I last wrote.

What kept me from it was, of course, that I was reading *Wahrheit*. And it can sometimes happen that when one is totally absorbed with a book, thoughts about the author can get in the way. Now that I'm through with it, the thought of the three thousand miles between us evokes a sad bitterness in me.

Lieber Verehrtester, to begin completely without inhibition, this is the greatest of your books and a very, very great book indeed. These movements of thought (and the whole thing is really written in the style of an andante) open up and make present and pace off the space and the whole multidimensionality in which "perception in concern," actually responsive perception, has established itself as reason. That is neither eclecticism nor a synthesis of opposites but, rather, a kind of synthesis and reconciliation of things at the greatest possible remove from each other. With the construction of this space—which can be opened only by the movements of thought or of an indefatigably thinking, omnipresent movement—each individual thought loses, as it were, its tie to a certain place and so its pedantry. It becomes free to be near what is most remote. Politically speaking, this is the de-provincializing of Western philosophy, which causes me to indulge occasionally in essentially inadmissible speculation as to whether this isn't perhaps the last book of Western philosophy, its last word, so to speak, and at the same time the first book of a world philosophy, its first word, so to speak.

I won't go into the figure on page 142,[1] because I'm afraid that my inability to grasp such things will lead me to protest against something that is simply too difficult for me to understand. Perhaps it's a good aid for people who can read and think more with their eyes. I didn't really like the introduction, not either introduction. They're written in a different style, though there are very nice things in them. But for me the book doesn't really begin until the sentence: "The one all-encompassing divides itself into modes of the all-encompassing."[2]

I liked your freedom essay[3] in *Der Monat* a lot—once again so completely in the style, or, rather, in the spirit, of Lessing.[4] For the rest, the congress[5] was not, I assume, altogether satisfying. I found some of Silone's[6] remarks very good and moving.

Commentary has presumably sent you Elliot Cohen's speech in Berlin about Jews and Germans[7] and will send you my report from Germany.[8] I wonder what you will say to the report. I tried to be fair, and I hope you'll be able to see that I'm more sad than bitter. About Cohen's speech: the Berliners, apparently under the question-able guidance of the cultural congress, issued to Cohen, or via Cohen, an invitation to the Jews to take part in a discussion. The agenda: restitution questions, DPs,[9] and a few other banalities about "Old Injustice and New Misunderstandings" (sic!). In short, the gentlemen intended not to talk about the German problem but about the Jewish one and at the same time to start in on everything that displeases them. Among the Germans who were invited there wasn't a single one (except

157

for Heuss[10] perhaps) who ever took an unambiguous position on this issue. You weren't even mentioned, nor was Kogon or Sternberger or anyone else. And on top of all that, the time set was Christmas. Perhaps that was just a dumb oversight, but there was explicit reference to its symbolic meaning. In short, a mixture of gall, tactlessness, and ineptness. For Elliot Cohen it was quite awful, because everyone naturally said: I told you so.

Helene Wieruszowski told [me] about your experiences in Heidelberg. Of course, they should go ahead and read you. But you should go regularly to give lectures if you can. The encounters with students really are wonderful, and I was delighted that the auditorium was full to overflowing. What the professors seem to have learned and retained from the Nazis is that hypocrisy is totally superfluous and that government by people with dirty hands can be set up quite openly. I'm of the opinion that that is a mistake because it presumes an assurance of one's own power and a lust for power that these weak little creatures don't have at all.

Yes, Germany—yesterday, when I was already thinking that I wanted to write to you I heard *The Abduction from the Seraglio* on the radio. And suddenly the whole so-called real and present-day Germany seemed to me to be a bizarre and nasty hallucination.

Rüstow: I'll write the publisher a few friendly words one of these days soon. Your recommendation, or nonrecommendation, was absolutely right. It's strange how everything that is real is ultimately destroyed by this kind of abstract comparison, and with it the reality of thought as well. Everything becomes boring. This method is most highly developed in Toynbee. In the end, nothing is left but challenge and response or superimpositions or whatnot. The worst of it is that no matter what system of categories someone uses, everything "comes out right," because, just as in cooking, you can't take out anything that you haven't put in.

Things are fine with us. Monsieur has begun his teaching at the New School, and he's enjoying it. I finished correcting the proofs for my book, with loud complaints, and I've shoved the index off on somebody else. So I'm having a lovely time—reading Plato: Politikos, Nomoi, Republic. My Greek is slowly reemerging. Listening to a lot of music. Seeing friends, too. Koyré[11] called out of nowhere this morning; great glee.

I haven't heard anything from Herbert Read. Perhaps you should inquire again.

I don't quite dare think about St. Moritz next year for fear of jinxing it. If I had wanted to, I could have "had" to go to Europe again this fall. But I didn't really want to. I want to go all the more next year. I'm still negotiating with Monsieur. I'll send you a good picture of him soon. He has become balky and suspicious of anything that upsets his work schedule.

My very best wishes to you both. Regards to Erna.

Your
Hannah

106 Hannah Arendt to Gertrud and Karl Jaspers

December 25, 1950

Dear, dear Friends—

A year ago today I was with you, and if I knew that I would see you next year as planned I would feel easier. But in the meantime so-called world events have taken on that tempo so unpleasantly characteristic for this century that you hardly know whether you'll be able to write the next letter, much less make plans for late summer. But you never know, of course, and as long as the world isn't going up in flames, everything can turn out more or less all right again.

So today more than usual I'm thinking back gratefully on my days in Basel and on the lovely, uniquely lovely brightness of them, on all those many hours that resembled each other "like sisters but none exactly like another." To Monsieur's amusement, I've bought a little tree for the first time since my childhood, really to remind me of my days with you. For that reason it is no longer an embarrassment to me but gives me pleasure and has real meaning for me.

I still owe you thanks for the Curtius,[1] which I read with great pleasure—like a welcome greeting from a past world. Gottschalk brought the book by your brother[2] and friend, but we haven't started it yet. Thank you for thinking of it. I was in the Midwest for the first time at the end of November—at Notre Dame[3] and Chicago to lecture. I enjoyed it a lot, particularly the students at Notre Dame and the faculty members, too, who were very open to my material. Gurian had invited me, in fear and trembling, because at this Catholic institution a woman had never mounted the podium before. He was literally sweating with fear despite the murderous cold, which tickled me so much that I completely forgot my customary stage fright.

159

When I came back, *Der Monat* with your excellent piece on Marx and Freud[4] was waiting for me. It became clear to me once again in reading it how much *Von der Wahrheit*, as an expression of your philosophy, de-tyrannizes thinking, how much communication as a form and a way of thinking stands in contrast not only to "advocatorial" but also to purely logical thinking. (I've read Plato and thought a lot about the affinity between philosophy and *tyrannis* or the partiality philosophers have for rational tyranny, which is, after all, the tyranny of reason. That is inevitable if one believes in being able, through philosophy, to discover *the* truth for man as such.) I would like to try to rescue Marx's honor in your sight. Not that what you say about him isn't right. But along with that (and not just along with it) there is Marx the revolutionary, whom a passion for justice has seized by the scruff of his neck. And this separates him most profoundly from Hegel and unites him, it seems to me, in a not entirely visible but very powerful way with Kant.

Otherwise there's nothing new, except that the atmosphere in which we live has changed radically again. For the first time, this country is affected by unrest. Things don't look very good, as far as one can judge the general mood. People may be for the war but think (or hope) it can be taken care of with atom bombs. It's impossible to know how the mood will change when people finally realize the insanity of that idea. But still, this war mood is crazy and dangerous. One symptom of that is that the percentage of young men who are not registering for the draft is unusually high. Here, where there is no obligatory general registry for all citizens, it is very easy simply to withhold your name. I have always thought the American army was an army of volunteers.

This, I'm afraid, has become a rather dismal New Year's letter.

My very best wishes and good-bye for now!

Your
Hannah

---

107   *Karl Jaspers to Hannah Arendt*

Basel, January 7, 1951

Dear Hannah!

If I didn't know how kind and patient you are with your friends and others as well, I would have to despair. Two precious letters—of

Oct. 4 and Dec. 25—are here in front of me and no reply to them yet! I offer no excuses but count not only on your great and dangerous temperament's being extravagant in forgiveness this time but also on your not drawing any false conclusions, knowing how much you are loved, how irreplaceable you are for us, and how present you are in our lives at every assessment we make of the human situation today. Perhaps we are taking the prospect of seeing you again all too much for granted. But now I want to respond to the points in your letters, in random sequence.

I liked your Report from Germany[1] and had no reservations about it. It is indeed characterized by unspoken sadness, not by bitterness. You see the realities and interpret them—showing of course no special concern for the Germans, because that is not your task. It would be more mine, but I too am at a loss there—until I publish my Germany dream someday. I did not much like Elliot Cohen's remarks.[2] That's a form of dealing with each other, of tactical dealing between one major power and another (alas!): between Jews and Germans. Talking that way strikes me as pointless. It's so without affection for human beings, despite its "rightness," so much rooted in the consciousness of being Jewish. No one will respond to it with anything but counterargument. The tactlessness and gall of the Germans there[3] (and so often elsewhere) is obvious. The right response, it seems to me, is either to ignore those things and try to get past them, asking reasonable questions—or righteous wrath. But this tone of calm "negotiation" I find an embarrassment. As far as the "rightness" of it is concerned, the question is whether the mere passage of time—five years—isn't a reality. Situations change despite the reality of what has been done and of what has happened. One can't ignore time and speak today as if it were still 1945. Germans in great numbers have not in fact reacted. Those who have—you name only a few names—refuse to see "the Germans" as a collective. And where the fact of no reaction, of a refusal to take guilt upon oneself, exists—a dreadful fact with grave moral and intellectual consequences for us—one cannot constantly demand a reaction. That doesn't help, and it doesn't change things. All one can do is come to some kind of terms with these Germans, since there are 50 million of them, and deal with them on a human level—or resolve to kill them. As for what comes of discussions about "guilt," the private sphere throws some light on what would be possible in public. I've held back in my correspondence with Heidegger ever since his "confession of guilt"[4] because it was not genuine and

161

contained no real understanding. It was superfluous and without consequences. Somewhere in life—because of the passage of time—one must, reluctantly, let things fade out of sight (but not forget them). The joy of infinite, uninhibited, and never completed illumination can join only true friends together. One mustn't mistake the one mode for the other. It seems to me that Elliot Cohen, with all good will, was confused. I wrote a response to him, many pages, but then didn't send it. I realized that I was making the same mistake he was and could not really speak publicly on that still so unclear common ground between us. I recalled Halpern's criticism[5] of my *Schuldfrage* too, and thought: Speak your piece once and then keep your silence. That is probably the best thing to do in this case.

Your imperialism essay in *Der Monat*[6] is wonderful. I'm eagerly awaiting your book. Your analysis of the minds of these Englishmen taught me something new and was fully convincing. It's clear that things could not continue that way in the long run. Do you touch on the other side of the story in your book? Namely, that if we are going to have world empires—and they seem inevitable ever since Sargon[7] in the third century B.C.—then no empire has been as humane, as benevolent, as liberal as the English empire—much better than the Roman one, not to mention all the despotisms!—since the English gave people the intellectual and, ultimately, the material weapons to liberate themselves and put the question to them of a free confederation in the Commonwealth. If that fails, it is nonetheless a noble and honorable mistake. But perhaps that is all irrelevant to your book.

You have read my book *Von der Wahrheit*. And have such kind things to say about it, things with which I would like to agree—yes, you have grasped very well what I *meant* to accomplish. With your generous and charitable eye, you overlook that I fell short of that goal. I was happy, of course, to read what you said. Praise from your mouth is most welcome. But please, don't neglect the failings.

I'll be sending you my Heidelberg lectures[8] shortly. You read the first of them in *Der Monat*.[9] There's nothing new in them, just old material presented "pedagogically" for my German students. A little point of interest: In connection with the lectures, I held a colloquium and asked for written questions. I got more than a dozen relating to the first lecture, but all of them about psychoanalysis, *none* about Marx. I was surprised and mentioned this to Rossmann. Very simple, he said. No one dares to talk about Marx here, not positively, because of the occupation authorities, and not negatively, because the Russians may be coming. I don't believe that, despite Rossmann. It's probably the lack of interest in *anything* political. How different from the old days of battling the Marxists in my Heidelberg seminar!

Plato and the "tyranny of reason"—yes, how rightly you see that! In a doctoral examination recently I asked a candidate who had given Plato as one of his fields: How is it that de Gruyter in Berlin could publish a book in 1933 called *Plato and Hitler*?[10] —But what Plato did *once* in error, and only tentatively at that, one cannot, for that very reason, repeat without being un-Platonic. Finally, when things got serious, Plato's first act of "terror" was to instruct Dionysius[11] in mathematics.

That seems to me to be the radical difference between Kant and Marx, too. You speak favorably of Marx's passion for justice, which links him to Kant. If you were here, we could begin a long talk, and I would hope for support from Monsieur. Marx's passion seems to me impure at its root, itself unjust from the outset, drawing its life from the negative, without an image of man, the hate incarnate of a pseudo-prophet in the style of Ezekiel.[12] The workings of this justice are evident, for instance, in the discussion with Weitling,[13] with Lassalle,[14] and with many others. I don't see a trace of Kantian spirit there. That's different with Engels. I would agree with you there. Do you know the first draft of the *Communist Manifesto*,[15] which Engels wrote? Marx's editing took out all the humane passages and made the text propagandistically much clearer and vastly more powerful. I can't see anything else in him but an "evil" person. Lenin understood him correctly; the German Social Democrats didn't. But you can find plenty of pages in Marx to support your favorable view. But even there I usually find the tone suspect.

Monsieur has started teaching. You wrote that he was enjoying his first classes. Is that still the case? The picture of him you promised has still *not* arrived. I still know so little about him. But I think of him as a true ally.

Now to the world situation. We know as little as you. I read with some dismay what you write about the American population's leanings toward war and the folly of believing that the matter can be settled with technology. Acheson[16] does not seem to hold that opinion. What we read about him, about Marshall,[17] bolsters my confidence. The United States mustn't let itself be lured into the Russian trap. All the "evidence" seems to suggest that Stalin can't want a war now (but your Jew is still right: I don't know whether he knows that). If negotiations on long-term arms control succeed, then we *could* have peace for a long time, though that is unlikely. Perhaps the greater danger at the moment is that the Americans will lose patience. They'll have to get out of Korea, maintaining in the worst case a bridgehead there in a permanent state of war. How would it be if they continue to indict China and declare that they will occupy and keep Formosa until China allows Korea her independence and settles all their differences "legally"? Then they will have saved face but won't be caught in a continuing war. It will hardly be possible to hold on to Indochina either. But a permanent blockade—which would annoy no one but English business interests—is possible, along with the organization of all forces against Russia for the long haul.

If the Americans dig themselves in too deep in Korea, they could bleed themselves to death the way the Athenians did at Syracuse.[18] The Chinese can sacrifice millions of men; their population will still be too large. They're starving anyhow. A war with China is sheer madness.

Let's stick with our hope for your visit along with Monsieur this summer!

There's nothing for it. We have to live again with the awareness that everything that constitutes our world can be wiped out in a month. I can't quite believe that will happen, in spite of everything. Whether things fall out one way or the other, nothing changes in terms of what one can *do*.

Warmest greetings and best wishes for the New Year. Stay cheerful and clever, both of you, and keep on loving people—in spite of everything!

Your Karl Jaspers

Your success at Notre Dame struck me as such a matter of course that I didn't even write about it. Gurian deserves praise for "sweating" on your behalf. Perhaps that's what the envious demons demand.

108 Karl Jaspers to Hannah Arendt

Basel, February 15, 1951

Dear Hannah!

Your book[1] has just arrived. Even before I read it—which I'm very much looking forward to—I wanted to thank you right away and let you know the book is in our hands.

Beautifully produced—and such a reasonable retail price!

You know how proud I am, no, how happy about the bond that you make known with the epigraph.[2]

I enjoy seeing in the biographical notes about you that I am always mentioned as the man with whom you took your doctorate, despite the fact that I don't deserve so much credit.

Warmest greetings to you
and Monsieur
Your Karl Jaspers

I've just read the foreword quickly: masterful, it seems to me—I've never yet seen the situation and task of our time presented so clearly, simply, and vividly.

And the final chapter, which I already know in part. Wonderful in its demand—which is, in any case, altogether right and necessary. But how do we get to the point where everyone will accept it? It will no doubt take more than merely making the demand to accomplish that.

Hasn't Jahwe faded too far out of sight?

109 *Hannah Arendt to Karl Jaspers*

March 4, 1951

Lieber Verehrtester—

This was supposed to be a birthday letter when the flu got me (you know: "A cold lurks outside the store, nailing victims who come out the door"[1] and made me totally useless for nearly two weeks. I thought of sending a wire but then thought you both have so many relatives in this country that an overseas telegram might alarm you.

I'm glad that the book was ready for your birthday. It's not in the stores yet, not until the end of the month. As long as I didn't have the epigraph, I knew that something was missing; and then the mood of the epigraph prompted me to write the foreword very differently from what I had originally planned, as if I were freed by your sentence.

Your question "Hasn't Jahwe faded too far out of sight?" has been on my mind for weeks now without my being able to come up with an answer to it. No more than I've been able to find one to my own demand from the final chapter. On the personal level, I make my way through life with a kind of (childish? because unquestioned) trust in God (as distinguished from faith, which always thinks it knows and therefore has to cope with doubts and paradoxes). There's nothing

165

much you can make of that, of course, except be happy. All traditional religion as such, whether Jewish or Christian, holds nothing whatsoever for me anymore. I don't think, either, that it can anywhere or in any way provide a basis for something so clearly political as laws. Evil has proved to be more radical than expected. In objective terms, modern crimes are not provided for in the Ten Commandments. Or: the Western tradition is suffering from the preconception that the most evil things human beings can do arise from the vice of selfishness. Yet we know that the greatest evils or radical evil has nothing to do anymore with such humanly understandable, sinful motives. What radical evil really is I don't know, but it seems to me it somehow has to do with the following phenomenon: making human beings as human beings superfluous (not using them as means to an end, which leaves their essence as humans untouched and impinges only on their human dignity; rather, making them superfluous as human beings). This happens as soon as all unpredictability—which, in human beings, is the equivalent of spontaneity—is eliminated. And all this in turn arises from—or, better, goes along with—the delusion of the omnipotence (not simply with the lust for power) of an individual man. If an individual man qua man were omnipotent, then there is in fact no reason why men in the plural should exist at all—just as in monotheism it is only God's omnipotence that makes him ONE. So, in this same way, the omnipotence of an individual man would make men superfluous. (Nietzsche, it seems to me, has nothing to do with this, or Hobbes either. The will to power always wants simply to become more powerful and so remains within the comparative, which still respects the limits of human existence and does not push on to the madness of the superlative.)

I suspect that philosophy is not altogether innocent in this fine how-do-you-do. Not, of course, in the sense that Hitler had anything to do with Plato. (One compelling reason why I took such trouble to isolate the elements of totalitarian governments was to show that the Western tradition from Plato up to and including Nietzsche is above any such suspicion.) Instead, perhaps in the sense that Western philosophy has never had a clear concept of what constitutes the political, and couldn't have one, because, by necessity, it spoke of man the individual and dealt with the fact of plurality tangentially. But I shouldn't have written all this. None of it is thought through at all. Excuse me.

Your good, long letter of early January has gone unanswered for an inexcusably long time, too. I was particularly pleased to have your excellent critique of Elliot Cohen's article, because the whole thing left me feeling uneasy, but I could never quite put my finger on why. Now the way you have spelled it all out makes the entire room warm and bright again. You're absolutely right. All the responses were "counterarguments."

English imperialism: The best thing about it was how it was liquidated and also how in spite of everything the still-intact national institutions of the homeland always thwarted the real intentions of England's imperialistic party. It's hard, it seems to me, to compare it with the Roman empire because, though Roman rule was presumably much crueler and intemperate, it was still a genuine empire and not merely imperialism, because the Roman conquerors forced Roman law on foreign peoples and by doing so avoided the disastrous bastardized governments of modern times.

Marx: I immediately called Monsieur in for consultation, and he agreed with you completely. He thinks Marx had no sense of justice but did have one of freedom. I've thought the whole thing over again, and the (very early) *Debatten über das Holzdiebstahlsgesetz*[2] came to mind. There he analyzes the de-naturing of man and of nature by the economy of commodities; how it is no longer two people who need wood who stand face to face but a wood owner and a wood thief (human needs are not the crucial point anymore) and how wood is not crucial anymore either. In the eyes of the law, it could just as well be plastic. These two things together—the de-humanizing of man and the de-naturizing of nature—are what Marx means when he talks about the abstraction of society, and a rebellion against these things seems to me to be still alive in the later Marx as well. I don't mean to defend him as a scholar (although he was a great scholar, scholarship is the very thing he destroyed with his ideological overlay) and surely not as a philosopher, but as a rebel and a revolutionary.

Piper has written to Harcourt, Brace. Many thanks. A German edition would please me, and to appear with the same publisher you do would be particularly nice. Perhaps something will come of it.

Heidegger: You write that you feel inhibited in your correspondence with him, and I am sorry for that, because I was the innocently guilty cause of his "confession of guilt." You're right with your phrase "no real understanding," but for that reason I think it is indeed "genuine" this time. Explanations would not have been genuine, because he really doesn't know and is hardly in a position to find out what devil drove him into what he did. He would be only too glad "to let things fade out of sight." I've obviously prevented him from doing that. You're right that he has written as one can only to a true friend after thirty years of unbroken friendship. But don't forget how cautious and evasive his original reactions were. As you can see, I have a guilty conscience.

The world situation doesn't look any better. I'm always uneasy as soon as it looks like there won't be a war, because I'm somehow convinced that war will come when we're least expecting it. (That reminds me of my friend Kurt Blumenfeld,[4] who used to say that he was sure he had cancer because he had no symptoms whatsoever.) The insane course of history makes us all into that kind of hypochondriac. —I cling fanatically to hope for a united Europe, and I'm totally convinced that one single correct move could stave off the worst and give us time. At any rate, I think there will still be time for my next visit, about which I think a great deal. I argue endlessly with Monsieur and can't budge him: If he goes to Europe, he maintains, he'll have to go to Germany, too, and that is the last thing he wants to do. Ergo, he'll stay where he is. And his general principle: One should only travel when one is forced to.

An essay by Karl Barth on America and Russia[5] came into my hands. Maybe you've seen it. Very typical for European intellectuals (and it is difficult enough to maintain any distinction between the intellectuals and the mob) and possibly the most dishonest thing of this kind I have ever had the displeasure to see.

This letter has gotten much too long. Now it will have to stand that way. I would so like to come for a little visit.

Always your
Hannah

110　*Karl Jaspers to Hannah Arendt*

Basel, March 11, 1951

Dear Hannah!

What a joy your letter of March 4 was! Yes, it would be nice to talk again right now. Every paragraph demands it. Your "childish" trust in God, isn't that philosophy? Somewhere we are children; otherwise we couldn't live—and we are grateful that all reflection, which sets no limits for itself, always ultimately goes back to an unintellectual impulse from which all truth basically comes.

Your husband's success as a teacher is fine. A singular man who does not want to come out of himself hides his treasures. I would so much like to see him and speak with him together with you. And now you have sent for the first time a good picture of him. I'm seeing him now for the first time.

I'm writing today because I've been sorting out old manuscripts and notes. Among some seminar notes (for a Schelling seminar) I found a sheet of paper with a few words I had jotted down in preparation for discussing your seminar paper. And a letter from you about the same seminar.[1] I'm sending them because you might enjoy recalling this. Many people don't like such things, because recollections show them only what they don't want to be or what they have failed to do or what they have repressed. You affirm yourself and will like to have memories, it seems to me. So I'll take the chance—besides, this is pretty harmless stuff. From your letter I see that it must have been in 1926.

Warmest greetings to you both!

As always, your Karl Jaspers

My marks on your letter are from that time. I haven't added anything now.

111   *Hannah Arendt to Gertrud and Karl Jaspers*

May 14, 1951

Dear Friends—

I've been wanting to write for so long that your letter dropped into or, rather, out of my mailbox almost with a thump. The reason for my not writing is the same as yours for writing: I, too, wanted to know whether anything would come of my trip to Europe—and I still don't know. It really depends on whether our naturalization goes through quickly or slowly, because traveling without a passport has begun to look a bit risky, though neither of us seriously expects war to break out. So don't count on me at all. About all I can say with much certainty is that my job will prevent me from getting away any earlier than September. Monsieur will not come. He is teaching summer school, and then the winter semester begins in mid-September, leaving him with not much more than five or six weeks off. That makes

169

it impossible for him to travel. But then, he's having so much fun that we shouldn't feel sorry for him. ("A man who hides his treasures"? Not any longer, at any rate. His students have given him a tape recorder so that his lectures can now be recorded on the spot. All you have to do is be consistent in something—for instance, be consistent about not writing—and some way out will always present itself.)

What I've been meaning to tell you for a long time, however, is this: Tillich will be giving a seminar at Yale this winter on existential philosophy and has asked me to take over more or less completely the sessions on Jaspers. I was terribly pleased. Now Columbia has made the same request, and on the next two Wednesdays I'll do my best there to spread around as much wisdom as I can. Neither of us would have dreamed of this at the time I wrote you that first letter (for which I thank you very much. It called up so many memories in a concrete way, and with the necessary correctives applied; that is, it refreshed my nearly lost recollections of how gawky I was then).

I'm glad you had such a good time with your brother and brother-in-law.[1] Please give him my regards, even though I have never met him personally. I haven't read his book[2] yet. I glanced at it, and it seemed to me such a serious and important work that I wanted to leave it for vacation or some other time when I didn't have other pressing things on my mind.

One more thing: Kaufmann[3] from Princeton asked, without further explanation, whether you "knew English." I somehow managed to say neither no nor yes, but more yes.

I've been reading a lot of Marx and Hegel lately, but I'll save that for another time. I haven't heard anything from Piper. *Der Monat* and probably *Hochland* will publish large excerpts. I haven't had any luck with *Merkur*. Paeschke's dishonesty got on my nerves because it's typical and not individual. So I wrote him a somewhat ill-tempered letter. He seems to have taken it amiss. —The book has received more attention here than I expected. Did I write you that I was elevated to the station of cover girl[4] for a week and had to look at myself on all the newsstands?

Monsieur sends warmest wishes. My best and fondest regards to you both

Your   Hannah

(temporarily) St. Moritz, August 6, 1951

Dear Hannah!

You and Monsieur[1] have both written such kind letters in May and still haven't received a reply. There is no excuse for me, unless you allow as an ameliorating circumstance that I fell hopelessly silent for all my friends and relatives (and wrote only to publishers!) because I can only barely keep up with the day-by-day demands. Please, please don't feel in the least put off.

We're in St. Moritz now—magically beautiful and peaceful. No obligations, no duties, no deadlines. One dreams and then opens one's eyes. This noble landscape impresses itself anew on one and will continue to exert its influence through the year, as it has before. It emanates a demand, as if a response of a high order should necessarily follow. And Nietzsche's soul lives here.[2] Each year we think you ought to be here with us. Perhaps we'll manage it someday after all? (If both requirements happen to coincide: your trip and the invitation from the owners of this house.) Or will you feel that this place suits only old, sedate folks?

I was delighted to read about your husband's lectures. Now they'll be fixed on paper. Yes, it's strange. By not writing, he forces his ideas to find expression but, as in the ancient world, in spoken form. May he continue to get the same response he did the first time.

And what a joy it is to me that you will be speaking about my philosophy at American universities! Thank you. I would love to be in the audience. I'm still so deeply involved in the process myself that I feel I'm only now beginning to articulate what I really want to say. It's almost crazy. Perhaps Kant was right: Just when you're far enough along that you can really begin your work in earnest, you have to die, and it's the same for whoever comes next. I'm still presumptuous enough to start over and over again. The shadow of the end doesn't paralyze, but it does lend a salutary note of unimportance to the whole enterprise. Thinking about that does one good when, in one's zeal, one loses a sense of proportion. In spite of all this, the work goes forward slowly.

I read the chapter of your book that appeared in *Der Monat*[3] right away. Excellent! The success of this book seems assured to me. Modernity combined with an "old-fashioned" seriousness that cannot be taken for granted anymore at all today. It always makes me happy when I think about it.

Piper[4] wrote me many weeks ago about your book. He was worried about the length. The book would have to cost at least DM 25. That high a book price in Germany would prevent large sales. I wrote back that he should ask you whether abridgment by leaving out a few chapters would be possible. In any real sense, it is not possible. But better the main chapters than nothing at all—or do you feel differently? DM 18 would be the highest price—say two-thirds or half of the book. Barbaric! Are you angry that I would even consider such a thing?

Thanks to your ambiguous reply about my English, I received through Kaufmann a marvelous invitation from Princeton University. For nine months in Princeton, with *no* teaching responsibilities, only private talks with colleagues and work on my books, $9,000, or, for a shorter stay, $1,000 per month. Unfortunately, I had to refuse it. Not just because of the language. I also need my strength for the things I still want to accomplish. The visit would be a lark, and I would love it, but such things are no longer for me.

I thank your husband for his kind letter. I understand why he will not be able to come this year. I hope that won't always be so. You have some prospects of making a trip to Europe this fall yourself. That would be wonderful for us. I mean, we haven't really even half begun to talk yet—deeply satisfying as it was in human terms when you spoiled us with your earlier visit.

Warmest greetings
Your Karl Jaspers

113   Hannah Arendt to Karl Jaspers

September 28, 1951

Lieber Verehrtester—

I've waited inordinately long to reply to your wonderful letter from St. Moritz. But I am now able to report that I will presumably have my citizenship in December (all the preliminaries have been taken care of)[1] and will then arrive on your doorstep sometime. —Piper hasn't written to me, so I'll just let it go. I don't really believe that "too long and too expensive" stuff. We know the story on that.

You wrote so well about the "far enough along that you can begin in earnest"—it made me so happy. It is still true that the gods let their favorites die young, not literally true, but in the sense that they don't allow them what is supposed to be a comfort of old age, that is, feeling "old and tired of life." The ambiguous, ironic gift of the gods is that death always has to find something that it can destroy, that it remains, in other words, what it was to us in youth. So we don't grow into it the way the Jewish patriarchs did until death dangled above their mouths like the ripe fruit of the fig trees they sat under, waiting. That's the price that one pays for remaining involved in life for as long as one is alive. Then it is death that cuts us off from life, not the burden of the lives we've lived.

Although I knew better, I was still harboring a small, guarded hope about Princeton. You've made the right choice, though I don't think it would have been a pure lark. My reservations were primarily about the climate. The Americans have forgotten about it, but this continent was never meant for human habitation. Too hot and humid in the summer and too cold and humid in the winter. But this country is, despite all that, still incredibly interesting, even though—and precisely because—stupid things are done here. I'm eternally grateful that it was here I was washed ashore. For my citizenship test, or, rather, in celebration of it, I've learned a little American constitutional history. Truly wonderful, right down to every last formulation. Much of it is still alive, and it would have been very obvious to you, though Americans know hardly anything about it on a conscious level, so much is it a part of their flesh and blood. So I'll have to come see you and tell you about it as best I can.

We had a nice holiday in the mountains near New York (i.e., four hours away by car). I'm just about to go there again for a little supplementary vacation (Jewish holidays). I've grown very fond of the landscape there.

I had a letter from Schilpp[2] a few weeks ago. He asked me to contribute to a book about you. He said you had given him my name, and I will of course agree. He suggested "Jaspers as Citizen of the World" as a subject.[3] It startled me a bit at first, but now I quite like it. Please let me know if it's all right with you or whether it strikes you as a bit too heavy-handed.

All best to you both.

With warmest greetings
Your Hannah

Basel, January 12, 1952

Dear Hannah!

I'm delighted to know that you and your husband are now American citizens. That is a wonderful thing, and not only because it makes traveling easier. We too will profit from that. You'll write as soon as your plans are firm. Mine and my wife's pleasure at the prospect of seeing you is great indeed. You don't know how often I think of you and find encouragement in that.

You have sent me a book about America. I still haven't thanked you for it and haven't found the time to read it yet. But a look at it has convinced me that I have to and want to read it—if I want to risk a short paragraph on American philosophy in my "Weltgeschichte der Philosophie."[1] There are some books that have been standing on my shelves unread for ten years. But if they're there at the right moment, that proves how good it was to own them, though of course I can't count anymore—or can count less than ever—on having ten more years.

Golo Mann was here recently. He wrote a review of your superb book in *Die Neue Zeitung*[2]: very respectful but very critical. You "exaggerate"—and he gives his reasons for saying that. Because Golo has written such good reviews on Burnham,[3] Koestler,[4] and others and because I feel wounded with you if you come under attack, I turned my guns against him. My case went something like this: "Exaggeration"—of course she exaggerated. What she set out to do was reveal relationships among ideas. Once that is done it's easy to show where those relationships don't apply. No one can ascertain how great a bearing they had on the actual course of events. Hannah never claimed that English imperialism produced Hitler and Stalin, nor did she claim that there was any intellectual identity anywhere among them. But the analogies in the phenomena, which ultimately made the whole disaster possible, would still be there even if there were no causal relationship at all. What she has done is perceive those relationships and present them with remarkable vividness.

Then I said: The few who know what freedom is have to stick together. There aren't so many of them. Respect isn't enough. Should it be only the crooks who stick together like burrs and instinctively support each other all over the world? His response: Yes, I admit that I was angry, and it's easy for me to go too far in my reviews. I'm excessive in my condemnation and my praise.

Golo and I were not in complete agreement. He is an honest, likable, talented person with a great historical awareness. I've liked him very much ever since his student years in Heidelberg. It would be nice if you could get to know him. You could manage it. He is bristly, shy, sharp-tongued, and unhappy, but always decent. He has inherited talent from his father, but he is far superior to him in character. His unfavorable review of your book was an error on his part, but still not reprehensible. The main thing is that an uninitiated reader will still see from his review that your book is a major one.

I've written this by the by, just to tell you a little something. Because I have so much else to ask and say that I don't even want to begin. And that's why we're so eagerly looking forward to your visit.

Warmest greetings, also to Monsieur
Your Karl Jaspers

*

115 Hannah Arendt to Karl Jaspers

Yaddo,[1] January 25, 1952

Lieber Verehrtester—

Your good letter. I am of course pleased when you defend me, and I'm sorry that I haven't read the review. (I learned about it only by way of a crazy letter from a DP who wrote me that if I would send him an affidavit[2] for the States he would eradicate all of my "enemies" there, like Golo Mann, for example. Because the man was obviously mad I wasn't even sure that Golo Mann had really written anything.) It seems to me there is so much we have to say to and hear from each other—and that seems particularly so when I'm out of the New York whirl for a few days as I am now—that I can't even make a start at it. So I'll just respond with whatever flows into the typewriter.

I once met Golo Mann very fleetingly and liked his face, but I was overwhelmed and embarrassed by his shyness. Now I would like to meet him, and since he was so annoyed about my book, the meeting will surely go better.

"Exaggeration"—of course. "Relationships between ideas," as you say, can hardly be presented any other way. And then they are not really exaggerations either. They're products of dissection. It's the nature of thought to exaggerate. When Montesquieu says that republican government is based on the principle of virtue, he is "exaggerating," too. Besides, reality has taken things to such great extremes in our century that we can say without exaggeration that reality is "exaggerated." Our thinking, which after all likes nothing better than rolling along its accustomed paths, is hardly capable of keeping up with it. My "exaggerated" kind of thinking, which is at least making an effort to say something adequate in a tone that is, if possible, itself adequate, will of course sound wildly radical if you measure it not against reality but against what other historians, going on the assumption that everything is in the best of order, have said on the same subject.

He was probably angry because of his own neoconservatism, which I do not share. But I hope he wasn't angry the way many academics are, namely, at an outsider who dabbles in their trade, doesn't quote them with the appropriate reverence, doesn't go to congresses, and doesn't even aspire to the grandeur of being a professor. That kind of anger is usually easy to combat, even though the means for combatting it are not quite fair. I don't see why one should only suffer the disadvantages of being a woman and not bring the advantages a bit into play as well.

Did I write that I had an invitation to Harvard? I'm accepting it with mixed feelings of irritation and fascination. They're organizing a conference on totalitarianism for next fall. It can't possibly yield anything of interest, but I'll go this time.

I'm so much looking forward to Basel. And while I'm happily anticipating my visit (and have time for happy anticipation), I'm reading Kant and Schelling, *Menschliche Freiheit*.[3] I read that for the first time in my first semester at Heidelberg, for a paper in your Schelling seminar.[4]

I'll write to your wife about all the practical matters.

All my very best, and until soon!

Your
Hannah

116 *Karl Jaspers to Hannah Arendt*

Basel, January 29, 1952

Dear Hannah!

Great delight reigns here in anticipation of your visit. Today I'm just quickly sending the review[1] by Golo Mann. It was sent to me from Germany, hence the underlinings. I never see this newspaper otherwise. You're quite right in what you say about Golo Mann. Only one thing, I think, is not correct. He is *not* an academic and has no professorial competitiveness. His shyness is a symptom of his difficult legacy, and on top of that he is the son of a famous man. He has freed himself from that in, I think, a truly forthright way.

Warmest regards Your K. Jaspers

117 *Hannah Arendt to Gertrud and Karl Jaspers*

February 18, 1952

Dear, dear Friends—

This is really a birthday letter, though a bit ahead of time. I can't write any more, can only send the very best wishes.

Erna: as far as I know, she can't get an immigration visa if she has a firm job lined up.[1] That sounds absurd but isn't; it's just obsolete. The point at an earlier time was to prevent people from importing slave labor in immigrant guise. This law is still in force, and it seems to me she should inquire into it further. I've spoken with a few friends but can't, of course, get any firm commitments. Either they have servants and have no reason to let them go, or they can't very well wait. Once Erna is here, I can give her good recommendations. What she will have to have in any case is an affidavit, and she can't get that from people for whom she will then work. No one here would be willing to do that, because it would give Erna the legal right to remain in that household. I could give her an affidavit, but I'd rather discuss that with you in person beforehand. It means assuming heavy responsibilities.

I'll leave here on March 21, and on the 27th I'll be in Paris, where I'll stay for a few days. But this isn't very important, because I'll be in Paris for a somewhat longer time in April anyhow before I go to Palestine. I can make my plans to suit your preference, so I'll wait and see what you write. If things should change here—and that is always possible, because I'm traveling for the organization[2]—I'll let you know right away. Is it all right if I come for a week, or is that too long? Please, please write frankly what is best for you. I really will understand no matter what the circumstances. I had thought I would go from Paris to Germany by way of Basel, then via Paris again to Palestine, and via Switzerland on the way back, about the end of

May. I'd love to spend at least a week in Greece. And maybe I'll treat myself to it.

Thank you for the Mann review. More on that when we can talk. (How nice that I can write that so casually.) If I weren't so excited and happy, this letter wouldn't have turned out to be so stupid.

Always your
Hannah

118 Karl Jaspers to Hannah Arendt

Basel, March 5, 1952

Dear Hannah!

Just a quick word before your departure. Every day my wife and I say to each other how delighted we are with the prospect of your visit. It's wonderful that you can stay for a week, and perhaps again on your return trip from Israel, if that works out.

Be patient! We'll talk about all sorts of things together, one after the other.

Give my regards to Monsieur. It's a great shame that he isn't coming, too. But I still hope to have the chance to meet him.

Warmest greetings
Your Karl Jaspers

119 Hannah Arendt to Karl Jaspers

March 16, 1952

Lieber Verehrtester—

How good of you to write again. The prospect of Basel gives everything I'll be doing a firm footing, without which I would feel quite lost on this world tour. Of course I will come again on my return trip.

Now a suggestion: I received a telegram from my family[1] in Palestine asking me to come as quickly as I could. I don't know why, and because of the censorship I can't find out. So if it's possible I would like to go there earlier—that would mean Palestine and then Greece. In that case I would like to limit my stay in Paris to a minimum (I'll be coming back there anyway) and come to you on Monday, March

31, and stay until Sunday morning. If that is all right, I'd arrange on the return trip to be in Basel on Saturday, May 3, to stay the weekend. Please let me know right away in Paris if that doesn't suit you. Then we'll go back to the original plan, and I'll come on Thursday, April 3. Perhaps it would be best if you write to my friend's address (instead of American Express): chez Mme Anne Weil, 1 Avenue René Samuel, Clamart/Seine. I'll be in Paris on the 27th. If I don't hear anything from you, I'll be in Basel on Monday, that's two weeks from tomorrow. —I won't believe any of this is happening until I'm in Paris. I keep thinking to myself all the time how I'll tell you this or that, what you will probably say to this or that. The list starts, very concretely, with domestic politics in America and ends with Plato. What are you lecturing on in the summer? I'd very much like to hear a lecture of yours again.

Fondest regards to you both—Your
Hannah

120 Hannah Arendt to Gertrud and Karl Jaspers

Paris, April 8, 1952

Dear, dear Friends—

Thank you for your letter, and thank you for the invitation.[1] Heinrich, with whom I have checked in the meantime, wrote back that I shouldn't let a "once-in-a-lifetime" opportunity like this escape me. So I think, if you're really sure that it would not be too much for you in any way, that I could easily come for at least a week around August 1. Now I'd like to ask a favor of you: Please let me share the household expenses with you for this time. That's only fair, and you know I'm very well able to do it.

My schedule finally seems to be reasonably firm, though I always have to add a cautionary *sauf imprévu*. From the 25th to the 27th I'll be in Lugano, then, on the return trip, in Zurich briefly. If it's still all right with you, I could be in Basel on the afternoon of Wednesday, May 28, and stay, unfortunately, only a short time, until Friday morning (but then, you're also in the middle of your semester). Just enough time to catch you up on things. Everything else we'll have to postpone for St. Moritz. (Too wonderful to be really true.)

I still don't know where I'll be staying in Munich. Drop me a line c/o American Express, Munich. I'll leave here on Saturday and will probably be in Munich on Tuesday, the 13th.

Warmest greetings
Always, Your
Hannah

121 Hannah Arendt to Gertrud and Karl Jaspers

April 10, 1952

Dear, dearest Friends—

Just a quick hello and my thanks and the news that I'm finally settled in the Hotel d'Angleterre, 44 rue Jacob, Paris.

I found a telegram from Heinrich here in which he swears he has written regularly (who do you believe more? the post office or your own husband?) and also appraises me of a mysterious happening, which I assume to mean that I got a Guggenheim[1]—the fellowship that Golo Mann had. If I'm right about that—and it seems likely—that would be very nice and would mean that starting this fall I wouldn't have to worry about earning money at all for one or two years.

My friend[2] met me at the train. Now I'm expecting Kazin along with his nice young American girlfriend. I imagine we'll christen the Guggenheim a bit.

Now I can describe to you what French phenomena I can see from my window, which looks out onto a courtyard. For example, a man with an umbrella leaning out of an attic trapdoor to repair the roof. Things like that happen only in Paris.

With warmest greetings
Your
Hannah

Regards to Schmuel.[3] And to Erna,[4] too.

122 Karl Jaspers to Hannah Arendt

Basel, April 12, 1952

Dear Hannah!

That's wonderful about the Guggenheim! You'll have the chance for some undisturbed work: two years of leave. The new book—from the "heights" of the history of philosophy[1]—will no doubt be the product of this time, but better still is the freedom to work and think in the company of your Heinrich.

I'm still feeling as if my mind is fresher, newly inspired, and as if my soul were stronger. My wife and I speak every day of the days spent with you. These two among the Noahs[2] have seen each other again. How much better seeing and speaking are than letter-writing. The back and forth in the present, minute by minute. Only then do you really see what the other is and what was lying ready in oneself.

Gertrud was reading to me from J. Burckhardt last night. He said he wouldn't want to live this life a second time. How differently I feel. This affirmation has never left me entirely—may it continue to be granted to you and to me.

I've written to Jeanne[3] to let her know you're coming.

Warmest greetings
Your Karl Jaspers

123 Hannah Arendt to Karl Jaspers

Paris, April 17, 1952

Lieber Verehrtester—

I'm happy to have your letter, and my living and thinking are still completely in the grip of our talks in Basel. It's nice to continue them mentally on walks in a spring such as I have never seen before in Paris. It's like a dream world filled with blossoms.

The Guggenheim—I've received the official confirmation in the meantime—is a great relief. It's not a lot of money, but I don't need more. With what Heinrich has, it's quite enough. We won't have to dip into savings, but we won't be able to save much either.

Jeanne Hersch and I hit it off instantly, from the first moment on. We've seen each other twice again since. She got me together with a friend of hers, Milosz,[1] a Polish refugee, whom I was very eager to meet. I'll tell you more about her later perhaps. In any case, she attacks me a lot and upbraids me even more thoroughly. So you see, we get on famously. She is valued highly here, and she is thoroughly delightful. Astonishing, how young she is. I feel like a real old lady.

I saw François Bondy[2] and got the impression from Jeanne Hersch, Milosz, and him that the Congress for Cultural Freedom is something quite different and very much better here than it is in the States. That was a comfort to me. I'll see them all and speak with them all again.

181

I've just read (and this is the real reason for my writing) the pages "Uber meine Philosophie" in *Rechenschaft und Ausblick*.[3] That's the nicest summary anyone could ever want. I'm overwhelmed by it. Why don't you tell Schilpp just to translate that? It seems to me it is wonderfully suited as an introduction to a volume of selected readings.[4] Or do you feel too great a need to write something new for it?

Warmest greetings to you both

Hannah

124   *Karl Jaspers to Hannah Arendt*

Basel, April 20, 1952

Dear Hannah!

I'm glad you are getting on so well with Jeanne Hersch. I didn't expect it could be otherwise.

The Guggenheim is confirmed. And you sound on such a firm financial footing when you write about savings.

You'll tell me more about the people from the Congress circles later. So it's something worthwhile after all.

What you wrote about my self-portrait of 1940 was very kind. But I will have to write something new for Schilpp, probably with some partial repetition. I don't really feel like it yet, because anything that diverts my attention from the history of philosophy is an annoyance to me.

My lecture course begins tomorrow.[1] I always have some stage fright. But being obliged to speak usually acts as a stimulus for my work.

We just had a visitor from Tel Aviv, an old doctor from Berlin. His tone, reasoning, and assessments of the situation were those of a good Prussian officer. It was bizarre: The Arabs are shutting off Israel's life breath; therefore, they have to be "forced" to make peace. A new war is the only way, without territorial conquest, but with enough force to bring about a peace treaty—perhaps that goal can be achieved peacefully by means of threats alone. People are being shot along the borders every day. More Jews have died since the cease-fire than during the war, and so forth. Bizarre because this man is clearly an admirable person, decent, open, helpful, and because he seems to me to be one of the best German Prussian types but happens to be a Jew.

We think of you often, grateful for your existence.

Warmest greetings

Your Karl Jaspers

182

Paris, April 28, 1952

Lieber Verehrtester,

Thank you for your letter. I always write as though my financial footing were a bit sounder than it really is. There's a lot to tell from here, so I don't even want to begin. What you wrote about your visitor from Tel Aviv is, I regret to say, all too familiar to me. I keep telling myself: Be cautious in your judgment of the Germans; we're just like them.

Joe Frank, an American friend living in Paris, told me yesterday that he has suggested a modern-philosophy series to Yale University. Of your works, he suggested *Existenz und Vernunft*,[1] (the Dutch lectures). Frank impresses me as a good person of real substance. I'm mentioning this in case you should hear something from Yale. They seem to be interested.

My plans are beginning to look a little more settled. It's very likely—*sauf imprévu*—that I'll have to go to Lugano and Zurich in the last week of May. I'm not absolutely sure of the dates. Would a brief catch-up visit suit you then? I'm going to Lugano because the publisher of Broch's literary remains[2] invited me to discuss the project with him there.

Did I write that I have an invitation to the University of Manchester for the end of June?

I saw Jeanne Hersch again and will surely see her once more.

I'll definitely be here until May 10. I'll send you my address from Germany once I'm there.

All my very best to both of you.

Your Hannah

Basel, May 3, 1952

Dear Hannah!

You are always welcome here. If, contrary to expectations, a conflict should arise, we can make some kind of arrangements—because with you complete frankness is possible.

The "children"[1] are coming from Oldenburg on May 20 and will go on to the Jura a few days later with my sister,[2] who is coming tomorrow.

So just write us as soon as you know when it is convenient for you to visit.

I look forward to what you'll have to tell us.

Warmest greetings
Your Karl Jaspers

127   Hannah Arendt to Karl Jaspers

Georghausen, July 7, 1952

Lieber Verehrtester—

Just a quick line to tell you that I spoke in London with Herbert Read, who is planning to bring out *Ursprung und Ziel der Geschichte* soon. I had a long talk with the translator [Michael Bullock]. He made a good impression. He has studied the translation of *Der philosophische Glaube* closely so that he can maintain a uniform terminology in his English translation. Best of all, he had just completed the work and gave me the manuscript. I'm afraid I won't be able to look through it before August. We both have one or two questions for you, which we can talk about in St. Moritz.

I can't write about England this time; I'll save it all up to tell you. I'm here half for a rest and half to finish up some work for a deadline. A very beautiful baroque castle, hotel, very comfortable and pleasant.

I tried to reach Jeanne Hersch in Paris, but she had left her hotel without leaving a forwarding address. Maybe they just didn't want to give me the address. At any rate, she probably wasn't in Paris.

Next Sunday I'll be speaking here in Cologne to a small group, then next week in Heidelberg—very strange somehow. Around the 20th I want to go to Berlin for a week. Lasky wants to arrange for a lecture, and I want to have seen Berlin. It doesn't seem to me there is any danger at all at the moment, because the Germans haven't signed the treaty[1] yet. After that, I have something else to do in Germany and expect that I'll join you on July 31 or August 1. For the last days of July, the best address will be Frankfurt, c/o American Express, Taunus Anlage 9.

I'm a little concerned about how you are both tolerating the heat. In Paris it was quite brutal. Maybe it's better in Basel.

All my best wishes, and my regards to your brother-in-law and brother [Ernst Mayer].

Your   Hannah

Basel, July 9, 1952

Dear Hannah!

Your letter of July 7 from Georghausen has just arrived. Many thanks. Now you'll have more work with that history book. In St. Moritz I'll be available to help. I hope you'll just read sample passages that will prove so good that you can leave the rest unread.

I had my last lecture a few hours ago. Now I have nothing do but look forward to St. Moritz and our time together there. Gertrud has sent you the address already: Villa Nimet, St. Moritz (Engadin). The house is on the road from the village of St. Moritz to Suvretta, not far from the village. It would be best for you to take a cab from the railroad station, either a horse cab or car. The name of the house—Nimet—was that of an Arab or Abyssinian woman, whom a Swiss married. I'll tell you the story.

This letter will reach you in Heidelberg. Yes, it is strange. I hope you have a good audience. There are still some good people there. And the city remains wonderful, the most beautiful in Germany.

My wife—you asked about this—does not tolerate the heat well. I manage fine if I don't have to work. One does grow lazy during a long warm spell and is entitled to. But today it's cooling off beautifully.

Berlin—I don't like the idea of your trip to Berlin. I read in the paper today that a jurist (from the League of Free Jurists) was kidnapped right out of the city. The pursuers couldn't catch the car. At the border, the Russians had already raised the newly installed gate, and the kidnappers' car made it out of West Berlin. The man was pulled into the car right off the street. But Lasky will be delighted if you do go. Give him my regards. We haven't heard from him in a long time.

Warmest greetings
Your Karl Jaspers

Basel, July 21, 1952

Dear Mr. Blücher!

We have never met, yet it seemed as if you were here with Hannah at our house.[1] Before, you were only Monsieur; now Hannah often says Heinrich. She may say little about you directly, but you are present with her. And she has told me some things: about your lectures, your mode of work, the factual details of your life. When I told her that I wanted to lecture on four major figures (crucial in the history of the world), she exclaimed with pleasure: just like Heinrich. The basic idea behind the lectures seems similar for both of us, though the names are not the same. Along with Socrates, Buddha, Confucius, and Jesus, you are also discussing Abraham and Moses. In the past I've spoken about the latter two only in connection with the biblical idea of God. Perhaps you are right to single them out for special treatment also. I'll reflect more on that. I'm glad that you take Abraham's reality as established fact. Someone like that can't possibly have been invented.

Hannah has, it seems to me, undergone an evolution in recent years. Her great rage is almost gone. She is becoming more just, tolerant toward what is most alien to her. She shows greater detachment toward Germany. I haven't progressed as far, and so there is sometimes a desirable tension between us, not a hardening into unreconcilable "positions" but an ability—for me very enlivening—to speak to each other on a common ground. Through her I am better able to understand, in the context of present reality, the way writers and men of letters are obliged to live today, the horrible aspects of it, which she by no means overlooks but understands and makes into an object of study in a wonderful way and with affectionate eyes. She may sometimes deceive herself but this self-deception itself is lovable.

My wife and I are very grateful to you for so readily agreeing to the extension of Hannah's stay in Europe. We are hoping for a happy time together in St. Moritz, working, resting, talking in accordance with our moods and fancy.

I was impressed by Hannah's distinction between a high and a low road in modern history. Her book traced the low road, hence not a word about Marx. The new book will complete the picture with the high road. Her respect for the mind kept her from making the great thinkers partially responsible for the horrors that occurred in the reality that her book analyzes. The view she has opened to us is wide and impressive. I don't go along with everything she says. Marx's thinking and his personality, with its sense of outrage, its violence, and its dictatorial character filled with hate, have not only had, I think, an influence that can hardly be overestimated but also bear responsibility for what has happened. I have not up to now been able to meet this man with anything but hatred on my own part (as I do Luther and Fichte). I hate his unique insight into an incredibly influential, though also limited, realm of reality, and I hate his penetrating intelligence. He uses his insight and his intelligence to satisfy his will for justice, a will that from the beginning was both a will to power and a desire for vengeance. Marx does not use his hate and his love as organs of cognizance and then put them on ice, turn away from them, play them off against each other in order to achieve through self-criticism a maximum of truth. Instead, he falls victim to his own hatred and follows it, in the name of justice, into an abominable vision. So I see in him a distortion of philosophy and absurdities that are both glaring and pernicious. I'm very eager to see what Hannah will make of this. I'm ready to correct my view of Marx. In any case, Marx is still a blameless human being, a "respectable citizen," compared to the literati, to whom Hannah does not deny her high regard and her human tolerance, a tolerance that I feel I am capable of only if I slip into the role of a psychiatrist.

I hope that life will last long enough for us to meet here in Basel. Sometime, I think, the aversion that keeps you away from Europe will fall away—and you are still young enough to travel.

With all best regards and wishes

Your
Karl Jaspers

130 *Karl Jaspers to Hannah Arendt*

Basel, July 24, 1952

Dear Hannah!

We will be driven to St. Moritz on the 26th. You are welcome to join us from July 30 on—a few days of lazing about, which are always essential for us at first because of the altitude, will see us fully rested. We're so much looking forward to seeing you. If a letter won't reach us in time, let us know by telegram, as you have before, when you will be arriving.

Thank you very much for the Malraux[1]. The text is fascinating, the pictures, wonderful. Important insights and brilliant commentary are intermixed with associative talk. I want to read further. It's particularly rewarding for the basic view of art. There is an element of greatness in that.

Rossmann reported from Heidelberg about your uncommonly powerful lecture[2] and your great poise during the discussion. I was happy to hear it. I've stopped worrying about Berlin. If you don't give any public talks and if the plane doesn't have to make an emergency landing, there's little risk of anything happening. There can be no doubt that you are known there and are public enemy No. 1. Who has ever seen so clearly what was going on behind the scenes as you have? The old Communists perhaps, but not so lethally, because they were still tied into the system. The way you speak, from the perspective of a truly different, free world—they surely won't forgive you that calm vision, even though you do have an American passport now.

Until soon! Warmest greetings
Your Karl Jaspers

131 Hannah Arendt to Gertrud and Karl Jaspers

Frankfurt, July 26, 1952

Dear, dear Friends—

Thank you for your kind letter expressing such concern for me. I didn't go to Berlin after all. I couldn't quite fit it in, and I took that as a sign that I probably shouldn't fly in there. And I don't want to be taking on extra stresses and strains at this point.

I'll tell you about Heidelberg when I see you. Without you in it, the city is empty and lacks a center. That is simply a fact. Otherwise, there were some pleasant things and some unpleasant. That for later. Rüstow was actually less interesting than I had expected but then much nicer.

This will reach you in St. Moritz, I hope already a bit caught up on your rest. The operation in Holland[1] will be over by now. I hope everything went well, and you can breathe easier.

I'm counting the days, so excited about seeing you. If I don't hear anything further from you and everything is still all right with you, I'll arrive in St. Moritz on Thursday, the 31st, at about 6:30 in the evening and will take a taxi right to you. I visited Frau Dr. Waltz. What a charming and lively person!

If you want to get in touch with me, I'm staying at the Eden Hotel am Zoo, Waldschmidtstr. 61/61a.

With warmest regards
Your Hannah

New York, August 5, 1952

Lieber und verehrter Professor Jaspers,

It pleases me deeply that you feel I have in some sense been with you; and the opportunity to be with you in reality is, as far as I can see now, about the only thing that could lure me back to Europe again.

Difficult as it is for me, I'll willingly wait a little longer for Hannah,[1] to allow you more time with her and her more with you. From my perspective of great distance, the gathering (how good it is when word and concept correspond so well) of you, your wife, and Hannah strikes me as a rare family celebration among elective affinities, and how appropriate that it is in those high mountains to which Nietzsche once went and preceded you.[2]

Yes, I too am planning to talk on prototypical human figures. But Hannah must have made a mistake in reporting this plan to you, because I don't count either Moses or Paul among them. They are great statesmen, and in that category I am drawn much more to Solon, to whom you erected a truly Greek memorial tablet in your short essay on him.[3] His gentle, irresistible power is portrayed as quietly and simply there as are the eternal figures of the dead on the reliefs of Greek tombs. I'm not really sure about Buddha, although in his Asiatic way he has much in common with Jesus. In place of Confucius I'm inclined to put Lao-tzu, who looks more and more Socratic to me the closer I study him. And then of course Jesus and Socrates. Abraham seems to me utterly unique. It is not so important to me that he is supposed to be the father of the human race, in historical terms. He seems to me rather to be the father of what is humanly possible and of the possible human being, who, by virtue of this human existence, has found the one God, in other words, the possible God, the God for whom you are trying to establish the unending ritual of your transcendence. I found this concept of the possible God and then I found Abraham, and yet I owe the concept to him.

In an introductory course in philosophy here I have drawn on your book[4] and found confirmed something that I have been saying to Hannah for a long time, which is that you could be of great importance to young people here in America. Your exemplary distinctions between science and philosophy are as urgently needed here as daily bread. The Americans have a sure nose for professional competence, and in you they feel they are hearing both scientist and philosopher. They breathe a sigh of relief when they see that here someone is concerned for the purity of both, and they are grateful to be given criteria by which they can distinguish and discard the murky, modernistic pap of pseudo-scientific and pseudometaphysical ideologies and philosophies. They also feel that they are in the presence of a liberal thinker, in the best sense of that term, and they quickly develop trust in you. What has always separated me from the Germans is that none of them, with a few major exceptions, have ever been seriously concerned about freedom; and, if you'll excuse me for saying so, that is what separates you from the Germans, too. And for that very reason you are a German who can speak to good effect in America.

Despite my requests, Hannah has not written to tell me how you are progressing with your project on the philosophy of history. You are probably putting all other things aside in order to concentrate on the second volume of your major work.[5] I am slowly developing here for the New School a major project "for intercontinental understanding," a crucial matter for America right now. In this regard, I make constant reference to your initiative[6] envisioning a dialogue with Asia on basic issues. I'm more concerned with a possible dialogue of this kind between America and Europe, but your important initiative seems to me indispensable in considering the problem of intercontinental understanding. I've already suggested inviting you to come here or sending someone to visit you there. We haven't been able to convince the rich folks to finance this yet, but we'll keep after them.

I've just been hired by a small elite college[7] here to carry out a new educational project. I'm planning to attack progressive education and its catastrophic consequences here by means of something I'm calling communicative education in your honor. For this project I'll be drawing a great deal on the source that I consider the true primal source of all your philosophy, i.e., your theory of communication; for it sometimes seems to me as if you had succeeded in elevating pedagogy itself to truly metaphysical relevance. We plan first to show the beginning students the crucial importance of ultimate questions in terms of the problems of their own lives and then to lead the students organically into their respective disciplines. I would like to try to replace the no longer realizable system of universal education with systematically communicative activities and to guide the students into an ongoing habit of self-orientation. You can well imagine how valuable your works in these areas are to me in these efforts.

I wish you and your wife a good rest. I too am beginning to pack my bags for a vacation here in the mountains with Hannah. At the

190

moment she is still with you, and you are both working diligently at the intercontinental understanding that we all need so urgently.

Warmest greetings
Your Heinrich Blücher

If Hannah is still there, please tell her that she will have no duties whatsoever at Bard College. They agreed to all of my conditions. She will be able to stay peacefully at home.

133 Hannah Arendt to Gertrud and Karl Jaspers

August 23, 1952

Dear, dear Friends—

Just a word of hello and thanks for everything. It is all still so wonderfully palpable and vivid to me that I can recount it correctly and well and over and over again.

And thank you for your warm, wonderful letter,[1] which Heinrich will answer from Palenville.[2] I have your two books on the university[3] after all; they were just where they were supposed to be. Schelling and Fichte are already in my suitcase. I'm off tomorrow. So stupid that I have to go to Buffalo first.

I'm writing in haste and only to confess my sins right away. How I managed to pack all those things in together is a mystery to me.[4] They just emerged fom the papers that I had sent in my traveling case before I left St. Moritz.

I hope the gorgeous weather continued for you up there. I keep thinking back on it all the time. I wanted to write you from Zurich but couldn't get to it. I read Lou Andreas-Salomé's *Rückblick*.[5] She had this to say about the Nietzsche business: In the early '80s a mutual friend, with Rée[6] and Lou Salomé's prior approval, wanted to bring about a meeting and reconciliation between them and Nietzsche. Nietzsche's response was: "No. No one can forgive what I have done in that matter." So, I concluded, you were absolutely right. Dignity preserved even in the face of one's own "calamity."[7]

Stay healthy, both of you. Warmest greetings and thanks

Your
Hannah

Basel, August 23, 1952

Dear Hannah!

I've read your *Rahel*[1] straight through and with great interest. There is no doubt in my mind: this book is powerful and significant. Much of the writing is excellent. It contains pages of extraordinary profundity.

An external failing, it seems to me, is an excess of repetition. The whole book could be tightened up, all to the benefit of the already existing dramatic structure. The lack of a detailed chronological table listing all the biographical facts strikes me as another such failing. The reader does not want to go to another source for orientation. An overview of this information would let him know where and when in Rahel's life whatever you are discussing in a given passage actually took place.

Is it coincidence that the title page is missing from the manuscript? The book is only in part a biography of Rahel. You adhere by and large to a chronological sequence, but in such a way that a series of essays discusses the total phenomenon, with penetrating analyses and sound judgments. The presentation is completely objective. The reader is not obliged to think about the writer. But this work still seems to me to be your own working through of the basic questions of Jewish existence, and in it you use Rahel's reality as a guide to help you achieve clarity and liberation for yourself. Because that was so, it made possible these analyses that now have an objective existence of their own. But because that was so, it also made possible the peculiar mood of the whole work, as if Rahel as Rahel seems to have wakened neither your interest nor your love, or as if the book takes Rahel as a point of departure to then deal with something altogether different. No *picture of Rahel* herself emerges but only, so to speak, a picture of the events that chose this individual as their vehicle. I think it likely that you could do Rahel greater justice today, mainly because you would see her not just in the context of the Jewish question but, rather, in keeping with Rahel's own intentions and reality, as a human being in whose life the Jewish problem played a very large role but by no means the only one.

It therefore seems to me that everything you cite from "enlightened" thinking is illustrated with negative examples (Dohm,[2] Friedländer[3]) and then leads to pejorative presentations. But it was the greatness of the "Enlightenment"—of what made Lessing what he is and, ultimately, Goethe, too—that carried Rahel. And it was part of Varnhagen[4] too, though in an even more denatured form. I wonder if the way in which you present the "Enlightenment" not only underplays it but also distorts it. Basing your view on "Die Erziehung des Menschengeschlechts," you see Lessing's "reason" as historically based and set it over against Mendelssohn. That seems wrong to me. Even in Lessing, the origin of reason itself is—thank God—above history, and his thinking with history goes beyond history. The bewitchment of historians by a deified history was still in the future. Mendelssohn is doubtless flatter, more complacent than Lessing, naïve and dogmatic. Even though he may not stand comparison with Lessing, the impulse that linked them as friends is common to them both and an undeniable truth.

Another point: Your view of Rahel is, I feel, loveless. Only on isolated pages does the depth of Rahel's soul become evident: where you develop a wonderful fantasy about the possibility of a relationship with Gentz,[5] where you speak about the tie with Pauline Wiesel,[6] perhaps too in your interpretation of her withdrawal from von der Marwitz.[7] The great figure of this woman—who trembles and bleeds, without home and homeland, without a world and without being rooted in her one love—who is so honest, reflects ceaselessly, understands, misunderstands, and casts off that misunderstanding—who constantly loses her way, loses track of herself, and has to re-create herself and deceives neither herself nor others about that—who reaches that mysterious territory where lies can appear as truth—you let this figure speak, but not from her core, that is, not as this human being herself who is not in her nature a Jew but who passes through this world as a Jew and therefore experiences the most extreme things, things that happen not only to Jews. You convey that Rahel does not lose herself but remains true to herself. But that does not become clear in the structure of your presentation. On the one hand, you let Rahel dissipate herself in disjointed experiences; on the other, you force everything under the rubric of being a Jew. You make the reader feel the emotional impact of all that, but you don't let Rahel's brilliance appear in all that confusion and achieve its full glow. Again and again you judge isolated actions in a way one should perhaps not judge if one feels one has at some point seen Rahel whole ("childish"—"behaved revoltingly"—"stupid and witless with ecstatic delight over the fact that she was permitted to take part," and so on). With Rahel, the very thing you cannot do, as a moralistic judgment would, is isolate individual facts, turns of speech, opinions, and actions and see them in the abstract. Rahel thrashes about, goes off the deep end, forgets herself, approaches basic human questions in a way dictated by fantasy yet one that contains a kernel of truth. (Why, for example, are you so angry over the pacifistic impulse in her fantasy of a women's strike against war? What idiots have made of such ideas later does not negate what Rahel originally thought for a moment back then, prompted by the naïve heart of a person not oriented to reality and without being altogether serious about it.) You have to permit Rahel her errors, just as you have to permit everyone, even Goethe, his errors; and you have to perceive those errors in the context of the individual's stature, as the darker sides of truth. And in the case of an "exception" like Rahel, justice and love demand this of us even more.

What starts to take shape in your work but is then lost in sociological and psychological considerations (which should not in any way be omitted but should be incorporated into a higher level) is the unconditional aspect of Rahel (for example, with Finckenstein[8]: only once in a lifetime, such a love cannot happen twice), the quality of her personal influence, the totality of her insight, her secret knowledge of things, the timeless in the temporal, all the things for which being a Jew is only the outward guise and only the point of departure.

Your book can make one feel that if a person is a Jew he cannot really live his life to the full. It is surely infinitely difficult as soon as the Jew is no longer firmly rooted in the faith of his ancestors. But it can be done, as Spinoza showed us once and for all: rejection of the Jewish belief in the synagogue and the law; refusal to become a Christian; a life with God, seeing all things *sub quadam specie aeternitatis* and in *amor intellectualis*, in love and kindness toward mankind and toward oneself. In this book, you deny such a possibility with a derogatory reference to the Robinson Crusoes, but you acknowledge it today under the rubric of the Noahs. Rahel was no Spinoza, but she lived in eternal restlessness, working her way toward what he achieved, led a richer and livelier life than he did, though without arriving at the clarity of fully formulated insights. Her unanchored soul dwelt in a bright profundity, even without the peace granted by philosophy.

A few errors can be easily corrected. For example, page 105, "the Arnims' "[9] anti-Semitism. Despite her husband's disgraceful views, Bettina produced one of the finest things ever written about the Jewish question.[10] She was never anti-Semitic. Your presentation of Humboldt[11] strikes me as almost grotesque.

You wrote this book before Heinrich Blücher came into your life. Perhaps your work on Rahel made it possible for you to keep your heart and eye open for the new direction of your life, which in no way resembles Rahel's. But now, I think, you could reduce Rahel's Jewishness to one element in your presentation and let the greatness of her soul stand in the foreground. What the Christian world imposed on the Jew and what disappointments, errors, and distortions in the Jew followed from that should not be minimized. Nor should it be denied that this was of the greatest importance for Rahel at all times. Your book emphasizes what Dilthey[12] in his typically evasive way keeps at arm's length when he writes: "One takes fright at the passion with which Rahel, in her private correspondence, suffers the fate of being a Jewess, feels herself to be an outcast."[13] (By the way, this same Dilthey was "frightened" himself later when his daughter wanted to marry a Jew [Misch].[14] Lujo Brentano[15] told me about his intense discussions with Dilthey at the time, the upshot of which was that Dilthey gave in.) But that shouldn't be the primary focus. What is important is that Rahel was a human being, liberated by the Enlightenment, who traveled individual paths that didn't work out for her and ended in blind alleys, but she also remained on the one true way, and that persists despite her failure.

Now to the question of publication. It's such an important work that there is no doubt as to its right to be published. What keeps me from urging you to publish it is my wish that in the public eye you be a sovereign figure for the Jewish question and that what you publish on it be able to stand up over time. It is also my wish that you not be so unfair to Rahel and the Enlightenment. Finally and most important of all, that true, profound "Jewishness," which is so uniquely historical in its effects without being aware of its historicalness, should be made clearer in Rahel, without its being called Jewish, for that always has an equivocal effect. In any case, it seems to me, you have to rework the book before it goes to print, tighten it, polish some sentences, perhaps add a detailed chronological and biographical table. If you want to publish it, I'll be happy to recommend it to Piper, warmly and with good supporting reasons (although my recommendation is unnecessary in view of the high regard Piper has for you).

I can't, of course, know whether Piper will take it. From a publisher's point of view, the question is whether subject matter like this—problems of inner actions and subtle judgments—will interest many buyers in Germany today. That your book in its present form is a bonanza for anti-Semites will neither harm nor help its sales. Your essays published by Lambert Schneider seem to me much more interesting for the contemporary world. If Piper had published them, they would probably have been a great success. Lambert Schneider has no talent for promotion. The commercial fate of your essays has made me regret that very much. But we couldn't know that when we all published with him. His failing in that regard is responsible for my *Schuldfrage* nearly disappearing from sight, too.

My ambivalent attitude will be a bit of a disappointment to you. I was convinced that I would agree to publication without any reservations, and I'm surprised at my own hesitation. The book must not under any circumstances remain unpublished. There is so much that is wonderful, true, and fully worked out in it—material that has never come to light in previous studies of Rahel—that it has to be made public, no matter what. It is my hope that you will rework the whole book at such time as inclination and circumstances prompt you to. If that is not possible, then it has to be published as it stands, at the risk that in the light of the highest standards a shadow will fall on you, a shadow that does not really strike you yourself but the work in its present form.

We've been home again for a week now. My wife is much relieved because Ernst is finally doing much better. I'm working on the third chapter of my history, which will also be my lecture course[16] for the winter semester. You are in the mountains, taking a rest from your strenuous months in Europe.

Our best wishes to you both, and warmest greetings from my wife and your

Karl Jaspers

135 *Hannah Arendt to Karl Jaspers*

Palenville, September 7, 1952

Lieber Verehrtester—

Your good, long letter. Your wonderful thoroughness, your illuminating patience, your listening and responding at the same time and both at once. I didn't want to answer right away because I have learned to mistrust my first reactions. But if I had replied right away, I probably would have come up with the same answer.

I was not surprised at all. I had expected your objections, and if I had recalled the book more closely, a book that has been very remote to me for years now, I would have at least guessed, if not known, what your detailed response would be. You're right. Except for the last chapter, the book was finished in 1933 or even 1932. I completed it, rather grumpily, in the summer of 1938 because Heinrich and Benjamin kept pestering me about it.

Regardless of what I will have to say here in response to your letter, our agreement remains in force: I won't publish the book. You recall that I told you my decision to publish or not would hinge entirely on your reaction. (Whether a publisher for it can be found is another matter.)

It's my view that many of the things I say in the book should have been said publicly before 1933 (perhaps even as late as 1938). They could have been said, at any rate, and they would not only have done no harm but might even have done some good. I think, too, that at some time, perhaps when this generation of German Jews, which will not be followed by any more, is dead, it will be possible to say these things again. But right now it is probably best not to. I'm not at all afraid of anti-Semites. They turn everything to their own purpose anyway, and they can still make better use of Disraeli or Rathenau[1] than they can of me. But I am afraid that people of goodwill will see a connection, which does not in fact exist, between these things and the eradication of the Jews. All this was capable of fostering social hatred of the Jews and did foster it, just as it fostered, on the other side, a specifically German breed of Zionism. The truly totalitarian phenomenon—and genuine political anti-Semitism before it—had hardly anything to do with all this. And precisely that is what I did not know when I wrote this book. It was written from the perspective of a Zionist critique of assimilation, which I had adopted as my own and which I still consider basically justified today. But that critique was as politically naïve as what it was criticizing. Personally, the book is alien to me in many ways, and perhaps that's why I feel it as particularly alien to me now, especially in its tone, in its mode of reflection, but not in the Jewish experience, which I made my own with no little difficulty. By virtue of my background I was simply naïve. I found the so-called Jewish question boring. The person who opened my eyes in this area was Kurt Blumenfeld, who then became a close friend and still is. He was able to do that because he was one of those few Jews I've met who was as naïvely assimilated and as unprejudiced by his background as I was myself. He is also one of my few Jewish friends who knew about Heinrich and then, completely free of prejudice, became very friendly with him. It's a pity that you don't know him. He is a prematurely old man now and very ill. He used to say: I'm a Zionist by the grace of Goethe. Or: Zionism is Germany's gift to the Jews.

You're absolutely right when you say this book "can make one feel that if a person is a Jew he cannot really live his life to the full." And that is of course a central point. I still believe today that under the conditions of social assimilation and political emancipation the Jews could not "live." Rahel's life seems to me a proof of that precisely because she tried out everything on herself without attempting to spare herself anything and without a trace of dishonesty. What always intrigued me about her was the phenomenon of life striking her like "rain pouring down on someone without an umbrella." That's why, it seems to me, her life illustrates everything with such clarity. And that's also what made her so insufferable.

The picture of Rahel that you put up against mine is in all its essential features the one drawn by Varnhagen. You know what I think of Varnhagen. But aside from that, one could have demonstrated, as long as the Varnhagen archive still existed (it has disappeared; I searched for it all over Germany,[2]) that this picture is totally false. He falsified it doubly—he eliminated the altogether insufferable side of Rahel and at the same time the altogether lovable side. Both can still be seen in six volumes of letters[3] between Rahel and Varnhagen, which came out without emendations after Varnhagen's death. The bad thing about this falsification is that it is basically done in a way in which Rahel herself would have liked to falsify. But of course never would have falsified. As far as the falsifications are concerned, they consist of the following, as far as I can recall without having the material at hand: Three volumes of Rahel's letters (*Ein Buch des Andenkens*[4]) 1. always change the name of the recipient—Rebekka Friedländer[5] is called Frau v. V. etc., 2. always omit passages that refer to the Jewish question, which creates the impression that Rahel was surrounded by a large circle of close non-Jewish friends and that the Jewish question played a relatively minor role in her life, 3. certain people who either do not belong to "good society" (like Pauline Wiesel) or whose relationship with Rahel does not conform to the standards of good society (like Gentz) are either completely left out, or everything of real importance relating to them is eliminated, 4. relationships with other people that reflect prestigiously on Rahel are presented as more important than they in fact were (e.g., the relationship with Caroline v. Humboldt[6]).

As far as the Enlightenment is concerned, I probably didn't express myself clearly. My focus was only the Enlightenment as it was relevant to Rahel, and by that I mean to her as a Jewish girl who had to bring about her own assimilation (that is, had to do consciously what others at a later time would have simply handed to them). Under those special conditions the Enlightenment played a highly questionable role. I illustrate it with "negative" examples because in this historical context there aren't any positive ones. Mendelssohn and Friedländer were the key figures, not Lessing. And unlike you, I see Mendelssohn as nothing but flat and opportunistic. Spinoza is as absent in him, it seems to me, as he is in Rahel herself. Spinoza was a great philosopher and as such *sui generis*. He was indifferent—or at least in every essential respect indifferent—to the fact that he was a Jew. It was his background, the thing that he left behind. He was not yet confronted with a Jewish problem in his time either. Everything was personal history. That he was a Jew and as such stood outside society was just one opportunity more for him. Mendelssohn's and Rahel's primary objective was to enter society, which one can hardly hold against them. The first who would be able to find his place outside it again was Heine, because he was a poet the way Spinoza was a philosopher, and he was a revolutionary as well.

That brings me to the really central question. You assume something like a more or less unbroken tradition of Judaism in which Rahel would have her place the way Spinoza and Mendelssohn do. But Mendelssohn is the only one of the three who has a place in Judaism, and that for reasons that are quite unimportant here. He translated the Bible into German with Hebrew letters, that is, he taught the Jews German. He also played a role as a representative of Judaism in the "learned circles of Germany" and even became in Mirabeau's[7] eyes the example to show that Jews are not necessarily barbarians. As a philosopher (?) Mendelssohn is completely without significance in Judaism. And if we were thinking only in terms of Jewish tradition, Spinoza would be completely forgotten today, not remembered even as a heretic. (I couldn't talk Schocken into publishing a Spinoza volume because "Spinoza wasn't a Jew.")

Judaism doesn't exist outside orthodoxy on the one hand or outside the Yiddish-speaking, folklore-producing Jewish people on the other. There are also people of Jewish background who are unaware of any Jewish substance in their lives in the sense of a tradition and who for certain social reasons and because they found themselves constituting a clique within society produced something like a "Jewish type." This type has nothing to do with what we understand under Judaism historically or with its genuine content. Here there is much that is positive, namely, all those things that I classify as pariah qualities and what Rahel called the "true realities of life"—"love, trees, children, music." In this type there is an extraordinary awareness of injustices; there is great generosity and a lack of prejudice; and there is—more questionably but nonetheless demonstrably present—respect for the "life of the mind." Of all these things only the last one can still be shown to have a link with originally and specifically Jewish substance. The element of Judaism that has persisted longest simply in the way people live is family loyalty. That is not an intellectual quality, however, but, rather, a sociological and political phenomenon. The negative "Jewish" qualities have nothing to do with Judaism in this sense and all derive from parvenu stories. Rahel is "interesting" because, with utter naïveté and utterly unprejudiced, she stands right in the middle between pariah and parvenu. Jewish history, to the extent that it is an independent history of the Jewish people in the Diaspora, ends with the Sabbatai Zwi movement.[8] Zionism marks the beginning of a new chapter; perhaps, too, the great migration to America since the end of the last century. Perhaps there will be still another renaissance of Judaism (I hardly think so).

You reproach me for "moralizing" about Rahel. I may well have slipped into moralizing, and I shouldn't have. What I meant to do was argue further with her, the way she argued with herself, and always within the categories that were available to her and that she somehow accepted as valid. In other words, I tried to measure and correct the parvenu by constantly applying the standards of the pariah because I felt that was her own method of proceeding, even though she was perhaps often not aware of it.

On the externals: The lack of a title page is no doubt an oversight. Heinrich sent the copy that was bound and easy to put his hand on. The title was to be simply *Rahel Varnhagen: Eine Biographie*. There must be a chronological table in one of the copies. But perhaps it, too, has been lost with many other notes. Repetitions—absolutely. I never went through the book again to prepare it for print, hardly ever even checked it for typos. Despite the unseemly length of this self-protective (I hope not!) epistle, this whole project has not been very important to me for a long time, actually not since 1933. My reason is not so much, as I first recognized with the help of your letter, because I see the entire subject itself differently now (I might see some points differently if I read the book again, but not the essentials) but, rather, because I feel this whole so-called problem isn't so very important or at least is no longer important to me. Whatever of the straightforward historical insights I still consider relevant are contained in shorter form and devoid of all "psychology" in the first part of my totalitarianism book. And there I'm content to let the matter rest.

It's wonderful here. A lovely, clear, early fall. Heinrich was very tired but is well rested now. He began at Bard College last week and came back very well pleased. It's not very far from here, so he can get there easily by bus and taxi and can stay here until the end of the month. He'll write to you himself about what he wants to do and how he will handle his theme in detail. "Grenzen pädagogischen Planens"[9] just arrived yesterday. Thanks very much! Heinrich has it; I haven't read it yet.

I'm really very happy to be home again, and I say that without a trace of irony. I was in New York only for a few days last week to see the Guggenheim people and see that everything was in order at the office. I'm reading your Cicero[10] at the moment, also Rousseau. I'm doing some real work. Piper has not written, by the way. But I did have an inquiry from Kösel. I still haven't signed a contract with Rentsch. So I can think about it all some more. If they offer to publish the book in Germany with the first part included, I might change over to them even at this late date.

How good to hear that your brother-in-law [Ernst Mayer] is well on his way to recovery now. Give your wife my warmest regards. She mustn't be angry if I speak badly of the German Jews. More important, she mustn't be hurt by it. As you see, in this regard and in others as well, I'm much more afraid of her than I am of you.

I'm enclosing a little essay by Blumenfeld on Rathenau.[11] He just sent it to me, and it happened to arrive together with your letter. You'll be able to read it quickly. There are a few nice observations in it. Blumenfeld himself is much more of a person than he has ever been able to get down on paper. You'll see, perhaps, what I mean.

Your semester will begin soon. All best wishes. I'm enclosing a letter from the translator in England[12].

With warmest and fondest greetings
Your
Hannah

October 16, 1952

Dear Hannah,

Uneasy at heart as I have been for a long time, I went to Heidelberg and found that any work is better than talking to people in such cases.

Soon after my return my brother Ernst died, on October 10.[1] We were hoping for his full recovery and that spring would find us reunited again here in lectures and seminars, in work, in conversation. We think he contracted pneumonia.

Karl had only this one friend. For 45 years.

Ernst's death hit me very hard. Because my sister-in-law[2] is very close to me, there is much I can do for her, a task in which Karl will be of great help to me.

You are not familiar with the depth of the ties one has with brothers and sisters.

With warmest greetings
Your Gertrud

Jeanne Hersch was here for a day. She knew and loved my brother and saw to it years ago that Ernst and his wife were invited to the Rencontres[3], Ernst as a contributor. That was a wonderful reunion after the Hitler years. Jeanne is in top form, fully engaged in her work. We were delighted to see her.

137   *Hannah Arendt to Gertrud Jaspers*

November 1, 1952

Dear Friend—

I've been meaning to write every day since your sad news arrived, but I haven't had a quiet moment. You know how much I am thinking of you both and of your grief. I see you in your room, at your desk, looking out the window, and I think that now you have a little peace after all, though it is the peace of mourning. You're right; I didn't have any brothers or sisters, but I know how much strength it takes to survive, that is, the double strength to live through and hold fast to one's grief and yet remain alive.

I haven't been able to settle down properly and get to work ever since we've been back in New York, and so I'm a bit restless. First I had to renovate the apartment, and then New York life began to come down on me. Somehow I've got to extract myself, but I don't know how yet. Swarms of people I like a lot. That's just what makes it so difficult. —Hanno Waltz[1] was here with us for a few days. A nice young man, but not in his mother's league at all. With the endurance of youth, he ran around in the city for twelve hours a day. I didn't make any fuss over him. I hope he didn't take it amiss. One gives up certain conventions here that are still taken for granted in Europe.

There'll probably be a lot of talk about you this evening. Stefan Andres is coming and Kristeller,[2] who told me about his visit in Basel when I ran into him on the street just now, and Leni Wieruszowski,[3] whom I haven't seen at all yet and who is of course a bit miffed. Also an American friend, Mary McCarthy,[4] who writes novels and is quite well known and who is staying with us at the moment and doesn't know a word of German. *Qui vivra, verra.* I'm busy cooking, an endeavor whose success really depends entirely on me.

Heinrich is well, but he is really very busy. Which doesn't hurt. He's working too hard at his religion course, but it is better than it was last year, and I'm happy about that. This time we're recording the whole course, and we also have a girl to write it all out. This is the first time I've had time enough to go regularly.

11.5. At this point the phone rang, and from then on chaos descended. On top of that came widespread nervousness about the election. Now we know, and it's not good. Stevenson's campaign was excellent right up to the end, and it was some comfort that somebody tried for once to do nothing else but talk sense.[5] Eisenhower is a dangerous idiot, and the combination with which they won—Taft like Hugenberg,[6] big capital plus Eisenhower like Hindenburg,[7] dim-witted military men plus [Joseph] McCarthy or [Richard] Nixon like . . . (but that I'd rather not even say), at any rate, the mob appeal—is not very encouraging. As you see, I'm hung over. We've voted again, for the first time in twenty years, and all we can do is hope that it won't be the last time.

Good-bye for now, dear Gertrud. Write and let me know how you both are. I had good news from Piper.

All my best to you both. As always

Your   Hannah

P.S. Please ask your husband if he has received Voegelin's[8] new book *The New Science of Politics*[9], which contains an extended study of Max Weber. He is quoted frequently. If not, I'll send it right away. I think the book is on the wrong track, but important nonetheless. The first fundamental discussion of the real problems since Max Weber.

Basel, December 29, 1952

Dear Hannah!

When one has the intention of writing a *thorough* reply, the consequence can be that one doesn't write at all. So it has been with me with your letter responding to my remarks on your Rahel book, a letter deserving of serious consideration. Blumenfeld's essay, which you sent with your letter, made me feel that more acutely still, and my stronger impulse was to say something about the German Jewish question rather than about Rahel. In doing so, I wanted to defend against you and Blumenfeld the many remarkable people who have lived as German Jews, if that were necessary. Very many pages in your book contradict in your own words—I'm happy to say—your claim that Rahel is "insufferable." Granted, she has an "insufferable" side, and you have felt it more strongly than I have with some Jews of the modern period. Should one project that back onto Rahel? — But this would bring me to a discussion that is beyond my powers at the moment. I hope we will see each other once more. I would like to talk with you at length again about this. What it comes to in the end is that I will never cease claiming you as a "German" (you know that, of course), although, as Monsieur would say, I am, along with you and many other Germans, "not a German," namely, not in the political sense (even though I am a German according to my passport, but that gives me no pleasure).

There was good reason why I did not write. Shortly after Ernst Mayer's death I fell seriously ill with my old complaint (very severe hemorrhages, which we keep concealed here). After five weeks, I was fine again, contrary to the doctor's expectations but not to my own. I feel almost better than I did before. But for a while I could neither write nor talk nor read. And so I did not write to you. Now I have a lot to catch up on. My work, given the goals I have set myself, eats up my time—that would be quite all right actually, if I weren't neglecting so much else.

For that same reason I have to ask your husband to be patient. I was very taken with his good, long letter.[1] I will be following his intriguing project with the liveliest of interest. It is still not clear to me. But your husband's enthusiasm immediately convinces one that something good is in process.

The Christmas holidays were wonderfully peaceful for us. We made a point of having no visitors. My wife was in need of quiet and time for reflection and some good sleep. Things are good with us now. The attacks of vertigo, weakness, headache remain ultimately harmless. Her soul is as alive as in her youth. The bad time she had this summer is over. (These periods of depression and irritability have recurred during her whole life. Awareness of them and experience with them have helped her to keep them under control for the most part, but she still suffers from them. The good times are by contrast all the more carefree and happy.) Ernst Mayer's death has of course cast a shadow on our lives, more so for my wife than for me. That is to be expected.

When I think of you, I imagine you eagerly at work. On the "high road": You will make sudden discoveries, find connections, and take pleasure in working on this intellectual level. For my part, I harbor the hope that you will in the end find Marx the intellectually responsible originator of what prepared the way for totalitarianism. Intolerance, indeed terror are exemplified in his personal character. There is an unbroken continuity from him to Lenin. The question is whether the gap between Lenin and Stalin is as great as you perceive it to be. I think you are right about that, but even here, where actual Marxism has disappeared, something remains of what in Marx's character was the mood and motivation prior to all of Marxism and all Marx's ideas. He was probably a figure of destiny, like Luther, not as important for his ideas as for the character that carried those ideas. Demons don't exist, but there is something like them in people like that. We have to recognize them, as far as that is possible, in order to rid ourselves of them. But, most important, we have to oppose them as much as we can.

Warmest greetings and all best wishes—from my wife, too—to you both for the New Year

Your Karl Jaspers

139 *Hannah Arendt to Karl Jaspers*

December 29, 1952

Lieber Verehrtester—

We heard nothing from either of you for a long time; then Lotte Waltz happened to write to me that you had been ill. I hope that her addendum, which was that the illness was over and that you are back to teaching again, is right. Was it very bad? One of your usual bronchitis attacks? How are you now? Very tired? Very much torn out of your work routine?

This isn't a letter, just a New Year's greeting with all the very best wishes. Everything is going along well here. I've really dug into my work and am very pleased that I won't have to take a job in the foreseeable future. Heinrich is, actually was, somewhat overworked —New School plus college. But he's managing. I dread the next semester a bit when he will be home only three days a week and will have classes at the New School on one of them.

Now we're in the middle of the holidays and seeing a lot of people. Politically things are as dismal as they possibly could be. I don't even want to write about it. —I heard from Heidegger after long silence.[1] He wrote about your letter[2] and said he didn't know how to reply and still hoped for a talk with you.

Lieber Verehrtester, take good care of yourself!

With warmest greetings
Your
Hannah

140 *Hannah Arendt to Karl Jaspers*

New York, February 19, 1953

Lieber Verehrtester—

I'm picturing to myself that it's Monday and that I'm in your house, which is so dear and familiar to me, and that I have a few minutes alone with you and feel free to say to you in the spoken word what in the written one sounds stupid and pompous.

I want to thank you for the seventy years of your life, for your existence, which would be cause enough for gratitude. I want to thank you for the early years in Heidelberg when you were my teacher, the only one I have ever been able to recognize as such; and for the happiness and relief I found in seeing that one can be educated in freedom. I have never forgotten since then that the world and Germany, whatever else they may be, are the world in which you live and the country that produced you.

I want to thank you for your friendship; you know what it means to me. It is such a great gift precisely because the mere fact of your existence would have been enough.

I feel funny sending wishes, because everything I wish you I also

206

wish for my own sake. I hope you'll remain healthy and live to be very old (I promise to come for your eightieth birthday!) and in full possession of your powers, so that you can complete everything you mean to do without haste and live your life fully to its end. And I hope, too, that the world will honor you as much as I would like to honor you, because it seems to me that everyone would do well to put ceremony aside and examine his life in the light of yours. The part of the world that does honor you will then partake of the light that comes into a room when you enter it.

I don't want to respond to your last letter today, but I think I can promise you that I will never cease to be a German in your sense of the word; that is, that I will not deny anything, not your Germany and Heinrich's, not the tradition I grew up in or the language in which I think and in which the poems I love best were written. I won't lay false claims to either a Jewish or an American past.

Heinrich is at Bard, will probably send a few lines tomorrow or the next day. He has sent you some Cézanne watercolors,[1] and I—to introduce a mundane note into all the ceremonies—a few ties. I hope the package arrives in good time and you won't have any trouble with customs.

Give my warmest regards to your wife. This is a great and wonderful day for her, and I wish I could be there to help with the dishes or whatever.

In respect and gratitude and friendship I am

Your
Hannah

141 *Karl Jaspers to Hannah Arendt*

Basel, April 3, 1953

Dear Hannah!

How much I have to thank you for! Your kind letter, your wonderful contribution to the Festschrift[1]—and thanks to your husband for his birthday wishes and the beautiful Cézanne watercolors (which I can enjoy while lying on my chaise longue, thanks to a reading stand artfully constructed by my nephew [Enno Dugend]—and lastly, thank you for your ties. I'm wearing one of them today for the first time as I write to you. Is there any danger that with this tie around my neck you and America will collar me? It's a risk I'll gladly run. The ties, I should add, are of the finest quality. I take real pleasure in them, and I delight once again in your extravagant streak, which I admire in you, although it is not part of my own nature at all.

Your essay is again so well done that after reading it I thought: Fully rounded and true. You have put the basic idea of your book, no, *one* basic idea, into the most easily comprehensible of forms. I am happy to have it in the Festschrift, whose purpose it is to honor me and of which I am now genuinely fond (with some few exceptions, of which I will not speak). I'm curious to know how you react to it as a whole.

Now, as you know, when I read you or listen to you, I'm immediately prompted to talk with you, which is to say, argue with you. I always want to put my finger on the forces present in an intellectual product, just as I do with the things that come into my own head. If we try to remain purely objective, we will have trouble getting hold of the "demons" that get hold of us. So now you'll hear the concerns I have after reading your essay. I know you enjoy this kind of discussion and are of one mind with me in it. I wonder if you are not seeing this new element,[2] which you in fact do see and which you develop beautifully, in an exaggerated form that prompts you to take a position against everything in history that remains fundamentally the same, i.e., against continuity. You are afraid of any analogy whatsoever because it obscures the new impulse. What begins to take shape in your essay is a sense that there is a mysterious history inherent in a totality of events that is calling completely new forces into existence. These forces are melting down everything that has preceded them and are themselves absolute in nature. Over against that you also see, of course, the one great opportunity, human existence itself, that is continually being reborn, and you suggest that briefly and movingly.

What would you think if I adapted your insight in the following way: You have convincingly portrayed this type of rule, which indeed and by its very nature no longer conforms to Montesquieu's types and cannot simply be placed in a row with them. Here I would ask, first of all: What are all the things in the real world that do not conform to this type? There seem to me, at this particular moment, to be a great many. Second, what is it that perhaps dominates this type itself instead of being dominated by it? The next question is: What has made this type possible? Your book provides a number of important answers to that question. But all of this, the entire insight that emerges from it, is limited by the same sentences that Max Weber wrote after completing his painstaking and convincing studies on the spirit of capitalism[3] (seen archetypically) as a product of the Calvinistic ethic (also seen archetypically): "I consider it proved that this factor plays a role; how large a role it plays cannot be proved. I consider its role large." In other words, you have opened up a line of investigation but not explored the reality of the totalitarian mode to its full extent within the overall human reality. For that is an unattainable goal, indeed, an absurd one. If we do not keep reminding ourselves of these limitations, we're in danger of falling prey to a new demon of the philosophy of history.

Once the new phenomenon has been revealed, we may then inquire after the analogies to it in history. That will certainly not be easy, and we must certainly not underestimate the difficulty of it. And no matter what, we may doubt that this new phenomenon—in its entirety as you have delineated it—will now or ever become reality. Such a total realization is possible only in borderline cases, which remain mere exceptions.

Don't be angry that I have dictated this letter. I've sent out almost 400 printed thank-you notes. I want to thank my friends personally, but I can't keep up. Daily life, my job, and my writing exhaust my limited strength. So it seems better to me to write at least this kind of letter rather than none at all.

Give my regards to your husband. To you both, my warmest wishes for your happiness and success in your work.

So you want to come for my eightieth birthday! Let's be presumptuous. I am with you. That does not prevent us all from knowing every day how things stand with us. My wife joins me in sending warmest wishes

Your Karl Jaspers

142 *Hannah Arendt to Karl Jaspers*

New York, May 13, 1953

Lieber Verehrtester—

I've been wanting to write you for months, to thank you for your letter, to let you know that the foreword for Milosz arrived too late,[1] alas, alas! because it is wonderful—devastated and devastating—(but Knopf[2] will find another use for it; Hadas,[3] professor of Greek at Columbia and very good in German, and I translated it together), to say how delighted I was about your honors[4]—and yet I didn't write because what it is I have to tell you weighs so heavily on us every day now that it takes away all desire to do anything.

You probably know a lot from the papers. Can you see from them how far the disintegration has gone and with what breathtaking speed it has occurred? And up to now hardly any resistance. Everything melts away like butter in the sun. Most important of course is the disintegration of the governmental machinery and the presumably quite conscious establishment of a kind of parallel government, which, though with no legal power, possesses the real power. And this takes in far more than just the civil service. The whole entertainment industry and, to a lesser extent, the schools and colleges and universities have been dragged into it. It is essentially impossible to consider any specific parts of the society as set apart from it, for even where the Congressional investigating committees[5] aren't sticking in their dirty noses, an extremely effective self-censorship takes place. The editor of a newspaper or a magazine, for example, or the director of a business or the professors at a university will quietly conduct a "purge." (No professor will write a recommendation for a student anymore in which he fails to mention the student's "unquestioned loyalty." If he doesn't do that, the recommendation is useless, and the young man needs a job!) In this self-censorship, everyone actually censors himself. It all functions without any application of force, without any terror. Basically, nothing at all happens—and yet the whole thing eats its way farther and deeper into the society.

Of major importance is the role of the ex-Communists, who have brought totalitarian methods into the thing (not methods of government but methods used within the party). Because it is obvious that no one can know whether another person has really broken with the party or is only acting as if he had, everyone—and that includes really good people!—has accepted as a principle that the only proof of such a break is for the person in question to give the names of people he saw or met fifteen or twenty years ago. This forces into public view just about everyone who at any time quite innocently sympathized with the party (usually at a very young age or in outraged opposition to fascism or in agitation over the Spanish Civil War) and who has long since forgotten it all. That takes in a large number of people, particularly among intellectuals. And so the originally small number of genuine ex-Communists is constantly growing. Important in this regard is Chambers's book,[6] which played a key role in the election campaign here. Biographical research plays a role here quite similar to

210

the one that ancestral research did in Germany. (But there is no trace of anti-Semitic or other kinds of racial influences here. On the contrary, the Jews are playing a prominent role in the whole mess simply because they make up a major percentage of the intelligentsia.) The great danger that the ex-Communists represent at the moment is that they are introducing police methods into normal social life. Because, without exception, they name names, they make police agents of themselves after the fact, as it were. In this way, the informant system is being integrated into the society. I'll spare you a description of how that works in detail. The trap into which they are lured is built like this: One of the committee members asks the person in question if he is now or ever has been a Communist. If he answers this question, without taking the fifth amendment, which provides that no one is obliged to testify against himself, then he has to answer all further questions under oath. If he doesn't, he can be cited for contempt of Congress and face a jail sentence. The whole thing has become a farce: 1. Anyone who refuses to testify does himself the greatest harm because he appears guilty in the eyes of society, even if not in the eyes of the law, and his job, position, etc. can be affected. It is standard practice at all schools and universities, even the private ones, to fire immediately anyone who takes the fifth amendment! 2. When people have refused to testify—i.e., in the few cases where they have really refused—they have done so because that was the only way to refuse further testimony without making themselves guilty of perjury or contempt of court. In other words, the original intent of the fifth amendment has been stood on its head; it no longer protects one's own interests but is instead a kind of self-incrimination; and it is used deceptively because the witness involved uses it—and has to use it—for purposes other than for what it was intended. Anyone who does not take the fifth amendment (and taking it is of course very difficult for people who are writers, because everyone knows what they thought ten or twenty years ago) has to name names. Or go to prison. The remarkable thing is that nobody has gone to jail yet. Several people have slipped through the committees' fingers by lying. The minimum sentence for lying is six months.

The really disastrous consequence is that lawlessness continues to spread. Everything that is going on is taking place outside the law. First and foremost is the fact that the Communist party is not prohibited by law. That is disastrous—and a kind of trap in itself. (Anyone who advocates forbidding it will be told that he is "anti-democratic.")

The CP is not forbidden, but anyone who belongs to it will not be able to get a job, will be defamed, etc. The only person who has understood this is George Shuster, the president of Hunter College in New York. If the party were forbidden, then there would be no more equivocation about it: anyone who belonged to the party *now* would be violating the law. But what he did in the past would be nobody's business—provided the law was not made retroactive. And there are some charming examples of retroactivity. Not in the laws themselves, but in the administration.

The administration itself, with the golf-playing president at its head, is as helpless as you have no doubt gathered it is from the papers. It is a government of big business whose sole concern is to make big business bigger. That doesn't necessarily mean a depression, but it probably does mean the liquidation of small, independent businesses. This is an extremely important point. The really healthy thing about the development of the economy here was that even under the stress of war production major government contracts were awarded to small and medium-sized industries in spite of their higher costs. That has come to an end completely, and the power of the trusts grows every day. The danger in this isn't so much the increasing power of the big concerns (that power is quite effectively controlled and held in check by the very real power of the unions and by the fact that all the big companies are ultimately dependent on government contracts) but, rather, that the small *independent* man is disappearing as a political factor. In other words, this administration is making this society day by day into more of what it already is anyway: a society of jobholders. And by doing so, it plays directly into McCarthy's hands, because the blame for this total lack of resistance in the society can be laid squarely at the door of these jobholders. And in all this, prosperity, in which everyone has unlimited opportunity and is therefore obliged to get ahead because everyone is getting richer by the minute, plays exactly the same role here that unemployment played in Germany. Six of one, half a dozen of the other.

At the moment, the ex-Communists are playing a sorry and key role in the process of disintegration. I think their importance will diminish in the long run. Good old American know-nothingness will take their place because it is the only thing that can go hand in hand with the ideology of Americanism that is just beginning to emerge now. This is all quite plain to see already. (The president of Brooklyn College, known citywide as an idiot with an important big job and as

212

what people call a "reactionary" here, said to me in a public discussion that he was born and raised in Iowa and therefore didn't need to think or read anymore to know what was right. He, along with Sidney Hook—a comical team—then told me that it was un-American to quote Plato and that I, just like Tillich, suffered from being Germanic. Sic!) Some of the more intelligent people are beginning to disassociate themselves from all this. It's symptomatic too that the Congress for Cultural Freedom,[7] which, God knows, has never lifted a finger in this country for either culture or freedom and has become a kind of collecting point for these types, is not very active here anymore. But the depressing thing is that the by no means small number of really good people who joined this organization years ago, when things looked very different, have not been able, despite much deliberation, either to leave the organization or to move that it issue a protest against the methods of the investigating committees. It would amount to the same thing, because such a motion would produce a split in the organization. As individuals, they lose interest, fade out of sight, etc. But the power of public opinion is so great in this country that nobody does anything, although for the time being it's absolutely clear that speaking out would have no dire consequences at all! (Although, to avoid painting a false picture, I should add that Hook—the very man who told me eight weeks ago that the Congressional investigating committees were the only way to preserve academic freedom!—disassociated himself from the committees in the strongest of terms a few days ago. In an open letter in the *New York Times*.

As you can see, I feel that we're looking at developments that are all too familiar. Naturally—or, rather, not so naturally at all—in totally different forms and under totally different circumstances. I'm constantly reminded of a quote from Huey Long,[8] who was the petty dictator in a Middle West state in the 1930s and widely regarded as a fascist. In response to the accusation that he was a fascist, he said: "You are wrong, I am not a fascist, I am a local boss; fascism, if it ever should come to this country, will come in the guise of democracy and it will start in Congress, not in the government of the states." All that is very "interesting," especially the fact that public opinion can remain unorganized, that it needs no "movement," that everything proceeds almost automatically. For example, almost all of the western states have followed the example of the federal Congress and formed their own investigating committees. And there is much more, all of it brought about without violence and only through pressure. Concentration camps are highly unlikely, even if the present course continues to be pursued. Much more dangerous is the role of the so-called psychiatrists and the social workers, all of whom have psychoanalytical training and who give their clients only "psychological guidance," not material aid. (The material aid is regulated by law; one has a right to it. But anyone who makes use of this right has to accept psychological guidance!! In other words, there is already obligatory psychoanalysis for anyone who is in financial need. For the moment this is of no importance because of the current widespread prosperity.) When prisoners of war from the Korean War were expected home a few weeks ago, the army issued a statement in all the papers saying that the first thing that would be done with any of the prisoners who had been "infected" with Communism would be to put them in psychiatric clinics! I don't believe that was actually done. But the thinking is typically American. Another "interesting" thing, too, is the curious reversal of the relationship between the executive branch (the administration) and the legislative branch (Congress), particularly in a country in which the executive has almost dictatorial powers. Congress represents public opinion. And only God knows what that really is.

To give you a more complete picture I would have to tell you about the role the major foundations play in the universities. The Ford Foundation is in a perpetual panic about how to get rid of its money, which under no circumstances can be left alone to accumulate profit that would then be taxed away. The foundation's millions have accelerated a development that was already underway. Support for individual independent scholars, even if they belong to a university, is out of the question, because the foundations could never use up their money paying out such small sums. So everything goes into organized research, and the ancillary institutes gobble up the universities, which is to say, free research. This promotes types that are familiar to you but that are appearing in such great numbers here that they are becoming more dangerous than ever. They are the incompetents, the ignoramuses, who put a staff of college boys to work reading books for them. The whole business operates in a vacuum and produces no results. It is interesting only because by these means the intellectual proletariat is able to acquire positions of power or make positions of power out of ones that never had any power before. This was all evident with the Rockefeller Foundation, but never to such a degree, because such vast sums were not involved there. Culture simply can't make

214

use of so many millions. It suffocates under the weight of them. This new generation, whose company I had the opportunity to enjoy at the last political science convention, is undermining "morale" at the universities. And the foundations are not "free" either. I have heard from a reliable source that McCarthy let the Ford Foundation know that he would find ways to sabotage sales of Ford cars if the foundation stuck by its decision to give 15 million for the study of civil rights. (Nothing would come of it anyhow, unless some people should suddenly and unexpectedly get together and decide to offer some determined resistance. That's always a possibility.)

Just about anything is possible here at the moment, among other reasons because neither free speech nor a free press are de facto prohibited. It is not the case either that one cannot publish. On the contrary. For the time being, we are not isolated in the least, perhaps less so than ever. I've taken potshots at the whole mob and haven't suffered in the least for it. Perhaps a few of my friends, very good journalists, will be able to start up a magazine[9] that will not content itself with pious protests couched in general terms (that kind of protest is common here but doesn't mean a thing), but will report in detail what is really going on in this country. What is typical in this situation is that one can very well express one's "opinion," but editors will as a rule refuse to publish straight facts and reports. So everything happens half in the dark. And that in a country where people give credence only to facts and can be convinced only by facts.

I'm telling you all of this in detail in spite of my fear that you'll think I'm exaggerating, because it seems important to me that you be informed. I feel it is no longer possible, as it was only a few years ago, to stand up for America without any reservations, as we both did. That does not mean that we can join in the European chorus of anti-Americanism. The dangers are clear and present. What will come of all this no one knows. If McCarthy does not become president in 1956, there's a good chance things will be all right again. But we're seeing now what is *possible* here. Perhaps you'll remember that we spoke last year about the Congress for Cultural Freedom. I know very little about its activities in Europe, but it troubles me a bit that you are still so prominent in it. Perhaps the situation is different in Europe. As you may know, the Congress is going to publish a new magazine, in London, with Spender and the director here, Kristol[10][. . .] as editors. Kristol told me that it's going to be a kind of English *Monat*. One

215

cannot work for it of course, but can occasionally publish there. That would not matter. What troubles me is any kind of organizational connection.

Things are going very well for us personally. Heinrich is enjoying his teaching, also the fact that philosophy has suddenly become popular at Bard. Not, of course, with the faculty, particularly not with his colleagues in philosophy. But you know all about that, and it's always the same old story. He is home only from Friday through Sunday, so I'm playing the grass widow and not liking it much. As compensation, I'm working contentedly and getting a lot done. Please don't think that we're personally depressed. Quite to the contrary. We never had it so good—as our good old Truman used to say.

I'm preparing my Princeton lectures[11] and a lecture for Harvard.[12] At Princeton I'll talk about Marx in the tradition of political philosophy. The more I read Marx, the more I see that you were right. He's not interested either in freedom or in justice. (And he's a terrible pain in the neck in addition.) In spite of that, a good springboard for talking about certain general problems. I taught a little at the New School this spring and enjoyed it. About forms of government.

Don't be angry at me for not responding at all to your kind letter. All this other stuff has been on my mind for so long, and now this letter has grown so dreadfully long. And at the moment I'm examining this connection between the "new" and the "beginning," which is everywhere, and I would go on at too great length if I got into it. May I remind you of a statement of Nietzsche's (from the *Wille zur Macht*)? "The evolution of learning dissolves 'what is known' more and more into an unknown. But it *wants* to do just the opposite and takes as its point of departure the instinct to trace the unknown back to what is known."[13] I've just written a little essay on the difficulties of "understanding," which will probably appear this summer in the *Partisan Review*.[14] I'll send it to you then—without the expectation that you ought to read it right away!!!

How is the semester? What are you lecturing on? How I would love to drop in on a lecture! What are your plans for the summer? St. Moritz again?

We're planning to be away for July and August, first, as usual, at our little hideaway in the mountains here, the hills really, then at the shore. I'll write again then.

For the distant future we're planning to go to Europe in 1955, if things stay the way they are now and we can afford it. Heinrich would like to travel through Italy, too. Just thinking of it is like a dream! All my best to you both.

As always your
Hannah

P.S.: I forgot to mention that Kurt Blumenfeld is in Germany for a few weeks. He may go to Switzerland and give you a call. I told him I wasn't at all sure you could see him, etc. You shouldn't hesitate to say no. —The same goes for an old friend of mine, Julie Braun-Vogelstein (widow of Heinrich Braun,[15] the member of the Reichstag, and the editor of Otto Braun's literary remains[16]). She is an extremely talented art historian and archeologist. You'll see right away what's wrong with her. You can always say no!! I couldn't very well not give her your address. She has been very good to me, and we are friends —though with some reservations on my part. With Blumenfeld, on the other hand, I've argued a lot in my lifetime and sometimes parted ways, but I am his friend without any reservations.

143   Karl Jaspers to Hannah Arendt

Basel, May 22, 1953

Dear Hannah!

Strange. In recent days I've wondered several times why Hannah hasn't written at all. So much is going on in America. It's a little frightening. She has always let me know before when something serious was happening. Now your letter has arrived at just the right moment. I'm very grateful for it.

The newspaper reports here are such that one constantly wonders why Eisenhower is putting up with all this, why he doesn't clean house with McCarthy. They suggest that he is afraid of the Congress, but they also lead one to think that things have to reach a certain point before he will act. At any rate, we are presented with a bleak picture that is being viewed optimistically here.

You delineate the situation with your customary perspicacity. I'm convinced that you are seeing it correctly. One is clearly unable to judge the extent of the danger. But it must be great when a cross section of Americans is behaving, as you see it, in a cowardly and stupid way. They have never been like that before. And the course the world will take for a long time, affecting us all, depends on what these Americans do.

We can still hope that something will stir in America. You imply as much and mention people who understand the situation. It's wonderful that you want to work on a journal that will help clear the air with factual reportage and clear judgment. That you can speak and publish freely there and speak with people who are in large part people of goodwill by virtue of their legacy and tradition—that gives you a great opportunity. In a situation like that what is needed is a spark; then perhaps a great many people will see the light and follow your example. If they see clear signs of the tide turning, they may regain their courage, especially since they will not run any great risk in doing so.

I'm remembering how you prophesied correctly in 1931 and how I didn't believe you. I thought the majority of our fellow citizens rational and humane, as they are capable of being. But they were utterly defenseless against, and succumbed to, the tricks of the power manipulators and their own fear of the fait accompli. That could happen in America, but it is less likely than it was with us. What a wretched and despicable end that would be to a great and honorable human venture! You are obviously more hopeful now than you were then in Germany. You can do something. Journalism has a different function there than here. Make haste with your journal. It is clearly high time for it. German immigrants have done America great service on a number of occasions. Wasn't it a German-American—Zenger[1] or a name like that—who fought for freedom of the press in the eighteenth century? It must be exciting to be in this fluid situation, this melting down of the nation's substance, a melting down which, however, can be halted and reversed at any moment by cool clarity. How much your husband must share your agitation. The two of you together—I see you as a real intellectual force. All the more so because, in this great game of existence, you both speak with voices of calm dependability against overblown, self-important stupidity, and also because you are able to enjoy the present moment by moment.

You are uneasy about my being a member of the honorary presidium[2] of the Congress for Cultural Freedom. I am too. The problem is that I don't have sufficiently numerous and clear reasons to articulate why I should resign the post. Niebuhr[3] recently took the late John Dewey's place in the honorary presidium. I read in journals here in Europe about a certain stir of activity in the Congress, and there are reports on work accomplished. Up to now, I've been struck only by a kind of dullness and slackness of spirit but not by anything actually "wrong." Your report makes clear what I felt a long time ago with Koestler's success in this circle, namely, that the Congress is primarily opposed to Russia, not to the principles of totalitarian methods in general. Inspired by you, I would have to find an explanation that takes into account the current situation in America, a situation that has become almost a personal cause for every thinking person today. It would have to be stated that one cannot belong to this world congress if, by doing so, one's position can be misrepresented in America. But things will have to come to a head. I will be grateful to you for further information and for your advice. The business is annoying because it forces one to take one's own importance too seriously and because, once I have publicly taken part in something, I am reluctant to break off the tie.

I'm glad you were satisfied with my foreword for Milosz. Once again I owe you thanks. You did the translation as if you were always available. I wrote the foreword at the request of Jeanne Hersch, whom I find it hard to refuse anything. I was reluctant at first but then got caught up in the work and enjoyed it. In spite of the excellent preparation of your insights, I still found the reading a new experience because Milosz writes so concretely and with a psychology that only someone who was there and who both had to and was able to work his way out of that experience could develop.

I'm delighted to hear about your husband's success at Bard College. It's much more important for philosophy to become popular than for his colleagues in philosophy to be pleased. I hope to hear more in the future about his activities.

Of course I would like to see Kurt Blumenfeld, no matter what. It would be nice if he could let me know in good time when he will be coming through Basel. Saturday and Sunday are always the best days for me. I might do without Julie Braun-Vogelstein. We older people weigh the prospect of every single visit very carefully. Neither of us can complain really, but my wife has frequent attacks of vertigo and tires easily, especially in conversations, because she always takes such an active part in them. And, as always, I have to treat myself with kid gloves. But if the situation is *favorable* I'd like to speak with Frau Braun, too. With you, I'll leave that decision up in the air for now. The semester has gone well so far. I'm lecturing on "Wissenschaft und Philosophie" ("Science and Philosophy") and giving a seminar on "Das Problem des Bösen" ("The Problem of Evil"). I'm also giving three lectures, one for Swiss pastors,[4] which I've already done, one in the department of art history, scheduled for next week, on "Leonardo as Philosopher,"[5] and in two weeks one for Swiss physicians on "Die Idee des Arztes."[6] As you can see, I'm still very presumptuous. But I can do it only with clever husbanding of my strength and with careful hygiene.

I hope you will in fact both come to Europe in 1955 and that we will see you again then. It's wonderful that your husband wants to go to Italy and you are sharing that dream with him. From my wife and me, warmest greetings and wishes for you and your husband

Your

Karl Jaspers

Yesterday and today the paper had reports[7] about McCarthy again: Wechsler's case[8] (*New York Post*) and numerous protests, especially that of a New York journalist[9] who does not want to testify anymore (but will hardly be able to refuse because of contempt of Congress, as you wrote).

An unimaginable stupidity must have taken hold in the USA. It frightens us because we are familiar with it.

144   *Karl Jaspers to Hannah Arendt*

Basel, June 5, 1953

Dear Hannah!

I'm returning your Rahel manuscript to your New York address by registered mail and posting it at the same time as this letter. Forgive me for delaying so long. Permit me to repeat that in my view this book is so important that it must be published even if you do not rework it. You should in any event make preparations to publish it sometime, even if that moment should be in the distant future. I would also like to repeat that another final checking of the manuscript by you could well turn up some important corrections and seems to me very desirable. That will be difficult because the book comes from a phase in your life, the tendencies and feelings of which are no longer current for you, even though you have no reason to repudiate them in your past.

For today, just this brief notification. Warmest greetings to you both

Your

Karl Jaspers

Palenville, N.Y., July 13, 1953

Lieber Verehrtester—

I've held off a bit with replying to your letter because I wanted to wait and see how things developed here. But first of all let me tell you how excited I was by your Bultmann essay,[1] which, oddly enough, arrived just as I had finished and sent off a paper for Harvard on religion and politics.[2] I'll read it at a conference there next week.

Now to Bultmann. Your essay seems to me to provide the first serious basis for discussion I've seen yet. As you know, I learned a lot from Bultmann and owe him a lot. I don't want to forget that debt. It seems to me, too, that you don't quite do him justice as a person. Perhaps I'm prejudiced because I simply like the man. I think his honesty, which you mention, is more firmly rooted than you suggest. Then, too, the objective difficulties he faces are greater and for him worse, not solely as the representative of a religion or of a faith, but of an institution, which is as flawed as any other institution. But that isn't important. He will probably respond, and I hope that you have opened a dialogue.

The key point seems to me to be this: the justification of myth as a basic capability of reason and the rejection of the confusion, shared by the orthodox and the liberal alike, between myth and magic—you speak of a drifting off "into the materialism of the palpable and utilitarian."[3] Another is the conspicuous neglect—not only in Bultmann—of Jesus' preaching as opposed to Christ as "God's work of salvation," also the narrowing of Christianity into a radicalized Paulinism. It seems to me that something similar is evident in both cases, namely, an exclusive regard for the functional and a pushing aside of the real "substance." Jesus thus remains interesting only in his function within God's work of salvation on earth, not as a "preacher" who says: You should or should not do this or that. To sum up: faith communicates itself, wants to be understood and so understands itself.

There are some other points I would like to talk about with you (right now, the geographic distance between us is and remains a real stumbling block). Among them theology. It seems to me that theology is a science. In other words, it is basically different from philosophy, because it assumes that the revealed existence and acts of God are as palpable a reality as the reality of animals is for zoology. (Augustine was not yet a theologian.) The theologian is, in your formulation, someone who "*knows* the mysteries of the divinity" whereas "in the

221

liberal view there is no belief in the revelation."[4] That is why theology and philosophy cannot become one. Theology is not the philosophy of faith. (That is one of the problems facing modern theologians who want to remain theologians. They believe in a certain sense, but not in the way a theologian has to believe if he is to have a solid basis for his science.)

You show precisely and very convincingly how all these efforts "make the enterprise itself appear doubtful to the believer."[5] That, it seems to me, has been true since Pascal and Kierkegaard, who both made the leap from Descartes' doubt into belief. (That is very clear in Kierkegaard's little essay "De omnibus dubitandum est.")

You say that if Kierkegaard's position were correct, that would be the end of biblical religion. The difficult thing for theologians is that modern science doubts everything as a matter of principle, though not the individual results of science, and that theologians as scholars can't participate in this modern development of science without depriving themselves of their field of research. Now they are carrying doubt over into faith, where it has no business whatsoever, for the only possible outcome of that is either Kierkegaardian absurdity or obvious superstition.

In other words, the difficulty that Bultmann faces—and all of modern theology with him—is that on the one hand the institutions of the churches share with all modern public institutions the dubious nature of the political; and that on the other hand the development of modern science has made it impossible for theology to be and remain a science. None of these difficulties directly affects religion and faith, but they do of course draw both of them indirectly into the problems those difficulties raise.

Basically, you are suggesting to Bultmann that he read and interpret the Bible as if it were a philosophical text. Or: when you say in your conclusion that philosophy and theology could become one again, what that really amounts to is philosophy taking theology back under its wing. In any case, theology ceases to be a science, and yet that's precisely what it has been for many centuries. What takes its place then is philology on the one hand and philosophy on the other. Contemporary theologians who are good, that is, good in a scholarly sense, are without exception philologists already. Bultmann is a truly great scholar. It seems to me that if he is to satisfy your quite justified demands for honesty, he would have to step out of his own skin. (You see what my prejudices are.)

You'll note that I'm writing you from the country, which is very lovely now. I'm remembering last year and St. Moritz. You'll soon be there again. How did the semester go? I'd like to hear more about the problem of evil.

Heinrich is a bit tired from his work at Bard but very pleased with how it went. He managed to win over 75% of the faculty to his plans and 90% of the students. (Such a thing is unheard of at Bard. It's an old established tradition there for the students to criticize everything.) And he has even been elected to the key faculty committee that decides on appointments and so forth. That too is astonishing, in view of the very short time he has been there.

I don't feel like writing about politics; the situation is too dismal. You'll have heard about the farce with Cohn and Schine.[6] You can best understand it by reading Shakespeare on Rosenkranz and Guildenstern. The central point here and everywhere is that we are living in a society of jobholders. We see that all too clearly every day. We still don't know yet whether our magazine will get off the ground. We have $50,000, but that is too little here. We need twice that much. One can still print anything one likes. —As far as the Congress for Cultural Freedom is concerned, Messrs. Hook and Counts[7] (I think Counts is an alcoholic and I know he's a complete fool) have behaved shabbily again. Einstein urged intellectuals to risk contempt of Congress and refuse to testify.[8] Politically that is the only correct thing to do; what makes it difficult on the practical level isn't the legal implications but the loss of one's job. However that may be, the two aforementioned gentlemen, writing on behalf of the Congress, instantly fired off a letter to the *New York Times* in which they called Einstein's suggestion ill considered and irresponsible[9]—this after never having deemed it necessary to publish anything at all against McCarthy, except occasional denunciations in other contexts. The interesting thing about the adjective "irresponsible" is that it's the only one they have ever used to describe McCarthy. Ergo: McCarthy and Einstein are equally irresponsible. I've never thought much of Einstein's political statements, yet this time he's right. In no case should he be subject to attack from this quarter, even if he was wrong. These people have kept silent in the face of so much wrong that it wouldn't have made any difference if they'd let a little more go by. But this time they rose to the occasion instantly. McCarthy published remarks at the same time, saying Einstein was a bad American or no American at all or some such thing. —I'm passing all this on because I want to keep you up to date on developments here. For this same reason I've had all their publications from the last year sent to me. Too pathetic to bother talking about.

Thanks for *Rahel*, which has already arrived. At the moment I can't even look at it, much less prepare anything for publication. She hasn't seen the light of day for so long that a few decades more won't make any difference. Maybe I'll feel more drawn to it at some other period in my life. And thank you for your trouble and your kind concluding words, which I was of course happy to hear.

All my best to you both.

As always
Your
Hannah

146   *Karl Jaspers to Hannah Arendt*

Basel, August 25, 1953

Dear Hannah!

Many thanks for your good letter of July 13. It reached us in St. Moritz. I'm sorry that I haven't been able to reply until today, even though the memory of our time together last year in St. Moritz often came to mind. Frau Waltz was there again. And so I am writing to you only now, unforgivable negligence!

My reason for writing is that I received your contribution[1] from Schilpp a few days ago. I read it with great pleasure and found it even better than I imagined it would be. I have no objections at all, except perhaps that in your noble fashion you grace me with your own ideas in the process of reporting mine. And so I come out looking better than I am. I'm glad that this essay will appear in Schilpp's volume. There are 22 articles so far. I'm reading them all at once now and have to respond to them.[2] That's not easy. If you were here, I would discuss this at length with you. It is interesting to see how these many people—all very intelligent yet remarkably different—encounter my work and say something about it that at first seems to be a confusion of voices coming from totally different intellectual quarters but perhaps ultimately comes together in a unified picture after all. Despite the many contributions, I feel the lack of some things I would have liked to have reported, and I also find much that strikes me as superfluous. But all in all, I'm satisfied and stimulated—if I were somewhat nasty,

I would say: Just as in a seminar. There are a few essays, such as yours, which give me pure pleasure. That's not the case with most of them.

In St. Moritz I wrote the philosophical curriculum vitae.[3] I would like you to read that too, but there isn't time. The question is whether I have taken the right approach. What I have written rises from personal encounters in my life to the extent that the thinking of certain individuals bore directly on my own thought. Ludwig Curtius and Alfred Weber don't appear at all, but Rickert,[4] Heidegger,[5] and Ernst Mayer do, and of course Max Weber time and again. I would have liked to have your judgment on the few words I permitted myself to write about you, too. But that can't be, because Schilpp will be coming in person to pick up the manuscript from me in September.

You write about Bultmann. If I have the opportunity to reply to responses, I will cast Bultmann's personality in a more positive light. You're quite right about that. Your definition of theology as a science is overly simple. I'm afraid it isn't adequate to the task. I very much agree that Augustine was still not a theologian. But who was the first one?

I was happy to hear that Monsieur is having such great success at Bard. From his long letter of a year ago[6] I have only a vague notion of what he is doing. I can't quite picture what concrete form it is taking. That it is working is obvious. I wish him continuing success.

What you write about Hook and Counts's letter to the *New York Times* about Einstein is dreadful. Do you have a duplicate of that letter? I could perhaps use it to stir things up a bit in the Congress here in Europe and then see what develops.

Warmest greetings to you both, also from my wife

Your
Karl Jaspers

147 *Karl Jaspers to Hannah Arendt*

Basel, September 15, 1953

Dear Hannah!

Schilpp visited me last week. We discussed all the details of the book he is preparing for publication. There are 23 articles now. My autobiography is finished (Schilpp has read it and is delighted—he is a boyishly naïve, thick-skinned person). I'm writing every day on my replies to my critics. I've read all the essays. —Now of course you will wonder what my reason for writing is, and you'll be expecting me to come up with another request. But please, don't hesitate to refuse it if it is in the least inconvenient for you. This is what it's about.

Schilpp is translating my autobiography and my responses into English himself. The autobiography is 140 typewritten pages long. I'm afraid the responses won't be much shorter. My question is whether you would check the translation when it is done. That is once again, of course, an irksome burden for you. It's possible that you will determine quickly that the translation is bad and that you will have to suggest engaging another translator. (You could perhaps suggest Fritz Kaufmann.[1]) Or the translation is tolerable and requires only a few corrections on your part. This would have the additional advantage for me that for whatever reasons, personal or political, you might find it appropriate to omit one passage or another from the autobiography. Changes of this nature can of course be agreed upon only between the two of us and without Schilpp. I'm particularly eager to have the Heidegger chapter come under your critical eye. Schilpp won't complete his translations until sometime in the course of this winter, first the one, then the other, probably not before January. If you are willing to do this and want to—that last condition is an absolutely essential one—then please write me, and I'll pass the word on to Schilpp.

Not long ago I sent you a few lines at your vacation address. I assume you're back home now.

Warmest greetings to you and your husband, also from my wife

Your
Karl Jaspers

148 *Hannah Arendt to Karl Jaspers*

September 21, 1953

Lieber Verehrtester—

Of course, and with the greatest pleasure! I'm particularly eager to see the Heidegger chapter. Fritz Kaufmann would certainly be an excellent translator, although I don't think much of him otherwise. Schilpp, whom I do not know, quite rightly kept pushing me and reminding me to send in my manuscript; then, oddly enough, he didn't even acknowledge receipt of it.

226

I'm a little behind in sending my thanks for your vacation letter.[1] I so much want to talk with you again, and especially at moments like this one feels what a poor substitute letters are. How long is the Schilpp book going to be? And who all is in it? If you really find some of the essays superfluous, wouldn't it be possible to omit them? The good material can be obscured by excess baggage. But Schilpp probably wouldn't go along with that.

Nothing new has happened here. I'm enclosing the Committee's attack on Einstein.[2] I'm sorry that I don't have Einstein's letter.[3]

You no doubt know that Renato de Rosa[4] has turned up here. At first he was extraordinarily "unhappy." Now things seem to be a bit better. I did my best for him, introducing him to a very charming and pretty American friend[5] whom we have taught German during our many years of friendship. I like him a lot, but I fear that his problems in Naples,[6] on account of which I sympathize with him, will not find solutions in either Germany or America.

I'm sending you under separate cover a few essays[7] I've published here in the last few months. Read them as you find time, without feeling any obligation. One of them is the English (and expanded) version of my contribution to the Festschrift.[8]

The semester has already begun for Heinrich, and I've taken up my life as a grass widow again. We are both well. We had a wonderful vacation. I'm preparing my lectures for Princeton, which will begin in October and which will then be followed immediately by two more here at New York University.[9]

With all best wishes and warmest greetings to you both

Your
Hannah

149 *Karl Jaspers to Hannah Arendt*

Basel, September 25, 1953

Dear Hannah!

Thank you very much for your letter and your willingness to help. I'm writing Mr. Schilpp right now that once he is through with his translation he should send it to you along with my German text. Schilpp is indeed a strange fellow. I had a few days to get to know him. He emigrated as a boy before the First World War to become a missionary. He studied theology in America, was a Methodist minister, and is now a professor of philosophy. His style is a mix of youthful enthusiasm, liberal naïveté, insensitivity, and cloddish behavior. Despite all this he struck me as a decent sort. That he didn't even acknowledge receipt of your manuscript is scandalous but typical, and I brought this lapse to his attention.

His efforts on behalf of these fat books (900 pages on the average; mine is not to exceed 1,000) are, it seems to me, praiseworthy. The business end is not altogether clear to me, even though he speaks very openly about it. I didn't want to inquire into everything. At any rate, he hasn't yet earned anything himself that would adequately compensate him for the great amount of work involved. None of the contributors receive anything either. He has recently felt much more satisfied with the sales of the whole series because a house with a competent advertising department has taken it over. His contract with Kohlhammer for the German edition provides for an honorarium. He very willingly showed me the original contract. I felt that the contributors and I too should receive half of that honorarium. He then proceeded to explain to me all the difficulties, which I will not recount to you. All in all, I came to the conclusion that in view of the actual effort involved in publishing such volumes one should forgo any claim to an honorarium. If anyone stands to gain at all by them, it can only be the publisher. Still, there's something not quite right here, though it seems customary in America to provide contributions like this gratis. —I don't believe I've written you about the German series yet at all. The Einstein volume[1] is supposed to be the first. If and when mine will appear has not been settled yet. Mine will be easier, relatively speaking, because some of the articles are already available in German, and so the translation costs will be lower. But it will be a good while before all that comes to pass.

You ask who the contributors are and how the volume is organized. The contributors from America are Collins, Earle, Kurt Hoffman; also the emigrant Americans Manasse, Walter Kaufmann, Fritz Kaufmann, Lefebre, Golo Mann, Helmut Rehder. From Germany: Latzel, Thyssen, Kolle, Johannes Pfeiffer, Eduard Baumgarten, Gerhard Knauss. From Basel: Kunz; from Geneva: Jeanne Hersch. From Israel: Julius Loewenstein. From Copenhagen: Holm. From Dublin: Hennig. From South Africa: Lichtigfeld.[2] —The subjects touched on are: basic concepts, relationship to science, the all-encompassing, borderline situations, communication, failure, evil. My relationship to Max Weber, to the Bible. My view of Kierkegaard, of Nietzsche. On psychopathology, on psychology, on anthropology (where my illumination of existence is reduced to anthropology). Relationship to history, meaning of tradition. Freedom. Relationship to religious faith. On art and literature. —That must strike you as a huge stew. It's not so bad in reality. My response, which I have just put into final form today, attempts at least a kind of grouping and ordering. I confess that this response has given me some real pleasure. I perked up doing it, the way one does in seminar discussions. One could easily say of it all: What self-aggrandizement! But one has to put up with that if one wants to reach a larger readership. If I'm not totally mistaken, a book like this could make a few people here and there in America take notice, however alien and un-American this whole philosophy may be. I can see that from the critiques written by the native-born Americans, which are superb in their form but haven't the faintest understanding of the subject.

Thank you for the statement against Einstein.[3] I'll have to give it some further thought.

I'm looking forward to your publications very much. Good luck with the lectures in Princeton.

Your short remarks on Renato were wonderfully acute. In my mind's eye I can see him sitting in your apartment. I and even my wife, who has been very critical of him, have remained very fond of him all these many years.

Warmest greetings and best wishes for your husband's work from my wife and

Your

Karl Jaspers

I can take care of my letters quickly now because I can simply dictate them while lying stretched out on the sofa. I have an assistant[4] who knows shorthand very well. This makes my letters undisciplined and somewhat shapeless. Please excuse me! Better this way than not at all, I feel.

I'm going to drop the entire Heidegger section in my autobiography. It seems to me that I can't speak just biographically there but also have to offer a critical discussion of substance. I can't do that now. I haven't the time. I would have to read all of Heidegger first. So I'll keep my silence for now.

New York, November 15, 1953

Lieber Verehrtester—

Your good, long letter I have left unanswered for so long because I was so caught up in the Princeton lectures that I didn't want to look at anything else. That has to do with the totally irrational panics I experience in such cases and that oddly enough get worse when I'm successful but fade away entirely once I realize that I'm not reaching my audience. Then I become completely calm and reasonable. But in the opposite case . . . Now I have two more lectures here in New York at New York University and one at Harvard in early December, and then I'm going to retire.

I guess I can say that the Princeton lectures were what is customarily called a success. I tried to show what is actually going on in the political sphere and to what extent the traditional definitions of concepts, which I illustrated using the definition of governmental forms as a model, are inadequate. All very tentative, but I made a little progress anyhow. —I got to know Walter Kaufmann,[1] who attacked me furiously— which was his perfect right. What do you think of him? I'm not sure what I think. He is not (please keep this completely entre nous!) very well liked there because he is given to the German and German-Jewish mode of discussion, which is so very intent on having the last word. He struck me as very gifted but limited and not very profound, and, above all, too ambitious.

Schilpp sent me a long letter—a letter from him must have been lost, etc. Very likely, given the state of the postal system here. Now I'm curious to see the biography and your response to the contributors. It seems to me that the business side of the project is in order. He isn't doing this to make any money out of it. That can't be why he's doing it at all. Things work like this here: To get ahead at a university, i.e., to be promoted, say, from assistant professor to professor, etc., you have to publish. This obligation to publish weighs on everyone here like a nightmare. The academic journals are full of nonsense that not even the author believes but that is necessary for his career. None of these journals pays a red cent; very few of them are read. One way out is to become an editor and let other people write a book for you instead of writing one yourself. Then you appear in the card catalogue as the author. The book is listed under the editor's name. —You'll appear only as a subject heading, and we, the contributors, not at all. This isn't fraud either, because it's common practice. It's even better, of course, to be the editor of a whole series. You publish one book after another and never need to write one. The contributors, who live in this academic milieu themselves and are used to this circus, don't expect an honorarium either. (This all sounds more sarcastic than I mean it to. C'est comme cela, and if this were the only thing in the world or in the academic world that isn't in order, this would still be the best of all possible worlds.) I didn't know at all about a German edition. If I had known in time, I would have written in German and had Mr. Schilpp translate. The obliviousness of the Americans: of course, but the obliviousness in this official milieu is greater than anywhere else. I don't know the other contributors: Kurt Hoffman[2] is, I think, a German. I think I know who he is, but I'm not sure.

I wanted to write to you about Renato, but now it's late in the evening, and I can't remember anymore what I was going to say. At any rate, we grew very fond of him. And I beg your wife not to be too critical of him, no matter what, because "Aunt Gertrud" is a major, major figure in his life. The greatest compliment he can pay women, whom he may admire for any number of reasons, is that they remind him of "Aunt Gertrud." This young man knows what honor is, and that is considerably more than I can say for the vast majority of men I know.

I don't want to write about politics today. You will certainly know the facts there as well as we do here, and perhaps better than we do. There is a chance that the Democratic party will wake up and understand that the essential issues are not economic ones or class interests, not now or in the next election. There is some likelihood, though not a great one, that that will happen. Unfortunately, Stevenson, of all people, seems to be hopelessly obtuse in this regard. Unless I'm mistaken, everything will be decided here by the voters. And how the voter will vote in his booth no one can say in advance. Despite all the Gallup polls. Precisely because everyone is so intimidated that no one dares to speak openly anymore, it is possible that many people will go the other way in the voting booth—and balloting here is truly secret! We'll just have to wait and see.

I'm glad that you have an assistant and that letter-writing can be taken care of from the sofa. That is such a great help. Please don't ever think that you have to write me by hand. One of the greatest advantages of getting older is that one finally acquires traditional rights to comfort. I'm beginning to make good use of those rights already whenever I have to deal with younger people, and I take the greatest pleasure in making them aware of my gray hair. If you can do so in comfort, let me know soon how you both are! I hope this letter makes it clear to you that we are both fine. Heinrich is very busy and is always a little overworked, but it isn't bothering him so far. He's having fun; he could have things easier if he would give up his two-hour lecture and his seminar at the New School—which is precisely what he doesn't want to do.

All our very best
Your
Hannah

151 *Karl Jaspers to Hannah Arendt*

Basel, November 27, 1953

Dear Hannah!

Thank you very much for your letter of November 15. Worried because I had not heard from you, I was just about to write to you. Now I am happy to hear that you enjoyed a great success in Princeton, that you are working, making progress, and enjoying yourself. Your offprints[1] arrived yesterday, too. I've read a little in one of them. Wherever I sense your worry about fanaticism, I always go along with you instantly. But I can't say anything yet. I have to put off reading these essays for the moment. Lecture preparations[2] and writing are absorbing me completely. I'm treating myself almost like a machine that one keeps running by careful preventive maintenance. It's working. One could almost say that my wife and I are in excellent health, although my wife suffers from attacks of vertigo and other infirmities of age and I have my usual complaints. But my wife's spirit is livelier than ever.

I enjoyed reading your delightful description of the American system of academic advancement in which Schilpp is caught up. In the last analysis, you seem to be of the opinion, which I share, that a project of this kind is meaningful and that we owe its author a debt of gratitude.

Walter Kaufmann visited us here in Basel once. Then, too, I'm familiar with some passages from his Nietzsche book[3] and with his essay—in the Schilpp volume—against my Nietzsche interpretation.[4] In my response, I left him and Eduard Baumgarten[5] for last and didn't take him altogether seriously. Because I am almost entirely lacking in humor and in the light, ironic touch as well, the sharpness of my response will, I'm afraid, offend a bit. You will presumably have a chance to see this text, and you can delete whatever strikes you as unduly harsh. One mustn't allow these two lightweights more importance than they deserve. Walter Kaufmann has an incredible memory and has read everything. Your description of him matches perfectly my view of him. In his eyes, Kant's writings before the *Critiques* make him a great philosopher, for in that period Kant was a European and enlightened. After the *Critique of Pure Reason*, he started wandering on German byways. That shows how little Kaufmann understands of philosophy. For him, I am a German, of course, a non-European, with only one foot in the Enlightenment, and therefore a highly suspect figure. None of that kept him from extending a very kind invitation to me to come to Princeton.[6] I doubt that he would do it again now. I consider a mind like his not undangerous.

My wife and I were very happy to hear that you and your husband grew fond of Renato. You hit the nail on the head when you said that he knows what honor is. My wife's criticism of him is only an expression of her affection for him. Renato was here again a little while ago. He was ecstatic over Aunt Gertrud this time because she wasn't critical at all and showed nothing but concern for all his problems. He doesn't have it easy. A man like him rouses envy and jealousy in normal Germans, with disastrous material consequences for him. For his part, he is completely unprepared to subject himself to any kind of sociologically normal life. It's as if he sprang directly from Greek antiquity: as humane as he is heathen, he refuses to sell his life for any silly trifle. And so, without meaning to, he has become an adventurer. His talents are so great that external hurdles like examinations are child's play for him. Despite all his cleverness, despite his constant activity, despite his constant searching and worrying, he is basically lazy. He lacks the tenacity necessary for any real accomplishment. That isn't an unsympathetic trait, on the contrary. But it is painful to see what it may cost him in the end.

Your husband mustn't drive himself too hard. In that, he seems to be just the opposite of Renato. If he takes on too much, he will lose that meditative tranquillity from which everything of intellectual value comes. In America, that is surely a much greater danger than it is here. The hectic pace of work eats people up. —You make only brief reference to politics. I'm sorry to say that I didn't understand what you wrote about Stevenson, that he is "hopelessly obtuse" as far as the central themes of the next elections are concerned. Despite my faithful reading of newspapers and magazines, I still don't know enough about America. You mention the key issue in the elections. Yes, that's it, and we will see then whether the majority of this national population, given the favorable historical premises and reasonable traditions behind it, will choose to remain on a sensible course. If not, then the consequences will be unthinkable. The imagination can barely comprehend them. The fact that Stevenson got almost half of the popular vote is a promising sign. How wonderful it is that you are in the thick of it all with your fingers on the pulse of world history. Here in Basel we watch world history as if from a private box in the theater. In my old age I'm perfectly content to sit here and don't wish it were otherwise. But we mustn't forget that we are spectators in a box and not participants.

Give your husband my best regards. I wish him all the best in his work. What will you do now that your time is your own? Continue to analyze the "high road"? Warmest greetings, from my wife, too

Your

Karl Jaspers

Now that I have your permission, I can chat away with you from the comfort of my sofa.

152   *Hannah Arendt to Karl Jaspers*

New York, December 21, 1953

Lieber Verehrtester—

Your letter about Kaufmann and Renato did me so much good. It's always like coming home—finding that somewhere, with you, there are still standards that make sense, standards that are clear and so wonderfully independent of chatter and conventions. You did me a real service with Kaufmann. I didn't quite know how I should judge him. What he said was flat and dogmatic and extremely strident in tone. I obviously rubbed him the wrong way, and I felt he shouldn't be made to suffer for that. On one point you're mistaken: Not only would he invite you to Princeton as cordially today as he did in the past, but he hasn't the faintest idea that he has written anything that could rub you the wrong way. He told me about his essay because your name was mentioned in the discussion in Princeton, and I said you had carried Kant's political position further. He was very proud of the fact that he too had recognized you as a "Kantian." One more

234

misunderstanding: It was Princeton, not Kaufmann, who invited you—Princeton is the snobbish university par excellence in this country. He is only an assistant professor there. On the contrary, it was a feather in his cap that he knew you and could write to you. They let things be handled that way so that they can feel someone out on an informal basis. C'est tout! Your name is well known here; you're regarded as a major figure. That has nothing to do with the sales of your books in English. All the university libraries have them, and the students read you. Heinrich has just made *Tragedy Is Not Enough*[1] obligatory reading for his students, by the way.

Heinrich has been home since the end of last week and has two months off now. He has recovered from the semester already; for the time being this overworking isn't bothering him. But one still has to be careful. He'll be 55 in January. Since I came back from Harvard, where I gave two lectures, I haven't done anything, and I don't intend to do anything before next year. I can't stand to look at anything. One of the lectures at Harvard was a real disaster. The sociologists, whom I've been irritating for years, finally went into a rage and let me have it. It was a lot of fun. I take great pleasure in a good fight. Now the holidays are upon us with a lot of people and housework. We're having an immense New Year's Eve party. That's not so easy without help, but we'll manage. Then at least we'll be quit of all obligations.

You'll have seen, of course, how Eisenhower has gone along again in the McCarthy business. That was to be expected. But McCarthy's appeal to the "masses" to send telegrams supporting his foreign policy against Eisenhower—a kind of plebiscite!—was a failure. There were way too few telegrams to be of any significance in a population this size, and then a good third of them were protests against McCarthy. It's a bad sign in the long run that the elections are our only hope and that we have to set all our hopes on them. It's become clear that within the government itself the judiciary branch (I don't know the German terms for these things anymore) has ceased to function and that everything hinges now on the opinion of the people, which is theoretically represented in Congress. That means that the continuing existence of the republic is at the mercy of the majority, which is precisely what the Founding Fathers very wisely wanted to preclude when they wrote the Constitution. The republic, which should define the framework and the limits of democracy, is being dissolved from within by democracy. Or one could also say: The society is overwhelming the

235

republic. This process is underway, and whether it can be stopped is very, very questionable, even if McCarthy is defeated. But his defeat is crucial, the conditio sine qua non. Then, at least, one could start fighting for the republic again. The confusion over these matters among intellectuals is immense. The blame lies with the sociologists and psychologists in whose conceptual swamps everything founders and sinks. They, too, of course, are only a symptom of the mass society, but they play an independent role as well.

Did I write you that Wiese[2] is coming to the States and has, rather red-faced, got in touch with me? I sent him a very friendly reply and will see him here in early February. He is unchanged. And he is still afraid of me. Very funny.

Renato doesn't just "esteem" your wife, he loves her. That is quite a different thing. Her criticism would never hurt him as long as he felt himself loved by her. On the contrary. The good thing about him is that he knows so clearly what is really important. —Give Jeanne Hersch my very best regards. I would have liked to see her again last year but couldn't locate her in Paris.

All my best wishes for the New Year! I long so much for you both. Be well!

Your
Hannah

153 Karl Jaspers to Hannah Arendt

Basel, February 7, 1954

Dear Hannah!

Gertrud gave me this letterhead stationery for Christmas. Formal enough for official letters and suitable for airmail. You sent us such a nice Christmas letter and New Year's wishes. It is too late to send ours now, but still, let me say—because it is always so—that our thoughts are always with you both, and our worries about you, too, worries which you, with your wonderful high spirits and cheerful nature, never admit having yourself. Please don't be angry that we didn't send a holiday letter. There is no excuse. But it was a sign that we were both debilitated from work and actually still are. I'm afraid, too, that a few recently printed little articles have not been sent off to you. I'm in arrears with all such matters. Things are fine with us. Gertrud has her infirmities of age, the old things, and sometimes

236

vertigo as well. But she is in good spirits, and day by day we are both as happy as Philemon and Baucis.

Now I want to take up a subject you will not like, but please honor this wish as a favor to me, as you have always done in the past. I want to send you $1,000. When you were not well off financially yourself, as I realized only later, you made sacrifices to send food to us in Heidelberg. That was such an extraordinary and unforgettable act of kindness that it seems totally inadequate now, in times of peace (for how much longer!), to acknowledge your generosity with a mere payment of money that will serve as at least partial compensation for your expenditures. Poor thanks at best. The reason why I did not do this long ago, but limited myself to—and soothed my conscience with—planning to will you a number of valuable books from my library (I've dropped that idea since), is that our own financial situation was weak in 1948 and remained so for a while. We started out with debts here in Basel and could save only slowly. Now we have saved enough to dispel any worries about the financial aspects of possible illness. I am, contrary to law, still holding my professorship and drawing a full salary.[1] As the president of the administration informed me, I can continue to do so *ad calendas graecas*, that is, as long as my health permits me to fulfill my teaching duties adequately. We have enough for ourselves in spite of help we are providing for relatives. I know you will believe me when I say that, because you know how anxious I am about material security. You mustn't pain us now by letting your one-sided, loving generosity prevent you from accepting what is only right and proper. But I have no doubts about your "reasonableness." So please send me your bank account number so that I can make this transfer. Let the same affection for us that motivated your wonderful generosity help you overcome your resistance to my proposal!

Schilpp is taking his time. There's nothing I can do about it. He'll finish sometime. He has had all the texts since October. The translations take time, particularly his own.

The Berlin conference[2] is not raising any new hopes. At least the Western powers are proving to be of one mind. I'll be very pleased if the EDC[3] is formed and Germany consequently does not develop its own independent army, which would mean nothing but trouble.

Warmest greetings to you both from us both

Your Karl Jaspers

New York, February 19, 1954

Lieber Verehrtester—

This is, first and foremost, a birthday letter for you both. Whenever I think of you at this time of year I am so grateful and happy, joyful actually, that you exist. And then I think back on all the years, and I think that if you were not here anymore it would be as if standards had disappeared from the world, and we would indeed be surrounded on all sides by what Kant called dismal imprecision. Stay healthy and strong. (In Yiddish one says: Be healthy and strong as a goy, but that is only 50% applicable to you, and even then it isn't altogether appropriate.) This birthday should be quieter for you than it was last year, provided your well-wishers haven't already made this day into a habit. But I don't wish that for you.

Now I guess I have to respond to your suggestion, and I'll do it with as much reasonableness as I can possibly summon up. First of all, you exaggerate! I can offer you hard and fast proof of that, and I'm amused no end that for once our roles are reversed. You have just about doubled the sum involved. (I don't have my record book of packages anymore, but I remember that fairly well.) You exaggerate in another respect, too. What seems to you so extraordinary from your perspective of an absolutely secure existence is simply a matter of course from my perspective of frequent emigration and exposure to so-called world history. I always thought that your existence too was less secure than it looked, and that's exactly why I could imagine very well how things were when the fuses actually blew. Those of us on the other side of the fence, to the extent that we weren't hopeless bourgeois types, had become used to maintaining a little solidarity, and without it every last one of us would simply have gone under at some point or another.

Can't you—and this is Heinrich's suggestion—regard this as a matter of hospitality, which, because of the extreme constraints imposed by the times, could be offered only in the kitchen?? And must I remind you of recent years, when you both offered me your hospitality in such grand style, hospitality that included not just the kitchen, God knows, but the whole house and all its territories? Do we really want to keep such strict accounts on each other?

To prove to you how reasonable I am and also how much I have learned in the Anglo-Saxon world, I would like to propose straight off an appropriate compromise. Let's assume that at some point in the future I won't be able to afford to go to Europe and won't be able to finance the trip through some organization or another, but that I absolutely have to see you again. Then I'll tell you so, and we'll work something out together somehow, if you would like to. Agreed?

I'm writing in a bit of a hurry because I'm working on a lecture series for Notre Dame University that unexpectedly had to be moved back from early May to early March. The subject: Philosophy and Politics. I'm working furiously preparing everything in written form, because the people there would like to print this material, and perhaps I will give it to them to print, but I'm not sure yet.

Then there is a possibility that I will "have to" go to Europe this year after all. My organization,[1] which I had laid to rest, may all of a sudden have the opportunity to undertake a microfilm project for all of Western Europe (Hebrew manuscripts and Jewish documents in libraries and archives). I should know in about a month. Then I would have to go to Rome, France, Austria, and Germany to negotiate permissions before the experts could be sent over. I would much prefer to go in the fall (September or October). It's possible, however, that I may have to go as early as May or June, if I go at all. I want to be here in July and August no matter what, because Heinrich has his vacation then and I see precious little of him during the semester. All this is still completely up in the air, but I thought I'd tell you anyhow.

As always
Your
Hannah

155 Hannah Arendt to Karl Jaspers

May 9, 1954

Lieber Verehrtester—

I want to thank you for the "Leonardo,"[1] which I forgot to do because I was just about to leave on a trip when it arrived. I also want to ask whether all is well with you both. It seems I haven't heard from you in a long time. Schilpp, by the way, still hasn't sent me his translation.

There's not much to report here except what you've been reading in the papers. I'm in the process of translating my book and at the moment a bit at sea because the Europäische Verlagsanstalt has all at once offered to publish the whole book and not just an abridged edition, as Rentsch wanted to do. Now I have to make a quick decision. It's a pretty big job either way, and annoying, because it is more of an interruption for me now than it would have been a few years ago. Because I can't write German and English at the same time, I've refused to give any lectures, or papers, as they're called here, except for two short ones, one for a philosophical society on the modern concept of history and one for this year's meeting of the American Political Science Association, which it would have been stupid to decline. I do want to inform you, however, that I've just received out of the blue one of this year's literature prizes,[2] from the National Institute of Arts and Letters (a mighty official outfit). A thousand dollars. A so-called honor, and really very funny.

The Europe trip is postponed for the time being. The funding required for it did not come through. Whether our organization will get what we have asked for isn't certain either, nor do Baron and I know yet whether we will refuse to work with a reduced budget or not. I'm assuming the trip will materialize sometime soon, but this summer is out of the question, which is really all right with me, because I want to put this stupid translation business behind me first.

This is just a brief hello. If your secretary is still functioning, perhaps you can dictate a few lines so that I'll know all is well with you.

My very best to you both,
Your
Hannah

156 Karl Jaspers to Hannah Arendt

Basel, May 14, 1954

Dear Hannah!

You would have every right to be angry that I haven't written for so long. What I can offer by way of an excuse is totally inadequate: my self-imposed work load, which is almost indefensible at this point; the daily tasks of a professor—the need to answer your kind letter only by hand, not by dictation; my trust: Hannah knows me and will not believe, even if she heard some nonsense told about me, that *that* is the way it was, and she will not misinterpret my silence—and then tomorrow, or the day after tomorrow, I'll finally write to her. Such were my thoughts week after week. Now *you* have written to me again and confirmed my trust. But that cannot excuse me.

Your decision on the financial question isn't altogether to my liking. But the fact of your and Heinrich's noblesse does my heart good. What a lovely, aristocratic interpretation you put on the facts: "hospitality, because of the extreme constraints of the times, in the kitchen"! Your husband was truly inspired when he thought of that one. And then, on top of that, the "Anglo-Saxon readiness to compromise," and what is truly Anglo-Saxon about your suggestion is that three of its terms make it highly unlikely the suggestion will ever be acted upon. Yet there is still a vague chance it will (although the condition that you not be able to afford a trip is such that I have to hope very much it will never come to pass). Anyway, I have now added to my bank account ledger (which has columns for funds on hand, current expenses, held back for taxes, reserve) a new column: Hannah, 4,000 francs. They await your call.

Because there are so many things that require comment I've dictated a letter, which is enclosed.

Warmest greetings to you and Monsieur
Your Karl Jaspers

A long time ago you mentioned that Blumenfeld would be visiting me. He has never come. Should I still expect him? I would like to talk with him about Rahel, among other things. But more important still, I'd like to meet this man to whom you owe so much and whom you value so highly.

Do you know anything about Leo Strauss,[1] who has written about Spinoza, an orthodox Jew of strong rational powers? Is he still alive?

157 *Karl Jaspers to Hannah Arendt*

Basel, May 14, 1954

Dear Hannah!

It's a great shame that your trip to Europe has to be postponed. We were very much looking forward to seeing you and speaking with you, and I was thinking you might even be in Ragaz on September 20, where some Swiss philosophers will be holding a Schelling conference.[1] We could have seen what is being said about Schelling these days, and you could have heard my lecture,[2] which would take us both back several decades to that seminar[3] in which you took such a lively part.

That's wonderful news that your book will come out unabridged in German. Of course it is inconvenient for you now. But I think that

241

it's worth it. The book can't but find a wide audience in German. It contains the most profound insights yet into this phenomenon that is discussed every day.

I am extremely pleased about the literature prize of $1,000 and about the honor connected with it. I don't find that funny at all, but only appropriate. Further things of this nature should come your way without your having to lift a hand for them. How happy this must have made your husband! According to your foreword, his involvement in the book was substantial.

I've been working very hard. I vastly underestimated the scope of my project two years ago (the world history of philosophy). I am taking increasing pleasure in the work; and, in that happy megalomania to which authors are subject, I think it extremely important. I can't predict yet exactly how it will develop. For the time being, I foresee three books: World History of Philosophy. The Great Philosophers. The Mission of a World History of Philosophy.[4]

My health gives me little cause for complaint. On the contrary, given my condition, I'm doing better than I could reasonably expect. My wife is suffering real pain in her knees, a consequence of so-called arthritis deformans. On level ground she can, thank God, walk without any problem, but when she climbs stairs, she sometimes has pain so severe that she cries out. That is in keeping with her emotional nature. Getting into a car, let alone a streetcar, is so difficult that it borders on the impossible. But she is in good spirits. We have visitors and are making new acquaintances among younger people. Thanks to my wife, these occasions are very lively. Unfortunately, I'm rather a clod because I'm always tired from my work.

The university here is quieter than ever. There are no catastrophes and no big problems. My wife and I continue to feel content in this atmosphere. We had no reason to expect we would have this tranquillity in our old age. In addition, the university has decided that not only I but my wife as well, if she should survive me, can continue to rent the house for life. Such gestures of friendship toward us, who are, after all, guests here, are very gratifying to us.

Warmest greetings from us both to you both

Your
Karl Jaspers

Palenville, July 24, 1954

Lieber Verehrtester—

These last months have gone by so quickly that I've just realized how long it's been since you last heard from me. Thank you for your kind letter. Believe me, my fears do not stem from mistrust but only from this Jewish anxiety about your and your wife's health, an anxiety with which you probably cannot fully identify. Let's let the matter rest at that. There's nothing much one can do about it. Reason doesn't help much.

Your cheerful outlook on your work made me feel very happy. Three volumes, in view of your subject, do not strike me as excessive at all. How will you go about it? Will you publish the first volume soon and then the others? Or do you want to wait until all three are done? I've just finished my "paper" for the Political Science Association this fall. It's called "Concern with Politics in Recent [European] Philosophical Thought,"[1] and in it I've made cautious mention of your world history of philosophy. That's called "work in progress" here. Do you have anything against my doing that? Whatever else I say about you is in connection with the essay for Schilpp. What is he up to anyhow? I haven't heard anything more from him.

We have, as usual, fled here from torrid New York and established ourselves happily in our usual bungalow. We're both working, Heinrich on a new course for the New School, I on the German edition of my book. It is odd to immerse myself in it again, and the work has a certain appeal on the level of pure craft. I'm finding it very pleasant to be finished with political philosophy and my growing heap of manuscripts for a while and to gain a little perspective on it all.

It is very disappointing to me that I couldn't go to Europe, and now something else has come along to get in the way of it. Over a year ago the University of California in Berkeley offered me a chair, and I told them that though I did not want to become a "professor," I always had an open mind for temporary arrangements. Now they have invited me to teach for one year on very good terms. After many telephone calls (all negotiations here are done by telephone at a distance of three thousand miles, and it sounds as if the other person is in the next room), we agreed that I would come for one semester in the spring and would lecture on the history of political theory from Machiavelli to Marx and give two seminars, one for beginners and one for advanced students. It will be very salutary for me to have to express myself for a few months in such a way that the children will understand me. The separation of 3½ to 4 months is very painful, particularly given the present atmosphere, in which people like us are quite isolated and are therefore more dependent on each other than ever. But on the other hand . . .

I forgot to write you that [Benno von] Wiese turned up here suddenly for a guest lecture in the Midwest and that we of course made peace with each other. He is completely unchanged—entertaining, pleasant, likable, and still a bit dissolute. And he still has his old fear of me. His lack of all sentimentality and his self-irony were sympathetic. The meeting was really nice. He was very enthusiastic about America and was toying with the idea of coming here permanently. He presumably has some prospects. The German departments at the universities here have gone completely to the dogs because hardly anyone has shown any interest in German literature since World War I. That is changing, and the universities are desperately searching for competent people to build up their departments again. We spoke a great deal about you, hence the card.

Blumenfeld didn't get in touch with you because he had to go back to Israel directly from Berlin. He has just written that he will be going to Switzerland this year and will get in touch then. To give you an idea of the man: a number of articles appeared on the occasion of his seventieth birthday, and an anecdote in one of them has stuck with me because it was so typical of him. When he was a young man he tried to make a Zionist out of someone who objected: "But you have to admit that this cause has no prospect of success." Whereupon Blumenfeld said: "Who ever said I was interested in success?" That he nonetheless managed to become president of the organization could, of course, happen only in Germany! You must know that quote from Cato that Gentz always cited: *Victrix causa diis placuit sed victa Catoni.*[2] That is the spirit of republicanism.

Leo Strauss is professor of political philosophy in Chicago, highly respected. Wrote a good book about Hobbes[3] (as well as the one about Spinoza). Now another about natural law.[4] He is a convinced orthodox atheist. Very odd. A truly gifted intellect. I don't like him. He must be in his middle or late fifties.

I was sorry to hear that Krüger[5] is so ill. Do you know more details?

Yes, rheumatoid arthritis is a nasty and painful business. Is there nothing that can be done? Mud baths used to be the treatment; they probably didn't help much either. How is her heart?

Will you go to St. Moritz again? We'll stay here until the end of August. The address is: Chestnut Lawn House / Palenville, N.Y.

All best wishes to you both

Your

Hannah

159   Karl Jaspers to Hannah Arendt

Basel, August 29, 1954

Dear Hannah!

Kurt Blumenfeld and his wife were here with us three days ago. It was wonderful. From the first moment on our conversation was open and trusting. There was no need to be cautious. Among other things, I tried to counter his dreadful accusation that loss of character was the price Jews paid for assimilation in Germany. My own experience leaves no doubt in my mind that there were people of the finest character who were Jews through and through and totally German at the same time. Jewish-German culture was a noble thing for a century and a half, stained, of course, like everything in history, with many ills as well. As an example from among my closest associates and as a symbol for many other Jews, I can cite the difference between my wife and my best friend, Ernst Mayer. My wife, incredibly sensitive, her feelings wounded as a Jew at the mere possibility of an insult, and ruthlessly consistent, yet entirely German and sustained by Jewish substance, both inseparable and not at all as in Heine, in whom an element of incongruity persisted. And then there is Ernst Mayer, completely insensitive to slurs from childhood on, impossible to insult as a Jew. When he was a boy, his schoolmates stuck pigs' tails in his pockets and insulted him in other ways, none of which ever happened to my wife. But people who did things like that just didn't bother him. It never occurred to him to make a generalization to the effect that the world he lived in was anti-Semitic. As far as I can tell, neither of them suffered any character damage. Yet their attitude toward the world around them was different. They loved each other with an intensity that seemed to go beyond the bond between brother and sister. The beginning of our relationship was remarkable. When Ernst met me in a medical course, he persisted in seeking out my company even though I, a North German block of ice, responded with no more than routine courtesy. He told Gertrud: I've finally met a German student. Gertrud said: Leave him alone. He may be anti-Semitic. Don't push yourself on him. Ernst didn't let himself be dissuaded. After four weeks we were friends. And when I met Gertrud, at the end of the semester, after she had held out against a joint visit for a long time, our fate was decided within an hour. And I'm supposed to decry assimilation? My feelings go in just the opposite direction. When I'm with Blumenfeld, I'm dealing with a German who is also a Jew and who even in his formulations thinks completely differently from the way I do. But it is thanks to our common German heritage that we immediately understand each other so well. He is as German as you are. What is German? you'll ask. Either I don't know, or I could write whole books in response. In any case, it is something that unites us. A Russian Jew—like Frau Blumenfeld—as likable and valuable a person as he may be, is not German. You know, of course, that in stressing this German quality I do not attach any significance to it. This is not a question of will but of reality. Blumenfeld told me that he had spoken with Niebuhr in New York. They started out in English, then switched to German in the middle of the conversation. Niebuhr spoke German as if he had just left Hamburg. His forebears emigrated to America in the 1840s, but the family held onto the language generation after generation. Perhaps he too is a man whom I would immediately perceive as German, even though he is completely an American as well. My wife and I like Blumenfeld immensely. We spoke often of you, of course, to whom we owed this meeting. He has great affection and admiration for you. Mine are, I think, even greater, but quite different.

Blumenfeld's eyes shone and were so kindly. His strokes seem, however, to have taken their toll on him. That may account perhaps for a certain slackness, a certain tendency toward sentimentality and exaggeration. But none of that mattered in the least. What he said, how he said it, and his glance, all that was so remarkably pure and honest. Thank you for sending them both our way.

Now thanks are due for your letter of July 24. Your vacation is no doubt over by now. I should have written long ago. But I fell ill in mid-July (infection), then we went on vacation. We have been back in Basel for a few days now, and I am all well again.

It's wonderful that you were offered a professorship in Berkeley. That you refused it is just like you. If it weren't for your husband, I would consider it a form of hubris. Blumenfeld expressed his concern that sometime in the future you might do something very stupid. I responded that that might have been so in your youth, but in the meantime you have become so realistic, experienced, and clever that you would keep yourself under control and not insult the Americans. And I added that you are able to write and speak in such a way that you are not insulting and so are not forced to be silent. After Blumenfeld said what he said, I felt somewhat nervous for you again myself and so I am writing this to you. Your guest semester in Berkeley in the spring will be instructive for you without a doubt, because of both the teaching you will do and the responses it evokes. But it will be hard indeed without your husband.

You write about the current situation in America. I don't understand it. A very prominent Jew in America recently wrote to Blumenfeld: Now things are getting critical for us, too. Did he mean that seriously? Or do you have something completely different in mind?

What you say about Leo Strauss interests me. An atheist now? In his earlier books he appears as an orthodox Jew who is providing justification for authority. The style and tone of his books put me off, but what he writes is very informative.

You ask about Krüger. He had two strokes, one in January '53 and another in the fall of '53. The cause is medically unclear, but his condition is bad, especially the aphasia. His working or teaching again is out of the question. He is in a sanitarium in Heidelberg at the moment. He hasn't been pensioned yet. People there are, understandably, still keeping alive the fiction of a possible recovery. A bad situation. His retirement is, in my view, the most dire loss for German philosophy. Krüger is the most decent, the most solid, the most serious of them all. Ill fate seems to be hanging over German universities.

My wife's knee and rheumatism have shown amazing improvement, and we are very happy about that. Her heart doesn't exactly pose a threat, but it makes itself felt in a loss of stamina. Her intellectual vigor and spiritual vitality remain unchanged. We are very happy together. We were in Valais for our holidays this time, near Lake Geneva. Frau Waltz took us around the countryside in her car, from the Great Saint Bernard to Evian and Mont Pelerin.

There will be a Schelling conference in Ragaz at the end of September. I'm working on a talk for it.

For you and Monsieur from my wife and me, the warmest greetings

Your

Karl Jaspers

A quick dictated letter, as you have permitted me!—but better than nothing.

October 6, 1954

Lieber Verehrtester—

This letter won't be much of a letter at all. I've been meaning to thank you first for the Bultmann book[1] and go into that in some detail, but somehow I haven't got around to it, and so I've put off thanking you for your wonderful letter about your meeting with Blumenfeld. I'll do that now and postpone the Bultmann a bit. On top of that I'm beginning to yearn so much for you both that each letter only makes me angry that I can't be with you and talk with you.

On the question of Jewish assimilation: Blumenfeld is basing his case—and I think correctly—not on individuals but on his historical and social experiences with a group of people. You say: Jewish Germans, but people usually say (wrongly?) German Jewry. The only way Blumenfeld, as a Zionist, can describe the situation is to say that there was a German Jewry, which represents one part of the Jewish people scattered all over the world. That's right historically, that is, from the standpoint of Jewish history. As far as assimilation is concerned, the situation was politically and socially impossible and would have resolved itself—either by disappearing or by way of Zionism. But precisely because it was politically and socially so complex it offered, on an individual level, remarkable opportunities of a human and intellectually productive sort. In this sense, German Jewry was truly a great thing. The story you tell is altogether charming. All Mediterranean peoples suffer from this same kind of misunderstanding, immediately interpreting northern reserve as rejection because, given their temperament, they can't imagine so much restraint. Your little Neapolitan friend [Renato de Rosa] would not have reacted any differently.

Blumenfeld has been having these strokes for 13 years now. Everyone who knows him says he is only the ruin of his former self. I thought you would see past the "ruin" and fill in, and I'm grateful to you that you did. Of course he is very "German." He used to say: I'm a Zionist by the grace of Goethe. Jenny, as your wife seems to have recognized more clearly than you did—"I left her in peace" is wonderful[2]—is quite another story and not necessarily a pleasant one.

America: Things have been very much better here for the last few months. It looks as if McCarthy is finished. The historians will no doubt busy themselves someday writing about what has happened here and how much extremely valuable china got smashed in the process.

But what the "prominent Jew" wrote to Blumenfeld isn't true at all. It was characteristic of this show that it had no anti-Semitic twist to it at all. What I see in it is totalitarian elements springing from the womb of society, of mass society itself, without any "movement" or clear ideology.

The trouble with Jews, particularly now, is that they are firmly convinced that disaster always has to appear in anti-Semitic guise. On that point, Blumenfeld and the little Jew who sells newspapers on my corner are in complete agreement. If I say to him that McCarthy has proved that he isn't an anti-Semite or that there has never been so little anti-Semitism in the United States as now, he concludes from that that I'm for McCarthy.

Thanks very much for the magazine.[3] The photograph is excellent, one of the best of you that I've seen.[4]

Leni Wieruszowski told us a little about you, which only made me wish to have been there, too. It's hard to know how to deal with her, but also impossible just to drop her. It's good of you to keep seeing her. It means a lot to her.

I've had a letter from Blumenfeld already, all enthusiastic and happy. He says he left your house "a better man," and that one could "speak better about the assimilation of the Jews with you than with . . ." and then comes a list of names, which I will discreetly keep to myself, but they include just about all the professors at the University of Jerusalem. —I'm not quite sure exactly what he means about my "stupidity," but because he has a good eye for people, he's probably right. Besides, there's nothing one can do about stupidity but wait patiently until one does something stupid. One survives stupid mistakes. Anyway, don't worry—but thank you for worrying.

We didn't come back to New York until early September, and Heinrich is already back at Bard again. He comes home every Thursday either early or late in the afternoon and goes again on Monday. Things are going fine. I was in Chicago for the meeting of the Political Science Association and am living very much to myself now, finishing up the German edition of my book, which is a beastly job, and giving a few talks, Harvard and Oberlin College and a few other little things.

I wanted to write about your article in *Foreign Affairs*[5] too, and about the one in *Confluence*,[6] but really only to say that I'm in complete agreement and that I particularly enjoyed the one in *Foreign Affairs*.

I feel a little different about "Bultmann." I don't agree on a few points. But in your second piece you have recast all the personal issues very nicely. All in all, I like the second article almost better than the first.

I'll write again soon, and forgive me for babbling on in this letter.

Be well, both of you, and accept, as always, warmest greetings

from Your
Hannah

161 *Karl Jaspers to Hannah Arendt*

Basel, November 27, 1954

Dear Hannah!

I still haven't answered your kind letter of October 6. Permit me to dictate a letter to you so that you will at least have some word from me.

Blumenfeld sent me a few essays. I still have to read them and reply to him, but I will definitely do it.

Your comments about the Jews in America were a great comfort to us. In this area, too, we can rely more on your judgment than on all the rumors. As for your worries about totalitarian developments stemming from mass society, they are surely very justified. You and your work are in the thick of the intellectual struggle against such developments. Ultimately, no one has control over the course of history, not even in a theoretical view of it or in a prognosis. In the battle of opposing forces which no one can really survey, all one can know is what one wants to live for oneself. The perspectives that our understanding and external experience almost force on us today are dreadful. Intellectually, the main task is to develop the ideas and the critical positions that can dispel the irrevocable character of those perspectives.

Please tell me sometime, when you feel like it, what your reservations, objections, and dissatisfactions with my Bultmann criticism are. I give great weight to your judgment and viewpoint. You can prompt me to make corrections. It will no doubt cause you some work to write that out. I hope that a time will come when the impulse will seize you to make your position on this clear to me. This little book is finding an astonishingly warm reception. The first printing was 6,000 copies. A second printing is planned for January.

You've given a number of talks, and you'll soon be heading west. I enjoy imagining you there, talking and discussing, waking people up and making them think about the great questions of politics and free human existence. I didn't send you my two American articles because I received only two complimentary copies. But you discovered them for yourself and read them. Thank you. I'm glad that you agree with them. I'm a bit annoyed with myself in retrospect that I qualified my praise of your great book with a reservation.[1] I should have either left it out or gone into more detail. I hope you weren't annoyed by it.

One of these days, Peter Waltz[2] will visit you. I would imagine, since you know his mother well from St. Moritz, that you'll be interested in meeting him. We're fond of him. He has passed his exams at the ETH[3] in Zurich, is doing studies on tobacco problems in America at the moment, and will eventually move into a top management position of a group of Swiss cigarette factories, since he belongs to the family of the owners. He is a nice young fellow. He may take too much pleasure in the luxuries of modern life, but he is unspoiled. He has a dangerously pessimistic view about the possibilities of love and a good marriage. They're things he'd like to have, I think, in a form suitable to him, but he hesitates, grows melancholy, and writes literary things and fairy tales that aren't too bad (this is confidential, because he shows us these things, and no one else is supposed to know, of course). I can imagine that you could open this lad up a bit. But that would depend on an opportune moment, and you will have little time for him in any case. He is not expecting anything.

Warmest greetings to you and your husband, and best wishes to you both

Your Karl Jaspers

My wife sends her best, too. Do you know yet when you'll make your trip to Europe?

162 Hannah Arendt to Karl Jaspers

Berkeley 4, Cal., February 6, 1955

Lieber Verehrtester—

You probably think I've disappeared. And that's partially true in the sense that I've arrived safely at the extreme tip of our Western world, namely, at the point where the Orient (China) is no longer in the east but in the west. The trip here was incredibly exciting and beautiful beyond all expectations. Across the Great Plains, out of which the Rocky Mountains suddenly rise up, the most amazing stone formations. The plains unbroken, except by rivers, which are the most important features in the landscape of the continent. The way the whole continent unfolds in front of you (I traveled by train, three days and three nights) makes you feel as if you are a witness to the creation. And when the sun rises over the reaches of snow or the mountains, then it's just like: "Da erschuf er Morgenröte, Die erbarmte sich der Qual."[1] I was in San Francisco today, a very beautiful city, like Lisbon but on a massive scale. The Pacific! Quite different and much larger and more dangerous waves than in the Atlantic, and dark sand as well.

Otherwise, I'm sitting here a bit alone and wondering how this is all going to turn out. Classes begin in a week. The campus is incredibly wealthy, marble in the library, and so forth. I don't know yet how the students are. The faculty appears to be pretty sleepy. Philosophy has gone the way of semantics, and even that is third-rate. But despite that, the university has a good reputation here.

My quarters in the faculty club are pleasant, and they take good care of you here. Everything very comfortable but not luxurious. Luxury is for the students and the Board of Trustees. The faculty isn't spoiled. The students are the donors of the future and therefore considerably more important than the professors. That isn't fundamentally any different in the East; but you don't notice it there. I'm enclosing a questionnaire that the students here are encouraged to fill out about their professors.[2] There are similar things in the East, but I haven't seen anything like this yet. You can really see from this how easily a democracy can turn into an ochlocracy.

After many, many years away from it I've just been reading again, with great pleasure, in your little Göschen book.[3] I'm going to use it in my beginners' seminar here, in which I'll be dealing with the basic political experiences of our time, beginning with the First World War. I wonder what the children will say about it!

There was a letter waiting for me here from Brandeis University (a Jewish university that was founded a few years ago and has come along well). The letter asks me whether you might be willing to go there for a year. Because this isn't Princeton, where an offer always carries a certain prestige with it, I'll decline right away for you so that you won't have to write an extra letter. I hope that's all right with you.

I can't write a decent letter now. I have to settle down first. The past few months were awful. I had to finish the German text of my book and edit two volumes of Broch's essays,[4] all in great haste, as well as prepare for here. —Peter Waltz didn't call, by the way. Maybe he'll turn up here. I remember his mother very well. How wonderful that whole time in St. Moritz was.

Despite all these goings-on I am planning a trip to Europe. Heinrich says that if I don't have a look at the world now and travel around in it while I can still enjoy it, I'll get like him and go under in my work the way he has. So if it is at all possible, I'll go to Europe this year, too. Now he absolutely refuses to come. And so our original plan will come to naught again. But in September, when his semester begins, perhaps I'll fly over after all. And with great plans that include Rome—Athens—Jerusalem. Then in one year I'll have taken in the whole Western world. And that presumably will put my heart at rest again. The world is just so lovely.

It all seems so far away, and this semester is like a huge mountain I have to climb over first. But I'd still like to ask now when and how a visit would suit you. I thought I might come to Basel before the main part of my trip, so I wouldn't crash in on you during the semester. What do you think? Then I would fly directly to Zurich and from there on to Rome.

I had word from Schilpp. He wanted to send part of his translation to me in New York. I had to tell him that he would have to wait a bit and that I'd prefer he send the whole thing here. First he drags his feet, and now he wants somebody else to put everything in shape for him from one day to the next. I couldn't do it before I left, and I haven't heard any more from him since. Well, sometime even that project will see the light of day.

Perhaps you can find a free moment with your assistant and drop me a line to say how you both are. Your birthdays are coming again soon. How I would love to come for them sometime. All the very best.

Warmest greetings
Your
Hannah

163 *Karl Jaspers to Hannah Arendt*

Basel, February 18, 1955

Dear Hannah!

Your letter gave my wife and me great pleasure. How wonderfully you described your trip and your state of expectation. You are still able to see the world fresh and new, as in youth. That is truly astonishing after all that you and we have experienced. How right you are to want to go to Rome, Greece, and Jerusalem, and how good your Heinrich is to encourage you. Nothing we let slip by can be made up later. It will be nice for us to see you again. I'm planning to take a leave next winter, except for a seminarlike colloquium once a week, assuming the leave is approved. Then you would be welcome at any time, either before or after your Mediterranean trip. Our plan to be in Cannes in September is up in the air because of a sudden and severe heart ailment of Dr. Waltz's. But all our plans are only tentative. When the time is closer, we'll make firm arrangements. I often carry on inner dialogues with you. I have a lot to share with you. I hope we'll have a lively talk when we sit down together.

I happen to know two people in Berkeley who have some stature intellectually but who you probably will feel have none in human terms. I'd like to describe them to you, because both of them evoke the Heidelberg atmosphere here. —One of them is Olschki.[1] He visited us recently. He is apparently a first-class research scholar who brings philological ingenuity and a vast store of knowledge to bear on matters of intellectual significance. At the same time, his outlook is that of the complete skeptic who is impressed by nothing. What he writes about Leonardo is almost scornful; Galileo, on the other hand, is a great figure.[2] A while ago he clarified the meaning of "veltro" in Dante[3] in an extremely complex but also, according to knowledgeable sources, definitive way. There can be no doubt any longer about the way Dante felt himself to be a prophet. When I asked him about this recently, he said, "Yes, I think that by using relevant astrological material I've come up with the definitive interpretation of this matter. If there is any mystery at all in Dante, then it is solved." He has taken a different tack with Marco Polo[4] now but again discovered something completely new and crucial. In the course of this project, he learned Chinese and can write Chinese poems. "I just happen to have a gift for languages," he said, when I expressed amazement over this. I also knew that he was among the professors in Berkeley who refused to sign a loyalty oath[5] and lost his post as a consequence. Asked about that, he said: "I can't brag about that, because my papa left me so much money that we can live modestly but very decently from it. And the Americans weren't paying me much anyhow." I've known Olschki for many years and have friendly feelings for him, though they have their limits. Have I ever told you the way he behaved when he took over the chair that

254

Ernst Robert Curtius[6] had held before him? That's a somewhat complicated story I'll have to tell you in person. Later, Gundolf and I weren't so pleased that we had pushed his appointment through, for when it was time to make another appointment in his field and we wanted Auerbach,[7] the best Romanist there was at the time, he argued passionately and successfully for an absolute nobody. I said something rude to him at the time—I sometimes let things like that slip out, I guess; and after that he wouldn't say hello to me for a while. In 1933 he grasped the situation immediately, set up a guest professorship for himself in Rome, and had Berlin confirm somewhat later that his return to Heidelberg was not expected. That way he received his Heidelberg salary in Rome, and he's still drawing his full pension as professor emeritus from Heidelberg, sent to him now in America. He's married, without children. He doesn't want to live in Europe anymore, or in America either. "The Americans are afraid of the mind," he said. "But I don't know a better library than the one in Berkeley. The Americans collect the books, and there's nowhere else I can work better."

The other is Bukofzer,[8] full professor of musicology, a student at Heidelberg and from my part of the country, an Oldenburg Jew from Achtern Street, from a family that had a superb clothing store. He went to Basel in good time, took his doctorate here, was engaged but couldn't marry because the Swiss, adhering to international agreements, respected Hitler's laws governing Germans. So he emigrated to America, and now he says in jest, with a big grin on his face, "Heil Hitler." The course of his life couldn't have turned out better. I understand he's been very successful. He's interesting to talk with, but I have to admit that I don't care for him. It seems to me that a contemptuous, egotistical attitude has the upper hand in him. But perhaps I am mistaken.

The questionnaire you sent me is a remarkable document indeed. I'll show it to a lot of other people. Do you know Golo Mann's new book on the American mind?[9] If not, let me know, and we'll send it to you. I think it's worthwhile, though it certainly won't contain anything new for you. I like his mode of thought a lot. What he has to say about America's China policy seems excellent to me, but much else as well.

You'll have begun teaching by now. That will surely make for a very busy time. I'm eager for your next report.

I won't write about myself today. I'm being diligent, but my plans seem ambitious and much more. Well, it's better to live, even in old age, with the assumption that you've got plenty of time. And this writing of books is an enjoyable business in any case.

Schilpp is a slowpoke. I prodded him a little while ago. He comes up with excuses but no clear commitments. He's hoping to finish this year. But I've heard that kind of talk before. All that apparently remains to be done is the translation of my two essays, which he has taken on himself and that you were going to correct. He won't be through with them in the very near future. You're absolutely right to want the whole thing in one piece and to want to look through it at a time convenient for you. It's all well and good for me to talk about "convenience," but I do realize this task is an imposition on you and will never really be convenient. How much simpler it would be if Schilpp would spend the money to have Dr. Manheim, whose work you have found so good before, do the translation. But Schilpp does not want to put any money into this project.

You'll be up to your ears in work by now, as I know from my own experience. But if you should have a spare moment, make use of it to write a line or two.

With all best wishes

Your Karl Jaspers

164   Hannah Arendt to Karl Jaspers

February 28, 1955

Lieber Verehrtester—

As you can see, I went right to the Olschkis'—an oasis in the desert. You were much in our thoughts.

Your Hannah[1]

165   Hannah Arendt to Gertrud and Karl Jaspers

Berkeley, March 26, 1955

Dear, dear Friends—

It was so good to have both your letters[1] right at the start here when I was still feeling very much at the ends of the earth. I've waited a bit to reply because I first wanted to get an idea of how things really are here. (The questionnaire I sent apparently isn't used after all. It has suddenly and mysteriously disappeared from our department, where it lay around in great piles. That, of course, in no way changes the significance of it.)

Before I report on things here: No sooner had I decided to go to Europe, as I wrote you, than I received an invitation from the Congress for Cultural Freedom to a meeting in Milan in September[2]—all expenses paid! You see: truly more good luck than good management. I can't leave New York before September 6 and have to be in Milan on the 12th. It's really up to you whether I visit you first thing (how sad that the plans for Cannes probably won't materialize, and how sad for Frau Waltz,[3] whom I remember so fondly), or in November. If you get your leave, and I assume there isn't much question about that, then perhaps November would be better. There's no hurry on this, and you can take your time deciding. If I don't come to you first, I would fly directly to Italy and spend a few days in Venice, which I don't know at all. And I'd also very much like to have an introduction to the philosophy professor in Athens,[4] because I don't know a soul there. But that doesn't have to be!

I got to know Olschki right away after I wrote to him at your suggestion. He really is a scholar and has written a few very good things. And I'll see him again. But the postcard I wrote there wasn't altogether honest. I wrote what he, and she in particular, so obviously wanted me to write.

That happens to me sometimes. And then, it is also somehow true that this is a beautiful desert, of all deserts the most beautiful. The only problem is that the Olschkis can't be an oasis for me anymore. I can't return to that world of pure culture, which isn't even very pure. Frau Olschki said—after the card had been written!—that she felt as if she were in an "African village" here, and I was really outraged by that. I sent Bukofzer the same kind of note as to Olschki but got no reply. I did meet him then at Olschki's. You're right about him. More on him perhaps when we can talk together. But Olschki is a real scholar, and I do respect him.

On the subject of oases: the first real oasis I found appeared in the form of a longshoreman from San Francisco who had read my book and was in the process of reading everything of yours that is available in English. He writes himself—and publishes, too—in the manner of the French moralists. He wanted to know everything about you, and I mean everything, and we were friends right off. He showed me San Francisco the way a king shows his kingdom to an honored guest. He works only three or four days a week. That's all he needs. With the rest of his time he reads, thinks, writes, goes for walks. His name is Eric Hoffer,[5] of German background but born here and without any knowledge of German. I'm telling you about him because his kind of person is simply the best thing this country has to offer. And don't forget that I met him through a colleague, and he has lots of friends at the university. You couldn't take him to Olschki's house, and that speaks against Olschki.

The second oasis is my little neighbor[6] here in the club, very young, hasn't done her doctorate yet, and her whole room is stuffed full of Plato, Aristotle, Kant, and Hegel. She comes from the West, the child of very poor parents. She's bright and good, and as familiar to me in her makeup as if she came from a neighboring village.

My lectures and seminars are actually going very well. The students are satisfied, at any rate, and I'm drawing a lot of them from other departments, particularly from history. But philosophers, too, and even theoretical physicists. Unfortunately, the faculty in our department is particularly bad. It's not worth wasting any words about my colleagues, with the exception of one young instructor. And the students are from the same mold. I'm having much more fun with my beginners' seminar than with the advanced one. The beginners are still willing to take some chances and are unspoiled and intelligent. Unfortunately, though, all my classes are too full. For one reason or another. And I'm a little overworked already, which won't do me any harm. I'm having the beginners' seminar read your *Geistige Situation der Zeit* and *Ursprung und Ziel der Geschichte*. The students enjoy the reading a lot once they've got over their initial shock and realize that they can understand it perfectly well if they just exert themselves a little. But there are 80 students in this beginning seminar, and I sometimes feel like a circus director in the ring. The subject in the advanced seminar is limited to totalitarianism. In that seminar, by the way, there are several German students who are here on scholarship, one of whom seems to be quite good. And then there's the usual quota of Jews, some of German, some of American background. Altogether there are only 25 students (that's a lot for an advanced seminar here) and about 20 auditors, about whom I don't have to trouble myself.

I don't know Golo Mann's book. I want to read it very much, but not now. I don't have the peace of mind in this madhouse. One thing is very clear to me: in the long run I couldn't tolerate teaching for the simple reason that it is almost unbearable for me to function in a public world all the time, one in which I am "somebody" and served up as on a platter. I just can't handle it. Every Sunday I call Heinrich, and we chat away across the whole continent as if we were in the same room. Nice.

All my warmest regards,
Your
Hannah

166 *Karl Jaspers to Hannah Arendt*

Basel, April 8, 1955

Dear Hannah!

My wife and I were delighted with your letter. What wonderful descriptions of American possibilities your sketches of the longshoreman and the girl "as if from a neighboring village." How right you are to be outraged over the expression "African village." When I read a letter of yours, I'm encouraged by the fact that you are able to live the way you do—speaking with your husband every week across a continent and acting as a professor, as if one could live in eternal youth, without being pressed into a mold, seeing things always with the freshness of first perceptions!

What you wrote about Olschki put my mind at rest. The card did in fact surprise me a bit. Your judgment of them both is surely correct. People like us can't but respect scholarly accomplishments that are of such use to us ourselves. But scholarship is truly no oasis.

You should decide when you would prefer to visit us. Perhaps it would be better after the conference in Milan, because there is still some possibility that we may go to Cannes after all. I don't really think we will. Stouthearted Lotte hopes for it and wants it. But I'm afraid that she could be deceiving herself somewhat about the difficulties of the coming months. A heart attack like that is a serious matter, and only if she is present and constantly in charge of everything, not only of the taxes and the household, but also of his assistants, nurses, and the practice itself, is his mind at ease. Things just can't run without her, unless there is a radical and unexpected improvement in his condition. She was here a few days ago. I admired her again for her strength of heart and her rationality in making provisions ahead for the care of all five children and her own parents and for the calm faith with which she is facing these dreadful irruptions into her life, which has up to now been so happy.

Unofficially, I've been granted full leave for next winter. I still have to keep it a secret, though, because the application is still formally under consideration, and that will take quite a long time. I'm very pleased.

I read in *Der Monat* that Lasky was at the Leipzig fair. He saw your great work prominently displayed in the book exhibit. He was quite surprised, because undesirable books, though on display, were tucked away in an obscure corner. The exhibitor clearly had not grasped the thrust of your book, which is now being grandly exhibited and extolled in the East, probably with no practical consequences, because every sale is controlled by the state.

For today, only this hasty letter, warmest greetings, and our best wishes to you and your husband

Your
Karl Jaspers

167 Hannah Arendt to Karl Jaspers

July 1, 1955

Lieber Verehrtester—

After I wrote you last the circus began in earnest. I've been home for a week now and glad of it. It was all very nice and somehow a lot of fun as well. But I don't ever want to go through that again! Curiously enough, the thing about it I really can't tolerate is, of all things, the political aspect—being in the public eye every day. But otherwise it went very well and has helped me a lot with things I want to do in the coming years. I had two unusually gifted students: one a man from Texas, son of the Salvation Army general there. The other really did come from Mrs. Olschki's African village. He is from Kenya and from one of the tribes that started the Mau Mau movement.[1] I'll tell you about him when we can talk. The most perfect proof of the existence of Herder's "new examples of the human race."[2] —I didn't form any other friendships beyond the "girl from the neighboring village" (my neighbor in the faculty club) and the longshoreman.

I started organizing my trip here right away. If everything works out and early November is still all right with you, I'll fly directly from here to Milan on September 1 and from there to Venice, where I've never been before. The way I'm planning now, I'd be in Basel on

260

November 4 and will fly from there to Frankfurt and Cologne via Zurich. Is that all right with you? What are your travel plans?

Thank you very much for the report by Starliner,[3] the first part of which I found terribly distressing because of what it had to say about Königsberg. The second part was wonderfully suited for my seminar. I had several students who could read German.

Somewhere along the line I read—and fully agreed with—your lecture on Schelling,[4] which was reprinted in *Merkur*, if I'm not mistaken. But it was too short. You should make a short book out of it, or is it excerpted from your world history of philosophy?

There's something else I want to tell you, because I think it will please you. Frau Lemke, Bultmann's daughter in America, whom I don't know, wrote to me suddenly because she had read your essay on totalitarianism[5] on those continents where people are fighting against it and thought that the essay simply had to be published here. At first I didn't know what she was talking about, then wrote her that it had already appeared. I got quite a kick out of it all.

I've seen this vast and not yet completely settled continent, the deserts and the Grand Canyon, and many places in the West that look like something out of Chinese landscape painting. There's no doubt that the geographical dividing line between Europe and Asia runs somewhere through this continent. I see New York altogether differently now, like a ship clinging to the continent or anchored here. You haven't really left the European landscape until you've put the Rocky Mountains behind you.

I found Heinrich in fine fettle. We'll stay here for July, although it's already very hot. In August we'll go to Palenville again.

I'm not much in the mood for writing anymore. Everything has suddenly become so close. As I write this, I can see everything so clearly: your wife in the rooms downstairs and you upstairs on your sofa. I feel as if I could count the steps on the stairs.

My warmest regards to you both.

Your—
Hannah

Basel, July 15, 1955

Dear Hannah!

I've left my wife's letter[1] lying here for days now, and yet I was and am so much looking forward to your visit. It would be nice if you arranged your schedule in such a way that you could work upstairs at our house for a while and we could continue our "discussions" in peace in the spare hours in between. Ever since your departure from St. Moritz and our talks there and since my critical remarks on your insightful Rahel book, and now—this I mention only parenthetically—given an apparent shift in the political situation of the world, I realize that we perhaps still have a great deal to say to each other. It seems to me as if a conflict has emerged that, in view of the basis of reliable solidarity we share, could be even more significant and stimulating. I haven't grasped its nature yet, and perhaps I am mistaken about it. We'll need some leisurely hours to explore this matter. We can't force it. In any case, our next meeting will be a rare pleasure for me. The only other conversations I have that affect me profoundly are with my wife. Other talk with well-meaning people may not be sheer idle talk, but it remains very much on the surface. These people aren't fully present themselves, and then I'm not either. Or there are a few irreplaceably valuable people who visit us and whom I love very much—but no discussion takes place. —Well, I don't want to get ahead of myself here. Perhaps I'm too old to do battle with you anymore. If so, then we'll enjoy our time together some other way. You bring with you shared memories of a lost past. You bring the wide world as it is today. You hear from us two old people how we are spending our quiet years and how we have not forgotten the past, and above all you bring something I cannot express in words and which cannot be expressed in words: a human reality that you, together with your husband, have built for yourselves in this world and in spite of this world.

Warmest greetings to you both
Your
Karl Jaspers

Until August 20:   Palenville, N.Y., August 6, 1955
Until August 31: New York
I'll send addresses for the trip later.
Lieber Verehrtester—

What a wonderful letter of welcome. Basel will once again be my
home in Europe, as it always is; and this time, when I plan to be
traveling about so much, this center will be even more important than
before. Your good letter arrived in the midst of just such thoughts.
Thank you! And it was not answered promptly because of the heat.
That will sound strange to you, because you simply don't know what
heat is. I didn't either until this summer, which is surpassing everything
we've experienced before. Today was tolerable in the morning at least;
now it's 90 degrees again, as usual. A week ago we fled the city, where
we had been able to survive in our one air-conditioned room, Heinrich's study. But that meant living, working, and sleeping in one room.
We have it better here in our bungalow. It's still hot, but not intolerably
so.

It's still not entirely clear when I will come, that is, it's possible
that I'll come a few days earlier. Does that make any difference to
you? I think I'll fly directly from Istanbul to Zurich and not via Rome
again, which I will have seen on the trip out. How long I'll stay . . .
how long do you want me?

You write about our "conflict on a basis of reliable solidarity"—it
seems to me both have always been there. That's also a bit a matter
of temperament, more than you are probably ready to admit. The basis
remains always the same, and then we both enjoy doing battle, though
that is changing. But, please, don't take me too much to task about
"Rahel." I'll give you other opportunities enough for that. "Rahel"
is so far back in the past, and I never read it again after I finished it.
That's about twenty years ago now. I'm so glad that it's all right with
you if we do argue a bit again. And then, I'm so much looking forward
to your Schelling book![1] —I'll save the changes in the world situation
for when we can talk. The shift that took place within a few weeks at
the beginning of the year here in America is one of the most interesting
and strangest phenomena I know under the heading "public opinion."
Only Tocqueville had the slightest inkling of such a story. And changes
like this, which occur overnight, spread immediately throughout the
entire continent. Heinrich and I related exactly the same stories to
each other from our respective institutions, separated by the whole

continent. The atmosphere in the country is again what it was before, hardly changed at all; extremely pleasant and reasonable. Even Eisenhower, who, as an individual, is truly/just a plain idiot,/is as rational as anyone could hope for. The political tradition of the country has come through again; and we—thanks and jubilation be to God—were wrong.

Heinrich sends you his best. He left yesterday to spend two days at Bard, which is only a few miles away from here, for some stupid conference with the president and a few faculty members. He's in fine form and holding up well under the constant excessive workload of teaching at two institutions. —I'm working at a melancholy task. Before I leave, I have to take care of the editing and introduction for two essay volumes left after Broch's death. A final act of friendship. I had a similar task to do some months ago, writing a memorial article for Gurian.[2] I don't think I sent it to you. Would you be interested in it? It's simply a portrait, and as such successful. But only for people who knew him.

Yes, I would like to bring the wide world to you this time. I've begun so late, really only in recent years, to truly love the world that I shall be able to do that now. Out of gratitude, I want to call my book on political theories "Amor Mundi."[3] I want to write the chapters on work this winter, as a lecture series for Chicago University, which has invited me there in April.

All this can wait. What can't wait is this: May I send my winter coat to your address in Basel? (You can't and shouldn't decide this, of course. The question is meant for your wife, to whom I send my warmest thanks for her good letter.) You don't have to do anything with it except hang it in a closet. I won't need it before November, because I'll be in warm countries.

I forgot: It would be nice if I could do some work at your house at odd hours. I may have to give a few talks in Germany, and for that purpose I want to translate into German the talk I've prepared in English for Milan.[4] It's about totalitarian, tyrannical, and authoritarian forms of government.

My warmest wishes to you both, as always
Hannah

Basel, August 13, 1955

Dear Hannah!

To your good letter, only a brief and hasty reply on practical matters:

You are, of course, welcome a few days before Nov. 4. We would ask, though, that as soon as you are sure of your plans, you write and let us know the day and approximate time of your arrival.

We would both love to have you here as long as you want to stay, weeks on end. We are not expecting any other visitors in November. You decide what is convenient for you; or, if you prefer, leave the question open and decide here as your inclinations dictate.

I would very much like to read your memorial essay about Gurian.

Send your winter coat to our address. However, we won't be here from August 21 to September 4. The house will be closed; our Erna will be with her parents. Perhaps you could send it so that the package will arrive *after* September 4. With a declaration of the contents because the customs people are so fussy here (the package will, however, be brought to the house, so it won't cause us the least inconvenience).

Don't forget that you have 4,000.–fr. waiting for you here.

I like your "Amor Mundi." A nice title.

Totalitarian, tyrannical, authoritarian—given your way of thinking, those terms promise some important insights. I look forward to hearing more.

Warmest greetings to you both
Your Karl Jaspers

Ravenna, September 8, 1955

Just a word of greeting and thanks for your letter. I've been gadding about for a week now. —Until yesterday in *Venice*!, where I'll return again tomorrow. I've become completely inarticulate from all this gawking. And: no typewriter. [. . .]

How was your vacation? And where were you?

Regards—
Hannah

Basel, September 11, 1955

Dear Hannah!

Thank you for your card from Ravenna. Fresh from Berkeley and New York and now immersed in Byzantine piety! But in the meantime the conference has begun. Your talk doesn't come until the end, so you have to live with the suspense. I'm curious to hear about it all.

Now something different. I hope that Europäische Verlagsanstalt sent you my "foreword."[1] The publisher wrote me that you had given him "a free hand." I told him I had no objections to that, but I insisted that you be shown the text, not so that you could agree (you can't do that when you're being praised) but so that you could strike out, for whatever reasons, sentences or paragraphs, or simply turn down the whole thing. Then, on the title page, I struck out "With a foreword by Karl Jaspers." *If* they want to print a foreword in *Germany* for advertising purposes, then it should at least be done discreetly in the work itself. The title page of so superb a book should remain uncluttered. —From my point of view, I'm very happy to associate myself publicly with you—but it could have been done in a different way. What all this adds up to is simply this: Please drop the whole thing or parts of it, as you see fit. I won't be angry at anything you do, because all I want to do in this case is serve you.

I read in your book again with great pleasure. It should have appeared in German four years ago, at the same time the English edition was published. Now some of your things have reached literary circles here, though they are far from being generally known. The crucial points in your work are not at all easy to understand, because everything reads so well that the reader imagines that he's grasped the main point, the *one* major and basic idea, which, however, cannot be formulated briefly and at the same time understandably.

Wishing you enjoyable days for the rest of your trip!

From my
wife warmest greetings.
Your Karl Jaspers

Milan, September 13, 1955

Lieber Verehrtester—

I'm delighted that you are writing a foreword. I don't want to see it in advance. I told the publisher, who put the question to me only in general terms, that I would give him a free hand because there wasn't much else I could do but that I was basically against the idea of a foreword. There was no mention of you, and the thought never occurred to me at all. Now it's turned out wonderfully, and this is just right, because it was you who really made a return to Germany possible for me. Also because of the solidarity that unites us even in those things on which we don't agree. And because of the past in Heidelberg, which started me on my way. Thank you.

I'll tell you about the conference when I see you. We're living in a luxury here that I find scandalous. So far the conference has been tedious unto death. I played hooky today. Tomorrow I give my paper. I hope I'll still be able to stir myself up a bit. Without that, things don't go well. I'm afraid that my contempt for almost everyone here is all too plainly written on my face. Consequently, I'm overly friendly.

Met Milosz yesterday; he is a bright spot. And some of the Americans whom you don't know, like Dwight Macdonald, who in his total naïveté is smarter than all the literati put together. Lasky also better than some others. The French are the most degenerate.

In Venice I stayed with an American friend [Mary McCarthy] who has an apartment there for a few months. That was indescribably, magically lovely. But in just about every other way, too, I'm enjoying myself shamelessly.

I'll send you my talk here by separate post. Thursday I'll go to Genoa, where Blumenfeld is making a stop on his way to Badenweiler.

I'm enclosing a little something[1] for your wife.

Always,
Your Hannah

P.S. Apropos of Athens: You were going to give me an introduction to a former student[2] there. Do you still want to? Or not?

Basel, September 16, 1955

Dear Hannah—

My wife usually finds better formulations for putting friends in touch with each other, and she has written what seems to me an appropriate letter to the Theodorakopouloses. I will add to it, as I am doing here with you, only a few lines. Theodorakopoulos is a very simple, thoroughly decent man, philosophically very diligent. He takes philosophy seriously. As far as I can see, his accomplishments are not great, but that is not what ultimately matters. As a professor in Athens, he will, I think, be doing an admirable job pedagogically. I'm glad that you will be meeting these people, and I'll be curious to hear what you have to report about the meeting.

Warmest greetings
Your
Karl Jaspers

Rome, September 20, 1955

Dear Friends—

Thank you for the introduction! Rome is overpowering. The grandeur of the historical world, revealed in its many strata.

Blumenfelds: I didn't know how very much changed he is. If I had, I would not have sent him to you. But for me he remains unalterable. —They don't know that you will be in Badenweiler, too. And it's probably best if I don't tell them. You will certainly be able to arrange things there so you will remain undisturbed.

Milan conference:[1] boring. Everybody[2] talked in clichés. All about that when I see you. I liked Silone.

I move on again day after tomorrow. I'm writing with a ballpoint pen—without a typewriter I can't express myself anymore.

From Thursday on: Athens, Hotel Acropolis. I'll probably gad about in Greece until October 12.

All my best—.

Your Hannah

The publisher wrote about your "wonderful introduction."[3] But I'll wait for the finished book before I read it!

Athens, October 7, 1955

Lieber Verehrtester—

Just a line to let you know that I'm not lost for good. The enclosed[1] is unfortunately not a good reproduction. A good one is almost impossible to find. The actual grave stela is incredibly beautiful and impressive: the dead youth looking off into the distance, the little slave and little dog mourning at his feet; and then the old man—*not* mourning but his whole form a single question incarnate!

Everything here means more to me than I ever knew. I can't, I simply can't tear myself away. I'm going to cut the Israel visit short and stay here another week. I came back from the Peloponnese yesterday, and tomorrow I'll go to Delos and the world of the Greek islands, which call and lure one from all sides. Just think of it: the sea *shaped by land*. On the face of it, a contradiction in terms but here a reality. Whenever I can, I go swimming. Swimming always gives me a feeling of being at home.

I saw Theodorakopoulos before I went to the Peloponnese. He and his beautiful, charming wife invited me on a trip to Daphne. Very kind and nice. Thank you very much!

By the way: My letter from Milan was written in haste. But you must have understood: What I wrote about Blumenfeld was "objective." For me, he is unchanged!

Until soon. How nice that I can say that already.

All my best to you and your wife

Your
Hannah

Basel, October 12, 1955

Dear Hannah!

Thank you for both of your letters, from Milan and from Athens, and the wonderful monument. You are finding what you always knew more beautiful than you had ever imagined it to be. When we read your few lines, we are inspired.

Your coat has arrived. Your room awaits you.

We were in Badenweiler for two weeks. Gertrud, horrified here at meeting people there that she knew (Blumenfelds), rushed out once we were there to search for them: "We can't slight that worthy man —he might find out that we were here . . ." I looked at the guest list and found his name and his hotel. And then Gertrud went there and arranged meetings. They visited with us twice. I think it was very pleasant. Of course I understood your view: "objectively" changed by the illness. I wrote you in this vein after he was with us in Basel. His condition has *not* worsened since then. His bright eye, some gestures, his formulations, all make quite clear what he once was. And one can still take him completely seriously, even if difficulties of organic origin sometimes make him appear a bit helpless. He was visibly pleased about your dedication, about which you had told him. Germany: Freiburg and the Black Forest were of concern to him. He had vivid memories of his youth. Perhaps he does not see Germany's present situation and its people correctly. He is simply benevolent; he takes decency for granted, and all these other things hardly seem to touch him.

I came down with a cold on the second day, got bronchitis, and therefore couldn't go to visit Blumenfeld. Now I'm getting better, but I'm still not working—you can probably see from my handwriting how tired I still am. It's getting better every day. By the time you come, I'll be healthy again.

Warmest greetings and until soon
Your Karl Jaspers

178 *Karl Jaspers to Heinrich Blücher*

Basel, November 13, 1955

Dear Mr. Blücher!

Hannah left yesterday. These were wonderful days: an extraordinary three-way meeting of minds, a continuation and intensification of previous meetings. As on earlier occasions, you were present this time, too. Not that Hannah spoke of you—she apparently can't do that. But in response to our questions she communicated so much concrete information about your life and work in New York and Bard that I have a picture of it. And through and beyond that picture I always feel I can sense in you—despite all the differences in the courses our lives have taken and in our talents (I have a wretched memory, for instance, you, a fantastic one)—a remarkably kindred spirit in your allegiance to independent and, despite their radicality, primarily conservative minds; in your predilection for the real substance of the eighteenth-century Enlightenment; in your method of using great personalities to show young people what really matters. I think that you will yet come to Europe with Hannah. The reasons why you have not done it so far are only half valid. When your sabbatical year comes up, they will have no force at all. Berlin will not, of course, be free or accessible to you (except for West Berlin).

Germany will be no pleasure for you. But it seems to me that you can still meet excellent individuals there and, also, that Europe has more to offer than Germany. It would be wonderful for us if you would decide to come sometime. I would very much like to meet you in person and not just in the way I have met you so far, extremely gratifying as that has been. Then, too, I would like to ascertain, with you, what the important thing is to us in the fact that we are German, which is our heritage and to which we somehow ultimately belong.

Hannah was, as always, lively, high-spirited, intense in discussion, helpful. She enlivened our home. Even Erna, our good maid, was happy. She still beams whenever she speaks about "Frau Doktor."

I hope Hannah's book will become a major event in Germany. If it does not, then that is Germany's fault.

All my best regards to you, and warmest greetings from my wife as well

Your Karl Jaspers

179 *Hannah Arendt to Gertrud and Karl Jaspers*

New York, December 29, 1955

Dear, dear Friends—

I'm afraid this New Year's greeting is going to arrive too late, but my first days here were more unsettled than I expected them to be. Holiday time along with all the people one can't very well put off is about as inappropriate for a homecoming as one can imagine. So I haven't got around to anything, and I've even fudged writing this letter.

We talk about you so much, and I have put my pictures of both of you on my desk now because my visit with you is still so present and vivid. I had a lot to do with publishing matters in London, and I accidentally agreed to give the little book[1] for Piper, which still hasn't been finally agreed to yet, to an English house that has been asking me for something for a long time. My publisher here is content, too.

Because I haven't published anything more for such a long time, it apparently doesn't matter to him whether he has to translate this text or not.

Then there's Schilpp. The stuff should have been waiting for me here, but it hasn't come. I hope it'll arrive right after the holidays. — It came as quite a surprise to me that my little student in Berkeley just turned up on your doorstep like that,[2] particularly because she is really a very shy child, but you can never know with these Americans. They are so accustomed simply to going anywhere they please. I hope it wasn't too much of an imposition on you. I'm greatly relieved, and pleased too, that you liked her. She'll surely follow your advice. She's really quite all right. I was also pleased that you had a presence straight from the American Far West in your house. That will make Berkeley retrospectively more familiar for you. And in this way, the circle of my acquaintances, which is always rather dangerously far-flung, draws closer together.

We're going to see *Macbeth* tonight. There's a small group of actors here who play Shakespeare in a small theater more beautifully than I have ever seen him played anywhere else in the world. With great understanding for the purely poetical and lyrical elements, too. All in all I'm having it very good in this regard. A record player and some wonderful records were waiting for me here, and I'm playing a lot of them. It has added another whole dimension to my life, because ultimately the power of music is the greatest there is. I hadn't wanted to have a record player yet, for one thing because it is always much too great a temptation for me, and I thought it would be an ideal gift for my fiftieth birthday. But Heinrich felt I was being too pedantic and should finally have it and right away at that. So there it was, and I'm treating this most wonderful of technological miracles with great tenderness and care.

I've thought a lot about your peaceful Christmas. If my time calculations don't deceive me, you're both sitting upstairs right now, in your study, and reading together. I think a lot about that wordless quiet, in which you are both so much in tune with each other when you're together in the evening, a quiet that was palpable when one came into the room and that is always there as a background.

I am with you in all my wishes and thoughts. Have a good and healthy and productive year!

Your
Hannah

Basel, January 31, 1956

Dear Hannah!

Your visit was so wonderful and enlivening, so natural and open, so affirming, that I felt the impulse to write you a "special" letter right away. I postponed it from one day to the next, waiting for the opportune moment, but then I became more deeply involved in my work, first some more on Plato, then on Augustine, and now on Kant. Either I was working, or I was very tired. But now I mustn't wait any longer and, minus the opportune moment, I'm finally writing to thank you.

First, let me thank you for the gifts you left behind for us to discover: it was good of you to shower me with gifts from the sea, for I love the sea more than anything, more than landscapes. Did you know that, and that these items will be a benevolent reminder of their place of origin?

And then your Byzantines: I enjoy looking at them, with their, to me, alien grandeur, their sanctification of power, their piety in which a claw seems to be hidden (as in Augustine). What you are telling me with this book[1] is that we have to know about everything—and, most important, if I know you as well as I think I do: we have to know that what is beautiful is beautiful, and you are surely not mistaken about that.

And then your book, much of which I read again to lift my spirits, even though I am already familiar with it. I'm more convinced than ever that this book, convincingly developed out of your clarity of vision, represents a major breakthrough for our political world, the first of its kind amid all the current talk about totalitarianism. Every politician active today ought to read it and understand it. It's like the diagnosis and symptomatology of a fungal disease that spreads and eats up everything in its path. The carriers of the disease are intelligent the way fungi are because they do instinctively what is required of them; that they are capable of what is required is also a consequence of their basic nihilism, which overcomes all human resistance. They therefore have the talent of being able to obey the law of this disease without comprehending it as a whole. The result is the self-destruction of man and of these fungi themselves, which die when the body they have taken possession of dies. Now you have come along with this book in which you proceed, with admirable clarity, to elicit this insight from your horror; and anyone who wants to understand you will now have to make that insight, with its ramifications, its multiple facets, and its consequences, the object of thorough study. Your brilliant, dramatic presentation, your vivid observations, seem to have made it easy for the reader (Lotte [Waltz], who, I think, understands the book properly, read this marvelous book in a short time and "like a novel"), but that quality of the book can lead one to deceive oneself.

Then, too, as with significant insights, the reader who has these intellectual accomplishments before him can think (as I am thinking now with Kant) that the author was cleverer than he realized himself. It's as if the author retained an instinctive quality which, by means not of intellectual machinery but of a constant attentiveness turned afresh on the most diverse objects, brings to light the hidden system underlying the whole, without really knowing what that whole is himself. This is not much different from the way the instinctive vision of a clinician discovers step by step all the elements of a new disease, without quite knowing how. If another author should follow you, one who will put what you have grasped into a logical structure that is simple and easy to teach, one will still always have to go back to the source in you to participate in that power that enables others to see.

But I feel an even greater debt of thanks when I think of what I find difficult to express. Through you I was reassured of that community of reason that no one can describe. Will this reason be capable, like hormones, of subduing that fungal disease? The similes cease to apply when one is in touch with the things of which Plato, Kant, Spinoza, and Lessing make us aware. There, there are no laws we can point to except for rudimentary ones that cannot guide us to the most profound levels, no descriptions except ones of individual personalities. There, there are no institutions or organizations by means of which one can acquire power. The covenant is made without a contract. But where this something exists, it is so binding that all our hopes on earth rest on it. No prescriptions can help against the fungal disease or any other disaster, however many remedies we may rightly turn to. But what is crucial is this positive force, that cannot be expressed in words as a truth, but that buoys up our trust when our reason sees everything in a negative, pessimistic light and beyond salvation in the rising tide of calamity and ruin. The beauty of the natural world is a sign we should not value too lightly. It will remain, even if humanity destroys itself—but for whom will it be there? It is only of some aesthetic comfort. But that human beings can be united in reason and, through reason, in that love which generates the power to resist all ruin—that very fact sets limits on reason, which sees only hopelessness. You took my words about "being wholly in the present" as your epigraph.[2] You know how pleased I am about that. Perhaps I should add to it that we must never give up hope. The quote advises us to seize every possible opportunity; the addition to it, not to give up action where action appears to be meaningful. You have shown by your practice in your life that activity, reconstruction, reversal can still be carried out as long as destruction is not total. And if in a hundred years no more human beings are alive, or only a few that are without continuity with us, which is probable but by no means certain, then, if the fungal disease has made possible this last disaster of physical self-destruction after political self-destruction, this something will still have retained its meaning to the very end, this something to which these—for us— few people, who are perhaps many in real numbers but who remain silent, belong and who meet and recognize each other in the present world.

Anyone who philosophizes can speak, here on this border, only of time and space as outward phenomena and of whatever follows from that insight (as hinted in Plato, oddly wonderful and distorted in Augustine, bright and clear in Kant, and perhaps in a few Indian philosophers).

To do our part as long as we live, as you have demonstrated in your life, and to speak when we can, as you do—that has no meaning that can be defined in terms of practical results. I am picturing now, in a happy mood, how you and Heinrich Blücher are thinking and working over there—and Gertrud and I are happier in our work because of a few unsentimental people scattered here and there, cheerful in their seriousness, whom we have come to know and among whom you have become so irreplaceable for us. We do not form a circle, do not accept and reject or say who belongs or does not belong to it, but we some- times lose heart because the circle is small.

This letter has taken on something of that tone I had in mind some weeks ago, but I'm unable to recapture it wholly.

I still have to thank you for your two letters[3] and for sending me the passages and their interpretation. I have written to Oakeshott[4] but haven't received an answer yet.

It was entirely in order that you gave your Piper book to a publisher in England for translation, because you retained all the translation rights in your contract.

I haven't heard anything from Schilpp either. I did hear from Stuttgart, however, that the German edition of the volume should be set in the spring and appear in the fall.

Now I have another favor to ask of you. Read the enclosed letter from Dr. Knauss[5] and return it to me at your convenience. If you see any prospects for him anywhere, please let me know. Because you don't know him personally, you can hardly vouch for him directly. I think it is worthwhile to help him if possible. He took his doctorate with me in Basel, summa cum laude,[6] and is a German from a simple background. If I remember correctly, I told you at some point that he had no luck in Germany with the Forschungsgemeinschaft (research society) or with Gadamer[7] (habilitation), presumably because he is my "student"—but he is completely independent.

Gertrud and I wish you both success in many more endeavors— and for ourselves that perhaps one more reunion will be possible.

Warmest greetings
Your Karl Jaspers

181   *Heinrich Blücher to Karl Jaspers*

New York, February 14, 1956

Dear Mr. Jaspers,

Please excuse me that I am replying so late to your good letter. It made Hannah's visit with you both so vivid that I felt I had been there myself, and it strengthened my wish to be part of the next gathering of this kind. My vacation time did not go as well as I had hoped it would. Some protracted dental work and administrative chores that had been heaped upon me kept me from writing. And then I gave myself up to reading your *Schelling*.

Thank you for this book and for the handsome edition of Goethe's letters.[1] It is good to read a bit in his letters at the same time that one is looking at Kant in the clear light in which you place him in your *Schelling*. Erich Frank's essays[2] are particularly welcome, too, because they can be of great help to me in my work with our students.

I've sent off as a birthday gift to you a book with beautiful reproductions of the Buddhist frescoes in the Ajanta caves.[3] Just as the Chinese Buddhist reliefs of the Wei period are probably the only ones that can compare to the Parthenon frieze, these frescoes of Indian Buddhism can hold their own next to Michelangelo's. The truth and permanence expressed in their beauty express my birthday wishes for you, and they are also a token of my thanks for your *Schelling*.

How much more freely and easily one breathes when one reads this book. What you are discussing in it emerges in bright, clear form. Distinctions are drawn sharply and precisely. Positions are laid out in a surveyable fashion, and the position you take among them is unambiguous.

Your method of both analysis and exposition is derived completely from your subject itself and through your grasp of its inner structure. The sharp curves of Schelling's circling thought are so vividly presented that this eminently critical book stands as the best real introduction to an understanding of Schelling. This precise cross section through Schelling's constantly shifting perspectives brings into clear focus the persistent basic theme underlying his infinitely splintered thinking. And, finally—and this is like a seal on the value of your method of communication—your book about Schelling becomes a living introduction to the thought of Jaspers.

That was also the case in your *Nietzsche*, but here you achieve it with much greater clarity and immediacy. For that reason alone I wish that both books would finally be available in English so our students could read them. But that would be even more important for a crucial pedagogical reason. Your statement that you had philosophized with Schelling from your youth on[4] is so very evident in your book that it shows every reader how he can philosophize with a great thinker of the past as if that thinker were still alive. I have struggled constantly to convey this very experience to my better students, and now your book will be a great help in doing that, at least for me.

But the historical meaning of this work, as you would call it, or the political meaning of it, as I prefer to call it, is that you have found the point of leverage that has enabled you to roll the stone away from Kant's tomb. By systematically confronting Schelling, Fichte, and Hegel with Kant on crucial questions, you draw a sharp line that separates Kant from his "followers" and frees him from them so that he can again emerge with full clarity. Because German idealism is an important element that was absorbed into the amalgam of almost all modern mass ideologies, its separation from Kant is an important step in dispelling this false picture.

From a purely philosophical perspective, the heart of the matter seems to me to lie in your discussion of "creating self-sufficiency of the spirit." The dialectical, sleight-of-hand transformation of Kant's concept of reason into the concept of spirit, compounded of course by another dialectical somersault into the concept of matter in the period of Romanticism and Naturalism (the two cannot be separated), was the most potent tool for depriving people of reason, which is the only thing that can preserve the integrity of the person, and for transforming them into those pure individuals who, either alone and ghostlike or rolled together into those disgusting clumps of social masses, have staged that aimless, apolitical drifting of society that has since been called history in accord with the Romantic-materialistic concept of history.

That brings me again to your old question to me: How do I perceive myself as a German in these times? My answer has to be: not at all. As Hölderlin once said, the time of kings is past; and now the time of nations is past. The French Revolution began as a transformation of the state (the nation-state) and degenerated into a social revolution in which the state started to founder. But society, in neither its revolution nor its evolution, can guarantee to people what only the state can assure them: the right to hold one's person inviolate. The state and the citizen alone are capable of drawing from the undercurrent of random human events, both societal and individual, that small stream that deserves to be called historical because it irrigates the fields on which human beings can cultivate a civilization. But the random undercurrent of human events is a maelstrom,[5] driven by interests, that sucks us down into the depths. For an interest is not the cunning of reason but the obfuscation of reason.

This societal maelstrom has smashed into European history and flooded it. The deluge rises higher and higher, and it becomes less and less possible to draw off from this headlong rush a fruitful stream of the historical. Genuine political life is even less possible.

Instead, this boiling mass society of ghostlike, isolated individuals suffers from the delusion that history is being made directly here. They want to move directly from the past to the future by leaping over the present, as if a future could ever open up for human beings who have lost sight of eternity.

The Romantic-Naturalistic era exerts fascination because of its overpowering rush of events. With superhuman, demonic efforts on the part of ghostlike individuals and robotlike masses, all manner of forces are turned loose. Things are not simply allowed to take their course; rather, they are actually propelled into that course, and their pace in

278

the maelstrom is deliberately accelerated because the sorcerer's apprentices think this deluge is a historical process that will lead us to salvation. But it is only a frantic, circular, and empty epoch, filled with mere "current events." That is precisely why its course could be predicted better than a genuine historical course of events ever could, one in which reason generates events and so influences the course of history. Goethe, Heine, Tocqueville, Burckhardt, and Nietzsche have proved to be genuine prophets in that respect. Grillparzer stated the case most succinctly: from humanity to nationality to bestiality.[6]

In no instance where the people took control of the nation-state or where it was taken over in their name have national free states emerged, except in the United States and in England. Instead, the nation-state, regardless of the form of government it adopted, has been made into a mere façade for the competing interests of the national society. Romantic intellectual nationalism, solidly embodied in national naturalism, was the means used to disguise the appetites of national society as the metaphysical will of a genuine state, of a true fatherland.

But none of these façade states has ever been able to keep the person of its citizens inviolate. And so, everywhere in Europe, the First World War represented that real betrayal of fatherland of which no one ever speaks. National societies, pretending to be fatherlands, betrayed their sons and delivered them up to the purely industrial slaughter of the war.

That is when many young people in Europe, and I among them, stopped ever wanting to perceive themselves as German, French, etc., again.

Betrayal of the fatherland in this sense occurred in Germany for a second time with inflation and for a third time with Hitler. Under these circumstances, which, except in the United States and England, hold sway everywhere in the world and particularly among the colonial nationalisms, including Israel's, what old, genuine national culture is passed down to us serves only as a nationalistic mask to disguise society's greed. No grass can grow in such soils anymore, and any attempt that is made to discover true national possibilities anywhere is immediately drawn into the swindle of nationalism.

The United States is not a national state but in every sense a federal one. But, like England, it is still enough of a state to guarantee people the fundamental right of holding their persons inviolate. Both countries could be destroyed if their citizens became a social mass and no longer desired that protection. The social deluge swells higher day by day both here and in the English Commonwealth, but one can still fight for genuine political values.

I don't know how the great federative state Atlantis will come into being, but everything national seems to work against such a future. To want to become good Atlantic citizens in anticipation of that goal, just as Nietzsche once wanted us to be good Europeans, is the only goal I think worth striving for.

Nationalism began when every individual, every small spirit, saw in it his chance to embody something higher than himself and to feel himself, as a German or whatever, to be greater than he could feel alone. What now marks the end of nationalism is that it has become impossible to be both a human being and a German, a Frenchman, or a Jew (in Israel, in any case) or whatever. On the contrary, as a representative of this or that nationality, one will be forced sooner or later to become an inhuman monster.

So we are obliged today to try to become human beings only as ourselves—aided by those friends who have been moved to make this same decision and supported not by the "great spirits" of Romanticism but by the great human beings of all our national pasts. And one's own as well as all other "nations" should be judged solely by their constitutional forms, that is, in terms of the question: Where is the human being's person held inviolate? If the metaphysical thinkers of our time would see themselves and their friends in this way, that might well be a preparatory step toward a new, genuine politics that would leave the historical delusion of pure historical occurrence behind and would busy itself with future possibilities for forming governments.

Your *Schelling* would, I think, be an encouragement for "friends" of this kind, and they would all join me in wishing you at your birthday that the bold, original spirit you have made manifest in this book may long be with you.

With these and many personal good wishes, I am

Your
Heinrich Blücher

February 17, 1956

Lieber Verehrtester—

Thank you for writing that letter! It was and is such a wonderful confirmation of what I have always felt, too. It has always been so good to be with you that I shied away from saying both to myself and to you that it had never been the way it was this time. It buoys me up in my work and in the loneliness that my work, though not only my work, imposes on me. You have always given me courage, and now that you're deliberately encouraging me, I'll have to watch out that I don't get overly ambitious and cocky. But that is not what matters the most. The important thing is the immediate communication, and the most important thing about that is the immediacy. What you call the "fungal disease"—a wonderful parallel—is everywhere, and because this disease is caused by fungi, it also attacks otherwise good and sensible people of whom I am often fond. Once one has become allergic to fungi, one sees them in the smallest, apparently most harmless of things; and that makes communication difficult. What is so beneficial in your "bright rooms" is the reliable purity of the air.

Now for some news items that aren't so good. First of all, Schilpp. He has, of course, staged still another Schilpp show. When I got home, there was no manuscript to be seen. Instead, there was a letter from late January with a thousand excuses and saying that the manuscript is only half done. Should he send it anyhow? Etc. and so forth. I had to reply that I hadn't any time before Chicago and that he should send me the whole manuscript in April—by the grace of who knows what gods.

Things are no better with me, and I'm about to stage my own Schilpp show on you. I can't translate the English manuscript of my contribution[1] into German now. I just can't manage it. In part it's a lack of time. After such a long time away it took me longer than expected to make my way back into my work and into writing English. But more important still: I can't afford at the moment to write in German again. So, what should we do? Should I send the manuscript to you or to Kohlhammer and just hope that someone will turn up there who will do a decent job with it? Or should we, can we, wait until the end of April?

We were both very, very taken with the letter from Mr. Knauss. Heinrich is actually very much interested in finding a young philosopher for Bard, but at the moment that is highly unlikely, because there is no money for the post. But he wants to show the letter to various colleagues here in New York and see if there isn't an opening somewhere. It is truly horrendous that this man can't get a job in Germany, where they are absolutely desperate for people to fill their chairs. What I liked so much was his political interest and the sureness of his judgment and the openness reflected in his descriptions. I'll keep the letter here until Heinrich can see the man to whom he wants to show it. Perhaps Mr. Knauss can find something in California. That would be good actually, at least in terms of his further career in the States. On the other hand, perhaps he might well feel a bit lonely and abandoned there.

I've just realized that Heinrich immediately made off to his study with the new edition of *Psychologie der Weltanschauungen*[2] but forgot to thank you for it. I haven't been able to look into it yet and will have to watch out now that it doesn't wander off to Bard. The semester starts again there tomorrow, and I'm a bit sad. We were together all the time during these two long months, and it was very nice. I cooked diligently, a lot of new things that I ate on my travels.

Yes, Byzantium—before I forget it—is alien and yet so immensely impressive. So thoroughly spiritual, though of a spirituality that makes one shudder. I'm curious about how the India book will strike you, whether you both will like it.

My birthday wishes for you both—here people say: Many happy returns. And I wish that for you and myself and us.

I'm reading a lot in Goethe's letters, and I've read a great deal of Max Weber in recent weeks. And with great pleasure. I wanted you to know that! "Agrarverhältnisse im Altertum"[3] is a wonderful piece of work, and "Die protestantische Ethik und der Geist des Kapitalismus"[4] is one of incredible genius. I knew it already, but only now am I able to grasp everything he perceived. There's nothing in the literature after it that begins to approach it.

With gratitude and admiration

Your
Hannah

April 7, 1956

Lieber Verehrtester—

I haven't heard from you in a long time, and so I am, as always, a bit uneasy. I imagine that you received both Heinrich's and my letters around the time of your birthday. I've heard from Kohlhammer in the meantime that they won't need the translation until May 1. And at the same time a friend here who writes well has translated the essay, so everything will work out right after all.

Tomorrow I fly to Chicago for two weeks, to give six lectures over two weeks. I have my manuscript more or less in shape, but it is far from being ready for print. I'm going to call the whole thing *Vita Activa* and will be focusing mainly on labor—work—action in their political implications.

The autobiography and the answers[1] have arrived. Curiosity prompted me to look into the German text, and I've read it with great interest, though not thoroughly and not all of it. Once I'm back from Chicago, I'll really check through it. Our Schilpp has gone off to India on a government mission, so once again there's no hurry.

I wrote to Piper and got a reply, though a rather odd one, from one of his editors, somehow as if I had offered something and with ideas about the little book that in no way agreed with mine. I'll write to Piper directly when I get back and try to remind him of our conversation in Basel.

How are you both? I'm thinking that it is evening now in Basel and you are both sitting together in your study, that is, you are lying down, and you are reading and are together. I have hardly ever been so powerfully struck with what true being together is as I have in the silence and the calm that you share in your room in the evening.

My very best wishes to you both and warmest greetings to Erna.

Your
Hannah

Basel, April 12, 1956

Dear Hannah!

Now you are in Chicago, giving your lectures that I'm sure are very good and having some new experiences. It gives me pleasure to think of you there.

I'll answer Heinrich's very kind letter soon. It is not good that I have delayed so long. Today just a short response for you: First of all, thank you for your introduction to Broch's essays. It must be good because it provides a vivid picture. I read it, fascinated, right through to the end, but with a growing antipathy for its subject. Oddly presumptuous yet really at sea in his "theory"—and casting about for an anchor of "help." An unhappy human being. He pains me. —And I thank you too for your lecture on authority.[1] I was familiar with most of it already. Thinking it over now after reading it again, I'm undecided about it. Your separating the general concept from the specific Roman foundation seems justified at first but then, I think, cannot be carried through. Perhaps there is still much more authority in the world than there seems to you to be. Still, your overall view of the loss of authority and the significance of the "foundation" is important. I wish that we could be in touch with the essence and in such a way that we would immediately feel we were living in it. A holding onto and a growing affirmation of all the authority we can find is to be desired. Your view is almost entirely bleak. Your reference to Heidegger[2] seemed to me symptomatic of something in this mode of thought that I can't follow (although the reference was only parenthetical). I find the fact of Heidegger's distinction between "correctness" and "truth" excellent. But the *way* he arrives at that distinction strikes me as deceptive. He takes as Plato's "idea" the commonly held doctrine of ideas that has been incorrectly attributed to Plato. Plato uses the "idea" in the *Timaeus* for the last time where he relates the "probable myth."[3] He doesn't use it in important dialogues at all. You have to think the second part of his *Parmenides* through to get a sense of what he means. The simile of the cave is a wonderful, fruitful invention of Plato's, a game for thinking to the point where the simile no longer applies. And then you have to have the sixth book[4] in mind too, where Plato develops what then comes to formulation in the simile. Plato as the cause in world history of the disaster of correctness, which takes the place of truth, and truth as "openness," which Plato fails to achieve, all that you find wonderful. In my copy of the essay I wrote in the margin in 1942[5]: "a bit ridiculous."[6] It's too bad that I gave you the later printing a little while ago. I had forgotten the old one with my notes from that time on the margins, so I didn't look for it. We could have had a good talk about this. It can't be done in the brief format of a letter. I see it as a similar error in your reading of Plato when you understand Plato's views on the state and on laws as if they constituted a program and were not tentative derivations from the primal image, the meaning of which can be understood only if one does not forget that the premise of Platonic politics is philosophical education, the kind of education Plato began with Dionysius[7] by teaching him mathematics in order to make the *first* step toward liberation from the senses. We mustn't forget either that the best state, led by philosophers, does not need laws (because laws "always say the same thing," while governmental activity in its true form can never be circumscribed by general principles—I think that's what the *Politikos* says).[8] How one sees Plato is in itself a measure of one's own philosophizing.

The whole Schilpp business *appears* to be coming to its conclusion. He will be back in Chicago before the end of April and wants to start printing right away. Things with Kohlhammer seem such that the American and German editions will appear simultaneously. For Kohlhammer, I read through the two essays[9] again that I had written three years ago, and made a number of small corrections but no substantive changes. We'll just have to put up with the discrepancies between the two editions. The only question is whether you want to change the passages in the new version that are about you (there are a few additions in the "Antwort," a few changes in the autobiography) and about my wife (in the autobiography). If you like I'll send you the pages involved. You'll see immediately what is new, because it is handwritten.

My wife is worried about a "heart attack" I had, and her worry is not *totally* unjustified. But even if one can't know for sure whether one will live or not, it makes sense to live cheerfully and do what one can. It was by no means life-threatening. *Immediate* danger to me is unlikely. The thought of leaving my wife alone in the world is, however, dreadful to me. You will be among those good friends whom memories of the past will draw together around her. That is a thought that gives me pleasure. —But for now I plan to teach, and I'm preparing my lecture course[10] and my seminar.[11] And I'm in good spirits. I've dictated this letter to a new assistant[12] today. Huber has become a professor at the ETH in Zurich.

Warmest greetings to you both.

I plan to write to Heinrich soon. My thanks to you, too, for the wonderful Ajanta pictures you sent for my birthday.

Your Karl Jaspers

Piper's manners in dealing with you leave much to be desired. I think you have responded quite properly. He cannot let an editor carry on discussions that the two of you initiated person to person. But that is not a sign of ill will on his part. He leaves a lot of work to his three editors, whom he has had for some months now, and is away traveling a great deal himself. Then, if something important comes up, he writes excellent letters, as he did recently to Jeanne Hersch. Last fall, in connection with a foreword for selections from Amiel,[13] he shunted me off to one of his editors, too. The results were catastrophic. Afterward, *that* editor was transferred to the "production department."

Vita Activa is a nice title. Labor—Work—Action awakens great expectations.

185 *Hannah Arendt to Karl Jaspers*

April 30, 1956

Lieber Verehrtester—

This is no real answer to your letter. I just want to let you know quickly that I have just finished comparing the two manuscripts with the originals and will send everything on to Schilpp tomorrow morning. Corrections can still be made on the galleys, and I thought it better to dispose of the business with all dispatch. If you like, I'll be glad to make the final corrections for you when the galleys are ready.

I made more corrections than I expected to. What I could not change, of course, was the style in general. It is not very fortunate; it's convoluted and often lacks all understanding of the original. In the latter case I was able to make changes, i.e., correct outright errors. To deal with the other problem would require a complete rewriting—not possible in the short time available, nor (to use a Jaspersian expression) seemly.

It all seems excellent to me. Your replies to your critics are especially good, at least those in philosophy. I'm glad that you let Kaufmann have it.[1] [. . .] I felt a little sorry for Baumgarten,[2] assuming that this is the Baumgarten I know of. There is somebody here by that name on whom the fates have played some dirty tricks.[3]

In substantive matters, I found one sentence that I did not think meant what you wanted to say. You wrote: The statesmen will tell the people of their countries what the people are supposed to think. . . . [4] That is a dangerous formulation, especially in that brief form. But this isn't very important.

I was much relieved to hear that the electrocardiogram didn't reveal any problems.[5] I know that one can never know. But still, it's better to know this much. And nice to know that you will be teaching again.

Rencontres Philosophiques: I got the invitation and wrote back: Maybe! Whereupon they put me on the agenda. The truth of the matter is that I took the invitation to the Rockefeller Foundation and asked whether they would treat me to the trip. It's very, very unlikely. But if they should come through, I would be in Europe for a few weeks in October, and I'll write right away, though I'd come without Heinrich, whose semester will be underway then.

All my best to you both,
Your
Hannah

186 Karl Jaspers to Hannah Arendt

Basel, May 11, 1956

Dear Hannah!

Now you've had all the trouble of checking the translations and making some corrections in them. Thank you very much.

I'm sending you a few pages here that include major changes or additions or deletions in the German edition, especially in my reply to you and in the short autobiographical discussion about my wife. I could send still other things, but none are important enough to bother with.

This in haste for today. I hope to write to Heinrich soon. My lectures and seminar are going well so far.

Warmest greetings to you both
Your Karl Jaspers

Eduard Baumgarten is *not* the person in the USA whom you mean. He is on the faculty in Freiburg, occupied Kant's chair as a philosopher in the Nazi years, and made a radio speech (from Berlin) as late as 1945 urging that Königsberg be defended to the last man. He is a distant relative of Max Weber, has something of the indescribable charm of this family, and is quite a character. Because he is in a certain sense impudent—but in an eternally boyish way—he has to have his wrist slapped every once in a while.

July 1, 1956

Lieber Verehrtester—

I've put off writing to you from day to day because I kept thinking I would have some final word from the Rockefeller Foundation about whether they would pay my way to the Rencontres Philosophiques after all. Unfortunately, it doesn't look as if they will. Early in June, I met with a man I know well there: They would gladly finance a stay of several months in Europe, first of all, because it's hardly worth their while to give me the little pittance I want and, second (and probably more important), because they're obviously a little uneasy, in view of these crazy Congressional investigations, about supporting me for a French event they don't know much about here. (This just between us, please!) My suggestion was to stay five weeks in Europe (I really couldn't stay any longer this year) and to bill the whole thing as a research trip. But that apparently won't work. So it looks like it will be next year until we see each other again. That is sad. But no decision has really been made yet. I still don't have an official refusal, and it doesn't sit well with me to ask.

By the time your galleys for the autobiography and the reply arrived here, I had already sent back to Schilpp the manuscript with my corrections. So I just sent the galley pages on to him, too. I hope that doesn't result in any more Schilpp-ups.

It's difficult to respond in a letter to the questions you raised in yours. But we could quickly come to agreement on Broch, with the one difference that he was a friend of mine. I wrote the introduction with the greatest of distance and what I describe there is really very alien to me. There was simply nobody else who could do it.

We'll have to talk about Plato. In the short space of a letter everything leads to misunderstanding, as did, apparently, what I wrote in my authority essay. It seems to me that in the *Republic* Plato wanted to "apply" his own theory of ideas to politics, even though that theory had very different origins. Heidegger, it seems to me, is particularly off base in using the cave simile to interpret and "criticize" Plato's theory of ideas, but he is right when he says that in the presentation of the cave simile, truth is transformed on the sly into correctness and, consequently, ideas into standards. I have to confess too that I see Plato's political experiment in Syracuse differently. I can't help it: there's still something ridiculous about it even today. (Please don't be *too* angry!) Ever since Socrates' trial, that is, ever since the polis tried the philosopher, there has been a conflict between politics and philosophy that I'm attempting to understand. Plato talked back, and what he had to say was so powerful that we have measured against it everything that has been said on this subject since. What Socrates presumably had to say on the subject has been almost completely forgotten.

No, we'll have to let this be for the moment. I'm in the midst of my *Vita Activa*, and I've had to put completely out of my mind the relationship between philosophy and politics, which is really of greater interest to me. The Chicago lectures were all right; a few very good students and otherwise a normal success. I'm enjoying writing now, but I still don't know if it will come out right.

I got a reasonable letter from Piper, just as you predicted I would. We're still not entirely in agreement about the royalties. He wants to pay only 8%, and I don't want to accept under 10%. Not very important, but I don't see why he should pay less than is the general rule.

How is your heart? Are you taking digitalis? And how are your lectures and your seminar going? I would so much like to be sitting there again, and I'm really angry with the Rockefeller people—unjustifiably—when I think that it would be so easy for them to make that possible with all their money. Things are going well for Heinrich. He is still enjoying teaching immensely, and his students are responding enthusiastically. Now, at last, he's home for the whole week, and we're having a wonderful time together. —We won't leave New York until August. The summer has been very nice so far. Next month I have to go to Harvard for a few days to a seminar of young political scientists who want to consult with me. And so one grows old and "venerably gray," in spite of all one has done to prevent things from reaching this sorry state.

I don't know whether the publisher has sent you the reviews of *Totalitäre Herrschaft*. Very favorable, and always with mention of the introduction. If you haven't received them and are interested, I'll be glad to send them along sometime. Let me know. Sales seem to be satisfactory, too.

Where will you be going for vacation this year? To St. Moritz again? Or Badenweiler? Or perhaps Cannes? And what is Lotte Waltz up to?

All warmest wishes to you both—

Your

Hannah

289

Basel, July 7, 1956

Dear Hannah!

That is a disappointment for me. I have little hope about the Rocke-feller Foundation. Someone told me once that if a well-meaning Amer-ican says, "I'll do what I can," what he leaves unexpressed is: "But it can't be done." Well, perhaps that won't be so after all. But if not, then I think that next year Heinrich will come with you. I'm hoping for support from him in our discussion of the Plato question and of what philosophy is, could be, and ought to be. You write that we have to let this be for now. Although I would like to write one or a few pages right now, I will let it be. Otherwise what would come of it would be that the professor always wants to have the last word. So, in a future conversation we will come back to Plato, his "ridiculous" project in Syracuse, to "correctness" and "standards," and to the cave simile. That could yield a gratifying discussion because it will be phil-osophically a *very* fundamental one. How good that I needn't fear you will "slip away." For me, you are among the solid "guarantees" that all is not lost with humankind. I was glad to read that you have spent such happy weeks with Heinrich. May your lives together continue to be so happy and productive for a long time.

I wish further good progress with the *Vita Activa*. You're absolutely right to reject Piper's offer of 8% instead of 10%. Piper is an excellent publisher. But, like every other, he has to be a businessman, too. I've had the same experience and had repeated gentle "battles" with him. I get a bit annoyed in such cases, especially when the discussion takes a sophistic turn, as it did recently: He calculated for me his complicated operations, with their "general costs" and so forth, whereupon I re-plied: It is impossible for me to check these figures, but it seems to me that everything hinges on the publisher's goodwill, his willingness to run some risk. And the author's royalties hardly constitute the major part of that risk because they are paid only after sales. Piper: Yes, but no publisher pays in advance, because payment *after* sales is figured in from the start. Jaspers: I just received 3,000 marks from de Gruyter in a lump sum for 10,000 copies of the new edition of the little Göschen book. Because the retail price was raised to 2.50 since the time of our contract, de Gruyter voluntarily increased my royalties from 2,000 to 3,000. Piper: Yes, that's a lot, 30 pfennigs per copy. —Well, I'm more than willing to pay you the royalties in advance—the sum has to be paid in any case—. At this point I dropped the whole matter, because

I felt embarrassed about bringing it back to the original issue, which was the royalty percentage. —But none of this matters. Piper is an excellent publisher and a man I like personally. All you have to do is insist in a calm and friendly way on your 10%. —And so I wind up writing not about Plato but about publishing details.

I would very much like to see the reviews. The publisher in Frankfurt did not send them to me.

I've tried digitalis. It has a deleterious effect on my heart. Heart ailments are very varied in their origin and type. But I haven't had another "attack." Lecturing has done me good. My theory is that the calm but intense effort of those 45 minutes has an invigorating and regulating influence on my body and heart if I rest completely afterward until bedtime. And in this way I finished the semester in fine form without having to miss a single class.

We won't be going away for vacation but will stay in Basel. I want to finish the first volume (1,000 printed pages) of "Die grossen Philosophen."—

Warmest greetings to you both from us both

Your Karl Jaspers

189   Hannah Arendt to Karl Jaspers

Palenville, July 23, 1956

Lieber Verehrtester—

As you see, we are already in our accustomed and much beloved summer retreat. The Rockefeller Foundation just called to tell me that everything has finally worked out just fine. I already knew that I had been mistaken: the delay meant nothing; someone had just been sick. Now all that remains to be done is to find an organization that will pay me the money. I didn't involve myself in that at all, but they asked Chicago University, and Chicago was happy to do it and to get a little something out of it themselves as well, namely, that the foundation give them money next year so that I can go to Chicago for two weeks and do a little seminar with the older students. I'm agreeable, and everyone is happy.

I'm very happy and wasn't really expecting it to come through. But that seems to have been a misunderstanding on my part. These mammoth organizations have become so awkward and unmanageable that nothing can be done quickly anymore, even if everyone is in favor of it.

I've just written to France. I'll have to spend the week of October 11–18 there. Before that I'll probably meet my cousin,[1] who is just coming to Europe from India, in Paris. When would my visit be convenient for you? My only real commitment is the Rencontres Philosophiques, and I can make the rest of my plans to suit you. I don't want to stay in Europe any longer than into the first week of November, but even on that point I can of course change my plans to suit you. My cousin will stay in Europe until December. At some time and in some way I'll also go to Germany, but as of now I haven't any commitments there.

So there isn't the slightest possibility of my "slipping away." I'm eagerly looking forward to our conversation, and I'm glad that we don't have to "settle" this issue in writing.

We're enjoying a wonderful summer here—swimming, taking walks, picking raspberries, working. Not too hot and not too cold. And we're getting big ideas; we're looking around a bit and may buy a little house here because we've become so attached to this place.

I'm sorry that you won't be going away. It is always refreshing, even if one's circumstances at home are as pleasant and comfortable as yours are. But I do understand: a change of place is never salutary for one's work. You are no doubt teaching in the winter semester. I would so much like to come to a lecture and a seminar.

We'll be staying here until the end of August. The address: Chestnut Lawn House, Palenville, N.Y.

Until soon! And with warmest wishes
Your
Hannah

190   *Karl Jaspers to Hannah Arendt*

Basel, August 1, 1956

Dear Hannah!

What good news. When a foundation pays for your ticket, the long journey is no problem for you. And we will be delighted to see you again.

I have to begin teaching on Monday, October 22. I teach on Monday, Tuesday, Wednesday, and Friday (seminar). But it is the case more than ever that on days when I have to lecture I can't do any other talking. My subjects for the term—not that I know yet how I will handle them—are introduction to philosophy for my lecture and the philosophy of politics for the seminar. If you came on October 19, we would have two free days. I'm also considering the possibility of taking leave for the first week and beginning on October 29 (however, I'm not so sure whether the strictures of academic "protocol" will really permit that). If I did do that, then I would have nice free days to spend with you. The other possibility is that you come to see us *before* October 11 and meet your cousin later. Then we would be completely undisturbed by my teaching duties, which oblige me to take so much physical repose. Well, you can see what the situation is and can choose. Whatever you decide is fine with me as long as I can be left entirely to myself on teaching days.

You are leading a pleasant life in Palenville. How glad we are to hear that—at a time when most people are complaining. And you are even "putting down roots." There is something important in having a roof over one's head that is one's own property. It would be wonderful if you could find something that would continue to be comfortable for you both, even when you grow older or if illness forces you to alter your circumstances. And then, of course, one can always sell again, though that is not always certain.

I'm working on "Die grossen Philosophen," planning to complete the first volume and send it to the printer in October. It will take some concentrated work for these final stages. Then, scattered in between, I have to do three radio lectures (20 minutes each on the atom bomb[1] and on immortality![2]—and then an hour-long one on "the risks of public life"[3] and an essay on German universities for *Confluence*[4]— quite a lot of work. And then I have to see how I'll manage winter classes, which I should by rights be preparing now. Despite the workload my wife and I are in good spirits. And then, I do enjoy it all. I'm not feeling rushed—though I am letting too many letters go unanswered—and I don't get stirred up about what I don't finish. But the book has top priority for me now. I sometimes think of Heinrich as its ideal reader.

My physical condition is quite acceptable. Gertrud has visitors, Ella and Ernst and Ella's two grandchildren; and, at the moment, Paul Gottschalk as well.[5] Thanks to [Erna] Möhrle and another woman who is helping out with dishwashing and so on, things are going smoothly, and the visit is pure delight. I have my quiet, undisturbed realm in my two rooms. I take great pleasure in the two children (8 and 9 years old) and see again that children are "geniuses" in their growth and reactions. Unfortunately, they don't usually remain geniuses.

Warmest greetings to you both, also from Gertrud

Your Karl Jaspers

I've had a copy of the new edition of my *Philosophie*,[6] with the afterword you're familiar with, sent to you in New York.

Dear H.! Now that I've written, it just occurs to me that you will be fifty on October 14. Will you celebrate with Heinrich and leave for Europe only afterward? Or arrive in Paris punctually on October 11? Can't Gertrud and I invite you in that case to celebrate with us? That would give us *great* pleasure. In any case, you are invited to be with us.—

Please don't forget to bring the reviews of your book.

Warmest regards

K. J.

191 *Hannah Arendt to Karl Jaspers*

September 7, 1956

Lieber Verehrtester—

I'm writing in haste to thank you for your good letter and so you won't think I've disappeared. I'm touched that you thought about my birthday!—The stupid thing is that I still can't say exactly when I'll be coming, but I will come, of course, before the 20th. In the meantime, all sorts of things have happened here. First of all, the congress in France, which is to say the Recontres Philosophiques, was called off because it was impossible to organize the affair in such a way that *les penseurs du Parti* didn't constitute an overwhelming majority of those present. An amazing business. They weren't even embarrassed to say in their cancellation announcement that they were incapable of maintaining *l'impartialité.* Koyré wrote me, and from what he says it seems that the other Frenchmen who are not Communists were under such great pressure that they didn't dare to come if the party didn't get what it wanted. Tableau!

My first reaction was to postpone the trip. But the people footing the bill, that is, the Rockefeller Foundation, feel differently. I could perhaps have postponed the trip until later this year, but I can't do that because I've agreed to do a couple of lectures here at the end of November and can't cancel them. And I can't put the trip off until next year. So I'll be coming as originally planned.

For my so-called research in the libraries, I'll be going to Paris, Geneva, Cologne, and Kiel. The first thing I want to do is go to the Rembrandt exhibits in Amsterdam and Rotterdam, and then it would suit me best to come directly to see you. That would be around October 5. But I'm still not sure whether I won't have to go to Paris for a few days first. I'll know that for sure next week and will then write you immediately with firm dates, provided you don't write me in the meantime that that doesn't suit you. I could just as well go to Geneva or Paris for a week or so first.

I have to "confess" something that I keep forgetting. (Please take the word "forget" at face value; there are no psychological factors at work behind it.) A while ago a so-called Leo Baeck Institute for the study of German-Jewish history was formed. I am on its board here in New York, though it is based in Jerusalem. Several of its members were aware of my biography of Rahel Varnhagen, and because they have very few manuscripts at the moment, they have been after me constantly to let them publish it. I finally gave in. Voilà! But: I have reworked it, written an introduction, and prepared an appendix with some unpublished letters of Rahel's. The translator has the whole business now, because, absurdly enough, the institute publishes only in English. The book will appear here and in England next year. Now I would like to see it published in German too, and I've given it to a number of "innocent" people to read to see how they react to it. Judging from the responses, it is primarily a women's book and as such defensible.

Heinrich has just left to begin the new semester. He is well rested and really quite pleased that the academic year has begun again. The summer was lovely, but the house we came within a hair's breadth of buying we wound up not buying after all. We were advised to occupy a house on a rental basis first and then perhaps to buy it later. Renting is, among other things, much cheaper.

As if in compensation, though, Heinrich is toying with the idea of buying a car (the house was my idea), and we will probably both learn to drive this winter. Old-fashionedness seems to be a thing of the past. Too bad, actually. —Judging from all this, you might think we have become millionaires; nothing could be farther from the truth. But the college has introduced a halfway normal pension plan now, so we don't have to take saving so seriously anymore.

It gives me pleasure to imagine your many guests and the children in your lovely, quiet house. Yes, children are wonderful. I fell in love with a little niece[1] of mine in Palestine. She had just turned twelve, and she still writes me charming letters—in German, which she really doesn't know and in an orthography that defies description.

Tomorrow morning I'm going to Washington for a political science conference. I'm always a bit nervous before these things. It's not so much giving a talk as it is all the people and my physical inability to remember all the names.

Piper and I reached agreement, by the way. He granted me the 10% after all. An odd duck.

All my very best, and until soon! Warmest greetings to you both

Your
Hannah

192 *Hannah Arendt to Karl Jaspers*

September 15, 1956

Lieber Verehrtester—

All I want to do today is confirm the arrangements I outlined in my letter of last week, because everything seems to be falling into place beautifully. I'll fly from here to Amsterdam on September 30 and could, if that is agreeable to you both, be in Basel on October 5. But if you prefer, I can come later too, and will go to Paris first. If I do come on the 5th, I would like to be in Paris about the 9th. If you would rather that I come later, I would go directly to Geneva after I leave you.

As I've said, I can easily arrange to do whatever suits you best. But it would be nice if I could know in advance, because if I am going to go directly from Amsterdam to visit you, I would book a flight here to Basel or Zurich. It's hardly worth flying from Paris. I'm already booked for the 30th. In Holland, I'll meet an American friend [Mary McCarthy] whom I like very much.

Washington was very nice and even stimulating. Friedrich[1] from Harvard, who is teaching for the summer semester at Heidelberg now, is determined to have me for a semester in Heidelberg. I'm hesitant.

296

Heinrich is urging me to do it, if I would be there only for the three summer months. I have to talk this over with you. It wouldn't be a possibility until the summer of 1958 anyhow.

I'm already a bit excited but still so deep in my work that I can't really quite imagine the trip happening yet.

Heinrich has returned from the first week of the semester very much pleased. The faculty elected him unanimously to the chairmanship of the committee for academic standards and policies (promotions, new posts, changes in the curriculum, etc.). He's delighted to have the job, even though it does add considerably to his workload. The generosity of spirit in this country is really astonishing. His English is, of course, by no means perfect, nor does he have the academic degree that all the rest of them have. They couldn't care less.

Until soon, until soon. —Warmest wishes

Your
Hannah

193 *Karl Jaspers to Hannah Arendt*

Basel, September 17, 1956

Dear Hannah!

We're delighted that you are coming, and we await your final word on exactly when you will arrive. Perhaps you are expecting a line from us, although you wrote that you will assume our agreement if you do not hear differently from us right away. October 5 is fine with us, as is any other day around that time. You will stay until your birthday or longer, won't you? All matters of time and schedule are yours, not ours, to decide. I think you will be able to work at our house as you have before. We will be able to see each other in the late morning and late afternoon as well as at mealtimes. There is so much to talk about! I look forward to it. You will stay in the guest room and will have a desk in the library that faces on the street. Ella, Ernst Mayer's wife, who is very close to us, is living and sleeping in the library facing the garden. She will not disturb you or our conversations. She is helping with the book that *has* to go to Piper in (late) October.

I'll save everything important for when I see you.

To both of you, warmest greetings from us both
Your Karl Jaspers

Basel, September 18, 1956

Dear Hannah!

I just wrote to you yesterday, and I've just received your letter of September 15. If you write that it is just as convenient for you to come somewhat later rather than on October 5, we would appreciate your making that change. The reason is that we have just heard today from Flora Mayer[1] that she wants to come from London to visit us (she lives with her son[2] in South Africa). Under no circumstances can her visit overlap with yours. That would be a disturbance for us. So please write us what date you have in mind for later—after Paris. *Any* day after October 10 is fine for us. I begin teaching on October 29 (I did take a week's leave and had no difficulty getting it). You should dispose of the days or weeks as you like. Will you be with us for your birthday? You can of course be with us when I am teaching, too—the only problem then is that I can't talk with you, or as good as not. We'll look for your word of your schedule, first of all on when you'll arrive. I'm looking forward to seeing you.

Warmest greetings
Your Karl Jaspers

September 22, 1956

Lieber Verehrtester—

Your second letter has just arrived. (Preparations for a trip—the best thing about them is that the mailbox has letters from Basel in it so often.) How glad I am that I wrote again. How will you manage all these visitors now when Piper is supposed to have your manuscript by the end of October? It seems to me my visit will be a bit too much, and you *must* tell me—first, on principle, and second, this time in particular—if it is too much for you and if I'm staying too long. Please!

Perhaps we had best forget about the birthday in any case. If it's all right with you, I'll come around the 20th or 21st, that is, from Paris I'll go to Geneva first, where I have to allow a little extra time because I don't know what I'll find in the library or how long I'll have to stay. But of course I can also do whatever would be best for you, i.e., I could come to Basel first, and that would mean about the 15th.

Mail probably won't reach me here anymore, or at least it won't be a sure thing. I'm flying from here on Sunday, the 30th. Mail will reach me in Amsterdam c/o American Express. And from October 5 on in Paris, also c/o American Express. I'll send you word as soon as I have a hotel room in Paris (my cousin [Niouta Ghosh] is reserving one for me).

It is possible that mail for me will start arriving at your house in early October. Perhaps Erna can be in charge of forwarding it this time so that it doesn't make more extra work for your wife. Just send everything on to Paris.

Warmest greetings to you both,
Your
Hannah

196   Karl Jaspers to Hannah Arendt

Basel, September 27, 1956

Dear Hannah!

Now the dates are finally firm. How nice that you will be with us on October 20 or 21. Write to let us know which it will actually be.

How long you stay is entirely up to you. The way our daily routine is set up it will in no way be "too much." The only thing is that starting on October 29 I will be available to talk with only rarely. Among equals there can be, especially in practical matters, only openness and no "indirect communications." Hence, what I have just said.

I've been working all day—and now it's getting boring, because all that remains to be done is editorial work. I want to move on, and I have to force myself not to be careless (which I am doing anyhow). A thousand printed pages are an awful lot. When you come, I hope to be just about done and starting on preparations for my lectures.

Your mail will be sent on to Paris.

Bon voyage, and have a good time!

Warmest greetings from my wife and
Your
Karl Jaspers

Paris, October 7, 1956

Lieber Verehrtester—

Thank you for your letter to Holland. I'm still planning on the 20th or 21st. Your letter—it made Europe feel like home again right away. Holland was very lovely. Not only the Rembrandt exhibits. The country too. I was there with an American friend [Mary McCarthy], and we were both completely surprised at how much we liked the country and the people. The Dutch are very solid and very friendly. In a four-day stay we went to Amsterdam, Rotterdam, The Hague, Delft, and Haarlem. A wonderful tour.

I'm sitting in libraries here and finding a great many things I could not find in America. I'll arrive in Geneva on the morning of either the 15th or 16th, and then I'll write right away exactly when you can expect me. I'll know that the minute I've seen the catalog in the library.

If anything should come up in the meantime: I'm staying in the Hotel Carlton Palace, 207 Boulevard Raspail. I don't know yet where I'll stay in Geneva, but I will surely stop by at American Express every day.

How wonderful that it will be so soon.

Warmest greetings to you both—

Your

Hannah

198 Karl Jaspers to Hannah Arendt

Basel, October 13, 1956

Dear Hannah!

You say you don't want to celebrate your fiftieth birthday. But now it is here. When I think about this day, I feel both grateful and moved to celebrate. For you are one of those people I count among the great gifts of this world. What a life you have led, a life given to you and earned by you with a steadfastness that has mastered the evil, the horror that has come from without and ground so many others down; also, with a wonderful strength rooted in noble impulses, a strength that has transformed your vulnerable softness, your precarious vacillation, your tendency to let your passions run away with you into the in-forming forces of your being.

This strength stems in part from your physical vitality. Health is a wonderful thing, and beauty, and the ability to delight others. But those are not the things that have truly carried you. They were put in your service. Now you are facing the decade that, for women more than for men, brings those physical changes which you probably face with some apprehension. I am sure they won't touch you. You are one of those women who demonstrate the truth of what Kierkegaard said: Women become more beautiful with age, that is, in the beauty that shines through all the wrinkles and infirmities and is all the more beautiful because it no longer relies on the physical glory that is the gift of youth, and so this beauty is altogether different, more reliable, more real.

All I need wish you is that happiness will follow you, that your husband will enjoy good health with you, and that external circumstances will give you in your age what they denied you in your youth. Everything important you will make for yourself—on through the decades and into the more quiet ways of advanced age, in which your temperament will remain unchanged, responding, as always, to the true substance of things.

My wife and I are with you in our hearts, wishing you nothing but good.

For now, good-bye until next week, *before* you embark on your old age, the pleasures of which I am so eager to recommend to you.

With warmest regards,
Your Karl Jaspers

My wife's heart is bothering her again, and she is lying down and cannot and does not want to write. She hopes you will excuse her and sends you her warmest wishes. She will discuss with you when you are here the idea she had for a birthday gift for you—an accessory for the car you are planning to get.

199   *Hannah Arendt to Karl Jaspers*

Geneva, October 16, 1956

Lieber Verehrtester—

You're right. I was reluctant to celebrate my birthday, and then your letter came, and that was a celebration in spite of me. What I really wish for myself is someday to be the person you think that I am.

What I dread about my fiftieth birthday is perhaps in part the im-

301

minent physical changes, but, more important, it's the necessity of taking on "dignity," and with the best will in the world, I don't know how I'll manage to assume that. And one does not exactly want the alternative of being ridiculous either.

The nicest thing about the letter was that it came by special delivery on Sunday, when I wasn't expecting any mail at all.

I hope your wife's heart is giving her less trouble now. If anything should come up, I'm staying in the Hotel Touring et Balance (that's what the place really is called), and I can easily be reached by phone. The best times are before 9:30 in the morning and in the evenings around 7. Tel. 25 13 80.

I'll be through in good time here, but I still won't come until Sunday, because I want to meet with the wife of Heinrich's old friend[1] in Bern. Heinrich will want to know how things are with them. So I'll come from Bern on Sunday morning. The train arrives in Basel at 11:17. I can—but please, only if it suits you—stay until Saturday. I want to leave Saturday night to meet my friend [Mary McCarthy] in Brussels on Sunday, and from there on to Cologne.

I'll try to catch Jeanne Hersch here. She won't be back in Geneva until the 18th. I hope it will work out.

Geneva is pleasantly quiet and very restful after my days in Paris.

Warmest greetings to you both—

Your

Hannah

200   Hannah Arendt to Karl Jaspers

Münster, November 5, 1956

Lieber Verehrtester—

Things have taken as bad a turn as you feared they would, a much worse turn actually, for the whole delicate order created in the postwar years has been destroyed now.[1]

I toyed with the idea of flying home right away but decided against it for the time being. It seems to me as if it will be a few months, perhaps years, before the worst comes down on us. I really don't know anymore how it can be held off now. When it comes, it will come the way this present situation has—without a declaration of war, and the start of hostilities, as they are so euphemistically called, will occur too soon for us to learn about them in advance.

My heart is heavy. Will we see each other again?

I needn't say what you and your wife and your home have meant to me in the last ten years of my life. Our friendship and its "permanence" will remain in our hearts.

Your
Hannah

If I should quickly change my plans, I'll write. Otherwise, I'll be in Kiel until Saturday, Park Hotel. Then Frankfurt, c/o Europäische Verlagsanstalt, Goethestr. 29. On the 15th, back in Cologne, where I'm supposed to make a tape recording. On the 17th, Paris. Carlton Palace, 207 Bd. Raspail.

201 Karl Jaspers to Hannah Arendt

Basel, November 10, 1956

Dear Hannah!

Thank you for your kind words. For the same reasons and in the same way the shadow of dark clouds burdens our spirits.

Yes, reunions are always uncertain. We both feel we still have a great deal to say to each other. I still have much on my mind that needs its own good time to find expression. My hopes for 1958[1] are, despite everything, still high and not entirely unfounded as far as the political situation is concerned.

We remain, of course, completely in the dark about the most important factor (which we were not with Hitler): Do the Russians want a war soon, or don't they? It seems certain to me that the Russians act on clear decisions and will not bumble their way into anything. Everything is thought through there. Even in these years of friendly overtures, at the Geneva "summit conference,"[2] I wondered constantly: Is this a clever camouflage tactic that will allow the Russians to keep on arming themselves to the teeth and at the same time deceive everyone else and let them start arguing among themselves, or is it their real long-range goal to keep the peace, but where possible to strengthen their own position for a major showdown and to use that position of strength as a means to gain further advantages? Their continuing arms buildup, which is accomplished by exploiting the farm population in particular, and the existence of massive land forces are facts not much in dispute. The Russians are spending comparatively much more than the Americans. With the ground forces they have, they can take Europe whenever they want to without the atom bomb. But Montgomery[3] said about six months ago that a Russian attack on the borders of West Germany would *instantly* and *automatically* set off an atomic war. In their folly, the Americans think they can win security with their high-powered technology. But it will always remain true that in war the deciding factor is the willingness of the soldiers of an entire nation to run risks and make sacrifices, for avoiding conflict is, if not cowardice, at least a temporary yielding to self-deceptive complacency. Because the key people in Washington and Moscow *know* what the H-bomb is, while the people tend to forget it, the bomb is a massive obstacle to the outbreak of war. But what Moscow ultimately wants still remains obscure.

It would be nice if you were here for some talk every day. We would talk about Hungary and also keep silent. I wouldn't have thought it possible that a people could still do today what the Hungarians have done. It is dreadful that one must simply stand by and watch. The only help of any use to Hungary is military help, but it would almost certainly mean world war, and so it is not forthcoming. But this Hungarian struggle is something of which Kant would say: "It will not let itself be forgotten."[4] It will have consequences.

I'm very pleased with Israel's policies, behavior, and way of speaking. Just as the military leader Dayan[5] is the only one among the generals I see now who looks physiognomically reliable, unpretentious, unmilitaristic, and honest, so too are Israel's policies candid. And they are just, given that the Zionist decision to make a "homeland in Palestine" was achieved (there was much that argued against that earlier—since 1906, on that evening I told you about) and given that the state was founded and kept alive with determination and sacrifice when the English left it completely on its own in a state of emergency, without administration, order, or protection. Since then, it has formed a basis in reality that has precedent over law, indeed, has created law. If, then, the surrounding Arab world is provided with weapons for an attack whose explicit purpose is to destroy Israel and murder all Israelis, then the state has to do something. One cannot ask small states to take the danger of a world war into consideration, especially because they can never be the cause of a world war they do not want, but only the excuse. What is happening to Israel is—speaking above politics— symptomatic and symbolic for the continuing existence of the Western world. What Hitler did to the Jews was what, in a certain sense, was going to be done to all Germans (as you have brilliantly shown). What the Western nations are letting happen to the Jews will happen to those nations themselves. The connection is palpable.

But how unclear what will happen now is. There is at the moment in the Western world a certain willingness to see the truth and make sacrifices—small ones—for example, the willingness of all the countries of Europe to accept tens of thousands of Hungarians. Israel, unfortunately, is not benefiting from this kind of clear judgment. There are even people—this eternal anti-Semitism that is not able to perceive reality—who, outraged about Israel, blame her for the present trouble. One must be, and my wife is, very concerned for Israel. The great struggle simply to exist and make a claim on life continues to be fought, and with what great moderation and circumspection. Arabs are leaving en masse the territory west of the Jordan that belongs to Jordan—as they did in large part in 1948.[6] Despite this, Israel is *not* occupying this territory and is *not* occupying Jerusalem. That is self-control such as has rarely been seen even in the West. And how the Israelis have fought this war, compared with the pitiable hesitation of England and France,[7] which, had they been as forceful and soldierly as the Israelis, would never have let the whole situation get to the point it did. The occupation of the entire canal was to have been accomplished in a few days, as was promised on the first day. Now the business is by and large a failure. In any case the negotiating situation is one in which the Israelis, bolstered by their soldierly and circumspect behavior, can present their complaints to the world in a clearer and more forceful way than they could before.

It is evening and I am very tired. Excuse my handwriting.

Warmest greetings
Your Karl Jaspers

202 Hannah Arendt to Karl Jaspers

December 26, 1956

Lieber Verehrtester—

In all the confusion of my trip, departure, and arrival, I haven't written for a long time, and I see with horror that I'll have to hurry to avoid arriving too late with my New Year's wishes. I delayed because we reacted so differently to the political situation and because I wanted to wait and see what would actually happen. My fears were, thank God, unfounded. The Russians have obviously had much greater difficulties than I had dared to hope. The whole business may just turn out to be a total disaster for them after all, because the difficulties aren't cropping up just in the International and in the satellite states but very obviously in Russia itself. In any case, Hungary is the best thing that has happened for a long time. It seems to me it still isn't over, and regardless of how it ends, it is a clear victory for freedom. And once again, as in all the spontaneous revolutions of the last hundred years, the spontaneous appearance of a new governmental form *in nuce*, the council system, which the Russians have so violated that hardly anyone can tell anymore what it really is.

It seemed and still seems to me that the Suez adventure is a catastrophic policy that only became worse for not being carried through properly even on a military level. All that has come out of it for Israel is that the country could get war matériel in the cheapest possible way. The situation hasn't changed in the least. The reproaches aimed at America and that one hears here very often in the form of self-reproach don't seem justified to me, either. America is committed to the United Nations and due process of law. If it, too, starts to wage and support wars without a previous declaration of war, chaos will result. The way this stupid Mr. Dulles[1] handled the Suez question before the English-French adventure is another thing. At any rate, the upshot is that the States are attempting to back off from Europe a bit and to stress their world-political responsibilities more. Given the right circumstances, that can become very dangerous, but it isn't yet. I'm happy about the closer ties with Nehru,[2] the only Asian politician of stature and with an essentially Western outlook.

There's nothing new here. Prosperity continues to prosper, picking up in pace all the time. Now everybody and his brother has not just two cars in the garage but three, and I'm not talking about rich people but, for example, a Negro family in which the husband is a chauffeur and the wife a maid for a family in the country. I find it troubling, and I can hardly imagine how it can be for the good. But perhaps those are prejudices on my part and a lack of understanding of modern economics.

Things are going well for us. Heinrich is enjoying his holidays, during which he's finally getting some work done. These two winter months are really very nice. I'm getting ready for our New Year's Eve party.

It worries me a little that you heat with oil. But I guess nothing really bad has happened, and you're not freezing. When I left Paris, the hotels and all public buildings were heated only in the morning and evening. Perhaps things have improved. I haven't heard anything. One feels at a very great remove here, and the danger always exists that one forgets the everyday realities.

I think back with pleasure on this past year, which saw the completion of the first volume of your great work.[3] May it continue thus for a long time. And I hope we will be able to speak with each other again very, very soon.

Wishing you both happiness and health in the New Year, and please give my best to Erna.

As always, your
Hannah

203 Karl Jaspers to Hannah Arendt

Basel, December 29, 1956

Dear Hannah!

My last letter, in reply to your kind, agitated, and concerned letter in that critical period, was sent in care of the Europäische Verlagsgesellschaft in Frankfurt a. M. I hope things have gone well for you both in the meantime. The new year has begun under a dark cloud. Given the course of the things that determine the fates of all of us, we have to wish each other well more earnestly than usual.

My mentally ill "friend" in Bonn, whom you know, wrote to me then that "world peace is more certain than ever." I wondered if this was a case like that of a mentally ill patient in Heidelberg who walked into the clinic garden in a downpour and said: The sun scorches and burns. —Or is this an example of that perspicacity he has sometimes revealed?

What seems to me almost the most dangerous thing now is that the world is without leadership. Truman and Stalin were at least men who knew what they wanted and who exhibited a political "logic." Eisenhower is, by contrast, a civil servant or general who is actually waiting for "orders," and the Russian leaders are at odds with themselves. Their situation becomes increasingly hopeless all the time, but they still have at their disposal a massive and intact military machine that lives off the exploitation of the people. It is impossible to foresee what may hatch from the muddled passions of a leaderless governing body (Khrushchev[1] to the Western diplomats: You don't like us . . .

we'll bury you all!) or from the world-historical adventurism of a general. At any rate, we still have, instead of fear of hellfire, fear of the H-bomb.

I am rewriting an essay[2] that you are familiar with and that I have been dissatisfied with for a long time. I hope to make it into an expression of political consciousness in the shadow of the H-bomb. I still haven't written the pages I wanted to send to you for comment. I make slow progress because teaching demands much, indeed, most of my strength during the semester. Sometimes I think to myself that you are at work on your two political books and that we perhaps, or almost certainly, coincide in our outlook (derived from Kant) and complement each other in the subject under discussion. My pamphlet deals primarily with the "suprapolitical" dimension. It ranges from the technical facts on up to the idea of immortality. It seeks to test the concrete political facts of the day against the standards that come from that dimension. Yesterday I wrote about Gandhi. Well, you'll see. I'm a bit afraid of you both—of the stupidities and errors I may commit. I am, after all, a "dilettante" in this field, and you are both "experts."

Israel is becoming the touchstone of the Western world. If the West abandons Israel, it will suffer the same fate as Hitler Germany, which let the murder of the Jews happen. The danger remains frightful. For now, I think, we can be satisfied with Israel's actions—moderate, intelligent, and courageous, as the best Western countries are. Now they are building a pipeline from Akaba to Haifa and have sent a warship all the way around Africa to station it near Akaba. Well, these are small things, but important, crucial, because they are displays of courage. The people are growing into the tasks set for them.

Warmest greetings to you both
Your Karl Jaspers

204   *Hannah Arendt to Karl Jaspers*

February 17, 1957

Lieber Verehrtester—

When the book came from Kohlhammer[1] I wanted to write right away. The autobiography reads so beautifully now. It's strange how print always changes things, either adding or detracting. In any case, I hope very much that Piper will seize on this instantly and publish it as a separate little volume. Monsieur, who has read some in the book, too (more than I have), was amazed to see that there could still be such a pure biography in our century. The story has a pull toward the mysterious that is reminiscent of Stifter.[2] Just wonderful! But it is lost in this fat volume. Do see to it that it appears on its own.

Both your birthdays are here again, and I think that next year I'll come and help you celebrate them. If the world is still at peace—perhaps your mentally ill friend is right after all. Basically, everything depends on an unspoken agreement between America and Russia that is more reliable than the propaganda noise. Perhaps the real danger won't really come until small nations have the H-bomb, too. The danger that they will resort to this solution is greater not only because they are more chauvinistic and irresponsible, but also because, objectively, a war in which existence is at stake can erupt so quickly among them. But it will no doubt be a while before we reach that stage.

Yes, the world is without leadership and will remain so because no one can lead the world. As a consequence, all problems become more international in scope (when someone at the South Pole coughs, someone at the North Pole catches the cold), and this makes national leaders increasingly helpless. The present foreign policy of the United States is a scandal. What happened here with the lousy little king of Saudi Arabia[3] defies all description. Eisenhower, who has never met a guest at the airport during his presidency, turned up there promptly because the louse king had said he wouldn't come otherwise. Gestures like this are unfortunately revealing of the reality behind them. But I still don't think things will get to the point of imposing sanctions on Israel. The public mood here is very much against that. The so-called Eisenhower doctrine is very dangerous, because what it says, essentially, is: We will intervene only if the Russians are the actual attackers but not if you start squabbling among yourselves there. It is, in short, carte blanche for aggression. And this at the very moment when England and France have shown the world that they aren't world powers anymore. We knew that before, of course, but it hadn't been put to the test.

You'll surely have finished your pamphlet on the atom bomb by now, and we're both very curious and eager to see it. The pages you mentioned have never arrived. —I received galleys from Schilpp a few days ago, along with the news that anyone who wants offprints will have to pay for them himself. I'm going to be curious to see if he'll think it necessary even to provide the contributors with a copy of the book. An odd fellow.

All is well with us. Heinrich's winter break—two months!—is, alas!, over next week. We always enjoy it very much. His courses at the New School have begun already and are very well attended. —I'm working on the final chapters of the *Vita Activa* book and hope to be done with it by May. Then I have to go to Chicago for a few weeks, and then I'll begin the little politics book for Piper. [. . .]

We sent a book on Chinese painting for your birthday. It has the first translation from the Chinese of the famous handbook of painting as well as all the illustrations that go with it.[4] I gave it to Heinrich for Christmas, and we thought you might enjoy it. It is dreadfully heavy, but with your reading stand you'll be able to leaf through it from your sofa.

All our best wishes and warmest greetings to you both,

Your

Hannah

P.S.: [. . .] My publisher wrote me that the German Book Guild will publish a cheap edition of my *Totale Herrschaft* for its members.

205   *Karl Jaspers to Hannah Arendt*

Basel, February 24, 1957

Dear Hannah!

I was very happy to have your letter, which arrived punctually on my birthday, and the precious gift from both of you—and to hear such good news from you: exceptionally well-attended lectures, a cheap edition of your wonderful book, completion of the *Vita Activa* in the near future, and, most important, the "happiness" you are both enjoying.

Then there is politics. We would seem to be of one mind. Ever since November I've been affected by politics in a way I haven't been since the Nazi period. The main reason is no doubt that we are finally seeing something again that we can respect, perhaps admire: Israel's bearing and policy.[1] It is clearly winning the approval of all decent people. In Switzerland, public opinion is obviously on the side of Israel, after some slight initial hesitation here and there. The "greatness" of Israel's accomplishment is the uniting of moderation and intelligence with boldness, self-sacrifice, and the capability to match words with deeds. Here we see realized a moral-political force such as appears in the founding periods of states that have content and permanence. Israel is not behaving foolishly, but it is betting its existence on its actions. And the world is still capable of seeing and hearing that. Since November, Israel's situation has changed completely. Faced with a lethal threat, the possibility of attack any day, it dared launch an action that the world at first saw as "aggression" but that has now come to be recognized more and more as defense against aggression bent on Israel's total destruction. The lethal threat has not disappeared; in that respect there has been no basic change. But the world is gradually learning more and more about what is going on there. The UN has compromised itself by misusing the term "aggressor,"[2] which can be applied to Israel here only in a purely momentary, formal sense. Your American people—and we all feel in some sense like potential fellow citizens of America, no matter how far away from it we may be—are showing their mettle once again and are a second bright spot in the world. True, Eisenhower has been [re]elected, which is a disgrace, just as Hindenburg's election was, earlier, in Germany,[3] but the Americans aren't listening to him. He represents a great danger in these years, with his arteriosclerotic stubbornness and his senile need for quiet and his doddering propensity for irritation; for he is the most powerful man in the world, constrained only by his term of office and very little by the Constitution. But I am counting on the Americans. There is nothing they can do in the face of sudden events, but in the long run they display a natural decency that functions almost as an independent force. And I have hope for Israel, too. My feeling is something like this: The destruction of Israel would mean the end of humankind—and probably in fact bring about its destruction. One cannot, of course, substantiate a claim like that, even though it seems to me—subjectively—so obvious.

My "atom bomb" is still far from finished. It will be a small book—more or less an expression of a present-day, integrated political consciousness. That's why the pages I wanted you to see are still not written. What leads up to them has become an ever longer path.

The lecture wound up taking too much of my time. The strength I have available for work has never been great. The first volume of my "Grossen Philosophen" is being printed (almost 1,000 printed pages, should appear in May). It seems to me that this political essay stands in the same kind of relation to my "Grossen Philosophen" as in 1931 the little Göschen volume did to my *Philosophie*. But that sounds a bit pompous.

[. . .]

I am not, of course, familiar with your *Rahel* in its reworked form, but what I do know of it (and what will not have changed significantly in the new version) is enough to tell me that it will probably please no one, not the Jews or the anti-Semites or even me (except that in one way or another I like everything you do, even if I disagree with it). The book does not tap into any live vein in Germany's present-day reading public. So it will be a chancy enterprise: the book *can* stir up what is lying dormant, even if it evokes opposition. It needs a publisher like Rowohlt who dares to slap the public in the face and who makes a success of doing so. But because your book is so important in terms of its subject matter and of its high literary quality, Piper ought to assume that risk. [. . .]

I did, of course, immediately leaf through the extravagant gift from you both. A beautiful book! I was aware of this book as a late work in which the philosophical thinking of the painters gradually transformed itself into a "cookbook" of painting. From a book by Sirén,[4] which the editor of this one also used, I have excerpts containing *translations* of more profound formulations from earlier periods. It is a phenomenon of the highest order that has a parallel in the Western world only in the person of Leonardo (Dürer is in a different category): philosophizing in the process of artistic creation itself and conscious reflection about this philosophy. I was interested in this for a chapter in my "Weltgeschichte der Philosophie"[5]—but I doubt anything will ever come of that now. So far I've read only isolated passages of the editor's text.[6] The subject matter is so profound that it comes through even in a poor treatment. But our author, even though he is Chinese, seems to speak about it only from the outside and without clarity of thought—merely piling up Chinese ideas. The text is similar to Lin Yutang's Lao-tse translation.[7] His comments are based on Tschuang-tse,[8] the substance filtered through a brilliant literary man, and the resulting picture makes one wonder if he had the vaguest idea of what Lao-tse was really about. And then I was saddened by the bibliography. Our German contributions have no existence in the world anymore. The most important translation, which has never been equaled for its commentary, is by Viktor von Strauss,[9] and it is *not* listed. All the English and French ones are, however.

But enough for now. I have detained you much too long, and made things even worse with my terrible handwriting.

My best wishes for your work—and with hopes of seeing you in February 1958—warmest greetings to Heinrich

Your Karl Jaspers

206   *Hannah Arendt to Karl Jaspers*

New York, April 14, 1957

Lieber Verehrtester—

Your wonderful long letter, I am getting around to answering only now. I felt I should write at length about Israel and the Jews, yet I didn't really feel like it in recent weeks, probably because the reasons for immediate concern had dropped away. But you express your "feeling" that "the destruction of Israel would mean the end of humankind," and that doesn't seem justified to me even as a feeling. I often have the feeling that it would mean the end of the Jews, and yet I'm not really certain that even that is so. We're also not in agreement about the significance of the Jews for Europe, their political significance right now. That has changed decisively in the last twenty years. Today, the Jews are no longer an important and integral component in the European nations. Will they become one again? I don't know, but I don't think so, even though it is astonishing how quickly the number of Jews in Germany is growing (the estimate is about 70-80,000, of whom barely 40,000 have been statistically accounted for). And without a German Jewish population there can be no European one, at least not if we look at the matter historically.

How are things going with the "atom bomb," which we are eagerly looking forward to? What do you think about the statement of the German physicists?[1] I'm very pleased, almost grateful. There's finally some sign of life. That could lead to very crucial changes in the whole matter. One important thing it accomplishes is to call attention at last to the incredibly important role into which physicists have suddenly been thrust, for without their implicit or explicit cooperation, no one can conduct foreign policy at all anymore.

Heinrich was very happy to have your comments on the book about Chinese painting, because they concurred completely with his own view of it. They impressed on me again to what a disastrous extent German influence, actually the German voice, has disappeared from the intellectual life of the Western world. Names like Humboldt, Schlegel, and Brentano are completely unknown among younger people here, i.e., those under 45. Literally unknown, never been heard of, and that even among educated people. I was just reading a relatively old book by Whitehead, *The Concept of Nature*,[2] in which space and time are discussed at great length without one single mention of Kant. He does cite Schelling, but how—by way of a Russian philosopher whose work has been translated into English. That's the way things have been here since the post–World War I years. To be educated here means to know French, Russian, and Italian literature—in just about that order.

It just occurred to me in this connection: Has Walter Kaufmann's article on "German Philosophy [*sic*] Today" in the *Kenyon Review*[3] made its way into your hands? Big and really very snooty-snotty attacks on your inability to communicate and on Heidegger's inability to express himself clearly. I was very angry for a moment, also delighted in retrospect that you had taken such a sharp tone with him in your response in the Schilpp book. The guy is as typical (therefore, one shouldn't get worked up about him) as he is insufferable (and so one gets worked up anyhow).

Blumenfeld wrote me a few weeks ago that an effort is underway to get this year's peace prize awarded to the Jugendalijah and that he would very much like to have your signature for that purpose. Have I written to you about this? I don't think so. The Jugendalijah is an institution that was founded in Germany in 1933 and financed from America for the purpose of sending young people to Palestine and educating them there. It originated in the German-Jewish youth movement and did very good work. I was active on its behalf for years in Paris. I assume that Blumenfeld has written directly to you. There is perhaps good (political) reason at this time to award the prize to a nonpolitical institution in Israel.

It's vacation time for you now, but the semester will start again soon. I think of you both so often, more and more of you together, because your being together has become the quintessence of something completely alive.

With best wishes, as always your
Hannah

Basel, April 22, 1957

Dear Hannah!

Thank you for your greetings. Blumenfeld has not written to me. I would of course sign, gladly, on your recommendation—because I really know nothing about the matter.

The "atom bomb" is still not finished, which I regret a lot, because it means a great deal to me and shouldn't be put off. But I have to put it off because my teaching (lecture on Aristotle, Thomas, Hegel — Seminar: Nietzsche's *Zarathustra*) demands it, and I don't want to and can't retire yet. In July I'll get right back to it, with hopes of being done in August so that it can appear in the fall before Christmas.

The statement of the German physicists? I was excited about it *at first*, despite my mistrust of all these people (based on personal experience). At last, I thought, all the physicists of consequence in Germany have declared that they will not work on the bomb. They understand that Germany (as a small state) can afford what would be impossible and criminal in America. And I was pleased in any case to see the "mind" declare itself disobedient to the state. But then I was very quickly and totally disappointed (I still don't have the *exact* text, which I immediately ordered from my bookstore) because:

The physicists were not asked to work on a bomb at all; there aren't even plans for one—therefore the whole issue is purely academic, meaningless—

They did not take into account Germany's situation as one of innumerable small states but put their statement forward as a representative one for the world—

None of them has worked on the bomb yet—under Hitler, they were never confronted with the question; they haven't put themselves to the test at all (and how would such a test have turned out?); they thought making the bomb was so difficult, indeed, so unlikely a project that they didn't even begin—a Nobel Prize winner, Bothe,[1] *calculated* that the bomb was *impossible*—

Their action is a censure of everyone who has worked on the bomb and is working on it—a scandalous act on the part of people whose real situation was and is that they were never able to work on the bomb (because they saw no practically possible way of building it) and after 1945 were not permitted to.

So, all in all, typically German nonsense—and I, as a typical German, fell for it—and, so it seems, Hannah (also typically German,

315

excuse me, but you are, whether you like it or not) fell for it, too. And now the whole thing just looks ridiculous because the clever chancellor was apparently more than a match for the physicists, and they became "obedient" again where disobedience was childish in the first place.[2]

What are you doing? The first book of *Vita Activa* will be finished soon.

Is Piper going to be reasonable about *Rahel*? Without your consent, I have, of course, not written to him. Perhaps W. Kohlhammer Verlag in Stuttgart would be likely? Kohlhammer published an excerpt of yours from the Schilpp volume in its "house publication." So you are known there. Their production is very good. They're more generous because they have their own printing plant.

My wife joins me in sending you both warmest greetings

Your Karl Jaspers

208 Karl Jaspers to Hannah Arendt

Basel, June 26, 1957[1]

Dear Hannah!

When I told Gertrud about the murder,[2] her immediate response was: Winckelmann?[3] Like him, Bob was murdered by two stabs from behind that struck his heart. The murderer must have had an army knife and understood how to use it. The talk now is in part crude insensitive stuff. —I'm delighted about your success in Chicago and the publisher's enthusiasm.[4] —But please don't—as Gertrud thinks you should—burden yourself with my book.[5] It can wait for years until you have occasion to read in it. Heinrich may want to sooner: for Kant.

Warmest greetings to you both

Your Karl Jaspers

209 Hannah Arendt to Karl Jaspers

Palenville, August 29, 1957

Lieber Verehrtester—

I didn't want to write before I had read *Die grossen Philosophen*.[1] It arrived at a perfect time, right during my vacation—that is, in the weeks I was meaning to give myself between finishing the book for Chicago[2] and beginning the introduction to politics for Piper.[3] You might think I was prepared for this book. I wasn't. It is a genuine textbook, and I never could have imagined that such a thing could even exist, and up to now it never has. The book fascinates for many reasons, but most important is the mode of presentation, which forces the reader to discuss problems with the philosopher, joining him in the movements of his thought and in the pros and cons of his argumentation. In a certain sense, this book is the exact opposite of the *Psychologie der Weltanschauungen*, where opinions, views, and doctrines are developed. That isn't present here at all, and for that reason the reader always feels himself in the thick of the discussion. This is the first textbook of philosophy that has ever been written, and as such it is of an unparalleled originality. And for that reason too, as you say somewhere (I don't have the book here; Heinrich left for New York a few days ago and took it with him), it is "infinitely correctable." And I would add, infinitely variable. That you could succeed in doing this was possible only because you turned away so decisively from Hegel's history of philosophy as a philosophy of history and held so firmly to the notion that there is no real history of ideas, even though the central concerns of philosophy, more than in any other field, seem always to be the same. I haven't read the whole book, only about three-quarters of it, but I'm still quite certain that its real center is your wonderful analysis of Kant. When you go to heaven—and if things are there the way Socrates pictured them, with all of us continuing our conversations but now with the best minds of all time—then old Kant will rise from his seat to honor you and embrace you. No one has understood him as you have.

There are small points on which I disagree. I was pleased, touched, and honored by your remarks about our conversations, where you half quote me as an opponent[4]—but I'm not convinced that bringing in specific personal traits is such a good idea. That is particularly true of Augustine,[5] who comes off so badly with you and others only because you know so much about him. For which you are indebted to no one other than Augustine himself. The lines of Plato's poetry[6] (not very good) that have come down to us make me doubt that you would have treated him any differently if we only knew more about him. Here, too, it seems to me, Kant is your point of departure, or you always have Kant in mind. And in Kant, it seems to me, his vast experience of the world is equaled only by his completely impoverished experience of life. It's not his personal life that accounts for that, because he knew the world without ever setting foot outside Königsberg. But the power of imagination, which is as great in Kant as it otherwise is only in poets, left him in the lurch as far as life is concerned. But your presentation of Augustine is another high point in your book, and it remains undiminished by what seems to me an unjust judgment. So in the end it doesn't matter. Then, too, one could say: The fact that someone judges at all is enough. Even unjust judgment is wonderfully refreshing compared with fake Alexandrine respect. The overall atmosphere of the book is one of wonderful freedom. That isn't a product solely of the freedom and courage of its judgments but also of the discussion of questions and problems.

When the book arrived I had just reread your *Descartes*.[7] Since I hadn't really read Descartes until just recently, I hadn't understood the masterly quality of that little book until now either. Will you include it somewhere, just as it is? And what will you do with the Schelling book? I needed Descartes for my Chicago book. At the moment I'm reading the *Kritik der Urteilskraft* with increasing fascination. There, and not in the *Kritik der praktischen Vernunft*, is where Kant's real political philosophy is hidden. His praise for "common sense," which is so often scorned; the phenomenon of taste taken seriously as the basic phenomenon of judgment—which it probably really is in all aristocracies—; the "expanded mode of thought" that is part and parcel of judgment, so that one can think from someone else's point of view. The demand for communicativeness. These incorporate the experiences young Kant had in society, and then the old man made them come to life again. I've always loved this book most of Kant's critiques, but it has never before spoken to me as powerfully as it does now that I have read your Kant chapter.

I'm very curious to know what you've done on the "atom bomb" in the meantime. I have questions and objections that I hesitate to raise because you're in the process of rewriting it. I hope you will put in boldface and in some prominent position the sentence "This matter must not be allowed to come to rest."[8] Now it is only in the preface, where it is easy to read past it. For to accomplish that alone would be a lot, and that alone will be difficult enough to bring about in light of the prosperity of the whole world. What struck us in the latest developments in Russia was that Malenkov[9] thought the danger posed by the atom bomb is a danger for the whole world, but Khrushchev thought it a danger for the capitalist countries. This has been nearly overlooked, and yet it is the crucial point. I'm about to write the introductory theoretical article for an American magazine that is conducting a symposium on the Russian question.[10] And I'm really happy to be expressing what I've been avoiding saying for years. Now we can see with utter clarity where the journey is heading, and we have enough information to risk a judgment. The prospects are not cheerful.

We've had a long and very lovely summer in the country. We left New York at the end of June this year. Tomorrow this time of splendor is over. Heinrich, who wanted to visit some friends near New York, has gone on ahead. He sends his best regards. He is going to use the *Philosophen* right away in his teaching, and he was planning to write you right after he had finished reading the book, which he has not done, of course. I am, as always, sad to have to leave here. To make things easier for me, this unpredictable climate has decided to bring on a new ice age. It has suddenly turned as cold as it usually is only in October.

Say hello to your wife for me. I think of her so often with love and real tenderness. It just occurred to me that I left her last letter[11] about Bob Oboussier unanswered. It arrived during the last weeks of finishing the Chicago book, a time cluttered with the usual irritating technical matters. And it occurs to me that I wanted to clear up a misunderstanding. In *Aufbau*, where I read about the murder, there was nothing about homosexuality. Either I made that up or assumed it or came to that conclusion on the basis of other details.

Are you teaching in the fall? Do you have a seminar? And how was your summer vacation? Another son of the Waltz family has turned up here. I'm getting them all hopelessly confused, but that didn't get in our way at all. Please give Lotte Waltz my best when you see her.

My very best wishes to you both, and let me know what the "critics" have to say about *Die grossen Philosophen*, how it is received in Germany, etc.

Warmest greetings, as always
Your
Hannah

Basel, September 8, 1957

Dear Hannah!

We have just returned from vacationing in Locarno to find your good letter here. I'm glad that you are so pleased with my *Grossen Philosophen*, and I'll allow myself the pleasure of basking in your excessive praise. All I want to do today is thank you very much. I'll write about details another time. You have noticed the wonderful ideas in the *Kritik der Urteilskraft* that for me too have been a source of permanent insight from youth on. I would like to give a seminar on it with you right away and together with you bring to the attention of today's youth all the other treasures in it and the significance of the whole work.

I am very eager to hear what you will have to say about Russia after years of silence on it. I'm afraid I will not receive your essay before I have completed my "atom bomb." Unlike you, I do not see at all clearly where things in Russia are going. The possibilities of interpretation are always legion. When you compared Malenkov's and Khrushchev's remarks on the danger of the atom bomb for the world or for the capitalist countries, did you have in mind Khrushchev's fantastic statement a few months ago about the effects of these bombs, a statement that was later dismissed as "made in his cups"? Is it Khrushchev or Zhukov[1] who really wields the power? Khrushchev does not have a police force, as Stalin did, to set against the generals. Zhukov or other military men could be laying monstrous plans. The internal struggle within Russia is not over.

My wife and I send our warmest greetings to you and your husband.

Your Karl Jaspers

211   Hannah Arendt to Karl Jaspers

September 16, 1957

Lieber Verehrtester—

No, my praise was not excessive. But it would be fun to do a seminar, one on the beautiful, as Kant understood it, as the quintessence of the worldliness of the world. For every single human being. And on his so closely related concept of humanity, which only becomes possible through the ability to "fight" over the things about which one cannot "debate," because hope is "finding agreement among ourselves," even when one cannot finally convince the other.[1]

Your letter arrived just as I was about to write. You know that Kurt Wolff is in Europe now. And before he left we had a long talk about the American edition of *Die grossen Philosophen*. He and his wife are good friends of ours, and I'm sure you will enjoy meeting him. His publishing house is one of the best, also one of the most successful, in this country today, and he himself remains something that really doesn't exist anymore, namely, a publisher-personality. That's what he always was, of course. The astonishing thing is that he has remained so here and has been able to succeed as such.

But to *Die grossen Philosophen*: It would be a wonderful thing if the book could appear here and manage to become a success. It could mean a kind of revolution in the teaching of philosophy. Kurt Wolff asked for my opinion on how this very German book could best be presented to the Anglo-Saxon public here—and I say Anglo-Saxon intentionally, for in America, philosophy has been dominated, for better or for worse, by the English tradition. I talked the matter over at length with Heinrich, who has much more direct experience with these things than I do. On one thing we are agreed—though that doesn't mean a thing!!—: It would be good if the book could be abridged in such a way that the reader could be brought to the great philosophers more quickly. This abridging in the "Introduction" and the "Paradigmatic Individuals" should not be done by omitting whole paragraphs, but should, rather, aim at picking up the pace of the book. To a much lesser extent, one could perhaps do the same with Plato—Augustine—Kant, where one could omit here and there things that will mean little to the reader here, such as the discussion of neo-Kantianism. Your use of small print in some sections might provide some guidelines for the abridging process, although that would by no means always hold true. (For example, pp. 292ff. Plato's theology, which is in small print in the German edition, has to be retained.) The following sections on the metaphysicians are so much shorter anyhow that they should be left as they are. The greater part of the "Seminal Founders of Philosophical Thought" should be kept. If the abridging is done as I envision it, it would amount to cutting about 100 pages in all (20–25%), most of which would come out of the "Introduction" and the "Paradigmatic Individuals."

The reason for this suggestion is not the length of the book but the difference in American and European reading habits. People are used to getting things in a more rapid sequence here, and I think we could make this concession without changing anything in the character of the book. It would be a kind of transposition and not merely a translation. As far as the length itself is concerned, it would be much better to publish the book in two volumes: the "Introduction," the "Paradigmatic Individuals," and Plato—Augustine—Kant in the first volume; the metaphysicians in the second. In that case, it would be important for you to provide the promised sections on Eckhart and Cusanus. Then the two volumes would be of just about equal length. The subsequent volumes can then be easily added on, with each German volume probably corresponding to two in English.

It would be very advantageous if you could write a new preface for the American edition. It's true that everything essential is in the introduction, but certain points that would make things easier for the American reader appear there almost tangentially. What needs to be done is to outline the nature and structure of the book in a few pages, to get down to business more quickly than you do. I have essentially three points in mind: 1. It has to be said that nothing like this, that is, an introduction to philosophy in this form, has ever been done before; that this is not a history of opinions or ideas; that the philosophers are, rather, brought into direct confrontation with each other; that, indeed, 2. "the thinkers can truly speak only if we take them out of their historical contexts" (p. 45). And 3. the connection between science and philosophy, between separation and connection, of which you speak in regard to the relationship between philosophy and art, poetry, myth, etc. (p. 38): "close to science, fruitful for it and sometimes productive of it, but reaching infinitely far beyond it." The important thing here would be to point out right from the start the inadequacy of the usual alternatives, that is, philosophy antipathetic toward science (as embodied in German idealism or modern existentialism) on the one hand, and the positivistic identification of philosophy and science on the other. What I have in mind is something very short and very apodictic, because all these points come out afterward in the text. All you need do is give the reader a clear orientation.

I hope you won't misunderstand me: this is all just my opinion and not in any way binding. Perhaps one can't even "fight" over it, much less "debate" it. I let Kurt Wolff know what my ideas were because time was short. Under other circumstances, I would have preferred to discuss the matter with you first. But I had the feeling that it didn't matter, because Kurt Wolff is truly a friend of mine to whom you needn't hesitate to say that I'm completely off base. It was his idea that I take on the editorial work, which I will gladly do. But remember, please, that you are not in the least bound by that either. You will no doubt see him, and this letter is only to fill you in briefly on what we discussed together here.

I'll save Russia for another time. I'll send you a copy as soon as I have the essay written—early November.

What are you lecturing on this winter?? How far along are the next volumes?

Warmest greetings to you both,
Your
Hannah

212 *Karl Jaspers to Hannah Arendt*

Basel, September 24, 1957

Dear Hannah!

Here I haven't written the letter I was planning to write, and now I already have your next one with the wonderful and surprising news about the English translation. I'll respond to that right away.

You will "gladly take on the editorial work"? That is once again extraordinary and touching assistance rendered on your part. And an expression of how much you value my book. I'm a bit afraid that you are underestimating the work involved, but I am of course delighted. Obviously, I am more than agreeable. Nothing could improve the book's chances in the Anglo-Saxon world more than to be examined and abridged under your supervision and in accord with your views on it. Your suggestions seem excellent to me. To take them up individually:

1. A new preface for America presents no problem. Your comments have already set my thinking in motion, but I'll put off the writing of it until it is actually needed.

2. I can't do the abridging. I would be very averse to returning to this text I have already worked on so long. I can't even tolerate reading it. Also, I am very eager to move on to other projects.

3. As far as the abridgments you contemplate are concerned:

It makes sense to me to cut a great deal in the "Introduction." It is no doubt typically German preparation and self-justification, and like all introductions, it puts off getting down to business much too long.

And readers don't just skip over it, which they could of course do.

I'm reluctant to see the sections on the four paradigmatic individuals cut much. You should perhaps reconsider in abridging them. These four figures were important to me. I feel—perhaps foolishly—that they make a strong impression on the unprejudiced reader. Contemplating their lives leads one to the very roots of philosophical thought. That basis seems essential to me. Also, these sections tie in with things that are generally known but show them in a new light. Jesus seems to me particularly important for everyone in the Western world. I felt I was saying something there that went beyond what the theologians have to teach us and that is not so easy to come by. And then Socrates is the saint of all philosophy in the ancient world. Confucius made a great impression on me. I wanted to rescue him not only from the banal presentations he has suffered even at the hands of sinologists but also because I found him so fruitful for us. Buddha is the most alien. He has to be there as a link to Nagarjuna,[1] who in his turn is a link to modern symbolic logic, to the extent there is philosophy in it. Through these four figures the possibility of communication among all human beings is created. This section is not very long. It does not seem good to me to cut too much here. But that is not a decision on my part, rather, a request to you to think this question through again.

4.   Cuts are certainly possible in all sections, and therefore in the four paradigmatic individuals, too. I don't object at all to what you say about pace. On the contrary, I admire American literary discipline in this area.

The small print cannot unfortunately be taken as an indicator of what can be cut. I often used the difference in print size only to make the sections more surveyable. Small print marks off blocks of thought as self-contained units, but familiarity with them is often essential for understanding what follows.

5.   I would be glad to write sections on Eckhart and Cusanus. It's just a question of time. I have the materials I need (excerpts and notes)—for Cusanus, enough so that I could start writing immediately; for Eckhart, only in part. I'll start on this only when I know the American edition is certain. I recently suggested to Piper, by the way, that if there is a second printing (the first is 6,000 copies, of which 2,400 have been sold to date) we fatten up the volume by adding Cusanus at the least.

6.   Piper wrote me that Faber and Faber are considering the matter,

324

and that T. S. Eliot,[2] who is an adviser to the firm, is reading my book at the moment.

You ask what I'll be teaching in the winter. I have leave to write the second volume of the philosophers. In the summer I'm planning to lecture on Descartes, Pascal, Hobbes, Leibniz, in other words, work for the second volume. The earliest the manuscript can be done is the end of October 1958. But how uncertain that is at my age! It is a gamble, and I'm not, I think, being presumptuous.

At the moment I'm still working on the "atom bomb." From a literary point of view the book is, unfortunately, a whole philosophy *in nuce*. That seems to me unavoidable, given the subject matter. I finished a short while ago the pages I meant to send you from the section titled "Reason." And I still mean to do that once they have been copied and corrected. I'm eager to be done with it. I probably won't include Churchill, who could be useful to me as a type, or Gandhi, about whom I have written (how Churchill despised him!). I've looked through his ten volumes on the Second World War, and I felt great admiration. But this book is getting too long.

When I spoke with Piper a few weeks ago, I brought up the subject—without prior authorization from you—of your *Rahel*. He felt that the book was not really a biography, that there were too many repetitions in it, and that it would not appeal to a broad public. You can imagine how angry I was. I replied that it is much more than the mere story of a life, which anybody could write. It is a new mode of remarkable biographical illumination, constantly backed up with detail. The repetitions are necessary as recurring reflections of basic character. New material, real discoveries. Piper was clearly taken aback, but he did not say he would publish the book. That is too bad for Piper, not for you. For you will certainly find a publisher.

Your remarks on Kant always awaken in me a happy feeling of agreement. And I think at such times that perhaps you will tolerate or indeed approve of the fantasies that I have incorporated into the chapter on reason as it bears on politics and the atom bomb.

Warmest greetings, to Heinrich, too, and thanks from

Your

Karl Jaspers

My wife sends her warmest greetings and her thanks, too.

213   Karl Jaspers to Hannah Arendt

Basel, October 4, 1957

Dear Hannah!

Kurt Wolff was here last Sunday. We reached agreement in no time at all, and I have already written you what the essentials of that agreement are. It would be wonderful if an American edition should become reality. I've just heard from Piper today that Faber and Faber has declined. That leaves Routledge as the only remaining possibility in London.

Kurt Wolff brought me the enclosed review from *Neue Zürcher Zeitung*.[1] I'm sending it right on to you.

Warmest greetings
Your
Karl Jaspers

214   Hannah Arendt to Karl Jaspers

November 4, 1957

Lieber Verehrtester—

What do you think of our two new moons?[1] Can you make your peace with journeys to the moon? And what do you suppose the moon thinks? If I were the moon, I would take offense.

Forgive me for delaying until today to answer your detailed letter. I'm in complete agreement with everything in it. I had no time, and so I didn't look at the "Paradigmatic Individuals" again. You are certainly right on that point. Kurt Wolff called yesterday. You must have received the contract in the meantime. The flu has delayed everything here. Even I got it this time, and because of it I had trouble meeting the deadline for my manuscript about Russia. Now I'm done with it all—both the flu and the manuscript. I'm having an extra copy made to send to you. The essay won't appear until February, and I would like to have your reaction to it.

Piper did in fact write to me that he had reconsidered the *Rahel* project. I thought right away: He was in Basel. How nice of you to be angry with him. But I'd prefer to stay away from Piper. I just don't have any luck with him. It was the same story when we offered him *The Origins of Totalitarianism*, too. And then, I'd already sent the Rahel manuscript to Kiepenheuer. They've been trying to get something from me for years. They asked me for *The Origins of Totali-*

tarianism just after I'd signed a contract for it with Europäische Verlagsanstalt. Piper sent me Jeanne Hersch's book.[2] What do you think of it? Very sympathetic, and the critique of social democracy is really very good. But—

I have something I have to confess to you. This summer I put together for Europäische Verlagsanstalt some theoretical essays written in recent years. I wrote them all in English, and after having someone do a rough translation, I've reworked them carefully. The title of the volume is *Fragwürdige Traditionsbestände im politischen Denken der Gegenwart.*[3] They are all transitional essays, and I'm afraid you won't like them because they are entirely negative and destructive, and the positive side is hardly in evidence. Then, too, a much expanded version of the authority essay with the Heidegger quote in it is included.[4] As soon as this little book is out, I'll have a copy sent to you, of course; but I wish you were already familiar with the *Vita Activa*,[5] which you will surely like better but which will not be out until spring.

I don't know whether I told you that I had firmly resolved to come for your seventy-fifth birthday. I'm terribly unhappy to say that I won't be able to make it after all. The Chicago book has been held up so long that I can't expect proofs before February, and I can't wrap the project up if I'm in Europe. My contract stipulates a deadline; I need my books to refer to; I have to work up an index after I've seen page proofs, and so on. I just can't manage it. As consolation, though, I have an invitation—still not firm—for the city of Munich's 800th-year celebration next summer,[6] and I'm almost sure that I'll be able to come early in the summer. It pains me that I won't be there for your birthday, but I'm sure you'll understand.

I'm writing in haste. I have another deadline—the situation in the South.[7] I'll write more and better soon. One more thing: Wolff assaulted me with contract suggestions for the work on your book. I didn't like that, and I didn't have the time to give the matter any thought. Please, please make changes if you find the contract will cost you too much. I had thought he would assume the costs, or, rather, I didn't think at all because I couldn't care less about this side of the business. Now I can't even remember what he suggested and what I agreed to. We couldn't meet because he had the flu; then I did.

I hope you both have a healthy, productive winter. With warm wishes, as always,

Your
Hannah

327

Basel, November 15, 1957

Dear Hannah!

Your manuscript[1] has just arrived. I'm eager to read it. That broad sweep that I have almost come to expect from everything you write is present on the first page. I'll write you after I have read it.

I have to write today about the translation. I received Kurt Wolff's draft of the contract yesterday. I'm in agreement with all the key points, but I'm very uncomfortable with this long, printed form. I'm sending a short draft in German that follows the pattern my contracts usually use. I'm grateful to him for moving ahead on this project even though he doesn't have an English publisher firmly lined up. I am of course pleased and happy about a percentage of my royalties going to you. Kurt Wolff feels that the percentage figure should be determined after you have completed your work. Obviously you are not taking this on for the honorarium, which is always pathetically low for all work of this kind, and you are not even concerned about it. But you will not, any more than I, pass up what is our due. Kurt Wolff and I had already agreed to this here in Basel.

I enjoyed Kurt Wolff's visit very much. I don't believe I have written you about it yet. I could agree to everything he suggested. He did not go into detail about the amount of the honorarium and such matters. What I find in his draft now strikes me as respectable. There is something impressive about the man. This style of his, which used to be a familiar one to us in Germany, mixed in with American energy, I found very engaging. He is, of course, a publisher, and as such he is perhaps cleverer and more cautious in financial matters than we need to be—otherwise he couldn't survive. In view of the risk involved in my case, I find that only natural. I have no reason for complaint. No mention was made of a story from the 1920s. I don't hold it against him, and he probably thinks I don't even know about it. Frau Gothein[2] had translated Tagore.[3] Kurt Wolff had the manuscript for a long time without coming to a decision about it. Then, out of the blue, Frau Gothein received a telegram from him: "For a single payment of 1,000 Marks, the publisher will acquire all rights." Frau Gothein was delighted and accepted the offer immediately. Two weeks later the newspapers reported that Tagore had won the Nobel Prize. Kurt Wolff must have known about it. Max Weber was outraged and intervened. Kurt Wolff agreed to other more favorable terms; I don't remember, any more, exactly what they were. I needn't say that this should remain between us.

Now to your plan. I find it staggering and almost incomprehensible that you, who are—if you'll forgive me the term—among the leading minds of our time, want to invest your energies in such a project (but then, you have made so many sacrifices on my behalf). As for the project itself:

Your instincts and your editorial principle as expressed in your recent letter I found immediately convincing: Cut what would be distracting for American readers, what is interesting only for Germans but not necessarily interesting per se, what is superfluous. Revise with an eye toward effectiveness there. If my tale is as good as you think it is, then radical cutting and trimming is permissible provided that the final product works.

But once I'd reflected some more about how you would go about this, I thought: Maybe Hannah has taken on something here that is almost impossible to carry out (after all, we know she tends to let her horses run away with her). She is underestimating the work, which could amount to almost a complete rewriting of the book and which wouldn't be worth the effort in the end and probably can't even be done. Because a reworking of this kind would demand such complete immersion in the whole work of each philosopher and in the specific problems each presents, it seemed to me that this was just much too big a task. To do less would produce only superficial changes, such as cutting passages that are obviously too long—and I don't see any such passages—or the cutting of things that are not in themselves superfluous but for which you expect no interest from your readers. This latter approach I consider possible. That would not be a revision but, rather, an abridgment, based on the instinctive understanding of the American reading public that you have acquired and also on your instinct for the material.

You should, I think, do a trial passage and see how it goes. I think it possible that you may not want to take this project on after all. You should feel entirely free to proceed as you suggested in your first letter. We won't be able to reach a decision until you do this trial passage and see how things go.

I'll again have to put off writing you all the other things I want to tell you. They don't lend themselves well to dictation. But one thing I can say: Both Gertrud and I are delighted that we will see you again early in the summer. My birthday is really not important; the five-year ones aren't supposed to count anyhow. It might even have been a disturbance, because other people may come and I would prefer to speak with you alone, that is, you're the only one with whom I want to speak alone. It would be nice if we could know as soon as possible what the dates of your visit in Basel will be. Then we can adjust the dates of other visits accordingly. Unfortunately I'll be teaching (from April 22 to July 10). That is a great interference because I don't have much strength left over from teaching anymore. I'll be free only on Thursday, Saturday, and Sunday.

Warmest greetings
Your
Karl Jaspers

216   Hannah Arendt to Karl Jaspers

November 18, 1957

Lieber Verehrtester—

Your letter has just arrived. I'm answering it right away because I am much relieved that you haven't signed the contract with Wolff yet. I was planning to call him up today anyhow. I found the whole business so revolting that I chose not to think about it at first. What he is suggesting is absolutely uncustomary, and I will not agree to it, regardless of your reaction to it. Payment was the last thing on my mind. But if there is to be any payment at all for editorial work, the publisher is obliged to provide it, just as he does for translation. It isn't up to the author and editor to work out a "deal" between them. Wolff took this route because he can't possibly offer you less than a 7½% royalty. But with the 2½% difference between a normal honorarium and one for translated books he can still calculate in the price of an editor, because 7½% is rock bottom here and 8 or 8½% is often paid even for translated books. What did he have to suggest if a certain number of books are sold? At what point do you get an increase in royalties? To give you an example: I have a contract with my publisher for the German book I'm writing for Piper. I'll get 10% up to 10,000 copies; that means that the publisher will simply absorb the translation costs because a book of that kind will not sell more than 5,000 to 6,000 copies. One can't ask Wolff for terms like that for such a large work, because the costs will in fact be very high, but he really didn't have to behave quite so shabbily as he has. I hadn't heard the Tagore story, but I have heard similar ones. I thought he was becoming a little more respectable with age.

As far as the work is concerned, I have never contemplated a new version of the book. That is impossible and quite pointless as well. All I would do is cut and, in the Kant chapter, possibly suggest some minor changes in formulations where the going gets very difficult and where the translator is otherwise likely to make a mess of things. The experience that I can bring to the project includes not only an awareness of the Anglo-American reading public but also perhaps a knowledge of both languages. What I am suggesting is often done here by translators, but in this case that strikes me as dangerous.

And I ask you—we will fight about this one—how can you speak of "sacrifices"? This book will find its audience no matter what, and if I do it "for" anyone, then it isn't for you but for the American students whom I know and can help. You have your reservations, and I can understand that very well. Let me do a trial passage; then we can judge whether this plan will work out or not. From a publishing point of view, Wolff is right in wanting to publish this volume in two volumes and somewhat abridged. This approach seems viable to me, and if it is viable, it will be appropriate for the market here. If I'm wrong, then we'll drop the project.

I'm afraid, for the first time actually, that your estimation of me is too high. However, there's no point in fighting about that. But if I may speak on a "personal" level: When I was young, you were the only person who educated me. When, as an adult, I found you again after the war and a friendship grew between us, you provided me with a guarantee for the continuity of my life. And today I think of your house in Basel as I would of my homeland.

Trip to Europe: I want to sit in on your classes anyhow and look forward to that. I will also arrange things so that I will "really" come only after the semester is over, that is, in July. Everything is still very much up in the air. I had an invitation to Munich's 800th anniversary celebration, and I accepted it, in principle. Then I heard nothing more. If that all in fact happens as it is supposed to, it would be in early July. I also have to give a series of lectures in Geneva at the end of May. If everything works out, I would come so that I can give my lectures in Geneva at the end of May, run around a bit afterward, come to Basel to hear your lectures, and be back in America at the end of July.

Warmest greetings to you both, and my best to Erna,

Your
[Hannah]

217   *Karl Jaspers to Hannah Arendt*

Basel, November 23, 1957

Dear Hannah—

Your good—and angry—letter came yesterday; and today, Kurt Wolff's contract, simple, shortened, and with the terms I had approved included. So everything is in order except for one point:

"The author agrees to relinquish to Frau Hannah Arendt-Blücher for editorial work a percentage of the income due him from the publisher. This percentage will be determined on the basis of the work performed by her."

You wrote me: "I will not agree to that, regardless of your reaction to it." And your reasoning was that this was not a matter to be worked out between author and editor.

I certainly agree with you on that last point. I didn't think the matter through clearly when, in my conversation with Wolff in Basel, I agreed to accept less for my share in order to provide an adequate honorarium for the editor. My thinking went like this: The publisher will have to figure out how to do this. A business relationship exists only between him and each one of us, not between us. What that meant to me then was: Hannah has to receive an appropriate honorarium. Given the size and the nature of that book, I will therefore receive less than usual. So I am at fault—or partially at fault—because I was not mentally alert enough to think the matter through to the end and in concrete terms. I'm also at fault for accepting Wolff's concrete suggestion.

But even now there is *no legal* relationship established between the editor and the author. In fact the matter is such that by my agreement I have wounded your generosity—*very* unwittingly. *I* didn't mean to pay *you* anything. Rather, I wanted to allow the publisher to pay me less so that he would have more leeway to cover his expenses for translator and editor.

So please, don't be angry, but take this all with the humor that is essential to dealing with publishers. Don't be concerned about *me* in this matter. Because your business relationship is *only* with the publisher, work that out with him without worrying about me.

I feel that Hannah's intransigence will not let this slip by so easily, and so I am not in complete agreement with her. For your noblesse oblige will not want to put *me* in a position where I will have to break my word to the publisher or agree to your coming off badly in this arrangement.

I'm going to let the contract lie for now, and I'll only sign it when you no longer forbid me to (you don't have to agree to it). I would appreciate a prompt reply so that I don't have to keep K. Wolff waiting too long. K. Wolff can show you the entire contract, but you needn't be familiar with the whole thing, because you would then immediately start arguing for my rights instead of arguing independently of them for your own.

This is all unnecessary fuss. I'm annoyed that you're annoyed, and I'm afraid that you will want to cut through the knot rather than untie it. Please don't!

I'd like to write about many other things that are more important. But I'll put that off because I have to work on my "atom book" if I'm ever to be done with it. It keeps presenting me with new problems all the time.

I read your essay[1] with great interest. Thanks very much for it. That it is brilliant from a literary point of view goes without saying. What you said about the "events" in Hungary and how you said it was excellent. It was particularly meaningful to me because I had just written a foreword[2] a few weeks ago for the German edition of Lasky's document collection [on the Hungarian revolution]. I like what you said about it better than what I wrote. But our basic views are similar. You were with us back then when it began. How we reacted at the time was characteristic of each of us. You shouted out with joy. Gertrud was somber because it could not succeed and all she could see was the suffering the Hungarians would have to undergo. (Her immediate reaction on July 20, 1944,[3] was similar: "People shouldn't attempt something like that if they're not sure of success," because all she could think of was the consequences—the persecutions and murders.) And I: I was startled because something that was considered impossible was actually happening. I had some hope it could succeed, though I was without that "emotional warmth" that took opposite though "complementary" directions in both of you. Or are my recollections incorrect? —One thing that pleased me in your essay was that you held onto your old illuminating thesis for its truth, not out of mere stubbornness: The principle of total rule forces everyone who lives under it into acts that are in keeping with it. If he engages in such acts, as Khrushchev is doing now—whether by instinct or by insight—then he gains the upper hand, because the principle reasserts itself through him. You then ask: What is the source of power if there is no police force or army? Your answer is surprising: the new invention of generalized spying among the "comrades," in adherence to the most ruthless party ideology. I still don't understand completely, but I do see that there is a puzzle as to where the real power that holds the machinery together comes from. Your view that anything can happen, even a sudden, dramatic collapse, is convincing. Can the totalitarian principle, which your major book was the first to illuminate and define in all its aspects and in a logical structure, function without a dictator (or in such a way that the person of the dictator is interchangeable) and without the dictatorship of a collective that is constantly purging and reconstituting itself? The old tools of politics (Machiavelli) are surely as much in force in Russia today as they ever were but, if you are correct, in a subordinate role. It is an eerie business, as if a principle were, so to speak, alive and as if everyone, including the dictator of the moment, had become mere functionaries of it. I agree with you in your rejection of the usual sociological aspects (Djilas's "new class"[4]), because a shift in the meaning of all of them has taken place. It is certainly correct too that the governmental machinery in Russia, as a self-sustaining power, plays a role, but you put your finger on the point that makes that all completely different from the way it has been seen in the traditional forms of sociology. I'm far from comprehending this, although I'm convinced that you are revealing a truly new reality here. Individual aspects (such as the lies in which totalitarian rulers entangle themselves) are much discussed by other writers, but these things all take on another dimension in your work. And then, I find it wonderful that you neither demonize this mystery nor dispel it with rational clarity. Rather, you home in on it by way of the rationally perceivable and factual, and, finally, you take into account the possibility that it may explode, taking humanity down with it, or that it may dissolve into nothing, opening the way for humankind again. I found your essay less dogmatic than your book (in which you perhaps border on the dogmatic here and there). I'd like to hear more from you about certain details; for example, the difference between China and Russia in terms of the mass purges (in China "only" 15

334

million out of 600 million). Starliner's thesis[5] that China did not collectivize the peasantry is apparently wrong. That the "principle" took a very different form in China is clear. Mao,[6] who is obviously very cultured, writes poems (they seem very impressive in their German translations) in the old Chinese tradition but with new content (the famous "long march"—with the airplane over the whole, huge empire), written, so to speak, in a dialogue with the great emperors of past millennia. Mao appears to be one of a kind and not a type. Your "principle" is the major force here too. But enough of this.

You feel that I overvalue you. It was a turn of phrase for which I apologized immediately. None of us knows.

I was happy to read your "personal" remarks about my role in your life, of which you have made mention before. Is a "principle"—in a very different sense, of course—at work here, too? In the personal realm more than in the individual, the private, the principle that we serve or through which we exist, not, of course, as functions of a machine, but as incarnations of something that we, following Kant, call reason? The reason that allows us to achieve substance in history?

Warmest greetings from Gertrud
and your Karl Jaspers

Give my regards to Heinrich. When I think of him, I think too of his close ties with Kant and of his remark that Germany does not interest him anymore. I interpret him as meaning by that: Germany's present political structures, not our Germany.

218   *Hannah Arendt to Karl Jaspers*

New York, December 3, 1957

Lieber Verehrtester—

Your letter was a real joy. The precision with which you responded to my Hungary essay. There's a line in one of Rilke's poems: "Freier durch Widerruf freut sich die Fähigkeit" [Made freer by response, talent takes delight][1] in which "Widerruf" means echo. That says what I mean more concisely than I could.

Now some quick lines on the contract business. I feel I arrived at an amicable and friendly compromise with Kurt Wolff yesterday. He will send you a new draft of the contract, to which I have agreed and which I hope you will not find unfavorable. If you do, please say so. We tried to figure out as best we could how things would fall out financially, but that is impossible because Wolff still doesn't know what price he will set for the book and I still don't know how much work it will cost me. More on that in a minute.

Instead of one contract there will now be two, one between Wolff and you and another between Wolff and me. The one with you contains some changes in the graduation of your royalties. For the first 5,000 copies, you'll receive 7½% as previously agreed. Wolff doesn't think greater sales are out of the question, but he's not counting on them. If the book is more successful, however, you will not get 10% for 5,000 to 10,000 copies, as previously stipulated, but will have to make do with 8½%. If the book should enjoy very great success, though, your royalty will climb to 15%, which was not the case in the original contract. The contract gives me the 1½%. In order to have something on hand for editorial work in case of a smaller printing, Wolff will suggest that you receive only 40% of the secondary rights (reprints, etc.) instead of 50%, which means that I would then receive 10% from secondary rights.

This means, of course, that my honorarium will depend in large part on the success of the book. To spread that risk around fairly, Wolff has agreed to pay me a nonrefundable advance on royalties when I deliver the manuscript.

Because I don't know how much work the project will entail, the limit on my honorarium will be determined only after I have delivered the manuscript. That means that it will be contractually agreed between Wolff and me that as soon as a certain limit is reached, my share of the royalties reverts back to you. This will not be included in your contract because, without firm figures to work with, the formulation of it becomes too complicated.

I don't know how you will react to this. The arrangements strike me as fair now. What was important to me was that Wolff assume part of the risk and that under no circumstances your royalties be less than 7½%. On the other hand, it seemed justified to me from Wolff's point of view that your royalty not rise as rapidly as it ordinarily would if the book does better than expected.

If you don't like these arrangements for some reasons that I have overlooked, please, please say so and sign the old contract if that's what you prefer. Then we'll figure out later what we want to do.

Wolff was pleasant and open to all my arguments. He seemed to me like a cat who keeps on mousing out of firmly entrenched habit but who really doesn't care all that much about mousing anymore.

Perhaps I'm mistaken. I'll write about other things soon. I'm somewhat hurried today but wanted to tend to this matter quickly.

Just a word about your recollection: It was just as you said it was, and I too had the feeling at the time that your wife's reaction and mine were complementary to each other—like two sides of the same medallion. —Heinrich sends his warmest regards.

My best to you both

Your
Hannah

219 Karl Jaspers to Hannah Arendt

Basel, December 19, 1957

Dear Hannah!

Thank you for bringing this contract business to a satisfactory conclusion. I inquired of K. Wolff and have heard from him that he will pay you an advance of $500. It seems to me we cannot ask for more. As he sees it, the matter has been settled "fairly." It seems unlikely that enough copies will be sold to make further payments to you a reality. Your skillful maneuvering has once again ensured that nothing will be subtracted from my share. So in reality I am probably a bit in disfavor with Wolff. Now he will be paying what should have been taken from my share. Your speculation on future possibilities—with fictions—reminds me of a story I heard recently. An old German professor, in order to garner some immediate and very tangible advantages for himself, gave someone, all duly notarized, a share in his inheritance of major landholdings in Saxony (in case the East German state ceased to exist and old ownerships were restored!). The difference is that you have done just the opposite: you assure me immediate financial gain and rob me of shares in a fictional income, and very small shares at that. But since you have done this, you must also allow me to find it inadmissible for you to want to pay me back something from that fictional income. I'm *very* happy that the matter has been settled and sealed by contract. And in addition, I've had great fun in watching your unself-servingly unbusinesslike business acumen in action. If you wanted to be, you could be a winner in business too. But I fear that the point would always come somewhere at which you would, in a very unbusinesslike way, knock the underpinnings out from under your most elegant constructions.

Of the many observations in your essay,[1] one in particular has preoccupied me: What you say about the emergence of "councils" in all the revolutions of the last hundred years and what you view as very positive. I can recall the period of the workers and soldiers' councils in Germany.[2] What was astounding was that for that short period absolute order prevailed, as if by itself. Max Weber was a member of the Heidelberg Workers and Soldiers' Council, and he asked one day: Who, I'd like to know, is actually governing here? So often (though not always) councils are characterized by inspired and competent leadership and actions, but the moment a government emerges from them, they lose their significance. Wouldn't a "corporative state" be the result if things were different, that is, if the mass elections that reduce everything to the lowest common denominator and do away with the councils did not form a government? Much as Mussolini[3] abused the concept of the corporative state, it had remarkable power: as if expertise, personalities, the spirit of those called to a political vocation could triumph over the brutal, plebiscitary spirit that produced Eisenhower's victory over Stevenson! An aura from the Middle Ages that easily deceives us. What exactly did you have in mind in valuing the councils so highly? —But I don't want to steal your time. I'll ask you in person—and I won't write other things I could write. How much we would have to talk about if you lived in Basel!

Enjoy happy holidays with Heinrich! Warmest greetings to you both
from Gertrud and your Karl Jaspers

220   *Gertrud and Karl Jaspers to Hannah Arendt*

Basel, January 14, 1958

Dear Hannah,

First of all, we are well. The only reason I'm writing is that the mess Karl's papers are in makes it difficult for me to find out exactly what you wrote about your summer visit. My youngest brother is coming from Tel Aviv with his wife,[1] and I'd like to arrange things so that your visits don't overlap. And we have of course forgotten the dates you mentioned. We hope to see you again, hale and hearty, at our home. We look forward to it. My husband is making good use of this winter's delightful work leave, slaving with dogged persistence on his little book that is rapidly becoming a big one.[2] I hope he will finish it soon. He is reckoning a few more weeks. But he is often mistaken in these estimates. Then I'll give it a critical reading. I've typed it already, but not sequentially in one piece. I still haven't established any relationship to this topical book. There will be many sensitive questions to settle. Very different from Augustine,[3] which just seemed to come together of itself toward the end. —We have gotten through the winter without any flu or colds, though we have lived entirely to ourselves. Because you can't celebrate with us and also because one really can't celebrate in a big way every five years, we plan to keep quietly to ourselves and count our blessings on Karl's 75th birthday. I remain superstitious. It's a great help.

As for myself, I am content. And so it's best if I send Heinrich and you my regards and close for today.

Your   Gertrud Jaspers

Dear Hannah! I've just found your letter of November 18—so there is order in the disorder after all! There you write: "I will 'really' come only after the semester is over, that is, in July. Everything is still very much up in the air . . . invitation to Munich . . . early July . . ." Before that you would like to hear me lecture. So we can expect you twice. Wonderful! *If* you can give us firm dates—for Munich and whatever else you will do—we would be grateful, so that we can make our other arrangements accordingly.

Your essay volume[4] arrived yesterday. I started reading it and am eager to get to the rest. You'll hear from me as soon as I have time. I *have* to finish my atom book now. Perhaps I took on too much with it. It demands more than I can give to it. It is becoming a "volume." The fact is I'm a born professor and write textbooks.

Warm regards
Your Karl Jaspers

221 *Hannah Arendt to Gertrud and Karl Jaspers*

January 17, 1958

Liebe Gute,

The only thing you forgot to tell me was when your brother is coming. How should we arrange things?

Things look like this for me: I'll arrive in France in early May, will go from there to Bremen,[1] and have to be in Cologne and Frankfurt in mid-May. Then in the last week of May I will definitely be in Geneva from May 27 to 30 for a lecture series. I could very easily come for a weekend either before or after that. I can also stay longer, but during the semester that wouldn't be so good.

I had the idea of working in June. I have the chance to live in Zurich in the apartment of a friend[2] who is in New York at the moment, and I thought I could easily come from there to Basel for lectures and seminars without being a disturbance to you. If the Munich thing in fact happens, that will be in early July. I thought I would come to you right after that, after July 12 to be exact, the day the semester ends in Basel, and then I would go home directly from Basel. I think I'll come by ship this time.

As you see, I'm very flexible. At some point in all this I do, of course, have to go to Luxembourg to see Anne [Weil]. I can make my plans to suit you. But it would be good if you could let me know what is good for you so that Anne can make her plans accordingly.

I've just given *The Great Philosophers* a place on my desk—Kurt Wolff had the pages copied, and I need Heinrich's help to move this monster package at all. I haven't been able to begin on it until now, but now I do have adequate time. I'm thinking of giving it a couple of hours every day. And I'm looking forward to it. I've just about wrapped up all my projects in English and can give my full attention to the Piper book.

We have just put a socially very active time behind us. That's why I didn't even write at New Year's. I'm terribly ashamed of myself. The New Year's Eve party was especially enjoyable, a grand blast.

There's not much else to report, except that I've received and accepted a fantastic offer from Princeton for next spring: a semester as visiting professor with the salary of a full professor and without any duties aside from delivering three public lectures during the semester! and being in Princeton for 4 or 3½ days each week. That is no problem for me, because those are the days when Heinrich isn't in New York anyhow. Totally puzzled, I finally asked them what they were paying me this money for—about $6,000, though I don't know the exact amount yet. The answer, typically American: We thought you would be a good person to have around. And in the Department of American History and Civilization of all things, a field in which I really know next to nothing. So we'll be rich once again.

I'm eagerly awaiting the atom book. What do you think about the scientists' Göttingen Declaration?[3] Heinrich is home for his two months of winter holidays, much too much of which always goes into having to see people. New York is too big, and we know too many people.

Lieber Verehrtester, one more question: You will recall my little American protégée Beverly Woodward, who turned up at your house one day. She is in Basel now and will be attending your lecture and seminar this summer. She is planning to return to the States in the fall of 1958 and take her doctorate at Columbia University. She needs a fellowship and is applying for one. She has recommendations from Ricoeur,[4] very positive, and presumably from Karl Barth, too, with whom she is studying now. It would be good if you too could write a few lines, but this is a real imposition, because you hardly know the child and don't know whether she deserves this. She is living in Binningen bei Basel, Blauenweg 2, c/o Ratti. The recommendation should be addressed to Columbia University, Office of University Admission, 322 University Hall, New York 27, N.Y. I'm writing a few words for her, of course. That makes some kind of sense, even though I'm really not directly involved.

To both of you, all very best wishes for the New Year from both of us,

As always your
Hannah

222 *Hannah Arendt to Karl Jaspers*
New York, February 18, 1958
Lieber Verehrtester—

I'm really very sad now that I can't be in Basel. A seventy-fifth birthday seems to me even more important than a seventieth, three-fourths of one hundred years, and I made a firm resolve at your seventieth to make a special celebration of this one. So I'm doing it by myself by reading your *Autobiography* again, and thinking: What a thoroughly happy life! What you do not write about and perhaps could not write about is the splendor of age, of which we are perhaps well enough aware but in which we don't quite believe. Both of you have made me conscious of it again and again. One encounters it so rarely, but when one does, it is like the crowning of a lifetime. And the nice thing about it is that it is surely only possible when we live as couples and grow old together.

You have surely given yourself as a birthday present the completion of your atom book, and you are celebrating that along with your birthday. And that too is another clear sign of the harmony of your life and work. I've already started work here on *The Great Philosophers*, and I'm racking my brain over which translation to choose for the Plato quotes, which for the Kant, and what I should probably translate myself so that your meaning is not lost, what I should add to the bibliographies for an American audience, and other such matters. Most of the passages you cite I've been able to find without any trouble, but I will have to ask you for a few here and there. The translator mustn't translate directly from the German in the quotes, so he'll have to know where to find what. I haven't begun to think about the cutting yet. I promised Wolff that I would complete the first volume before I left, mainly so that I would be able to discuss everything with you directly and also because the translator [Ralph Manheim] lives in Paris and I want to talk with him. —Will your atom book be out when I come to Europe?

I've just returned, after great delay, on a flight from Toronto that turned into quite a little adventure because of the winter storms here. I'd gone to take part in an idiotic but well-paying television program. The moral is: One just shouldn't try to come by money easily. Heinrich was worried; I lost time—in short, a real nuisance. I'm in the middle of my Piper book,[1] which is going to be longer than I thought and take longer than Piper thought. Well, he's no doubt accustomed to woes of this sort. I'll write to him in the next few days.

Just a brief acknowledgment of, and reply to, your wife's kind letter: I'll arrive after the semester ends, on July 12. I have to be back here no later than August 1, and I want to go home via Paris to speak with the translator after my visit with you. I'll probably fly after all. On an overpopulated ship I feel as if I'm in a first-class concentration camp. As you see, then, I can make my plans entirely to suit you, so please tell me how much time you have for me.

Jeanne Hersch will probably come to America. The Rockefeller Foundation wants to bring her over for about six months or something like that. I was asked about her (please keep this between us) and recommended her highly, of course.

Dear, dear friends, I'm reluctant to produce mighty phrases. You know what I wish for you and for me.

As ever and forever

Your Hannah

223 *Karl Jaspers to Hannah Arendt*

Basel, March 5, 1958

Dear Hannah!

You celebrated my birthday in such a friendly, close, and unselfserving way that your letter provided me with one of the lovely moments that have stayed with me from those days. I am grateful to you for everything you have done for us both, but even more for this friendship. It makes me feel confident that it will withstand every test. I send back to you your own words: "as ever and forever."

Then the potted blue hyacinths arrived, a whole bush of them. They filled the room with their fragrance (I'm very fond of it. Hyacinths have been my birthday flower since early childhood). Extravagant, this huge basket, as what you do so often is. Your American friend [Beverly Woodward] brought it in a car. It would have been impossible to carry it. I liked the girl, by the way, although I don't really know her yet. She struck me as free, unselfconscious, "modern," "rootless," and yet not confused despite that. She seems to be pursuing an ideal; she respects you, without excessive emotion but obviously very deeply, as if you were her model and gave her courage. I'm enclosing a carbon of the letter I sent to Columbia.[1]

It's really a very good thing you were not here on my birthday. I don't tolerate all the activity and talking well, and my wife doesn't either anymore. Anyone who is close to us therefore doesn't get his due. My physical being offers a kind of resistance I cannot overcome but have to deal with diplomatically, paying my due respects to the body. How different and wonderful physical vitality is which needn't set itself any limits.

The celebration was different from my seventieth birthday, too. You can't repeat these things. There's only *one* birthday of old age, and that is the seventieth. The eightieth is, for those who experience it, a quiet straggler. One is almost not there anymore, at best a memory for the world. The seventieth is like a focal point for one's whole life. As the Bible says: "The days of our years are threescore years and ten. . . ."[2] That is a qualitative statement, not a quantitative one. That charming game you played with three-quarters of a century sprang from your irrepressible impulse to put the best possible face on reality for your friends' benefit. One could make wonderful observations on biology and history and time here.

The flood of letters and telegrams (about three hundred altogether) and flowers was greater than it was five years ago. One is pleased to know the world respects one (very strange actually), and that there are more than a few whose regard one enjoys. I have to resort to a printed thank-you note, which I'm sending out by the score. But among those many messages were some that were touching, some even deeply moving. My sister and Ella [Mayer] were here and are still here.

Basel did not join in the celebration. Only the ten-year celebrations, not the five-year ones, count here, quite reasonably.

The invitation to Princeton is wonderful and fully deserved. The best of America is coming to your door. But then, you will have to put up with Mr. Walter Kaufmann as a partner in discussions. I suspect that you will be more than a match for his rationalisms and sophisms. Then he will just keep still. He will not himself be convinced, because he is a person capable only of positions, not convictions.

I still have not read your essays.[3] The end of February was the deadline for my "atom bomb," and I had no choice but to finish it. I finally sent the manuscript off yesterday. I just checked by telephone with Munich to make sure it arrived. It is, I fear, much too long for Piper. Well, we'll see. The manuscript pages I was going to send you before, I haven't sent after all. I struck out the one sentence that came from our conversation. The whole passage no longer has any concrete tie to our talk and is not a continuation of it either. Rather, it has been separated from it and moved into the realm of the "general." I am enclosing the omitted lines[4] here.

So now you are working on *The Great Philosophers*. What a task you have taken upon yourself! You are, of course, going about the business thoroughly, as is your wont, and are finding it much more of a job than you expected. If you get sick of it, you must give it up. I can think of this project with pleasure only if we share the same impulse: to make these great men accessible to those readers who are willing to think. I feel sure that your introduction to the book will help it find its audience in America if anything can. We believe there are people in America who have not yet had their say. —The book has sold quite well in Germany (4,000 copies from a printing of 6,000). Only one of my books has been commercially successful in America so far: *Reason and Existenz*,[5] published by the Noonday Press and translated—apparently very well—by Earle.

How nice that you are coming to see us! We'll expect you on July 12, and for occasional visits from Zurich before that. Plan to stay for as long as it suits you. If you want to be in America on August 1 and to see Manheim in Paris before that, maybe you can stay with us until the 24th, perhaps even longer. As you know from experience, you have to have something to do when you are with us. I can speak for only a limited time each day. I hope the atom book will be out by then. Publication is planned for June.

Give my regards to Heinrich, and my thanks for his birthday wishes.[6]

Warmest greetings
Your Karl Jaspers

224 *Hannah Arendt to Karl Jaspers*

March 16, 1958

Lieber Verehrtester—

Your wonderful letter. I sometimes think back on my youth, and then it seems to me like a dream that everything has turned out as it has. The omitted sentences that you sent me are very fine, and I found them completely convincing. My reaction—"You shouldn't have said that"—was wrong. I reacted from the outside, so to speak. It was good, of course, that you did not keep silent about it. Perhaps we should return to this subject again when I'm there. To write about it is too complicated for me at the moment. Unfortunately, something really stupid was affecting me, namely, the German atmosphere at the universities with its "here Jaspers—there Heidegger." I encountered it in its most pronounced form in Dolf Sternberger. It reminds me of the rivalry between the ancient schools of philosophy. None of that has anything to do with what you said, of course. I'm just mentioning it here to clear it out of the way of our discussion.

My main reason for writing today is to report about work on *The Great Philosophers* and to make some suggestions to you. The

345

suggestions follow from two basic assumptions: 1. The publisher feels that the book has to be shortened by about 20% for the American market. 2. The publisher and I both feel that American readers will not take well to the long "Introduction." They want to get to the heart of the matter more quickly. The conclusion I draw from that is to revise the "Introduction" radically. That is the only option we have anyhow if we are going to cut the book, because it is almost impossible to do any cutting in the major presentations—perhaps some can be done in the "Paradigmatic Individuals," I think, but next to none in Plato—Augustine—Kant.

So my suggestion is to limit the "Introduction" to purely technical matters and to leave out the entire section on greatness. If we include it, then we'll hardly be able to cut at all.[1]

I'm glad that you like my little Beverly Woodward. She sent me a very respectable paper she wrote in French on Plato's doctrine of the soul, along with a somewhat wild but intelligent commentary in English. "Rootless"—unfortunately true in the most literal sense, that is, without family. Her mother left her father [. . .] a decent man but without any understanding of a child like her. I guess I'm something of a mother figure for her, although she never tried to get close to me; and I think all the better of her for that. A talented youngster who doesn't have it easy. She wrote a delighted letter about her visit with you.

Piper wrote very enthusiastically about your atom book. I'm very eager to see it and will no doubt be able to read it before we really get together. Yes, Zurich in June, if nothing gets in the way. At the beginning of July I'll be in Munich for the 800-year circus. They're paying for my trip! Otherwise I probably wouldn't have accepted. I absolutely hate that kind of affair.

On July 12, I'll be with you. The first thing I mean to do is try to convince you that you're mistaken about old age. (Now your wife will say: "Hannah is getting impudent.") The Bible quote may be right, but all that has in fact been pushed up about ten years. Just think of the many eighty-year-olds who are more active today than seventy-year-olds were thirty years ago. Besides, we shouldn't have any prejudices in such matters but should just take things as they come. You are unchanged, not only in what is commonly called intellectual vitality but also in your ability to take in new information, in your alertness, in your openness to the world. That's not just me "putting the best possible face" on anything. That's just a statement of fact.

346

I'm working on proofs and doing other such business. I also have to work up my lectures for Europe. I'm writing secretly, as it were, on the book for Piper and enjoying it. Princeton—the best thing about it is that it's so well paid.

I'll be with you soon.

> Warmest greetings to you both, and regards to Erna—
> Your
> Hannah

225 Karl Jaspers to Hannah Arendt

Basel, March 25, 1958

Dear Hannah!

Again, my warmest thanks for everything! I can write only a short reply today because the "atom bomb," administrative chores, and now the coming semester have me in such a whirl that it costs me energy to maintain the balance I need to do anything properly.

Today, to deal with the main thing: your work on *The Great Philosophers*. You have, now and for all time, a completely free hand for the entire project. I trust you. The responsibility cannot be divided. These answers I'm sending you are merely opinions:

Doing without the "Introduction" is probably good for America. The "German professor" always has to "introduce" things, to justify himself, to lay out his plan. I've always done that. In this case, my intention was to create the "mood" for studying great philosophers, to ward off feelings inimical to my project, to strengthen respect while making a maximum effort to achieve honesty and realism. And so the omission of the introduction strikes me as somewhat strange: as if the connecting link and the foundation were swept away. But I am not disagreeing with you. Go ahead and drop the "Introduction." My only question is: Could it be published in another form at the same time? Isn't it, after all, an independent whole that can stand on its own? If that can't be, then I can make my peace with that, too. The American reader, once he has read my major presentations, will perhaps come by himself to the things I have said in the "Introduction."

The publisher told me personally at an earlier date that he didn't want to cut the book for cutting's sake but, rather, that he wanted to make it more accessible for the American reader. Indeed, he wanted to lengthen it by adding Eckhart and Cusanus (which I cannot provide at this time). Now you write that he wants an abridgement per se. That troubles me a little.

The specific cuts you have suggested all seem good to me. They clearly provide a justified smoothing of the way for the reader.

In Plato: the attractive force of being[1]: *The Republic* 523a. There it says of the subjects of instruction that lead to reason (νόησις): ἑλκτικῷ ὄντι παντάπασι πρὸς οὐσίαν.

How much I'm looking forward to seeing you!

Warmest greetings
Your Karl Jaspers

226   Hannah Arendt to Karl Jaspers

April 24, 1958

Lieber Verehrtester—

Your "I trust you" struck terror into my heart—or, better, as people say here, it put the fear of God in me. I gave the book through Augustine to Kurt Wolff two days ago so that he could send it on to Manheim. I turned the business about the introduction over in my mind several times again but finally settled on my radical solution after all. The reader here has to get into the book more quickly. What tipped the scales for me was that several people here who know the book well and are delighted that it will appear in English shared this same opinion. I spoke with Wolff about a simultaneous publication of the "Introduction." He basically supports the idea of a separate publication, but he wants to delay it until after publication of the first volume (up to and including Kant). I'm not sure whether this isn't just a diplomatic response on his part or if he's really serious about it. Without his agreement, one can hardly offer the introduction to other publishers. We'll have to talk further about this.

There's one thing I don't understand. You wrote that the publisher didn't want to cut for cutting's sake and told you that himself. From the very beginning he asked me whether I thought cuts were possible—primarily because of the very high costs of production. But this is not important; he is giving me free rein. He saw that there were hardly any cuts after the "Introduction," and he had no complaints. He knows, too, that I think the Kant shouldn't be cut. The work lies in finding the appropriate translations for the texts you cite and not

348

to leave this to the translator. Also to tell him where the passages from the New Testament are so that he won't waste too much time. This is the reason why I haven't been able to finish the Kant yet. I just don't know the existing English translations well enough to sort that all out. I want to discuss this with Friedrich (Carl Joachim) of Harvard before I begin. He has translated Kant and very well, though far from all of him. —Eckhart and Cusanus can wait because Wolff wants to make two volumes out of the one anyhow and, if I understand him right, wants to publish them separately.

I've heard from Manheim, will see him in Paris now and also arrange something with him for the end of July, when he'll have seen the book and will know what the difficulties are likely to be.

I'm about to board the ship, and I'm already in a bit of a tizzy. I suddenly found myself with a lot to do in the last few weeks, and I'm tired. I'm looking forward to the boat trip. I'm traveling with an American friend, Rose Feitelson, whom I want to show around a little in Germany. Then she'll go on to Yugoslavia. I've told you about her—she has been checking all my English manuscripts for more than twelve years now.[1]

One more favor: Could you tell me when your lectures and seminar are? I so much want to come! I won't bother you at all but will go right back to Zurich again!

To be able to do that—how wonderful!

Until soon, until soon!
Always your
Hannah

I'm very eager to read the atom book. I hope I'll have it before I come to Basel. The new essay volume[2] is very handsome. Piper sent it to me.

227   *Karl Jaspers to Hannah Arendt*

Basel, May 1, 1958

Dear Hannah!

You'll have started off on your big trip by now. Thank you for your last lines from America and your good news.

For today, just a quick response to your questions: I lecture on Monday, Tuesday, and Wednesday afternoons from 5 to 6 on Descartes, Pascal, Hobbes, Leibniz. There will be no lecture on May 14 and on May 26. I have a seminar on Hegel's philosophy of history on Fridays from 5 to 7. But please, the trip from Zurich is much too much trouble. It isn't worth it, except for you to reassure yourself that my mouth is still functional!

My atom bomb book is supposed to be in the bookstores on June 30, but for publicity purposes Piper is having some copies printed on poor-quality paper to distribute to book dealers and radio stations. As soon as these provisional copies are available, I'll send you one. Then you'll get the real thing early in July.

I'm very eager to have your response to the atom bomb book. I'm quite worried about it because I've taken a chance here with a subject for which the extent of my knowledge is inadequate. The point is to show the problem in all its perspectives and to say that only by viewing the whole picture today can the basic strength of human beings emerge and perhaps become our source of salvation. The key point is to show where all "doing" and "planning" come up short but still follow a guiding principle that comes before doing yet is not irrational or alien to thought. My attempt can have value only as an attempt to go the whole way in a fundamental way, and it will be meaningful only if others do the same thing better and soon. —My wife and I send our warmest greetings. And please give our regards to your friend.[1]

Your Karl Jaspers

228 Hannah Arendt to Gertrud and Karl Jaspers

Luxembourg, May 10, 1958

Dear, dear friends—

Thank you for your letters[1] that were here to greet me. I won't be in Switzerland before the end of May. I'll be in Zurich on the 21st, am giving a lecture there on the 22nd, and will try to come to your seminar on the Friday after that, the 23rd. Please let me. It's one of the things I've come to Europe expressly to do. In the two weeks after that I can't come. I'll be in Geneva first, then in Heidelberg and Frankfurt. Then after that, my Zurich address is:

Minervastr. 26, c/o Britschgi. Telephone: 24/67/45.

I've had a wonderful week. It will, alas, alas! be over on Monday. My friend here has her own apartment, and the furniture is from the time when I got to know her. And I sometimes feel as if nothing had ever changed. And in a certain sense that is true.

When is the atom book coming out?? I am waiting so eagerly for it.

I can't write about Europe yet. Paris is always like a dream that lies outside of time. And Luxembourg too lies outside of time in another sense. This is a totally godforsaken place except for the presence of the Coal and Steel Community.[2]

If you want to reach me before I'm in Zurich, I'll be in the Hotel Bristol in Cologne from May 16 to 20.

How excited I am! So soon now—

Warmest greetings
Your
Hannah

229 *Hannah Arendt to Gertrud and Karl Jaspers*

Until September 10
Chestnut Lawn House
Palenville, N.Y.
August 8, 1958

Dear, dear friends—

I'm so many miles away again. I can hardly believe it, for I am still reverberating to the harmonies of my weeks in Basel, that "most alive, lively of times." And with those reverberations still so present to me, I am thinking about writing my eulogy of you.[1] Unfortunately, that's no guarantee that I'll write a decent one. And if I start thinking about that possibility, then, of course, I can't write at all.

Blumenfeld was immensely pleased with the atom book. He is in much better health. We had a few days entirely to ourselves, and that was a real strain but very nice as well. And then the drive down to Geneva with dear Zilkens,[2] who came to pick us up. And then on the same evening the plane to New York. I still find the suddenness of flying somewhat unsettling, the speed of it: you're still here and then you're already there. Flying itself doesn't bother me at all. One feels much safer than one is.

I didn't find Heinrich feeling very well. He had a peripheral neuritis, nothing serious at all, but unpleasant and irritating. He's feeling much better already, but it was good to get out of New York and the oppressive heat quickly. I had to sit down right away and read proofs for the second edition of *Totalitarianism*—now the galleys on the radiator in the study upstairs can be thrown away—unpack, and pack again for Palenville. I hardly managed to get caught up on sleep. But I've made up for that here, where things are the same as ever—for us just right—where we know every tree and therefore know exactly what is happening, both with the trees and with the houses and people.

The main thing I have to report is that Arthur Cohen[3] from Meridian Books, who asked after you and whom I naturally told about the "atom bomb," was instantly very, very keen on acquiring the rights. I told him how things stood. He thought he could offer better terms than Chicago Press could. He has surely written to you in the meantime. It seems to me it can only be to the good for you and your negotiations if you have a second offer. My experience with Meridian Books has been good, but personally I have much more confidence in Alex Morin[4] at the Chicago Press than I do in Arthur Cohen.

And then there is Arlosoroff[5]: It's best if you not include him at all. His murder has never been cleared up. It's almost a sure thing, but not absolutely sure, that the murderers were Jewish. The English were still in the country then and were responsible for police, etc. Blumenfeld gave me a detailed account, but the upshot of it all was simply that one has to let the matter rest. More on your other questions later. Blumenfeld thinks they wanted to murder Weizmann[6] but didn't get him. That was Weizmann's opinion, too.

I'll write about things here another time. American foreign policy is completely topsy-turvy, and the only thing the president is interested in is golf. If only we were rid of this administration. No one here is interested in the Middle East, and because prosperity is breaking out all over again, the Republicans, unfortunately, have a very good chance of winning the next election.

Last but not least, the dream dress:[7] I've asked at every place in New York that sells fabrics from France, but no luck. In a shop where an older man waited on me they could at least recall the material. . . . I'm afraid it just doesn't exist at the moment, and we'll have to wait until it comes back into fashion. My guess is that this material, which was very light, was too durable. I spoke about it with an old friend of mine who is wealthy and between 75 and 80 years old. She still has a dress of this material and has had it for over thirty years. Indestructible. She couldn't be of any help either. It's unlikely that the material is available in Paris. We get everything here that the Continent has to offer in the way of elegance. Anne [Weil] will not be in Paris before September, and the Koyrés[8] aren't there either. So you see, lieber Verehrtester, my best efforts to share in the profits from your atom bomb book have proved of no avail. There's one more possibility in New York. I'll try that when we're back in the city, and then I'll report to you again.

All best wishes for the holidays. Regards to Erna, and, of course, to your brother [Fritz Mayer] if he is still there.

Warmest greetings
Your
Hannah

230 *Karl Jaspers to Hannah Arendt*

Basel, September 16, 1958

Dear Hannah!

You'll be wondering why I haven't answered your letter of August 8 yet. It is terrible, all the more so because I was very happy after your visit with us.

One reason was that I had two spells of fever occasioned by my bronchiectasis. They took some of the pleasure out of Locarno.[1] Now I'm completely recovered, but because I couldn't work for a long time, I'm feeling pressed with the two lectures.[2]

Are your friends in Paris really unable to locate the velvet? I'm going to be really disappointed if nothing comes of this. Excuse this quick dictation. I wanted you to have at least a sign of life from me.

Until we meet in Frankfurt!

Please thank Heinrich for his note added to your letter. Every word from him is a pleasure for me.

From Gertrud and me, warmest greetings

Your Karl Jaspers[3]

231 *Hannah Arendt to Karl Jaspers*

September 19, 1958

Lieber Verehrtester—

A week from today we'll be sitting together in the Frankfurter Hof. I can't wait!

Your letter just arrived. I thought you were probably ill. I hope you are really fully recovered, so that the travel won't be too much for you. When will you be in Frankfurt? Sometime on Friday?

Chicago Press: I've just written to Morin. He wrote me a few weeks ago that everything was in order, that they had the book, and that all they needed now to get the project under way was a quick word from me saying that I approve Marjorie Grene[1] as the translator, and that I will check the translation. I assume that she has already begun work. The reason for Morin's not replying may well have been that he was away, but I suspect the reason is this: he can't send you a signed contract until a university committee responsible for the university press has met. I don't believe they meet until October. I didn't understand this procedure at first either. But Morin has, de facto, carte blanche. The semester doesn't begin there until October 1. The university has holidays before that. Work at the press goes on as usual, of course, but there are no committee meetings.

Heinrich was delighted to receive the nihilism book[2] and sends his thanks. He has started to read it and is much impressed by the precision of the formulations, the conciseness of the writing. His semester has begun already, and his work for it is demanding a lot of him. At least the New School hasn't begun yet. They wait, very reasonably, until the Jewish holidays are over.

It's true, the silk velvet has come to naught, even though all kinds of people, myself included, have run themselves ragged looking for it. So please, both of you, please don't forget to bring along the dress that I left hanging in the big wardrobe upstairs in Basel.

I'm writing this in haste so that it will be sure to reach you by Monday. I'll fly from here on Wednesday and will be in Frankfurt on Thursday.

My very warmest regards to you both—

Your
Hannah

P.S. It just occurred to me: Given the incredibly bad postal service here, it's unlikely that I'll have a reply from Chicago in good time.

232 *Karl Jaspers to Hannah Arendt*

Basel, October 12, 1958

Dear Hannah!

We arrived home in Basel two days ago. We spent a delightful week in Heidelberg, walking old paths, everything full of memories of happiness and sorrow. During our last night there I dreamed—for the first time in my life—that Gertrud and I were arrested by the Gestapo. Heidelberg was wonderful. But it's a thing of the past now. We can't go back to it. Gertrud too was content to return to Basel. Neither of us had the faintest desire to live in the new Heidelberg. Alienation and rootlessness—mitigated by friendly surroundings—are everyone's fate. The newly elected mayor of Heidelberg (a socialist) visited me and brought a big bouquet of carnations for Gertrud. He had heard that we were in Heidelberg, and he offered his help if there was anything we wanted. Now we're resettled in our quiet lives.

The hubbub, which has penetrated as far as Basel in the form of about 500 newspaper clippings, will soon pass. What will remain is your eulogy.[1] Hearing it brought me an unexpected joy. Everyone recognized your objective accomplishment. But I heard more than that. In your words I saw reflected the deepest impulses of my life— indirectly, despite all your brilliant formulations—and in such a way that I feel confirmed and encouraged. And your declaration of solidarity with me (particularly in your acceptance of the simile of the spark of light,[2] which you did not put in quotation marks—that was for me the most meaningful such declaration I could imagine). It's strange: can we say things in public that we are reluctant to say in private? Does the public arena have a hidden aspect that can assume visible form only in public, an aspect that is comprehensible despite its not being explicit? I was happy, and was embarrassed, knowing that others were looking at me.

I don't know any other type or example of a eulogy comparable to yours. The only one that occurred to me—and the comparison is of course inappropriate—is Thucydides' praise of Pericles. Because Thucydides saw Pericles as reason itself, there was no character left to describe.[3] He portrays Nicias, Demosthenes, Alcibiades, and others as eccentric characters who come to grief because of their clearly defined and limited natures. The only thing that brings Pericles down is the plague. He would have won the war if he had lived. There is nothing to say about him. He does and says what is true, not what his individual nature prompts him to do. He doesn't laugh anymore once he assumes rule over Athens, and so on. That is the greatest of praise. The only thing that can be compared to it is what you have said. But of course the comparison is not right.

Because I take your tribute very personally. Hannah is speaking to me in public. What I do is visible in a new light. That your eulogy, conceived as it is in the grand Roman style, puts what I do into a light that declares humanly unattainable goals to be real ("unachievable," "unswerving") is to its credit and to the credit of the concept that anticipates what the goals of a human life should be.

You have understood me, together with Gertrud—no one has done that before. And it is entirely and absolutely true.

Piper wants to publish both our talks right away.[4] I have agreed for my part, but at the same time I said and wrote that he could not go ahead and print without your explicit approval. I already have the galleys of your talk in front of me. But I still don't know if you have agreed yet.

Give my regards to Heinrich. I thank him for encouraging you to take this on and then for finding the talk good. I have to include him here as well: the eulogy comes from him, too.

Warmly,
Your Karl Jaspers

233   *Hannah Arendt to Karl and Gertrud Jaspers*

November 16, 1958

Lieber Verehrtester—

It is difficult to answer your letter because it is too beautiful and strikes too well the heart of what I wanted to achieve. I agree with you that in a public situation something can emerge, become palpable, that otherwise can or may exist only in a hidden way. I have, if you will, used the public arena to say outright things that, had I been alone with you, face to face, I would otherwise have dared only to suggest. I did that not only because this was an occasion, and you, if you'll permit me to say so, were helpless in this situation (even more helpless than on walks, when you are not allowed to talk), but also because what I was speaking about is truly your public appearance, that about you which appears in public or that which *appears*.

I reread your speech several times, and I liked it more each time. Heinrich wanted to write to you because he agrees with you completely in your view of the European role Germany could possibly play (and now he says you should write your Germany book, and I had given him false information before). He hasn't written, of course, and he's been so busy since the semester began that one can't even blame him this time. But in mid-December he gets a two-month holiday.

356

It's nice that Piper is publishing the two talks together. I think back on Heidelberg sometimes, and it is all still very vivid to me. And when I think of this joint pamphlet, it seems to me as if I were dreaming.

It has been hard for me to find any peace and get back to work this time. That's why I haven't written for so long. The Princeton business stirred up an inane fuss because some witless student suddenly found out that I'll be the first woman to teach at Princeton with the rank of full professor. The boy passed that on to the newspapers, and I'd just as soon remain silent about everything that followed from that. The upshot is that I've been doing battle with every newspaper in New York. One thing I've learned at any rate is that it's impossible to kill a story and that if you bar your house to photographers they'll still find a way to get hold of some pictures. But this was just the straw that broke the camel's back. I've stumbled into a lot of extraneous claptrap anyhow because I was away for so long and because a book[1] of mine has come out. At any rate, the book is suddenly selling so well that the publisher has to get out a second printing after only four months. Exactly why, nobody knows, not even the publisher. But the direct consequence of that is more lectures; and because they're well paid I can't very well say no.

I'm immersed in American history and preparing my Princeton lectures on the concept of revolution. (I'll incorporate this material into the book for Piper.)[2] It's breathtakingly exciting and wonderful, the American Revolution, that is, and the founding of the republic, the Constitution. Madison, Hamilton, Jefferson, John Adams—what men. And when you look at what's there now—what a comedown.

I'm glad that you both were content to return to Basel. Alienation and rootlessness, if we will only understand them aright, make it easier to live in our time. And we certainly should allow ourselves that little bit of relief. They keep things from pressing in too close on us. They're like a skin that grows onto us from the outside. And because of that skin, we can afford to remain sensitive and vulnerable. The 500 newspaper clippings may well have faded in the meantime, but I've heard here from all quarters what a deep impression you made on the Germans. I was glad to hear it. I would almost have thought that wasn't possible anymore.

You're in the midst of your semester now, and I'm glad that I was there in the summer so that I know exactly how it all is. Why isn't Switzerland the fiftieth state of the United States? It would be quite suitable, and that would make life much nicer.

A few days ago I came across the sheet of paper on which I'd noted what you wanted to know about Israel. I'm enclosing the circular letter of the rabbinate[3] apropos of the immigration of Jewish refugees from Poland with their non-Jewish wives (to whom most of them owed the fact that they survived the Hitler years!). A friend said to me a few days ago that there are more and more people in Israel now who are finding the theocratic rule of the rabbis intolerable. Another point: The name of the village where an army regiment staged a massacre on the day before the Suez Campaign is Kfar Kassim. The story is this: A state of siege was declared for all the Arab villages in Israel, and all the inhabitants had to be in their houses by 5 PM. Violators, whether men, women, or children, would be shot. This announcement wasn't made in Kfar Kassim until 4:30, however; and the villagers were in the fields and couldn't be notified in time. The village was consequently almost completely wiped out—everybody, women, children, etc. When the soldiers were given this order, they asked what they should do with the people who couldn't be notified in time. The Jewish officer's answer was: May Allah have mercy upon them! —The matter was finally settled in court a few weeks ago, and the soldiers were all sentenced to life imprisonment. A decision has finally been made, too, to try the officer who gave the order. People are afraid about this, because nobody knows where the order originated; that is, people are afraid because they probably in fact do know. The public does not know. —And finally: The first Arab village to be wiped out at the beginning of the Arab-Jewish war (about 1947) in order to set an example was called Deir Jassim.[4] The mass exodus of Arabs from Palestine was largely prompted by this massacre. It was widely characterized then as a second Lidice.[5]

Warmest greetings,
Your
Hannah

I forgot: number of Arabs before and after the war. Much debated. In my opinion, the most reliable figures are: of 580,000 Arabs, 150,000 stayed in the country, and 35,000 returned. At the moment there are about 200,000 Arabs in Israel.

November 16, 1958[6]

Liebe Gute—

Just a quick hello. It was all so wonderful. Every time I think of you, and that is every day, my heart grows warm. Thank you for your letter. It's good that your brother[7] had such an easy death. I wanted to write you right away, but things were in such chaos with me that nothing was done as it should have been. Have you gotten caught up with your backlog of mail? I had a few letters, too, one of them from a real mental case. Your husband would have been delighted and would surely have begun a correspondence. But I didn't dare to. I've read a marvelous book: *Anecdotes of Destiny* by Isak Dinesen (or Karen Blixen),[8] a great Danish storyteller, a grande dame and a wise old woman. It isn't available in German yet; otherwise I would have sent it to you. I'm sitting here surrounded by things you have given me. Cigarette case, handbag, watch—all things that I use constantly. That's very nice.

Greetings and kisses from
Your
Hannah

I had a very nice letter from Mr. Heuss[9] along with some offprints.

---

234   Karl Jaspers to Hannah Arendt

Basel, December 31, 1958

Dear Hannah!

Your lively November letter brought such good news! Already a second printing of *The Human Condition*. That is a truly great success for a theoretical book, especially in America. And then came the "circus," which pleased me, too. That is the way one acquires a name in America, and anywhere in our world. And, as with advertising, these things have to be repeated every now and then. But you don't like that and balk at it instead of taking it calmly. Perhaps you fear developing the repugnant qualities of some famous women. You're in no danger of that. It is your accomplishment, indeed it is in keeping with the motives for that accomplishment, that you are heard and a visible presence for people.

Your lectures in Princeton will surely be excellent. I'm using your Hungary book[1] in my seminar. I'm finding confirmed there what I felt in my first reading of it: a masterpiece, especially where it moves one to raise questions and objections. Political thinking can never, as mathematical knowledge can, be sealed off against every objection. Even where I feel you are in error the impulse behind the error is still true (as with the "councils"). My students respond with innumerable written queries. They are fascinated not only by the facts. In thinking your book through, they become philosophical, as you are yourself, and they ask: What is history? What is freedom? What is total domination? I don't know whether these young people perceive the hidden respect at work in your thinking, but I think they do. There have been no impudent remarks so far, and Hannah Arendt remains an authority for these students, even when they attack her sentences.

I'd like to join you in your studies of the American Revolution. I have only vague memories from earlier reading. I found Hamilton the most admirable: knowledgeable, an aristocrat, bold and perhaps arrogant but a statesman without illusions and with the power to see things through in a recalcitrant world. Jefferson struck me as much more of an American as one imagines Americans to be, clearly admirable, with goodwill of an average sort, not without cunning and not without illusions. But perhaps my recollections are deceiving me. It's a great thing to study men like that and to see what they brought about. That all that was possible gives one courage.

You are now at your peak. You will choose only great subjects appropriate to you, and there will be no lessening in the energy of your thinking or formulations, no yielding to the danger into which success wants to seduce us.

Thank you for the book on the Palestine refugees.[2] You have clearly had some hand in it and authorized it with your name. I like the presentation and diction very much. The suggested solution, along with the conditions, makes sense to me. No one point can be separated from another; the whole thing forms a unity. This complex and yet simple, concentrated, and clear study strikes me as a study preparatory to the moment when the Arabs will choose to make peace with Israel. Before that, it may perhaps be a factor that can make reasonable Arabs more willing to have peace and the unreasonable people among the Jews readier to make concessions. The spirit of this solution is, as should be the case with good political thinkers, a thinking through of the concrete situation from the perspective of pure reason and humanity. It is our hope that the moment will come when what has been thought through here can become reality and that this thinking through itself will contribute to that coming about. It is a beautiful, decent, and great document. It will probably convince more Jews than Arabs at first, for the peace settlement will be the key point, without which the central principles of the solution will be pointless.

Thank you too for your other communications about Israel. When you are here again next year I will have to interrogate you about those matters in which, as you said, I am blind concerning Israel. Unfortunately, I let the subject drop too quickly in our conversations this time.

The quiet of philosophizing has reestablished itself here with us. Gertrud is feeling very well. She is enjoying seeing the children from Holland,[3] and I am sharing her pleasure. We celebrated Christmas here with them, their mother,[4] and Ella.

I'm encouraged by Heinrich's feeling that I should write my Germany book. I can't do it yet because *Die grossen Philosophen* has a greater claim on me now. If I manage to finish the second volume, then I'm considering fitting the German book in before I start on the third. As you know, I don't want to annex Switzerland politically, but I would like to annex Hannah substantially and also her husband, though with him I suspect that is quite unnecessary. Gertrud has already been annexed, almost more than I like to see.

Warmest greetings to you both

Your Karl Jaspers

Please excuse the dictation. I would otherwise have had to postpone this letter again.

235   Hannah Arendt to Gertrud and Karl Jaspers

January 31, 1959

Dear, dear friends—

Your telegram[1] followed me home from Princeton. (I won't move down there until next week, and since I'll be in New York every weekend anyway, it's best if you continue to write to New York and forget Princeton.) Yes, a Lessing Prize,[2] and at the very moment when you are lecturing on Lessing.[3] It was you, of course, who got me into this pickle: your introduction to *Totale Herrschaft* and then St. Paul's Church.[4] What can I do? I don't really feel quite up to all this. It makes me a bit dizzy, and so I just don't think about it. Otherwise I would already have written you. I just don't want to trouble myself with it. I am, as you quite rightly said, "balky." Probably just because I am, of course, terrified of this Princeton stint. And then, I do have a horror of "famous women." Whether I'll eventually learn to handle all this "calmly" seems questionable to me. I take comfort in the fact that such things are short lived in our time. It will soon pass.

Much more important is that you can make use of my Hungary pamphlet in your seminar. That is a genuine honor, and I get red in the face when I think about it. American Revolution—Jefferson better, I think, than you recall. John Adams is perhaps the greatest figure. But what a group! And how this country has gone to the dogs if you measure it by nothing but its own standards. In the meantime I've wound up in the French Revolution. I have a lot to say about that, about Robespierre in particular. But I'll save it for another time.

I envy you your quiet at this point. The weeks around and after Christmas are always busy for us, and this time the Princeton business comes on top of that—too many people, too big a city, and always something that has to be done. Heinrich had his sixtieth birthday, which we celebrated properly—with caviar and champagne and an evening with friends. It was a nice party, and he enjoyed it this time. His astonishment at really being 60 years old is comical. Because he can think only in decades, this even came on him without any transition, as it were.

I took particular pleasure in your cheerful letter, dear Gertrud.[5] I hope you really like the scarf. I had looked for a cashmere scarf like that for you in Europe, but I couldn't find one, and then I happened on one here. It's wonderfully light and very warm, and it's very handy on trips, too.

It's already time to start talking about plans for Europe again. I wrote to Hamburg that I couldn't come before this fall, and the people there are extremely friendly and flexible. How do things look for you? I'll probably have to be in Hamburg in the first half of October. What time suits you? Before? After? Anything after September 25 is fine with me. But I would like to have your thoughts before I make a firm commitment.

Warmest greetings
Your
Hannah

236 *Hannah Arendt to Gertrud and Karl Jaspers*

Princeton, February 21, 1959

Dear, dear friends—

Both your birthdays, and one of them an eightieth,[1] and I'm afraid I'm too late. The past year was, it seems to me, a good and rich one for you both. I hope things will remain so for many long years to come. This will remain an unforgettable year for me, that pure, clear harmony at a public event in Frankfurt after my weeks with you and that lovely conclusion to it in Heidelberg.

I can blame my tardiness on Princeton. It's just the way I expected it to be. The most important thing is the so-called parties, at which one meets droves of new people whose names one cannot remember and whose faces one struggles to engrave on one's memory. Of the students, I have only fleeting impressions so far, and they are not very good. I hear the same thing from all quarters. This is the last of the old universities that still uphold the ideal of the gentleman, for whom it is unseemly to know too much. Under the pressure of progressive education, which has reached Princeton too, of course, the danger is that "not too much" becomes "nothing at all." This is the first place in my American experience where class differences simply cannot be overlooked, especially as evidenced between professors, who are mere employees, and the gentlemen students, who are about to mature into alumni and become the future trustees of the university. Unfortunately, I have very little contact with the students, but the atmosphere is palpable everywhere. The idea of speaking here, of all places, about the concept of revolution has something ineffably comical about it. I couldn't have picked a better topic if I had tried.

Heinrich, with whom I talk on the telephone every day, just told me that the manuscript of the "atom bomb" just arrived from Chicago. Unfortunately, I couldn't go to New York this weekend—solely because of these parties!—so I won't get to see it until the end of the week. Ralph Manheim didn't start on *The Great Philosophers* until the beginning of the year. What can one do? It is perhaps more important that Kurt Wolff will definitely leave America in the spring and settle in Zurich. He wants to continue to run the firm from there. Whether he'll succeed in that is another question. This all became possible because of the fantastic success of the Pasternak novel,[2] which has made publishers in any number of countries filthy rich. And for all that, it's neither a very good book nor a truly great novel.

The parties aside, things are going well for me here. I have a very nice little house with two big rooms, all brand new, furnished by the university for guest professors without children. I'm the first to use it, so I'm breaking all this splendor in. The head of the department, my so-called boss, a pleasant and highly influential gentleman in his late sixties, just stopped by to bring me a carpet sweeper. Something like that would be almost impossible in Europe. We tried the thing out together. He left, promising me a vacuum cleaner. What I wouldn't give to be able to come see you right now for a little while and talk, about Lessing, for example. But we'll simply have to wait until fall again, despite all the miracles of technology. I'll have to be in Hamburg sometime in the first half of October for the prize. When can I come? What's better for you? Before or after? I can easily make my plans to suit you. I can get away anytime after the middle of September.

With all best wishes to you both—
Hannah

237 Karl Jaspers to Hannah Arendt

Basel, March 26, 1959

Dear Hannah!

I should have written you long ago and thanked you again for everything: for the forest of hyacinths for Gertrud's eightieth birthday. It blossomed and spread its fragrance and gave us great pleasure.

And I should have written of the disappointment I felt that Dr. Manheim had not begun translating *Die grossen Philosophen* until January. The effort you put into the preparatory work will not be in vain in the long run. We will just have to wait and see.

And then the translation of the "atom bomb"! More trouble for you. I hope a few sample passages were enough to let you determine that the quality of the translation is good. I hope too that nothing has been cut from it. Have you sent the manuscript back already? The publisher wrote me that it is being set and should appear in the fall. I look forward to that with some suspense, wondering whether a book of mine will evoke a response in America this time.

The reason I did not write was the lethargy induced by a flu that caused no fever but dragged on for weeks. I was particularly plagued by the loss of my voice and then by hoarseness that I still have even now but that is slowly improving. But my overall health is good again. I'm working again and finally writing to you.

In the meantime you will have made progress on your political book.[1] I'm eagerly awaiting it. Though I do not want to let myself be diverted from *Die grossen Philosophen*, there is certainly nothing next to that project that interests me more than politics.

Russia does not seem to see the time as ripe for a war yet. This respite will probably continue. Is that what you think, too? But a respite is really all it is. What I fear is that finally, at some point, America will hide behind the UN's skirts and, without openly abandoning Berlin, will gradually abandon it by means of apparently harmless agreements. That would be awful: one simply can't do that to those two million Berliners who have stood so firm. My mood vacillates between fear and faint hope. Eisenhower has made so many different statements that one can't put any stock in any of them. It *seems*, however, that the American people are thinking more and more about Berlin and are firmer in their resolve about it. Or are we in Europe mistaken about that?

Give my regards to Heinrich!

Warmest greetings
Your Karl Jaspers

238   *Hannah Arendt to Karl Jaspers*

Princeton, March 31, 1959

Lieber Verehrtester—

Instead of a letter a question: I received an invitation from Tradition and Change[1] to take part in a seminar in Basel at the end of September. I gave them a noncommittal answer. Only after doing so did I learn that you had agreed to participate. That changes things for me. I received a long essay by Raymond Aron[2] that I couldn't make much of. That may be my fault. Perhaps I'm just a little too deeply involved with my own projects to be open to others. I'm not sure about that. I made a real effort.

From my point of view the situation is this: It's possible for me to go because I'll be in Hamburg on October 9 anyhow. But I can't possibly prepare anything. Do you think it makes any sense for me to come under those circumstances? Do you want me to come?

I hope you are both well again. Your wife wrote that she was "overhappy."[3] What a wonderful word! It keeps popping up in my thoughts. About Princeton another time.

I'm not really writing in haste, but this is general letter-writing evening, and I don't want to write to you in that mode.

Warmest greetings to you both
As always
Your
Hannah

Basel, April 6, 1959

Dear Hannah!

Our short letters crossed in the mail.

In response to your question: This winter I told Lasky that I would attend the seminar in Basel, and I recently confirmed that again with Paris. But just a week ago I backed out again. My major reasons were that I had taken on too much and that we want to spend September in Lotte [Waltz]'s mother's wonderful apartment in Cannes. Lotte will take us there in great style and comfort.

Declining was made easier for me because I found Aron's essay, which I received a few months ago and which will set the agenda, acceptable enough as a survey of points of view—of the loci communes of current sociological talk—but not at all as a point of departure for discussions. What usually results from that sort of thing is just endless palaver. My first impulse was to give a more aggressive, provocative talk myself. I answered with a long, friendly letter. The secretary replied that she had passed my letter on to Aron. Then I heard nothing further. I didn't like being dealt with by the secretary while Aron himself said not a word. That's the kind of behavior one expects from prime ministers. I received no reply either when I said I would not attend, and that confirmed my feelings. But the *reason* for my declining was quite another.

So there is no reason for you to quash your resistance and come despite it. But it was nice of you to consider it on my account.

Warmly
Your Karl Jaspers

Basel, April 16, 1959

Dear Hannah!

Please don't be annoyed if I inquire once again how things stand with the translation of my atom book. I'm concerned about it. Is Marjorie Grene's translation not good? Is it at least passable? Has it gone back to the publisher?

You know how much the publication of this book in America means to me, and the sooner the better. That's where this book really belongs, although it seems fantastic to be giving Americans something like that to read.

I've just read that the Nobel Prize winner Max Born[1] has said of my atom book that it is "an example" of "the mindless perpetuation of traditional attitudes."[2] I'm taking consolation in the fact that I'm reaching out to America. After sixty years of all possible variations of that response from my German compatriots I've gotten used to it.

Warmest greetings to you both

Your Karl Jaspers

You did get my letter about "Tradition and Change" saying I will *not* attend?

To a request from *The New Republic* in Washington, I wrote a brief response[3] to W. Lippmann's series of articles "Today and Tomorrow" (about the Berlin crisis).[4] I would like to have been able to refer the reader to passages in my atom book. But that would surely have been out of place in the American press.

241 Hannah Arendt to Karl Jaspers

Princeton, April 27, 1959

Lieber Verehrtester—

Your letter just arrived. I had hoped I wouldn't need to tell you about the atom book until everything was more or less in order. I received Marjorie Grene's translation about two months behind schedule in early or, rather, in mid-March. One reading revealed that there were a great many basic mistakes in it, which is to say that she had apparently forgotten much of her German. I can't recall the details now, because my papers are in New York. I don't think any of us was prepared for that. If I'd had the manuscript at the beginning of January, as originally planned, I might have been able to straighten things out myself, though I'm even doubtful about that. With my being in Princeton, that was unfortunately out of the question. So I called Chicago and had a long talk with Morin. The upshot was that he didn't know anyone he could depend on to do the revision right. Every line of the English text has to be checked back against the German—no mean task. After much casting about and discussion with

American friends, I suggested commissioning Ashton (a former German).[1] I found his work very good when I was working for Schocken, and he speaks and writes excellent English. It was important to me to have someone whose mother tongue is German, because in this case that is the only way we can guarantee that all the errors will be eliminated. At that point Morin decided to fly to New York to talk things over with Ashton at my place. We gave Ashton the manuscript, and he promised to let us know by May 1 when he can deliver it and what he thinks of it. He was not able to put everything else aside from one day to the next and take this on. I didn't want to write to you until I had heard from Ashton. This means additional costs for Chicago, of course, but they can be absorbed. Morin was almost as unhappy as I was about the delay, but not about the costs! You'll have to take my word for it that it was really impossible to print the manuscript in the condition it was in. The pity is that there are so few good translators from German, and the few there are are always overworked. In other words, if Ralph Manheim (the best) doesn't have time and Richard Winston (who is less suitable for philosophical texts) doesn't, and if Denver Lindley can't do it either—then it's very hard to know where to turn next. That was the reason Morin thought of Marjorie Grene in the first place. A point against Ashton, whom I was considering at the time, was that English isn't his mother tongue. Morin would surely have had his reservations. Then too, I didn't know that Ashton knows your books very well and is very familiar with your thinking. But he did not know the atom book. —As for the publication date: Morin had originally wanted to have the book in the bookstores in October. That means it would have to be done in August so that it could be distributed at least four to six weeks in advance of publication to critics and others with influence on public opinion. The earliest possible publication date now is, I believe, January 1960.

Your letter about Basel and Aron came as a great relief to me. The whole business put me off, too, and I'm glad that I don't have to take part in it. His behavior toward you is really quite outrageous. That's the kind of manners these people take on without even realizing that they're doing it.

I start my public lectures today, and of course I'm scared, which is only right and proper. We're having the kind of lovely spring we very rarely have in America, where one usually tumbles from winter into the heat without any transition.

Lieber Verehrtester—what can I say? Your reservations proved correct, and we should have listened to you. And I think I would have listened to you if I had known who else to choose.

Rather unhappy, but otherwise as ever

Your
Hannah

242   Karl Jaspers to Hannah Arendt

Basel, May 2, 1959

Dear Hannah!

Your letter has just arrived. What trouble you have taken on yourself and what haven't you done to straighten things out. As always, I am grateful to you. Without you, the book would certainly have been published as is. Now I hope things will work out with Ashton, about whom you have reported so favorably. I'm eagerly awaiting his response of May 1. The delay is a pity, but please don't be "unhappy" about it!

I wish you good luck with your lectures. It's good that you have stage fright. If that disappears, it means that you're content with yourself. Then you fall into routine and become your own imitator.

So you'll come directly to us from Hamburg in October? Stay as long as you like. I have leave then and will be working on *Die grossen Philosophen.*

Warmly
Your Karl Jaspers

I just saw that Ashton translated three lectures from *Rechenschaft und Ausblick,*[1] which were published in 1952 by Russel F. Moore Comp., New York. Acting out of excessive amiability, I gave the translation rights to an emigrant, Hanns E. Fisher, whom I didn't know. Then he didn't do the work himself at all and gave the book the title *Existentialism and Humanism* (plagiarized from Sartre![2]). But none of that was Ashton's fault.

243   Hannah Arendt to Karl Jaspers

Palenville, N.Y., July 20, 1959

Lieber Verehrtester—

By now the semester is over for you, and we are once again in our delightful summer place and have been for a week now. Neither of us is in dire need of a rest, but we are still glad to be out of all the hustle and bustle. We'll stay until mid-September this time, at least that is my plan now, so that I'll be in New York for only a week before I fly to Europe.

I don't even know if I've told you yet that the people in Hamburg have moved their award ceremony up. I have to fly from here on 9/23 and will probably stay in Hamburg for almost a week. You wrote that it doesn't matter to you when I come to Basel this time. I'm still not sure, because I want to get together with relatives from Israel, probably in Zurich but possibly in Italy. If things turn out the way I picture them now, I would come in the second half of October. Is that all right?

Princeton—the lectures went well; the University Press wants them; and I'm in the process of making them into a book, a project that's giving me much more trouble than I expected it to. The fact is that the material is really quite new for me.

A Mr. Hubbard[1] got in touch with me about the atom bomb book, but he hasn't written again, although he said he would let me know what he thought of it. In the meantime I've received a letter from the publisher, i.e., a copy of the final text of the agreement with Mr. Ashton. I don't know whether the publisher wrote you that Morin left Chicago University Press quite abruptly. He couldn't get on with the director, Mr. Shugg.[2] I know Shugg only slightly. I'm corresponding with him now and don't even know if there will be someone to replace Morin, who was a very able fellow. This is one of the most aggravating things that happen in all one's dealings with publishers here: the so-called editors, who have complete authority and conduct all the business with authors, leave the houses, and you have no one with whom you can maintain any continuity. At the moment, I literally don't know a single person at Harcourt, Brace anymore, and yet I'm bound by contract to them. I'm in exactly the same situation with Chicago Press. So far, I haven't had any bad experience with them— which can't be said for Harcourt, Brace—and the letter to Ashton, which I'm enclosing here in case Chicago neglected to send you a copy, leaves me with a favorable impression.

What do you think of the political situation?[3] I have so often wished in recent weeks that we could communicate quickly. Adenauer's behavior strikes me as totally inappropriate, and lots of people here are downright scared. If this is possible, what might happen next time? But at the moment, other things are at stake. I'm afraid that East

Germany will indeed become a satellite like the others, and that can mean only that Berlin will be lost in the long run, too. The bad thing about the situation is, it seems to me, that for the Western powers Berlin has only prestige value, high though that prestige value may be. For the Russians, however, it has clear concrete significance.

How are you both doing as far as health goes? All my best wishes!

Warmest greetings
Hannah

244 Karl Jaspers to Hannah Arendt

Basel, July 30, 1959

Dear Hannah!

Many thanks! The letter from Shugg is relatively reassuring. With some dismay I see and am calculating by how much Chicago wants to cut my book. Morin made no mention of that to me. But now there's probably nothing that can be done, and I hope Mr. Ashton will treat the book with understanding.

Because Dr. Hubbard[1] offered to stop in at Chicago Press on his trip to America, I asked him to do so. He spoke only with a secretary because Morin was out sick. That was no doubt a superfluous gesture, but I thought it a good idea to demonstrate once again to Chicago Press the degree of my interest in this project. His reason for not calling you again was probably a desire not to intrude or a misunderstanding. He was there to learn the particulars for his visit to Chicago. You met him here in Basel. I consider him a man of intelligence and excellent character. He has a position here with Ciba as the editor of their English-language house publication.

I think your brief political remarks about Berlin are, unfortunately, altogether accurate. The situation is cause for anxiety. We'll talk it over in detail in the fall. Adenauer's behavior is every bit as bad as that of his party. I almost wrote an article earlier, but, following Kant's example, I had a maxim to hand that I made up for myself in 1916: Never inject a word into a current political issue; speak only to the political situation in general. Since last fall I've had an odd relationship with Bonn, but I'll tell you about that later. I assume that the moving up of the prize ceremony in Hamburg is not troublesome to you. As I wrote before, we are at your disposal for October. As soon as you know your exact dates, please let us know at what time we can have

you with us. I would like to have another week in October free for
Rossmann, with whom I'm preparing a new version of my *Universitätsidee*.[2] It would be good if I could set a time with him, too. His
semester begins, I believe, on November 1 (mine, on October 28), but
for now you have a completely free choice (I'll ask Rossmann to come
either before or after you in October).

Enjoy the rest of your holiday with Heinrich. Congratulations on
your successful lectures in Princeton. Things are continuing to go
wonderfully for you.

We are both well. The semester is over. We're having a lot of relatives
visiting. First from Oldenburg, then from Israel and New York. We're
both happy to have them.

Warmest greetings to Heinrich and you from us both

Your

Karl Jaspers

Dear Hannah![3]

One other matter that I don't want to dictate because it is at the
moment confidential. A Dr. Martin,[4] a member of the Bundesrat, has
visted me repeatedly since last fall. He is planning publication of a
magazine on university affairs. I liked the idea, and advised him on
it. Now his "friends" have bought the *Deutsche Universitätszeitung*.[5]
That is still not public knowledge. An editor, who I gather is quite
capable, will take care of the technical matters and arrange for articles
(somewhat the way Dr. Thiel[6] does for Springer's *Studium generale*[7]).
A board chaired by Dr. Martin will handle the finances. A number of
people will make up the "editorial board": Raiser[8] (jurist in Tübingen),
Popitz[9] (full professor of sociology in Basel as of October 1), Büchner[10]
(pathologist in Freiburg). I suggested Golo Mann and Kurt Rossmann.
And I will be a member, too.[11] Everyone except Popitz has already
agreed.[12] Dr. Martin has asked me to write to you and ask if you will
be on the editorial board, too. I did not suggest you because I did not
want to add to your burdens at all. But it means a great deal to Dr.
Martin, who is an admirer of your books, to have you join us. And
so I did not refuse his request. If you are willing, he will extend an
invitation. He didn't have the courage to do so on his own initiative.
An occasional essay is all that will be expected of you.

You will ask what I think of the project. The first thing I said to
Dr. Martin was: A prerequisite for a journal like this is the active
intellectual participation of an interested group. That group does not

exist but is being somewhat artificially created. Still, the mission of the publication is both real and important in light of the fact that university reform is imminent, that large sums will be raised to effect it, and that those monies must be properly used. And so I agreed to participate, with the reservation that whether and when I would contribute an essay would have to remain uncertain.

One asks, with a politician: What is his real motivation? I don't know. I can only offer a hypothesis for which I have no supporting evidence. Dr. Martin is currently a member of the Foreign Policy Committee of the Bundesrat. *Perhaps* he is grooming himself for the post of federal minister of culture, which will probably be created soon. (I personally favor state administration of the universities. If the federal government contributes a lot of money, it will also want to have a say in things—that's not good.)

The journal as such is clearly meant to be without political bias. It should, however, have intellectual stature.

I don't dare urge you to do this. I don't feel there is any danger of being politically misused. Unless Heinrich has a "nose" here for something I have not thought of.

But it would please me, of course, to see you become an increasingly important voice in German intellectual and political life.

I had already begun on a revision of my *Universitätsidee*, the first version of which was, unfortunately, miserably written. Now this project is coinciding with my interest in this journal.

When I read all the nonsense that is written about the German university and when I look at the present reality of the university, I think more often than not that we are fighting for a lost cause. That would be honorable enough in itself. But you can never know!

Warmly

Your Karl Jaspers

245 *Hannah Arendt to Karl Jaspers*

Palenville, N.Y., August 11, 1959

Lieber Verehrtester—

You no doubt know that Morin left the Chicago Press quite suddenly—up and out. Hence the letter from the director, Shugg. I think I recall talk of some cutting from the outset. Translators do that here with all or almost all German books. But what Marjorie Grene then went ahead and did was neither expected nor understandable. Dr. Hubbard called me after his visit in Chicago. I do remember him now. On the telephone, too, he made a very pleasant and solid impression.

I'm glad that we seem to be in complete agreement again about the political situation and judge it similarly. Now that Dulles is dead the chances of an understanding between Russia and America are good— the two major powers that have the H-bomb. From the Russian point of view, it is good that China is not a third such power. When we see each other in the fall, we'll know more. It was probably right for you not to make a statement. This business with Adenauer showed at a stroke on what shaky foundations everything official, everything that does not have to do with economics, stands in Germany. One should regard that as a symptom. The thing was almost too comical to interfere in, unless one wanted to be simply rude. Or am I wrong and too "polite"?

Dates: The ceremony in Hamburg is on September 28. After that I want to meet with relatives from Israel with whom I can't connect at any other time. Probably in Italy. I am very eager to go to Florence. So I can say with certainty that I won't come until the second half of October, if that is all right with you. I can't give you an exact date yet. I want to look up some friends in Rome, too, and possibly the publisher in Milan who is doing *The Human Condition* in Italian.

Now about the journal. Heinrich and I both have our reservations. Am I correct in understanding that the federal government is behind it? We both have a deep-seated prejudice against government enterprises, and I don't think that I would be willing to be an editor or serve on an editorial board for such a journal here in America. The quasi-official nature of the Congress for Cultural Freedom was always such a stumbling block for me that I refused even to be a member. Though not, of course, to speak under their auspices or to publish in their journals. In the case of a German publication, however, these reasons weigh even heavier. But here too I would be glad to publish in the journal if I have something suitable for it. As far as the subject itself is concerned, namely, the idea of the university, I consider it extremely important, and I'm glad you have decided to prepare a new edition of your *Universitätsidee*. We'll have to talk about that, too. Things can't go on as they are, neither in Europe nor in America. The Princeton experience in particular made that very clear to me. The whole educational system needs radical reform. As a young secondary-school teacher from Germany who visited me here said, it simply won't

374

Hannah Arendt, around 1930

Hannah Arendt in New York, in the early 1950's

Heinrich Blücher at the time of his first trip to Basel, 1961

Hannah Arendt in New York, 1963

56

30%

965

Gertrud Jaspers in Basel, 1968

do anymore, for example, that secondary-school graduates don't know what the American Congress is but have their heads stuffed with the dates of innumerable battles. Similarly, my students in Princeton didn't even know that there had ever been such a thing as Austria-Hungary! But then they learned it quickly enough. At the moment, Heinrich is really doing nothing else but trying, at least experimentally in his college, gradually to change the direction of things. Under the rubric of General Humanities. I'll tell you about that when I'm there. Unfortunately, he'll have to give his two months of winter vacation to it, and it is costing him much of the summer, too, because he is constantly going to meetings at Bard, which is just a short run from here by car. For a long time I've tried to avoid these problems by simply sticking my head in the sand, but I do realize that a great deal will depend on how we go about educational reform. And how, above all, we prevent the reduction of all education to the purely technological. Which is very tempting because it becomes increasingly difficult even to run the machinery of modern life and keep it functioning.

I'm glad that you're taking so much pleasure in your visitors. I'm sitting here contentedly with my *Revolution* and not letting myself feel pressured despite Piper's justifiable impatience. I want this to be good. But now I have to get my speech for Hamburg out of the way first—on humanity.[1] And because I've just been reading a little Lessing it occurs to me to ask if you know Kommerell's book on Aristotle and Lessing?[2] I came across it by chance in the library.

It's nice that I can already say "until soon." A year is, after all, a long time. I'm very much looking forward to seeing you.

All my best wishes to you both. As always

Your
Hannah

246 *Karl Jaspers to Hannah Arendt*

Basel, August 26, 1959

Dear Hannah!

It gives me pleasure every time I think about your Hamburg Lessing Prize. No better man than he! A permanent revolutionary who cultivated "reason" in himself constantly from boyhood on and who was unfailingly humane in his nature. *That* humanity is so much greater, so much truer, than later humanity. Only Goethe and Kant stand comparison with him: Humboldt, only in his goodwill (by the bye: Humboldt was not at all anti-Semitic, contrary to what you remark tangentially somewhere in your Rahel book. I've just read Humboldt's memorandum on developing a legal constitution for the Jews,[1] 1809, I believe, wonderfully sober and unrelenting in searching out all the hidden reservations and shortcomings and inimical attitudes in the people who were writing this law). You will be speaking about humanity. I don't doubt that you will do it well. You really know what it is you are talking about there, just as Lessing knew. How few do know!

The university: your "no" is the right choice for you. As you no doubt noticed, it was the answer I expected. But I didn't want to fail to ask when I saw how much the people who are putting this journal together value you. It is not a government project. A Christian Democratic Union representative is financing it with funds from a bank that is interested in it. More than that I don't know. The representative,[2] who has been visiting me on and off since last fall and providing me with information of interest to me, is perhaps reckoning with becoming the federal minister of culture at a later date (that is *pure* hypothesis on my part). Such an office is in the works. For his part, he obviously has only political ambitions, not intellectual ones, has some education, a medical man. I don't know all the ins and outs of the whole thing. But as long as an open, nonpartisan discussion takes place in the journal, I don't think I am personally running any risk. If things turn out differently, then I can always resign. But I really don't expect that to happen. —I'm beginning to fantasize about all this: how one should go about founding a new university, a federal university along with the state universities (new universities are the obvious choice because of the massive demand). One would not have to make any allowance for "vested rights," which have constituted such a formidable obstacle to "reforms" in the past (and which I consider inviolable). But enough of this. I'll soon stop indulging in this fantasy. After our holidays, *Die grossen Philosophen* will be my only major project. I've rewritten my *Universitätsidee* and written a new and longer introduction; and I mean to add a second part: with concrete suggestions for reform plans. Rossmann is working with me on this and may write the second part. We'll publish the book jointly. Rossmann has a lot of experience in these matters. We have been in agreement on the fundamentals for decades. He has contributed ideas this time that seemed important to me. By virtue of my age I may be able to soften his tendency to make harsh judgments (a tendency that I am doubtless given to myself). We have to move our "colleagues" to cooperate, not refuse to offer them our hands, and so we have to write as if they were in basic agreement with us. Their problem is, I suspect, more ignorance than it is ill will. "Humboldt is no longer relevant" is their pet response. But most of them haven't read him at all. Everything is there in the official papers and memos on the founding of the university in Berlin.[3] Those writings are simply marvelous, not because of the specifics pertinent to the time but because of the "principles" that guided Humboldt in his dealings with the given practical matters. Those principles are still "relevant" today, *if* we want a university. If we deny them, then it is plain we do not any longer want a university. One truly radical difference is that Humboldt looked around and found the important people who, as professors, were creating reality. He called Fichte to Berlin, praising him to the skies,[4] even though he had had from him an officially solicited document (an almost totalitarian plan for the university), which he quietly put aside as nonsense. He wanted a plurality of forces and obviously trusted the university as a whole not to succumb to the absolutist impulses of one philosopher (by way of comparison: Goethe's behavior toward his friend Schelling. Goethe advised against calling Schelling to Jena in 1816 because Schelling's *demands* seemed unacceptable to him, amounting, Goethe thought, to a blueprint for dominating the university).[5] —But the historical aspect is of *secondary* importance. We have to want a university *today* or not; we can't imitate. The idea itself is "eternal."

If only Heinrich and I could get together now and then! He is in the thick of bringing about reform on a practical level; my involvement is purely theoretical.

We are very much looking forward to your visit; the second half of October it is then! [. . .]

Gertrud joins me in sending you both our warmest greetings

Your Karl Jaspers

247   Karl Jaspers to Hannah Arendt

Cannes, September 11, 1959[1]

Dear Hannah!

Yes, how nice that we will see each other and have a chance to talk—once again there is so much worth talking about. [. . .]

You are certainly correct that Lessing has not found a place in world literature[2]—and that there is much in him that is historically obsolete and rationally contrived. Perhaps the only writers who take a place in world literature are the creators of great symbols or of a humanity that remains forever representative in its every last detail. But the crucial thing about Lessing, he himself, when one looks at him, this "tramp," as he would ultimately call himself, this man pursued by misfortune, this man who was also a bungling hothead, is still, as no other has been, the incarnation of reason in its persistence and constant self-renewal. This unceasing work with and on himself in his perceptions and his judgment is indeed in itself without "shape." He was not able to give eternal expression to his love. He had hardly a single "new" basic idea to pass on. But despite that: for us Germans he numbers among our great ancestors and examples.

The printing of the first volume of *Die grossen Philosophen* comes as a great and unexpected pleasure. Thank you for traveling to Paris. I hope your impression will not be a poor one.

You have to be "afraid" about the talk you'll give in Hamburg; otherwise it won't be good. I'm familiar with that fear. But for my part, I don't feel the slightest fear for you. I'm just curious to read what you will say and what will happen in Hamburg. By the way, your name is known in Germany. There is no doubt about that. And your reputation grows the better people understand your great book.

Warmly

Your   Karl Jaspers

248   Hannah Arendt to Karl Jaspers

Paris, Wednesday[1]

Lieber Verehrtester!

I'm assuming you're back in Basel again, and I'm writing today only to let you know right away that the translation[2] is excellent. Much work remains despite that, but it is a lot of fun. For philosophical texts, Manheim is probably the best man there is today.

Paris is lovely, as always. An autumnal beauty. Tomorrow evening I move on to Hamburg. I'll be staying in the Senate guesthouse there, Neue Rabenstr. 31, Hamburg 36. Then Berlin, from the 30th on,

Hotel-Pension Regina, Kurfürstendamm 37. I'll write from there. Just these few lines to keep you posted. I hope your domestic difficulties[3] have abated somewhat.

Warmly
Your
Hannah

249 *Hannah Arendt to Karl Jaspers*

Berlin, October 3, 1959

Lieber Verehrtester—

The telegram[1] from the three of you gave me such pleasure, and a little courage as well. Everything went off very well, of course, and Piper wants to print my speech in the Piperbücherei. It was not, believe me, written "for eternity." It sounded better than it is, and has to be reworked now.

Now I'm tied down here in Berlin with restitution business,[2] and I won't know until next week when I can get away. Surely by the middle of the week. I'll probably fly directly to Florence, without a layover in Zurich. Then I'll write right away to suggest, at last, a firm date.

Did you get my letter from Paris? I sent it to Basel, and Piper thought you would surely be back. I hope it all worked, that is, with the letters. I wrote that Manheim has done a beautiful translating job, and I'd like to add now that it would perhaps be possible for him to meet you sometime. He would like that. But I didn't promise anything.

Piper told me about the honorary doctorate at the Sorbonne.[3] He hoped you would in fact go there. And he is right that only your presence will give the affair its due importance. Will that be possible? And how would that affect our plans? Can you drop me a line in Florence—c/o American Express?

Berlin is a real delight. Hamburg was, too, in its way. Not at all stiff, very unconventional, the senator downright touching. But Berlin: grown back together again, or at least in the process of healing. A major city again, in some ways more pleasant than before. One can't even imagine that something could happen here. But there were so many things we couldn't imagine. I like being here, feel myself at home, even in the government offices. I've gone to the East Sector, too, which is very easy and uncomplicated to do now. People from the East are here all the time too, especially in the theater and the opera, where they can pay in their currency so that it remains affordable for them. All very rational and pleasant. I wander about, don't work at all, and thoroughly enjoy being lazy.

Until soon—oh, how nice that it's working out again.

Warmly
Your
Hannah

250 Karl Jaspers to Hannah Arendt

Basel, October 6, 1959

Dear Hannah!

Thank you for your letters from Paris and Berlin.

Hamburg was another success for you. "Everything went off very well, of course, and Piper wants to print my speech in the Piperbücherei"—Gertrud and I are delighted. You'll have to tell us all the details.

I can't go to Paris. Everything has been arranged with the rector in Paris. It would not be good to change things now, even if I wanted to. It would mean a loss in credibility. But that's the way things really are. I have no desire for a repeat of my "helplessness" in Frankfurt—unless it be for some extremely important occasion. I don't mind saying it pains me not to go. Paris and the Sorbonne—living on their past glory—still represent something extraordinary.

And now your happy wanderings in Berlin, where you feel "at home." What you report about the present state of affairs in Berlin sounds wonderful. In permitting this freedom in Berlin, the politicians in the East must have something up their sleeve. Is this just a soothing, seductive, and deceptive maneuver on the path toward "a free city of Berlin"?

Of course I would like to meet Manheim. But the trip to Basel is a long one for him. For my part, I'm agreeable to a meeting at any time, provided it is arranged beforehand. I'm delighted to hear that he has translated so well. You have never passed such a favorable judgment before.

We returned from Cannes a few days ago. It was wonderful. Lotte

[Waltz]'s solicitude and patience are beyond description. Now I'm recovering from the trip. [. . .]

Your visit is welcome at any time. We are waiting for you to set the date. We'll decide whether you'll stay in a hotel or with us when the time comes. I think you'll stay with us.[1]

We're very much looking forward to seeing you!

Warmly
Your
Karl Jaspers

251 *Hannah Arendt to Karl Jaspers*

Florence, October 13, 1959
Hotel Helvetia and Bristol
Piazza Strozzi

Lieber Verehrtester—

Florence is too beautiful and exciting for me to be able to write. With great difficulty, I persuade my legs to take at least a few hours' rest every day at home, i.e., in my hotel, so that I can deal with at least my most pressing work. We will see each other and talk together soon, soon. This is definitely a city for men, by the way, and to such an extreme that even today almost everywhere there are only good men's shops, which I find very amusing.

My time in Berlin was taken up with restitution business. Beautifully taken care of—thanks to your letter,[1] you remember? So I'm rich, or almost rich.

Thank you for your letter. Please, both of you must agree that it's best this time if I stay in a hotel. That won't bother us. I think I'll come on the 23rd, Friday of next week, in the evening, and I'll call first thing on Saturday morning. Piper recommended the Hotel Krafft, but it's a bit far, though with a taxi nothing in Basel is far. I'll see. I thought I would stay—if it's not too much for you—until the 29th, so that I can be in Frankfurt on the 30th and 31st. After that, two days with Marianne Wendt,[2] who is dying of cancer. Then two days more in Cologne (lecture) and Brussels (Annchen [Anne Weil]) and then home. You can reach me here for sure until the 21st. It's possible that I'll have to go to Locarno for a day on the 22nd before I come to Basel.

I didn't call from Zurich because I arrived late in the evening and dog tired—I couldn't make my flight connections in Frankfurt—and then I had to leave again very early the next day.

Warmest greetings to you both and best regards to Erna

Your
Hannah

252   *Hannah Arendt to Gertrud and Karl Jaspers*

[Florence], October 18, 1959

Dear, dear Friends—

I'm not sure which date I gave you. Florence has sent me into a complete tizzy. In any case: I'll arrive on Friday night and will call Saturday morning, the 24th. Is that all right? If not, please telegraph here—Hotel Helvetia and Bristol—because I'm leaving here on Thursday morning and will spend a day in Locarno.

Warmest greetings
Your
Hannah

253   *Karl Jaspers to Heinrich Blücher*

Basel, October 28, 1959

Dear Mr. Blücher!

Hannah read aloud to me the sentences which, in your letter to her, you addressed at the same time to me. I was delighted. You are working in the real world and making an effort to accomplish something there. I just think a little about these things. What you say to me is important to me. Where you agree with me, I am encouraged. Where you raise questions, I too reconsider.

I was especially pleased that you could agree without any reservations on the distinction between science and philosophy. To carry that distinction through in practice is immensely difficult. It would change the spirit of the university, bringing it closer to what it should be. It would permeate all the disciplines and purify them, while at the same time imbuing them with a newly emerging meaning. Its consequences would be the unmasking of superstitious belief in science and the creation of serious awareness for that other mode of thought that is truly life-sustaining. "Reform" cannot be accomplished here with any

382

kind of measures, only within people's heads. Anyone who under-stands that will find his teaching and research transformed.

You note, certainly correctly, that my distinction between religion and philosophy is not sharp enough. I hope that you will be somewhat better satisfied in this area by a new book of mine, "Philosophischer Glaube angesichts der christlichen Offenbarung."[1] But it is only half done (this half is already being printed for a festschrift).[2]

You speak of the role of art in the university. I have really never thought about that before, for art history and art theory are different from the teaching of art in an academy. Should such an academy be incorporated into the university the way an engineering school is? In the Federal Republic of Germany (I won't say "Germany" because that is a much more inclusive concept and another reality) there is (in Ulm) an Academy for Visual Arts that is recognized as a university-level institution. I have no real sense of what is involved there. The program, the subjects, the teachers all strike me as a strange muddle. But I don't know. In general one could say: Any field that requires knowledge and research and that has an idea that shapes its knowledge into a whole belongs in the university.

You speak too of *"premature* plans for the reform of the university." I understand you this way: Without an intellectual change of direction all material, institutional, and statutory reforms will be in vain. When you then add that that is "no reason to become impatient," I don't understand you entirely. Perhaps you mean we should not expect the best right away—we should not give up the fight under any circum-stances and no matter how pessimistic we are (even if all we achieve is to leave a sign indicating that another path was possible)—in both respects I agree with you.

Having Hannah here is, as always, a great pleasure. We talk together in carefully measured-out hours. This time we have taken to insulting each other mutually, like students. I can still manage it—but as an "old fellow" I'm at something of a disadvantage.

Hannah is full of her travel impressions, especially from Florence, which was a real revelation for her. She sees it differently and more correctly than it is usually seen: "a man's city," "unsentimental passion"—politics, architecture, sculpture, painting—but no literature (except for Dante early on).

From Germany—which in her conversation she likes to confuse with the people visible in the Federal Republic today—she has pulled away even more, is more indifferent toward it. That pains me somewhat. I feel she is mistaken about herself, even though she truly has, together with you, achieved a state in which she exists with her feet on the ground, even though deprived of the ground of her origins.

Warmest greetings
Your Karl Jaspers

Hannah has copied this letter because my handwriting would be so difficult for you to read. We are both grateful to her for this.[3]

254 Hannah Arendt to Gertrud Jaspers

New York, January 3, 1960

Dear Friend—

Two good letters from you,[1] redolent of Christmas spirit, and I can't even manage to write in time for New Year's. Yes, we're already so thoroughly settled in, so used to our new place,[2] that we've almost forgotten the old apartment. It was, of course, quite a lot of work, and Heinrich was at Bard and very busy. Still, I enlisted him to hang the pictures.

But let me start at the beginning. When I left you, I went to see Marianne [Wendt], who died about two weeks later. From uremia, which was probably a relatively merciful end. She was still very glad to see me, but I really came too late. She wasn't able to grasp any longer what her real condition was, or could only for seconds at a time. The medications, primarily hormone injections, I assume, and morphine too, of course, induced a kind of euphoria in her. And at the same time the physical degeneration was not as obvious as it usually is in the final stages of cancer. It was eerie. I was able to take her out of the hospital every day. We spent one evening with relatives of hers in the Taunus. Having to lie and put on a performance creates that wall that separates the living from the dying. I did that, though not in any major way, but I was uncomfortable with it.

Then home by way of Cologne and Brussels. The time in Cologne was quite pleasant. I spoke to a packed auditorium at the Husserl Archives. But I couldn't ever feel quite at ease in Germany this time. A very perceptive woman of my age said to me in Frankfurt: It's as if we were walking on swampland again. I'm afraid that is only too true. We talked about the abyss between official Germany (Bonn, universities, radio, newspapers, etc.) and the people. The so-called people are profoundly unhappy despite the wildest prosperity; they're malicious, secretly hoping that everything will fall apart, even if that means they have to suffer. They're full of resentment against everybody and everything, but especially against the so-called West and democracy. This is all unarticulated; there is no movement, no focal point, but the atmosphere it creates is dreadful.

Then when I came home from the airport two little thirteen-year-old Negro boys snatched my purse from me in the hallway of our building. It was no great loss. I didn't have any papers in it, and I was fully insured besides. But I decided to read this as a sign from heaven and to look for a different apartment. And to demonstrate to Heinrich the seriousness of my decision, I took him along on my first apartment inspection, including him really only for psychological reasons. But when we left the building we were both ready to take the apartment right away. It was really funny. Heinrich had made up a list of requirements that seemed to me impossible to fulfill, and on top of those I had my own demands. So I dragged him along to prove to him that he was demanding the impossible. And then what did we find but everything we had hoped for. Two studies with a fantastically beautiful view of the river. Completely quiet, no noise from either the street or the neighbors. Four large, nicely proportioned rooms and a small room. Very nice kitchen with pantry. Generous closets, huge ones, some of which you can walk right into. The building very well kept up and with a doorman day and night. The doorman is a kind of private policeman that one has to pay for here now because the city police can't cope with juvenile delinquency anymore. The price is just what we had set as our maximum, but for what we are getting it is not too much. All the "equipment"—kitchen stove, refrigerator, kitchen sink, bathtub, etc.—is brand-new. And there are two full baths and a toilet with a small bathtub.

Moving wasn't too bad because we had two apartments for a whole month. Our contract on the old one bound us until January 1. On moving day itself, everything was so well organized (I'm bragging, you see) that I was able to go to the movies that evening with a friend who was helping me. We had literally gotten everything done. Granted, we had had the library and the shelves needed for it set up ahead. I had a lot of help and didn't pinch pennies anywhere. If you're going to do it, then do it right. And it didn't even cost as much as I expected. Now we're comfortably established, and I've started working again. We had our usual party on New Year's Eve, only more people than usual. Word had gotten around, and people don't wait to be invited anymore. They just call me up and ask if if they can't please come. What can you do? There were more than 60 people, but Esther (my cleaning woman) and I managed it just fine. We were in bed at seven in the morning, and the apartment looked as if nobody had been there at all.

Würzburg:[3] How did you know about that? Was it in the papers? It came right in the midst of our move, and I promptly forgot the whole thing. (This just between us, please!) And so I was a little late in declining. I was so preoccupied with curtains and a new carpet that I even forgot to tell Heinrich about it. As you can see, I am really "unworthy."

But something that will perhaps give your husband pleasure: I told him about the big squabble I had here last year over my heretical views on the Negro question and equality. I said, I think, that none of my American friends had agreed with me and that very many of them were really angry. Now out of the blue an American foundation has given me an "award" (a kind of prize) of $300 for this very article.[4] Presumably because it was so unpopular! That is very typical of this country. That reminds me of a story from the war. The high schools in New York gave all the students of the senior classes the assignment of thinking up an appropriate punishment for Hitler. A Negro girl wrote: He should have a black skin put on him and be forced to live in the United States. The girl won the first prize and a four-year scholarship for college!

Manheim sent the rest of the manuscript in the middle of all this, and I sent it back to him in Paris with some suggested changes, all of which he accepted. Now Sauerländer[5] (a native German) at Pantheon is reading the whole manuscript through again, and then we will put the finishing touches on it together. It ought to appear in the fall.

A good and happy New Year!

Your
Hannah

I'm eagerly awaiting the "Epikur"![6]

255   Hannah Arendt to Karl Jaspers

February 29, 1960

Lieber Verehrtester—

We haven't written to each other for a long time, and I feel rather to blame. Both your birthdays and no hyacinths for your wife! It just didn't work out this time. Nobody in Switzerland, and the florists' international orders aren't reliable.

I hope things are going well for you and that you are working. We are happily established in our new apartment and enjoying our view and comfort. Heinrich has stumbled from one semester into the next without a single day of vacation. But he seems to tolerate it very well indeed. I'm living very quietly, going to the theater or a concert only now and then but hardly ever to parties. I'm seeing only friends, and I'm glad I don't have to do any socializing. I'm working on my translation of *The Human Condition*, which is supposed to be done in April and will perhaps be done in early May. Now and then I go, or, rather, fly around a bit to trade a lecture for a few dollars. But I'm not doing even that unless it's really worthwhile. Otherwise, I'm in the process of refusing all my invitations to Europe for the summer (three of them; that's counting only the ones that would pay my way). I'll never manage to meet all my obligations if I don't just take a year and sit still for once. Then, too, it's not so easy to leave Heinrich alone. He doesn't like it so much anymore. We're both thinking about coming somehow, either at the end of the year or in early 1961. That is, if it's possible for Heinrich to take leave for a semester. Then he would have vacation from June until February of next year. That would be something anyway, even if he has to use the time to work, which I can understand.

The reason I'm writing today is because the people at Pantheon Books have told me they still don't have the preface, aimed at the American reader,[1] that we discussed. You'll recall it. We spoke about it, and you thought you could have it ready by the end of the year. We are in the last stages of preparation for printing. The whole manuscript has been checked through once again, and now I have to make some additions to the bibliography. Sauerländer, who is about the equivalent of what is called a *Lektor*[2] in Europe, is coming on Thursday so that we can clear up with each other technical matters for the printing.

I heard a few weeks ago from Ashton, who told me, to my dismay, that the atom book still isn't finished. He sent a few chapters, which are excellent and without a single error. But the project is taking an eternity, and I don't really know why.

This has turned into a dreadful letter, and we won't even count it as one. How is Erna? Is she continuing to improve?

All my best to you both
Your
Hannah

Basel, March 5, 1960

Dear Hannah!

Thank you very much! But I am at fault for falling silent after your visit. I can't excuse it. I'll tell you sometime why it happened. It has nothing to do with you.

And about my dragging my heels with the preface. Your letter arrived in the evening yesterday. I wrote the preface today. Gertrud will copy it tomorrow, and then I will rework it. I hope to send it off to you in a few days. I dug out your old letter and felt oriented to the job right away. I'm using a few of your words and I feel a bit "Americanized" already in my attempt to accomplish for Americans a task to which I am not accustomed but that has been very correctly set for me. Against my nature, I've adopted a somewhat light tone. Please check through this preface, make corrections, and send it back to me if necessary.

The philosophers [Eckhart and Cusanus] that I was supposed to supply to fill out the second volume have gone by the board. But perhaps that can wait until summer.

I'm troubled to learn about the delay in the translation of the "atom bomb," particularly because no date has been set for completing it. But I'm glad that Ashton is producing such a good translation.

You write with satisfaction about your wonderful apartment and the peace and quiet in which to do your work. That you found the right place so quickly—you told us you were *planning* a move—and that you could convince Heinrich completely and instantaneously seems like a miracle after the worries you expressed here about the apartment.

It is becoming more difficult for you to travel to Europe. I'm afraid that if Heinrich plans to come he will change his mind again at the last minute. Tell him that he has to make this trip for *our* benefit too. Otherwise we may never see each other and speak together in this life. And Hannah—once a year—has become indispensable to us. So I will continue to hope very much that you will come at the end of this year after all.

In the session of the Bundestag (February 18) devoted to anti-Semitic acts, the government statement included a long quotation from your Lessing talk[1] (where you speak about the state of "being at a loss," about "knowing and being able to bear the fact that things were this way and not otherwise, and then seeing what results from that." Because Adenauer was ill, Minister Schröder[2] delivered this statement and spoke of the "Jewish emigrant," of her "very profound insight," and concluded by saying: "I think, ladies and gentlemen, that these are thoughts very much deserving of our reflection."[3]

I'm sending you as printed matter the offprint[4] that contains the first half of the book for Nanda Anshen. You don't need to read it. Perhaps I'll rework this section too later. —Everything progresses slowly. Too much claptrap!

I put in for my retirement, effective October 1. I was asked "to remain formally in office" for one more semester and to lecture for *one* hour until April 1, 1961. I of course accepted those terms. But it has to be confirmed yet by the various authorities. I'll tell you another time how all this came to pass.

Warmest greetings to you and Heinrich

Your Karl Jaspers

257 *Karl Jaspers to Hannah Arendt*

Basel, March 8, 1960

Dear Hannah!

I'm enclosing the foreword here. I've tried to transform myself into an American. Please give this a *ruthless* going-over and, if necessary, send me the pages with your suggested changes.

The question remains as to whether the table with the grouping of the philosophers into three volumes should be included somewhere. If so, I would have to change something, because a few names from III have been put in II.[1]

How good that you are turning away from the many distractions for a while in favor of further undisturbed work. The world, hungry as it is for lectures, ceremonies, and shows, would eat you up and pay you well for it and provide you the pleasure as well of being publicly effective, which is by no means mere fraud. And in Germany the number of those who want to hear your voice is growing. They have great respect for you, and what you say is welcome to many Germans' ears. They are aware that for all your criticism, your thinking is not at all nihilistic and that behind it is a great love, which is the true essence of the philosopher. If people cannot hear you for a while, they will later be able to read, in addition to all the good things you have written, still more good things that have been thought through calmly, thoroughly, without haste. Then at some time, if you feel like it, you will be there in person for them again.

I'm in the process of writing my talk for Basel's 500th-year celebration.[2] I'd like to have it more or less finished before the semester begins.

The appointment negotiations[3] are burdensome to me. I suffer more than I used to from the lack of human stature, the conventionality, and the closed minds of those involved. These proceedings have a somewhat eerie quality. Very much in keeping with them is the story of a young woman, a privatdocent, who has written a few philologically striking and remarkably insightful studies. She knows Greek, Latin, and Arabic well, was recommended by Wilpert,[4] and received an invitation from us. She then in fact came to Basel, but once here she called me up at noon in total panic and, without notifying anyone, did not appear for the lecture she was to give in the afternoon. When I visited her later, I found her in bed, calmed down with the aid of a nurse. Behind the foreground of hysterical panic I thought I sensed the initial stages of schizophrenia. But then, calmed down, she got right up after I had left and went that evening, having just received the invitation, to Salmony's[5] for dinner. The poor creature was simply wonderful. You say that only pariahs are human. I would say the mentally ill are, too. But both those statements are correct only within narrow limits and in a larger sense not true. I'm afraid that rather than take a potential mental case we will get a puppet or nonentity instead. But then again, perhaps not. I think Salmony is better than that, but he is the last person anybody else seems to want.

Warmest greetings!

Your Karl Jaspers

I don't have your exact address. I'm lacking the number that comes after New York (the one that gives the section of the city). I hope my letters are arriving despite that. Please send me the exact address in any case.

258   *Hannah Arendt to Karl Jaspers*

March 25, 1960

Lieber Verehrtester—

Frau Singer[1] just called—just as I arrived back from a lecture trip. I'm in arrears. Not entirely my fault. But first to business: The preface is superb; I passed it right on to the publisher, who felt the same way and sent it on immediately to Manheim—that is, a copy of it. We'll have the translation here in a few days.

My delay: Apart from the lecture trips and the logistics connected with them, a very good American friend [Mary McCarthy] of mine turned up here suddenly ten days ago with divorce and marriage troubles. She is living with us for the time being, which is going very well. But at first we had a certain feeling of unrest here, which was aggravated by my having, at this of all times, these lecture obligations. And so one is given to heel-dragging!

The philosophers to fill out the second volume: will it be possible to send a carbon copy when you have finished the manuscript for Piper? So that we won't have to wait until the book is available in print?

The offprint[2] has arrived, too, but I haven't read it yet. Nanda Anshen happened to be here just then, saw the offprint, and took it away from me. I'll get it back, of course.

I'm very, very eager to hear more about your retirement. That comes as a great surprise, and I have the feeling that you've had some kind of run-in with the faculty. I'm really very sad about it but take some comfort in the weekly lecture. Perhaps you may decide nonetheless to give a seminar now and then. What you write about the hiring difficulties sounds somehow grotesque. But that truly awful story about the girl confirms me in my prejudice against women as professors. I may not have been able to manage a performance like that because I lack the uninhibitedness of the hysterical, but I can understand how fear would drive someone to simply lie in bed. That takes a certain courage, too, that I don't have. You thought: early stages of mental illness. You are probably right, but I don't think single women need to be crazy to do crazy things. —Apropos of university calls: The faculty at Würzburg wrote an exceptionally friendly reply to my refusal, which pleased me because I'd been late with my answer.[3]

Another thing on *Die grossen Philosophen*: Once your preface is translated we'll have to go through the "Introduction" once again, and the publisher here wasn't sure whether he wanted to present the plan of the entire work in such detail. But in any case: could you please drop me a line telling me what the changes are? I somehow recall Epicurus and Lucretius in the second volume of the German edition, but I'm not sure.

Address: the number after New York is 25, but never essential. It just makes things easier for the post office.

Heinrich sends his best regards—he just hollered in at me not to forget. It's almost certain that I'll come at the end of the year, and I hope very much I can bring Heinrich. He won't make the trip for the sake of Basel "too" but exclusively for that reason. And to see an old friend of his youth.[4] Unfortunately, everything else strikes him as merely a nuisance, and my hopes of a Mediterranean trip with him, for which he still showed some interest a few years ago, are more or less dashed. He will probably come for only two weeks. That is grotesque—after nearly 20 years away from Europe. But he is not open to such arguments. But more on this when I see you. I don't mean it as criticism, but it doesn't cease to astonish me.

There is much to tell you about political matters here. The Negro question is turning out to be as serious as I judged it to be from the start. But that for another time. The household is calling, and "the necessities of life" always have a certain urgency about them.

All my very best to you both

Your
Hannah

259 *Karl Jaspers to Hannah Arendt*

Basel, April 2, 1960

Dear Hannah!

Thank you very much! The delay was in no way due to your loafing. How kind you are to open your house to your American friend!

First of all to the *Philosophen*: Of course you will receive a carbon copy as soon as the first philosophers of the second volume are completed. They are the philosophers grouped together under the heading "Weltfromme Anschauungen": Xenophanes, Empedocles, Anaxagoras, Democritus, Epicurus, Lucretius, Poseidonius, Bruno. You were quite right in assuming that Epicurus and Lucretius have been taken out of the third volume and put in the second.

Perhaps the publisher is quite right in not supplying the plan of the entire work in the same detail I go into in my German "Introduction." The plan of the whole is, after all, still very uncertain. I'm delighted that sections of the "Introduction" have been translated and will be printed. I thought the whole "Introduction" had been omitted. It is a product of my unshakable professorial view that everything has to be a textbook, and that textbooks have to have introductions. I can understand that they can be cut or placed just as well at the end, but my feeling is still that I want to inform my readers in advance about my plan and tone and basis of judgment. You know that I am agreeable to any way you decide to do things. It gives me real pleasure that this book is appearing in America. I'm eager to see if it will be well received. That you will appear as editor on the title page seems to me, quite apart from everything else, an excellent entrée to America.

Give Heinrich my best regards, and tell him how happy I am that I will have the chance at the end of the year to meet him with you.

Now a word about my retirement: no, no problems with the faculty. That would not be sufficient reason. I have just gradually come to the unavoidable conclusion that it is time. In the spring of '59 I was hoarse for a long time and was constantly worrying during the summer semester, asking myself after each lecture: Will I be able to manage the next one? People were telling me that my voice changed toward the end of the hour, but that is all better now. In a faculty meeting with 50 people in July I not only spoke but also responded to an interruption with the same volume I had had before. But strangely enough, the feeling of having grown older remained, and it was reinforced when, from August on, I had continual intestinal bleeding. When you were with us, I thought that the bleeding was certainly not hemorrhoidal (that much medical acumen I still have) but must be due to a cancer. Because that would be inoperable at my age, I was in no hurry to find out for certain, but finally I wanted the matter cleared up. It turned out not to be cancer but a so-called diverticulosis. But the experience left behind something like a sign for me. I can't say that there's any compelling reason for my decision, but I am reminded of something my father[1] used to say: You should leave a job when other people think you are still in good form. And then, I don't get the same kind of pleasure from lecturing that I used to. Reflection, study, and writing are more enjoyable to me. But the really deciding factor is that I can no longer satisfy the demands of my job. Meetings are more exhausting for me than before. The smoking in them causes me more frequent bronchial episodes with fever, and then I suffer from them for several days. And I have been neglecting the meetings anyhow, often simply not going. That just won't do if you've accepted the responsibilities of a job.

When I made my wishes known, the president told me he regretted my decision very much and suggested to me that I stay in office for at least one more semester and lecture for one hour so that my retirement would not begin until April 1, 1961. I could not refuse that, especially since he kindly said, Basel owed me a debt of thanks. Now, this suggestion has to pass muster with the various authorities. But it is certain that I will retire either on October 1 or on April 1.

My response to your kind question has gone into such detail that it seems self-important, but I know that you are not annoyed by it and that you indeed understand that such matters cannot be decided and justified with rational arguments. They signify instead simply a stage of maturation in life at which what is clear admits of no further discussion. All I know for myself is that I am happy at the thought of being free of official obligations.

The political situation is dreadful again. Everywhere. Adenauer seems to me, however, one of the most clear-sighted formulators of foreign policy, one who sees the simple things. The solidarity of the West is crumbling at an accelerating rate.

Warmest greetings to you both

Your Karl Jaspers

Gertrud sends regards to you both. Please excuse the dictation. Without it, this letter would have been put off too long.

260   Karl Jaspers to Hannah Arendt

Basel, June 17, 1960

Dear Hannah!

Today just a quick question: The University of Nebraska Press in Lincoln would like to translate my three-volume *Philosophie*. They are making a respectable financial offer. The only problem is the translation. Professor Keller[1] at the university there might take it on. I asked whether the Press could send a translation sample to you, only for your judgment, not for any corrections. You mustn't be burdened once again with matters of this kind now. If the translation turns out to be more or less tolerable, I think I should agree. It is in itself unlikely that one could convince anyone else to undertake the translation of this large work. So my request to you is to read this translation sample and judge it. Would you? I have already given the Press your name and address. But you can of course refuse.

You have, I hope, in the meantime created the peace and quiet you need to be completely free for work on your political book. Dr. Martin has visited you. I suspect he did not make a good impression. He is useful to me for the communications he can provide, and so I maintain the relationship. He is very pleased that you are allowing him to reprint in the *Universitätszeitung* a section[2] from your translation for Kohlhammer.

Warmest greetings to you both from Gertrud and me.

Your
Karl Jaspers

261 *Hannah Arendt to Karl Jaspers*

New York, June 20, 1960

Lieber Verehrtester,

It's a scandalously long time that I've gone without writing. Heinrich has been wanting to write you about the university offprint[1] but hasn't been able to get to it during the semester. This week he will finally be coming home and will have his long vacation before him. We have decided not to go away this summer. The apartment is too pleasant. At the most for a few weeks in Vermont in August.

When your letter came, I was terrified at first, then could breathe easy again. How are you now? Perhaps it is good after all that you retire. You will have more than enough opportunities to step forward and speak if you really want to.

Now I want to give you a quick report, even though there isn't too much to tell you. For about two weeks now I have, thank God, been quit of translating my *Human Condition*. It was real torture, and now I'm having trouble getting back into English. My American friend stayed until the end of April, the whole business a fantastic story, in part very American and in part that change-of-life syndrome about which you warned me in such kindly yet emphatic terms, one with which I have trouble empathizing, given all its panic, anxiety, etc. This episode took its toll on me because I like her a lot and am very concerned. But what can one do—except offer one's house? Now she is in Rome in a rather unhappy situation.

In the midst of all that and following it I had to make a couple of decisions that were not easy for me either. In any case, I'll go to Northwestern University for two months next spring and to Wesleyan University for a semester next fall. Wesleyan has just opened a kind

395

of Institute for Advanced Study. I'm accepting both offers essentially for financial reasons. You know what the retirement situation here is. One has to save a bit, and both these appointments pay very well for relatively little work. I'm not at all concerned about the fall semester, because I can always come home for weekends. Wesleyan is very close by. And for the two months in the spring things will just have to go on without me.

Then too, Heinrich's overall situation is much better again, and not being at home seems much more possible to me. It is as good as certain that we will come in January. He has to start teaching again in mid-February. If he wants to teach at the New School again, he has to be back as early as February 1.

What do you think about the political situation? Isn't it hair-raising? And I haven't the least confidence in the presidential candidates.[2] It isn't enough, after all, merely not to be senile—which Eisenhower is without a doubt. I heard and saw him recently on television. But despite that, I have the feeling that for now the situation is still not dangerous. The real upshot of the Geneva summitry[3] is that nothing in Berlin has changed. Though I do not mean to say by that that it wouldn't have been considerably better to arrive at that same point without all this summit-conference posing. The business in Japan[4] is much more serious, but even that I can't take quite seriously, because I've always been of the opinion that all these American bases aren't worth much if, in a showdown, there aren't enough troops on hand to occupy the countries involved and protect the bases.

By the way, I received an odd letter about your *Philosophie* from a Professor Keller. Does Nebraska Press want to publish it? Does he want to do the translation? Is it all right with you if I ask him to give me a sample? He'll be in our area in the summer and will presumably come to see me.

And while we're on the subject of visits: don't be shocked when you meet Nanda Anshen in person. Despite all appearances, she is a decent, solid person. Her only problem is that philosophy has gone to her head, which is more funny than it is bad.

Warmest greetings to you both

As always, your
Hannah

P.S. How is Erna? Is all well with her? And what are your summer plans?

396

Basel, July 30, 1960

Dear Hannah!

Our letters crossed in the mail. Your letter already contained the answer to mine.

The University of Nebraska Press has sent me a draft contract I see no need to change: 6% and an advance of $200.– on signing and $200.– on publication.

Professor Keller has not replied to three letters from the Press. He is teaching at the moment "in the eastern USA." I recommended Manheim. The Press will ask you directly, I assume, whether you can recommend another translator.

The offer appears to me to be a serious one. I would be delighted to have a good translation of my *Philosophie*.

I'll be happy to have a visit from Nanda Anshen. It will be good to see her, especially after your description and after her irrepressible initiative. She is obviously a very decent person. I am, however, completely reworking my book.[1] I don't like the half that was published in the Barth festschrift[2] at all anymore. I'm refining and expanding it now, and it may be getting too long for Nanda Anshen.

You both have vacation, but you're staying home because it is so pleasant there! We are happy to read that. At last you have quarters in which you are truly comfortable.

My wife and I send our warmest greetings.

Your Karl Jaspers

263   Hannah Arendt to Karl Jaspers

Haines Falls,[1] August 22, 1960

Lieber Verehrtester—

Kurt Wolff sent me the clipping from the *Neue Zürcher Zeitung*, which I received a few days ago. And I have since read a somewhat longer summary in *Aufbau* (which you surely have already and which I am therefore not sending along), and then on Sunday the *Times* had the little article, enclosed here.[2]

Wonderful! Wonderful, too, is the obviously provocative formulation you used, because what really matters is just what you've said: The important thing is not reunification but freedom, understood for what it is, namely, as an alternative that represents a basic principle. One can of course blur that principle by arguing that freedom (understood as self-determination) would lead to reunification. And that argument has no doubt already been stated emphatically. Whereupon the reply is that self-determination as a right of nations applies to constitutional form and domestic political arrangements and by no means needs to include the so-called right to national self-determination, which has consequences for foreign policy. At any rate, this is the heaviest blow that has yet been struck against German nationalism. And it could lead to a clear division between the camps, whereby it would quickly become evident that the so-called right and the so-called left are in the same camp.

You also seem to have suggested neutrality. Even if the Russians were willing, which they of course aren't (and can't be because of their satellite states), it could be guaranteed only under the condition of neutrality for West Germany as well. I would think that a good solution, because I don't set much stock by NATO in the long run, and neutrality would not stand in the way of European integration.

I'd very much like to know what the follow-up on this is, whether there are any positive reactions to it. Cries of protest are bound to go up, precisely because no one seriously believes in reunification any longer.

We've been here since the beginning of August, this time somewhat higher in the mountains than usual, which is agreeing with us well. We're in a beautifully situated Swiss inn where the innkeepers and the guests speak only Swiss German and it smells just the way Swiss inns are supposed to. We go back to New York at the end of this week. Nebraska Press wrote a few days ago. Because the translation[3] by Mr. Keller arrived just as we were leaving, I didn't get a chance to look at it, and then I stupidly forgot both manuscript and original at the last minute. But these few weeks won't make all that much difference. I've written to the Press. I heard from Pantheon that they have the manuscript[4] ready for composition. It will probably appear in the spring. I also had a short letter from Nanda Anshen that I couldn't make much sense of. She apparently wasn't either in Munich or in Basel. Has the contract been signed, at least?[5] She said she wanted to draw it up with me. I'll call her as soon as I'm back in New York.

Unfortunately, I am obliged to go to two congresses in New York that I couldn't very well extricate myself from. And I've spent half my time here preparing papers for them. But now in this final week

I'll make up for that by doing absolutely nothing at all. In July we entertained ourselves with the big party conventions at which the presidential candidates are chosen. In all seriousness, it was interesting, and I've come to realize that television is good for something after all. [Nelson] Rockefeller made by far the best impression, and his speech to the party presented the best program. It is very possible that his turn will come in 1964. As for the rest, it's interesting to see that no one has the slightest idea what the different candidates' chances are. It seems to me beyond question that because of television the number of "independent voters" (who are not bound to either party) has risen vastly and that an extraordinarily large number of people are still undecided. Unless something highly untoward should happen, we will wind up voting for Kennedy. Nixon would be quite awful. I don't think much of [Henry Cabot] Lodge, but I suspect he wouldn't be an outright catastrophe either.

How are you both? Is Lotte Waltz driving you around a little in the countryside again? Or have you decided to stay at home for the whole summer? We've had the coolest summer in memory here, which is very nice for a change.

All best and warmest wishes,

Your
Hannah

264   *Heinrich Blücher to Karl Jaspers*

New York, October 4, 1960

Dear Mr. Jaspers!

In the burgeoning tide of sound and fury that world history serves up every day, genuinely political acts and words have become rarer and rarer. Hammarskjöld's actions in the Congo[1] and your speech to the Germans (that is, the interview and the newspaper articles following on it[2] that I have seen here) are the only events since I don't know how long that have political significance. Success is not the the important thing here. Hammarskjöld's course of action, the success of which is in no way certain, and your talk, which seems to be bearing so few consequences, are political, as it were, because they both have the character of genuine events and so stand apart from the world-historical sound and fury in which all deeds and words are only occurrences. In the midst of the new "nations'" assault on the United

399

Nations, Hammarskjöld has tried to bring the demands of freedom, those eternal demands, into a new relationship with the constantly changing demands of the nations. Your talks have the very same intent.

Even though in politics the voice of wisdom can always speak only through the mouth of a reasonable man and a decisive, wise act be carried out now and then by an individual man, a genuine event remains a genuine event. That is, it remains visible for a long time, hovering above the rush of occurrences, and people can look up at it again and again and orient themselves by it. Just as every lie has to establish itself as an abyss directly under its corresponding truth, so does every truth have to hold itself suspended above its corresponding lie. And the applause of the masses, indeed even the powerful sound waves of the loudspeaker, can easily precipitate its fall into the lie.

The role that national forces will play in the future is the crucial political question of our time. That a basic assessment of this question should come from Germany, of all places, and, on top of that, from a German philosopher, of all people, came as such a marvelous surprise to me that I almost felt that freedom, in its despair, was resorting to miracles.

If even only a single German so clearly rises above the nationalistic madness, then one can't know what else might be possible. It seems that many German politicians have gravitated hesitantly toward your view and turn away from it now presumably only for partisan reasons and with divided minds. I heard here that very young people in Germany were moved by your talk. A single public act in this direction on Germany's part would amount to a warning lesson to new, small nations, backed by the authority of an old nation that has often been defeated. I think that your basic distinction between alienable and inalienable rights bears a relationship to the distinction, mentioned above, between genuine political events and historical occurrences. Inalienable rights, I would think, can emerge only from freedom. Social and historical occurrences produce only interchangeable and alienable privileges.

I wrote to you once how we as boys during the First World War became aware of the national hoax. The nation-state is the genuine political community transformed into a lie; the nation is the lie that special-interest groups use to make themselves appear as something better. Nationalism is just as dangerous an ideology as capitalism, socialism, racism, imperialism, and it has been mixed with all of them to produce the most poisonous of cocktails. This broad-scale muddling together of ideological lies goes merrily on, and I am afraid that Mao will soon be telling us that white people are born capitalists and yellow people born communists.

With the aid of the national concept, genuine attachment to one's native people and land was distorted into the lies of racism and national superiority—a massive abyss of lies yawning directly below the truth. That genuine attachment I spoke of has nothing to do with such lies, and it can be protected only by means of a political community based in freedom.

Nationalism has always led to imperialism by way of jingoism and chauvinism. The new, small nations that are springing up out of the jungle soil like mushrooms are, by their nationalistic shrieking and all manner of mass hysteria, being driven into the hands of the imperialists. Before they have the chance to stumble ahead in their own national imperialism, transfixed all the while by the old imperialism and co-lonialism of their former oppressors, they can be gobbled up by social imperialism or by some new race imperialism, because these imperi-alisms have developed totalitarian methods. And so the necessary struggle for freedom, namely, the struggle of the federative principle against the imperialistic principle of all stamps, is made almost im-possible by the fog of social and national drivel.

That is why reflection on the "national" is so necessary and is in itself a political event. With your talk, you take the bull by the horns. Just as you confront nationalism with freedom, so must all these ide-ological "bulls" I have just mentioned be confronted with freedom. That is the politics we have to pursue. And that is the reason why politics is in such dire need of philosophy today. But where is phi-losophy's and especially German philosophy's understanding of free-dom? Now such an understanding is beginning to take shape in German philosophy. Shouldn't it be grounds for hope that even the Germans suddenly want to do something for freedom? The East Berliners have done something already in any case[3] and have not left all the glory to the Hungarians.

If Germany were a member of the United Nations,[4] then you could do no better than to read your thoughts there publicly and for the record, thoughts that do not constitute "Speeches to the German Na-tion,"[5] but, rather, addresses to the nation per se. In any event, you have my wholehearted support.

I look forward very much to being able to discuss all this with you soon. Because Hannah is teaching at Columbia at the moment[6] we cannot leave until the beginning of January. We want to fly from here on January 10 and go to Rome for about a week. We thought we would then go directly from there to Basel—on about the 20th. If that does not suit you, then we could come to Basel first thing or also a week later than I've just suggested. Unfortunately, I can stay in Europe only until about February 4. Hannah intends to stay longer, but at the moment all her plans are still in disarray. She will write you herself.

Until early next year, with warmest greetings

Your
Heinrich Blücher

265 Hannah Arendt to Karl Jaspers

New York, October 4, 1960[1]

Lieber Verehrtester!

Just a quick greeting and the good news that the atom book not only will appear at the beginning of January but also that Ashton has restored all the cuts in it. The book is now just like the original. The Press has handled everything beautifully. Ashton is slow but very good. The publication date, it seems to me, is even better than last year's would have been. —Heinrich wrote you about my confusion. I cooked this mess up myself and I'm not sure yet whether I'll have to eat it as well. I want to go to Israel for the Eichmann trial,[2] and *The New Yorker*, a very well-known magazine here, has said it will send me. The problem is that no one knows when the trial will begin and how long it will last, also that I'm committed to being at a university for April and May. Not to mention all my other commitments. I had hoped the trial would be in March. Then I would have stayed in Europe after Heinrich went home, translated my revolution book for Piper, and then flown to Israel. But it seems those plans will come to naught.

Until soon, and until then, all my best regards.

Your
Hannah

Basel, October 14, 1960

Dear Mr. Blücher!

What a pleasure to get a letter like that from you! You write like one youth to another, enthusiastically exaggerating the importance of the "event." But you do that because the issue, nationalism, is in fact so important. We are both convinced the devil is at work here, and, so it seems, everywhere. Your agreement has inspired me to complete the additional essays that, together with the five earlier ones from *Die Zeit*, Piper will publish as soon as possible.[1] I hope that you will be satisfied with the others, though perhaps not to the same degree. Politically you are far my superior, and by way of Hannah you have sometimes instructed me in the past. Now I've gotten myself into this field, and I'm having trouble knowing where to stop, but with this publication with Piper I mean to make a clean break from it for the time being.

Your image of history—the hovering of genuine events above mere occurrences—is very apt, also the analogous one of the danger of falling into the applause of the masses. I run no risk of the latter danger at the moment. But your warning is good nonetheless.

The odd thing is that I haven't said anything new but am really drawing on an old tradition. The literary people who are annoyed and are jealous of the effect I've had reproach me with that. The effect has clearly been due to a constellation no one could have predicted. It is perhaps risky for me to exploit it in order to tell my Germans so much more in addition. If you were here, I would give you each of my new essays to read and so would surely guard myself from many an error. I feel now that what matters is not errors in details but, rather, the mode of thought, which at a time like this should lead to ultimate consequences.

You are proud of the East Berliners, and with good reason. They took the chance, but only briefly, and did not find an echo in the population as a whole. The Hungarians accomplished much more and remain the model for a future moment that we cannot foresee. I am very happy that we will meet in Basel at the end of January. It will be almost like a miracle if it comes about. I won't believe it until it is a reality.

Warmest greetings and thanks.

Karl Jaspers

Basel, October 14, 1960

Dear Hannah!

A letter from your husband is always a remarkable event, and a letter like that especially so.

You have taken on a great deal but have the equanimity to cancel those things that you cannot manage properly. The Eichmann trial will be no pleasure for you. I'm afraid it cannot go well. I fear your criticism and think that you will keep as much of it as possible to yourself.

It comes as a great surprise that my atom book will appear in early January now. You can imagine how pleased I am, also that all the cut passages have been reinstated. In the last analysis this press has proved to be excellent. It has taken a chance with a lot of money. I hope for both the press and myself that the book is a success. It has perhaps lost hardly any of its timeliness.

My wife and I recently spent two happy weeks in Heidelberg in the Schlosshotel. She sought out all the many decent people from the Nazi years and took pleasure in that old solidarity of spirit. Now, for the last ten days, we have had a new task to deal with together. My wife's hearing troubles have taken a sudden turn for the worse, and she is almost deaf. Conversation is possible only with the aid of a very powerful hearing aid. We are searching out technical improvements and receiving good advice. With the common, comfortable devices, like the ones built into eyeglasses and a device one hangs over the ear, she can, unfortunately, hear hardly at all. They are too weak. Her relationship with the world will inevitably change. My wife is taking it well, and we are thinking how good it is to grow old together. My retirement is coming at just the right moment.

With the warmth of old friendship and in happy anticipation of seeing you again

Your
Karl Jaspers

November 9, 1960

Dear Friend—

I've been wanting to write since I got your husband's letter telling me about your deafness. But I was sick and in bed—nothing at all serious, but I was without a typewriter, which is to say, only half there. I'd like to have further details. I experienced something similar here with an elderly friend who was very hard of hearing. After some days the problem took care of itself. Then, too, I have confidence in the latest hearing aids, which are surely as readily available in Basel as they are here. But, dear friend, please write me. And don't get too down. There are many possible routes of communication.

We spent nearly 24 hours in front of the television at the presidential election. We are both very relieved that Kennedy won—by about half a percent! I don't think anyone here had ever seen anything like it. There will be some significant changes. There would have been changes with Nixon, too, but not fundamental ones. Kennedy is a different type, and having looked him over from every angle for weeks now, I have to say that I'm impressed by him. The voter turnout was massive. In the afternoon the street where our poll is was literally packed with people. The participation was 90%! The campaign was, with a few exceptions, almost free of mudslinging, and the exchange of the customary congratulatory telegrams between the losing and the winning candidates particularly cordial. Eisenhower is the only one who's upset, which I suppose one can't blame him for, because he had gradually talked himself into the illusion that all he had to do was suggest a man to the American people, someone whom he had selected himself and who was "his boy," and the voters would snap him up. That's not even senility at work; it's just his native stupidity. Television played an immense role. What was always so evident to us, namely, that Nixon is a hypocrite and a liar who cares only about his career, became clear to a great many people during the 4 television debates. And what counted among the so-called independent voters was general human quality. It is a good sign, too, that such an incredibly large number of voters voted independent of party affiliation. Kennedy won with a large majority in a number of states that then blithely elected a Republican congressman or senator on the same ballot. And vice versa. It's very good, too, seeing that Kennedy has won after all, that he won by such an incredibly small margin. That should help dampen a measure of innate arrogance in him. This election may have unfavorable repercussions for Adenauer. The fact that another generation is coming to power here will have consequences in the international arena, too. On top of that, as a Harvard product and at least to some extent an intellectual, Kennedy belongs to the circles in America that are influential in intellectual and academic life and therefore look to England and France, not Germany, and are oriented to those cultures.

We'll see each other soon! It seems like a particularly long time since our last meeting, even though that was only a year ago.

A whole letter full of nothing but election talk. You'll have to forgive me. It is very important after all.

And all I meant to do was say: Please drop me a line!

As always and with warmest greetings
Your
Hannah

269 *Hannah Arendt to Karl Jaspers*

New York, November 21, 1960

Lieber Verehrtester!

Your wife's letter[1] telling me that you're lecturing in the main auditorium,[2] that your book[3] will appear any day now—all that gives me such great pleasure. I think sometimes of Max Weber's phrase about the pianissimo of advanced age[4] and that in your case almost the reverse is true. How wonderful!

But today I am writing only to send you the contract[5] from Harper (Nanda Anshen). You'll recall that you refused to sign the excessively long printed contract. I subsequently pared the contract down to what seemed to me to be the essentials and then negotiated with Harper again. Whether you will sign now is another question, but as far as this series is concerned, things are, I think, in order. I made very few substantial changes. The only important one was in a paragraph providing that you would receive only 5% (instead of 10%) royalties if the book should ever sell less than 500 copies per half-year. That struck me as unacceptable. Assuming that you find everything in order—the contract is in easily surveyable form now—you should sign both copies and send them back to Nanda Anshen. Harper will then sign and pay you the advance of $500.

All very warmest regards
Your
Hannah

Basel, December 1, 1960

Dear Hannah!

It's bad that I haven't written at all. I won't try to find excuses.

I recently received from Kohlhammer your *Vita Activa*,[1] the German translation of *The Human Condition*. I have read in it a lot these days, because I wanted to and found great pleasure in it. I was familiar with a number of chapters from the English edition, the beginning and some later material, the chapters on forgiving and promising in particular. But in German I can read so much more quickly and easily and grasp the overall picture so much better that I feel I'm really getting to know the book only now. What appeals to me so strongly in this book is that the things you explicitly state you will *not* talk about (right at the beginning and repeatedly thereafter) exert such a palpable influence from the background. That makes the book in some strange way very transparent for me. There is nothing else quite like it today. All your important and concrete discussions are carried by another dimension. Therefore, despite their great seriousness, they become "light" in all their reality. Your many pertinent insights and illuminations and the historical profundity of your explanations provide concreteness and solidity.

It isn't worth specifically listing my fairly numerous objections. They all touch on surface matters, for instance, your habit of constantly using "Greek," "modern," and so on and classifying positions in those terms. Or I stumble at the short sentence about Weber's Calvinism:[2] "In part corrected."[3] I would have liked documentation on how and where it has been corrected. If there is any work of Max Weber's marked by that scholarly subtlety that the world has such difficulty in comprehending, it is this one. What I have seen in the way of "correctives" (apart from the feeble German efforts that Max Weber was able to respond to himself) always seizes on ideas that Max Weber did not put forward at all and that others simplistically read into him (as in Scheler,[4] as in Tawney,[5] whose book, which is really not bad, I read decades ago and who annoyed me with his distorted reflection of Max Weber). This point is not unimportant to me, because what is involved here is the essence of Max Weber's scholarly achievement. Max Weber may be subject to correction in many other works, if one cares to express it that way, and I have my objections to raise with him, too, as I did during his lifetime. But in this one work (and this is not the case with his other volumes on the sociology of religion) one has to point up the error after total immersion and after following Max Weber step by step in his cognitive process. I doubt if scarcely one of the critics has understood what is contained in Weber's statement that goes something like this: "I believe I have demonstrated that the Calvinistic ethic was a causal factor in the rise of capitalism. How significant this causal factor was cannot be proved. I consider it of great significance." It seems wonderful to me, because it is so scholarly. Max Weber conducted this kind of research in such detail and from such heterogeneous sources only to achieve results that claimed to be so minimal. The modern sociologists, who claim so much so quickly and so blatantly, may say: *parturiunt montes, nascitur ridiculus mus.*[6] That is simply what scholarship is all about. And the mouse isn't just a mouse either, but an exciting insight, caught by the tail. That is true with you, too, though in a different way: The other dimension stands in the background but is not given explicit expression. Unfortunately, I am so much less cautious and probably so lacking in shame as well that I want to articulate what is there because I think that has to be done, too. I think I told you before about the conversation that Thoma[7] and I had with Max Weber in which I was so bold as to catch him up for his caution (in his *Wissenschaft als Beruf*). Turning to Thoma, I said: He doesn't know himself why he does scholarly work. I told you what his reaction and his answer were.

Thank you for the recent trouble you have taken with the contract with Nanda Anshen. She will leave neither you nor me in peace. The contract will just have to wait until the book is done. Even the very first lines of the present draft, the ones about the length of the book, are impossible for the author to sign. Nanda Anshen knows that; at least I wrote and told her. I don't know how long the book will be, but as soon as it's finished we can come back to the contract. I promised her that. Perhaps the book will be too long then. My work on it was interrupted for a few weeks by *Freiheit und Wiedervereinigung*, to which its publication by Piper should put an end. These essays are being published today and sent directly from Piper to you and Heinrich. At the moment I'm finishing up the new version of the *Universitätsidee* (with Rossmann); then I mean to finish the book *Religiöser*[8] *Glaube angesichts der Offenbarung*. I'm quite far into it. I interrupted work on it in early September. But I can never know when it will be done. I hope in the spring.

We are very much looking forward to our time in January with the two of you.

Give Heinrich my warmest greetings. —I should also mention that my wife, equipped with a new hearing aid and sitting right up front, was able to hear my lecture yesterday. She was very happy.

Thinking of you in faithful friendship

Your

Karl Jaspers

Will my "atom bomb" really appear in January? And what about *Die grossen Philosophen*?

271 Hannah Arendt to Karl Jaspers

New York, December 2, 1960

Lieber Verehrtester!

The Eichmann trial, against which you voiced your reservations at the outset, has now happily or unhappily knocked all our plans into a cocked hat. I had a teaching obligation for April and May that I couldn't very well just call off, and that I thought at first I would be able to fit in around the Israel trip. But that has become so unlikely that I have decided for safety's sake to move the teaching stint up to January-February, which of course means that we cannot come. I thought for a moment that Heinrich might go alone, but he doesn't want to, mainly because we had wanted to go to Rome for a week together. Heinrich's semester starts again in February, and he won't be free again before June 20. He would then come right away. My situation is such that my plans will depend entirely on the trial. If it really begins on March 6, I would have to fly directly from here without making any stops. But if it is postponed again, which is very likely, I would travel by way of Zurich, making a stop in Basel, then fly on. No one knows how long the trial will last. In no case am I likely to indulge myself in this "pleasure" for more than a month. If it doesn't begin until April, I would probably not fly back to America but would wait in Europe for Heinrich.

If this all sounds muddled, that is in part because I am very unhappy about not being able to see you for so long and in part because I'm ashamed of myself for having gotten into a genuinely confusing situation. Because now, of course, I have to cancel all sorts of things, change plans, and so on. It's quite dreadful.

But for all that, my dear and honored friend, I would never be able to forgive myself if I didn't go and look at this walking disaster face to face in all his bizarre vacuousness, without the mediation of the printed word. Don't forget how early I left Germany and how little of all this I really experienced directly.

Chicago Press called a few days ago. They want to publish the atom book in January with a lot of fanfare, and they have invited me to come to the official sales conference and talk with their representatives, that is, the very important middlemen who sell to the book trade. I don't know whether I can yet, but I'll try to do it.

I don't know whether you can see over more than 3,000 miles how down in the mouth I am!

Warmest greetings
Your Hannah

272 Karl Jaspers to Hannah Arendt

Basel, December 12, 1960

Dear Hannah!

Not a word of explanation is necessary. Of course the rescheduling of your joint trip is unavoidable if you want to hear and see for yourself what goes on at the Eichmann trial. We'll see each other a half-year later—for we always live with the conviction that we'll still be here then. And in the summer it will probably be more pleasant. When you are clear about possible dates, I'd appreciate hearing from you. We're expecting Fritz [Mayer] from Israel sometime. We would like to avoid a collision.

The Eichmann trial is unsettling, I feel, because I'm afraid Israel may come away from it looking bad no matter how objective the conduct of the trial. Just as actions like Eichmann's—you said it beautifully—stand outside the pale of what is comprehensible in human and moral terms, so the legal basis of this trial is dubious. Something other than law is at issue here—and to address it in legal terms is a mistake. The kidnapping from Argentina[1] was itself illegal. In my view it is fully justifiable, but not by legal arguments. It is in itself a political act. There are so many embarrassing aspects to this case!

Israel didn't even exist when the murders were committed. Israel is not the Jewish people. Fortunately, Goldman[2] is a match for Ben Gurion.[3] The Jewish people are more than the state of Israel, not identical with it. If Israel were lost, the Jewish people would still not

410

be lost. Israel does not have the right to speak for the Jewish people as a whole.

Eichmann could say: Here I stand. It can happen that an eagle falls into the hands of clever trappers. You are acting neither in the name of the law nor in the name of a great political conception. In my eyes and in those of the world and of history you are vengeful (which is understandable for the kind of creatures you are) or ridiculous. Do with me what you will. I will say not another word. I do not want any defense. I know what I have done, and all I regret is that I wasn't able to kill you all.

Well, this creature won't speak like that because, given his nature, he can't have enough class. But if he were to speak like that, Israel would be in an awkward spot, all public outcry and especially all the rage of the Jews notwithstanding. World anti-Semitism would have its "martyr."

The trial presumably will take place. Its significance is not in its being a legal trial but in its establishing of historical facts and serving as a reminder of those facts for humanity. The hearing of witnesses to history and the collecting of documents on such a scale and with such thoroughness would not be possible for any researcher. That this is being done in the guise of a trial is, granted, unavoidable, but it is shot through with incorrect attitudes, because of everything connected with it. Or will the Israeli judges succeed in shaping the trial in such a way that these tangential factors fall away? That would be a remarkable accomplishment. I'm nervous about this, because I fear harm to Israel. That can be avoided only if the judges can develop that unpredictable, rationally not constructible perspective that goes beyond legal thinking and shows them, in the eyes of the world and beyond any question or doubt, to be thinking men. And if the Israeli press, at least its major papers, can do the same. What I fear, too, is that remarkably intelligent reflections, complicated discussions that lead off into limitless fields, and a lack of simplicity will not let the human greatness needed to deal with such facts emerge. What is needed is the spirit of the great old prophets—Amos, Isaiah, Jeremiah—but that can't be expected from Jewish orthodoxy, from Jewish total assimilation into modern nationalism (and from the abandonment of the Jews for the sake of the Israelis), or from highly trained minds.

What you will hear will, I fear, depress you and outrage you. How wonderful if I should be proved wrong! In any case, it seems to me, one has to take care that as little shadow as possible is cast on Israel.

Who has the right to judge harshly where only a prophet would have such a right?

It will stir you up, but you are always eager to see with your own eyes and hear with your own ears. If I could, I would like to be like you. The risk to one's self is not small here. But I will have the pleasure of hearing from you, having your reports and judgments in personal conversation, and perhaps becoming a bit more enlightened about this business in the process.

I have a cold for the second time this fall (with its embarrassing side effects) and am canceling another lecture. Despite this the administration is asking me to lecture an hour a week again this summer (the president of the board of trustees told me I could begin in mid-May and stop in mid-June). They want, it seems to me, to go on "displaying" me, but also do me the kindness of paying my salary for another half-year because I am still formally in office. [. . .]

You write that my atom book is to appear in January helped along by special efforts on the part of the publisher. I'm very pleased about that. That the book is now appearing in America is, objectively, probably of little consequence, as is most of what is written. It strikes me—perhaps foolishly—as a faint possibility that this book may make a difference. We are constantly up against this minimum of chances —and sometimes a "miracle" occurs. And you have been asked to talk with the powerful people in New York! An imposition! You can do it if you want to: convince people, quietly persuade them, show visible seriousness without pathos—and perhaps most important: I think you know the Americans better than they do themselves.

I'm immersed in Max Weber again after not having read him for a long time, because I want to lecture on him for one or two hours.[4] It is strange how remote the content and concrete tasks of politics are for us today and how close this man's mode of thought. I see this particularly in the case of the German national idea. As early as the 1920s I said: Max Weber was the last national German. But at the same time he had gone beyond that himself.

Warmest greetings to you both, also from Gertrud

Your Karl Jaspers

Basel, December 16, 1960

Dear Hannah!

The Eichmann trial really presents a massive problem. How it is solved will have consequences not only for Israel but for the world—as a model or antimodel, as a precedent for a way of thinking and comprehending.

I have already stated my view that this trial is wrongly conceived at its very root. Now I have this foolishly simplistic idea: It would be wonderful to do without the trial altogether and make it instead into a process of examination and clarification. The goal would be the best possible objectification of the historical facts. The end result would not be the judges' sentence, but certainty about the facts, to the extent such certainty can be attained. And then what?

I think Israel could then declare as follows: It does not want to pass sentence. The events lie beyond the scope of any one state's legal jurisdiction. Also, the situation is such that Israel would be passing judgment on its own behalf in a case whose substance is of a different order. This case concerns all of humanity; Israel places the evidence and the criminal at the disposal of—whom? The UN? —The probable consequence: Nobody will want to have anything to do with the case. But that would be a new and important fact that would weigh heavily on the UN and be troublesome to it in terms of the public's perception of justice and human dignity. The UN would cite legal objections to wriggle out of this situation.

Judgments passed by the victors on the vanquished have, in the past, been regarded as political actions and distinct from legal ones. That was the case with the German commission established in 1919 to investigate the "war criminals" after the Western powers had declined a neutral investigation that would have included opening the archives of both sides.[1] The political realm is of an importance that cannot be captured in legal terms (the attempt to do so is Anglo-Saxon and a self-deception that masks a basic fact in the functionings of political existence). In the case of Eichmann this dimension is not involved; a dimension that in being "political" has, as it were, dignity, is larger than law, and is woven into the fabric of fate. Something else is at issue here, something less important but still something of genuine concern to humanity. It has no dignity, but for the sake of truth and clarity it too has to be lifted out of the merely legal framework. A

413

legal proceeding as momentous as this is the last place where the *premises* should be left unclear.

Well, I'm just writing this all down, really quite at a loss. If Heinrich shares my view, you and he, provided you agree, should work out the concrete suggestion and the ramifications of the possibilities. I can't manage it. But since you are so intimately involved and will bear responsibility as a reporter, I wanted to write this to you in any case, even if it is nonsense and off the top of my head. I feel that I am dimly aware of more than I can render with conceptual clarity and vital force, things that ought to be emphatically stated immediately, now, *before* the trial, *provided* what I'm saying has any truth to it.

Warmest greetings
Your Karl Jaspers

274   Hannah Arendt to Karl Jaspers

December 23, 1960

Lieber Verehrtester!

I'll put aside all else and all the other questions your letters touch on and will address only the Eichmann case. Heinrich and I have discussed your two letters at length. But now that I'm writing you, he isn't home; I'll hang onto the letter until he's had a chance to protest.

I'll respond first to your first letter—Israel could come off badly, etc. I am not as pessimistic as you are about the legal basis of the trial. Granted, Eichmann was kidnapped, just plain abducted and hauled off. But the Israelis can say: 1. We kidnapped a man who was indicted in the first trial in Nuremberg. He escaped arrest then. The Nuremberg court dealt with cases of crimes against humanity. Eichmann was an outlaw—a *hostis humani generis*,[1] the way pirates used to be. 2. We abducted him from Argentina because Argentina has the worst possible record for the extradition of war criminals, even when extradition has been requested. And that in the face of repeated insistence not only of the victorious powers but also of the United Nations that anyone accused in Nuremberg be arrested and extradited. 3. We did not take the man to Germany, but to our own country. Germany could have demanded his extradition. What we would have done in that case is uncertain. The man should have appeared before the Nuremberg court, a special court. There is no successor court to carry on the special court's mission. If the Germans were of the opinion that their regular courts were such successors, then they should have demanded Eichmann's extradition. As things stand, there doesn't seem to be anyone but us eager to bring a wanted criminal to trial. So we'll go ahead and do it.

As far as this aspect of the matter is concerned, it seems to me there would have been only one alternative to kidnapping. Somebody could have gunned Eichmann down on the street and then immediately given himself up to the police. That, too, would have produced a trial. The whole story would have been rolled out again just as it will be now —only with a different hero in the leading role. This is not an alternative I just made up. Shalom Schwarzbard[2] did precisely this in Paris in the early 1920s when he shot the man who had been the ringleader of the Ukraine pogroms[3] during the civil-war years in Russia, then immediately went to the nearest police station. After a two-year trial, during which the history of these pogroms was detailed, Schwarzbard was acquitted. I knew him well in Paris, a wonderful fellow. But that was Paris, which was still a world center in those days, had a halfway reliable judicial system, and offered a guarantee of the greatest publicity. The chances for an enterprise of that kind in Argentina would not have been exactly good.

Israel may not have the right to speak for the Jews of the world. (Although I'd like to know who really does have the right to speak for the Jews qua Jews in a political sense. Certainly, many Jews don't want to be represented as Jews or only want to be in a religious sense. So Israel has no right to speak for them. But what about the others? Israel is the only political entity we have. I don't particularly like it, but there's not much I can do about that.) But in any case Israel has the right to speak for the victims, because the large majority of them (300,000) are living in Israel now as citizens. The trial will take place in the country in which the injured parties and those who happened to survive are. You say that Israel didn't even exist then. But one could say that it was for the sake of these victims that Palestine became Israel. It was nothing other than Bevin's[4] refusal to give the necessary immigration certificates to the survivors that set off the revolt against England and led to the founding of the state. In addition, Eichmann was responsible for Jews and Jews only, regardless of their nationality. In other words, other issues and jurisdictions don't come into play here at all. That would not be the case if, for example, it was Bormann[5] who had been nabbed.

As far as this aspect of the matter is concerned, I have to say that the most troublesome thing for me is how the Israelis keep stressing that Eichmann "voluntarily" agreed to go to Israel and appear before a court there. Something is obviously not quite right there. (Torture? Threats? God knows what they did.)

As to the conduct of the trial itself, I share your fears. Still, they have decided not to let the thing run for a year, which would have been sheer madness. But I'm still uneasy about the trial all the same. It's a pretty sure bet that there'll be an effort to show Israeli youth and (worse yet) the whole world certain things. Among others, that Jews who aren't Israelis will wind up in situations where they'll let themselves be slaughtered like sheep. Also: that the Arabs were hand in glove with the Nazis. There are other possibilities for distorting the issue itself.

As for an international court or an investigative proceeding that would then lead to the establishment of such a court, attempts of this sort are not new, and so far they have always failed. In the UN, because of resistance from the General Assembly. The only possibility seems to be to attach to the International Court at The Hague a criminal court for *hostes generis humani* that would be competent to try individuals regardless of nationality. As long as such a court does not exist, international law holds that any court in the world is competent—so why not Israel? Legally, Israel *couldn't* even claim it isn't competent. The argument that Israel is passing judgment on its own behalf doesn't seem pertinent to me. Let's assume that somewhere in the world some Americans are beaten to death out of a general hatred for America, and somehow or other the murderers wind up in New York. Should a court here not be competent to sentence these gentlemen? Legally, this is called the "passive nationality principle." The country or state to which the victims belong has jurisdiction, as distinguished from the active nationality principle, by which the Germans would have jurisdiction, or from the territorial principle, by which just about all of Europe would have the right to take up this gentleman's case. Don't misunderstand me: I would be all in favor of an international court with the appropriate powers. But the only reason, it seems to me, that Israel could declare itself incompetent is because it committed a kidnapping, not because it is passing judgment on its own behalf. And I don't find the kidnapping so bad in this case. Furthermore, an international criminal court would not alter the fact of the kidnapping.

You fear an increase of anti-Semitism. From here, these fears seem groundless, but I could be wrong. Even the "defense" you imagined Eichmann making, or, rather, his refusal of any defense—I am an eagle that has fallen into a trap—wouldn't impress anybody here. It would, I think, not so much provide the anti-Semites with a martyr as it would convince the whole world that these people were just plain crazy or suffered from interesting neuroses. That kind of stand might impress me a little—but then, I'm not from here.

Let's assume the trial is conducted impeccably. In that case I'm afraid that Eichmann will be able to prove, first of all, that no country wanted the Jews (just the kind of Zionist propaganda that Ben Gurion wants and that I consider a disaster) and will demonstrate, second, to what a huge degree the Jews helped organize their own destruction. That is, of course, the naked truth, but this truth, if it is not really explained, could stir up more anti-Semitism than ten kidnappings. It is unfortunately a fact that Mr. Eichmann personally never harmed a hair on a single Jew's head, indeed, that neither he nor his accomplices even took part in selecting those who were sent to their deaths.

All this may strike you as though I too was attempting to circumscribe the political with legal concepts. And I even admit that as far as the role of the law is concerned, I have been infected by the Anglo-Saxon influence. But quite apart from that, it seems to me to be in the nature of this case that we have no tools to hand except legal ones with which we have to judge and pass sentence on something that cannot even be adequately represented either in legal terms or in political terms. That is precisely what makes the process itself, namely, the trial, so exciting. The question is: Would things be different if we had a law against *hostes humani generis* and not only against murderers and similar criminals?

But I am going there as a simple reporter, not even for the daily press, but for a magazine. That means that I bear no responsibility whatsoever for what goes on. If I should attempt the kind of thing you are suggesting, the Israelis would probably respond instantly by barring me as a reporter—and rightly so. I still haven't even heard the reasons they will give to substantiate their competence. As a reporter, I have the right to criticize their reasoning but not to make suggestions to them. If I wanted to do that, a reporter is the last thing I could be. How great a distance I want to put between myself and these very questions you can judge from the fact that I will be reporting for a non-Jewish publication. As I see it, the only thing I could do is offer something by way of a conclusion: the Eichmann case has shown that we need a court for criminal cases in The Hague.

The German pamphlet[6] arrived two days ago. I haven't been able to read it yet. Because I will be going to Northwestern in January, I've had to double my seminars at Columbia this month and so I haven't gotten to anything else. Have you received the Chicago book[7] yet? It looks very respectable. The publication date is the end of January, so there's enough time for book reviewers.

December 24

Monsieur has read this letter and finds it more or less all right. I've just now managed to get him to have his picture taken. I consider this the greatest victory my seductive arts have ever been able to win. If the picture turns out to be halfway decent, I'll send it. Now we have to change clothes—put on our festive duds, the Berliner would say— and go eat goose.

All best wishes for the New Year! And in hopes that we'll all see each other again in good health and with the world in not too dreadful circumstances

As always
Your
Hannah

275   *Karl Jaspers to Hannah Arendt*

Basel, December 31, 1960

Dear Hannah!

Your legal considerations seem altogether correct to me, but only within the legal sphere. The political basis of the power that enables the law is, I believe, another matter. You perceive clearly the present realities, such as the nonexistence of a UN criminal court.

The difficulties can be circumvented by invoking the sovereignty and power of a national state like Israel. And that is presumably what will be done. And the likes of us will prefer to keep our peace in public about the embarrassing situation this puts Israel in.

What you would like as much as I would remains utopian at the moment. When I wrote recently, I felt the desire to see it realized;

and I still harbor a foolish yen for my idea: Israel does an exemplary job of historical investigation and documentation and then closes with this demand addressed to humanity, which is represented formally today by the UN: Here are the facts. It is a task for humanity, not for an individual national state, to pass judgment in such a weighty case. We have the perpetrator of these crimes in our custody and place him at your disposal. What he did concerns all of you, not just us. Create the means by which humanity can mete out justice (possible consequences I am thinking of are, for instance, appeals to this highest, supranational authority from people whose human rights have been violated by their own countries). You have the same thing in mind with your idea of the *hostis humani generis*. That would be a fitting expression if it was not so reminiscent of the *odium humani generis*[1] of which, according to Tacitus, the Christians were accused. Also, the word "enemy" strikes me as too positive. An enemy is still a some-body. A "perpetrator of crimes against humanity" has a different tone but isn't ideal either. What you have in mind here—and I am influenced by its appearance in your earlier writings—is more crucial than ever for humankind's self-awareness. Historically it was rooted solely in the Old Testament and, despite the appearance of "stoic cosmopolitan thinking," was expressed in its original form nowhere else on earth. But it was absorbed into Christianity, which in its New Testament form is Jewish through and through.

We differ somewhat (though not ultimately) in our views of Israel. I see in the founding of this state only a necessary stopgap measure in an age still under the sway of nation-states. It is profoundly alien to the Jew, a form of assimilation in these times and one in which other things are lost than were lost in the earlier so-called assimilation. It may happen that Judaism will be lost in Israel if Zionism prevails (which, by the way, Ben Gurion adheres to strictly: the only person who can be a Zionist is one who comes to Israel and settles there). If Israel is an emergency solution for these times, an army of Judaism, so to speak, which is so vastly much more than any sovereign state, then perhaps the state of Israel has possibilities different from other states'. But only as long as this "more" makes itself felt, it seems to me, does Israel remain of interest for Jews. And, this is my perhaps erroneous thought, this "more" could, by way of an extraordinary, stirring act that would bring the greatest embarrassment to the world, waken from the drabness of present formalism a serious consideration of the idea of humanity. The Jews would bring this about, the people who derived from Adam's beginnings the impulse to protect the stranger, neighborly love, and the solidarity of all human beings.

Unfortunately we can't speak to each other about this. We'll make up for that this summer.

Warmest greetings
Your
Karl Jaspers

P.S. Could you give us your reports for the American magazine by having a copy of the magazine sent to us from the U.S.?

276 Karl Jaspers to Hannah Arendt

Basel, January 3, 1961

Dear Hannah!

Still another thought I forgot to add to my last letter:

In the context of human affairs Eichmann deserves to be executed —but on the basis of a sentence pronounced by humankind, not by a single state.

If my utopian suggestion were adopted, Israel would keep Eichmann in custody and at the disposal of the governmental authority of humanity, but Israel would not have to pass sentence and carry out the execution in the state of Israel itself.

Because what was done to the Jews was done not only to the Jews but essentially to humankind, the death sentence would thus originate from a place that would give it a very different significance and one appropriate to the case. Humanity would show what its response to such behavior is. That response has to have historical impact. If Israel carried out the execution, that would, so to speak, trivialize Eichmann's actions in people's minds and not allow them to stand out in bold enough relief.

Well, I won't bombard you anymore. Rather, I'll wait expectantly for what you will write and tell me.

Is the future doomed and all of us with it? I sense something symbolic in this Eichmann trial and in the course it will take. There are moments in which everyone gains new insight, or they can simply slip by unnoticed.

Warmest greetings to you both, from my wife, too, who is discussing this issue with me, with more excitement because she is more involved.

I am becoming aware through this what I, being without her Jewish soul, would never understand otherwise. But I still have not articulated my ideas and demands clearly.

Your Karl Jaspers

There was a wonderful picture of you in the *FAZ*, along with a well-meaning essay by Sternberger[1] that did not match the quality of the picture.

Heinrich's picture, which we are eagerly awaiting, has not arrived yet. Years ago, at my insistence, you showed me a picture that was too small and too hard to see anything from.

277   *Hannah Arendt to Karl Jaspers*

Evanston, Ill., February 5, 1961

Lieber Verehrtester—

I haven't written for so long, and there is so much to discuss that I don't quite know where to begin. First, the atom book: It's off to a good start, reviews in all the papers. *Time* magazine, very important, had it among its recommended books, and you have probably already received the review I'm enclosing.[1] The review in the *New York Times Book Review*[2] was, unfortunately, by Niebuhr. It was friendly enough but showed not the slightest understanding of the book. Yesterday in Chicago I spoke with Morgenthau,[3] who has reviewed the book for *Saturday Review*[4]—apparently a very good and reasonable review, but I haven't seen it yet. The book is lying about everywhere here and being read by all.

The publication time is excellent. Kennedy's election has worked a major change in the atmosphere here within a few weeks. Everything he has done so far is very good. The question is whether he will be able to convince the country of the urgency and danger of the situation. Most important, whether he will be able to check the growing incompetence in all fields, put an end to corruption, etc. It gives one a feeling of reassurance that he at least knows how things stand. The bizarre thing about the Eisenhower era was that really everybody thought everything was pretty much in the best of shape. Kennedy has already succeeded in winning back into the political arena people, intellectuals, who had pulled back from such things entirely during the last 10 years. Lowell[5] (an American poet, very famous), who had been invited to the inauguration in Washington, wrote me: The world is green again.

This new atmosphere is also making itself felt among students at the universities. At Columbia I was beginning to see some of my students, very gifted ones, who wanted to leave philosophy and get back into politics by way of political theory, or at least wanted to remain in close touch with politics. Here, too, the political-science students are very much better than the philosophy students. That wasn't the case for a long time, but it can be explained by local circumstances here (where philosophy went to the dogs under Mr. Schilpp[6]).

For now I meant to stick with "business." The most important thing here is *Die grossen Philosophen*. Pantheon claims they are printing the book now and have scheduled it for publication next fall. This project has had me worried because Kurt Wolff suddenly left Pantheon about six months ago. They simply drove him out in the most outrageous way. He wrote to let me know but did not give me any details. Helen Wolff was in New York in the fall and told me more, most important, that they were negotiating with another very large publisher with whom they may be able to publish their books under their own imprint. This was all in strictest confidence; I couldn't write you about it. I hadn't heard anything from Pantheon for months—because everything there was in chaos, among other reasons. I wrote to Wolff at the end of the year and asked him to write to you. He refused, with the excuse that he couldn't tell you anything as long as he was "John Lackland."[7] He thought everything would be straightened out by the end of January, but I haven't heard anything from him.

So I decided to write to you without Wolff's knowledge. It seems to me the best thing to do is to leave the book with Pantheon. Whatever shape Wolff's plans take, giving him the book would mean a further delay of 6–12 months in any case. The man responsible for the book at Pantheon is Mr. Wolfgang Sauerländer, a former German, with whom I have worked together most agreeably so far. But I hardly know the present director at Pantheon; also a former German. [. . .] Sauerländer wrote me here, sent me the bibliography—which has to be enlarged for use here—and mentioned next fall as the publication date. That is, of course, 6 months later than projected, but that can happen. I'm concerned about how these people will launch the book without Wolff, who had a particularly keen interest in it. The Chicago Press did a really superb job with publicity and clearly took great pains with it. The preparation for the books Pantheon has put out since Wolff left has not been as good as it was before. The credit for that goes less to Wolff than to his wife, who is incredibly able.

I still haven't replied to your two letters about the Eichmann trial. You probably know that it has been put off once again, this time to March 15. And a few weeks ago the press here was reporting that it would be postponed still again until May. That would be wonderful, but it has not been confirmed yet. That would make it possible for me to stop in Basel before the trial. I very much want to do that and not speak with you only *post festum*, for this business is not really clear to me at all. My pirate theory won't do. For the definition of piracy to apply, it is both factually and legally essential for the pirate to have acted out of private motives. And therein lies the rub. The concept of *hostis humani generis*—however one translates it, but not: crime against humanness; but, rather, against humanity—is more or less indispensable to the trial. The crucial point is that although the crime at issue was committed primarily against the Jews, it is in no way limited to the Jews or the Jewish question.

I think we are in basic agreement on these points, but how they can be presented both politically and legally remains the question. We are not in agreement, I think, about the State of Israel, which, it is true, was finally born of necessity but which in no way arose exclusively from that necessity. That relates to a number of questions bearing on the so-called Jewish problem, questions on which we have never been in total agreement. It seems to me they don't need to be considered in this case. I am much more troubled by the Lavon affair,[8] which is, in its structure, a second Dreyfus affair[9]: what a clique does, it blames on someone who doesn't belong to the clique in order to cover up the methods it uses itself. The Israelis were motivated of course by so-called idealism; and the French general staff, which, down to the last man, sold documents to the Germans (then phony ones when they ran out of real secrets), acted out of pure greed. This affair shows how rotten this state is and what a dangerous "idealist" this Mr. Gurion is, who is of course ultimately responsible for the whole business. You will say that this has nothing do to with the Eichmann trial. I'm not so sure, because the Lavon affair has created the atmosphere in the country. And to conduct this trial in such an atmosphere . . .

So perhaps I'll be lucky and will be able to come before I go on to Israel. In no case will I write there. I have wonderful terms. I can write as much or as little as I want to, and, best of all, I can turn in the manuscript whenever I happen to be finished. I had a long talk that was really very gratifying with the editor in chief of the magazine.[10] Amazingly intelligent and generous. My plans now are to fly directly to Israel from here (with two days in New York) and then at the end of April or the beginning of May return to New York via Basel. I'll do my writing in New York and then go back to Europe in July with Heinrich.

All my warmest wishes to you both! How is Erna, by the way?

Your
Hannah

278 Karl Jaspers to Hannah Arendt

Basel, February 14, 1961[1]

Dear Hannah!

From the very beginning we have been in complete agreement on the main point: the Eichmann case concerns humankind and should not be reduced to an Israeli issue. The only question is what are the proper political and legal forms for dealing with it. We are both at a loss for an answer.

One can propose concepts of international law. But you know that all of international law and natural law are not law in the same sense as the law that underlies normal court proceedings. They are not backed up by a power that is able to conduct a trial, the results of which could be acted upon without a war. Servatius,[2] who knows all the tricks in the book and has made the worst kind of impression on me, will press on in Israel from one sensation to another purely for the sake of sensation, and will not have a hard time of it legally. He can start right off by questioning the competence of the court.

Politically we have the UN and the International Court at the The Hague along with the courts provided for in the UN charter. If Israel would do what my simpleminded fantasy suggested in my first letter to you: reduce the trial to an inquiry into the facts; pass no sentence; keep the criminal in custody for a court that, as a representative of humanity, is competent to judge a crime against humanity—and today the UN professes to be such an authority—then, it seems to me, an action of the greatest integrity would have been carried out, the world called upon, the mass murder committed on the Jews recognized in the significance it has.

You have not yet, it seems to me, come up with any better suggestion. The possible objections to this idea are many. Even the UN would first have to create the appropriate court; it could base its actions on natural law—or it could, by its failure to act, leave this question to humanity hanging, this question that cries to heaven. It seems to me that would be better than letting the matter be "taken care of" in Israel. Dealing with it this way would have consequences that, because they would be confusing and would elicit endless reproaches, strike me as disastrous for this huge problem per se and presumably for the Jews and for Israel.

It would be good for Israel, I think, to display this *high-mindedness*, to prove true to the Jewish tradition. Perhaps the only practical disadvantage of proceeding this way is that the prisoner Eichmann could escape or be freed someday.

It would be nice if a postponement of the trial allowed you to come to Basel on your way to Israel. I don't have any wisdom to hand out, but sometimes in the course of conversation something no one had thought of before emerges.

You illuminate an aspect of the Lavon affair that is entirely new to me. I hadn't known before what to make of that "crime." The news reports made it appear that it was of no great importance and that the Histadrut[3] was the real issue. Gurion wants to dissolve the "state within the state" and is having a hard time of it because of his own party's involvement. Lavon seemed to me to be an unusually intelligent man, who, like Gurion, works with all available political means and who, in competition with Gurion, wanted to strengthen the Histadrut, to tighten their organization and make them more unified, to heighten rather than lower their demands. I'm not well informed, of course. But for years now I've had a prejudice against the Histadrut and for Ben Gurion (although I in no way approve of his conception of Israel).

Many thanks for your good news about my book. I know that I have you to thank primarily for this entire process, from your first recommendation of the Chicago Press on. Our luck with *Die grossen Philosophen*, which has made much more work for you, has not been as great so far. Your report saddens me for Kurt Wolff's sake. Your decision to leave the book with Pantheon because it would take much longer otherwise makes sense to me. In any case, I will go along with your decisions regarding this book, which has in part become yours.

Thank you very much, too, for the photographs. I have looked at them often, and my wife along with me. Those of you are fine; sensitivity, sadness, and strength, as we know you. Your great affirmation of life is not as prominent in these pictures. Heinrich I see here for the first time, with a great and immediate feeling of affinity. One sees the intelligence, the skepticism, the kindly sense of humor, the sharp edge, and something still of that Berlin energy and indestructibility, and residues of good Berlin barbarity. When I put the pictures side by side, I think: He can't always have found it easy not to wound this sensitivity. Our barbarity from the other side of the limes demands patience of others. I know that about myself.

Ever since his inauguration speech, Kennedy has emitted something for us, too, that we have hardly ever experienced: a hope that one man sees things clearly, simply says what needs to be said, surrounds himself with the best men, and with the power of a natural faith wants to make felt in the world the reasons why life is worth living. He is the first of the statesmen in power to say without conditions, without reservations: freedom "at any price." Perhaps he just possibly has in him what we have come not to expect: that one man gives others courage because his words and gestures and actions are so convincing that everyone makes a greater effort and is more open to the harshness of the truth. How much we need such hope!

Dodo [Singer-Mayer] and her husband (Egon Singer) are coming to Basel sometime in July. Will you be in Switzerland from July 15–31?? We don't know which days they will be with us. Could you telephone to Dodo if you have a chance? Or can you determine now for how long—as long as possible—you will be in Basel and write us so that we can make arrangements by letter with Dodo.

Erna is doing very well. We are sparing her, of course. No heavy work and no unnecessary excitement. She is in good spirits, and her presence is a blessing. To spare her, we would ask the Singers and you, if you come with Heinrich, to stay in a hotel. If you come alone, please stay with us. That won't be too much for Erna but will be a pleasure for her. Our cleaning woman will see to it that Erna's work load is not increased.

This summer I'll lecture *once again* for *one* hour.[4] The administration asked me in such a pleasant way that I didn't want to refuse. For this minimal work I'll continue to draw my full salary until September 30, money easily earned, but I'm absolutely determined not to continue this arrangement for another semester. I'm not interested in lecturing anymore, and I feel it's time.

Warmest greetings
Your Karl Jaspers

426

Evanston, February 21, 1961[1]

Dear, dear Friends—

This is a birthday greeting—not an answer to your long, wonderful letter. At this time each year I always think how nice it is that you both were born, that you found your way to each other, and that you then established this unique life together, which has now become a second home for me. What can I wish you apart from what I wish for myself—that this may continue for us for a long time.

As you know, the Eichmann trial has been postponed. So if it is all right with you, I'll stop by before I go to Israel. Though I can't say yet just when that will be. A friend has just written me that she will be in Rhodes and Crete over Easter, and that tempts me immensely. But I still don't know whether I'll really go or not. That will depend too on whether Heinrich will have a semester break, that is, an Easter vacation. He'll have some week in April off, but it may not coincide with Easter. That would ease the decision for me.

I'll get in touch with Dodo Singer in New York. But it seems to me there'll be no difficulty in arranging things so that we'll come before July 15. In any case, we can certainly avoid being there at the same time. Yes, of course we'll stay in a hotel. I would never have dreamed of the two of us crashing in on you. Could you please send me the Singers' address? I don't have it anymore, and there are a lot of Singers in New York.

All my best wishes
Your
Hannah

---

280 *Karl Jaspers to Hannah Arendt*

Basel, February 26, 1961

Dear Hannah!

Kurt Wolff and his wife were just here to tell me that he concluded a contract with Harcourt, Brace[1] (your publisher) three days ago. Now he would like to move "our" book (which is what it has become by virtue of your editorial work on it) over to this other house.

My reply: I have always decided publishing questions after discussing them with you and have usually followed your advice. Therefore, I wanted to know first what you thought about this change (I ignored your last letter on this matter and had him present it to me anew—only with the understanding that I had known from you for some time that he wanted to part ways with his publishing house).

I found Kurt Wolff and his wife very likable. He seems to have been treated very shabbily: breach of faith on the part of the man who, when Wolff was an emigrant and enemy alien, made agreements with him that are now turning out to be so unfavorable. Such was my impression.

But what we have to arrange between us is a business matter, too. I said it made me nervous if I as author were to ask to have the rights returned to me and so made myself legally liable for the costs to date (which must be considerable). I would not be willing to assume that risk myself.

Kurt Wolff replied (contradicting somewhat what he had said before): All I needed to do was agree once the transfer was arranged by contract between the two publishers, so that the contract I had had would now be with Harcourt, Brace instead of with Pantheon. I said it would be best if he discussed this with Hannah.

Kurt Wolff said further that part of the book but not all of it had been set. But that would not stand in the way of the other publisher taking the book over.

So you see, the decision is essentially yours. I said cautiously that I *usually* go along with Hannah's suggestions. So we still have a way out.

You wrote recently that there was some question about the time period within which the book would be published. You felt that Pantheon was a surer bet. Does the new contract, which I have not seen, answer this question differently?

All this simply by way of a report on what we discussed. The decision is, of course—between us—entirely yours to make. I'll do what you say. I know you won't commit me to a business arrangement that carries any risks for me.

If it can be done in a normal and easy way, you will no doubt be as pleased as I if we can leave the book in Kurt Wolff's hands, for it was his interest and initiative that set this project in motion.

Kurt Wolff told me, by the way, that he has a "heart block"—his pulse is 30. That is a very serious matter. It seems that the inevitable impairment caused by his illness gave his disloyal partner the opportunity to take advantage of him. Disgusting! Sudden death has to be reckoned with, although such an illness can *sometimes* last for a long time.

The Eichmann trial has been postponed again. Will you be coming through Basel first then after all?

Today your wonderful forest of hyacinths arrived once again. Gertrud's room is bursting with flowers, but yours are in the middle of the room—and your name is announced to every visitor.

Warmest greetings to you and Heinrich from us both

Your Karl Jaspers

281 Hannah Arendt to Karl Jaspers

March 27, 1961

Lieber Verehrtester!

I didn't write earlier because I wanted to speak with the president of Harcourt, Brace before I formed an opinion. You will see from the enclosed copy of my letter to Kurt Wolff,[1] who called me here once again from Locarno yesterday, that I strongly urge making the change and attempting to get out of the contract.

Reasons: The contract between Harcourt, Brace and Kurt Wolff explicitly states that its terms will remain in force for Helen Wolff in the case of Kurt Wolff's death. Given your reservations on this point, this provision seems to me crucially important. The contract holds "for both or either." Pantheon appears to be in a state of total dissolution. Sauerländer was the editor there who was responsible for your book. If he leaves Pantheon, no one will take any interest in the book—unless very good new people come on there. But I haven't heard anything to that effect. Harcourt, Brace is really excellent. The president (Jovanovich)[2] [. . . is] gifted and not without charm. He has fought his way to the top within the firm, one of the consequences of which is that a number of his editors left and with them some authors as well. I left him, too, for example. But then he behaved so decently and I found myself liking him so much that he now says with some justification: I lost an author and won a friend. The contract with the Wolffs is very favorable for both parties, and it speaks for Jovanovich that this arrangement with the Wolffs means so much to him. He even called me in Evanston. He apparently wants to add a European division to the firm, and that is the very thing that will be of great value to this house in particular. Harcourt, Brace is vastly larger and financially stronger than Pantheon could ever be. It is one of the largest publishing houses in the country and has specialized for decades in supplying texts for colleges and universities.

You'll find the details in my letter to Wolff. If you are in agreement, I would suggest that you let me know right away, possibly by wire, so that I can still catch this [. . .] Kyrill Schabert.[3] That would not, of course, make a letter from you unnecessary. I would say that you intended to write such a letter. Also: I would accept Kurt Wolff's offer to draft the letter because technical details could be involved that would not occur to either you or me. Wolff said on the phone that he would draft the letter and then send it to me first. In an interview, I would argue that the whole project owes its existence to the personal involvement of Kurt Wolff, whom I in particular have known well for many years. Further—and I would stress this—the delay in the production of the book (Pantheon apparently still hasn't begun to set it yet) indicates a lack of interest in it. Further still, Harcourt, Brace's college and university division makes it a particularly appropriate publisher. And, finally, Harcourt, Brace has already shown a clear interest in the entire work. But I will do this only if Kurt Wolff, too, feels it would be appropriate for me to talk to Schabert.

I'm writing in the evening and am tired, but I want to get this letter in the mail today. I won't be able to stop on my way to Israel after all. Heinrich will have Easter holidays, and the trial will begin on the 11th. So I'll fly directly from here and will be in Jerusalem on April 9, Hotel Moriyah, King George Street. I'll stay about three weeks, and if it's all right with you, I'll come directly to see you then. You'll see from my letter to Wolff that I don't want to fly back to the States in between because Heinrich will be coming over on June 24 anyhow. We want to go to Rome and Sorrento first (I've never been to Paestum and Pompeii) and will be back in Switzerland again around July 10. Then we can make whatever arrangements suit you. I'm still not sure whether in the interim I'll settle down to work in Zurich or Munich. Zurich is more pleasant, but Munich has a very good library and, besides that, in the Institut fur Zeitgeschichte, all the books that one could possibly want for the Eichmann project.

I'm sorry that I can't come before the trial, and I dread the hysterical atmosphere I'll be going into in Israel. Today an Israeli in the diplomatic corps, a decent, intelligent man, said in a discussion of the possibility that Eichmann might not be executed: That would cost significantly more lives; there won't be a village in Israel where heavy rioting won't break out immediately!

In any case—we'll see each other and talk together in about four weeks. And with that I'll console myself in the meantime.

Warmest greetings
Your
Hannah

282 *Karl Jaspers to Hannah Arendt*

Basel, April 1, 1961

Dear Hannah!

I just sent you a telegram saying that I fully agree to the change in publishers that you recommend to me with such good reasons. That goes without saying. And then I am glad if we can succeed in rescuing the book from this muddle.

I shall expect from Kurt Wolff a draft of the letter I am supposed to write—I still haven't understood to whom. That is an excellent arrangement. I couldn't possibly write it correctly. I will simply check to see that I am not assuming any new obligations and that I have no role in the process of transferring the book from one firm to the other. I would not take the chance of doing that. But I think, presumably correctly, that that will all be done directly by the two publishing houses and Kurt Wolff.

We're very much looking forward to seeing you, you alone first, then the two of you. Dodo and her husband will be here from June 4–7, so there will be no collision at all.

What won't you experience in Israel! The inklings you have are frightening.

Yesterday I finally did agree to do an interview with Bondy—for Swiss radio[1]—after having fended him off for a long time. 25 minutes. As usual, my "fantasies." I took the liberty of using your distinction between "crimes against humanity" and "crimes against humanness," with mention of your name. Bondy wants to print the interview. He presented me with seven questions that I was allowed to dictate to him in advance. Then I spoke like a professor in a seminar. In no case can it be printed as I spoke it because, when I speak extemporaneously, I make grammatical mistakes, repeat too much, tend to sloppiness. Speaking just isn't writing. So I'll revise the transcript and then see

431

whether I can agree to let it appear in print. If you prefer not to be mentioned by name (*solely* in connection with the distinction between those two terms) let me know *immediately*. But I can hardly imagine that you would have any reservations.

The interview is meant as an introduction for the daily reports that Bondy will be doing from Israel for Swiss radio. Martin Buber,[2] who was asked to grant the same interview, declined. Bondy will leave for Jerusalem at the end of this week.

The Eichmann trial has us all stirred up. It is not just a matter of sensationalism. It will, in its totality, become a major symbol of the life of the mind today. I *fear* only *one* thing: that Israel and the Jews will be judged badly in the world as a result.

I did happen to meet Halevi:[3] a rationalist, without any powers of concrete perception. He struck me (it was one visit years ago) as a decent man.

Warmest greetings to you both,
also from Gertrud
Your Karl Jaspers

283   Hannah Arendt to Karl Jaspers

April 1, 1961

Lieber Verehrtester,

Your telegram just arrived.[1] In the meantime Wolff's letter and draft crossed in the mail with my letter, the carbon copy of which I sent you. I spoke on the telephone again with Jovanovich (Harcourt, Brace), who also advised against my going to Pantheon myself and putting my cards on the table, as I had originally intended.

To simplify things I'm enclosing here Wolff's draft with my changes on it and his letter.[2] I think my changes are self-explanatory. The last paragraph had to be changed because I won't be at home, and Heinrich is in the apartment only on weekends. Once agreement has been reached with Pantheon, the manuscript can be picked up there and taken directly to Harcourt, Brace. The letter that should be forthcoming will be forwarded to me.

This is all for today. I'm writing this in an upset state. The young daughter[3] of very good friends of ours just called up to say that she's seeing double and that the ophthalmologist is sending her to a neurologist. I have to go there with her on Tuesday, after Easter, because both parents are on a kind of world trip. I'm very fond of the child and very disturbed by this.

Heinrich has been home for the Easter holidays since Thursday, so we're having a little time together. I'm trying to drum into him which suits he should take and which not, which suitcase, etc. It's a pretty hopeless enterprise, and I've just decided to put it all in the hands of our good Esther (cleaning woman and friend of the house). She will see if she can manage him.

My address as of April 9:
Hotel Moriyah, King George Street, Jerusalem.

Warmest greetings
Your
Hannah

284 *Karl Jaspers to Hannah Arendt*

April 3, 1961

Dear Hannah!

For the sake of the record I'm sending you this interview I wrote you about recently. I hope that you are not angry about it.

What won't you experience in Israel! I have bad presentiments, which I hope prove incorrect. One can, I think, ask a great deal of people in a general way but not in concrete situations. At any rate, I think one should not attack Israel and the Israeli court but should stress the human motives that are, unfortunately, so natural. One need not condone them for that reason. And then again perhaps something marvelous will come out of this in the end.

I've heard here that Servatius made the "condition" that Eichmann not name certain names (I hardly see how, in this crude form, that can be true). I read that Israel will be paying the legal fees. Now I hear that that isn't the case. The source of Servatius's fee is unclear. Hypothesis: People in Germany who are threatened by the trial have bought him off to keep their names from being mentioned. I don't believe that. But *if* that should be the case and *if* the Israeli judges avoid for political reasons the *complete* exposure of *everything* pertaining to this case, then the alarm must be sounded. But all of this is probably just more of the silly stuff that tends to surface on such occasions.

I don't fully understand what Ben Gurion's political aims are with the trial, but I'm troubled by them.

You'll be busy every minute now. Very interesting in any case, if only it did not touch on the nerve of the fate common to us all. *You* have to bring that out. I can't do it.

Warmest greetings from us both and all
good wishes
Your Karl Jaspers

285 *Hannah Arendt to Karl Jaspers*

Jerusalem, April 13, 1961
Pension Reich, Beit Hakerem

Lieber Verehrtester!

Thank you for the interview.[1] I won't write anything about it because it seems to me that I agree with everything in it. The only thing I'm afraid of is that we'll stand more or less alone with this view of things. I couldn't even get out of Bondy, with whom I'm staying in the same, very beautifully situated pension, exactly what he thinks himself. (Please note the change of address! Bondy arranged nice quarters for me here.)

The trial: you'll know all the essentials from the papers. Eichmann is no eagle; rather, a ghost who has a cold on top of that and minute by minute fades in substance, as it were, in his glass box. The chief justice—Landau[2]—superb! All three of the judges are German Jews.[3] The comedy of speaking Hebrew when everyone involved knows German and thinks in German. Landau speaks very good Hebrew (people tell me). The prosecutor,[4] on the other hand, a typical Galician Jew, very unsympathetic, is constantly making mistakes. Probably one of those people who don't know any language. His argument artificial, overly legalistic and with gross errors, interrupted by spells of emotion. But above all immeasurably boring and full of nonexistent precedents, on which the prosecutor focuses instead of stressing the unprecedentedness of the case. He does make occasional mention of that, but the right things he says disappear under the irrelevancies. The judges are already rather impatient. Perhaps Landau will manage to get the thing under control yet. Servatius—oily, greasy, clever, concise and to the point—he knows what he wants. The rumors you wrote about I've heard here, too, concerning Krupp[5] in particular. They are of course possible. But what is established fact is that the government here has paid $20,000, which Servatius thinks is too little.

Key point: The whole thing is so organized that it can last until Judgment Day unless some miracle intervenes. That is pure madness, which everyone here in this country understands fully—except for the prosecuting attorneys and, presumably, Ben Gurion. What the real purpose is I don't know, and I doubt that anyone here knows. If the prosecutor continues as he has begun, the trial could drag out for months without very crucial aspects of this devilish business ever coming clearly to light. For example, the fact of Jewish collaboration, of the overall organization, and similar things. In the meantime, the country is full of Germans. The mayor of Frankfurt is staying in the same pension I am. These Germans are displaying an unpleasant over-eagerness and finding absolutely everything wonderful. Enough to make you throw up, if I may say so. One of them has already flung his arms around my neck and burst into tears. I've forgotten the name.

The country's interest in the trial has been artificially whetted. An oriental mob that would hang around anyplace where something is going on is hanging around in front of the courthouse. A surprising number of children between 3 and 10. What I hear from the real youth is quite a different story. This is their parents' business, they say. It doesn't concern them. But if it interests their parents, then it is legitimate. What goes unexpressed: We have more important things to do. Court is not in session today, and I was able to sleep late for the first time since New York. I've spent the whole day here in the pension, sitting in the sun on my balcony. This evening I'll get together with some American colleagues. And on the weekend I'll probably travel around the country a little with my family.[6] The weather is wonderful, still rather cold, but the sun is bright and warm, the countryside greener than I have ever seen it.

My first impression: On top, the judges, the best of German Jewry. Below them, the prosecuting attorneys, Galicians, but still Europeans. Everything is organized by a police force that gives me the creeps, speaks only Hebrew, and looks Arabic. Some downright brutal types among them. They would obey any order. And outside the doors, the oriental mob, as if one were in Istanbul or some other half-Asiatic country. In addition, and very visible in Jerusalem, the peies and caftan Jews,[7] who make life impossible for all the reasonable people here. The major impression, though, is of very great poverty.

What have you done about Wolff's letter? I assume you haven't sent it as is because it seemed to you that you were assuming the costs to date. I don't think that there's any chance of that but assume that you've cleared that up with Wolff by phone in the meantime.

That's all for now. I'll write as soon as there's anything new to report. This is all just first impressions.

With warmest greetings and until soon
Your
Hannah

286 *Karl Jaspers to Hannah Arendt*

Basel, April 24, 1961

Dear Hannah!

Thank you very much! Your letter provides a picture that one cannot get from the newspapers here. You sketch things concretely and convincingly. Things surely are the way you paint them. Distressing. Let us hope the three German Jews[1] gain control. But the whole thing is threatening to blow away and disappear. Already the world's interest is totally focused on Cuba,[2] Kennedy, Khrushchev, and now on De Gaulle.[3] I heard his speech last night: wild, desperate accusations—total decline—resort to any and all means (but he didn't say which)—and finally: Men and women of France, help me! His voice was almost despondent, without the power of his earlier speeches. But perhaps that was the right thing for France in order to mobilize the whole population. I think he'll succeed. A subjugation of France by Salan and Challe,[4] like that of Spain by Franco[5] (who came after all to help stem the tide of Communists and barbarians), would be absurd. If one takes into account the material possibilities—which are very complex—the army would in the most extreme case no doubt fail because of the insubordination[6] of its own soldiers and the monolithic passive resistance of the entire French population.

I'm glad that we are in such agreement in our view of the trial. We have, I think, since my first long letter, which you argued against, corrected each other in our conception. Because no one had made any public statement in this direction, not one showing even the slightest tendency toward it, I let myself, after refusing at first, be talked into this interview without coming to a clear decision about it, so that the form it took was improvised. How much better it would have been if you, with your energy and still youthful intelligence and as a Jew, had developed this idea before the public. The chances would have been better that the intelligent German judges, after researching all the facts, would have considered the matter from this perspective, too.

I wrote immediately to Pantheon Books, following your recommendations. After I spoke with Kurt Wolff on the telephone, he gave me written confirmation in the name of the new publisher and on his own part that they would assume responsibility for the costs. Now, Pantheon Books doesn't want to go along. I put them off for the time being, saying they would hear more from me later after I had had a chance to speak with you, presumably early in May.

We look forward to your visit!

Warmest greetings
Your Karl Jaspers

287 Hannah Arendt to Karl Jaspers

Jerusalem, April 25, 1961

Lieber Verehrtester!

Everything important when we see each other. This is just to ask if it's all right with you if I come to Basel around May 8. It could be a day later; I still haven't looked into possible flights.

Things here continue to be very interesting, sometimes very impressive, often absolutely awful. I'm seeing more of people than usual, had a talk with Golda Meir,[1] the foreign minister, yesterday that lasted late into the night; before that with Rosen,[2] minister of justice, brother of a friend. Also (and this is between us because on principle he does not speak with the press) with Landau, the chief justice. Marvelous man! Modest, intelligent, very open, knows America very well; you'd like him a lot. The best of German Jewry. Blumenfeld arranged the meeting.

I've just come back from a luncheon given by the university. I'm speaking to two seminars and will also meet again with a selected group of students. I'm pleased about that, of course. This weekend I'll drive around in the countryside with my family. I've got to get out a bit. I'm waiting eagerly for our talk, keep thinking, in the midst of all this horror, that you exist and that I can go to you. Then I instantly become completely calm.

Kurt Wolff sent me your correspondence with Pantheon. I too think we'll come away better than we expected. The Wolffs want to come to Basel. That would really be the best thing. Then we can discuss everything.

One more thing: Wouldn't it perhaps be better if I stayed in a hotel this time? And couldn't Erna call the hotel where Piper always stays? I've stupidly forgotten the name. There is an easy, quick connection to Au Street. It seems to me that would be quieter and better for you both.

Send me a line here. I wrote you already that I have a different address. Next week I'll write or telegraph my exact time of arrival.

Warmest greetings to you both

Your

Hannah

288 *Karl Jaspers to Hannah Arendt*

Basel, June 8, 1961

Dear Hannah!

I have received *no reply* from Pantheon Books—Mr. Schabert. Now you will have to trouble yourself with this again. What does one do when people remain silent, offer passive resistance? I'm sad about this because I had hoped the matter was in order now.

Much has happened since you left. The world situation is growing worse. Our statesmen appear anxious. Khrushchev in Moscow is dancing with the Asiatics from Indonesia amid the applause of all concerned, even the female Indonesians. The Algerians are raising their demands (which have to be granted). Adenauer[1] makes stupid, soothing statements (as always, untruthful to the Germans, with the sole aim of winning elections). Kennedy has seen clearly that military strength is urgently needed and has to be increased but that it alone is not enough and not the main thing. Provost Grüber's[2] statements represented a bright spot (though one without political significance). They were simple, true, relentless, and without the faintest trace of scolding or even of pathos.

Ashton wrote me a letter, one of such good tone, personal, and in German, that I was much pleased. He is horrified by the consequences of the Cuban fiasco, speaks of Kennedy's and America's prestige "collapsing like a house of cards." I hope that he is greatly exaggerating in the moment when the world and we are still feeling the shock. I am not ready to withdraw my trust in Kennedy so quickly. The fate of us all lies with him now.

When you came to us from Israel, you were almost totally exhausted by the many people you had seen and all the excitement you had experienced. And then you had to have patience with me sometimes when I gave out. Now I'm looking forward to your and Heinrich's visit in July, not too short a one, I hope. It's strange: I feel that I know Heinrich well already and am almost his friend, and yet we still don't know each other at all. In expectation of meeting him, I have the happy feeling that I will be encountering a human being who as your husband already stands in the highest esteem for us but who has also been a felt presence for us for a long time in his own right and as a man who under all circumstances raises his head above the humdrum and has remained independent. Because *Die Idee der Universität*[3] has just appeared, I have sent it to him as one knowledgeable and experienced in such matters, but I do *not* expect that he will read it now. We have so much to talk about. May we enjoy many a happy hour together!

You will, I gather, travel to Israel soon. In the meantime, Eichmann has shown still other aspects of himself, among them some personally brutal ones. Such a functionary of bureaucratic murder cannot, after all, be without personally inhuman qualities, which under the proper circumstances come to the surface, even though under "normal" conditions he would not have become a criminal. It will not be easy for you to draw a picture of this man that represents his reality.

Warmest greetings, also from Gertrud, and bon voyage!

Your Karl Jaspers

289 *Hannah Arendt to Karl Jaspers*

Munich, June 9, 1961

Lieber Verehrtester!

Your letter just arrived. I hadn't written because my Israel plans were still not firm. Now it's almost certain that I will not fly from here until the 17th and will be back in Zurich on the evening of the 23rd to collect Heinrich on the 24th. I'll save Eichmann's "brutality" for another time. It has not been proved. The statement about that has to be taken with great caution.

I was going to write to Schabert in New York right away but then saw that Wolff will be in Zurich again on the 12th. So I wrote him and asked him to call me. He may well know something more that we should take into account. I'll write immediately after his call. How annoying!

There is much to report about Germany, but at the moment I don't want to. I had a lot of opportunities to speak with students and discuss things with them. The only hope is a European federation, regardless of how small this Europe is at first, a "federation for increase," as Harrington[1] puts it so well, one that other nations can join later with equal rights. The young people are often delightful, but what should they really do? There are only two things that would be important from a German perspective: accept your position on the two Germanys and recognize the Oder-Neisse Line. Then everything would start to flow again, and then one could talk very differently about Berlin. It's bad enough that Adenauer isn't doing that. That the SPD [the Social Democrats] won't touch it with a ten-foot pole either is far worse.

Kennedy—Ashton is just passing along what the general mood in America is and what, as such, can change. But Ashton is a good man! I've always harbored a secret fear that Kennedy is really a seriously ill man who cannot rely on his own body and nerves. But perhaps that is nonsense. He looks a bit that way.

Life is very pleasant here. Good working conditions, and I'm being massively spoiled by Piper, whom I like more and more all the time. And, if possible, his wife even more![2] Tomorrow my American friend with the back problem[3] will arrive. It seems to be only a fashionable illness after all. She doesn't seem to have quite understood what the doctors told her. But I'm not sure. At any rate, she's able to fly here from Warsaw. Annchen [Anne Weil], who sends her best, was here with me over Whitsuntide.

I've met Winfried Martini[4] here a few times—you'll recall that we spoke about him. At his house I met a Dr. Klaus Jensch, a psychiatrist, who made an excellent impression (which can in no way be said for Martini) and who is a real student of your *Psychopathologie*. I encouraged him to write to you sometime. As I said, he made a very good impression.

Heinrich wrote that your book on university reform has arrived and that he was hoping to be able to read it over the weekend. You write so wonderfully about meeting him, and I'm so pleased that it is finally going to happen after all.

When I come back from Israel I'll at least call you in Basel right away. If Heinrich won't arrive until the evening of the 24th or the morning of the 25th, perhaps I can come over for a little while, if that suits you.

All my best to you both and warmest greetings,

Your
Hannah

290 *Hannah Arendt to Karl Jaspers*

June 16, 1961

Lieber Verehrtester!

Kurt Wolff called but didn't have anything special to report. So here is a carbon copy of my letter to Schabert.[1] I hope it will help!

I'm off tomorrow morning, and on Saturday, the 24th, at 2320, or 11:20, Heinrich will arrive and will presumably be picked up at the airport by a large escort, because his friend from Locarno [Robert Gilbert] will come to Zurich for the day.

I'll call you as soon as I'm in Zurich. It could be the 23rd or the 24th. I have two possibilities, one via Athens, which I may have to take because it would enable me to make full use of the Friday morning session. Not to mention Athens itself! Then I would spend the night of the 23rd to the 24th in Athens and not arrive in Zurich until the afternoon. In that case, I wouldn't be able to come to Basel. But that doesn't matter. We'll see each other soon anyhow!

My addresses: Until June 23, Jerusalem, Hotel Eden. From the 24th to the 26th: Zurich, Waldhaus Dolder.

Just one more thing: I've given different people your address as a forwarding address for me because I didn't know quite what else to do. Nothing that comes will be urgent! I'll tell the people here, too, that anything that arrives for me after the 22nd should be sent on to you.

It was really very pleasant here and an extremely productive time. Piper has spoiled me so much that I've really had to watch out that it doesn't go to my head. Otherwise all I have to report is that I own a Minox camera and am already taking pictures of everything I see. When I'm with you this time, I'm going to make pictures of everything and everybody there, too.

Until then, warmest greetings to everyone!

Your
Hannah

Basel, July 31, 1961

Dear Heinrich Blücher!

You can't read my handwriting. Gertrud will copy this letter.

In the time since your departure there has been reverberating in me what was utterly clear and self-evident between us and what is so rare: a meeting of minds free of convention and on a foundation that one cannot exactly name. If we call it Berlin or Oldenburg, German, European, or Western, that says a lot in terms of background and suggests an inalienable heritage but is still not adequate. It is a deeper, firmer foundation that supports us. And a consequence of it is that one can say anything—on the spur of the moment and when one is fresh or when one is tired and the moment fails us—without danger of major "misunderstandings." We were, of course, well prepared and found what we were expecting. Now, I think, we have personally felt again underfoot our old foundation on which one can build and feel oneself at home in a spinning world. That came home to me with particular force because our lives, our paths and activities, have been so very different. That difference is fortunate if, within it, a common ground that was always there makes itself felt. If we had met in our youth, we would probably have argued much more violently than we would now if we could get together often. This has made me think about Fritz zur Loye, a friend of my youth, who died in 1916 and with whom I fought to the point of anger; but we both knew: There will be no breach, for after our anger we will calm down, listen to each other. The friendship grows stronger because neither wants to lead the other but, rather, feels himself led with him from somewhere else and has trust. Our meeting was not, of course, so violent at all but only harbored that possibility. On the contrary, things went very quietly between us: you, a mature and experienced man, and me, now an almost ancient man. Only recollections of possibilities no longer open to us could emerge.

The plan and content of your educational enterprise impressed me greatly, though I could learn only a little of it in our short time together. It struck me as both conservative and modern: conservative, because based on what is eternally great throughout the millennia and with the aim of a more profound education, not the decimation of education —modern, because, within the context of our society and unprejudiced by the academic world, you speak to people as one human being to another, and try to satisfy those urgings that are innate in many, perhaps in most, people. Through contact with great, challenging works that convert and delight the soul, the works of great thinkers, poets, and creative human beings, you encourage those seeds to grow. We may hope (in moments of doubt) that ultimately, in our now deadening, technological world, humankind, some human beings, will come to self-awareness and self-assertion and control over the consequences of technology, because every human being, as Hannah has said so often and beautifully and movingly, is a new beginning. In your work, you want to see to it that young people become aware of great thought early in life, that the essentials are not crushed for them by the mass of nonessentials. These young people will be inspired when they perceive the demands you are putting on them and when they see a teacher who is obviously not putting anything over on them. Your life-sustaining acceptance of what is noble, undertaken at your own choice and on your own responsibility and your concrete experience of life give you the possibility of achieving your goals. What your students make of your teaching is not in our hands.

Almost every day will bring you, as it does us, renewed fears about the direction current politics is taking. I liked very much the style and tenor of Kennedy's last speech. I assume that he knows more than he is saying, and I fear that he may go wrong again because of inadequate information—information that we don't have either. That he wants to increase America's and Europe's conventional forces massively and is asking sacrifices of people now and is preparing them for still greater ones in the future—all that makes him credible. The standard of living in the Western world may well have to be lowered to make such an arms buildup possible. (That may not prove necessary at all, but still, people must be ready to accept it, because everyone has to realize what is at stake, that everything, namely, freedom, is at stake.) But for the Berlin question, the arms buildup is coming too late. The situation at the moment is probably such that in case of war America would have to use its bombs immediately and by doing so would step into absolute darkness. And would load shame on itself for all time. If the great arms buildup were already accomplished, the picture would be totally different, even if the losing side should ultimately resort to the bombs. The actual state of military power is the basis for the decision about Berlin. It is only the shadow of Russia's military power that accounts for all the talk about colonialistic thinking's being a thing of the past and so forth. Kennedy's insistence on rights is good, but he has to distinguish between rights for the sake of which the step into darkness should be ventured and the rights one can waive in the interest of stabilizing the consequences of the war (to use Khrushchev's phrase). The politically hypocritical Federal Republic is the last place where this distinction is made, but it is the Federal Republic that should be aiding America in its thinking instead of insisting on payment of the note that America was foolish enough to have signed. It seems to me that if we are to maintain any hope at all the step into darkness should be risked for only two reasons: the two and a half million West Berliners must not be robbed of their freedom, and East Germans must still have the possibility of emigrating to the Federal Republic. One need not cling to the city of Berlin (but then, the Berliners must be able to move to the West with their worldly goods). One can recognize East Germany as a de facto satellite state, but the Federal Republic should do this only on the condition that free elections under international supervision are held in East Germany, that is, only if an East German regime is thus legitimized; for there are Germans in the East who must not be sacrificed by Germans—though the Germans will of course sacrifice them. They have done worse: they gave up their Jewish Germans to the murderers without lifting a hand in protest. If Khrushchev can save face with a stabilization of the consequences of the war that includes the freedom of the West Berliners and the freedom of the East Germans to emigrate through that hole, then a surrender to totalitarian rule is a surrender to only half a murder. I heard someone say recently that Khrushchev operates on the principle: "What is mine is mine; what is yours we can negotiate about." That is of course not negotiation but extortion, and one puts up with it only if one isn't powerful enough to oppose it. And even then it would be in no way certain that an airtight guarantee for this new stabilization could be achieved through negotiations. But the attempt seems necessary to me, along with the abandonment of the German fictions (primarily, Berlin as the capital and therefore as a symbol for claims that, by the very nature of things, represent a threat of war for the future), necessary so that if the worst should happen we can at least be clear on what our sole reason for fighting should be and why we should risk absolute darkness.

Things will probably go, despite Kennedy, the way you recently suggested they would, and I agree with you: Under the pretense of maintaining freedom and of treaties guaranteeing freedom, freedom will in fact be destroyed step by step. I can't deny that this prospect horrifies me. Because Kennedy's current arms buildup comes too late, it unfortunately has the effect of mere show, and Khrushchev will *not* be duped by it if, assuming that Berlin is not surrendered, he wants war. Or are we ignorant of basic military facts favorable to the West? The number of divisions in the East and the West is occasionally mentioned. The difference suggests that, if atomic weapons are not employed, Russia would occupy Europe in 4 to 6 weeks.

Enough of this! Warmest greetings

Your Karl Jaspers

292 *Karl Jaspers to Hannah Arendt*

Basel, August 1, 1961

Dear Hannah!

Now I'll write to just one of you at a time—but it will always be meant for the other as well.

For you I'm enclosing a letter from Mr. Schabert (Pantheon Press).[1] He has given in. I sent him a brief and friendly letter of thanks. You will no doubt have heard this directly by now. You'll now have the trouble of transferring the manuscript. I hope Frau Beradt[2] will help. Then other cares will follow but no new annoyances, I hope.

Warmest greetings! It was so good seeing you—even if we two spoke more with each other by way of Heinrich, who stood in the middle. That had nothing to do with the privileged position of men but was unique to this first meeting. We are hoping there will be another.

Your Karl Jaspers

293 *Hannah Arendt to Karl and Gertrud Jaspers*

New York, August 6, 1961

Lieber Verehrtester! Liebe Gute!

Yes, it was wonderful! No matter how much one looks forward to things, the reality always surpasses one's expectations. It's a delight for me that Basel and your house, which for me have been like my old European homeland for so long now, belong to us both here, that we can call them up from memory into the present, that I don't have to tell about them anymore; that they are simply present. And then your offer of "Du"—which didn't even scare me and hardly surprised me (Heinrich isn't easily discombobulated anyhow)—like a seal on the fact that trust, no matter how great it is, can be elevated one more step into intimacy. I recognized the similarities between you, but I wasn't sure they would become evident because all the "externals" are as different as they could be. I often daydreamed about those "possibilities no longer open to us," not in a very sad way really but rather playfully. The way I sometimes play with the fact that Heinrich lived around the corner from me in Berlin. Just at the moment when all four of us were sitting around the table for the first time together and everything was so simple and utterly natural, I kept thinking: It's good this way, very good, actually. And this utterly natural way we are together, which in its utter naturalness is really ("objectively") highly unnatural, might never have come about. And when I see Heinrich with Robert Gilbert, to whom he is attached with the same bonds of friendship that I am to Annchen [Anne Weil] (who sends her regards; we met for a whole week in Paris) and with whom he shared his life until '33, then it becomes clear to me how good his youth must have been, even if it was hard and couldn't have the pure, unmuddled, unequivocal clarity of your life. When Heinrich came to Paris from Locarno, he was blissfully happy, and he said of the whole experience, that is, Basel and Locarno: It was an orgy of friendship.

I wanted to write straight off from Heidelberg but didn't get to it because of all the traveling around without a typewriter. Meeting with students and young faculty (assistants, etc.) was pleasant but nothing special. "Well-meaning" people—[. . .]—are boring. They just don't have any ideas. Rossmann with his very nice new wife[1] much better than ever before. I don't think his stuttering is any cause for worry. I paid close attention to the hitch in his speech. It's really not disturbing and isn't a stutter. But if he could be gotten out of there, it would, I think, save his life. The atmosphere is wearing him down, and one can't hold that against him. He is completely isolated. You can't live like that unless you have endless vitality and really enjoy fighting. Basel would be just right for him.[2] He could grow again there, somehow become free. He is helpless against Heidelberg viciousness. [. . .] The worst of it is that he has no friends, that the few people there who have not all but at least some of their wits about them don't have anything to do with each other. I also met the district attorney, Bauer,[3] from Frankfurt, the man who, as is well known, wanted to have Eichmann extradited to Germany. He doesn't amount to much. First of all, he is a Jew, so the whole business doesn't count for anything, and second, he's nothing more than just another good Social Democrat.

From Heidelberg I went to Freiburg after all, and that was a remarkable venture in more than one respect. First of all, Mr. Kaiser,[4] who invited me to his place. About 40, I'd say, homosexual (which doesn't bother me any! it was just funny how he tried to hide it), lives in an extremely luxurious villa he built himself, complete with floors of Carrara marble that he selected himself and had cut to size. He lives there with an Arab from Tunis (cf. André Gidé,[5] who couldn't leave the Arabs alone either), who is supposed to play the butler but who is so shameless in his behavior that it's downright comical, and no one can ignore what's really going on. And then, to round off this bizarre household, two real live sheep that are supposed to keep the grass clipped. He had invited high dignitaries from the university, and their ladies were quite beside themselves. That was very funny, too, because so provincial. He invites the students there, also, and gives big dance parties. The house really is very well built and truly unique. And academically his credentials seem impeccable. He could no doubt easily put a good baker's dozen of professors into his pocket. I had a wonderful time there, but I have to admit that I kept my pleasure to myself.

I was less amused by the following incident. I had written to Heidegger that I would be in town at such and such times and that he could get in touch with me. He did not call, which didn't strike me as odd, because I didn't even know whether he was in town, and the people I was with didn't know either. But then this happened: Fink[6] was among the people Kaiser invited to his house, because I had told Kaiser I had known Fink from our youth. And I did that because this summer I received an invitation to some university weeks that Fink was in charge of, and there was something in the invitation to the effect that Fink would be especially pleased and so forth and so on. And Kaiser told me that Fink had spoken very "positively" of me, so I said why not invite him, too. So what does Fink do but "brusquely" decline the invitation, saying he did not want to see me and referring explicitly to Heidegger, who apparently forbid him to do so. Why? I have no idea. The only conclusion I can draw from the whole thing is that Fink told Heidegger I was there and that he would see me and that Heidegger then said he didn't like that. That Fink put up with this is something else again. It sounds like the kind of thing that went on in the George circle.[7] I'm telling you about this in such detail because it is certainly possible, but by no means certain, that it has something to do with you, though I really can't see how. A year ago Heidegger sent me his recent publications with an inscription. I responded by sending him my *Vita Activa*. C'est tout.

The discussion there was primarily with assistants, privatdocents, and older students, who to a man saw Hitler as the embodiment of "fate" and as a "historical necessity," although they could not agree whether it had its roots in Bismarck or Marx or Nietzsche or Hegel. A discussion of the matter itself they declined as presumably too "superficial." Hitler apparently wasn't well educated enough for them.

Pantheon: everything in the best of order. Gerry Gross[8] will come to see me tomorrow. He very much wanted to talk with me. So the parting will take place on friendly terms. I have my old secretary [Bertha Gruner] working for me this week because I can't cope with my mail any other way. She can also get the manuscript and take it to Harcourt, Brace. Our place is so pleasantly cool that we'll stay here for the time being and then perhaps go to the Catskills[9] for two weeks later. There's only one thing I want: finally to be at home and not packing any more bags.

We are greatly concerned, particularly about France.[10] In Paris, people were almost certain there would be another coup. If things go wrong, all of NATO could collapse. And on top of that there is the dangerous development in Germany with all this reunification talk that no one takes seriously but that might be taken seriously someday. I still don't think there will be war over Berlin, and there won't be because Khrushchev doesn't want it and can't want it. Here and especially in Paris, I've talked with a few people who have been in Russia, who speak Russian, and were able to move about freely there. It continues to astonish me how badly everything there functions. The corruption is said to be incredible. Everyone steals, I was told by someone who still has close relatives there and a real insight into conditions. We let ourselves be impressed by the great achievements in space, which are much easier to organize than a country. The fear of China is widespread and a significant factor. My feeling continues to be that all Khrushchev wants is to maintain the status quo. Berlin, I still fear, is lost, but it will probably go in a gentle manner that will permit the Berliners in West Berlin to carry on their lives relatively unaffected for the time being. It is really a disaster that the West has no suggestions of its own, that it is putting no pressure on the Federal Republic, and lets it muddle on in its hypocrisy—because, among other reasons, the West doesn't even realize how hypocritical the whole state of affairs is. But all that is irrelevant compared with our worries about France. If that ends in a fascistic venture, what then?? Won't that immediately set a landslide in motion in Germany?? I thought earlier that Khrushchev might risk war if he saw himself confronted with the serious possibility of a federated Western Europe that would clearly be a major power. I don't believe that anymore. Even then he would probably try to develop some kind of alliances to protect his rear from China. In the meantime, we are losing the only ally[11] in Africa that the West has ever had. Furthermore, the Tunis affair is the worst thing that could happen to Israel—the last hope for splitting the Arab world. As far as Russia is concerned, they really don't need a war. If things continue to go as they are, everything will fall into their hands anyway, and all they have to do is watch out that the Chinese don't take too much of it away from them. In India, for example, people are extremely worried. (I spoke in Paris with my cousin [Niouta Ghosh]; she lives in Calcutta and is married to an Indian.) —In Russia, the hatred for Germany is still very great, of course. It's interesting that one makes no distinction there between East and West Germany. "One," in this case, is a newspaper editor! I consider it possible that Khrushchev is perfectly content to see Germans leaving the eastern territories and that he will probably send some other "settlers" there.

Enough of all this. I don't even want to look at the papers anymore. Kennedy leaves me feeling very uneasy. I just hope he doesn't crack under the strain. Heinrich isn't home, and I'm going to send this letter off as it is so that it won't lie around any longer. He will probably write soon, too. His view of travel has changed after all. I think we'll be coming again soon. And the two of you shouldn't be thinking you're "ancient," because that's what you have yet to become.

Warmest greetings

Your
Hannah

294 *Hannah Arendt to Karl Jaspers*

August 18, 1961

Lieber Verehrtester—

I'm sending the enclosed letter[1] so that you will have an idea of how delighted the people at Harcourt, Brace are to have the book.[2] But perhaps it would be good if I could have this letter back. Yesterday I also received a letter from Kurt Wolff, whom Jovanovich had already called. Jovanovich is the president of Harcourt. British rights: Unwin[3] was interested but asked that the book be abridged! I wrote him I didn't think that would be possible, and I considered it unlikely that you would agree to it.

As for other things, I am writing with a heavy heart today because of Berlin.[4] We could see what was coming, of course, but that still doesn't make the reality any more palatable. I think it's altogether possible that there will be direct German-Russian negotiations, and I have the distinct impression that Adenauer is beginning to change course. No one here, not even in the papers, seems to realize how serious the situation is, because there appears to be so little danger of war.

How are things with you? I'm trying to get back into my work and finally finish writing my revolution book. On Sunday I'll rejoin Heinrich in the country[5] for a few days. He will probably come home next week himself. I wish I could quickly skip over to Basel for a few hours.

Warmest greetings
Hannah

295 *Heinrich Blücher to Karl Jaspers*

New York, September 5, 1961

Dear Karl Jaspers,

When I got home again, it seemed almost incomprehensible to me that it could have happened, but reality just laughed at me and called attention to the certainty of my inner experience, about which philosophers should never have any doubts. And even seen purely pragmatically, it is hardly admissible to doubt an event that has changed one. It is one of the few great and crucial joys of my life that it was given to me to meet you and even that I could meet you, that I was with you and felt myself at one with you. I said to Hannah in jest that in Basel I would be taking my philosophical exam very late in life but that it was the only exam that I could take with real seriousness. But quite seriously: it is a wonderful thing that I, who in philosophical matters never even thought of looking for confirmation from the experts, have now received your encouragement. Because of it, I'll return to my students at Bard tomorrow with much greater pleasure and feeling a little more sure of myself.

That it was possible is a fact. Your letter makes clear to me how it was possible. Let me attempt "to name" that "deeper, firmer foundation." It is the foundation of what you have called transcendence, for transcendence is not only the goal toward which man should fly, but it is also the only firm soil from which he can take flight. Here the point of origin and the goal are the same. In my terms: We see and understand ourselves on the soil of a shared and unconditional will for freedom and truth. Or, no matter how different our opinions about categorical imperatives of all kinds may be, on the soil of an absolute impulse for the absolute.

You as a rich boy and I as a poor one, you as a Frisian with old, deep roots and I as a self-uprooted Berliner, were never as alien to each other as you were as an academic and I as an antiacademic philosopher. And it was you alone who built the bridge across that gap. I told you that I had no interest in the abstract freedom of philosophers and especially of German philosophers. There I am ready to admire and to learn but not to love and accept. But when I think about real freedom, then from the circles of German philosophy the name I hear today, after Kant's and Lessing's, is yours. (And I mustn't forget my beloved, desperate Nietzsche, who ran headlong after concrete freedom.) And so, since you have shown contemporary Germans how even a German philosopher can kick over the traces, we share not only a common ground but also a common goal: to stand up for the indivisibility of physically real freedom and conceptually real truth.

Politically, that means always standing for the free republic and its principles (as you did so well with your distinction between freedom and reunification) but never backing any specific government (as you wrongly did with your recognition of Adenauer). Yes, politically we are as horrified and as much at a loss as you. And so I want to begin, cautiously, to talk philosophically about politics. Just as it is philosophy's task to unite truth and freedom, so it is the equally herculean task of politics to bring freedom and justice together. In our dreadful anxiety and need, we like to hear people at least talk about freedom (Kennedy), though neither the world nor even American students are really listening. The word has become threadbare in their eyes, and too often they have seen social injustice hiding behind it. That is changing a little now but not in any major way yet, and people are mistrustful and attached to their old insights. They think, moreover, and they see confirmation of it often enough, that the mass of Americans are capitalistic ideologues; and poor people don't think much of

451

that. They find the socialistic Russian ideologues much more to their liking. They still think that a socialistic ideology will bring social justice with it. It is hard for them to see that behind a verbal curtain of social justice freedom is being slaughtered. Many still don't know what freedom is and what use it is to them. Others are quite prepared to exchange it for more bread and, ultimately, for a higher, industrial, standard of living.

The reality in America is that all too often ideology is determined by political opportunity and politics all too often by economic interests. And the reality in Russia is that the economy is determined by political power interests and politics by ideology. A dreadful state of affairs, because neither system is really concerned with justice or freedom, and so neither one really has to do with politics. It is of course a long way from Dulles's view that neutrality is immoral to Kennedy's propaganda for neutrality. Unfortunately, by the time neutrality was being advocated, no state had any interest left in an alliance with America. And now of course the present Bolschev[1] has put on atomic fireworks in Belgrade for the neutrals' benefit, has pounded on the table with his boot, and made clear to them that now the time has come when he, for his part, will declare neutrality immoral.

So as not to close on such a grim note, I want to return to the education of the young. I'm seeing everywhere among young people, but quite clearly here in America, signs of a growing disgust for and hatred of hypocrisy. Metaphysical interest is growing more and more, too. They are asking for the truth. If we respond correctly, can't we perhaps interest them in freedom?

My thanks to Gertrud for the clean copy, which was very helpful. Everything I have said to you, my joy and my thanks, is meant for her as well.

Warmest greetings
Your
Heinrich Blücher

296 *Karl Jaspers to Hannah Arendt*

Basel, September 13, 1961

Dear Hannah!

I owe you thanks for two letters. I am glad that *Die grossen Philosophen* will be printed now. And I was happy to read how pleased the new publisher is with it. So all your work will not have been in vain. As regards further abridgment for an English edition, I share your view. Kurt Wolff has sent me the new contracts. Everything is in order.

Heidegger's behavior: You have read Fink's letter. Therefore, one cannot have any doubts, which I would like to have. In a letter to me years ago he had great praise for your "magnanimity." Does his silence mean that he has given in to his wife[1] now? and has even become hostile? That your eulogy in Frankfurt[2] should be the sole reason for this present action is, after he sent you his works last year, not likely, but still possible, given the inconsistency of his thoroughly puzzling behavior. Thinking about his motives doesn't help. It just leads one to banalities, which does not assuage my anger. For you, the situation strikes me as simply ugly and totally undeserved. Your magnanimity, which you grant to anyone who does not outright murder or denounce people, will have given you some distance on this.

Heinrich wrote me a letter that moved me, and for now I'll thank him here. Our letters are a confirmation of reality.

September 16

I had to put this letter aside because we had visitors. Your letter of August 6, so good and detailed, requires much by way of response. I enjoyed immensely your wonderful description of that house in Freiburg and all that went with it. A university of philistines deserves to have something like that plunked down in its midst. But I fear that it is incapable of fruitful outrage productive of intellectual reaction and vitality.

Why do you suppose it is that the well-meaning people are, as you put it, "boring"? [. . .] This well-meaning business is a peculiar thing. That became gradually clear to me in the twenties from the example of the *Frankfurter Zeitung*. I really became aware of it only when the paper stopped printing Max Weber because he, so grossly out of step with the times, derided the revolution. There has always been a tradition of knowing better there, yet at the same time the paper has always been overly cautious. The *FAZ* of today, which we of course read, treats the hypocrisy of German public life with kid gloves and so is as guilty by association as the old *Frankfurter Zeitung* was in its time. And hence the tedium. No significant discussion is taking place, though there are sometimes charming essays by Sternberger (one at Christmas about women, for instance). These people can also be fanatics in pursuit of the truth where that is not at all called for. As now, for example: democracy requires a strong opposition party (correct). Therefore the Federal Republic of today must not have a coalition government that would be formed from the two major parties (which in the present situation and for the next four years is, in my opinion, wrong).[3] I would vote SPD, but I am not allowed to because Germans living abroad are not permitted to vote, with the exception of those who are abroad in government service (down to the last employee in an embassy or consulate), but not those who are abroad by choice. With a permit from the consul, I could very easily vote in Lörrach. For the last elections in Italy, 40,000 Italians went home from Switzerland to vote.

Your worries about France are certainly very justified. The danger for Europe is great. The Algerian situation seems to elude any solution. Rational negotiations are not taking place. All that remains for the French to do is return to Europe—those who want to—and for the French state to help them with a fresh start. But that is apparently so intolerable for the senior officers of the army that they have been unreliable now for a long time. De Gaulle himself helped to encourage this tradition of *gloire* and is its spokesman. But that he has recognized what is inevitable in the real world evidences, I think, an element of greatness in him. That is what distinguishes what is happening in France from all the other miseries Europe is experiencing. How satisfying that there is at least one man of stature on the horizon in Europe. However alien to me his positions are and however much he seems to be of another era, I still look to him with some hope. Perhaps he will be able to achieve what appears impossible. He is hesitating. He can't hesitate much longer. The people, except in Algeria, are with him. Whatever the upshot—whether he is victorious or goes down to defeat—it will not mean a loss of dignity, which seems to go along with everything that happens in Germany. For the sake of Europe, he must win. I have sympathy for him. His calmness and courage are powerful factors. Fate has set the most difficult of tasks for him: to win the upper hand over the officers and perhaps to build a new army.

But despite all this Berlin appears to me the greatest cause for worry. America's note of a few days ago about the access routes seemed excellent to me. But the situation is becoming all the clearer: rights are not really at issue at all but, rather, how much Khrushchev can gain for himself by extortion (the threat of world war). As a dictator, Khrushchev can always pull back at the last minute and appear as the magnanimous man of peace. Kennedy appears to me to be bluffing less and less. And it will not be so easy for him to pull in his horns. In important respects, "Munich"[4] is an inappropriate analogy. In Munich, France and England gave up what they had. Now, as I see it, the only chance is for the West to focus, very openly and with full credibility, on the one point for which it is willing to risk everything: the freedom of the West Berliners. Everything else it can let go: Berlin as the future capital of Germany, reunification, the political ties between the Federal Republic and West Berlin, all propaganda generated in Berlin, the RIAS[5] radio station, the palace for the president of the Federal Republic, the headquarters for organizations of the Federal Republic in Berlin. But the Allied troops, and, most important, the Americans, would have to stay. Berlin would become an international city under the protection of the Western powers, without any foreign office of its own but with a free internal administration. The Berliners, who are truly wonderful, would as individuals be freer than any other people in the world. They would not have any military service. It would be a gift from heaven for them if the UN moved its headquarters to Berlin. Instead of being the capital of the Reich, as it once was (and which it will never be again), it would be a world city. It would have the opportunity to develop an intellectual life that would radiate out into the world and draw from it. Politically, it would not be the slightest threat at all. It would fulfill its new role of being a unique, neutral, internationalized focal point—without any precedent in history, a totally modern phenomenon. The routes of access would of course have to be assured. The economy would doubtless have to be subsidized—for a while.

As for the two of you, I picture you nearing completion of your revolution book. Heinrich continues his educational work. —I am writing my "theological book."[6]

That there is nothing one can do! Complaining is really nonsense, and also "boring"—and yet I've indulged in it anyhow.

Warmest greetings to you both, also from Gertrud

Your Karl

The publisher's letter is enclosed.[7]

Perhaps I've already written to Heinrich what I've included in this letter. If so, please forgive the forgetfulness of old age!

Middletown, Connecticut[1]
November 1, 1961

Dearest Friends—

Heinrich was very ill. That's why I haven't written. After a bad cold that he probably got from me, he came home with a splitting headache that he'd put up with during a full week of lectures and seminars at Bard. Then his condition grew worse, and after being at a total loss at first (but presuming a tumor), the doctors ran tests on him in the clinic and discovered a congenital aneurysm that was probably present 40 years ago when he was hit on the head. He is still in the hospital, one of the best in the country, and I've managed to see that the head of the neurology department is personally in charge of his case. He's really doing very well. He had no real symptoms, no paralysis, only some paresthesia in his left hand and even that has already disappeared. His improvement is not due to any treatment. His condition improved just as quickly and, for the doctors, unexpectedly, as it had deteriorated. (His sleeping all the time seems to have helped!) The head neurologist reported to us that the arteriogram did not reveal any signs of arteriosclerosis. The blood vessels are those of a much younger man. But still, any arteriosclerosis is more dangerous for him than for other people. The lesion is evident but very small, the clinical improvement very rapid and truly spectacular. The doctor therefore advises against surgery, and very emphatically so. However, some risk remains. He can't say with any certainty what caused the rupture. He feels it was a spasm. Other doctors there, going by the results of the latest research, think the whole episode, including the aneurysm, might have been caused by an infection.

Since he's been feeling halfway decent again, he's been completely unconcerned. I told him the full truth, of course, if for no other reason than to make clear to him that he really had to lie still for the usual three weeks and couldn't just go back to Bard. I also told him that the mortality rate in such cases is 50%, to which his response was: Don't get all worked up. You're forgetting the other 50%. But we have managed to beat a little consciousness of his illness into his head. It was urgently needed, and difficult for the nice Jewish doctors to achieve because they usually deal with vastly more sensitive temperaments.

I forgot to mention that the aneurysm is located in the pia mater, and the case is one of subarachnoid hemorrhage. There don't appear to be any other aneurysms. I could tell some unflattering tales about doctors, but I'll postpone that. The head doctor is absolutely first class and doesn't produce the usual medical blah-blah that really got on my nerves during the critical days.

I've been back here again starting this week, but I go to New York regularly on the weekends. And get reports every day. It's only about two hours to New York. There's nothing I can do there at the moment, and he's not in need of consolation. He has his own room, can read, talks with the doctors, and is fascinated by neurology. On top of that, the nurses are nice and pretty, and he enjoys that. The hospital is the university clinic at Columbia and impeccably run. Very difficult to get a room there, but this time I had no qualms about making use of my so-called connections.

Well, now I want to respond to your September letter, which went unanswered at first because I had a very unpleasant cold. But I'm completely back to normal now.

I've been in touch with Kurt Wolff constantly by mail. He wants Manheim to start immediately with the translation of the second (American) volume. Can we still count on Eckhardt and Cusanus for this volume? Or have you changed your plans? I'd like to know that, and I'd also like to know what the next German volume looks like, how far along it is, and whether we should possibly be putting something else in our second volume.

Heidegger—yes, it is a most irritating story. The tribute has no bearing on it. I was back in touch with him again after it. And I don't think, either, that his wife is involved. That would explain silence or excuses or something similar, but not this open hostility, which he has really never displayed before. My explanation—putting aside for the moment the possibility of some kind of gossip—is that last winter I sent him one of my books, the *Vita Activa*, for the first time. I know that he finds it intolerable that my name appears in public, that I write books, etc. All my life I've pulled the wool over his eyes, so to speak, always acted as if none of that existed and as if I couldn't count to three, unless it was in the interpretation of his own works. Then he was always very pleased when it turned out that I could count to three and sometimes even to four. Then I suddenly felt this deception was becoming just too boring, and so I got a rap on the nose. I was very angry for a moment, but I'm not any longer. I feel instead that I somehow deserved what I got—that is, both for having deceived him and for suddenly having put an end to it.

And now for the political front, which hasn't exactly improved in the last month. Berlin as a UN city is, I'm afraid, out of the question. I don't see any solution at all, unless it is to evacuate the Berliners and build them a new Berlin somewhere between Hannover and Frankfurt. I can't imagine how Berlin's status can be maintained. And as I see it, the simple fact that the Berliners quietly permitted the wall to be built through their city—instead of calling out the fire department and using fire hoses to prevent its construction—shows that they know that, too. From what I hear, Kennedy is somehow not up to dealing with this. He vacillates, forgets, doesn't assume leadership, is more or less a football in the hands of his advisers, some of whom are good and others of whom are far less than good. De Gaulle—there, too, I fear he'll lose out. He puts too much faith in himself and his grand words. But perhaps I'm mistaken. The new atomic explosions have something horribly threatening about them. We will soon start them up again here, and God knows where that will eventually take us. For the time being, it's like a children's game in which each side shows the other how many sticks and stones it has accumulated, and this show of strength takes the place of actual fighting. Whoever turns out to be the first to detonate a thousand-megaton bomb is the winner. I assume that for the first time in Germany so-called illusions are bursting like bubbles, but they weren't even illusions, because nobody believed in them! That reminds me of the time an apparently retarded German student asked me: Don't you think it would be better if we young people were allowed to keep our illusions? That fits the situation perfectly. But then, I don't have anything much good to say about any Germans at all again. They've sent Holthusen[2] here to be director of Goethe House. Now it turns out that this noble soul was in the SS at some point. Then I, idiot that I am, tried to save his skin. But he apparently misinformed me. [. . .]

You'll see from this letter that I'm still in a bit of a tizzy. What I really need is a few hours in your house on Au Street—

Be healthy, and greetings from us both

Your
Hannah

Basel, November 6, 1961

Dear Hannah!

You waited until things looked better before you wrote to us about Heinrich's serious illness. Modern medicine, even when it can't help, is still very good for people like you and us. We want to know what's wrong. You understand, in principle, but you still don't know what really happened: whether the rupture of the aneurysm has produced a scar that will provide better protection than before against further ruptures. Heinrich's spontaneous and wonderful recovery can be explained only by a resorption of the blood and a closing of the rupture.

You had the anatomy of the case clarified for you right away. The site involved lies entirely outside the brain. If there was a recurrence and a hospital was nearby, an operation would be possible if he were in danger. A dreadful option, granted, but still by no means as bad as brain surgery. I would think it will be possible to establish later on whether the aneurysm is still there and is in any way changed.

It's wonderful to read how unconcerned Heinrich is and is making use of this opportunity and experience to learn a little about neurology. I shared his enthusiasm at one time. This field of medicine is, despite all its complexity, remarkably clear. Our knowledge of it is developed to a high degree yet still remains on the edge of the incomprehensible. Looking at microscopic pictures in this field, I always felt the way I do looking at distant galaxies. We are always increasing our knowledge, but in such a way that what is really "behind it all" becomes increasingly inaccessible to us.

You young people, we old folks are all too ready to think, should not be subject to such attacks. What a foolish assumption for old people to make! It never occurred to us that your long silence could have meant you were seriously ill. I thank fate that it made itself felt with no more than a reminder this time. The worry about a tumor—a very logical worry—is now in the past. But despite the favorable course things have taken, I am still eager for further reports. Quiet recuperation and formation of the scar still have to take place.

Your interpretation of Heidegger's behavior is so strange that I would never have considered it if it had not come from you who know him so well. He must have been aware of your books for a long time now because they have been discussed in all the papers, and one has followed on the heels of another. The only thing that is new is that he received a book directly from you—and then such a reaction! The most incredible things may well be possible.

The second volume of *Die grossen Philosophen*: My work plan is, first, to finish my book "Philosophischer Glaube angesichts der Offenbarung," then the second volume. So I can't possibly begin work on it before the spring of 1962. How quickly I'll move forward then I really can't say. I've done extensive preparatory work. But a coherent text—based on selections from what I've already done—remains to be written. As of now, I'm not planning to include Cusanus and Eckhart. We had planned to make the beginning of the second volume the concluding part of the first. This final section is 330 pages long. If the second American volume is to be as long as the first, then a little less than 180 printed German pages have to be added to it. They would come from the second German volume. I may be able to have those 180 pages ready in manuscript by the fall of 1962.—

I too have considered your solution for Berlin (emigration of all Berliners, of West-Berliners, as many as want to, with all their portable goods in an orderly, peaceful way). A centralized settlement in the form of a new Berlin seems impossible to me. The only possibility would be to absorb them throughout the Federal Republic and in the United States and wherever individual Berliners wanted to go and would be accepted. Berliners as a specific German ethnic type would disappear. I still resist that. The question is at what point will the West's willingness to give in become a political and moral catastrophe for the Western world. Somewhere and sometime the question will be: subjugation or the bomb. Subjugation will bring the bomb anyhow, of course; perhaps at a later point in a war between Russia and China. The only way we can spare ourselves from the bomb is by way of the spirit of the Western world. But then we mustn't let things become worse. Giving in to Russia drives the whole world over to Russia's side. We're seeing that very clearly now. All the fine talk, like that of this repulsive Nehru,[1] is just a smoke screen. In reality, all they believe in is power. Their behavior shows that. And so I am—and have been so far—for ridding ourselves of illusions but for maintaining the fact of West Berlin. We have to preserve that minimum of dignity, and without it a free political life cannot endure.

What you write about Kennedy is bad. In the foreseeable future, everything will hinge on a few moments for which the appropriate behavior cannot be calculated in advance.

As on August 13[2] in Berlin. In my view, the Berliners had no authority, but the Western powers could have commissioned the Berlin police to use the fire hoses, as you suggest after the fact. That strikes me as an excellent idea. Everyone was horrified and paralyzed, Kennedy included.

Holthusen is a friend of Piper's. Piper should know about what you've told me.

My regards to Heinrich. I'll write to him soon.

Warmest greetings

Karl

Gertrud will write tomorrow.

November 7, 1961

Dear Hannah!

I left this letter overnight, and in the meantime I've tried to think through further from a medical point of view this danger that you have just put behind you. What one really would like to know the doctors can't tell you. But one has to be prepared for the possibility that something like this could happen again, highly unlikely as that seems to me.

My thoughts: *When* did the hemorrhage stop? That is, *when* did the hemorrhaged blood close the aneurysm? How much blood escaped and how large was the "blood tumor" that caused the pain? The improvement in Heinrich's condition will have come about through the resorption of the blood when the hemorrhaging stopped of its own accord. . . . And so one question leads to another, questions the doctors don't like to hear because it is impossible to provide answers to them.

But now, *if* there is any indication of another hemorrhage, you'll know what to do: Lie down and remain absolutely still, raise the head, avoid any raising of pressure in the blood vessels (pass stool with the aid of enemas), and perhaps use drugs, which are probably better known in America than here (adrenoxyl or other anticoagulants). The hemorrhage Heinrich had certainly did not have to become as severe as it was. It had probably stopped by the time he came under treatment. The quick recovery resulted from the resorption of the blood and hence in the reduction of the pressure. When I think back over this, then the fear we thought we no longer need feel grows all the more. A long period of rest will be essential, on account of the pressure on the brain that he experienced as well as for the sake of the scar, which has to become completely solid.

Warmest greetings to you both!

Karl

461

Middletown, Connecticut
November 16, 1961

Dearest Friends—

I'm writing right away because we have just received the final medical report from the various doctors. Things look rather better than we had expected. The hemorrhage was minimal and was quickly absorbed. The aneurysm is there but is not at all bad. The likelihood of a recurrence is slim if the thing is allowed to heal properly. Everything else—circulation, blood pressure, heart, etc.—in the best of order. It would have been crazy to risk an operation. Heinrich is up and has already been out for a walk, to his great pleasure. He's not the least bit weak despite three weeks in bed. And he doesn't tire easily otherwise either. The head doctor's advice: Live very cautiously for two months and then forget the whole thing. The only thing he has to avoid is any great physical exertion, advice you really don't have to give Heinrich twice, because he has always felt that his ancestors did everything along that line that can be expected from one family. The attack probably followed on a spasm (they really don't know exactly). That seems likely to me because he has suffered from spasms all his life, due to a flaw in his vegetative nervous system. (When he was young, he had diarrhea for six months, and the doctors had given him up for dead. Robert [Gilbert]'s response to that was: If you're going to die anyhow, we might as well take a trip to Italy. Which they did—with the happiest of results.) The doctors will be able to do something about these spasms.

Your letters[1] gave me great, great pleasure. I don't have them here. Heinrich kept them. He just told me the whole story on the telephone, and I am of course much relieved.

Helen Wolff is in New York, and we had a pleasant afternoon together. Kurt Wolff seems to be better. The blood clot (I can't remember the German word at the moment) has partially dissolved by itself, and his pulse is considerably stronger. She showed me the galleys for the first volume, which delighted me no end. At last! I am preparing the second volume for Manheim right now—selecting translations, etc. I told her that we couldn't expect part of the second German volume until next fall at the earliest. We'll have to see. It's hard to get an idea of the length because we're not using the small print in the English edition. I could, of course, start counting words, but I can't quite bring myself to do it. Once we have Manheim's translation we'll see how things look.

Otherwise there really isn't anything to report, because I'm not in the mood for politics, having just read the *Times*. What I would very much be in the mood for is visiting and talking with you. I long for that. And when I read the letters from both of you—with Gertrud's "All flesh is grass, and all the goodliness thereof is as the flower of the field,"[2] which ran through my head over and over again in those difficult days—I realized once again how wonderful it is to have friends with whom one is so completely in tune.

But I have it good here. The college is academically good and the atmosphere very pleasant. A good seminar on Machiavelli that I'm having fun with.

Good-bye and thank you and warmest greetings from

Your Hannah

300   *Karl Jaspers to Heinrich Blücher*

Basel, December 26, 1961

Dear Heinrich Blücher!

Only after the worst was over did Hannah tell us about your grave illness, which was initially so inexplicable. Now it seems clear that after a few months of taking it easy, you'll be able to forget the whole episode. Our fright came after the fact, so to speak. By the time Hannah wrote, the happy ending was so certain that I—being rather slow to catch on—felt only in retrospect the full impact of what you have been through. Your response to Hannah: "You're forgetting the other 50%," was wonderful, but things are the same for you as they are for us: If one partner has to die, he can't be as much at peace as if he were alone. The one who dies second has it easier. Death itself is not such a disturbing prospect, but leaving one's partner alone in a world where only the most intimate companionship can still provide sustenance is another matter. This time your illness was only a memento. How much more precious it makes the time that remains to us!

Your letter of friendship in September is still very much with me. I have read it often and did once again just now. I needn't repeat how much at one we are by virtue of that transcendental ground that gives us both our point of departure and our goals. Instead, let me comment on a difference between us that probably is not one at all: that I was wrong to have given my blessing to a specific government, namely, Adenauer's. You're mistaken in saying I gave my blessing to this government. I gave my blessing only to the foreign policy of the past: unequivocal commitment to the West, recognition of the consequences of reunification actions undertaken with Russia, stalwart resistance to the Social Democrats' nationalistic foolishness, especially in the dreadful plan for Germany[1] of about two years ago. I never gave my blessing to the Adenauer government as a whole. My essay on Adenauer[2] shows that clearly. But in one thing you are right: none of that belongs in the realm of philosophical thought. Perhaps I can defend myself this way: It belongs as little to philosophy as does Plato's approval of Dion's campaign[3] or Kant's glorification of "the Age of Frederick"[4] (which he put in boldface type). But I am, after all, like all of us, first of all a human being of my time and only perhaps a little bit a philosopher. Moreover, the great philosophers were dealing with truly great figures; I, with a rather insignificant one as far as real substance is concerned. And now even Adenauer's foreign policy strikes me as very questionable, as far as one can survey it at all. I think what he is doing now is wrong.

This questionableness lies in your pessimistic assessment of the world situation as a whole. I can't object to what you say. You see things as they are, I think, in both the East and the West, the governing principles, the hypocrisy here, the massive lies there.

All Kennedy has done so far is give speeches—impressive ones, granted—and send excellent communiqués to Russia. But he has not drawn the West together in such a way as to make self-assertion and coexistence logical and honest. It seems utopian now: a common economy of the free world; coexistence, that is, breaking off economic ties to the East (while maintaining free intellectual exchange); special aid to and cooperation with only states and peoples that come together on the basis of agreements and solidarity; no "Peace Corps";[5] no gifts; but decency and openness in the interest of all. Kennedy's foreign policy seems to deal with each situation ad hoc. It seems to lack direction and now, in the Congo,[6] is perhaps as unintelligent as it was in Cuba. The task before America's president seems almost beyond human powers. So far, under his clearly well-meaning leadership, the solidarity of the West has only eroded further. He seems to give his speeches as much in vain as we write our books. Solidarity can be achieved only by reducing those hypocrisies you formulated concisely,

464

meaningfully, and clearly in your letter. There can be no "more" or "less" here. What is required is a complete reversal. We believe this is a possibility if there were a group of politicians and a president who could show the masses, who are no less receptive to the truth than they are to hypocrisy, what they feel, a president who could show them clearly what they only sense darkly, could tell them what they really want, and so could create willing assent by virtue of his credible personality. Charisma would become evident in speeches and actions, in courage and prudence, as the simplicity of the moment informed by a background of eternal truth, which is able to cope with every new moment. This charisma, the nobility of man as such, could become visible in the inner, unified form of a single individual, in whom others can recognize their own hidden potential. Pericles succeeded in this and remains proof of it for all time. His only mistake was that he neither saw nor trained anyone to succeed him. Caesar succeeded in it, and William of Orange. Jan De Witt managed it only halfway (because he lacked insight and thought he could achieve his ends solely by diplomacy and without an army). Cromwell had this quality in a perverted form. Kennedy has come a long way in recognizing truths that can be articulated. In spite of everything, I still place a little hope in him. In what human reality can one place hope at all right now?

I'm becoming more pessimistic regarding Berlin, too. I had thought the freedom of West Berlin could be preserved. And I still think it possible. But the West, divided in its interests as it is, will not be able to preserve that freedom. The Germans themselves are an obstacle to it because the nationalism the Social Democrats (Schumacher[7]) have revived, and that Adenauer has taken on for the sake of votes but against his better judgment, corrupts every reasonable idea. What is needed is abandonment of all German illusions, acquiescence in the existing political freedom of West Berlin, relinquishing all propaganda (the RIAS radio station, etc.) and all espionage based in Berlin, development of a flourishing economy and an intellectual life under a municipal constitution such as the world has never seen before: completely dependent in foreign policy on the Allies, who want this freedom, no autonomous foreign policy, proscription of any step in that direction; but free newspapers, without censorship; no army of its own, hence no obligatory military service—the only people on earth who need not and may not put on a uniform, except in the theater—eradication of the military spirit; limitation on immigration (as in Monaco today, because of tax benefits; there—that is, in Berlin—to escape from military service in one's own country); a model of peaceful life, the opportunity to be a glowing example of this for the world. There is, of course, the dreadful danger that it would become a morass of degeneracy, with all kinds of corruption, of mere hedonism carried to extremes. It would represent a chance for a free life, governed by the mind, that would act like a magnet, attracting the spirit to this place from wherever German is spoken. If this chance were wasted for the sake of vulgar advantages, then the whole venture would not be worthwhile anymore and could be abandoned politically, too. The Berliners could create a model for a world in which disarmament can take place someday. The world will have to live for other than military reasons, but no less heroic ones than existed during the era of wars, in which history began and which has continued to the present. I like to fantasize in these directions, and I even think you could too and in a very different way, while Hannah smiled a friendly smile at these German men, or children? [. . .] If all this is nonsense, then the best thing for all West Berliners would be a guarantee of departing freely with all their movable property within two years. There would be no pressure; the choice would be a free one for each individual to make—if they would be allowed to move to the Federal Republic and to other countries.

That things will probably work out differently—namely, the pretense of freedom will slowly be destroyed by the Russians—I needn't say. Foot-dragging and halfheartedness are our downfall here. At some point, one reaches the either-or. No one wants to run any risk or seize an opportunity.

Well, enough of this discussion, which we could carry on for days if we were together.

You will not have your traditional New Year's Eve party. That is probably good, not only out of regard for Hannah's strength but also as a symbol that we can't attempt anything on the grand scale anymore but—for the time being, and perhaps altogether—only on a small personal scale.

For both of you, a good New Year, health, pleasure in your work, and warmest greetings from Gertrud

Your Karl

I'm sorry to say that Hannah will have to read this to you! I don't want to burden Gertrud with copying this today, Christmas, when she is writing letters herself.

Saturday, December 30, 1961

Dear, dear Friends—

I had just written down the date when your good, long letter to Heinrich arrived. He was able to read it without any help from me. He will reply himself. He is doing very well. The doctor discharged him, and we have already celebrated and drunk to the occasion several times. At first he tired more easily than usual, but in recent weeks that has passed entirely. Now he has vacation until mid-February, and I'm very happy about that.

In the meantime, the Eichmann verdict has been reached, and I've just gotten all the material from Jerusalem. I'll start writing in the coming weeks, but the verdict is thoroughly disappointing. Instead of confessing that one has to mete out justice even when the law leaves one in the lurch, they've presented things in such a way that they may just pass muster legally but don't reflect the truth at all. Eichmann's concluding statement is not unsympathetic, without any self-aggrandizement. Only Mr. Servatius remains outrageous. In Jerusalem, he said this was the fairest trial he had ever seen, and then at some congress in Germany, he said the only criminal act connected with this trial was Eichmann's kidnapping from Argentina. But I haven't formed a final judgment yet; I haven't been able to look at the material carefully yet.

For today I'm writing only to be in time for New Year's. We all know what we wish ourselves, and that requires no repetition. Instead, I'd like to ask a question. The revolution book is almost finished, and I think it is quite good, at least in passages. What I feel I have been able to do is to clarify certain basic facts about America that people in Europe know very little about. I would very much like to dedicate the book to you both. Is that all right with you? There's no hurry. You can take your time to think about it.

In the back of my mind, I keep thinking about your suggestions for Berlin. I think they are highly realistic and could well be carried through, but the initiative for them would have to come from Germany, and I see absolutely no possibility of that happening. Reuter[1] would have been the only man with whom one could even have discussed such things. (Absolutely right! Heinrich)[2]

By the way—as regards the hundred German portraits[3]—with Buber in the lead—Heinrich is very displeased to see us in the same company with Strauss[4] and Krupp. The picture of you is wonderful. (I'll send you soon the pictures I took when we were with you. A few turned out very well.)

I've met a philosophy professor at Wesleyan by the name of Glenn Gray,[5] who is very much influenced by you, appears to have heard you lecture, and is a truly outstanding person. We're neighbors there and drink our aperitif together in the evening and talk about philosophy in general and Jaspers' philosophy in particular. I'm taking the "Heidelberger Erinnerungen"[6] to him so that he can get a somewhat more direct impression. He is married to a German woman and speaks excellent German.

Warmest greetings
Your
Hannah

302   Karl Jaspers to Hannah Arendt

Basel, January 5, 1962

Dear Hannah!

Your letter just arrived. Heinrich's illness, which seemed so ominous at first, is behind him. Good that he still has some vacation time to rest.

You want to dedicate your new book to both of us.[1] That requires no lengthy deliberation. It is right and meet that you take both of us as one. Who would have thought of it? Only you, and I am happy about it. What your gesture also expresses is not just acknowledgment of an intellectual debt, which would be inappropriate for you and us in any case, but a human bond that dares to show itself publicly.

Gertrud joins me in thanking you. She is not in good spirits—these depressions have plagued her periodically from her youth, a heavy burden. I hope it will be better soon—and for this reason she is pleased more "in potentia."

Gertrud's brother Otto[2] in Israel died recently. He was operated on for Ca [carcinoma] two years ago. This fall the metastases appeared. His brothers and his wife[3] cheered him every day, displaying a wonderful family solidarity. The doctor in charge of his case was superb. I think only Jewish doctors are like that: utterly realistic and competent and human at every moment. One probably receives better treatment in Israel than here. Gertrud was very fond of this brother; she raised him and Fritz like a mother and was constantly attentive to them ever since. Otto was not particularly gifted for life in the world, but a pure soul, always tactful, absolutely reliable, and a skeptic and pessimist. He was the only one of all the siblings who thought very little of religion. In Tel Aviv he won the affection of many people. More than a hundred attended his funeral, and some of the tributes people made following his death were uncommonly warm. Gertrud is sad but at the same time relieved that he was spared dreadful physical pain except in brief episodes. He visited two years ago and was very close to us.

There seems to be something new on the political scene. The Russian superbombs appear to have been so-called clean bombs,[4] which do not contaminate with radioactivity. The massive destruction of countries and continents can be carried out *without* killing all of humankind. Russia can destroy Europe with a few bombs and occupy it immediately—without worrying about radioactivity. If America does not have these bombs or does not have them in sufficient numbers, that would be very bad. Does Kennedy's hesitation to continue testing in the atmosphere mean that he has no "clean bombs"?

When I read the reasoning behind the Eichmann verdict my reaction was the same as yours: confusion on the part of the judges, who were able to distinguish between "natural law" and "positive law" in theory but failed to do so in practice. The seriousness of the trial is lost from sight because the political aspect of it was not taken into consideration. The Israeli law of 1950 or '51 is an act of political sovereignty, by which the law was established. Law among nations, natural law, cannot be created this way; and international law on the basis of treaties does not exist. In view of this, my interview[5] seems to me not to have made its point. Landau didn't read it or didn't understand it. The major role of English law, which is invoked so often, is understandable. But first of all it is law for the English under English jurisdiction; second, the English have created this marvelous phenomenon over the centuries: the method of precedents instead of codification, the vitality of creating law on the basis of a natural law that is in constant need of refor- mulation, the political struggle of great jurists to achieve justice. That doesn't exist anywhere else. One cannot use it as a point of reference. Today's situation requires a new mode of legal thinking that remains in touch with ancient law. This new mode could have found expression in the Eichmann trial, but it did not. Therefore, the trial remained only a sensation, not a real event. The Israeli judges were decent and very intelligent but without greatness and without philosophy. A pity!

Warmest greetings for Heinrich and from Gertrud

Your Karl

303 *Hannah Arendt to Gertrud and Karl Jaspers*

February 19, 1962

Dear, dear Friends—

This is an overdue letter of thanks for your letters[1] and a birthday letter for you both. I returned from a lecture tour a few days ago with the flu and stupidly let the doctor give me antibiotics for it, and now I'm having one of these allergic reactions which seem more and more common. It is really amazing how everything in nature's economy has adjusted to our inventions and is now fighting against them. One of the really uncanny phenomena!

I shared your sadness over your brother's death (and was very happy to have the good news about your sister-in-law,[2] whom I know and like so much). In human terms, not in "existential" ones, it really seems to be the case that one's own death, assuming that one is not affected by illness in youth, is prepared for by the deaths of others that belong to one, as if the world gradually dies away from us, at least that part of the world that we call our own.

Heinrich is back at Bard, truly his old self again. A week ago he received word of his restitution payment. They allowed him the highest possible amount for professional damages, which was very decent of them considering that he has had a normal job for so long now. At first he hadn't wanted to apply for anything, because it just didn't suit him, but now he is really very pleased that we (my lawyer,[3] who is a friend from my youth, and I) forced him, as it were. It is nice to get an outright gift once in a while.

Except for the technical end of it, the revolution book is finished, and I am glad that you will accept the dedication. But I have to enter a protest: An acknowledgment of an intellectual debt is involved as well, one that is so closely linked with the human bond that one can't really say anymore and doesn't care to say where the one begins and the other ends. And this, too, it seems to me, has been so for as long as I can remember. By the by, the first volume of *Die grossen Phi-*

losophen will come out in March. They are working very quickly and precisely there. I'm very pleased.

Discussion of the possibility of war has broken out in full force here with student demonstrations in front of the White House and all sorts of goings-on. It has to be said for Kennedy that he sent coffee out to the students who were demonstrating against him—against the planned resumption of tests and the shelter business,[4] which really does seem to be dreadful nonsense—because the weather was so bad. Unlikely that Adenauer would have managed a gesture like that. My lecture tour to a number of small universities and colleges in the Midwest was very interesting and could have been very enjoyable if I hadn't had a fever. As it was, I was happy to be home again. One finds "them that are quiet in the land" everywhere, and one comes home with a somewhat better view of America. You find a solid substance there that has not been eroded away by the widespread pursuit of amusement and pleasure. There are German Jews wherever you go. You see them instantly everywhere. They are clearly recognizable and yet are completely accepted. There is no question, at least not in other people's minds, that they belong to the society.

All best wishes for the year and warmest greetings

Your
Hannah

304 Karl Jaspers to Hannah Arendt

Basel, March 18, 1962

Dear Hannah!

The first volume of *Die grossen Philosophen*[1] has just arrived . . . from Harcourt, Brace. Kurt Wolff sent me a copy a few weeks ago. Now I can see once again the trouble and care you have taken with this book: abridgment, bibliography, and, what I of course cannot see, your checking of the translation. I thank you very much. It was no small task. Will the book draw American readers now? The great initial success of the "Atombombe" quickly subsided; the second wave of interest that follows only after the initial response to a book has presumably not come to pass. The production of this book is also first-rate. After the years of waiting, the printing was finally done with astonishing speed. I am grateful to the publishing house, with which I have had no dealings before this, but I have not written to them because Kurt Wolff is the actual publisher. Manasse[2] (in Durham) wrote that he found the translation excellent [. . .].

I'm working on my book.[3] The article in the Festschrift for Heinrich Barth[4] was premature, not finished, and in large part badly written as well. I succumbed to the pressure of the deadline back then. It has become a new book. Now I am at it every day and don't want to do anything else until I'm finished with it, by the end of May or June, I hope. As I am writing it, I often think of you both. Heinrich's brief sentence in his letter about our shared outlook (. . . transcendence . . .) is a constant source of encouragement.[5] Your hesitation in words and your reluctance to speak of such things set the necessary question marks but do not discourage me. I know as little as you, but it seems to me not unimportant how our ignorance is expressed and how what is contained in it finds expression. —In this book, I run up and down the ladder from drastic realism to that rarefied atmosphere where one has to draw breath with care. I don't know finally what I think of it all. But I am totally absorbed by it in any case, and Gertrud joins me in the work, though with her customary caution, sometimes amiably putting up with me, at other times quite satisfied. We are both living in this project. It determines the course of our days.

It was just announced on the radio that an armistice has been signed for Algeria. The dreadful predictions of what will happen now may not, I think, prove correct. Preparations have been made to deal with the eventualities that have been discussed at such length. There will not, of course, be instant peace and harmony. If De Gaulle succeeds in this, he will emerge as a great statesman and not merely as a larger-than-life figure. He has reportedly received every officer, from the rank of colonel up, to discuss the situation personally with each one, the necessity for this measure, and its goals. The intellectuals are spreading pessimism. I hope they'll be wrong this time.

Warmest greetings to you both

Your Karl

305 *Karl Jaspers to Hannah Arendt*

Basel, March 27, 1962

Dear Hannah!

Today's report from Frau Beradt brought us, along with news of your accident,[1] peace of mind as well. But Gertrud and I were still shaken by it. The reality of this serious accident was present to us, the borderline of life so close that it seemed for a moment as if darkness were descending on the world. But Hannah is still alive! She raises her head from the abyss and declares, although injured everywhere, that the whole business has been much exaggerated. How good for Heinrich and for us that you are still alive! May your battered body recover quickly. After such an event, it is like a miracle.

We will hear from Heinrich, I assume, how things are going. You cannot and ought not write. It was good of you to think of us and see that we were informed by someone close to you rather than left to learn of this from the newspaper!

Warmest greetings and wishes for you both
Your Karl[2]

306 Hannah Arendt to Gertrud and Karl Jaspers

March 31, 1962

Dearest Friends—

When I received your telegram I reproached myself for asking Lotte [Charlotte Beradt] to tell you the news. But with this damned press and publicity you can never know. I came home from the hospital yesterday and found your letter first thing. Great glee. And now I'll quickly tell you everything. Heinrich has written in the meantime.

The accident, which blocked all traffic for hours, was caused by a truck that rammed into my taxi. I didn't see it because I was reading, and I was instantly unconscious. Ergo: concussion with head lacerations, but no skull fracture, no broken nose, no broken jaw. My face, which is already quite normal again by now, was more or less black all over at first. On top of that, nine broken ribs and a cracked wrist—but it doesn't bother me when I'm typing, which I'm trying out right now. The brusque young surgeon who took charge of me right away said straight off—It looks pretty terrible, but there probably isn't anything seriously wrong. And he turned out to be right. I had to have a blood transfusion. We decided a second wasn't necessary. I'd rather eat steak. One eye took something of a beating, but the injury seems to have been only external. I can see and read as well as ever. No brain hemorrhage and no internal bleeding. Some abrasions, too, not serious. The pain was never unbearable, and I took codeine for only two nights. I crawled out of bed on the third day to see how

I could manage on my legs, with the result that I was neither dizzy nor weak, and the doctor let me get up, with due caution. From then on, everything was fine—no complications of any kind and an amazingly rapid healing that surprised even my brusque surgeon. They discharged me yesterday, among other reasons because I would have run away on them if they hadn't. The hospital, although medically very good, was a regular pigpen as far as the administration and the nurses were concerned, and, in addition, insanely expensive. Here at home I have my good Esther, who can take care of the household for me, and in a pinch I could do it myself. But I'm not supposed to yet. I'm being altogether reasonable. I'm not working yet, I go for walks, read. I'll go to the movies and take it very easy for a week.

As far as lasting damage is concerned, I'm, of course, primarily concerned about my appearance. At first I looked like a Picasso that turned out wrong. But that's over, and now I just glow in all the colors of the rainbow and have to wear a kerchief because of the scalp wounds (30 stitches) and my half-shorn head. I have a scar on my forehead and a small one over one eye. When I go out, I put on a black veil and pretend that I'm Arabian or a heavily veiled lady. Then, too, I lost a tooth, which doesn't exactly add to my beauty. All that will presumably be brought more or less under control in a few weeks. A detached retina and other things are still possibilities, but not likely.

Having caused you anxiety at first, I'm writing in such great detail now to reassure you. And with a light heart as well, because I'm really happy to be alive. In the first moment after I regained consciousness and quickly realized what had happened, it seemed to me for a second as if my life was in my own hands. I was completely calm; dying seemed quite natural to me, by no means a tragedy, or something to get worked up about. But at the same time I said to myself, if I can manage it decently, I'd really very much like to stay in this world. Then I tried my limbs out and found that I wasn't paralyzed. And then I sat back quietly and let everything take its course, didn't give Heinrich's address so that he wouldn't be notified by the police, had someone call Frau Beradt—I knew her number by heart—had her cancel all my appointments, and that was that.

I was very relieved to have the good news about Erna.[1] Give her my warmest regards. The advance sale of *Die grossen Philosophen* is astonishing. It just shows what this publisher can do. I'll close now. I still have to write to Annchen [Anne Weil], who was very worried, too, and a line to Mary [McCarthy], an American friend, who, unfortunately, saw me on the first day and burst into tears at the sight. She is in France now.

I keep thinking about your one sentence . . . "as if darkness were descending on the world," and I thank you and can't forget it.

Your
Hannah

By the way, I saw Jeanne Hersch, had a very nice evening with her.

307 *Hannah Arendt to Karl Jaspers*

April 1, 1962

Lieber Verehrtester—

Just read the *New York Times Book Review* with Frankel's review.[1] It couldn't have been better, and I'd almost be willing to say that it has launched the book. All the more so because Helen Wolff is very clever at exploiting things like this to the full. Heinrich and I raised our voices in a little duet of triumph. I'm all the more pleased because the reviewer and I banged heads together in a public discussion a few years ago, and I was a bit rough on him. But he didn't take it out on you. You really can depend on the Anglo-Saxon tradition in things like this.

It is nice to hear from Gertrud how involved you both are with your work.[2] I hope Erna's illness and absence aren't causing you too much trouble.[3] She'll be back soon.

Things continue to go well with me, every day a little better.

All best wishes
Your
Hannah

308 *Karl Jaspers to Hannah Arendt*

April 4, 1962

Dear Hannah!

After one of her operations, I think it was in 1914, Gertrud said, when we were all happy to know that the critical phase after the operation was past: "You all can celebrate, but write to Prenzlau[1] that I'm in terrible pain and feel utterly wretched." I think of that when you make light of your situation and say "every day a little better."

475

Is there a difference there? In jest: Jews and Greeks complain bitterly and aren't ashamed of it—Romans and Germans and uncivilized peoples do just the opposite. Do you and Heinrich and I belong to the wrong side in this point, to our own detriment?

What a pleasure it was for me to have your news about the book[2] and the pleasure you took in its prospects. I'm very encouraged and feel a new and stronger desire to work on the second volume, which I expect to attack again in August. I hope I'll quickly make progress, because I'm well along in my preparatory work and have already written many pages, though not yet in publishable form. A new assistant[3] will be coming to visit any minute, and I will be giving him work connected with this project.

Kurt Wolff wrote me that 3,000 copies of the book had already been ordered before publication, and today I heard from him that a book club will pick the book up in the fall, which will bring me $1,600 and you 400. I think that's wonderful, especially because of the wider distribution it means. Money we all have enough of for the moment. The boom in the world economy is washing up a little extra for us here on the edges, too.

My thanks to Heinrich for his letter.[4] My best to you both, and my special wishes for further quick recovery to you—the fright comes back to haunt me again and again: you were both on the edge of the abyss this year.

Warmly

Your Karl

309   Karl Jaspers to Hannah Arendt

April 5, 1962

Dear Hannah!

Your letter of March 31 with your report just arrived today. The ones you and Heinrich wrote later arrived earlier. Only now do I see the whole picture clearly. Once again it strikes me as a miracle. So many injuries and not one of them affected a vital function. I would dismiss the faint possibility of a detached retina. Without symptoms, that strikes me as medically unlikely. So all that remains is your concern for your beauty. I share that. But I suspect that your thick hair will cover any scars on your head. Only the one over the eye will remain. Is it large? If it is small and decorative rather than jagged in form, it can actually heighten beauty. The tooth can be replaced. Dentists can work magic. That you must remain beautiful I take as given, and you will remain so. Ultimately, your beauty will radiate under any conditions. It lies primarily in your movements and your glance and your expression. The course this terrifying event has taken could make one believe there is something indestructible in you. The devil dares only to scratch you but not to penetrate to your core. It's good that you are following the reasonable path of giving your body some rest for a long period. That is essential not only for the full healing of your injuries but also for recovery from the shock. The body demands that it be treated kindly; then it is willing to serve us and identify with us. If we treat it like a slave, it rebels.

May all continue to go well!
Warmly
Your Karl

310 *Karl Jaspers to Hannah Arendt*

Basel, July 2, 1962

Dear Hannah!

Jeanne Hersch and Helen Wolff brought greetings from you and told me how spry you are. The turban looks good on you. They couldn't report anything about the scar on your forehead because the turban hides it. The report was rather thin because they told me nothing about the content of their conversations with you.

All I want to do is send you a greeting before we go to Heidelberg for three weeks. My manuscript[1] has been sent to the publisher. I hope to get the galleys while I'm still in Heidelberg. Möhrle is very well; she is very much looking forward to Tonbach.[2]

I've been "retired" for a full year now. It is delightful. But I vacillate between presumptuousness and a moderation befitting old age. The former keeps tempting me to take on this project and that instead of focusing exclusively on *Die grossen Philosophen*. For example, a lecture for the Association of Swiss Bankers, which will celebrate its fiftieth anniversary in October.[3] Now of course I'm a bit worried about what I can and should say to these gentlemen. As a title, I've suggested "Freedom and Fate in the Economy." For the time being I've passed up the chance to write an essay on the Berlin question. I feel increasingly that I no longer have anyone's ear. Perhaps that's a consequence of not lecturing at the university anymore. German politicians can drive one into a rage. That the CDU still supports Adenauer with a large majority is more the fault of this society than it is of Adenauer himself.[4] It has always been thus.

You will be going on vacation soon. I wish you both pleasant weeks and contemplative work.

Warmly
Your Karl

311   Hannah Arendt to Karl Jaspers

Palenville, [July/August 1962][1]

Lieber Verehrtester—

Your letter arrived just as we were leaving to come here, and I wanted to write immediately to send you a word of greeting in Heidelberg. For months now I've been totally absorbed by the Eichmann business. There's no thought of articles anymore. What I have to see to now is that the book doesn't get too long. If I've spent more or less the whole day sitting at the typewriter, I find it difficult to summon up energy for anything after that. So now I am sending this to Basel because according to my reckoning your three weeks are up. I am very much ashamed of myself! How are things? Are you working on galleys now? That's such a dreadful business. I'll soon have to face it with the revolution book.

Things are going very well for us here where we know every tree and every stone and each of the many waterfalls. We're sitting in our old bungalow and are both working diligently. But we go for walks, too, and I swim every day. Heinrich will go to New York next week to spend a week there doing all kinds of things, but then he will come back here for another week or two. He is in excellent health, but I still prefer not to see him in the New York heat, although our apartment is on the cool side. I am in fine fettle, and I've dispensed with the turban now that my hair has grown back in so well. The scar on my forehead can be seen only with difficulty at the moment because I'm very deeply tanned. But it isn't otherwise disfiguring either—except, of course, for the insurance companies, which I hope to milk for a small fortune and so make this whole business worthwhile. Really, "the devil only scratched."

Yes, Adenauer and Germany as a whole, where they are finally, after the Eichmann trial, slowly going about getting rid of the worst people. The incredibly lenient sentences are a bad sign. For 6,500 gassed Jews one gets, I think, three years and six months, or something like that. We've seen all that before—when the Feme murderers[2] weren't punished. This so-called republic is really like the last one. And in the long run, economic growth will not help it get around these political matters. The stock-market crash[3] here hasn't done much yet to change the mood, which is astonishing because the losses involved are huge. Only people who understand something about it are worried. For the rest, lots of people tighten their belts but without complaint. On the whole, people take such losses the way they would losses in gambling, which is what they are.

I met Karl Barth here at some official lunch, and because I was his partner at table we had a chance to talk. The publicity circus had made an obvious impression on him. He said he regretted it very much that he saw so little of you in Basel. And why didn't I visit him when I was there. Mentally, though not physically, he struck me as being very old. But I didn't find him unpleasant.

Now I'd quickly like to sketch out my plans. In the fall the first thing I have to do is go to Chicago for two weeks, which I had to cancel because of the accident. After that, like last year, I'll go to Wesleyan for the semester. I've taken on too many lectures, even though they are nearby, and I'm a bit worried about my work schedule. In the spring Heinrich has a sabbatical, only one semester, but that still gives him about nine months of vacation. We're planning to go to Europe in February, first Basel, and then take a trip to Sicily and Greece. I hardly dare mention these plans for fear something will interfere with them. Not only does the "Eichmann" have to be done by then, but also the "Revolution" translated into German and the proofs for the English edition of it read. I have a great yearning for a real break from work, though I can't deny that I'm enjoying the Eichmann business. If I could stay here on into the fall without a telephone and without the household, I could manage it all easily. But the circumstances just aren't so.

Warmest greetings to you both—

Your
Hannah

New York, September 17, 1962

Dearest Friends—

I'm shocked to see how long I've left Gertrud's letter[1] unanswered. We came back to New York at the end of August. Heinrich has been back at the college since early September (completely recovered and without any fatigue despite a great deal of work), and I have finished the "Eichmann." It has become a book, but *The New Yorker*, which is extremely enthusiastic about it, wants to try to print the whole thing—which would be very nice financially, for my plans to use my head in a different way to make money will apparently come to naught. Insurance companies pay really high sums only for permanent injuries, and I don't have any to show.

First I'd like to know about your heart. Is it a coronary sclerosis? The phrase "back at my desk again" was very reassuring. We'll have to see about when we can get together again. Heinrich hasn't been wanting to leave here until March. I've thought that maybe we could turn up for the festivities.[2] I could, of course, come alone and help Erna with all the doings. I hadn't thought of a long visit on that occasion. We'll postpone that, if you want to and can have us at all, for our return trip. I can't say yet when that will be. We want to wander around for several months. It's a long way, and we're not bound by any dates. Heinrich, who doesn't like flying at all, wants to go by boat. The southern route with an Italian steamer would make most sense.

Now the main reason for my writing: I've just torn the whole place apart looking for your radio interview before the Eichmann trial,[3] the one that also appeared in *Der Monat*. I'm in desperate need of it for an epilogue to the book. Could you send it to me? I've lost it, or somebody has made off with it. It can't be found.

I'm eagerly looking forward to the *Offenbarungsglauben*. When will it appear? Manheim is already translating the second volume of *Die grossen Philosophen*. I'll have two more weeks of peace here, but then things will get underway in earnest, and I'm dreading it a little. First, to Chicago for two weeks, then to Wesleyan again, where I want to do a seminar on "Nicomachean Ethics." I'm looking forward to that, but unfortunately I'll have to fit a great many lectures in between because I had to cancel everything in the spring. And on top of that there are the galleys for "Revolution" and "Eichmann." And I still have to finish putting "Revolution" into German before we go on our trip. If I should turn up at your place before the trip, there probably won't be anything left of me but the buttonholes.

I'd like to know what you thought about the meeting of De Gaulle and Adenauer.[4] I didn't like it.

All my best and warmest wishes

Your

Hannah

313   Karl Jaspers to Hannah Arendt

Basel, October 25, 1962

Dear Hannah!

I've been meaning to write you for a long time. What has prompted me today is the minor mix-up that Kurt Wolff has caused. I had told him that Nanda Anshen has the moral right to my new book.[1] However, I thought it likely that its great length would be an obstacle for her, as it presumably would for Kurt Wolff. He wanted to see the galleys anyway, and I had no objections to that. In the meantime, Nanda Anshen had let me know that the length of the book was not a problem for her. And I passed that on to Kurt Wolff, too. Last week I wrote to Nanda Anshen, sending her a draft contract (which I improved upon in a second draft), and I asked Piper to send her the book by airmail. It's too early for me to have a reply from her yet. She has, of course, clear and uncontested right of first refusal. A letter from Kurt Wolff today seems to suggest that he has forgotten all that. He has sent you the galleys (please wait for the book, which must be on the way to you from Piper—and then let it lie for a while—there's no need for you to interrupt your work), why I do not know. I just received copies from Piper today myself. Things move slowly. The official publication date was last week. The contract with Nanda Anshen's publisher is short. She told me she was willing to accept this kind of contract and do without the long, printed form. She was very agreeable to all this in your presence here in Basel. So that would obviate our earlier agreement that you would draft the contract with her. I hope that I will not have to involve you in this and impose on you again.

Kurt Wolff was forgetful, too—why shouldn't he be? I am, too! Age!—about the second volume of *Die grossen Philosophen*. I told him a long time ago that I would not be sending Eckhart and Cusanus but the beginning of the second German volume. With that I have satisfied a request he has made repeatedly. I'm working on the Cusanus and *hope* to have it finished by the end of December. That would fill out the second American volume adequately. The Cusanus can then come out later in German. For the time being, we'll have to do without Eckhart. The material I've gathered so far isn't sufficient.

Nanda Anshen wrote me, by the way, that Ashton is willing to translate my new book. That would be wonderful. But I'm afraid that nothing will come of all this. The book is not, it seems to me, of a style that will appeal in America. But enough of this!

You asked a while ago what I thought of the Adenauer–De Gaulle performance. It has turned out to be of no significance. At the time, I was simply irritated by it. German-French friendship, as a community of interests, has long been taken for granted; it may do to stress it with a ceremony. That seems to me to be De Gaulle's style of propaganda. But to tie in with that a pulling-away from England and to stress, not just Europe, but continental Europe,[2] and on top of that the special bond between Germany and France, seemed to me a bad sign, a politically stupid move. I was outraged. But, as I said, the whole thing is of no significance. Gertrud shared my opinion.

What are you thinking now? Since Tuesday everything has changed.[3] It seems to me like the crossing of the Rubicon. A halt to Russian advance had to be called somewhere. Kennedy seems to me to have put it simply and correctly: Waiting involves a greater risk now than acting. He seems to have the American people behind him. The moment, it seems, is ripe. And South America concurs. I am afraid, of course, but satisfied with the political mood. This time I have not yet seen any maladroitness on Kennedy's part; rather, a remarkable political finesse, shored up by the seriousness of which Anglo-Saxons are capable.

I'm bitterly disappointed by European reactions. People make jokes, are superciliously clever, talk about details. A seriousness is lacking here that senses this is an an all-or-nothing venture and that everyone has to be behind it. The FAZ apparently lacks the capacity to comprehend such an event. On the first day, all it carried was a report, not a lead story, as if there were nothing special about this, and had not a word of comment. A total failure on the part of that journalist. On the second, there was one small article by Dechamps,[4] which was good. There has still not been an overall orientation commensurate with the importance of the situation, no reflection on its meaning.

People in Germany are calm, as if nothing significant had occurred. No sign of summoning up the Western world's disposition for clarity. Adenauer expressed his support immediately and without reservation. Once again I can sing his praises. But even he has not spoken a word of any weight.

It is no excuse for people to say: America is reaping now what it sowed with its abandonment of Europe from the Suez crisis to its pressure on Holland over the New Guinea question[5] and with its continuing support for Nasser.[6] The resentment in England is apparently great. The important thing today is to see that *these* American interests are also European interests. America's lack of solidarity with Europe was bad (but the help it rendered Europe in other things far outweighed that). For good or for ill, and despite past insults to them, the small nations have to show absolute solidarity with the major power, the USA, which is their only shield and on which their own existence depends.

It saddens me that everything appears so "petty" and is carried on in that spirit. If, as I hope, the seemingly impossible should come about: the halting of the Russians, dismantling of military installations in Cuba, and the withdrawal of the 5,000 technicians and military personnel in Cuba, then, I fear, a morally wretched condition will follow. I am relying on Kennedy, who at this moment is assuming real stature in word and deed. Only in him do I see real seriousness. But his most difficult tasks lie before him. And he seems to know that.

Today came the news that the Russian ships have turned back. There will be no attempt to break the blockade (Kennedy seems to me to be quite right, by the way, in saying "quarantine," because "blockade" is correct only when heavy weapons are involved). I hope that report will be confirmed. That would be a first step.

Kennedy's statement was superb: Freedom is worth the highest price, and we Americans have always been prepared to pay that price. That is the proper attitude of determination together with clear understanding.

Our first concern is for you if the end of the world is imminent. There will be no place to hide, of course, but you are so near the danger. Will the palaces of the UN afford New York some protection? But I have to confess that I am not yet counting on disaster. As an observer, who has no responsibility to assume, one can see hopeful opportunities: Khrushchev knows what he can expect. A series of hostile actions between the USA and Russia is conceivable in the course of negotiations. But both sides know that such actions cannot exceed certain narrow limits. I would think, hypothetically, that if America took Cuba, Russia would not start an atomic war. If Russia took Berlin, America would not start an atomic war. If Russia "attacked Europe on a broad front," America would respond with atomic war. Russia would behave similarly if America were ever capable of liberating the satellite states with European and its own troops.

One can go on endlessly with this back and forth.

If you care to, send us word of your mood.

Warmest greetings to you both from us both

Your Karl

314 *Hannah Arendt to Karl Jaspers*

Middletown, October 29, 1962

Lieber Verehrtester—

Your letter arrived just a half hour before Nanda's visit. She came armed with both contracts, of which of course she could not make head or tail. Her German isn't up to the task, not to mention her other capabilities. For the time being I've done as you suggested—that is, not gotten myself mixed up in this at all and told her she should go to Harper with the right contract and then see what comes of that. Personally, I don't think you'll get what you've asked for, but if you do, that would be nice. Their lawyers will probably stick their noses into this, and in that case we may have to come back to the suggestion I made earlier. The length of the manuscript is no problem at all. The copy Piper is sending has not arrived yet. Kurt Wolff, in his confusion, sent me the galleys, and Heinrich took them because I wasn't home anyhow. And now Nanda is asking for the book because she wants to send it to Ashton right away. Still another problem with the contract: As best I can recall, Nanda as editor is somehow entitled to a share, which you have not taken into account. Part of the reason why she says yes and amen to everything is that she doesn't understand at all what's going on. The other part is that she wouldn't know how to respond if she did. But in other respects she is a thoroughly fine and decent person. [. . .]

In the meantime, the Cuba crisis has ended happily. I have to confess that I didn't have the slightest worry this time. That's how sure I was that it would not come to war. I did think, however, that it could take weeks or months before this outcome could be achieved, namely, that the Russians would, first, send no more ships, then stop building installations in Cuba, and, finally, dismantle everything. This seems to be the new style in diplomacy, and we'll have to get used to it. It can always go wrong, too, but perhaps it won't as long as Khrushchev is at the helm. We have every reason to be satisfied with Kennedy, especially for his persistent refusal to invade as long as another possibility remained. His argument—it is unseemly for a major power to attack such a small country. Very reasonable. But this success does not mean in the least that all has been won. The important thing for America to do now is exploit this situation for a fundamental reorientation of its policy toward Latin America. This is its first real opportunity. It's very important, too, that Mr. Castro[1] has received a lesson in the reliability of his Russian allies, that is, that they are not conducting a policy of world revolution but simply Russian foreign policy. Very interesting and quite dangerous in the long run was a brief report today of enthusiastic demonstrations of solidarity for Cuba on the part of the Chinese.

The Cuba affair seems to me almost proof that if the Berliners had really just called in the fire department when the wall was built, they could have washed the whole thing away without much ado. That wouldn't have solved the problem of Berlin, but it would have been an important move nonetheless. It is exasperating to see with what equanimity the Germans obey, especially when they obey Herr Ulbricht,[2] of all people, the last Stalinist, who is where he is only because the Russians want to punish the Germans. The Germans just can't seem to understand that politics and the nursery are not the same. In politics, obedience to and support for a regime are one and the same thing. I just saw a letter from a young and extremely gifted jurist,[3] who had been offered an assistant professorship here, even though he is only 23 or 24, and who had gone back to Germany to try living there on the consideration that it was perhaps not right to leave one's "fatherland" in the lurch. He wrote that he is already packing his bags to return here. The minister for refugee affairs in Niedersachsen, a Mr. Schellhaus,[4] demanded in public that anyone who argued for recognition of the Oder-Neisse Line should be prosecuted in criminal court for high treason. When *Die Welt* criticized him, outraged readers wrote in that the minister should not be denied his right of free speech. The young man added: "Defenders of the oppressed can always be found in Germany."

I'm in Middletown again for the fall semester, just as I was last year, and have been here for two weeks now. The first two weeks of the semester I was in Chicago, where I read four times for two hours each from my revolution manuscript and met with truly astonishing success. I've read proofs for it now, and I'm in the process of writing the last chapter of "Eichmann." And along with all that is my seminar on "Nicomachean Ethics" with very nice, alert young men. A lot to do, but I'm enjoying all of it, and I'm not tiring easily. I always have some German students, too, who Americanize themselves more quickly than all other nationalities and so much so that one is never quite able to pick them out.

The mood here was never for a moment agitated. The people were, as one says, behind Kennedy, but not in a frightening way—there were great differences of opinion and open opposition, as there should be. No one was defamed. And now people are saying Whew!, but not with any triumphal bellowing.

We both read your lecture on economics[5] with great pleasure. It is so good to find confirmed again and again that we are in agreement in all basic matters. I have one reservation: your point of departure is the money economy. It is, perhaps, though I'm not sure of this, no longer very important in the overall economy. What is important is the coming automation, on the one hand, and, on the other, the conversion of private property into corporate property. In America at this point, it is stupid and dangerous to talk about the free entrepreneur, the master in his own house. Nobody can own more than the grocery store on the corner anymore. It has all become corporate property. But more on this another time. It's late; I'm sitting here with a very nice wine and a little chocolate—all brought along yesterday from New York, where I meet Heinrich over the weekends. He is very well, although he has a lot to do.

All my best and warmest wishes

Your
Hannah

315 *Karl Jaspers to Hannah Arendt*

Basel, November 2, 1962

Dear Hannah!

Wonderful—the liveliness, the capacity for work, and the joie de vivre that speak from your letter.

Cuba gives cause for uncertainty again. Kennedy will need all his alertness to avoid falling into all the new traps these Russians, who have the upper hand at the moment, are setting for him with their hesitation, their new arguments, their new demands. If he can hold South America together, he'll succeed. At the moment not even the missiles have been dismantled. Inspecting, to see that a large part of the matériel isn't hidden, is surely extremely difficult. It's unlikely that Cuba will permit any effective form of inspection.[1] Sovereign rights. The constant introduction of new complications drags this simple business out into an endless process, unless South America itself should decide on its own to invade. Then the whole matter would be cleared up in two days.

Cuba and Berlin seem to me to be completely different in one major point. Russia could do nothing with its conventional forces to stop an invasion of Cuba, nor could America do anything with its against an invasion of Berlin. If Russia wants to defend Cuba against America, it will have to resort to atomic weapons. If America wants to defend Berlin against Russia, it too will have to resort to atomic weapons.

But Cuba is an isolated forward post that is militarily very dangerous for America. Berlin is not a militarily significant forward post.

Berlin remains in great danger the more the American thesis of an atomic war only in response to a Russian attack on a broad front in Europe becomes reality.

Thank you for your comment on my banker lecture. What you say about automation and the corporative character of the large concerns is surely correct. That the money economy is "no longer very important in the overall economy" has been established since Stinnes.[2] But for human beings and their way of life, for permanence, tradition, it could be very important. This problem is the same in Russia and with us.

The key point that underlay the thinking of my lecture, but that I did not touch on at all because I lack the knowledge to say anything intelligent about it, is the transformation of the economy. Up to now the economy has been inseparable from capitalistic expansion, but now it must be transformed into an *expansionless economy that turns all its energies inward*, and an economic ethos appropriate to such an economy has to be developed. *This* transformation limited at first to the free West (and including Japan) is crucial to our survival. Expansion will have to end someday. And to achieve this transformation in freedom could be the salvation of freedom itself. Well, this is all very vague. I could add something more, but not work it through. Economics is a very honest, down-to-earth business, although it seems limited in its horizons.

November 12

Dear Hannah!

This letter was put aside, as you can see from the date.

I just reread your letter and was glad that the contents of your book on the American Revolution found such success with the students. Because of its dedication, it is, as it were, Gertrud's and my book, too.

What you say about Nanda Anshen [. . .] is convincing. In the meantime I've received another letter from her concerning possible *abridgments* by Mr. Ashton. I wrote her that I would agree to consider suggestions from Mr. Ashton and would probably accept them.

She wrote not a word about the publisher and the contract. On that score, I told her that, if it was desired, I would go back to a number of the sentences formulated earlier. At the same time I suggested Dec. 31, 1962, as the date when her option would run out. That is, I feel, a fair proposal. Kurt Wolff wanted that a few weeks ago. I had forgotten it and I mention it now because of the silence on her part.

We're having rain and snow and darkness here, the usual miserable fall weather. We're staying at home. It suits us here, and Erna too. Erna is all enthusiastic over some nice concerts. Today she is going to the first lecture in a series on novels. She will read in advance each work under discussion: *Ahnung und Gegenwart, Nachsommer*,[3] etc. A house companion who brightens the mood of the whole household every day.

At a university ceremony on Friday, I'll receive an honorary doctorate of medicine. I'm still simple enough to be pleased about it. My background is being recognized, and I like feeling at home; indeed, I feel more at home in the medical faculty than in my own.

Warmest greetings,
Your Karl

Basel, December 2, 1962

Dear Hannah!

Piper has written me that you have agreed to take part in a radio discussion with me in February in Basel. It is to be aired in the series "Politics of the Times in Dialogue." North German Radio. —Then his letter goes on: "Don't envision recording a self-interpretation of the interviewee but rather making a slice of contemporary history visible through him and through his encounters with others . . . with Jaspers, of course, a more or less philosophical slice of contemporary history" . . . So it is to be an interview after all and not a dialogue? Between us, a real dialogue is the only possibility. I did a routine radio interview with Klaus Harpprecht recently,[1] and I have no desire to repeat that. The only acceptable approach would be a political discussion of the present situation. What do you *really* think about this whole business? I assume that, prompted by your friendly nature, you once again just didn't want to say no. Can you picture what it would be like? A dialogue between us would be a minor sensation. Both of us equally well known in Germany now—and there we are on a first-name basis, "Hannah"! "Karl"!—and then, our basic outlooks in which we feel very much at one, but which will strike official Germany as absolutely impossible, while at the same time we part ways in particulars, in the experimental play of thought. What do you think? I won't reply to Piper until I've heard from you.

Piper is an excellent publisher. But his people seem to want to make as much commercial use of my birthday as they can. I have to stave them off a little. My new book, which costs 32 DM (too much; the price was set at 24 DM at the Frankfurt Book Fair, and the book was already finished by then), is going to appear in January in a "cheap" student edition for 20 DM. That strikes me as impossible: first, toward the buyers who paid the higher price only a few weeks earlier and, second, toward the book dealers who still have the more expensive edition in stock . . . The cheaper edition could be issued in another year or two.

What does Heinrich say to all this?

Warmest greetings to you both
Your Karl

When I picture our radio talk, I can imagine it as a wonderful thing in which I and not you ask the questions.

489

You still haven't received my new book. I requested it from Piper long ago. They are somewhat slow in getting to it this time. The German recipients got the book a few days ago, I, too, only recently (not counting five copies I received a few weeks ago).

Your predictions are surely correct regarding the contract, and my simple version will give rise to complications. You suggested higher royalties in your draft of two years ago[2] but there was also this irksome word "libelous."[3] Unfortunately, I didn't think to look at your draft when I wrote mine. Now I've taken it out again, and I could make a number of additions, which would be perfectly acceptable to me, but under no circumstances can I accept "libelous" (on that point I'm "fanatical").

Kurt Wolff would sign my contract on the spot. But of course I will wait and see what Nanda Anshen's house says. I would not refuse additional clauses regarding English editions, offprints, etc.

I think it wonderful that Ashton wants to translate the book. This time I will have to consult with him if he should want to abridge and if he wants to turn the overview of the contents into essay form (as in the atom book).

I'm working on the "Cusanus" for the second volume of *Die grossen Philosophen*, which you will edit. I'm enjoying it. Since the time of my preliminary work, excerpts, and overviews from the '20s a lot has been written about him, some of it useful, also for the swings in the political assessments of him, which change with Germany's situation. There is probably no other philosopher who remained politically active for his whole life, was almost constantly "on the job," and at the same time developed a philosophy of such high quality not in his spare time but in connection with his work. I do not, however, rank him as highly as a philosopher as I did earlier. He is not a "classic" philosopher, but metaphysically he is original and profound.

Germany is a madhouse at the moment because of the *Spiegel* affair.[4] A corrupt publication, corrupt parties, and corrupt government agencies are tangling with each other, and the knot appears to be impossible to untie. The whole thing is extremely interesting. The state compromises itself in an irresponsible game that such a state can afford because its domestic political life is protected by the last of the provisions limiting its sovereignty as stated in the general treaty of 1952[5]: If riots or public disorder gets out of hand, the Allies have the right to step in. And it is protected in the outside world by the miracle of America's aid. A state that has no real political responsibility and doesn't take

490

real responsibility on itself to become a respectable state with domestic political freedom will become a locus of corrupt party oligarchy and of total confusion despite the intellectual energy of jurists and other specialists.

Warmest greetings to you both from Gertrud
and your Karl

317 Karl Jaspers to Hannah Arendt

Basel, December 5, 1962

Dear Hannah!

Gertrud has told me a bit of news taken from her secret correspondence with you[1]—and it is truly secret—namely, that you have accepted a professorship at Chicago under the best of terms.[2] It's almost like a medieval sinecure. The work that you do there so brilliantly is limited to such short times that you don't need to make any changes in your life at all. I'm very happy about it and congratulate you and Heinrich.

I've received from Nanda Anshen a contract written as if our entire correspondence had never taken place. That is no way to negotiate. For the sake of brevity, I'm sending you carbon copies of my reply[3] and of my letter to Ashton.[4] I think I've written in such a way that things will yet fall into place. The trouble you have taken should not have been in vain. I hope you will agree with me and feel that you mustn't waste any more time or energy on this matter. It seems to me that everything is laid out clearly and the publishing house can make its decision.

I'm bombarding you with letters. Forgive me!

Warmest greetings to you both
Your Karl

318 Hannah Arendt to Karl Jaspers

Wesleyan University, December 13, 1962

Lieber Verehrtester—

Today, at last, I can get around to thanking you for your two letters. The Christmas vacation is about to begin, and tomorrow I'll go home. I've had an immense amount of work to do and couldn't fit in anything else at all. Partly because the students took so much of my time, and partly because I have two books going to press at once, the "Revolution" and "Eichmann." Then, too, Klemens von Klemperer[1] gave a lecture here on campus about Adenauer's foreign policy. To my pleasant surprise, it turned out to be a lecture on Jaspers' critique of Adenauer's policy. It was excellent and quite powerful. I gave him your article on economics,[2] which he had not seen yet.

The *Spiegel* affair: a "corrupt publication"—is that established as fact? It is without doubt a kind of scandal sheet, but it was also the only publication that was utterly outspoken in its criticism and exposed the corruption in government (Herr Strauss, etc.). There's no doubt that that's why the government is taking Augstein and Ahlers[3] to court. And in the meantime they're sitting in pretrial confinement without due process of law! As far as the indictment itself is concerned, a young jurist[4] I know well, a German who studied at Yale here, wrote me that in the issue of *Der Spiegel* in question there was not a word that he had not already seen in *Foreign Affairs*. The whole thing reminds me all too painfully of Ossietzky's case.[5] He too was charged with high treason to silence his magazine and put an end to its criticism of the government. I find Adenauer more sinister and insufferable all the time. And the craziest thing about it all is that the people don't get rid of him. But then, there is no successor for him, and that is 75% his fault. He can tolerate only yes-men. It's too bad for Germany. Now it's coming home to roost that no one listened to what you said—on the question of "denazification," on the question of reuniting Germany. I often meet German students here. They're either pigheaded, or they say: Once I've finished my doctorate, I'm coming to America.

"An expansionless economy that turns all its energies inward": I agree completely, but the problems are massive. As long as poverty persists in Asia and to some extent in Latin America, too, industrialized nations will have to export without profit. And then there is the development of Africa. In short, a world economy or, more correctly, a worldwide economy without expansion and without intentions to expand. But once this energy-laden economy is turned inward without outside markets, it will soon become evident that it simply has too much energy. That is, at that point it will be crucial to abandon the ideal of economic growth and try to achieve some kind of stabilization. Otherwise, consumer goods will be the end of us all. —There's a newspaper strike here at the moment, so we're getting no news. We're managing fine without.

492

On the radio talk: I've heard from Piper again in the meantime:
1. It would definitely be a "conversation," not an "interview" with
questions put to you. That would be out of the question for me because
that's a skill one has to acquire. 2. There are already two major broadcasts about you planned in connection with your birthday, so this
program would be broadcast later. 3. Mr. Reinholz[6] of North German
Radio wants to see me beforehand and would like me to come to
Europe via Hamburg. It's not clear to me from all this exactly what
these gentlemen have in mind. But if we can do this program the way
we want to, it would be wonderful. Then, too, I don't have any burning
desire to visit Mr. Reinholz, and certainly not before we have had a
chance to talk together. If he wants to see me, he should come to
Basel. As you see, I'm all for this, even though I have only a vague
idea of how we should go about it. I'm thinking back on our many,
many talks together. We should try to find some way to present the
process of conversation itself, so to speak. The subject matter is up
to you. Whatever terms you set will be all right with me—with
the one condition that I use only "Du" and not your first name.
Not even for the sake of the radio will I be able to bring myself
to say "Karl." But because you find the "Du" appropriate, we'll stick
with that.

I haven't heard anything more from Nanda Anshen. I hope she
understood what you said about the option. [. . .]

Now the only question remaining is when you'd like to do this radio
talk. Before or after your birthday or not until the summer, when we
come back from our trip. I would prefer not having to come before
your birthday, but that isn't essential. I can accommodate any and all
plans this time.

I'm having some difficulties with Piper because of the Eichmann
book. It may well be a risky thing for a German publisher to take on.
He hasn't read it carefully, and I have the impression that there isn't
anyone in the house who knows English really well. At any rate, we
still don't have a contract, and I've written him a very forceful letter
about the matter of translation, too. Once the thing appears here in
The New Yorker other publishers will probably inquire about it. But
I'm not sure. It won't sit well with the Germans at all. I've been
extremely outspoken in my opinions.

All warmest wishes to you both

Your
Hannah

Basel, December 19, 1962

Dear Hannah!

Thank you for your letter of December 13. If you find the idea of our radio talk wonderful, then I do, too. Of course, we will do it the way *we* want to. There is no hurry. We'll talk about it when you are here after my birthday. Then we'll see whether Radio Hamburg will want to do what we suggest. Neither you nor I will let ourself be ordered around by a radio station. I make a principle of being friendly with these gentlemen but ignore the symptoms of their need for power. In their eyes, we are dolls to be placed where they want them and easily replaced. But we will do what *we* want.

Nanda Anshen sent a telegram yesterday, saying that Harper [& Row] agreed to all the points and that the contract was on the way to me. Only when I have the contract in front of me will I see whether that is true.

I have to make clearer what I meant when I called *Der Spiegel* "corrupt." It certainly does *not* serve any interests in the sense that it takes money for such service. There is no indication—and it is presumably *out of the question*—that it extorts hush money. By "corrupt," I mean that it has no point of view, no political conception, no direction, and no goals. It arises from the masses' need for aggression, the need for exposés and sensationalism, in which the ministers themselves are caught up. The spirit is nihilistic but in the guise of assumed "moral" principles. It "uncovers" politically relevant matters and other things. It has developed a negativistic-arrogant style, which has spread even to the letters to the editor it publishes. Not a trace of decency, no nobility, no content. But I would not say that earning money is its main goal. One can see, in this case as in many others, how thoroughly it goes about its work, that is, extraordinary organized efforts are made to gather information, even on minor matters. Garnering fame by universal accusation, making people look ridiculous, calling things into question, feeling that one's very being is rooted in such negation—all that provides a certain kind of joie de vivre. But in my opinion you are absolutely right in saying that it is vitally important for the Federal Republic that *Der Spiegel* is there. *Because* our entire press (even *Die Zeit*) is in fact intimidated, though it doesn't admit to that, because it does *not* provide, with good style and a positive outlook, what is urgently needed in democracies today: the revelation of realities, convincing and well-reasoned judgments—*that* is why *Der Spiegel* is there. And under *these* circumstances we cannot wish it away, yapping cur that it is. But one needn't have anything to do with it oneself. Example: When my atom book appeared in 1958, Piper wrote me that Augstein[1] and two other editors had asked him whether they could come to Basel and interview me. Piper strongly urged me to do it because it would mean the sale of 3,000 to 4,000 copies more. I thought about it. I'm not at all against advertising. Without it one doesn't exist in these times. But *this* kind of advertising was repulsive to me. I had read several *Spiegel* interviews with other people, always the same: the *Spiegel* people remarkably intelligent and well-informed; a planned effort (three against one) to seek out weak points; the weapon of irony as a response to answers that convincingly toppled their thesis; sudden leaps to another plane of discourse instead of sticking with the speaker's subject. I pictured that to myself on the basis of the examples I could only dimly recall, and I thought: You will take a licking for the benefit of a public eager to laugh at people and see them made vulnerable. And on top of that the *Spiegel* people break off the interview when they have made a particularly telling point, and then no response can be made to it. A mode of discourse like that I call corrupt. I said to myself, it may not matter to me if *Der Spiegel* drags me too through its kind of mud, which it has already done a few times. But if I reach out my own hand to them and serve as a guinea pig for them to try out their sophistic methods on, then I do indeed make myself ridiculous. If my university or the state in which I live *charged* me with participating in such an interview (not Piper), then that would be something else again. Then I would be carrying out a "duty" and would not be ridiculous. *Then* I would even enjoy the encounter. So I asked Piper to make a friendly reply in the negative, giving as the only reason that I was overburdened with work.

You can see that I used the word "corrupt" somewhat carelessly, and now you know approximately what I meant by it.

"Expansionless economy"—and "energy turned inward"—those are, as you say, vast problems. They certainly cannot be solved in advance by reflection. There is need for philosophy to create an ethos that will inform economics as it creates drafts for the technical means to be employed, that will inform sociology as it finds possible ways to communicate to the collective mind—and more. More on this when we meet. I can't draft what it seems possible to me to construct here. In my seminars I sometimes tried to interest economists in these issues. One seemed to catch fire, but when he turned in his paper, I could see that he hadn't understood anything at all. He's a professor in Karlsruhe now. That is a discussion topic for us (but *not* on the radio).

It's annoying that Piper is creating difficulties about the Eichmann book—just as he did before when your major book[2] wound up with the Frankfurter Verlagsanstalt. [. . .] Your Eichmann book—with which he was deeply impressed and about which he had only positive things to say—will certainly draw the interest of a good German publisher once it has appeared in America.

Warmest greetings
Your Karl

320 Hannah Arendt to Karl Jaspers

Middletown, January 7, 1963

Lieber Verehrtester,

It's a scandal that the New Year has begun and I haven't been in touch. I was at home, but in a dreadful pickle. I had the galleys of the Eichmann book on my hands along with the page proofs for the revolution book. And on top of that a stream of visitors and the usual holiday chaos. You once said nobody overworks himself, and I recited that every day as my motto.

Your letter of December 19, our radio talk: You too have probably heard from Piper that North German Radio wants us to talk about the beginnings of your philosophy as the beginnings of existential philosophy. What do you think of the idea? I can't imagine it as anything but an interview, and for that, God knows, I am not the right person. Also, they want me to come via Hamburg to listen to the tapes with Bondy[1] and Zahrnt[2] and have a preliminary talk with them. I let Piper know that I thought it improper to take part in a preliminary talk of this kind before we had spoken together.

Everything you say about *Der Spiegel* is true, but it doesn't seem to me to pass muster at the moment. We'll talk about that. I'm still up against deadline pressure. And the most annoying thing about it is that I haven't had the time to give your book even so much as a glance.

Piper apparently wants the "Eichmann" after all, with some hesitation and, it seems to me, reluctance. We still don't have a contract, and I've taken the liberty of calling that to his attention.

Nanda Anshen: I met her at a party, and she told me, all aflutter, about the telegram. I hope everything is finally in order. I had the impression that she had understood what was going on this time.

January is here, and February is approaching. And the question is: When are you expecting me? I had thought of flying from here around February 20. Either direct to Zurich or by way of Paris to talk with Manheim. Hotel reservations, etc. are probably not difficult at this time of year. I was thinking of a hotel near the railroad station where the Wolffs always stay. The Rhein Hotel isn't so appealing in the winter. Also, don't forget that I've become wealthy. *The New Yorker.*[3] I'll explain when I come.

All best wishes to you both,

Your Hannah

I dictated this, and the girl doesn't know German very well. Misreads sentences, etc. Sorry!

321 Karl Jaspers to Hannah Arendt

Basel, January 12, 1963

Dear Hannah!

Having finished the enjoyable work on two books, you're now eaten up by the trivia. But, unfortunately, proofs do have to be read. [. . .]

Mr. Reinholz from North German Radio has written to you now, too. I answered him that the two of us would discuss the matter at the end of February and then send him word. An interview is out of the question. The radio people keep reformulating the plan. The series is called "Portrait of the Times in Dialogue." That is so general that it permits *anything*. I jokingly wrote to Mr. Reinholz that one could understand that title to mean that the times, like the sun in a drop of water, could be reflected in the minuteness of a dialogue. We'll have to see what we come up with. If Mr. Reinholz doesn't want to go along, then the very able Meyer-Gutzwiller[1] here in Basel is always willing to broadcast our talk and then pass it on to German stations. Swiss Radio pays, of course, only a fourth as much as the German honoraria.

Nanda Anshen's house is by and large agreeable to my terms. Harper has, however, lowered the royalties to 7% for the first 15,000 copies, 9% for sales above that. As compensation, they've raised the advance to $1,000. I've agreed to that. Only *one* point remains unsettled: a date has to be set after which the rights revert to me if the book is not published (the outside limits I have set are: 18 months for the translation, 15 months for printing), and I would forfeit the advance unless a new agreement is reached. If Harper accepts that, then the matter is settled.

I'm really very pleased that you are coming. Otherwise, Gertrud and I would look forward to the day[2] only from the perspective of whether my bronchial tubes and heart will act up or not. The celebration promises to be a quiet one. An eightieth birthday is different from a seventieth. In the consciousness of the general public, you're almost beyond this world. Then, too, I've alienated more than a few affections in recent years. I'm really enjoying the work on Cusanus. But the picture of him that I thought I had captured completely in my old notes has changed a great deal in the course of my new study of him, and details of it continue to change week by week.

Warmly
Your Karl

322 *Hannah Arendt to Gertrud and Karl Jaspers*
New York, February 8, 1963

Dearest Friends—

I'm still reading proofs—Eichmann without end. In between I entertain myself with Piper, who seems to want to go ahead now but is still afraid of his own courage. I've already had offers from Rowohlt and Kiepenheuer—don't like either one. But I've sent Piper a friendly threat, telling him to stop dragging his feet, without, of course, telling him the names of the other publishers.

He wrote about the radio talk, too. It seemed quite all right to me, but I don't know what you think. Heinrich is reading *Der philosophische Glaube* and will probably write soon himself. He is completely recovered now, energetic and involved in his work.

My main reason for writing is to give you dates. I'll fly from here on the 19th and will be in Basel on the 20th; however, I won't be halfway palatable until the 21st because I'll have to lose a night's sleep. I don't like that. As far as living goes, I'd like to suggest that I stay in a hotel this time. I'm afraid that my business will be a disturbance to you. I have to telephone, and I'll be getting calls—which all adds up to a completely unnecessary burden on you. I may come and work at the house, and I'll always be available. It's altogether possible that *The New Yorker*, which is half magnificent and half mad and has much too much money, will place an urgent call to me to ask if they can change a comma. If I'm not at the hotel, then I'm simply gone and can't be reached. And then the comma will not be changed, and the world will not end. I've written to the Euler and asked them to reserve a room for me.

My other appointments: I have a radio talk[1] in Cologne on March 6 that will pay for my trip. I have to prepare that still. After that, nothing—except that I have to look through Manheim's translation, and for that it's probably best if I go to Locarno, where Helen Wolff can help me. Heinrich has decided not to leave here until March 23. He is into his work, and he prefers that. He will take a boat by the lovely southern route directly to Athens. On April 5, I'll board his ship in Naples. We won't be back in the "North" until the end of May or beginning of June—four weeks in Greece, two weeks in Sicily, and then about another two weeks in Italy. Our ship will go back on June 29th from southern France, where we're thinking of traveling around a bit, too.

I have to get back to my galleys. I'm counting the days, and because I can't count, I keep miscounting all the time. By the by—I have the impression that the Wolffs would very much like to come to Basel for your birthday but don't quite dare. I pretended not to hear, but thought I'd pass it on. After Locarno, I think I'll settle down in Zurich and continue translating the revolution book. Then I can come over now and then if you like.

All warmest wishes, and until soon!
Your
Hannah

---

323 *Hannah Arendt to Karl and Gertrud Jaspers*

Strasbourg, March 30, 1963

Lieber Verehrtester, liebe Gute—

We were in Colmar, and I agree with you. Grünewald,[1] overpowering, but he left me cold. *But* Schongauer[2] reminded me all at once that the word *innig* [deeply felt] exists only in German.

It's late and Annchen has gone to bed. I've been absorbing some more culture. The cathedral here is *ravishing*.

Heartfelt greetings
Hannah

Athens, April 14, 1963

Dear Friend!

Thank you for your letter,[1] which was such a great reassurance for me. My thoughts return constantly to Austrasse. We have never seen each other for such a long and continuous period before; and precisely because there was a little of the everyday about it, it seems to me as if everything were still very present.

We arrived here a week ago, at midnight in Patras, where I somehow induced the owner of the village café, a huge, immensely fat, dark, and wonderful-looking fellow, to take us under his wing—there were no more hotel rooms available there—and so we drove to Athens, four hours along the Corinthian Gulf under a full moon. That in itself was incredibly beautiful. And since then it's been one splendor after another. It hasn't been really exhausting, but I'm feeling some muscles I haven't used for a long time. Yesterday we were on Aegina. The temple there on the peak of the mountain affords a view all around the island and was perhaps the most beautiful experience of all. We've just decided to go over there again before we leave. Longer trips begin next week, but we've decided to stay a week longer in Greece and not leave here until May 10, which means we'll spend a few days less in Sicily and Italy. I've reserved rooms for us in the Krafft in Basel for June 5. I think I forgot to tell you that. I can change that at any time. But the hotel people told me that something was going on in Basel at that time and that it would be impossible to get a room before the 8th without a reservation. They said I could always cancel because any free room will be snatched up in that period anyhow.

We found a wonderful place to stay. A large, very pleasant room, very good common rooms that no one ever uses, a well-kept house with a first-class library in German and French, very pleasant and well-educated people who speak French and English.

Revolution has gotten good reviews, and I'm enclosing the review from the *New York Times*,[2] which appeared, curiously enough, on the first day the paper resumed publication. There was a review in the *Washington Post*, too, by William Douglas,[3] a Supreme Court justice—"a classical treatise." That is an important comment for me, because even though I took great care with my examination of American institutions, which all go back to the Revolution, I never felt absolutely sure of myself. My interpretations are often very unorthodox.

Next week we'll go to Crete—but without Heinrich, who doesn't care much for that culture and wants to remain immersed in the purely Greek. So we (Lotte Beradt and I) will just leave him in the museum in Athens and will expect him to be able to explain every vase to us when we come back. We'll fly there for three days, and have friends there who have a car.

Every once in a while I pinch myself to convince myself that all this is real and we're really here. We read the papers at night in bed. Otherwise, we don't read at all, except for the guide. In short, we're living the "easy life" of the gods.

Warmest greetings
Your
Hannah

325   Hannah Arendt to Gertrud Jaspers

Athens, April 28, 1963

Dear Friend—

I'm battling with a typewriter that is suffering from battle fatigue and has a ribbon that keeps quitting all the time. Your letter[1] was waiting for us here when we came back from the Peloponnese, and tomorrow we head for Delphi. The landscape in Crete was magnificent. But Knossos, restored in the spirit of Queen Victoria, was a disappointment. Phaistos is marvelous, however, and the museum in Heraklion extremely interesting, particularly because of the vases and the very small, extremely sophisticated, and elegant small objects—seals, jewelry, etc. It's as if taste was discovered there. But it also becomes clear how little we have left from this culture—scraps, fragments, nothing more. We were there for three days, and that was quite enough. Whereas even the longest time isn't enough for Athens. The National Museum is simply inexhaustible, and everything in it a masterpiece. Today we spent the whole morning with the vases alone, where we —quite appropriately—met a German professor—Weischedel[2] from Berlin. Heinrich never tires of walking the long way from the Agora to the Acropolis by way of the Pnyx and the Areopagus. We are ecstatic and completely dizzy with seeing. We don't want to read at all anymore. Heinrich is constantly afraid he might forget some sight he has seen. But he never does.

After extensive telephone calls with my family [Ernst and Kate Fürst]

I've decided after all to fly to Israel for three days. My little niece [Edna Fürst] in the military can't get any leave, and I want to see her. She was extremely insistent on the phone. It would have been nicer to have her here. Lotte Beradt, who also has relatives there, is going in any case, so we'll fly together again, and Heinrich is quite content to wander around here alone for a few days. On May 11 we'll leave here by ship to Brindisi, and on the 13th in the evening we'll be in Syracuse. I've probably told you this before, but I'll repeat it for safety's sake: Hotel des Etrangers in Syracuse until about the 20th, then touring in Sicily without an address, and then Rome, c/o American Express.

One more thing: Heinrich just got a letter from his friend [Robert Gilbert] in Locarno. It turns out that it would be better for Heinrich to meet his friend first and then come to Basel. I might use those days for a meeting with Anne [Weil]. If it suits you, we wouldn't arrive until the middle of the month, between June 12 and 15. We would have to cancel our reservations at the Krafft am Rhein, or change them, but that presents no problem. Perhaps you can drop me a line in Syracuse to say how things are with you.

Have you seen pictures of the Aphaia temple on Aegina?? It's almost as beautiful as the Bassae temple.

We laughed a lot about "Karl would have gone along to Crete; I would have stayed in Athens." Heinrich's immediate response was: Yes, he is still so young and curious. Otherwise there's nothing to report, except that we are happy and with you in our talk and thoughts.

Your
Hannah

326 *Karl Jaspers to Hannah Arendt*

Basel, May 2, 1963

Dear Hannah!

Your letters are inspiring. I am living your "easy life of the gods" vicariously and enjoying in my imagination how and what you are seeing. I am impressed by Heinrich's concentration on the classical, on Athens. He doesn't want to forget anything. Our happiness lies there where the truth, beauty, and greatness of human beings is visible.

Your visit is welcome to us at any time. Your "German orderliness" will always let us know in good time.

Gertrud has not written anymore because she came down with the flu again ten days ago. She is recovering now. I was worried for a few days. She was so very weak, slept almost all the time, had no appetite at all, said once: Is it possible to just die like this? But things were bad for only one day. And even on that day her heart and circulation were fine. On the third day, a localized bronchial pneumonia was perceptible, but that is on the mend, too. Today she is bored and impatient, is getting up to wash in the bathroom and so forth, returns with a pulse of 110, but recovers again quickly. She has to be reined in. My worries are over for now. But experience has shown that convalescence can take a long time. By the time you come—the postponement of your arrival is a good thing—she will, I hope, be fully recovered. We remain very happy with Dr. Bernstein.[1] After you left, he examined Gertrud because of her heart, a severe arhythmia. The arhythmia disappeared after two weeks on small doses of digitalis. Möhrle was wonderful, touching in her concern and care, even in the unappetizing aspects, like a nurse. Gertrud said once: I still don't have any appetite, but it comes during mealtimes because the cooking is so good. She makes up the menu herself. She still doesn't feel like writing yet. She asked me to give you her very warmest greetings. This afternoon she'll get up for an hour for the first time.

Won't Israel be dangerous for you? The situation there is showing a dangerous face again. If Jordan fell into Nasser's hands, neither America nor England would do anything. Why don't the Americans finally guarantee the borders? In Israel, we hear, the mood has not changed; the country remains courageous and confident and aware of its own strength. Who knows what your impressions will be there. You can tell us about it in Basel.

Heinrich is right that I am still "curious," but "young"? I'm beginning to enjoy the beauty of age and the reduction of obligations, and I am still not suffering too much from the unavoidable embarrassments. But I look forward to seeing Heinrich as if I were young.

Warmly
Your Karl

Basel, May 16, 1963

Dear Hannah!

Gertrud has been rid of her fever for a week and has had her appetite back for two days. It seems—if our unreliable scale can be believed —that she has gained back one of the twelve pounds she lost. She is still weak, but she is really feeling better every day. When you are in Basel, she will be—we can hope with real justification—her old self again. I am back to normal again myself. I was in a sad state when you last saw me and spoke with me. I have dreadful recollections of it—to have put in such an appearance with you. It was after the fever *before* my birthday. I had still not recovered fully from it and could barely make it through the celebration and say what was minimally required. And then I fell ill again immediately, along with Gertrud. And so I had no real desire to talk and wasn't really present in conversation. Well, you can tolerate that, too. I needn't worry about that.

I didn't have the courage to read your revolution book either. The English language! But I picked it up a few days ago, and I've been reading with growing enthusiasm, as if the language were not English at all. I'm still far from having finished it. But I have grasped the basic thrust of your intention. I think it is a book that is the equal of, if not perhaps superior to, your book on totalitarianism in the profundity of its political outlook and the masterly quality of its execution. I sense nothing artificial in it, no forced rational arguments; I find no super-fluous digressions. Your presentation of a single idea is a powerful current that pulls me along. Your insight into the nature of political freedom and your courage in loving the dignity of man in this arena are wonderful. I sense the influence of Heinrich's character and life experience, and in reading this book I think of you both. I am com-pletely absorbed by it.

What you write about the American Founding Fathers and what you convey about them is completely new to me. You will have made historical discoveries here that will rouse the Americans out of their self-forgetfulness. Your comparison and identification of the meaning of the "workers' and soldiers' councils," the "small republics," the beginnings and the truth of all revolutions since the American one, were familiar to me from your Hungary essay.[1] That essay left me hesitant;[2] but now I am convinced of the parallels of meaning and of the opportunity you see in them, though that opportunity has so far always been lost.

In the course of your presentation, the greatness to which you give expression is a source of encouragement. Ultimately, the whole is your vision of a tragedy that does not leave you despairing: an element of the tragedy of humankind.

The great literature that you cite bears witness to the fact that what you are doing here and what is essentially so original, in your attitude as well as in your thought, is not just a random, personal inspiration. This literature comes to your aid, introduces elements that you incorporate into the simplicity and greatness of this vision.

I want to continue reading and not skip a single page. It is easy for me because I think I already have a firm footing in the central idea. I am reading with the sense that you are correct in everything so far. If I should have objections, they will come later.

And *this* book you have dedicated to the two of us! I'm very grateful.—

The most beautiful part of your trip is behind you now. Will everything else, despite all the other beautiful things you'll see, seem somewhat pale by comparison?

I sometimes think in reading your book that Greece is there for you: without your homeland among the Greeks you would hardly have been able to find the form, without them you could not have found the perspective that allowed you to perceive the marvelous significance of the American Constitution and its origins.

Warmest greetings to you both
Your Karl

328 *Karl Jaspers to Hannah Arendt*

Basel, May 19, 1963

Dear Hannah!

The enclosed letter came back from Syracuse. I hope that my other letter reached you before Rome. Gertrud is better again physically, with the exception of a general weakness, cardiac weakness, and a somewhat greater need for sleep. Psychically, she is plagued by fits of depression, which, in those predisposed to them, are particularly likely after bouts of flu. But by and large we're quite content. By the time you come in mid-June, I hope we will both be "in good form." I am already, and I am looking forward to talks with both of you.

I continue reading your book with a steady enthusiasm that never flags. I wonder if your dream and mine, different as they may appear to be, don't really belong together after all, and, in any case, have the same base: the dream of political freedom which, as your book so enchantingly shows, has indubitably appeared here and there in this world in thought and in reality.

Karl Löwenstein from Amherst[1] was here yesterday. An intelligent man but a rationalist, basically stupid, really incapable of discussion. He would like to speak with you, of course, as everyone does. To be on the safe side, I told him you would probably be here only a short time. But perhaps you'll be interested in his judgment of your two books. He still hadn't read the revolution book but had seen the "Eichmann" in *The New Yorker*. His opinion: "As reportage, too good; as intellectual work, without focus." At any rate, he has great respect for you.

Warmest greetings, also from Gertrud, to you both

Your Karl

329   Hannah Arendt to Karl Jaspers

Rome, May 29—no typewriter,

but I'll do my best!

Lieber Verehrtester—

We received all three of your letters only in Rome. And so the negligence of the hotel spared me a real fright. Perhaps the depression too has passed by now.

We are still overwhelmed by all we have seen. Sicily—Syracuse in particular—was very beautiful. First the strange cathedral with the most wonderful Doric columns incorporated into it, Romanesque, and a late Baroque façade that is one of the most beautiful I have ever seen, on a plaza that has in miniature the oval curves of the Piazza Navona (where we had our first evening meal in Rome)—in short, *proof of continuity*, palpably, visibly there! Then Agrigento, and a magnificent little theater in the mountains, untouched, completely preserved, Palazzolo. And in Palermo, the great things are Monreale and the museum. Selinunte—a very interesting ruin; *Segesta* very disappointing.

And then, to wind it up, Paestum, which can be compared only with the very great Greek achievements—the Parthenon, the Aphaia temple, the Apollo temple in Bassae.

You see how it is with us—we are slopping over, as Heinrich says. I've gone on strike here. All I want to do is see the collections of antiquities, buy clothes, drink Campari and wine, and eat a lot and very well. I've read almost nothing in all these weeks. Only Goethe's *Italienische Reise.* —On that there'd be a few things to say.

I can't tell you how much your approval of the revolution book pleased me. Not only because I was afraid you mightn't like it, but because every word you wrote strikes the very heart of what I meant to say. A tragedy that warms and lightens the heart because such great and simple things were at stake. Heinrich's experience, of course, *and* the experience of America. In America (letters and reviews), people are a bit taken aback but satisfied nonetheless. "Eichmann" has prompted a great outcry, but it leaves me rather cold. Israel: only my family, a really quite wonderful "niece" [Edna Fürst], who is very close to me—the daughter of my cousin [Ernst Fürst] and a friend of my youth—who somehow validates my own childhood and youth. She is a little lieutenant, nineteen and, praise God, also very pretty. We get on as if we had been together every day for years.

I just keep writing away here, but I should give you some dates: We'll go by train or plane from here to Zurich on June 4. Robert [Gilbert] (Heinrich's friend) will come to Zurich, and on the 7th I'll leave the men to themselves and will go to a meeting in Kronenburg, near Koblenz, of students supported by the Scholarship Foundation.[1] I think we'll be in Basel about the 15th. Perhaps I'll come earlier, but I won't disturb you. I'll translate "Revolution" and put my papers in order. In any case, I'll call you from Zurich, probably on the 5th. We want to stay at the Waldhaus Dolder again but don't have a reservation yet. I'll take care of Basel hotel reservations from Zurich.

All warmest wishes. How nice that I can write: Until soon!
With love—

Your Hannah

Provence, June 30, 1963

Just a quick word of greeting before we board ship. Paris was very hectic and, together with the strike and pouring rain, rather dreadful. It's pouring here, too, but the landscape is absolutely extraordinary. —We think and talk about Basel.

And coming back! I'll write on the boat. This is just so you'll know we aren't lost.

Warmest greetings, your
Hannah

331 Hannah Arendt to Karl Jaspers

New York, July 20, 1963

Lieber Verehrtester!

Our days in France were too full to let me write, and on the ship my typewriter broke. First of all, "business"—and to begin with, the peace prize.[1] I discussed the matter briefly with my very discreet American friend [Mary McCarthy], and she said to me that Dan Jacobson,[2] a Jewish South African writer, whose name and writings I know and admire, was in London and that we should ask him to come to Paris. She thought he would be the best person to inform me. So we called him up, and he came to Paris for a day, even though we didn't tell him anything on the phone. He made an extraordinarily good impression on me, absolutely honest and of course personally very much involved in these issues. I'm enclosing what he suggested.[3] As far as the matter itself is concerned, I'm more convinced than ever now that the next peace prize should go to a man (or woman) who is trying to make peace between the races. That's where, socially, here in America, all hell is breaking loose. Things are much worse than I realized. Most people of good will are very pessimistic. A Jewish friend who is very active on behalf of the Negroes said yesterday: We are all lost. I'm by no means so pessimistic. Much will depend on whether the Kennedys[4] succeed in getting their Civil Rights bill[5] through. That won't solve the problems, but it will open the way for progress. But if the bill does not pass, we had better brace ourselves for the worst here. There are already entire sections of the city that are no longer safe for whites, and in Chicago things look even worse. The mob on both sides is just waiting for the chance to strike out. Every day we read in the papers that either a car with whites in it has driven through a black section shooting wildly or a car with Negroes in it has driven through a white section shooting just as wildly. But those are still isolated cases; the country is big; and the police are still functioning. And I still think it would be a mistake to give the prize to an American. The only possibility would be the Kennedys, and they aren't really a possibility, because they are in power. It would look like direct interference in American politics. As far as the South Africans are concerned, I think Jacobson is right and that Huddleston[6] is the best candidate.

Now I'd like to tell you about the rest of our trip, and I can see your room before me and the two of you, and how calm everything becomes, and assumes the proper proportions so that one can say everything and receive an answer to everything. And how for each individual, particularly when there is disagreement, the same standards apply and everyone stands on the same ground. I think about that continually, and we speak very often about you. But that is obvious. You have assumed such a firm place in our life together that it seems as if you were walking beside us through the apartment.

Paris: not pleasant, although the freshly washed city has its original color back and looks more wonderful than ever. The people in their prosperity snatch up everything they can as if they had no faith in that prosperity. They don't invest, do everything only halfway at best (a bathroom with a tub but no toilet, etc.), are constantly run-down and complain all the time. —I was sitting in a taxi and hadn't shut the door properly. A driver passing by was kind enough to point it out: wild cursing, why is he sticking his nose into other people's business; that's the third time that's happened today. Of course, because the door doesn't close properly. Which is in part a consequence of the mad strike tactics that leave you never knowing whether the gas will go off in the middle of cooking dinner or the electricity or—to name a genuine catastrophe—whether the subway will go on strike or the airports or the customs police . . . And all the strikes come as a surprise and last only a short time so that they really can't do anyone but the public any harm. They don't represent a serious financial threat at all. This system has been thought up by madmen to create mass neurosis. My American friend [Mary McCarthy], despite her beautifully appointed new apartment, dreams of nothing but the reassignment of her husband[7] because, as a foreigner, even though she speaks perfect French, she is treated in a way that makes her paranoid. An old French

509

friend thinks the country is on the verge of civil war, which I don't believe. —Then on to Provence, where it was wonderfully beautiful. Perhaps the loveliest of many beautiful landscapes we saw. I'd like to live there, and the people are very different from those in Paris. Prosperity there has a meaning and is dealt with rationally. The farmers are finally having it really good for once, and they'll grudgingly admit it. The only problem is that their sons don't stay at home but go to the big schools in Paris, and a genuine life in the fundamentally still healthy provinces can't properly develop. —Finally, in Cannes, we boarded the ship, very handsome and luxurious, which we both enjoyed, but we also didn't regret seeing it end. One week, no longer, is fine.

In New York the whole apartment was literally filled with unopened mail and mail that hadn't been forwarded. Almost all of it about the Eichmann business. A lot of interesting letters, a few among them that made utterly clear to me the reasons for this seemingly incomprehensible uproar in Jewish circles. The explanation is so simple that I should have understood it myself. Without realizing it, I dragged out a part of the Jewish past that has not been laid to rest: former members of Jewish Councils[8] occupy high positions and sometimes the highest positions in governments everywhere, but particularly in Israel. Worse still, the Kastner case, which I mention in my report, was more serious than I realized. Kastner,[9] who holds a very high post in Israel, was accused by a journalist of having collaborated with the Nazis, and he in turn sued for libel. In the first proceedings, Halevi (later one of the three judges in the Eichmann trial) found that Kastner, who had worked closely with Eichmann, had "sold his soul to the devil" and cleared the journalist of libel. Kastner appealed the case and is supposed to have said that if he did not receive satisfaction at that level he would "spill the beans," namely, about links during this period to the Jewish Agency[10] and to Palestinian party leaders. Whereupon he was murdered; not by Hungarian survivors, as I had assumed, but apparently, or so people say anyhow, by the Israeli secret police. In short, we have circumstances very similar to those in Germany, but it is, if that is possible, even more dangerous to stir around in them than it is there. The smear campaign against me here continues apace. Conducted on the lowest level, it consistently claims that I said just the opposite of what I did in fact write. The Jewish press has reported that Hausner, the state prosecutor, came to America at the government's urging and for the express purpose of heating things up. At the moment, three or four large organizations, along with whole regiments of "scholarly" assistants and secretaries, are busying themselves with ferreting out mistakes I made. It is quite instructive to see what can be achieved by manipulating public opinion and how many people, often on a high intellectual level, can be manipulated. Among the Jews themselves there are very many who retain their independent judgment, but the reactions have taken such a turn (with rabbis who preach from the pulpit) that a friend said it's like the time of the Dreyfus affair. Families are split down the middle! I'm amazed and never expected anything like this, and I can see, too, that it's downright dangerous. (People are resorting to any means to destroy my reputation. They have spent weeks trying to find something in my past that they can hang on me. They finally gave up, but are going at it differently now.) If I had known this would happen, I probably would have done precisely what I did do. And in the long run it's perhaps beneficial to sweep out a little of that uniquely Jewish rubbish.

Week after next we'll go to Palenville, as usual. Mail will be forwarded from New York. It's quite hot here, but we hardly feel it in our apartment. Heinrich has had some unpleasant work done on his teeth, but he's quite amiable despite it. He has a tendency, though, to fly into a rage over the attacks on me, and his opinion of the Jewish people is not always what one might wish. (But that only in jest.) Write soon and let us know how things are, even if it's just a line.

All warmest wishes—

Your   Hannah

332   *Karl Jaspers to Hannah Arendt*

Basel, July 25, 1963

Dear Hannah!

Your good letter just arrived. You have really stumbled unsuspectingly into an ambush, and the enemy is conducting a vile campaign against you. I'm beginning to worry a little myself. I understand Heinrich's rage. Because you have touched an extremely sore spot for many people, shown their lives to be informed by a lie, they hate you. I once caught a thief in the act, and I can still feel his gaze on me: I have never experienced such terrifying hatred again. What you have communicated was, though hidden in books, in large part already known. Your power as a writer—like Lessing's—has made it widely

511

known now. Truth is beaten to death, as Kierkegaard said of Socrates and Jesus. Things haven't come to that and won't come to that. But these people are putting labels on you that are totally inappropriate and revolting. In the long run, of course, your nature will win out and shine through in triumph. But now? I see as you do the effects of "manipulating public opinion," the superficial judgment of people who haven't even read the book. If a similar fracas begins in Germany after Piper publishes the book, then I'll want to write something. Even if it doesn't do any good, anyone who has even a small reputation in Germany will have to rally to you publicly.

Apropos of that, let me mention something that Piper wrote to me and that I have heard about too in a letter to Gertrud from Emil Henk[1] in Heidelberg. Piper thinks what you mean by "resistance fighter" should be more precisely defined. I haven't found the passage in your book. In essence we are of course in agreement. Because it is Germans who are concerned here, the same rage is possible as among the Jews. At any rate, I'm assuming that you mean by a resistance fighter only someone who worked *actively* to bring about the fall of the Hitler regime. A hundred percent negation of the regime and daily suffering under it was not uncommon. A wild guess: perhaps 100,000 people in Germany. *Relatively*, very few; *absolutely*, a very large number. I knew such people, my friends. In your sense of the term, someone who conspired but did not act and who was ready to work on a new start after others had acted was not a resistance fighter. Emil Henk in Heidelberg, our loyal friend during the Nazi period, joined in 1933 with like-minded Social Democrats to keep an organization alive. He was put in prison in 1933 for quite a while. At that time, in Heidelberg at least, things were still relatively lenient. He maintained—without the organization, I think—contact with his friends, was a friend of Haubach,[2] Mierendorff,[3] and many others. During the war years I heard from him many of the names that became well known later. Through fortunate circumstances, he escaped disaster himself because his involvement was not discovered. Through him and through von der Groeben[4] I got to know *Gerstenmaier*,[5] also a *brother of Trott zu Solz*.[6] They visited me; we were of one mind in our conversation, but they asked nothing of me and said nothing about their plans. They also knew about my illness. *Haubach* (who by the way took his doctorate with me in 1923 [about] with a rather odd dissertation but one that showed real talent)[7] visited us in Heidelberg shortly before his arrest, gave us—Gertrud in particular—instructions, described the situation (that was late July 1944) with full awareness of its danger, and told us that he meant to go into hiding right away with a friend in Mecklenburg. He didn't do that because when he was in Berlin he let himself be convinced that no more arrests were being made. He died because of carelessness. He was not involved in the assassination attempt and didn't even know about it in advance, but he was on the list of ministers for the planned new government, and he was convicted of being an accessory to plans for the new government. Haubach was in a concentration camp back in 1933, too, for more than a year, I think. When he visited me afterward, he didn't want to tell me about his experiences there. Just thinking about them filled him with horror. "To talk about that would be like setting off a bomb here in your room."

For these men, Haubach, Mierendorff, Henk (all socialists), the national interest was not primary, and they did not change their opinion when the war started going badly for Hitler's Germany. The murder of the Jews was not the central problem for them. They saw that crime as one among other crimes. Henk and Haubach didn't know anything definite about the murder of the Jews. That people died in concentration camps Haubach knew from his own experience. He didn't *know* that the transport trains went straight to the gas chambers. He certainly would have told me.

You will know all this. I can confirm it from my memories. All that is required is to be as exact as possible in formulations relating to the resistance fighters so that no misunderstandings will occur. Emil Henk, who did not go into detail in what he wrote us, apparently arrived at such a misunderstanding from his reading of the English book (or of *The New Yorker*). He made his judgment on the basis of your text. Such people—I cannot forget their decency and their beneficent activity during the Nazi period—see the value of their lives, as it were, in their experience of their shared anti-Nazi position and in the memory of their essentially passive planning (in expectation of the great day of Hitler's fall). Emil Henk's life, which denied him completely, even after 1945, the political success he sought, takes its sustenance from those things, from being able to say: I was a resistance fighter. If clear distinctions are made, their contribution remains beyond question. But if activity is the criterion, as you have made it, then they were not "resistance fighters," nor were most who shared their position. Goerdeler[8] wasn't either. One sees in large degree the pathetic nature of their fate, not the heroism. Tresckow[9] (of whom von der Groeben told me during the war) was a completely different sort of man. First of all, he had attempted bomb attacks back *before* the war, and, second, he thought the risk of July 20 necessary explicitly as expiation for Germany's shame and crimes, not just as a means of rescuing Germany from its situation in the war. He insisted on action, even if it was doomed to fail. After the failure of the plot, he committed suicide on the front. I don't know of another case of that kind, at least not among the military (even Beck,[10] if I recall correctly, had reservations for a long time about murdering Hitler). And all these military men accepted the arms buildup in 1935 from Hitler's hands, but they didn't want a war. Things are very complicated here, too, because of the multiplicity of the motives at work, but ultimately they are simple. And one must, it seems to me, recognize the greatness in the willingness to sacrifice oneself after realizing one has made a terrible mistake (as I assume Tresckow did, though I have no proof of this insight and "conversion" from the extremely thin documentation that is left).

Thank you for Dan Jacobson's impressive suggestions. I'll pass them on, without naming the source for now. If the response to them is favorable, then the foundation can ask Jacobson for a letter. In that case, I assume I may mention his name.

But I have decided not to take any real part, not in the small special commission either. My situation is peculiar there because I can't participate. But I can pass along communications.

How disturbing your report on Paris is; how pessimistic that on the Negro question. Now, for the first time, the word "race" (not nation) has been used in Moscow, by way of a Russian reproach to the Chinese.

And now, for that about which there is not much to say, what you call the "self-evident" and the most important thing of all. We are not alone in the world. Your last visit is still present to us. Our spirits are better because we can reach out to you in our thoughts and carry on interior conversations with both of you and with each of you in particular and inexhaustibly.

Erna's mother[11] had lost a lot of weight. Her excellent doctor there took the initiative and diagnosed cancer of the colon. She underwent surgery, then died on the second day. The burial was yesterday. Erna was stunned. Only after twelve hours did she shed a few tears. She thought of everything—even the black dress—didn't want to see anyone except Bona,[12] and went to Tonbach. It is the hardest blow that could hit her.

514

We are taken care of. She'll come back in a few days, will show Medi Geitel[13] how to take care of the household here, and then will go on August 8 to her father[14] for a month's vacation. Then Irma[15] will spend her vacation with the father. He lives in the same house, with his son and daughter-in-law[16] and grandchildren. He has severe heart trouble, spends a lot of time lying down, but when he can, he inspects the wood supply and the machinery to see that everything is in order in the cabinetmaker's shop that he passed on to his son years ago.

Gertrud's ear and heart remain unchanged. In other respects she is feeling so much better that she feels fully alive again. She suffered once again, no doubt as a consequence of the flu, from the depression that she has had on and off again all her life. Only when she emerges from those depressions does she completely realize what her state has been.

Warmest greetings to Heinrich. Have happy weeks in Palenville!

Your Karl

It's wonderful that the governors, against their own expectations and contrary to the prepared agenda, declared their basic support (with only three dissenting votes)[17] for eliminating racial discrimination!

333   Hannah Arendt to Karl Jaspers

Palenville, August 9, 1963

Lieber Verehrtester!

I'm answering your wonderful, long, convincing and persuasive and encouraging letter at the worst possible moment, but I will answer it now because I can't see when I'll have another chance. An acquaintance[1] in New York, who has been ill for months with a lymphatic sarcoma, is suddenly in critical condition (lungs), and I have to go back immediately because there is no one else there who can tend to her—no family, no really close friends, no one who can speak with the doctor, etc. I like her, but she is not particularly close to me, and that makes the whole thing only more difficult. All her close friends are in Europe.

You're absolutely right. It really is as if I had stumbled into an ambush, and how fair this fight is you can see from the fact that *Aufbau* refused even to print a statement from me—something that in this country is completely unusual. It's also typical that the same people who are, if I may use the phrase, slinging mud at me come to me secretly, under cover of darkness, so to speak, to tell me I should sue, this is a hate campaign, the articles in *Aufbau* are "embarrassing" and give cause for alarm—all this from people who then publish in the next number of *Aufbau*! Very odd. On the other hand, the rabbi[2] of Columbia University invited me to speak to Jewish students.[3] That is usually a very small circle—about 50 students, especially in the summer. There were 500 people in a hall for 300, and the police prevented more than 500 from storming the hall. I was greeted with an immediate ovation, spoke briefly, then led a long, detailed discussion, during which people submitted their questions written on cards, because the thing couldn't be managed any other way. The questions were anonymous. And not one of them contained a single provocation. Afterward long applause and great difficulty in getting away because more than 50 students came up to the podium to ask this or that question quickly. It was very pleasant; some of the questions were excellent; and it all would have been more pleasant if it hadn't taken place in 90 degree heat and without air conditioning. Another, similar, instance: an old acquaintance, a Zionist, Hadassah,[4] from whom I hadn't heard in years, wrote to me: Come back to us (she meant: to Jewish life). We need you. Very touching and very simple. And then there are examples like the public-relations man[5] (an important functionary) from one of the big synagogue associations here, whose rabbis are preaching against me from the pulpit. He approached me to say that he worked on the side as an agent for lecture tours, and would I like him to arrange a lecture tour for me with fees of 1,000 to 1,500 dollars per lecture! He wrote quite unabashedly on the stationery of his Hebrew Congregations. In other words—the whole business is almost entirely the doing of paid functionaries, and they no longer have control of very large groups among the Jewish people. Also, it is exclusively the older generation that is involved. The parallel to the German situation is impossible to miss.

As far as the resistance is concerned you (and Piper) are right that I have to explain in more detail what I mean. The key point, it seems to me, is that in their official proclamations, which they prepared for the eventuality that they would succeed, they mentioned Nazi crimes not at all or only on the side or as crimes against Germans, even if those crimes disturbed them privately. As a man from these circles whom I like very much wrote to me a short while ago, they would have risked civil war if they had done otherwise—which is true, of course. But the fact remains that they weren't prepared to risk civil war—for national reasons. Furthermore, it is a fact that Himmler[6] was informed that Count Helldorf,[7] an SS man, was involved and, consequently, that they were preparing nothing more than a kind of palace revolution. But, it seems to me, one has to separate clearly this resistance movement, which led to July 20, from the earlier anti-Nazi efforts of the Socialists (Mierendorff) and also of some conservatives. By 1938, all that was, so to speak, ancient history, for by then there was hardly any real group resistance left. A completely different question is the unorganized activity of individuals, even if they belonged to groups. They often helped where they could, at real risk to their lives, but that is a matter of humanity, not of politics. Once they began to act politically, they thought they couldn't offer "humane" or "moral" arguments anymore. And this was, I'm afraid, not just a question of tactics (although it may appear so to them today), in order to win the generals over to their side. In my opinion, the only things one can use for orientation here are the measures and proclamations prepared for eventual victory. Goerdeler, for instance, undoubtedly with the agreement of others, didn't even want to abolish the NSDAP! That would have been undemocratic. If I'm understanding things rightly, the only convincing argument against my thesis is Tresckow's case—about which I know too little. I'll have to look into it more closely. But what characterized these people politically as a group was their lack of principles, and that can't be explained only as a result of the alliance of Socialists and conservatives and convinced Christians —as if the principles involved were too heterogeneous for people to agree on them. The explanation is, instead, that resistance to the regime itself never became a principle for them. As far as the question of how much they knew is concerned, the answer would probably be different for each individual. But in general we can probably say that the majority of them were themselves so very much involved in the regime, or at least had such close ties to important functionaries, that one can assume they knew what was, on the Eastern Front at least, common knowledge. Whether they wanted to admit to themselves that they knew what they knew is another question. It's very striking, too, for example, that the eradication of Polish Jewry did not fall under the "final solution" of the summer of 1941, but had been already agreed upon, right from the start of the war. Even those people whose consciences were roused later by the "final solution," that is, by the inclusion of all Jews, even German Jews, raised not the slightest objection to it. Everybody accepted it as a matter of course. What I mean is that everyone who had a political role—even if he was against the regime and even if he was secretly preparing an assassination attempt on Hitler—was infected by the plague in both word and deed. In this sense, the demoralization of the country was complete—the only people not affected by it were those who sat steadfastly in their hiding places. You set their number at about 100,000, and I think that's a fair estimate. If those hundred thousand had come to power after Germany's defeat, things would probably look very different now.

How are things with you? And how sad the death of Erna's mother was! Give her my warmest regards.

I had a long letter from Dan Jacobson, which I'll forward to you once I've answered it. You can mention his name anytime you like. He sent me some material about Mandela[8] (the Negro) and Huddleston (the English missionary), which I will send on to you by separate post and that is interesting in places and not readily available. I remain of the opinion that this coming peace prize[9] should proclaim expressly the necessity for peace between the races.

All best wishes to you both. Heinrich is well. He is working up some new lectures and is in good spirits.

Warmest greetings
Your
Hannah

334   Karl Jaspers to Hannah Arendt

Basel, August 12, 1963

Dear Hannah!

That's wonderful: at Columbia University, invited by the rabbi, an ovation from a packed hall of Jewish students—I can imagine how forcefully you answered their questions and how personally convincing you were. You are conquering the Jews and are the best Jew yourself. My worries are almost gone. Against the power of truth, carried now by hundreds of students, the functionaries and old people can do nothing, at least not in the long run. You won't be spared the lectures. You have to complete your victory. If only that can be done without physical danger! You'll have to be careful and have a "bodyguard." A son of Springer's[1] (the publisher) whom we knew as a young man, now a professor in the USA (medical researcher), was attacked by a gangster in Chicago and lost an eye. Now, I hear, he's thinking about returning to Germany and joining his father's publishing house after all, an idea he'd rejected earlier. It may well be just a passing mood. I tell you this for what it's worth: fear of America because of the threat of physical violence.

I'm very glad that you want to write about the German "resistance" in more detail and with finer distinctions. I am, as you know, in full agreement with your basic views. Because an issue central to German life is involved here, as it were—or a lie that German life has not been willing to do without up to now—maximum clarity is crucial. Your use of the documents as a point of departure (all the plans for a future Germany) is unassailable. You have firm ground under your feet.

Have we ever told you about the conversation that Gertrud had in 1944 with my uncle, Theo Tantzen?[2] He was an absolutely convinced democrat from his youth on, not in the least "national," and he had real political judgment. (For example, I recall his views during the Spanish Civil War. I was worried about the Communists, but he remained utterly clear in his thinking: Oppose Franco no matter what, even if you have to join with Communists to do it.) Anyway, the two of them were talking about what should be done after the Allied victory. Theo spelled out his ideas. Gertrud's response: But you have forgotten the Jews entirely! Whereupon he said: You're right. First sentence of the constitution: All citizens share in the same rights—or something like that. That shows the degree of "forgetfulness," even with Gertrud sitting right in front of him. That is typical. The Jews were of primary interest to almost no one. A professor of medicine in Heidelberg,[3] a specialist for ear, nose, and throat, one of the silent but passionate opponents of the Nazis who was outraged over the persecution of the Jews and who helped them in any way he could, said to Gertrud when she thanked him after 1945: But that wasn't because of the Jews. We were all at risk. The Jews were just the first to go; the rest of us would have followed. Only stupid people didn't realize that.

Regarding Tresckow, there is a last letter and descriptions in Schlabrendorff[4] and Zeller.[5] I can't find anything in my chaos. Unfortunately, there is little known about the man.

An example of how one didn't need to know anything, even on the Eastern Front, was Radbruch's son,[6] who was home last in 1942. A lieutenant, he was killed soon after that. When his parents told him about the deportations of the Jews and the murder of the mentally ill, he said: "What nonsense you're falling for! That's just not true; that just can't be true." He served on the Crimean front.

You touch on a crucial point with the risk of "civil war." Civil war was, for everyone, even my father, the political crime per se, so to speak (an idea that stems from the German tradition of historical thought). That became evident in a conversation in 1934 when my father said to Gertrud: ". . . what you want then is civil war; that would be the consequence of your demands"—and she replied: "Of course, if that's what has to be—there are limits, after all." My father was really horrified.

Your formulation that "resistance to the regime itself never became a principle" is not, I think, a correct generalization. It does apply to Goerdeler and many others. But the one unifying idea was: the regime has to fall. It was the questions of "how" and "what then" that brought an instant parting of the ways. A "program" we would have found satisfactory has never come to my attention.

You say correctly that the Socialist opposition (Mierendorff and others) gave up even their minimal activity after 1933. By necessity, they became spectators. The only real route led by way of the military, as early as 1933 and up until the last.

Most of my estimated 100,000 are by nature not people of action. All of us with *Die Wandlung* after 1945 were nothing but a group of political complainers. It was their own fault that they didn't come to power.

I'll tell you sometime what Heuss wrote about Hitler[7] in 1932 (!) and the gist of my conversation with him in Badenweiler in 1934 (when I still didn't know about that highly laudatory journalistic bit of hogwash in which he ironically rejected racial theory). He does *not* belong to the 100,000. And that is true of most of the politicians in Germany today. Who is responsible for this state of affairs? Those who allow it, the population, the 100,000, the public voice!

I passed on your materials from Dan Jacobson, along with his name. I will also pass on whatever you still have to send me.

Because of your help, your ill acquaintance will not feel alone in the world. This modern situation is dreadful.

Warmest greetings to you both.

Heinrich will be pleased that you, as a single voice, are making yourself heard, being the good "demagogue" to mobilize the young. But it's not worth running real danger for.

Your Karl

August 18, 1963

Lieber Verehrtester,

I'm enclosing the rest of the South African papers[1] so that you'll have them at hand if you need them. They include Mandela's speech in court, the book by Huddleston,[2] and an explanatory letter from Jacobson to me. If you don't want people there to see my name, you can easily make it illegible with ink. I didn't do it because I wanted to leave that choice to you. Unfortunately, out of habit, I used the back of Jacobson's letter for the carbon copy of my reply to him. It doesn't matter. You can make the name illegible there, too.

Your wonderfully prompt reply arrived yesterday. But I won't answer it now because I want to send this by surface mail because there is no particular hurry with it.

Warmly
Your
Hannah

336   Hannah Arendt to Karl Jaspers

Chicago,[1] October 20, 1963

Lieber Verehrtester—

Thank you for the Joly.[2] I was familiar with it as a source for *The Protocols of the Elders of Zion*,[3] but I had never really read it with an eye toward its own content. An astonishing book.

I haven't written for a long time because I didn't have anything but dire news to report. At the end of August, Heinrich suddenly had serious circulatory problems, presumably of arteriosclerotic origin, and even though he is better now—he is at Bard as usual—this has left no doubt that old age has suddenly become an extremely palpable reality. That I had to go to Chicago right now, of all times, didn't make matters any easier. We telephone diligently—but what is that? On the other hand, it would have been impossible for financial reasons to cancel, and that at the last moment. We are keeping all this secret —which means among other things that we can't talk with anyone. Alcopley, who is our medical adviser, knows the situation. It's possible that he will try to see you. He is a very dear person, and very devoted to us [. . .]. At least with him one can talk.

On top of all this comes the Eichmann scandal, which continues to grow to fantastic proportions. My success in Columbia was a Pyrrhic victory in the sense that all it did was cause the Israeli government and the Jewish organizations dominated by it to redouble their efforts. And so, at the moment, to make me persona non grata in the academic world too, they have sent Ernst Simon[4] here on a special mission. He's traveling around to the universities and speaking against me everywhere at Hillel societies. Hillel is an organization for Jewish students at all the universities and most colleges, and led by rabbis. He put on his show in Chicago last week—with incredible lies and great aggressiveness. The rabbi here was by no means happy, but what could he do? It was forced on him from New York. It would have cost him his job to say no. A few weeks before New Year's Day the Anti-Defamation League sent a circular letter to all the rabbis in the country (people have told me this; I haven't seen the letter), telling them to preach against me. They haven't done it, but still! People who have publicly taken my side, primarily non-Jews, are getting propaganda material along with a letter in the mail, and the letter is from the "Prime Minister" [Ben Gurion] of Israel. And then one of the big illustrated magazines here, *Look*, wanted to do a report on this whole business at the end of July. They suggested a well-known, non-Jewish reporter. My publisher, as well as *The New Yorker*, thought I should agree to do it (answering written questions under certain conditions). They thought the story would be handled in a thoroughly fair way. But when *Look* came to do the story, they had assigned another reporter to it, a Jew, who interviewed only people who had already spoken out against me. And he sent me a questionnaire full of loaded questions. I answered the questions, but then my publisher and *The New Yorker* thought it would be better not to cooperate. There is no question in my mind that the Jewish organizations got wind of *Look*'s plans and intervened. These are only a few examples. I could multiply them at will. It's a classic case of character assassination. The method is always the same: they say I said things I never said in order to prevent people from finding out what I really did say. The German edition is being represented as terribly dangerous because I have supposedly exculpated the Germans. The implication: reparation is now endangered!

A campaign like this has a large impact. There are always a lot of people just waiting for a bandwagon to jump on—either for or against something. Then, too, everybody who is "against me" for whatever reasons is getting his chance through the organizations. Not only newspapers like the *New York Times* choose reviewers of my book from among people either I have attacked (like Musmanno[5]) or who have attacked me, but all the magazines that are headed by Jews and can be reached by the organizations are doing the same thing. That can take various forms. Jewish literary types who have never in their lives taken an interest in Jewish affairs are put forward as "experts." Those who are for me write private letters. Nobody on my side dares to publish his views anymore. And with good reason. It's extremely dangerous because a whole very well-organized mob immediately pounces on anyone who dares to say anything. Finally, everyone believes what everyone else believes—as we have often experienced in life. The old story is as true as it ever was: the one about the guard who gives out the false news that the enemy is coming and then winds up running to the walls to drive him off himself.

You said it was as if I had stumbled into an ambush. And that is absolutely true. Everything proves, in retrospect, to have been a trap. Like the exchange of letters with Scholem,[6] to whom I responded in good faith—and who then went out to shout this whole sordid story from the rooftops in *Neue Zürcher Zeitung* and *Encounter.* Which accomplished nothing else, it seems to me, than to infect those segments of the population that had not yet been stricken by the epidemic of lies. And everybody goes along. I can't do anything about it. Scholem was determined to publish, and I assumed he would in the Tel Aviv *Mitteilungsblatt*, which seemed harmless to me. And he did that first, but then used all his connections to broadcast the letters to the world.

There is hardly anything I can do, at any rate nothing that would be effective. These people know very well I can't take them to court, because it would ruin me financially and because with their massive financial and organizational resources they would win the case easily. I'll speak on the campus here next week, the only consequence of which will be that my opponents will redouble their efforts. If I wanted to refute every lie, I could spend all my time at it and would need a research staff and secretaries to help me out. In addition, I feel I am not up to this struggle. It isn't just a question of nerves and also not just that the coincidence of this business with my worries about Heinrich are simply paralyzing me. I'm incapable of presenting myself in public because my revulsion at this ruckus overwhelms everything else in me.

Finally, the question remains as to why the Jewish "establishment" is taking such an extraordinary interest in this matter and going to such massive expense. The answer seems to be that the Jewish leadership (Jewish Agency before the state of Israel was founded) has much more dirty laundry to hide than anyone had ever guessed—at any rate, I don't know very much about it. As far as I can see, ties between the Jewish leadership and the Jewish Councils may be involved. That came to light in the Kastner trial[7] and seems to be the reason why Kastner was murdered [. . .] after the trial and before the appeal trial. He was the most prominent negotiator with the Nazis, especially with Eichmann. He traveled all over Europe without a Jewish passport and was received with top honors. After the war, he was given a high position in Israel after having submitted a very positive affidavit in Nuremberg for Becher,[8] Himmler's special emissary to Budapest. He sued a journalist in Israel for libel but lost. He appealed, and he's supposed to have said that if the appeal trial turned out the same way, he would "spill the beans." Well, they won't murder me, because I don't have any beans to spill. They just want to make an example of me to show what happens to people who take the liberty of being interested in such matters. It's typical too that letters from me and to me don't go through Israeli censorship. They just don't arrive at all! Only letters to people they're sure of—Hebrew University, etc.—and to my family go through.

And because, as everyone knows, misfortune never comes alone, I'm having problems with Piper over the translation. With my approval, he gave the job to a Frau Granzow,[9] about whom I had not known that she had never done any real translating. She works for the radio in Cologne and is a pleasant person. I told him from the outset that only a first-class man should be considered. Which was of course too expensive for our good Piper. Now we're left holding the bag. I saw the first three chapters and had to revise them completely—bad German and more mistakes than usual. Frau Granzow has sent more to Frau Beradt in New York, and that seems to have looked pretty impossible, too. After I'd seen the first chapters I asked Piper to find another translator but left the decision to him. He has, of course, just let things go on as they are. I won't see the text until January, but I'm very much afraid it will be unusable.

Lieber Verehrtester, you'll understand why I hesitated for so long before writing. Why should I burden you alone and both of you together? But if I was going to write, it seemed to me, I had to say the way things are. I am not doing that with anyone else, and I am, I think, halfway capable of maintaining my façade. I give my lectures, have a lot of students, and, on the outside, things appear to be going along normally. In the end, you believe, we believe, the truth will out. But that is a belief. And the question of whether one will live to see that day is not answered by it.

Warmest greetings
Your
Hannah

337   Karl Jaspers to Hannah Arendt

Basel, October 22, 1963

Dear Hannah!

Your letter to Scholem[1] was true and profound and open. You have reached a point where many people no longer understand you. Scholem certainly not. All the better that you are still able to speak there. This strikes me as a beginning. The situation you unintentionally created prompts you to say more than you are usually inclined to say. You prefer to be personally closed where final motives are concerned, think you can translate everything into the "objective."

Now you have delivered the crucial word against "radical evil,"[2] against gnosis! You are with Kant, who said: Man cannot be a devil, and I am with you. But it's a pity that the term "radical evil," in a very different sense that was not understood even by Goethe and Schiller, comes from Kant.[3]

Now I finally want to read your Eichmann book too, so that I can speak specifically. I know in advance that I am at one with you in all the basics. But when one hears attacks, one has to know exactly what you said and how you said it.

"Das Mädchen aus der Fremde" ["The Girl from a Foreign Land"][4]: You are experiencing that in a new way, not simply—not by chance. It's good that Heinrich is standing by you—and a great number of friends as well.

Between the fronts of attack and applause you will perhaps seldom feel content. I am glad—though also a little concerned for your hidden soul, which does not have a very thick skin at all—that you can go out onto the street and no doubt do more than just hold your ground.

There are people everywhere to whom you give courage, me among them!

Gertrud joins me in warmest greetings. She becomes ferocious whenever anyone attacks you.

All best to you both
Your Karl

Basel, October 25, 1963

Dear Hannah!

Our letters crossed in the mail. What you write worries us about Heinrich. I'm expecting Alcopley this coming week. What little he told me sounded harmless. I can't put any kind of picture together. It is no doubt a sign of age, so inappropriate to you both, and too early. It's bound to change your mood. I hope that it is nothing more and that what my sister experienced over the last ten years will prove to be the case with Heinrich, too. The worst kind of symptoms she had left her again after I had long since concluded that the end was near for her. She is quite lively now, stronger than Gertrud again, and she says: Even in old age serious illnesses can take turns for the good. But that is all talk on my part. What is difficult to cope with, namely, what has to be neutralized by a pleasant, rational way of life, remains.

The persecution directed against you is dreadful. It is certainly as you have described it: a frightful symptom of our situation, the situation of the Western world and of our role in it. Whoever speaks the truth is ostracized, unless no one listens to him. I am firmly convinced that this campaign to destroy your reputation will not succeed. Whoever reads you will be instantly convinced of the high quality of your thinking, your seriousness, and your honesty, and, on further reading, of the justice and goodness of this woman who writes with such acerbity and personal restraint. Of that I have no doubt. Whether you will live to experience that? I can't have much doubt of that either. All your work taken together is convincing as a whole. The Eichmann book is only a small part of it. I've begun reading the Eichmann book, from the first to the last line. The first two chapters alone seem to me magnificent. People *must* hear the tone of sincerity in them.

The arrival of the mail—and with it the current issue of *Encounter*—interrupted my writing of this letter. In that issue I found a review[1] (that is, Gertrud found it; I took it away from her and read it). The very style that you have described!

What is revealed here is a deep-seated sense of having been struck a mortal blow. In reading your book, I'm moved to reflect on that. I'm not quite ready to believe that it's motivated by fear that abominations arising from the traffic between Zionists and Nazis during the war will be brought to light, things that very few people would know about anyhow. If that were so, then people would have some knowledge of those things. Something in "Jewry" itself has been struck a blow. And perhaps you will turn up things far worse. Well, I'll see.

Along with that comes the organization behind the molding of public opinion. It is effective because it has struck a responsive chord in people. If that is the case, "the Jews" will disown you and say you are not a real Jew, just as some Germans disown me and say I am not a real German. It won't do them any good. A time will come that you will not live to see, when the Jews will erect a monument to you in Israel, as they are doing now for Spinoza in Israel, and they will proudly claim you as their own, but even then there will still be Jews who will reject you, Jews like H. Cohen[2] and Rosenzweig,[3] who not long ago, filled with hate, supported the synagogue against the "traitor." But they will never be "the Jews," even if not a single Jew dares to agree with you publicly yet.

Gertrud said she wanted to stop sending money to Israel if it is being used to persecute you. I replied: Hannah doesn't want that. In spite of everything, she supports the state. So Gertrud will continue to contribute.

Something altogether different: Hochhuth's *The Deputy*[4] has caused a great stir here. I'm having the book sent to you. Two days ago I took part, with him and six other people (Catholics and Protestants, Probst Grüber among them), in a radio discussion that was allowed to take what course it would and was very well led by a moderator who did not take part in the discussion himself.[5] Much hate on the Catholic side, otherwise a friendly conversation. I was delighted to see this thirty-year-old German, self-taught (that is, without a university education and without a gymnasium diploma), passionately engaged with the question of the murder of the Jews. In detailed knowledge he was so far superior to the Catholic professor[6] (for modern history and current affairs) that he silenced him with facts and questions. He was not at all fanatical (the last act of the play, "Auschwitz," has the heading: A Question to God). And despite a high level

527

of reflection, he remains basically naïve. Then, too, he looks good, glowing with youthful energy and disciplined intelligence. Another "German," I thought to myself. He is getting the same treatment you are, except that he has friends as well as enemies. The government of the Federal Republic has publicly distanced itself from him (unlike Ben Gurion, who did so indirectly with you).

I'll write again when I'm through reading your book. Be patient with me. Everything takes longer.

You are both living now behind a façade that you show the world. I am with you in my heart.

Your Karl

We read in the papers that Kurt Wolff died in an accident in Germany.

339   Karl Jaspers to Hannah Arendt

Basel, October 29, 1963

Dear Hannah!

Since your last letter, bits of news pertaining to your book keep cropping up so often that I am encouraged by outside influences too to read your book. I'm in the sixth chapter now and sometimes able to anticipate already what will come later. I don't need to say how clearly your inquiry goes to the heart of the matter or how marvelous your presentation is (your critics don't contest that latter point; rather, it frightens them).

The enclosed review of a book by Ben Hecht in the *FAZ*[1] presents a picture of a matter you touch on tangentially. You are certainly familiar with it. Perhaps you'll be interested in the way it is reported here. I come away from the review feeling I have been well informed. The critic is well intentioned. For a reader like me, his judgments are in part contradicted by the material he presents. For you to go into these matters would be inappropriate to the major issues in your book. It is up to others to clarify them. It is obviously nonsense that Hecht has put an obstacle in the way of what the reviewer sees as a necessary rewriting of the history of the state's founding and of the paths taken toward the founding.[2] But that is not *your* subject.

That you are keeping your silence is obviously the only proper thing for you to do *for now*. Wonderful as your response to Scholem was and wonderful as readers (e.g., Krupp[3]) immediately felt it to be in contrast to Scholem, it was wasted effort. On *that* level, Scholem

528

cannot understand you, and many others can't either. In this hulla-baloo, which is being raised by people who are seemingly paralyzed by some of the things you deal with and who instinctively feel them-selves humiliated by your mode of thought as a whole, you cannot get a meaningful hearing. Others have to do the talking now. A time will come when you will speak again—that is at least possible. First, people will have to continue to unmask themselves unwittingly.

I await Alcopley's visit.

Warmly
Your Karl

In the few reviews of your book that I've read so far, your book itself is simply ignored.

What happened with the letters to the *New York Times* that it did not print? All of them presumably wanted publicly to take your side. Doesn't your publisher want the voices on your side to be heard? You recall: "letters that the *New York Times* did not print."

340   *Karl Jaspers to Hannah Arendt*

Basel, November 2, 1963

Dear Hannah!

Alcopley was just here. Now I know more. You know all the details. The facts cannot be talked away: the temporary kinaesthetic distur-bances, the susceptibility to fatigue, the elevated diastolic blood pres-sure. It is more than just age brings. I can understand that you are concerned, for there is unquestionably an impairment of the vital pro-cesses. There is a rule: In the majority of cases, initial symptoms may well seem frightful, but they are followed by a long period in which things go well. Then the event appears as a temporary condition. An appropriate diet and living regimen are of course essential. There are also some medications. It's good that you're keeping everything to yourselves. Will you be able to write soon how Heinrich has been in the meantime? And how is he organizing his work? He will have to keep it in narrower limits than he has up to now. When six months have passed and all is well, we'll be able to put our minds more at ease. It's my sense that your work at Chicago will last only a few more weeks. The separation at a time like this is painful for you both. Alcopley is such a likable man. I like his description of Heinrich: "an identical twin of Socrates." Heinrich won't let this get him down. The neurological knowledge he gained during his experience with the aneurysm will prevent him from falling victim to *melancholia medicinorum*. In the textbooks, you find only the disastrous cases described, not the ordinary ones. That's why beginners in medicine interpret routine abnormalities in themselves as horrible diseases. Alas, these are not altogether routine abnormalities! Or perhaps they are?

I am reading on steadily in your Eichmann book. It is wonderful for me. The Eichmann portrait is clearly the creation of a definitive picture. The course of the trial with its tension between two forces becomes lucid. The subject of the Jews' cooperation with the Nazis is only one subject. The subject of the Germans has equivalent weight. I've finished the Wannsee chapter now. The book is unsystematic; it took shape as reportage, grew into illuminating perceptions of the way things were. But I sense more in it: a desire for veracity and for the contemplation of man, but you do not speak explicitly about that.

I think you should continue to keep your silence. If I should write something, I will of course show it to you in advance (in confidence and for your criticism). I'm not ready to do so yet. The publication of the German edition, to which you will be adding a few desirable amplifications, would probably be the appropriate moment.

All best wishes to you both
Your Karl

341 *Karl Jaspers to Hannah Arendt*

Basel, November 16, 1963

Dear Hannah!

When I think of you, of you alone and of both of you, I am uneasy. It was so wonderful for all these years to see you both in your intellectual vigor, in your indestructible energy, after enduring a fate that few came through. Now old age is upon you. You resist it, and we with you. Alcopley's report was reassuring in the sense that there is no neurological condition. But the kinaesthetic disturbances (while walking on the floor, on taking hold of a doorknob) are objective symptoms, even if it is only the patient who can detect them. I hope they have passed. Is that the case? There is still nothing life-threatening. But the approach of age cannot be denied, and the necessary change that brings to one's regimen has to be learned and accepted. That isn't easy. Under these new conditions, your happy life will continue, to our pleasure as well.

The "destruction of your reputation" is, compared with that, of secondary importance and something quite different. What Mannheim[1] once said to me in Heidelberg does not apply to you: Better devastating criticism than silence; one at least becomes known. You can't tolerate human baseness, and you prefer personally to avoid the public eye. Now you are experiencing both at once. Anne Weil wrote: It's always been that way with Hannah. She says something. People are shocked and start to inveigh against her. And she responds either with astonishment or horror: But that's the way things really are! —I have read your book now from the first to the last line. I consider it marvelous in its subject matter. It bears witness, in its intent, to your uncompromising desire for truth. In its mind-set, I find it profound and full of despair; in the way it is written, a further demonstration of your literary powers. And then I think with Anne Weil: how infinitely naïve not to notice that the act of putting a book like this into the world is an act of aggression against "life-sustaining lies." Where those lies are exposed and the names of the people who live those lies are named, the meaning of those people's existence itself is at stake. They react by becoming deadly enemies. I recall the look on the face of a man, during the First World War; he was the boyfriend of our maid, whom I caught in the act of stealing. This dreadful look, almost reminiscent of the frightened, evil, and hostile looks that are occasionally shown by schizophrenics, I saw recently in the eyes of an Israeli writer[2] who visited us on Ernst Simon's urging. The look was somewhat moderated, but in its transformation from the normal one impossible to ignore. We were having a pleasant conversation. He was telling about the kibbutz he belonged to. He was a man of good will who had found his secure place in the world decades ago; enthusiastic and clear-thinking. After an hour, I brought the conversation around to you. Then I saw that look. I was really horrified, and I treated him as a psychiatrist would have. I spoke about you and your book, without any aggression on my part, expressed great admiration, went into specific points. He listened, was obviously distressed by the fact that I thought the way I did, but inwardly he was not listening; he was immovable: We have been attacked as Jews, our state has been repudiated, our Zionism has been scorned, etc. He knew nothing about you but had read your book. I do not consider him a base human

531

being but a fanatic who lives behind veils of self-deception. If one accepts that about him, he is, it seems to me, a serious person capable of making sacrifices. And so we invited him back again. People like him are sent to me so that I can learn what I want to know in living form. If he comes again, I'll see what answers he can give. There is no possibility of my changing his mind.

When I told Erna a few days ago that a critic had written of you that you despised human beings, she laughed out loud. You should have seen and heard that.

Now you are experiencing what you have never wanted: the "risks of public life." You've stumbled into it, and you'll have to stick it out. It pains you. It is no help to you to wish you some of my "thick skin." That you keep your silence for a while at first strikes me as fully appropriate. I would like to write something now, but worry to what degree I am up to it. Mainly because what I can say is on a level that most people don't understand. I think I can feel already the onset of the solidarity that all those feel who sense that their own life-sustaining lies have been exposed. Even a non-Jew perceives as his enemy anyone who has subjected Jewish realities to the light you have cast on them. That is our common fate. Except that you are less cautious and less afraid of stepping on toes than I have ever been, and you have literary powers that I lack. Funny: you said to me once that I tell people the truth so naïvely. Now you have far exceeded me in that naïveté.

I have several reviews (*Encounter*,[3] *Midstream*,[4] *Das neue Israel*,[5] and a brochure, *Nach dem Eichmannprozess*, published by the Council of Jews from Germany with an essay by Ernst Simon[6] in it). Can you send me anything else? I'll send it back if you don't have duplicates. Or perhaps what I have is enough?

How little I made use of the otherwise so pleasant weeks with you this spring. I was at a low ebb and also still didn't know your Eichmann book, in which I had looked at only a few pages. Now an extended conversation about the problems it presents would be very important to me.

My *Cusanus* is almost done. Should I send it right to Manheim? It is longer than I had planned. I'm reading it through one more time to see what I can cut.

Gertrud remains unchanged in her outrage. Anyone who attacks you had better watch out. You know what her anger is like. I calm her down about the individual "mistakes" that are of no consequence for the argument: Baeck's title in Berlin,[7] the sequence of events in Rumania,[8] Antonescu's and Hitler's initiative,[9] etc.

Please send a few lines about how Heinrich is now!

Thinking of you and Heinrich with love

Your Karl

Gertrud found a letter for you in the linen closet. It must have arrived too late to catch you. We are both becoming very old people: forgetful, easily tired, a lot of annoying but not crippling complaints. But we are enjoying life.

And despite all my complaints, I am still contemplating making thirteen television broadcasts, a half hour each. "A Short Course in Philosophical Thinking."[10] It would be an attempt to make the leap from concrete problems to philosophical questions and in that way to reach "the masses." It's to be a kind of university via television. I'll sit at my desk. Here in our house. I'd like to do it. But it will cut into work on *Die grossen Philosophen*. 25,000 marks.[11]

Am I biting off too much?

342 *Karl Jaspers to Hannah Arendt*

Basel, November 22, 1963

Dear Hannah!

I'm bombarding you with letters. Perhaps you haven't even received them all. But now I have to send you and Heinrich a few words: I'm hearing about the attack on Kennedy right now.[1] There's one news bulletin after the other on the radio. He is in a state between life and death. Someone said: If the Russians are behind this . . . Gertrud's immediate response: No, it has got to be the racial question. Is this Lincoln over again?[2] But now with completely different consequences? I have the feeling that something major has occurred, and I don't know yet rationally what to expect next.

Krupp just called, then Ernst Levy[3]—all shocked. I don't think the reactions hysterical.

Just a word of greeting to you both! from Gertrud

and Your Karl

Chicago, November 24, 1963

Lieber Verehrtester, liebe Gute—

I'm writing still under the shock caused by Kennedy's murder. For days we've been sitting by the radio and listening to news reports that are not only horrible but also, and worse still, completely foggy. The murder of the suspect[1]—about whom one can't help thinking that he was caught purely by chance or, worse, not by chance—by this underworld character, of whom the radio was just saying, as though by the by, that he was well known to the police in Dallas (was on a good footing with them?), has made everything much worse. And in one's preoccupation with these perhaps—let us hope—quite unfounded suspicions, one forgets the most important thing—the death of the man. Heinrich, with whom I've been on the phone constantly, said it was as if the shot that killed Kennedy had really struck the center of things, the center, that is, that held everything, both in domestic and in foreign policy, in balance, and it was as if now everything could collapse like a house of cards. It was very clear here that the young people and the Negroes were most deeply affected. Our waiters here in the club, all of them students, wept quite openly when the news was announced as we were all at lunch. I was not alone. Mary (McCarthy, about whom you were so kind as to send me the clipping from the *FAZ*[2] and who has become very famous all at once) had come here from New York for the weekend. She was in the States for a few weeks but will fly back to Paris day after tomorrow. We are perhaps even closer than before, because of these days. She has just flown back to New York, because she wants to try to form a committee of nonpartisan people who will insist on a real investigation of the facts. Texas has already announced that as far as it's concerned the case is closed; and that without any really conclusive evidence having ever reached the public—assuming that it really exists. I can't imagine that Bobby (Kennedy, the attorney general) won't do everything possible to clear up the murder of his brother. But does he still have the power now?

[Lyndon B.] Johnson is not a bad man, but he is a mediocre one. A clever tactician, provincial, basically without any understanding of anything. Perhaps he can learn, but he is ill, heart problems. He is a provisional solution, and from now on everybody will be thinking only about the next election. The Texas story itself, with the double murder and the obvious attempt not to inform the public, sounds like an event in a police state. The incompetence of the president's security forces, who left a huge building from which you can see everything unwatched, sounds like something from a fairy tale.

Heinrich: It seems that he is teaching his classes better than ever before. Mary [McCarthy] was at Bard and told me that the students lit up with pleasure when they learned that Blücher was an old friend of Mary's. They said that in every class he always tops himself. But that doesn't mean that he is well. He complains now as before about very great fatigue, lack of energy. The kinaesthetic disturbances are almost gone—they are probably neurological symptoms after all. His blood pressure is back to normal, too. It seems beyond any doubt to me that he is suffering from a real depression. Mary told him of course what the students had said—he won't hear any of it. But then he goes and gives a brilliant class. I'll see. I'm flying to New York for a few days on Tuesday. It will be Thanksgiving here, and both of us have a few days off. I also have to try to get him to the doctor again. He balks at it, in part because it is all just too much for him.

The Eichmann affair continues on its merry way. I'm sending you a few of the English reviews that have undergone some manipulation, too—probably from Talmon[3] (Hebrew University) and possibly from Isaiah Berlin,[4] who is on the closest of terms with the government in Israel. I spoke on the campus here, with very good success. Even more students than at Columbia. The talk was taped because so many people couldn't fit into the hall. Then the rabbi played it several times that evening at Hillel House. [Ernst] Simon, the rabbi said, apologized to him the next morning. He met with no great success; the students were rather put off and disgusted. The only person here on the campus who is agitating against me is Leo Strauss, and he would have done it in any case. Oddly enough, my standing at the university has, if anything, risen. And what is going on in New York at the moment is taking place more in small circles, though within them the tone is that of a howling mob. What is serious about this is that all the non-Jews are on my side now and that not a single Jew dares to stand up for me publicly, even if he is completely with me. [Robert] Lowell, a very well-known American poet and a good friend, was here and told me these things. He is not a Jew, and for the first time in the many years I've known him, I heard him make critical remarks about Jews.

You said: "What is revealed here is a deep-seated sense of having been struck a mortal blow. Something in Jewry itself has been struck a blow." That is absolutely true. The Israeli consul here came up to me after a lecture, and we spoke together for several hours. He said over and over again: Of course everything you say is true. We know that. But how could you as a Jew say this "in a hostile environment"? I said: As far as I knew I was not living in a hostile environment here. And he said: But you know that any non-Jewish environment is hostile. It is unforgivable that I spoke of the division between Jews and goys, and that I didn't respect that division is even more unforgivable. Because of Hitler and Auschwitz two things have become virulent again, the ancient *odium humani generis* and the terrible ancient fear.

Your letter of November 16 went to New York first and reached me here only on Thursday. When I read it, I thought, what would I do without the two of you! The Israeli writer[5] was probably sent to you to sound you out, which does not matter of course. He has probably been ordered to report to Simon. He is not altogether typical. Among the younger Jews one finds nonfanatics, too. I had several Israeli students in my classes here. I could talk with them, and they stressed that they were more or less of my opinion. —Apropos of the "mistakes": they're inevitable in this kind of book that consists only of facts. But Rumania and Bulgaria are not among those mistakes! The United Restitution Organization[6] gave birth to that myth through *Aufbau*. I wrote *Aufbau* a letter correcting their error, as did several other people, but *Aufbau* refused to print any of our corrections! At the same time and on his own initiative, the man who sent information to *Aufbau*—a Mr. May,[7] I think—wrote how much he was disgusted by the hate campaign of the Robinson brothers[8] and others, and that that kind of persecution gave great cause for concern! This talking out of both sides of one's mouth is characteristic of this whole business to an incredible degree. The cynicism of the functionaries is beyond belief. They take it as a matter of course and think there's nothing wrong with it. They assure me of how much they "admire" me and my Eichmann book in particular! And when I say: Well, then how is this possible, they say: But really now, you must understand . . . I could tell you stories like that one after another. But it's too boring.

I've just heard on the radio that the murder of Oswald has been taken out of the hands of the police and the authorities in Texas and that the Justice Department (that's Robert Kennedy) does not consider the case "closed" at all. That is still no real guarantee that there'll be an investigation, but still it's much better than nothing at all. It seems that the reporters protested. The press has, thank God, some real power here. As far as Texas is concerned, I share the opinion that I heard expressed everywhere day before yesterday—that state should go back where it came from.

The television series—wonderful. You've got to do it provided your health permits. That way you really will reach the "many," and the many are not the masses at all. —Congratulations on completion of the *Cusanus*. Yes, please send the manuscript to Manheim first. He will then send me the translation along with the original. Helen Wolff is finally coming to America, in January, I think. She wrote a very calm and lovely letter.

I'll write about how Heinrich is doing as soon as I come back from New York. That will be the end of the week.

What are your complaints of old age? New ones? Your letters sound good, everything but "old," God knows. How awful that we live so far apart!

You've never written what happened with Rossmann's appointment. I'd very much like to know. Annchen's remark—yes, she is probably right; that's essentially the way it's always been. Except that in the public context things are significantly different. And of course I'm "naïve"—as I was writing, I really didn't think of anything else but presenting things as correctly and as fully supported by facts as I could.

With love
Your
Hannah

344   *Hannah Arendt to Karl and Gertrud Jaspers*

December 1, 1963

Lieber Verehrtester, dear Friend,

I've just gotten back from New York, where I found your letter. We all had exactly the same feeling—something dreadful has happened. And the equally dreadful accompanying circumstances—Dwight Macdonald (you recall that it was through his magazine *politics* that we first got in touch with each other again) wrote: "What a country we live in (assuming Texas is part of it); let's move to Guatemala or some civilized place, maybe the Congo"—that have not been explained at all yet make the whole awful business seem more ominous with each passing hour. My feeling right now is that the new administration really will try to clear this thing up. Whether it will succeed—in Texas, where the police are not only corrupt but also riddled through with supporters of the [John] Birch Society[1]—is another question. In any case, it will be weeks and perhaps months before we'll be able to assess what the consequences will be. It seems as if a mask has suddenly been torn off the face of this country. And behind it we see an abyss of potential violence and pure bloodthirstiness that we had not guessed was there to this extent. In the South, it's the accepted thing to call anybody a Communist who sides with the Negroes in their struggle for equality. That is the real key. I've heard that students at the University of Texas said, or, rather, screamed, "That's what happens to a nigger-loving president, and that's what'll happen to every nigger lover!" And schoolchildren reacted with wild, spontaneous applause when they heard the news. What's at stake is no more nor less than the existence of the republic. But the forces of sanity are very strong, and it can be that this murder will bring people to their senses after all. That a man from Texas, of all people, will be Kennedy's successor is ironic beyond belief. Kennedy's wife behaved marvelously, and what is irrevocably gone now, even if everything should fall back into place again, is this whole new atmosphere, the "Kennedy style"—an openness to the arts and sciences, a respect for the life of the mind, a conscious and consistent attempt to give intellectuals a voice in the political arena without influencing or exploiting them.

Heinrich: I'm feeling much easier about him. I flew home to see to it that he finally got to the doctor. The minute I saw him I felt relieved. He looks much better than he did two months ago. We went to see the same neurologist he had consulted when he had the aneurysm and who was very concerned then. He examined him thoroughly and thinks there are absolutely no neurological symptoms and, in his view, no indications of premature arteriosclerosis, no indications of premature aging. Heinrich has very slight kinaesthetic disturbances—only subjectively detectable—in his left hand, which make themselves felt when he is nervous. Objectively, he has made a "miraculous recovery." The doctor wants to do some follow-up work in the hospital on the symptoms of fatigue—blood tests. Perhaps Heinrich is slightly diabetic, which the doctor does not think, or slightly anemic, which he thinks possible. But that can all wait until vacation. The blood pressure is normal (140:80). The doctor was against Heinrich continuing to take this medication that dilates the blood vessels. He thinks the complaints in the feet (in both feet and appearing intermittently) are due to a slight

538

neuritis, like the one he had once six years ago. These symptoms have passed, and there are no objective findings. Alcopley will write to you; he spoke with the doctor right after the exam. —It's clear that Heinrich is depressed, a natural consequence of the Eichmann affair. Also of the fact that he can't punch a few of these people in the nose. He is really a very old-fashioned gentleman where I am concerned. But he also has to realize that he really isn't quite up to brawling with younger men anymore (thank God!!). And because he has lived his whole life in an eternal present without any consciousness of passing time, he is presumably realizing for the first time that he is getting older. Mentally, he is in very good form.

Hochhuth: Thank you! I had the book[2] in my hands at your house, but I hadn't really read it until now. *Osservatore Romano*'s first reaction is typical: If Hochhuth is right, then it's the pope who is to blame for the murder of the Jews, not Hitler and the SS. That's the very same distortion my Eichmann book ran up against. The same old tactics (which always seem ready to hand). Some nonsense you never said gets attributed to you; then people won't discuss anything but the nonsense so they can dodge the real issues. The book is very sympathetic but unfortunately not of much literary merit. That Hochhuth is right is beyond any doubt: after all, the Vatican excommunicated not only the Communists but also the Action Française[3] in the twenties. Only Hitler and racism were never censured! It should be obvious in purely theological terms that racism is a genuine heresy: if the sacrament of baptism can't make a Christian out of a Jew—and the fact that not even baptized Jews received any official protection demonstrates that it cannot—then the church might as well declare itself bankrupt.

Here in Chicago people tell me that the Jews have joined forces with the Catholics against Hochhuth and are claiming that his play is anti-Semitic!! They, along with the Catholics, have protested against a performance of the play here. And Heinrich just told me on the phone that he had read in the *Times* that a man from B'nai B'rith[4] (the very powerful organization that is behind the Anti-Defamation League and that is leading the campaign against me here) has announced that he will "refute" Hochhuth's thesis and show that the pope's intervention would only have made things worse. There are two motives behind all this: first, relations between the Jews and the Vatican are very good right now; and the Jews want to show themselves as duly grateful.

And, second, there is the community of interests among all bureaucracies: nobody is interested in looking at the matter too closely. So one hand washes the other.

I'll be here for two more weeks and have an idiotic amount of stuff to do. Too boring to explain.

Say hello to Erna for me!

With love
Your
Hannah

345 *Karl Jaspers to Hannah Arendt*

Basel, December 13, 1963

Dear Hannah!

Your two letters were a blessing to us in our worry and distress about Heinrich. I was afraid, because I had heard nothing more from you, that you wanted to "spare" us. Alcopley hadn't had any recent reports either. Heinrich's impact as a lecturer is vividly present to me, the power of his teaching and the seriousness his students sense in him. Perhaps both our worries—about his illness and about you—are of the kind that, if they don't kill us, intensify our mental activity. Thank you for your detailed reports. Now, thinking of you, I am in good spirits again, though I am by no means making light of what has happened. A tolling of the bell was clearly audible.

The Israeli writer (his name is Rübner or something like that) was here again. The subject of your book soon came up, of course. It was a good talk because both of us spoke at length and neither held a monologue. He proved to be accessible, obviously of goodwill, was open, seemed to gain trust in me. He began to suspend judgment about your book. He knew it only on the basis of excerpts in an Israeli newspaper. I sense his own disappointments and doubts. Like you he is rooted in the Jewish biblical tradition, but differently. He lacks, however, the proud contentment that some feel at having found a homeland. The next time we get together, he wants to tell me about the kibbutzim, which are his real world, and about the apparently insolvable problems that are arising there. This time, there was no trace of fanaticism. Perhaps I was unjust to him the last time (I wrote you about the "evil" look). I do not think he will remain your enemy, even if, after getting to know your book better, he should still disagree strongly with it. We'll see. I'm optimistic. Gertrud was not present because she didn't want to be and could excuse herself with a cold. Talks like this work only between two people. Her anger would have inhibited the young writer (who, by the way, makes no claims to being a writer. That is Ernst Simon's label).

Now something that makes me very sad. I understand Golo Mann has written a very harsh article against you (in *Neue Rundschau*).[1] I've ordered a copy of the issue, but haven't received it yet. What Rossmann wrote me about it is so bad that I don't know what to think. After I had read what Rossmann had to say, I lay down and gave myself up to gloomy visions: Are we ourselves destroying freedom by violating the bonds of solidarity that should unite us even when we disagree most violently? Are forces emerging in our midst that strike out with blind ill will? Is that solidarity giving way to the pseudo-solidarity of literati, which (despite all the squabbling among themselves that is really not taken seriously) comes to the fore when somebody writes not merely because he wants to write and perhaps can write beautifully and is looking for material on which he can display this talent, but because he is searching for the truth and has something drawn from heartrending experience to convey, experience that doesn't speak of itself but, as with you, is hidden in the style that some people reproach you for, calling you ironic, cold, heartless, know-it-all, misanthropic (I've read things like that in some reviews; exactly what Golo has said I don't know yet, but apparently it is of this order)? —Excuse my miserable style, this long sentence; it doesn't work even grammatically. . . . I'm reminded of Ernst Mayer: we had very profound disagreements, but something remained that never broke, probably more thanks to him than to me; of that I have no doubt. Or I'm reminded of Max Weber; our relationship was never put to the ultimate test. I have my doubts sometimes, but then recall his extraordinary willingness to listen, and I cease to doubt, but I really don't know. Something remained hidden with him. And looking back into the past, I thought about still other people. I thought: Could Hannah ever destroy the bond between us? We have disagreed so often and on crucial matters, or at least so it seemed. No, I said to myself, that is impossible. Even to voice that doubt is inadmissible. For it leads to the point where *everything* crumbles, and then it is the doubter himself who is at fault. You see, I'm reporting how the news about Golo Mann hit me. Then wild, extreme thoughts come over me. But between Golo and me something is torn. At a moment like this, one recalls moments from the past that seem to be precursors of this latest incident. It pains me. I liked him a lot. I still like him a lot.

Behind all this lie the big basic questions: What is it that's so important about "mind" after all (I find here a confirmation of my philosophy, in which I have not to this day quite succeeded in saying what mind is)? What is "literary life," this corruptible yet powerful force that has more to do with lies than with truth? How weak we are! Our strength is not adequate to make our insights prevail.

My feeling is that you needn't let this racket disturb your inner life anymore. You know what it's all about now. And Heinrich, whom I can well understand, might do better to laugh rather than threaten to beat up this pack. There are still some primitive instincts left in us "men" that I value very highly but don't take too seriously anymore. Our loyalty shows itself in other ways.

Alcopley told me that Heinrich suggested the phrase "the banality of evil" and is cursing himself for it now because you've had to take the heat for what he thought of. Perhaps the report isn't true, or my recollection of it is garbled. I think it's a wonderful inspiration and right on the mark as the book's subtitle. The point is that *this* evil, not evil per se, is banal. I wasn't altogether happy with your phrasing of this point in your response to Scholem.[2] *What* evil is stands *behind* your phrase characterizing Eichmann. And that question is indeed one we will probably never be quite able to answer adequately. Your answer in your letter struck me as too combative and too weak at the same time. Well, if you were here, we would soon be in hot debate over this—to our mutual pleasure.

How happy I am that I can think about you both again the way I could before, with the slight change that Fate has knocked harder on your door and that the quality of your life, in keeping with your age, has become less secure in an area you had not given much thought to before. That's probably why Heinrich—and you, too, I assume—are giving such good lectures.

Fondly
Your Karl

Basel, December 13, 1963

Dear Heinrich!

You are keeping silent, but through Hannah you are speaking to me, too. Perhaps you are thinking there isn't much to say. You refuse to let yourself be impressed by these stupid phenomena that nature, which is otherwise so clever, is turning loose on you with savage randomness. Because they are keeping themselves within narrow limits and you are not faced with anything truly threatening, the vital spirit that is the real core of our being can declare itself satisfied. The episode was, I think, only a superficial skirmish and a playful warning meant to remind you that nature's bad aspect is as much a reality as its good one. It does not grant us immortality. I am happy to have had such good reports about you from Hannah and from Alcopley. But please do not maintain a total silence toward one who thinks of himself as your friend—

Karl

Basel, January 29, 1964

Dear Hannah!

We were happy to receive your kind letter of December 29.[1] Your sovereign tone shows that you are no longer suffering the way you were earlier when you wrote: "I feel I am not up to this struggle."[2] That was meant only in an external sense, as far as the public of literati, politicians, Jews, and Germans was concerned. In the meantime, several people have come out publicly on your side—as in the first letters to the *New York Times*.[3] I'm thinking about writing a little pamphlet, if you do not object: "Uber die Unabhängigkeit des Denkens."[4] I'm making notes as they occur to me, but the thirteen television lectures hinder progress on it.

Piper wrote me today that you have Frau Granzow's translation. I'm thinking about your expanding a few sections, particularly those relating to the "German resistance." We have spoken about this and also corresponded about it. A clarification of what the different kinds of resistance were would obviate all embarrassing discussion. Won't you modify your view of Reck-Malleczewen and me[5] as the sole examples of our kind? You agreed, if I remember correctly, to an estimate

543

of 100,000; that is of course an arbitrary figure. It could as well have been 300,000 or 50,000. Sternberger volunteered the information to me a few days ago that Reck-Malleczewen had not been thought highly of in Theodor Haecker's[6] circle in Munich. There was doubt about whether he had been put in the concentration camp for political reasons at all. Such rumors are not to be trusted; perhaps Theodor Haecker isn't either. What you have read is decisive, assuming your ear has not picked up any false notes in Reck-Malleczewen's book. Citing these two names as the *only* ones has clearly struck some people as odd or as an eccentric perception, because they are so different from each other. Your basic presentation of the national motive as crucial I find correct. That's the way it was. Golo Mann's printing of a long quote from a letter from Goerdeler to refute you[7] is a low trick that he was probably not aware of committing. Goerdeler, by the way, in his plans for the time *after* Hitler's fall, had envisaged a Jewish state on Madagascar, which German Jews could of course choose. Or if they wanted to, they could remain in Germany! What crudity and thoughtlessness, and then at *that* time! I have to say that I found Ritter's book[8] wonderful because, as a good scholar should, he presented all the facts that spoke against his own position. His homage to Goerdeler is, quite against his own intentions, a damnation of Goerdeler. It reminds me of Meinecke's *Weltbürgertum und Nationalstaat*,[9] where—on a higher level—Meinecke provided material (on Gneisenau[10] and others, for example) that for a reader like me undermined his affirmation of the Bismarck state.

Warmest greetings to you both from Gertrud and
Your Karl

Heinrich has been to the doctor for examination in the meantime. Because we have heard nothing, we assume all is well?

348   Hannah Arendt to Karl Jaspers

New York, February 19, 1964

Lieber Verehrtester—

I didn't want to write until I could send you the enclosed pages[1] on the resistance movement, and now I see that it is February 19—exactly a year ago I was in Switzerland when that lovely, unforgettable flood of affection, respect, and love washed over you both. It seems as if it was just yesterday. This year your birthday will be calmer, and the messengers won't have to bring the telegrams into the house in huge envelopes. How much I would like to be there right now. It's particularly vexing to me that I don't have anyone in Zurich now who can order hyacinths. I don't want to burden Erna with that, so I'll make arrangements here. And I'm renewing your subscription to the *Zürcher Zeitung*. And what I wish you and us—that I do not need to say.

Perhaps you can take a look at the enclosed pages and let me know what you think. I've read a lot of stuff. The only useful thing was Ritter, who may be unsympathetic but is amazingly objective. Otherwise—what can one say? In one of Goerdeler's memos, he says in one paragraph that the German people are informed about everything (meaning that there is no danger; we can stage the coup at any time), and in the next paragraph on the next page he says the German people are not informed at all, for if they were, things could not have come to the sorry pass they are at (this he says to prove that all one need do is announce publicly what has happened and everyone will support the resistance, also to whitewash the German people). Exactly the same kind of thing occurs in Henk.[2] For example, in the memo you sent me. On the first page he says the Gestapo had absolutely nothing to go on on July 20; they didn't know a thing. And on the next page: the Gestapo had what it needed from the word go! Reck-Malleczewen: the book[3] speaks for itself. Nobody could invent that. The rumors presumably go back to the frequent defamations on the part of the Gestapo, which of course preferred not to make arrests on political grounds and so trumped up all kinds of charges. I don't believe that, and I don't care one way or another. I really haven't been able to do anything but present in greater detail what is in the English edition in somewhat abbreviated form, because in the context of the book this is a secondary issue or circumstance. That nobody knew about preparations for the assassination attempt on Hitler, as Henk claims, is simply untrue. It was common knowledge in Stockholm, and it has been demonstrated innumerable times that Himmler was informed. All these things are an embarrassment. I have mentioned your name again, but we can easily strike it if you think its appearance inappropriate. I won't send this material to Piper until I've heard from you.

The fuss about me has quieted down here, and people are gearing up to go after Hochhuth instead. I've written an article for the *Herald Tribune*.[4] The good Catholics are all on Hochhuth's side; the Spellman Catholics[5] have literally let the Jewish Anti-Defamation League (which led the campaign against me) prepare their attack on Hochhuth. And what the gentleman there has produced in the way of barefaced lies surpasses what they came up with in the Eichmann affair, if that is possible. As far as I am concerned, the universities have saved me. Wherever I go—last week, Yale Law School; this week, a college in the neighborhood, etc.—I'm received with ovations, and the demand among students and for courses is so great that we have to speed up publication of the paperback edition. In addition, the National Institute for Arts and Letters, a kind of Institut Française with great prestige here, has elected me to membership,[6] which is ordinarily not granted to people like me. There are no scholars, only artists, poets, novelists. They did it of course "aus reiner Daffke" [for a lark] (assuming you know what that means. If not, Gertrud can explain).

Helen Wolff has been here for a few weeks and has visited us several times. I like her a lot. I read your *Cusanus*[7]—absolutely wonderful. Helen took it with her again right away to get it translated. In exchange she left me your Max Weber essay from the *Drei Essays*,[8] which she wants to publish, and we have run into some problems with it. Helen and Manheim as well are troubled by some very nationalistic-sounding passages. I've looked at it and think the only passages to cause concern are as follows (references are to the German edition[9]): pp. 24–26, "Germany's Mission in World History," also on p. 33 the last sentence of the first paragraph and on p. 34—"the first Pole who dares to set foot in Danzig will be met by a bullet." You say in the preface: "Today, all politics stand in the light of new historical premises that, practically, lay outside the intellectual perspectives available to Max Weber."[10] I think it would be good if you could repeat this, phrasing it in a slightly different way, at each of the three passages I mentioned. Or perhaps in the foreword you could explicitly tie this idea to those three passages. What do you think?

In the last two months we have been leading here what you call our "nice life." All Heinrich's physical exams turned up nothing. Alcopley and I are convinced that the episode was caused by a spasm in the brain, which cannot be objectively verified and seems to have passed without leaving any damage behind. In any case, his health is excellent, and intellectually he is in top form. He is impatient with people, but otherwise no longer irritated by day-to-day things and no longer tired. His depression is gone, too. Of course I shouldn't be away for long periods anymore. But how can I manage that? All kinds of arrangements have been made in Chicago to accommodate me. How can I just turn around and walk out on them? Quite apart from the question of our own finances. I haven't heard anything further from Yale. They won't wait forever. If I could have here what I have in Chicago and if the students in Chicago weren't counting on me, then all my problems would be solved. In the meantime my so-called boss in Chicago—the chairman of the department, in effect my dean—was here, met Heinrich, and they immediately became friends. That doesn't make things the least bit easier. Heinrich and I came to the conclusion today that attacks may threaten to destroy you (which is really not so terrible after all) but that it's the expressions of approval that really do you in. This country is just too big.

I could write a lot about politics, none of it very encouraging. Kennedy shouldn't have been allowed to die or Roncalli[11] either. A friend wrote us from Rome that he had read Hochhuth, and someone had asked him what should be done. He replied: "What can one do against the truth?" Adenauer, on the other hand, is reported to have said of Hochhuth (to the Italian ambassador): "That idiot! He's a Communist."

Good-bye and be well!

All best wishes
Your Hannah

349   Karl Jaspers to Hannah Arendt

Basel, March 1, 1964

Dear Hannah!

I want to reply to your letter soon. But for today, just this one point so that there will be no delay.

I think your amplification—on the question of the German resistance—is good. I agree with it. It is harsh but true. The space limitations, particularly in the framework of this book, do not permit of much more. Bonhoeffer,[1] von Tresckow, and others would be deserving of close study (I don't know much about them either. I suspect examination would reveal very positive, though apolitical, factors). Your use of Ritter is a good irony: one has to praise these historians on the whole for their devotion to "objectivity," for not wanting to falsify, and for including information that runs counter to their own value judgments—all helped along perhaps by their own lack of awareness.

I think my name has to stay because Golo Mann has already referred to it.[2] Opponents will check what you have changed, and cutting is riskier there than adding. And furthermore, I consider it an honor that *you* give me this place, even though I am not altogether comfortable in it.

We are happy about the negative results of Heinrich's medical examinations.

For today, just this in haste
Warmly
Your Karl

350   Karl Jaspers to Hannah Arendt

Basel, March 24, 1964

Dear Hannah!

Excuse me for waiting so long and for sending the changes for "Max Weber" with a dictated accompanying letter now. I hope these changes will dispel your reservations:

First, I'm replacing one whole paragraph in the foreword with a new one, which is enclosed with the manuscript. "Basel 1958 and 1964" will also have to be added at the end of the foreword.

Second, I would suggest adding the short essay enclosed here. This essay is from the Salin festschrift.[1] I have changed some things and cut others because it has already appeared in my little Max Weber book.

I'm under pressure because I'm afraid I won't be able to meet the deadline for the thirteen television programs. I have to admit I'm feeling my age. And so, unfortunately, I'm putting everything else off or just letting it lie. But that does not mean that if you have further reservations that you shouldn't let me know what they are or that I won't make changes you request. It is perhaps somewhat untenable to elevate Max Weber to such a unique position in political thinking, given the fact that individual elements in him seem to correspond to the fateful political positions of those times. I consider that correspondence one of appearance only. When the young Max Weber joined the Pan-German Union,[2] he had completely different ideas. He left it again very quickly. He was never able to join with others. The apparently genuine affinity with Friedrich Naumann's National Socialist Union[3] was in reality a situation in which he was constantly instructing the party and defending himself against it. He didn't fit in anywhere. It is easy to point

548

out constant self-contradictions in him, which ultimately turn out to be reasonable—in that he is like you. But in spite of all that, I am not at one with Max Weber in my basic philosophical position, but cannot say what it really is that separates us. I could always reach agreement with him in conversation about specifics, but the abyss of his despair was of a kind that made me sense he was charged with something I was not charged with. There was an explosive force in him that I lack. In the field of scholarship and research, he had to bear something perhaps as unbearable as what Kierkegaard and Nietzsche had to bear. It is amazing how indifferent he felt about all of his passionate scholarly productivity. I do not think he could have functioned as a statesman. He would have failed, and probably quickly, because at some point or another he would have been too trusting or too chivalrous. In a real crisis he probably would not have been able to do what he knew was best.

Warmest greetings
Your Karl

Warmest greetings to Heinrich from Gertrud and me.

In your external life, the whole critical uproar ultimately only added to your prestige, rather than detracted from it. But in your inner life, you have had to swallow some bitter disappointments.

I read that Hilberg[4] had publicly taken your side. Is that right? Could you lend me his review for a short while?

351 *Hannah Arendt to Karl Jaspers*

New York, April 20, 1964

Lieber Verehrtester—

I am enclosing my reply to Henk[1] in the odd envelope addressed by Gertrud. I assume that you saw his letter, but if not, it is almost identical, word for word, with the letter he sent Gertrud months ago. He is clearly an excellent fellow, but not very bright. And this kind of language—"the honor of my dead friend," etc.—gets on my nerves, but people are no doubt so accustomed to that in Germany that they don't even notice it anymore. The man from the resistance that I mentioned is, by the way, Axel von dem Bussche, who once, much earlier, attempted unsuccessfully to blow himself up along with Hitler.[2] He said: You (meaning me) overestimate the courage of these people. The assassination attempt failed, and had to fail, because every one of the participants in it wanted a guarantee that he would still be alive on the evening of July 20. But this is really just between us! He told me nothing about himself; I learned that only later from other people. He must have noticed that I had no idea who he was. He left off all his titles and "vons," also in the letter he wrote to me. We talked mainly about the Jewish question, anti-Semitism, Zionism, and such.

Now something else: I've written a foreword for the German edition of the Eichmann book, as Piper asked me to do. And I asked him to send you a photocopy. I hate to burden you with all this—but I really need your advice. It seemed to me weeks ago in a letter from you in March that you were hesitant—you said: "I'm not altogether comfortable"—with being named by name. We can still cut your name from the resistance section. What people like Golo Mann have to say really couldn't bother me less. In the last year, I've grown a skin that would make an elephant green with envy.

Piper has grandiose plans. He's coming here at the end of the week. He wants me to go to Germany for the book fair in September and then—press conference, radio talk with Bondy and Ernst Schnabel[3] and an interview with *Der Spiegel*. I'm more than uneasy about it. I'm not good at this sort of thing, not quick at repartee, I fall into traps easily, etc. And on top of that, I just plain hate this kind of to-do. What do you think?

I originally meant to come for a quick visit in June, if that was all right with you. But now I can't because some university has come up with the crazy idea of giving me an honorary doctorate of laws.[4] Very funny. But my publisher says I can't refuse it because then the university will feel insulted. And this falls right in the middle of the month. I can't come in May, because then I'll be in Chicago again, and in July Heinrich's semester will just have ended. He'll be home, and I don't want to go away then. So maybe in September after all, but without the book fair? What do you think?

I haven't heard anything about Hilberg's coming out on my side. He's talking some nonsense now about the "death wish" of the Jews. His book[5] is really excellent, but only because he just reports facts in it. His introductory chapter that deals with general and historical matters wouldn't pass muster in a pigpen. (Excuse me—I momentarily forgot to whom I was writing. But now that I've said it, I'll let it stand.)

The Max Weber chapter is still giving us trouble. Helen Wolff discovered that there are more overlappings than you had noticed, and so we had a long conference today. I suggested using it as a kind of appendix after the chapter about Max Weber as politician and giving the date of it. Then it would conclude the discussion of politics in Weber, and that seems best to me. She was doubtful that readers here would be interested in the question of what Max Weber would have said about National Socialism. She is mistaken. That's the very thing students do ask about. It will all come together quite well. She is extremely reliable and asks me about everything.

How do things look for Rossmann?[6]

How is work on the television lectures going?

I wish we could talk about Max Weber—I just read your letter again.

Until we meet, and I hope that will be soon! A year ago we were wandering around in Greece, and then we came to see you.

All best wishes
Your
Hannah

352 Karl Jaspers to Hannah Arendt

Basel, April 25, 1964

Dear Hannah!

This letter will have a weary quality about it. Twelve days ago I had a bronchiectatic ague with several days of fever. I'm over the fever and up again. This episode was no cause for alarm. But my condition is as it was when you saw me last year (to put it presumptuously: below my usual level).

I hardly need write about Emil Henk. You are absolutely right. Gertrud is, where she is grateful, eternally grateful. The reason she sent him an envelope that she had addressed to you is this: She had sent him your address twice before. He kept asking for it again over and over. So she wanted to make things easier for him. It is disappointing that he had nothing more to write to you than he had said in his letter to Gertrud. Gertrud had hoped he would be able to put you onto some new facts. The dead friend is presumably Haubach, whom I knew well. He was with Henk at our place on July 22, after the assassination attempt. We discussed the dangers. Haubach and Henk were touching in their solicitude for my wife. She soon turned the conversation around: How was Haubach to protect himself? He was just as much in danger even if he didn't know about the attempt in advance. Haubach agreed. He planned to go into hiding with friends in Mecklenburg. But he didn't do it because he convinced himself that no more arrests were being made. He was caught because of sheer carelessness. What he then endured was horrible. Henk was informed throughout. Every feeling of sympathy with his fate was justified. But he was not a "hero." Oh, all the pain![1]

Henk, a great support to me during the war, particularly in regard to the military situation, very clever, made good and well-founded predictions. That was wonderful in those times when one could speak with hardly anyone and when almost everyone, even friends, like Radbruch among others (Dibelius and Alfred Weber were the *only* exceptions) were hoping for a German victory. On the day the Americans arrived in Heidelberg and as the American soldiers were still advancing cautiously, taking advantage of all cover, there were a few young, very young German soldiers, in uniform, beyond the garden in the park, also taking cover, behind the trees. It was midday, twelve noon. Henk was with us, and he opened the window and yelled out: "Don't be crazy. Put down your rifles and surrender!"—which the soldiers promptly did. But after that, Henk very soon began to curse the Americans, having discovered his national heart. Gertrud was horrified, and said: "Let's not talk about it! They have liberated us all!" And so the subject quickly became taboo. —But enough of this.

Wonderful, what you had to tell about von dem Bussche! Of course I'll keep it to myself. A pity that such men keep silent. They presumably do so out of pride, because they don't want to brag about themselves. Noble on their part, but bad for the public.

Thank you for your thoughts on the Max Weber chapter. The solution seems good to me. If Helen Wolff wants to cut some more because of duplication, she has my permission. But the cuts must be limited to the duplicate passages. Both of us liked Helen Wolff very much when she was here last. We were as sympathetic as possible because of the harsh blow she had suffered. But then we found ourselves drawn to her by real sympathy. She spoke openly, without sentimentality, emotionally very involved yet rigorous with herself, and with the confidence to go on living and in that way alone to be near her husband, whom she had clearly loved very much.

Now to the main thing: Your *Eichmann* and everything connected with it.

I find the foreword excellent in its content. It has the proper tone. From a literary point of view, a few changes could perhaps make your presentation more effective. The reader could have the feeling, after the initial tension you create and the clear, informative sections, that the foreword finally just peters out. That can be avoided by a clearer separation of the subjects:

On page 3 you have left a blank line to indicate the introduction of a new subject. You could do that, I think, in several other places:

At the beginning of page 5: "In the report of a trial . . ."

Middle of page 7: The sentence "Apparently more complicated . . ." is a transitional sentence but empty in the first two lines . . . The theme: "what kind of crime . . ." should not appear as if by chance as just another subject, but should stand out explicitly as the new and crucial subject that the foreword will now treat in more detail than anything that has come before. From here on, this is the single point of focus. Pages 7 through 15 concern themselves with it. Eichmann disappears from view entirely. The content of these pages belongs to the most important things your book discusses. The proportions in the foreword are not right. That will no longer be the case if you substitute a clear break for that transition in the middle of page 7.

But perhaps I am mistaken. The effect of changes—these are slight ones and could be made quickly—becomes evident only if one makes them oneself. I wouldn't presume to go so far . . .

The last paragraph with its "And . . ." seems an afterthought. With it, you come back to Eichmann, who has not been mentioned since page 7 (although everything in these pages has reference to him). The last paragraph has to have its own weight, which you can give it by again using a one-line break. The paragraph does not have to be any longer. It just has to be made clear that as far as the trial is concerned, your main intention is being articulated here once more.

What a schoolmaster, you will say. And for all that he can't do himself what he wants to see done. That is certainly true.

I'll play the schoolmaster again when I say I would like to see the language bearing on the question of guilt made clearer (here I am prejudiced by my own efforts in *Die Schuldfrage*). I would speak not just of responsibility where liability is the issue. As far as the sense is concerned, I agree with you. But my own scheme is stuck in my head (in this case the "four types of guilt"). But I don't really think you need to make any changes here.

Please leave my name in the German edition. My sentence "I'm not altogether comfortable" referred to how I should behave toward Golo Mann in this situation, which I perceive as a provocation directed against me, too—although my involvement is insignificant compared to the way he dared to treat you. This blatant crudeness demands a retaliating blow.

Piper wants to mount a big advertising effort for you. I am essentially always in favor of that. It would simply be stupid today not to make use of advertising. There is no intellectual public anymore, no "class" in which a writer of a hundred years ago was at home. We have to see how we can reach individuals; that is, we have to turn to the "masses." But of course each individual measure needs to be carefully thought through. I am always delighted when you speak to large gatherings of students or at congresses of any kind or at a ceremonial event, such as the awarding of the Lessing prize. What you want to take on in the way of press conferences and *Spiegel* interviews, there you'll just have to follow your own instincts. The question is whether one wants to expose oneself to ill will or the intent to achieve certain effects. Let me share some of my earlier thinking about these things. After my television interview about *Freiheit und Wiedervereinigung*,[2] a rightist institution in Berlin, rounded out by a few professors (Herzfeld,[3] Gadamer, and others) wanted to come interview me in Basel. Physically I could have done it, but I declined. Max Weber probably would have accepted. I don't like to go into a battle where goodwill is obviously lacking and where I am alone against everyone else. — After *Freiheit und Wiedervereinigung* was published, three people from *Der Spiegel* wanted to come to Basel. Piper put great pressure on me to do it (it would mean sales of "at least 4,000 copies" more).[4] I declined again, not because I was up against ill will from the outset, but because I would have been up against people who were out for sensation, who would, as you say, set traps for me, were three against one, who would end the interview arbitrarily, and cut from the tape what they didn't want to print. One should not, I thought, deal with people against whom one is defenseless and who can cut what you've said and then write what they like about it . . .

A radio talk is a different matter, but with only *one* partner. Bondy has proved himself in this capacity. Jeanne Hersch told me quite a while ago that Bondy thought Golo Mann was right. My telling you this would be tattling if it were not you to whom I was telling it. I don't know if the report as Jeanne passed it on is absolutely correct. (She had no opinion herself at the time because she had not yet read your book.) One probably shouldn't give too much importance to what Bondy might have said. In a talk with him, you could com-

554

municate to a broad public what it ought to know. For that, Bondy would be intelligent enough and altogether civil in manners.

Because you have asked, I would be inclined to avoid the press conference, the *Spiegel* interview, and a panel discussion, but I would accept a radio talk with Bondy.

Rossmann: The university administration is unanimously against him; the municipal "board of education," unanimously for him. Zschokke[5] is for him. The city council, which is responsible for the final decision, is still uncertain. The council wants to invite Rossmann and the other candidate, a man named Meyer[6] from Zurich (a fat book on Leibniz[7] published in 1948), for separate interviews with the entire council (seven members) so that they can get to know each candidate personally. I have heard that there is mention made in an administration document of the "Jaspers clique." The "board of education" is directly elected by the people and is responsible for the entire educational system; the administration, only for the university. Rossmann's opponents have dragged in at the last moment the slogan: "A Swiss, not a foreigner." So things are touch and go. If Rossmann gets the post, it will be because of Zschokke and the popular representatives against the university. All of this just between us, please.

The television lectures are uncertain. My illness interrupted everything. I can't just write the lectures off. It will depend on whether they can give me time. If not, I won't be unhappy, although I would like to do this: an attempt to reach individuals in the masses with the essential points. Philosophy as an esoteric enterprise has no future, nor does it do justice to the seriousness of people today. With Heinrich's help, I would probably move ahead more quickly. Our intentions are the same; our means are not the same.

The probability that we will see at least you this year is a hopeful prospect for us both.

Warmest greetings to you both
Your Karl

You can see from my handwriting how tired I am. Excuse me! I'll write another time about the wonderful Greek photographs from Heinrich. For now, just my warmest thanks.

Congratulations on your honorary doctorate of laws. That and your lectures at the Yale Law School show that Americans have a grasp of your thinking that bears on juristic principles. Your marvelous discussion of citizenship in the *Origins of Totalitarianism* is proof enough! You've earned it.

Chicago, May 14, 1964

Lieber Verehrtester!

Your letter arrived at the last moment before I left New York to travel from Maine to Georgia: lectures, all makeups for the lectures I had to cancel because of my accident. From that tour I came directly here, where I'm doing a Kant seminar I'm enjoying immensely. "Foundations for a Metaphysics of Ethics" with your "Kant" from *Die grossen Philosophen* as my only aid. I've just come home from the seminar. In the fall I want to do a lecture on the *Critique of Judgment*. Reading Kant is giving me a great deal of pleasure.

I haven't heard anything more from Henk. Certainly there's nothing more that can be done there. I've never wanted to believe that lying is "the rotten spot" in human nature, but I'm gradually beginning to realize the role that self-deception plays. I got the translation of the Weber article from Helen Wolff, and I've just looked through it and sent it back. It seems fine to me, but I have not gone over the whole thing carefully. I say this only because the translation is not by Manheim. I like Helen Wolff a lot too. It is hard for her to go on living. She loved her husband very much, and without any illusions. I've always valued that highly in her.

The Eichmann foreword: You're absolutely right in everything you say, but I won't be able to make the changes you suggest until I have the galleys. I'm writing to Piper today to alert him. It's strange that the word "Haftung" simply escaped me. I am *very, very* grateful to you for having read so exactingly and for making such specific suggestions. I wrote this feeling impatient with it. And I was aware that it petered out, but that happens often with me.

Now for Piper's grand advertising schemes: I half agreed—before your letter arrived—to take part in a press conference for which written questions would be submitted in advance, that is, if the questions suited me and if ill will wasn't immediately obvious in them. Whether that will actually happen is up in the air. *Spiegel* interview: I share your opinion completely. One is there only to confirm their preconceived notions for them. Everything else is left out or the interview is cut short. Piper understood that. A radio talk remains a possibility, but not with Bondy. [. . .] But more on this when I see you.

Rossmann: How is this going to end? Would it be good for him to take the post if the university doesn't want him? Or would it quickly adjust to the fait accompli—as is usually the case?

An exceptionally good and able man was here as a guest lecturer, Albert Wohlstetter,[1] who worked for the government for many years on war-related issues. He was very taken with your *Atombombe*. You, he said, are the only person who understands the scientists and the nonsense they talk both here and in Europe. I was very proud of myself because he had found the reference to your book in my revolution book. He started out as a mathematician, then moved into mathematical logic. He's also unusually pleasant. We became very friendly, and that includes his wife, who is a well-known historian. I hope very much that he will take a position at the University of Chicago.

Annchen [Anne Weil] wrote that Koyré died. I don't know whether you knew him. An old friend of ours. Sad. I saw him a year ago in Paris after he'd had a stroke that aged him a lot. Then, Annchen wrote, he had bone cancer. So—thank God.

Have I told you that I got to know Nathalie Sarraute?[2] French novelist and a Russian Jew—it was like old home week; we hit it off so well from the first moment. She was so taken with America, which reminded me of you. She had been in Berkeley, where the longshoreman Hoffer had just been given an appointment in the political science department. (I wrote you about him many years ago,[3] because he had read your books and we were good friends.) He will tell the students something about unions. He had done that before, but now he is too old to work on the docks. It's too hard for him, and so the university came up with a permanent appointment for him. Nathalie Sarraute was very impressed by that. It would never happen at the Sorbonne!

But I'm rattling on. I'll be here until May 30, then back in New York.

All my very best—
Your
Hannah

354 *Hannah Arendt to Karl Jaspers*

Palenville, July 23, 1964

Lieber Verehrtester,

We haven't heard anything from you for such a long time. But, to our great pleasure, *Cusanus* has arrived. I got the manuscript from Helen Wolff but so far haven't been able to read it. Heinrich, who, on principle, doesn't look at manuscripts, started reading it right away. As usual, we've received two copies—Piper sent us one—so that we can each underline as we please.

We're having an exceptionally hot summer here, and so we have fled to the Catskills relatively early. It's warm here, too, but very lovely and peaceful, and the nights are always cool. It will come as no surprise to you that we are very disturbed by the Goldwater business,[1] the completely spontaneous and hysterical revolts of the Negroes, and the very changed mood of the people. Goldwater is a fool, but a dangerous one at this point because he has put his finger on the real sore point of the civil rights bill—private property and the rights of parents to control which schools their children attend. On top of that, the movement among the Negroes is taking on an increasingly racist tone: We won't stand for advice from white people; with white liberals as our friends, who needs enemies; eighty percent of the world's population is colored: why shouldn't we govern in America? and so on. And it's not just young Negroes, many of them delinquent, who are propounding this kind of thing, but respected intellectuals as well. Eighty percent of twelve-year-olds in Harlem can't read properly! And the criminality on the streets of New York and Chicago is really frightful. It could happen that all the improvements and progress achieved in the last few years will be thrown away overnight. It seems quite clear that Goldwater stands a good chance of being elected. On top of that—and a point that is hardly ever mentioned—Kennedy's murder has never been solved. The only thing that seems established is that it couldn't have been Oswald. But the Warren Report[2] will, of course, maintain just the opposite.

I'm writing today to make some more concrete suggestions for my visit in September. Piper wants to have me in Germany about the 17th, and apart from that I have also accepted an invitation from Bavarian Radio for sometime between the 15th and 20th. It would be best for me if I could visit you before that, in other words, in the first half of September. How would that be? I'm having endless trouble with Piper, by the way. [. . .] Now he's suddenly decided he wants to publish *Eichmann* only as a paperback—God knows why. I won't agree, of course. Earlier, he sent me a lawyer's memo about possible lawsuits. That in itself is fine with me. But you should have seen this memo: page after page filled with the concern that convicted Nazi criminals who served under Eichmann and who are now sitting in German prisons could feel that their "honor" had been compromised. Abso-

558

lutely fantastic and unmistakably a document produced by Nazi sympathizers—which no one at Piper seems to have noticed! I almost have the feeling that, without even realizing it, he has people like that working in his own house. The memo is a muddle and not even clear in its intent: the fact remains that they haven't changed a single thing in my book (I've just gotten the page proofs), presumably out of sheer laziness.

I think we'll go back to New York in mid-August (about the 15th), unless it's still unbearably hot in the city. Heinrich is fine. We have it good; we work during the day, go for an evening walk, and stop in for a quiet drink at the village inn, where we know the innkeeper and where people from the area (no tourists) go. The young people from the village go there to dance, and the innkeeper dances with the girls he has known from their childhood on. And if anybody, young or old, behaves badly (passes on village gossip, for example), he gets a dressing down from the innkeeper. Then the innkeeper restores good feeling by dancing with the ladies again or buying a round on the house. He has a really good influence on village behavior. It's good to see that in all this craziness.

Write soon! Warmly
Your   Hannah

I'm enjoying *Cusanus* immensely, and it's a great comfort to me in the confusion of these times.

Thank you very much, and greetings

Your Heinrich

355 *Karl Jaspers to Hannah Arendt*

Basel, July 27, 1964

Dear Hannah!

There is no excuse for my long silence. I've been caught up in my "lectures" for television. Everything goes slowly. I had nothing pressing I had to tell you. So I kept postponing writing.

You wrote about your Kant seminar. How good and wonderful that the peace needed for difficult thought is still possible!—and that you chose Kant.

Your letter, as lively as it is concerned, just arrived. Heinrich[1] is a good influence on village behavior. So that, too, is still possible today. I'm glad.

Your view of Piper is surely correct. We have known that for a long time. And yet he is still the most pleasant of publishers, if one does not want to work with Rowohlt or Witsch or Fischer. He was here a week ago. About you, nothing but enthusiasm and pleasure at the prospect of publishing your book!

I was interrupted by a visitor. Gertrud saw this letter on my desk and added a note in pencil.[2] Now I'll continue.

Piper wants to advertise on a grand scale for you and with you. You have written me about that. With enough assurances—so there will be *no* Bondy—I find that excellent. Wherever you appear, you conquer, as long as you are not confronted by outright ill will, against which you are defenseless. I have great hopes for your book in Germany: it should evoke great unrest, perhaps more. We hear with increasing frequency about the demand of German students for the truth. They don't want to let themselves be deceived any longer.

I would like to be able to show you in September a manuscript, the intent of which I have already mentioned to you. Unfortunately, I can't possibly do that because all I've done so far is assemble notes and haven't begun to write at all: on the independence of thought, with you and your book as an example. Everything goes slowly for me. I'm not finding the television lectures easy. And work on them was interrupted by a radio talk about Cusanus.[3] Even though I knew everything I needed for the talk, it still took me three days to prepare it. Then, too, the lethargy of age is upon me. I'm retired, and I like to do what the spirit of the moment dictates. At the moment, it's reading Shakespeare, because the BBC would like a lecture from me. They wrote such a remarkably nice letter, referring to the few pages about *Hamlet* in my book *Von der Wahrheit*.[4] But I really will have to decline. This spreading oneself too thin: I'm seduced by a suggestion, feel strongly motivated to act on it, but then let the project drop after all—it's a dangerous thing when one's sense of duty wanes. I was thoroughly fascinated by *The Tempest* again. It contains the most wonderful, mysterious philosophy. Even if I could write it down, I would never achieve Shakespeare's profundity. But talking about it, interpreting, and then rejecting my own interpretation again gives me great pleasure.

From you, I'm hearing for the first time that Goldwater's election in November looks likely. Judging from our newspaper reports, I had

560

believed just the opposite. Well, the country has experienced McCarthy. The Americans could get themselves into a situation from which it might not be so easy to free themselves again. I don't dare really contemplate that yet. That would be the first step toward the collapse of everything that makes life possible for us. We'll talk about this when you're here. You sent me by way of Hochhuth the letter[5] to Justice Warren. A wonderful letter from an individual.

My health is good, *much* better than in those weeks that could have been so delightful, and I let us all down.

I send warmest greetings to Heinrich. I think of him often. He is a pillar among people today. That comforts me.

No one can take it amiss from him that he does not want to write any books, but if only he would write down his philosophical aphorisms, some of which I have heard from him directly!

I look forward to our talks and the chance to see you again.

Warmly, as ever
Your Karl Jaspers

A photographer was here, a man named Moses,[6] who works for *Stern*. His photos will appear there first, then in *Magnum* and in *Du* and then in book form in 1965. A lively, capable young man (about 40, I would think). When I mentioned you, he said right away: Yes, wonderful, but I can't get in touch with her! I told him that you were coming to Germany. He will write to you to ask if you're willing to be photographed and where he could meet you.

356   *Hannah Arendt to Gertrud Jaspers*

Palenville, August 12, 1964

Dear Friend!

Your letter just arrived. I haven't written because I'm still corresponding constantly with Piper about the dates for the various events he has planned. These will take about a week because they will be spread around in Munich, Frankfurt, and Baden-Baden (television interview) and will all be after September 15. So I thought that I would fly from here on September 2 and arrive in Basel on the evening of the 3rd or the morning of the 4th, because I have to spend a day in Zurich on money matters. Would that be terribly inconvenient for you? Then I would stay until the 14th. I have to be in Munich on the 15th, in Frankfurt on the 17th—and so on. I'm very short of time because the semester in Chicago starts at the beginning of October. I thought I'd fly home on the 23rd, probably by way of Brussels to have a look at Annchen's new apartment. Let me know right away if these plans are all right. If they don't suit you, I could try to move things up six days, that is, come on the 9th for four or five days and then again on the return trip and not fly home until the 29th. It seems better to me if we could have ten peaceful days together. My experience is that days of arrival and departure count only as half.

I'm delighted about the television broadcast and eager to see it. When will it be aired? After our first very nice, peaceful weeks here we're now having visitors every day and are a bit out of kilter. All good friends, but a bit much all at once. I'm not really reading anything but Kant—great fun! Am preparing my lecture and continuing to translate *Revolution*.

We'll talk at length about character assassination and other such amusing topics. Amusing because *Aufbau* has accused me of, among other things, what the Freudians call penis envy. Now I'm curious to see what the Germans will think up and if they'll have any new ideas.

But seriously—every time that your husband writes that he wants to write something about all this, I blush with the honor of it and turn pale with fear that he could be drawn into this so-called discussion, which is at times very dirty indeed. But for now I'm neither red nor pale in the face but only ineffably happy and relieved that we will finally see each other again.

Warmest greetings, Your

Hannah

P.S. Please write to New York. We're going home on Sunday.

357   Karl Jaspers to Hannah Arendt

Basel, August 17, 1964

Dear Hannah!

Your letter this morning put me in the best of moods for the television filming that followed. Wonderful that you'll be here for ten days!

Piper, it seem to me, is doing an excellent job of organizing your advertising campaign. Wherever you go, you will convince people, even if you are confronted with hostile questions. The fact is that you are credible. How rare that is today!

I have a favor to ask: Could you bring me your essay "Zionism Reconsidered"[1] (or something like that) from the war years (in a magazine called *Menorah*) and lend it to me to read? I would also like to see again the two issues of the *New York Times*[2] that you had last summer (Musmanno[3] and all the letters the paper printed).

To you and Heinrich, warmest greetings

Your Karl

How much I would like to speak with Heinrich, too!

---

358   Hannah Arendt to Gertrud and Karl Jaspers

August 22, 1964

Dearest Friends!

The letters from you both[1] have inspired great anticipation of this trip as well as trip jitters in me. I just booked my flight for September 2. I'll be in Zurich on the 3rd (unfortunately there are only night flights). If I'm tired, I'll fly on to Basel; or, if not, I'll stay in Zurich until the afternoon to take care of everything. Would you please see if I can stay in the Krafft am Rhein from the 3rd to the 14th? If that isn't possible, I can stay at the Euler or the Rote Ochsen. I'll bring "Zionism Reconsidered," *New York Times*, etc. with me.

Until soon, and warmly
Your
Hannah

---

359   Hannah Arendt to Karl Jaspers

September 29, 1964

Lieber Verehrtester,

It was wonderful to hear your voice again in Brussels. Brussels was very nice, too. Annchen and I went to Brugge, and I went on to Gent the next day (marvelous van Eyck), and then I finally flew home to New York in an almost empty plane, so it was very comfortable. Everything is fine here. Things are going well with Heinrich. They're a bit hectic for me, but not bad. Sunday I'll fly to Chicago.

All this to send you the enclosed documents that I wasn't able to have photocopied after all but that will surely arrive safely by registered mail anyhow. First, I'm enclosing material from the Anti-Defamation

League,[1] which was the real leader of the campaign here, with the support and cooperation of the Jewish organizations. I'm also sending the letter that [. . .] wrote to me when he sent me this material. He supplied me with the internal memoranda, and I'm enclosing my reply to him.[2] Please keep [his] name confidential. They've booted him out in the meantime anyhow, but I still don't want his name mentioned. Second, I'm sending you two letters from Siegfried Moses,[3] a high-ranking government official in Jerusalem, retired, also president of the Baeck Institute, the federation of German Jews that has offices in New York, London, and Jerusalem. As you can see, Moses is an old acquaintance of mine. The letter of March 24 refers to a long conversation I had with him in Basel. He asked for a sharper distinction between the later Jewish Councils and the aid work they did before the war. I added a clarification to this effect on p. 35,[4] paren. Third, I'm sending you a circular letter from the Jewish Center Lecture Bureau,[5] from which you can see how closely Musmanno and the Jewish organizations worked together. Finally, I'm sending a newspaper clipping from *Aufbau*[6] and my response[7] to it, which *Aufbau* never printed. *Aufbau* received other letters to the editor[8] about this same article. They attacked Mr. May's[9] representations sharply, and *Aufbau* didn't print them either. What I am *not* sending after all is the newspaper report on Hausner's[10] visit in New York in May 1963, because I can't find it in the chaos of my papers. The report said explicitly that Mr. Hausner had come to America because of the publication of my Eichmann book. As best I can recall, the report was in the *Daily News*, but I may be mistaken.

I think we've already spoken about the pamphlet that Nymphenburger Verlagsanstalt put out against the "Eichmann" at Moses' instigation.[11] I've just received a letter from Michael Freund (a historian in Kiel) from which I conclude that anyone and everyone with the remotest interest in these matters has been supplied with a copy of the pamphlet.

I've just been on the phone with people at Piper about the boycott of the bookstores. This is no secret. The booksellers have been telling Piper's representatives that they do not *want* to sell this book—a totally extraordinary thing.

All best wishes and greetings
Your Hannah

Basel, October 4, 1964

Dear Hannah!

I received your interview with Gaus[1] a few days ago. You can imagine how pleased I was to read it. The portrait of you that emerges from it is clear and convincing. Anyone who hears this interview and sees you will not be able to evade you. Even your enemies, if they try, unsuccessfully, to find new arguments against you in it, will be affected by it. Who else has this openness that you dare display? Your spontaneity—the fine nuances and your impromptu observations—no one will be able to say that that is not absolutely genuine. Who today can rely as completely on oneself as you have here!

And finally, without expecting it, I read what you said about me, to me. You did that many years ago, but now you are saying it in public, how you once saw and heard me, and how you chose me to help further your self-education because of what could come through me to you, as it could to every student, but mostly did not. You called what I did "bringing you to reason." Only if one knows Kant does one know what is contained in the word "reason."

Those few words are an extension of your Frankfurt eulogy. If one has been in public life, it is a happiness rarely given one to hear, in one's lifetime and in public, witnesses who confirm the value of one's existence. Praise and censure usually leave one indifferent. Their effect depends on whom they come from. Each time I have received such a gift I have been touched by it, and felt a little ashamed as well. Ernst,[2] my friend, once spoke of me publicly but very discreetly. And then Ludwig Curtius,[3] with a little too much pathos but still credibly and at the same time with honest objectivity. With you it is different. You are so much younger. You don't need to be cautious, as Ernst was, and you do not see me from a distance, as Curtius did. And then, you bear witness to me and to my contemporaries that my life as a professor was not in vain. And I won't begin to speak of everything else that has been given me through you, your existence, your work.

Your call from Brussels was a nice close to these happy weeks. Now you are in Chicago and lecturing on Kant's *Critique of Judgment*. The rest you are leaving to the Germans. What you told me about Kempner[4] I then read in *Die Zeit*[5]: Kempner "showed himself to be a complete idiot" . . . "Frau Arendt was wonderful. Without regard for rank or sex" (I assume the reporter means here: without regard for the fact that Kempner is a world-famous jurist and a man), "taking aim and

565

sometimes hitting the mark, she displayed a touching and extremely keen integrity of intellect that is not often seen in this country. Anyone whose conscience was not already clear as he sat there made a resolve: I really must get around to reading this woman's book."

Wherever you go, your listeners cannot escape the force of your arguments and your language. The hostility melts away. But now I have another worry: There was a review in the *FAZ*,[6] a half-page, of your book and three others on related topics (this constant and brazen reducing of everything to the lowest common denominator!). The review focused almost entirely on the Jewish question and gave practically no attention to the German problems. "Her judgment on the Germans is too harsh—even those who offered resistance are often lumped in together with the rest." My fear is that as far as Germany is concerned, your book will be quietly ignored at the same time that it is being respectfully noted. That is the easiest route out. For what you say so simply, scattered about in different passages—to discuss that and to focus on it *in its totality* is dangerous for a reviewer: either he sacrifices his self-respect if he writes what is untrue, or he offends the broad public on whom his journalistic career depends. Catching up on everything that was neglected after 1945 demands great courage. Sternberger, of course, likes to say: What do you mean, courage! No one is threatened with harm to life, limb, or property! We can write anything we like! We'll see. Silence would be dreadful and a new bad sign. Fear of the truth is growing. A recent experience of mine demonstrates that. Perhaps you recall that I told "German Radio" in Cologne that I would do a lecture for their series "What Is German?"[7] I was deluged with praise and respect. Then it was suggested that I send my manuscript to Cologne first, *then* tape it in Basel. Taken aback, I asked: Why? I would tape the talk right away, and they would receive the manuscript along with the tape. Answer: I was asked to adhere to the "established procedure." In my mistrust, I had demanded that nothing be edited out of the tape. I was assured of that for a tape made after the manuscript had been approved. —Well, I politely declined to participate.

Gertrud and I are living quietly and happily day by day. The touch of depression that Gertrud was experiencing when you were here has disappeared again completely. She has regained her natural equilibrium and does not blame herself for anything. She has experienced these swings back and forth her whole life long, a consequence of her genetic inheritance, which, measured against the effects it could have had, has

566

manifested itself in a mild way, but it has been bad enough. But the good, healthy times always come back. And then the complaints of old age seem inconsequential.

I'm attempting to write—without strain and in the placidity of age—my planned pamphlet on your book. My notes are piling up. It is inspiring for me to occupy myself with your work. But I repeat: I don't know yet what I'll be able to do.

You don't want to be a philosopher. Because none of us can define what philosophy is, I have to ask what "not a philosopher" really means. That reminds me of what Rickert once said to me. "It is your good right to make a philosophy out of Max Weber, but to call him a philosopher is nonsense."

Gertrud and I send you both our warmest greetings

Your Karl

Your package of documents just arrived by registered mail. Once I'm done with it, I'll send it back to you registered. And then later the other documents you left here for me.

361 *Karl Jaspers to Hannah Arendt*

October 16, 1964

Dear Hannah!

The news just now from Moscow.[1] —I am completely absorbed with your book and with you. My homage includes a critique, which is, I think, implicitly your own and which I only make explicit. It is good to talk with you. The more I consider your book in detail, the greater it seems to me. But my text is still not ready, only a lot of notes. I don't know whether I'll be able to manage it. —And now this news! The first thing Gertrud said was, "Completely without bloodshed." But more than that, the Supreme Soviet has the authority now, because neither Khrushchev nor any other individual has power anymore. The situation is stabilized. There is no battle among the Diadochi. Dictatorship by a small group seems finally to have replaced the tyrant. Why did Khrushchev have to go? It's likely that it came as a surprise to him, too. It's probable that Russia's relations with China played a part here also.[2] But how will Russia's policy toward China change? Will the Russians ally themselves with the Chinese against us after all and fall into a trap themselves in the process? I can't believe that. Those people aren't that stupid. But they'll probably act "as if." I think the Americans will be afraid and certainly won't elect Goldwater now. Innocuous romanticism fades when the threat of a Russian-Chinese alliance becomes reality. But then, the whole business is an "as if," like the atom bombs themselves, which nobody wants to use. That doesn't put my mind at ease. Stupid realities are made from those kinds of "as ifs," as they have been in the past. I feel uneasy. We are again a long way from what seemed to be a growth of solidarity in the Western world (including Russia, based historically on the Christian religion and white race).

I am returning to your books. What better thing can one do in one's helplessness—which keeps recurring over and over in one's lifetime and presses in on one on occasions?

Warmest greetings to you and Heinrich, also from Gertrud

Your Karl

362 Hannah Arendt to Karl Jaspers

Chicago, October 25, 1964

Lieber Verehrtester!

The first thing to greet me here was your letter, which brightened my first days and weeks here. I haven't gotten the Gaus interview (or not yet anyhow), God knows why. I'm relieved that you liked it. I had the feeling that I spoke too spontaneously, because I like Gaus a lot. But, in general, I doubt that my presence in Germany made much of a difference. For example, someone from *Der Spiegel* was at the press conference[1] and was, I gather, very much impressed. But then *Der Spiegel* chose someone else to do the review—presumably the same man who was in Frankfurt—a certain Joseph Wulf,[2] who is completely under the wing of the Jewish organizations. So, you see, so-called power counts after all. Perhaps you saw the report of the press conference in *Aufbau*—no one from *Aufbau* was invited, and the report was unsigned. Maybe Kempner[3] wrote it. He turned up uninvited and was allowed to stay only at my intervention. Piper wanted to throw him out.

Activity threatens to degenerate into outright work here, and that is why I haven't written until now. I had to laugh over your remark about me and philosophy. What I want and what I say don't do me the least bit of good here. The students from the philosophy department simply turn up; some try to sneak in with us,[4] and they explain

568

to me with that American lack of inhibition what they intend to study and learn with me—and that's that. I can't very well send them back to the philosophy department, because that's where they come from. So I sit here and teach the *Critique of Pure Reason*, and I've just promised to do a little Spinoza in the four weeks I'll be here in the spring. In addition to my lecture course, which I announced earlier, I also have a Kant seminar and a Plato seminar (*Gorgias*). Which is, however, in no way the university's fault. I could say no, but that is of course impossible as long as I can handle the work load. And the interest of the students is touching and encouraging. The students are really excellent, and the discussion on a very respectable level.

Sternberger is staying two doors away from me, and things are very pleasant with him. But as you know, he too is by no means in agreement with *Eichmann*. He doesn't really understand why I got myself into something like this in the first place. His lectures are all right but not excellent, and at first he was a little taken aback by the style of the students' discussion: in Germany students took that tone in discussions with instructors, perhaps, but not with professors. At his second lecture he was much better prepared. He's very adaptable. We see each other a lot, have meals together in the club, and our friendship is intact. His English, by the way, is excellent, and he does not make himself conspicuous with bad (German) manners. He is a superb observer, essentially a journalistic talent of a high order.

Now, finally, to Khrushchev. I'm writing later in time, and we know a little more now. The most remarkable thing at the moment, it seems to me, is that the old routine just doesn't wash anymore, that all the parties—from Poland to France—won't put up with Russian methods any longer. This is the first time that has happened—the French even sent a commission to Moscow to find out what was really going on there. It's not possible anymore to let a man disappear "into the garbage can of history" from one day to the next. Khrushchev was certainly as oblivious of his impending fall as the State Department, which had just published a detailed analysis drawing on the knowledge of all the "experts" and concluding that Khrushchev's position had never been more secure than it was now! That is really funny, particularly if you keep in mind that Khrushchev would have agreed entirely with that view. No bloodshed is of course an important point, but Khrushchev's purges were without bloodshed, too. The difference this time is that the smear campaign didn't work any longer!

You see a transformation into an oligarchy (collective leadership), not a battle among the Diadochi. That's possible, but we still can't know that. Suslov[5] could be behind the whole thing. That's even likely, because he led the attack, and he is, as far as I know, an old convinced Stalinist. What do they really want to do now—from a purely ideological point of view. They can't have one "heretic" after another on the throne. So either they have to side with Khrushchev and say that under Stalin things got out of hand, or they have to do just the opposite and declare Khrushchev the real villain and rehabilitate Stalin. But that is apparently the very thing that is no longer possible, because the non-Russian parties and the satellite states won't let it happen. But if the Russians don't want to rehabilitate Stalin, then they are really in a pickle: ever since Lenin, one usurper after the other!

In real terms, not ideological ones, one can only guess at what is behind it all. I think it has to have something to do with China, because that is really the most difficult problem Russia faces, and it is one that threatens to split the parties everywhere. And as far as China is concerned, Khrushchev was in fact pursuing a policy inconsistent in itself. On the one hand, he was prepared to let a breach take place and so bring the danger of war in the Far East closer, but on the other hand he wanted to lower expenditures for arms and heavy industry in order to increase production of consumer goods and to raise the standard of living. And that was to be done specifically at the expense of the conventional, nonatomic forces, which would be the crucial factor in any possible conflict with China. So I think it likely that the military was genuinely concerned and entered a protest. We mustn't forget that during the last major party purge, in 1957, Khrushchev was already faced with a vote of no confidence in the presidium. The only thing that saved him was that the army was on his side and made military planes available to him so that he could fly his adherents to Moscow for the plenary assembly.

We tend to think instinctively in parallels, and it could well be that nothing could be more mistaken. Khrushchev's successors were mistaken, for example, when they thought they could simply announce to the world—the Communist world, that is—that Khrushchev was vain and stupid (NB: I don't know the German translation, but those adjectives were taken straight out of Khrushchev's speech against Stalin) and that everyone would then just forget that there had ever been a Khrushchev. There is no doubt that Khrushchev opened a tiny crack to freedom, and what was the result? Nothing worked anymore the way it was supposed to. He was deposed because it was felt that all of history on the international level was on the verge of collapse—and all Khrushchev's opponents accomplished was to accelerate that collapse. Could it be that we are witnessing the second decisive defeat of totalitarian government, and this time one that required no external forces to bring it about?

But if we do want to think in parallels, then we have to consider that from the very beginning internal party conflicts were decided by factors outside the party. Stalin defeated Trotsky[6] because he controlled the police. Khrushchev won out because he had the army on his side. We don't know whether the army or the police had a role in this last coup or palace revolution. Contrary to my first assumption, it could be that the police were behind this. The poison-gas attack on the German engineer[7] would fit that picture, for that was surely a police attempt at assassination and one staged by the people who didn't want Khrushchev making visits to Bonn. The police can't have been very fond of Khrushchev anyhow, because he reduced their power significantly. And so all the Stalinists in the Soviet Union could count on the help of the police.

All sheer guesswork. When you put it down on paper, it all looks stupid. It's just what I would say if I could be with you. If only I were!

But you're not right about this influencing the election in America. Johnson's victory was assured before anything of this kind happened. And the reason is simply that Goldwater has cut his own throat. A fantastic business! It's comforting to know, in any case, that there is a degree of stupidity that will in fact put someone out of the running. But what is not comforting is that all the dangerous forces here, particularly those linked to the Negro question, are still with us. Goldwater was just not able to mobilize them; perhaps someone else could have. The whole civil rights movement is in a crisis. In Mississippi convicted murderers and arsonists may be sentenced, but then they are immediately released from prison again on probation with the justification that their acts were provoked!! In the trial of the murderers of the three young civil rights workers this summer the witnesses for the prosecution (Negroes) were arrested and charged while the accused were let off![8] And Washington doesn't lift a finger! Whether Johnson will be somewhat more active once he's reelected remains to be seen.

I have to close, have to get back to work. Heinrich just called, and he sends warmest greetings. All is well with him. He feels fine and is working; he sounded very content. We're having a wonderful fall here—sunshine and cool weather and absolutely clear air. But the trees are already bare because of the awful drought this year!

My best wishes, and be well!

Your
Hannah

363   *Karl Jaspers to Hannah Arendt*

Basel, October 29, 1964

Dear Hannah!

Yesterday evening we saw you in the interview with Gaus. The brother of Frau Weill[1] in St. Louis has a television set that brings in Mainz, and we watched at his house. The content brought no surprises because I knew it well from your manuscript. But I had pictured the television presentation differently. It was not good: always different camera angles, which were distracting; your face in extreme close-ups, which were annoying because one could see your neck muscles twitch sometimes, as in an anatomical demonstration, again a distraction—and barbaric. The fact that Gaus was never visible made matters even worse. And then the glaring whiteness of face and arms, which seems to be the norm in television. But despite all this your facial expression was sometimes, as I've become accustomed to see it over the years, magnificent, sometimes tense and somewhat nervous. The spontaneity was genuine and therefore credible.

Your farewell to philosophy[2] is a joke, however serious your declaration of it was. "Political theory," that sounds like economic or physical theory. There used to be a distinction between theoretical and practical economics. Today, people speak of political science. Philosophically, something isn't quite in order about all that.

It's good that you're being instantly punished for making that statement! Your students are demanding philosophy of you and are of course right to do so. You're lecturing on the *Critique of Pure Reason* now and on Spinoza next semester. I'm happy about that. If you look into all aspects of Spinoza you'll see that he doesn't have that enmity toward politics that you attribute to all philosophers except Kant. I would claim almost the opposite. All of them are very serious about politics and don't regard it as foreign to their interests, except Epicurus, who provides an example of what you mean, and except for the skeptics (not all of them).

What you write about Sternberger confirms what I think about him. Except that I find myself irritated again and again by his accommodating and his fundamental misunderstandings of the way things are in the Federal Republic. But you can get on pleasantly with him if you don't expect anything from the relationship. Conversations with him are almost always productive of the superficial fluff of "observations," but sometimes they have more substance to them (if, for example, the conversation has to do with elections and the techniques employed in them).

You have written in detail about Russia. When I wrote to you recently, I hadn't read anything but the headlines and had a short report from Gertrud. The news in the meantime hasn't increased our knowledge. There is more and more conjecture.

Suslov is seriously ill with his old TB. Modern medicines will probably cure him, but that will take a long time.

The facts of the world situation, not conjectures about it, seem to me to be these:

If Russia wants to get on with China, it has to help it. If Russia helps China, it will be nurturing its archenemy. But that will only delay the inevitable conflict.

Russia *can* overrun Europe with conventional weapons now. Now that it has become clear that America will not use the atom bomb as a weapon of first resort, and only if it is *directly* threatened itself, Russia can experiment to see how far it can go: perhaps reopening its campaign on Berlin, occupying Berlin, then going farther still . . .

The disintegration of the national Communist parties' ties to Russia, which you have observed for a long time, is a reality. I share your hope that it continues. I too consider this development extremely important. It stands as a counterweight to an existential premise of Communism: that it perceive itself as a unified movement everywhere in the world.

And now back to conjecture, which one can indulge in endlessly. It could be that the military is ultimately the crucial force behind the whole thing. It was the military that kept Khrushchev in power; it is the military that is keeping the present leaders in power. The military remains in the background. But what is going on with the military? As always, it wants to become larger and more powerful and make use of the whole state for its purposes. The farther in the past the last war is and the more the younger segment of the population forgets it, the more the military's urge finally to use its massive power and not lead an inglorious existence in retirement will grow. Europe is after all merely a peninsula, one peninsula among many in Asia. The Russians look at the whole earth and want what appears to them to be their due. I don't mean the population as a whole but the military, which, in a crisis, has the population at its disposal because in war the people's interest in victory coincides with that of the military. Everything seems to speak against that: the rebelling satellite states, the economic situation, the threat of China. But the moment can come when none of that will matter. From one day to the next, everyone will go mad. Anyone who is still hesitant will be murdered. The Social Democrats will approve war credits[3] (or, in the present situation, Communists everywhere will do what Russia wants). The *Berliner Tageblatt* and the *Vossische Zeitung* will suddenly favor the censorship of news themselves because that will be essential to maintain the "morale" of a people at war.[4] But I hope that is all irrelevant and just one more false historical analogy.

I much prefer to share your view that this is the first great defeat of totalitarianism. But I'm also afraid that could be wishful thinking!

Then too, *if* Brezhnev and Kosygin[5] are the new masters, it seems to me, judging from their biographies and physiognomies, that we have nothing to fear from them. They appear "reasonable."

I continue working on my essay about you and your book. I still don't know if I will manage it, although I have the whole thing before me in the form of an outline and notes. A *little* book!

Piper told me about the man [Joseph Wulf] who was supposed to do the review for *Der Spiegel*. *Der Spiegel*, which has read the article, as has Piper, prefers not to use it if I will write an article. I declined to do so. First of all, I write terrible articles. Second, I don't want to waste my powder on mere claims and so devalue the essay I'm working on. And third, Germans in the Federal Republic should be writing about this. Let them show what they think and not hide their opinions. And an article from me cannot obviate the only danger I see—the building of a wall of silence around your book and notices that come too late and are too unenthusiastic. If I can do anything at all about that, it will be with an essay that once again focuses on your theses, affirms them, and offers further support for them (so far I've done that for only two passages: the Scholls[6] and Eichmann's "philosophical" documents and execution).

Well, enough! My handwriting will have you irritated enough by now.

Warmest greetings to Heinrich. I'm glad that he's in such good form. I would so very much like to talk to him about all these political and philosophical things.

I wish you great pleasure from your students and from their and your philosophizing!

Greetings from Gertrud.

Your Karl

364 Karl Jaspers to Hannah Arendt

Basel, October 30, 1964

Dear Hannah!

I just had a telephone call from Dr. Rössner[1] at Piper (Piper and his wife are in Greece). Piper's staff saw and heard your interview. All of them, Rössner said, were deeply moved by it. "Unforgettable," he said. At first everyone just sat there in silence, marveling that something like that was possible. According to Rössner, Herr Gaus said he had never experienced anything like it in any of his other "portraits."

I wanted to tell you this right away. My concern about the impact of the interview was misplaced, and I'm very glad of it. It is clear to me what affected my judgment: I want too much and I know you too well. From my point of view, television mistreated you. But in what I wrote yesterday, that applied only to the visual effect.

Sales are between 6,000 and 7,000. The book is "gaining ground," Rössner said. The printing was 10,000. Once sales approach 10,000, Piper is prepared to do a second printing right away. I expected more. Germany keeps silent. The people there are becoming sheep and are interested only in ridiculous things. And the literary people there are afraid. Sternberger's "opinion" of your book is not just an opinion but probably arises from the "spirit" of the literary community there.

Warmest greetings to you both from us both

Karl

365 Hannah Arendt to Gertrud and Karl Jaspers

November 29, 1964

Dearest Friends—

I made a quick trip home on Tuesday for the Thanksgiving weekend. You have to allow yourself a treat every now and then. I found

Heinrich in the best of spirits but also very glad that I came. We've gone out in style, eaten and drunk well, spent the days chattering away. All very easygoing and restful. I enjoy Chicago a lot, but it is strenuous, not because of the work but because I'm constantly on a serving platter, as it were. And that is even more the case because of our good Dolf [Sternberger], with whom, however, I get on very well. He is staying in the same faculty club as I am, and we see each other all the time. I'm not used to it. I'll fly back there tonight. In two weeks I'll be home for good.

I have both your good letters in front of me now. I couldn't get around to writing, had too much to do. Mostly a lot of fun, but not without constant tension either. I've learned a lot, particularly in the area of method, in which you have always found me somewhat lacking. We'll have to talk about that. In connection with the *Critique of Judgment*. A possible conceptual structure for history and political science. And representative thinking in politics on the basis of judgment.

You're writing a book about me, and all I can think is "topsy-turvy world." Yes, people in Germany are keeping silent. They are "cautious" and don't want to step on each other's corns. I received a few very good letters—but all of them from women! Strange. The sales are supposed to be quite good. The book has been on the best-seller list for two weeks, but that doesn't mean much. The *Spiegel* business seems to be taken care of. Mitscherlich[1] is supposed to write the review, and that is fine, because he is independent. Apart from these things, I hear hardly anything—except for the story at the university in Berlin, about which I can most easily inform you by enclosing a copy of my letter of protest.[2] I wrote to the rector of the university as well. This Mr. Aronson from the university in Jerusalem apparently turned up there and said it was not possible to understand my book without knowing me personally. I've never seen him in my life. Then he made up whatever suited his purposes. It's really all very funny.

Russia: the squabble with the Chinese goes merrily on, and Mao or Chou En-lai[3] is supposed to have said that Khrushchev is the real betrayer of the Marxist-Leninist gospel and that Stalin has been slandered. All very logical. But the Russians can't take up that line now. What it all really comes down to is the incredible incompetence of the Russian bureaucracy, in which I gather nothing works any longer. I agree that the military is behind Khrushchev's fall, probably the police as well. I consider the police more dangerous. I don't think that Russian military men want war, but I do think they're afraid of China and want enough conventional weapons to be able to fend off an attack without using atomic bombs. Do you know Richard Lowenthal's *Chruschtschow und der Weltkommunismus* (published by Kohlhammer in 1963)? I'm reading the English edition[4] just now. Some of it is very intelligent, very well informed. If you have a little time, have a look at it, especially the parts about China. Lowenthal is an old Marxist; then he emigrated and became a very well-known English journalist—for the *Observer*, etc. Now he's back in Germany, in Berlin, I think. Chips of the Marxist shell he was hatched from are still stuck to him here and there, but that's not very troublesome because he has so many facts at his command.

Hochhuth wrote just before he set off to see you—with pounding heart, so he said. How are things going with him? And with Saner?[5] We were just talking about when we could stop by again. Heinrich's semester is over at the end of June. We could come after that for a short while. What do you think?? It's really just a stone's throw, even if the stone is a jet.

All our best, and be well!

Your
Hannah

---

366 *Karl Jaspers to Hannah Arendt*

December 23, 1964

Dear Hannah!

How nice for us that you are planning a "stone's throw" to us in June! So there will be some talk about Kant, the *Critique of Judgment*, and "method." I look forward to it.

Never before have I thought with you day by day and reflected about you. I progress slowly. I've complained often enough about age, forgetfulness, how easily I tire. I needn't repeat that. In addition, I have to read so much, particularly about the German "resistance." My essay is becoming a book—a "professor" doesn't seem able to do otherwise. The book is to have two parts: first, I will introduce my themes, which, given the subject matter and the interest it arouses in

Germany, will go beyond the scope of your report; second, your mode of thought, the critiques of it, and you yourself. I have ample notes for all the chapters. How they will all fit together into a whole I don't know yet. In my enthusiasm, I want to do you justice in a way that will make an impression on people and be credible. And I also don't want to make a fool of myself at the end of my life.

At the moment I'm writing a long chapter about Julius Leber.[1] I want to show in more detail the small segment of the resistance that will stand up to scrutiny and that you touch on on one page. In your characterization of the German resistance, this small segment of it that has greatness and truth comes to the fore. Leber makes me think constantly of Heinrich. I think he is Heinrich's man. The book[2] is out of print. I have a copy from the library. There are documents in it, not just reports. It receives little attention in the literature on the resistance. Leber is not given his due there and is treated as if he were just one among many Socialists. In the last year, he was friends with Stauffenberg.[3] They really had nothing in common except that they were "men" and understood each other. Stauffenberg wanted Leber, not Goerdeler, to be chancellor, and L. Beck let himself be convinced. But Leber, always too modest in his life, didn't want that. He wanted to build up the Ministry of the Interior and a police force. The latter was important, he thought, and he felt capable of doing that. It sounds grotesque. But I find the air bracing here—with Leber, I mean. With Stauffenberg I find myself, in spite of everything, at a *very* great remove. That he alone (aside from Leber) had the real courage and decisiveness does impress me. Your basic view of the whole issue I consider correct from our perspective. Following your lead, I am rescuing the few bright spots. I hope that when you read it, you will be satisfied with it and agree.

But these seem to me small tangential details when I think about the book that is to illustrate the independence of thought in you.

Our time is over. The worship of power is widespread in the Federal Republic at the moment. Criticism is harmless, even when it is most trenchant. The weight of opinion is as great as it ever was. We have not been able to tolerate the freedom we enjoyed after the First World War and after 1945. It has gone unused both times.

We will celebrate Christmas with Erna and her sister Irma. We'll see to it that those days take as quiet and normal a course as any other. These days are very enjoyable. The pianissimo of advanced age, of which Max Weber spoke,[4] with William Penn[5] in mind—at least as long as our creaturely decay remains gentle and tame and takes no malign form.

Your house will be full again for New Year's.

All our best!

Warmly, Your Karl

May I keep the documents you lent me, perhaps until your visit? I still haven't reached the chapter for which I need them.

367 *Hannah Arendt to Gertrud and Karl Jaspers*

Christmas 1964

Dearest Friends—

Just a quick greeting for the New Year!

I have not heard from you in quite a while, and I hope all is well with you. I've been home again for almost two weeks now and have gotten pretty lazy. But despite that I am working, with great pleasure, on correcting the Cusanus manuscript. —Manheim's translation is quite good. Helen [Wolff] said she wants to publish it in the fall because they have the *Three Essays*[1] ready right now, which, by the way, has come out very well in every respect, including the printing and binding.

There is nothing special to report here. We are fine and are leading quite a peaceful existence. There will be more of a stir next week because a number of friends are coming. Tomorrow we are going to the wedding of Gerhard Casper[2] (from Hamburg), who once visited you and whom you liked very much. I think I told you about his stormy love affair, which one would hardly have expected from a stolid Hamburger. Now the new couple is blissfully happy, and, as my mother used to say, wherever love falls, it makes a great crash. Well, the crash in this case is gargantuan. He has in the meantime become an assistant professor in Berkeley, and she is finishing medical school here. They're having their wedding here because our friend Frau Beradt very kindly volunteered to host the reception and because neither one of them has any other family here. Not that we are really family, but we have been adopted, which is all great fun.

Best wishes and be well, and drop us a line if you can.

Warmly
Your
Hannah

Basel, January 8, 1965

Dear Hannah!

Thank you for your Christmas letter. So you're saddled with my *Cusanus*. I'm glad that the translation is good, and I hope it isn't making too much work for you. It seems that you like the book a little.

I'm still engrossed with the literature on the German "resistance." You set this discussion in motion, and it should be heard in Germany. Your judgments strike to the heart of the matter. I am elucidating them. Anyone who has reached clarity here will see all the more vividly that the Scholls and Julius Leber are the truly pure bright spots in the picture. I'm trying to do Beck and Stauffenberg justice without impinging on your judgment. We know too little about Tresckow. Goerdeler is too stupid and ridiculous to waste time on. And then the general points: "conscience," "decency." Here too you have touched on the key issues, but your formulations can perhaps be recast more sharply. I make slow progress. I hope I will be able to make the note you have sounded endure so that it can be heard better and those who want to evade the issue are exposed!

Shortly before Christmas Gertrud was taken ill. Very suddenly, in the night, with shivering and a racing pulse that could not even be counted. Our good Dr. Bernstein gave her penicillin right away for a few days. Now she is well again, though her heart is weak and she is still shaky. She hasn't been out of the house yet. Her spirits are good. She sends her warm regards.

Frau Salmony[1] had a streetcar accident. The situation was dreadful. She came away without serious injury. Broken ribs and some lacerations here and there. She will be fine, but it will take some time.

Because of her accident my mail since Christmas has just been accumulating. After all, I think: I'm retired. I even mean to let "important things" pile up. But then I'll have to see about finding some help.

Warmly
Your Karl

February 19, 1965

Lieber Verehrtester—

I can't understand, myself, why I haven't written for so long and that this has to become a birthday letter now. I just received a letter from Meyer-Gutzwiller[1] about your radio interview with Peter Wyss,[2] and a letter from *Der Spiegel* just arrived, saying that you have agreed to an interview about the statute of limitations.[3] That set me, so to speak, in motion. I'm greatly pleased and relieved that you have agreed to the *Spiegel* interview. The statements made by the minister of justice[4] were really not just pathetic; they were an outrage as well. And then the dreadful tone—we're all philistines after all, and similar things— was absolutely shocking, quite apart from the content. I read Benno von Wiese's "Coming to Terms with the Past"[5] in *Die Zeit*—which was, in my opinion, equally egregious, one stupid platitude after another. I sometimes think: If only this whole generation were dead. Just so we wouldn't have to listen to this hypocritical drivel anymore. I wrote to Benno and reminded him that he did not succumb to the "Zeitgeist," but to fear of it. And that it would be smarter to admit that. In reply, more blah-blah in a wounded tone. It is hopeless. And so I'm particularly grateful to you for sending me this very intelligent and sympathetic review written by a student.[6] Something like that really does cheer one up. Have you seen the Göttingen student magazine on the subject of the past?[7] Also on the encouraging side. The German professors must really be on the verge of panic at this point. Young people in Germany finally seem to be turning outspoken and have stopped mouthing these stupid confessions of guilt. Not very pleasant. And not without its dangers. If the professors, instead of protecting each other, should start snooping around in their colleagues' pasts and denouncing each other, that wouldn't be a very pleasant spectacle either.

Dolf Sternberger is another of my personal difficulties. But please keep this to yourself! He is determined to have a job in Chicago, but the prospects there are practically nil. The university might offer him a post if he were truly exceptional, but that just isn't the case. Everyone there paid him the usual compliments, and they were all very nice. That is the custom in this country, and he didn't understand that. Now he's trying with might and main to enlist me in his cause. I got him the short guest lectureship—he wanted it very much, and so why not? Nobody anticipated this eventuality. Now he has written me that he wants to dedicate one of his books to me. But I don't want that—especially not given the circumstances. Furthermore, he refused twice to take a public position on my side in the Eichmann affair. The *FAZ* asked him to review the book for them, and Piper asked him to conduct my press conference. He refused both offers outright. He took a "cautious" line. So tell me: What should I do? I'm reminded of Panofsky.[8] Asked for his opinion about a picture, he said: "If I had to speak the truth, I would have to lie." Well, I'd very much like to lie, but I'm at a loss for what to say.

Those are all silly details I very much enjoy pestering you with. But now to your letter instead: German resistance. I don't fully share your view of Goerdeler. He was the so-called intellectual leader of the movement. It will never live that down. He was the only one in the resistance, as far as I know, who had concrete suggestions for what should happen after a successful putsch. The fantasies of the Kreisau circle[9] can't very well be regarded as such. If the coup had succeeded, the Allies would very likely have had to deal with Goerdeler or with his plans. Of course those plans were "stupid and ridiculous," but any other plans besides stupid and ridiculous ones didn't exist, and that seems crucial to me.

From your letter I concluded that you are planning something along the lines of your Germany book—or am I wrong? In a completely different form, of course, but still with that basic direction. I'm very, very curious. First of all to see the *Spiegel* interview. I'm absolutely delighted that you're doing it.

I have a lot of preparations to do for [public] lectures that I can blame only on myself. On "moral" problems—an extension of what I learned from Kant last year—or think I learned. But in a more easily digestible form than for my students. Heinrich leaves for Bard next week for the beginning of the semester. Things are going extremely well for him, and he is looking forward to the new term. I'm a little worried that he has taken on too much, but as usual there's nothing I can do about it. At any rate, he is in fine fettle.

Your *Great Philosophers* is receiving more and more attention at the universities here. It comes from all quarters. There is a great need for separate paperbacks on the individual figures, particularly Kant. The students can't buy the book in its present form, too expensive. I'm enclosing a letter I recently received from a student in California whom I don't know at all.[10] I was very moved by the letter, but I'm not sure whether this man is really altogether normal. The "paper" he enclosed is oddly erratic but shows real talent. Do you have any advice for him? As you see, he wants to learn German and that would not be difficult for him. Where and to whom should one send him when he is through with college? I'm also enclosing an old clipping from *The New York Times Book Review*,[11] which may be of interest to you.

What else can I pester you—both of you—with? I'm not enjoying the lectures. Wherever I go, the lecture halls are packed. I hate that. When I go to parties, I'm labeled—celebrity! It will all pass, but for now it's dreadful! I feel like an animal with all routes of access blocked off—I can't be myself any longer, because no one will take me as I am. Everyone knows better. Only the exits remain open, and so I don't go anywhere, or if I do, I leave again right away. Nothing is fun anymore. It's just as the president [Louis Finkelstein] of the Jewish Theological Seminary, who is not at all stupid, said to a friend of mine: "These fools have made her famous." It is laughable, but the impulse to laugh soon fades.

The most interesting thing happening here is the student unrest in Berkeley.[12] It grows from the civil rights movement, the first opportunity in decades that the students have had really to do something, and they have in fact done plenty with the greatest of pleasure. Their organization is superb. In Berkeley they've achieved everything they set out to achieve, and now they can't and don't want to stop. Not out of ill will or frenzy but simply because they've tasted blood and know what it's like to act effectively, and now that they've reached their goals, they don't want to just go home again. The student movement represents a real danger to the status quo precisely because it strikes at the heart of genuine political life. I can only say with Jefferson: *Ceterum censeo*[13]—the ward or council system of small republics where everyone has a voice in public affairs. Otherwise, the major cities everywhere else here are becoming real jungles. The subway is no longer safe, no streets either, really, no elevator. Bizarre conditions. Juvenile delinquency has assumed the proportions of a national disaster. Nobody knows what should be done. I sometimes think the students should be mobilized, but one can't very well ask them to go unarmed to chum around with drug addicts. It is truly a problem demanding the most urgent action.

You wrote of Gertrud's illness, and that she is better again. News like that always gives me a fright, and then I feel joy and gratitude over the fact that you both exist. Is Frau Salmony better again?

All my very best wishes on your birthdays!

Your
Hannah

I've reconsidered Sternberger. I'll agree to support him. That is simplest. I have no objective reason to oppose his candidacy. On the contrary, we are in agreement on a great many things. And finally it is really touching to see how very, very much he enjoyed living and working with people who are truly without malice. Forgive me for having troubled you with this. But now I don't want to rewrite this letter.

370   Karl Jaspers to Hannah Arendt

Basel, February 28, 1965

Dear Hannah!

Just a brief word of thanks for your kind birthday wishes in the form of hyacinths and chocolates! My hand doesn't want to write because writing aggravates the rheumatic pains that have been bothering me for a few weeks. Gertrud has recovered from her second bout of "bronchial pneumonia," which once again began very suddenly with chills (the diagnosis is not absolutely clear to me). But I don't want this letter to be a list of complaints. We are actually quite chipper and content in our advanced age

I haven't worked on my book about your *Eichmann in Jerusalem* since Christmas. I hope I'll be able to again soon.

In the meantime I have let myself be seduced into a few "talks" or interviews. That is much easier. One of them was last week with Augstein from *Der Spiegel* about the statute of limitations. I had not slept well the night before because of the rheumatism, and the interview did not go particularly well, but I was able to improve on the language of my part in it. They left a stenographer and typist to help me with that.

I found the interview exceptionally interesting because I was so impressed with Augstein, an amazingly small and unimposing man with a keen intelligence and an immense amount of information at his fingertips. A thoroughly "modern" man, absolutely independent, even from his own *Spiegel*. In the afternoon I spoke with him privately for another two hours. He was very free with information. I hardly had to speak, only to ask questions. I'll tell you about it later. I can't say that I trust the man, on the contrary. But my attitude toward him remains one of suspended judgment. I've never run across a man like him. I felt as if I had sensed an affinity with him, and then an abyss.

I found one thing embarrassing, and that is my main reason for writing. Augstein quoted from a letter from you and reported what you said as follows:

You could understand that people felt a need to close the books on the past. "She doubts that the Jewish people could ever understand how the books could be closed now, but world opinion could perhaps be brought to that point under one condition: If the books are to be closed at all, then let's make sure that they are closed on the question of Germany's eastern border, that Germany recognizes the Oder-Neisse Line, and that people who blather on about taking back the Sudetenland will be vigorously opposed."

I responded by saying that border questions and the question of the statute of limitations on war crimes could not be considered under the same heading of "closing the books."

Immediately following that I said that this part of the interview was not for publication. Your letter was a private letter, and we could discuss it only in your presence.

So that section will be cut, because it was stipulated in advance that *Der Spiegel* could publish only what I explicitly approved for print.

This attempt on Augstein's part to introduce a sensational element into the interview increased my mistrust. Maybe I was right after all to have politely refused interviews from 1958 on? I'll see what comes of this.

I've essentially felt that ever since the "*Spiegel* affair" the situation had changed. Somehow we are "allied" with Augstein. And, as a mass medium, *Der Spiegel* is much more effective than all the illustrated magazines and *Die Zeit*.

I picture your "tours" to myself—the way you speak and the impact you have—and that gives me pleasure.

Warmest wishes to you both from both of us

Your Karl

March 14, 1965

Lieber Verehrtester!

I keep reading the *Spiegel* interview[1] over and over and thinking there probably isn't anything that could make me happier. It turned out beautifully, and now it almost doesn't matter how stupidly the government and the parliament behave (the issue is receiving hardly any attention here, and I still haven't been able to read any German papers about the parliamentary debate). Yours is a voice that says everything and speaks for everyone. The conversational tone is precisely what makes this interview so incredibly powerful, politically the most powerful thing produced in the recent past. It will stand, even if Germany should sink into a political and moral swamp.

On specific points: Augstein is an excellent interviewer. His objection about the "legitimacy" of the people sitting in judgment in Germany[2] is serious. And he is right too about Israel's role in these matters.[3] You have probably read about the deal Adenauer and Ben Gurion made regarding the Eichmann trial.[4] I was always convinced that such an agreement existed, and I remain as convinced now as I was earlier that Ben Gurion kidnapped Eichmann only because the reparation payments to Israel were coming to an end and Israel wanted to put pressure on Germany for more payments—in the form of loans or weapons. What Ben Gurion did is understandable. His argument was: Our existence is at stake. But there is no doubt that he then promised Adenauer to conduct the trial so as not to embarrass the present German government, that is, without mention of Globke, Vialon,[5] etc. Israel conducts realpolitik and uses "moral demands" purely for propaganda purposes. And it shouldn't be forgotten that the very respectable reparations that Germany then paid never would have been paid had it not been for the great pressure from abroad that the Jews mobilized. But you were quite right to put that aside right away and focus on the existence of the Federal Republic, for that is the real heart of the matter. And there, I'm afraid, one has to say that there is not the faintest indication of a radical change in attitude. Adenauer cut off any movement in that direction, and quite deliberately, by pursuing a policy driven solely by self-interest. He said to himself: The majority of the people went along and therefore have an interest in letting sleeping dogs lie. The greatest danger of those dogs being stirred up comes from the Jews, because of their influence on public opinion in the world. So we'll do everything we can to ward off that Jewish influence. Even Lübke wouldn't have dared to refuse his signature[6] under Adenauer. And what is particularly telling is that the so-called leftist opposition in Germany, the Gruppe 47[7] and all these opposition intellectuals, left their government in peace on this issue. They blabbered on about capitalism and exploitation and God knows what else—all utterly harmless stuff. But they didn't attack the Nazis in the state bureaucracy, nor did they press for discussion of the border question, nor did they declare solidarity with you in the question of reunification. That is, for all their radical hue and cry, they have taken no part in politics.

I share your uneasiness about Augstein, but it seems to me more and more that *Der Spiegel* has really been the only opposition far and wide in these years (it has made its mistakes, but why shouldn't it?). And if I feel a certain discomfort with Augstein, I have to add that my feelings toward just about any other German who has a role in public life are considerably more negative. For some time now I've felt myself "in league" with him. He has done more than anyone else. I did in fact write him a "private" letter, because I thought and still do think that by rights only a German should or can speak to this question. He misunderstood my remark about closing the books. I meant that ironically—as a provocative remark in the vein of why not go the whole hog. I didn't mean it as a quid pro quo. He didn't fully understand my remark about retroactive laws either. I said that the minister of justice was hiding behind the argument of retroactivity. But the truth is that all these criminals are being judged retroactively because there is no question at all that at the time they committed their crimes those crimes were not punishable by law. In Germany, where no special law was created, people are acting as if criminal law had not been rescinded for certain categories of people, the murder of whom was permitted or even ordered. This lie is coming home to roost now. However one may feel about the Israeli law regarding crimes committed against the Jewish people,[8] it is still a great advance over Nuremberg, because Rosen explicitly stated: Yes, we in fact have here a law with retroactive force.

Most striking perhaps are your words about world opinion.[9] They are reminiscent of Jefferson in the Declaration of Independence. Unfortunately, all anyone in Germany sees in world opinion is pressure exerted by "foreign" countries to which Germany has to yield because it is powerless. That is very dangerous, because it generates resentment of the worst kind. In general it seems to me—on the basis of other indicators as well, particularly in the universities—that only now, twenty years after the end of the war, are things reaching a critical stage in Germany. The first generation of "innocents" didn't dare speak up, because former Nazis, if they weren't too seriously compromised, were firmly entrenched and real opposition was too dangerous. But the generation that's coming along now can afford to do more. The twenty-year-olds, in short, are dealing now with forty-year-olds who are not themselves compromised. So the youngsters can risk opening their mouths, and they pull the older generation along with them— the forty-year-olds, not the horrified people of my generation. So I think it is worthwhile today to speak to the Germans again. It's true that the nationalistic currents are much worse and more aggressive than they were even a few years ago, but—and this is the one key point— there is a minority today that is really all right and that one can talk with. You call them the quiet ones. Yes, they are always there, but politically that isn't enough. Now, however, the quiet ones are beginning to make a little noise.

I don't know how the debate in the Bundestag[10] turned out. Not very well, I assume. Don't fret about it! What matters is that you have spoken and how you have spoken.

Only now am I getting to what I meant to begin with—the bad news about your sister-in-law.[11] I'm very, very sad, mostly on your account but also on my own. I met her only once at your house. I liked her very much, and I always thought I would see her again sometime. She was such fun to laugh with. I hope your wife is completely recovered now. Rheumatic pain is annoying. Salicyl (sodium salicylate) helps sometimes. Can't you dictate letters? Oh, how good it would be if we only lived a little closer together!

Warmly

Your

Hannah

372 Karl Jaspers to Hannah Arendt

Basel, March 23, 1965

Dear Hannah!

A nice long letter from you on February 19 and now your prompt reaction of March 14 to the *Spiegel* interview demand a reply, but I still can't write because the muscular rheumatism in my hand hurts too much and because I'm recovering from a not inconsequential illness. I sleep a lot during the day; work is out of the question. But you are right. I can at least dictate something to you, and Frau Salmony is so kind as to take the dictation.

Well, first to the unavoidable rehearsal of complaints: Shortly after the *Spiegel* interview I experienced heavy rectal bleeding. At first it was so severe that I needed a blood transfusion. Then, with the aid of modern medications, it abated, and after a week it stopped altogether. Now I've been without bleeding for more than a week. But the muscular rheumatism has gotten worse, with the consequence that most movements are painful. It travels around. In some places it will disappear again. During the bleeding, it took the form of lower back pain. Now it has left that area. I'm at least up now, lying on the chaise longue. Gertrud is in relatively good health, and we're both in good spirits and think that after all nothing more should be expected of me in retirement. The diagnosis is very likely the same as in 1959, bleeding as a consequence of diverticulosis in the colon descendens. Fortunately, the X rays from that episode were still available. The only difference is that the bleeding that time was superficial. Visually, it was frightening, but the volume was not great. This time the quantity was not really life-threatening, but it came close. Carcinoma is unlikely. I don't need to go through all the reasons for and against that diagnosis for you. One can never be one-hundred-percent sure. But aside from the bleeding itself there are no other symptoms that would give cause for concern. Most important, I haven't lost any weight. My appetite and other functions are all in the best of order.

But this present state of inactivity isn't altogether to my liking. I so much want to finish the book I'm writing about your book. But nothing more has been done on it since January. I have in my head what I want to do. The material I need is in large part ready but needs to be shaped and refined. The actual text exists only as notes and still has to be brought together. From the following example you'll see how far afield I'm going: at the moment I'm reading from Voltaire and about him. I admire the man. On the side, he accumulated great wealth through speculation. With it, he ruled like a minor prince in Ferney, built housing, set up watch factories. That took very little of his time and energy. He earned nothing from his writings. His vitality is extraordinary, his abundance of ideas, his power of formulation, his instinct for creating effects, his feel for French taste, all that is remarkable. But now I think I am seeing in him something analogous to Descartes. Just as Descartes represents a mode of thought that is constantly bringing confusion into modern science and scholarship and robbing them of their greatness, Voltaire represents in modern humanity that literary element that is in its very core as inhuman as possible, in reality mean-spirited, but that is responsible for the moralistic tone, the grand gesture, the voice of protest, and so on that have remained so much a part of discourse until today. No one has yet understood what I think I have discovered about Descartes. It is even more difficult to work out what I mean by a literary type in whose tradition, for example, Thomas Mann belongs. Why am I spending my time with this? Because I think that among all the heterogeneous forces that marshaled themselves against you this literary element as such, without prior agreement, found itself by its very nature united against you. One of the points that is important to me is that you have nothing to do with this literary element. Well, this I mention only by the bye. For the time being, this project is on hold. How it will turn out I can't say yet. It may be an utter failure and will then remain unpublished. That would be too bad.

You write about your lecture tours in America and your discomfort. Of course you are constantly meeting your doppelgänger who is not you but is the person that people expect to meet and who is quite different. The only remedy is for you to appear in person. Then the doppelgänger is forced to take to its heels. But the situation is odd. It is probably always the case in public life.

I'm glad that you liked the *Spiegel* interview. It came about more or less by chance. If Augstein hadn't asked, I wouldn't have thought of it. And when he asked, as usual through Piper, I thought about you and your comments on *Der Spiegel*. I thought it over with Gertrud for a day and then agreed, fully conscious of the danger involved. I don't know how things will develop from here. Your political comments on specific aspects of the question of the statute of limitations are in complete agreement with my own views. I won't go into that today.

Piper has sent off to you my new little book: the thirteen television lectures.[1] I am vastly more fond of them, of course, than I am of the *Spiegel* interview and German politics. It is odd that the peripheral and chance things make all the stir in the world and that we remain more or less alone with the things that really matter. Piper has grand ideas as far as sales are concerned. He made a first printing of 11,000 copies and 4,000 have already been sold from the first distribution. But unfortunately that doesn't mean much.

For years now I've been getting letters from people I don't know, even more of them recently, that say what I think is strictly utopian. Some then go on to say that it is clearly wrong, and I ought to do better. The others (I just received one of this kind from an emigrant, a woman, in Stockholm) say, on the other hand: I'd like to hear from you what we ought to do, yet I know that you can't tell us. But she remains cheerful and won't give in to resignation.

And to close with an amusing item: This afternoon I received a letter: "You Jew lover, you traitor, you slimy reptile!" —It would be wrong to say that something like that makes me angry, but it is awful to have to see that there are people like that.

Warmest greetings to you and Heinrich, from Gertrud, too. I'm hoping my television lectures will find a sympathetic reader in Heinrich. I'm afraid that they may bore you a bit. But the reason for that would be that you know me already and that these things will be all too obvious to you. I want to dictate another letter soon.

Warmly, your
Karl

373 Hannah Arendt to Karl Jaspers

received on April 13, 1965[1]

Lieber Verehrtester,

Your letter arrived just as I was leaving for Chicago, and it was a great relief to me. A few days earlier I had received Gertrud's letter[2] saying that the bleeding had stopped. The fright is still with me, but oddly enough diverticulosis is a very common disorder here, which is managed very well by diet. What I can't quite understand is why you haven't been on a diet for years, considering that diverticulosis was the diagnosis from that earlier, similar episode. I have some experience with rheumatism myself, though I've never had it in a hand. For two years I was completely incapable of moving my right shoulder, and I taught myself all kinds of tricks to keep it from being noticeable. And then one fine day it was simply gone. Nobody knows why or how. If it pains you so much—it's particularly bad in the hands—has anyone thought of cortisone? I never took it, but it's supposed to help.

I received your *Kleine Schule der Philosophie* yesterday; and, as Heinrich has just told me, a copy arrived in New York today. My copy is an extra from Helen Wolff. All I have read so far are the chapters about love and death. The chapter on love is entirely new and somehow truer than anything I can recall your having written about it before. (I don't have any books here and can't compare passages.) I read the first chapter, too. Extremely lively, so much more concrete and direct than anything else. It will make a great impression on people. This is philosophy without magic ("Could I but rid my path of magic / Forget forever that hocus-pocus . . ."),[3] and compared with what you have written here all conceptual language is a kind of magic. Your book has an incredible purity, and the only reason I haven't read more right away is that I finally wanted to write this letter, and I never know here what may get in the way—namely, students. Heinrich just said he wanted to read the book immediately, and on Sunday (when telephoning is cheaper) we'll talk about it.

Heinrich told me about an almost-accident that is still haunting me. He and a colleague were riding in a taxi on the parkway when the driver, next to him, had a heart attack, fell over into his lap, and died on the spot. It's a miracle that nothing happened, because Heinrich couldn't even move enough to get the driver's foot off the accelerator pedal. But nothing did happen. Whew . . .

I'm very eager to see what you will have to say about the literati question. Unfortunately, it is very specifically a Jewish problem, but that is of course only by chance. I've never read Voltaire. You say he is ultimately mean-spirited. But what is so extremely irritating, it seems to me, is that the intellect here—and to some degree real intellect—takes its rise directly from the filth. I have often thought to myself, starting when I was young: What do I really have in common with these people? Far less, let us say, than with Erna or with my good Esther, and I mean that literally. From a purely technical perspective, the key thing seems to me to be the "bright idea." If you have some degree of talent, there is absolutely nothing about which you can't have a bright idea. And once you've had that bright idea, even if you have it at somebody else's orders, then it becomes "my bright idea." Karl Kraus[4] said in 1933: "I don't have any bright ideas on the subject of Hitler."[5] Coming from a literary person, that is a major statement. I quote it sometimes to suggest that even Jews would have gone along with Hitler if they had been allowed to. So how can one say who would not have gone along? Karl Kraus certainly wouldn't have, even if he hadn't been a Jew. But Adorno[6] surely would have—indeed, NB, he even tried to on the basis of his being only half Jewish, but he couldn't pull it off. What troubles me so much about all this is the alienation from reality, that people ignore reality in favor of their bright ideas.

Now to another question: Do you know Michael Landmann,[7] professor at Berlin University? I've gotten into a nasty squabble with him. He is the chairman of the Society of Friends of Hebrew University and staged an evening against my Eichmann book—which in itself doesn't bother me. But at this gathering a student from Israel stood up and claimed (a) that a reader could understand the book only if he knew me and my "history" personally; (b) he was such a reader, and he knew (1) that I didn't learn that I was Jewish until I was twenty (my grandfather was president of the congregation, which everyone in Israel knows), (2) that I had said I had never made my peace with that fact. I then demanded of Herr Landmann that he issue a correction to these bald-faced lies. Of course I don't know this man at all. He claims he "knows" me from a lecture he attended. Herr Landmann indignantly refused and stood one hundred percent behind this presumably pathological liar who just wanted to make himself look important. The student wrote a letter six pages long in which he claimed other things he had made up out of whole cloth. Now Landmann is pulling you into this. He says that he, too, knows me; that he was your assistant and got to know me through you. I don't recall him. Can you jog my memory?

There were two very good articles in *Die Zeit* about the "satirical magazine" *The New Yorker*.[8] I'm enclosing them, but you should read only the beginning of the first one. That would seem to explain Golo Mann's behavior.[9] *The New Yorker* published a portrait of Thomas Mann, much to his outrage, until people told him it was good publicity. His outrage quickly faded. Golo Mann has surely heard that I don't think his father is Goethe—so two flies with one blow.

And finally: Yesterday I received a play from a certain Wolfgang Graetz[10] about the July 20 conspirators. In my opinion, it's excellent, really the truth. I can't judge whether it is correct in every detail. At the moment the play is at the Munich Kammerspiele, and I'd like to encourage Graetz to send it to you, which I assume he doesn't quite dare to do. Hochhuth, Gaus, Augstein, Graetz—there's life in Germany after all. It gives one hope. The grandsons are better than the sons (Gruppe 47).

Here everything is following its by-now-familiar course. Good students. A Spinoza and a Rousseau seminar. *Die Grossen Philosophen* made Spinoza more accessible to me. Now I'm sometimes truly fascinated by him. I don't like Rousseau, but one has to know him. He was so important politically. —I've just come from a student protest meeting against our policy in Vietnam. I went with several colleagues. The whole thing was extremely reasonable and unfanatical. So crowded that one could hardly get through. No one shrieked; no one gave a speech, and that in a mass meeting. Real discussion and information. Very impressive.

With warmest greetings
Your Hannah

374 *Karl Jaspers to Hannah Arendt*

Basel, April 17, 1965

Dear Hannah!

Another dictated letter.

It really does seem a miracle that Heinrich came out of that situation on the parkway unscathed. Now, like you, he, too, has been touched by the Moloch of the technological age, but not seized by it. Fortunately, he managed to escape its clutches. If one judges the seriousness of religions by the number of sacrifices they demand and receive, then technology is the most powerful religion that ever existed—Kägi[1] once made that observation in the faculty lounge.

I am very happy about the success you are having in Chicago: the best teacher and "the most normal"[2]—yes, that's the heart of the matter. One is constantly distressed to see that that is so seldom the case.

We always assume that people are rational, and that is what gives rise to our great mistakes and then to our harshness. You are much less prone to that than I am, however. You have mercy in concrete situations with specific individuals. But on the more positive side is what you recently wrote: in America, reason is possible in a mass meeting about Vietnam policy. It is wonderful that a meeting like that can provide information and discussion and proceed without demagogy. So again it is the Americans: we have to set our hopes on them.

Five days ago Gertrud had another of her attacks with high fever. On the second day, rales were audible from the same place in her lungs. She has been free of fever since yesterday, probably as a result of the penicillin. She has been up for an hour now, and her only remaining complaint is that she is weak. We'll have to watch out that she doesn't again do something rash right away. Depressed as she can get in her feeling of helplessness, she is just as quickly cheerful and optimistic again, at least as long as we two are together. —My rheumatism remains unchanged.

It is good for our spirits to know that you both can come in August. Right after hearing this news, Gertrud was in the best of moods, though just before that everything had still seemed dreary to her.

You have written kind things about my *Kleine Schule des Philosophierens*. And Heinrich too is pleased with it. You want to stage a success with it right away in the United States with Helen Wolff. This kind of philosophizing will often strike the commonsensical mind as quite mad, even though it isn't mad at all. Is it possible to make such philosophy readable in America? If so, that would please me very much, because in the overall picture America is the most important element for us. What Russia and China may yet produce is so completely obscure to us that we cannot count on it.

Perhaps you will both have more to say about specific matters of content when we get together. What you said about the first lecture was very nice: "completely without magic." I would like to contribute to ridding speculative thought too of magic but without detracting from its power, that is, I'd like to see its power to overwhelm reduced, but not the power of the quiet truth that can be illuminated only in this way. [. . .]

Thank you for *Die Zeit* with the article about the "satirical magazine." Very important for me. It makes a great deal clear to me.

But now to something much more important: I would be very interested in the play by Wolfgang Graetz. I'm not at all certain that the young author will want to send it to me. But if he is willing, please ask him to. I am reasonably well informed on this subject at the moment.

Does Heinrich like the lecture on fundamental knowledge?[3] It's a matter I consider important. I first lectured on it in the winter of 1931/32[4] when my *Philosophie* was published. I was aware that I had made a major step forward with it (or so I told myself). It gave me a great boost. "Philosophy" was not a lost cause after all. I was able to go on working. Now I see in it the logical tool (Kant: transcendentally logical) for getting rid of all magic. The tool is only usable, of course, if knowledge is already available from other sources. Fifteen years ago I planned a book the outline of which was drafted: *Clavis clavium* (the key to the key cabinet). Then I let it lie. No one responded to these ideas, not even in seminars. Then I became unsure of myself. Were my ideas wrongheaded after all? I don't think so, but the extensive and less good presentation of these ideas in my book *Von der Wahrheit* did not work the theme through in a way to make it convincing and inspire anyone to work with this key, as I actually have been ever since.

But now enough. Warmest greetings to you both from Gertrud and

Your

Karl

April 21

Because of the Easter holiday I didn't get the typed copy of this letter until today. Gertrud has gotten much of her strength back in the meantime.

Christiane Zimmer[5] was here today. She told us how famous you have become. But also because of your other major books. She had just spoken with a salesman in a drugstore who had read your books. He asked her if she was Hannah Arendt; she looked so much like a picture of you! I did not consider that flattering, and it shows that the young man doesn't see very well.

375 *Hannah Arendt to Gertrud and Karl Jaspers*

May 28, 1965

Dearest Friends—

It's hardly worth it to write again—thank God. Today we booked our return passage—by ship from Rotterdam on September 7. Heinrich doesn't know Holland, and we want to spend a few days having a look at it before we leave. Since Erna won't be returning until August 8, it seems to me we shouldn't arrive until about the 15th to give you a chance to rest up and reestablish the normal routine. I may come a few days earlier. Heinrich wants to see his friend Robert [Gilbert] again and possibly ask Natascha,[1] his very nice first wife, to come from Paris to Zurich. For my part I want to see Mary [McCarthy], who will be in Italy in August, either in Zurich, too, or at her place in Italy. Thank God there's nothing going on in August, so that I won't have to cope with anything all of a sudden.

Piper is here and has told us how things are with you both. Could your rheumatism possibly be neuritis, which is only made worse by aspirin and salicyl? Many of our friends here have had that, and I know how very painful it is. It's treated here—successfully—with vitamin B1.

Has Graetz sent you his play about the resistance? If not, write me right away. I'll send you my copy—a mimeographed manuscript and not the final text. You will have seen from *Der Spiegel*, as I did, that the gentleman is in prison, apparently can't keep from stealing, and after a rocky youth feels much better and more secure in prison than out. Which doesn't bother me at all. —Apropos German writers: they're all here at the moment. I've gotten to know Grass and Johnson;[2] I'll tell you about that when I see you. And Enzensberger[3] is on his way. The lack of common sense is often enough to make one despair.

Politically, we are worried and disgusted. I was in Washington to sit on a commission on education appointed by the president. The nonsense talked there was indescribable. The chairman was a well-known physicist who was presumably finding life in the laboratory boring because he didn't have any more ideas. His reason seems to have left him, too. That we all pay taxes to support this mindless idiocy! The one hopeful sign is the strong opposition in the whole country, the direct way people express their opinions, the utter fearlessness.

Much much more when we see you.

Warmly

Your

Hannah

376 *Karl Jaspers to Hannah Arendt*

Basel, May 29, 1965

Dear Hannah!

I wanted to at least say hello after all this time.

To report on my physical condition: I have in the meantime informed myself as best I can. A great many tests have been done. It has become clear now that what is going on with me is that the body itself is producing substances that generate infection (hence the occasional rises in temperature) but have nothing to do with bacteria. The body then develops antibodies against these substances. The antibodies are present in the blood. They were present in force in me six weeks ago, and now two different institutes have confirmed the presence of these same antibodies again. The origin of this illness is unknown. There aren't any medications for combating the illness itself, but there do seem to be some for treating the symptoms, and I am using them now: Ponstan so far, Butacolidin next week, and cortisone sometime later. All these medications have inherent dangers, particularly where hemorrhages and lowered resistance to infections are concerned; in other words, the very things that are most troubling in terms of my chronic illnesses. And so the level of treatment is dictated by the degree of risk one is willing to run. The illness has been clearly progressive so far, both in extent and in the severity of the pain. Americans have apparently assembled statistics showing that in 25% of the cases the disease can disappear as rapidly as it comes on, or at least that major remissions occur. The disease is not regarded as fatal. The physical state that it can induce is not, however, exactly comfortable. It makes itself felt in moments of helplessness when I'm getting dressed and always whenever I have to do something with my arms. Another symptom, if that's what it is, has been present for a week now, too, namely, that I am always tired and often fall asleep during the day. Day and night have come to resemble each other. From my subjective perspective, the night lasts a long time. Work is out of the question at the moment; I can't even make notes. But every day still brings much to enjoy. The meditations that one does not put to paper are worth a great deal. The world comes to me in so many ways that I am still very content. An example: During the early weeks of this rheumatic attack I wrote a radio talk called "What Is German?" and I recently reworked it and improved it. I sent it off (to German Radio in Cologne) fearing that they would not want to broadcast it. Although the language is very restrained, it is still, I think, a clear and thoroughly convincing rejection of the basic view of Germany on which the Federal Republic rests. I expected some kind of excuse for not accepting it, especially since I had overstepped the deadline by two days. So what happened? The young literary editor in charge of these things wrote me a very enthusiastic letter. He was not in total agreement with what I said but felt it had to be publicly aired. He thought this essay would make a real impression. And to top it off he raised my fee quite out of the blue from 1,000 to 3,000 DM. So there is still a lot of freedom left in radio, and there are still people in Germany who want to think, and a literary type, it would appear, can even feel solidarity with me. That made me very happy. But what the two of you will say to this talk I don't know yet. Since an answer to the question the talk asks is impossible, all it can do is create a mood and cite many relevant facts.

Hochhuth brought me the issue of *Der Spiegel* that has a report on Graetz and his new play that you wrote me about.[1] Your positive view of it is mentioned. Unfortunately, Graetz has not sent me the play. Going on the basis of this report, I have my reservations. What is given there as statements by Ludwig Beck puts one off so very much. The precision and the differentiation of Beck's language is lost. In the play Beck makes accusations, and that is precisely what he did not do. He tried instead "to hold the ranks together" and attempt the coup with all possible means. I'm no great partisan of Beck's, for other reasons. But I sense a crassness of presentation here. That could, of course, lie in the report, and I can't venture a judgment on the play yet. Only one thing can be said: With the exception of Julius Leber (and of course with the exception of the magnificent Scholls as early as 1942–43, who do not belong in this context), every one of these resistance fighters remained indecisive and did not reach a clear either-or position. And then, it is certain that a number of them, with their great seriousness, clever ideas, and fine formulations, didn't understand what they really were doing. They consciously sacrificed their lives. It is very difficult to present all that properly. Politically, the honoring of the resistance fighters, with those few exceptions, is a disaster. It stands in the nationalistic tradition and perpetuates it.

Yesterday, with Saner's help, I bought a dictation machine I can talk into. I want to see if that offers any possibilities. A text may come out of it, muddled, aphoristic, but perhaps usable as a basis after all. Saner, who is remarkably kind to me on a human level and comes to my aid with bright ideas, so to speak, gives me courage. Two weeks ago, a literary man from Paris was here. He wants to do a kind of publicity article for the magazine *Réalités*[2] about my atom book and in connection with the prize I received in Belgium for this book.[3] I was given questions in French that I could read, and I recorded my responses to them on tape. According to Saner and the man from Paris, it turned out well. But of course there's not a single idea there that I haven't presented long since, and the whole thing never left familiar terrain. At the moment I'm giving in to this mode, half tongue in cheek, and allowing that Saner may be right. After all, I'm still able to babble.

This all sounds rather dreary. Please don't think that that describes our mood. Erna is wonderful. Realistic, unsentimental, full of ideas, always cheerful. Gertrud strikes me as very reasonable, despite her tendency to find it intolerable when her beloved suffers. Thanks to the hearing aid, we can speak with each other and laugh together quite a lot.

Frau Salmony, who is taking the dictation of this letter, is a delight to us every time she comes. She never indulges in empty phrases. She is always helpful. Without her I could not dictate a letter like this. With anyone else I would be embarrassed.

Now I see in fact what the consequences of babbling are. With ink and the bother of writing, I would have been inhibited. Now I'll send this off without a care in the world and in my old trust in you both.

Warmest greetings, from Gertrud, too

Your

Karl

P.S. Your letter of May 28 has just arrived.

Wonderful that we will see each other. The prospect makes me happy.

I would very much like to have the manuscript by Graetz. It is in any case interesting to see what a man from such a background and with such an interior makeup sees and thinks important. Of course, it is ultimately unimportant whether he steals or not. But one first has to see whether his stealing is truly of no consequence.

Have you received the translation of my *Nietzsche*[4] from Wallraff in Tucson? He wrote me a few weeks ago that the book had been sent to you. Perhaps you could read a few passages and see how the translation is. If it is good, I wonder if Wallraff mightn't be a possible translator for my *Kleine Schule* with Helen Wolff. His enthusiasm is touching, and he is, it seems to me, an honest American sort. A child who is touched by the most profound things, delights in them, teaches, and is modest. Now of course he is eager to see his great project, this translation, have the utmost success. Only 800 copies of the book were printed, but it has gone into a second printing right away. A major publisher—I've forgotten the name—wants to bring it out as a paperback.

Yesterday I had a consultation with a rheumatism specialist together with our Bernstein. The diagnosis of arthritis chronica was confirmed. I was examined from head to toe. Besides the swelling on the back of my left hand, he found swelling of the left knee. The therapy is planned as a series of experiments, conducted with the caution that befits my age and other illnesses.

377 Hannah Arendt to Karl Jaspers

Palenville, June 11, 1965

Lieber Verehrtester—

Thank you very much for your precise report. Now I have a clear sense of what your condition is and how bad it is, even though I won't be able to gather more detailed information about it here. It wasn't clear to me that the pain had gotten worse, and I'm full of admiration for the calm sovereignty with which you endure it and describe how it is. Remaining loyal to reality through good and through ill is what all love of truth really amounts to and all gratitude for the fact that one was born in the first place. I wish I were already there and that we could spend what time you have left in your day talking. But then perhaps the medication will help, or you will be among the cases that experience spontaneous remission.

I've sent you the Graetz play, and I'm curious as to what you'll say about it. I've also enclosed a letter[1] that struck me as characteristic. I'm eager to see your radio talk.[2] I know, the radio people are by far the most refreshing lot in Germany today—alert, critical, well informed, and courageous as well. I don't know why they've all wound up in that field. Apart from them there is only *Der Spiegel*, which keeps getting better all the time. It even printed Hochhuth,[3] who made very good use of your concept of property. I just read the long essay about De Gaulle.[4] I'm sorry to say that I think Augstein is absolutely right. That's just the way it is. Essentially a big swindle. And as far as the Federal Republic is concerned, we don't need to waste any more breath on it. Its decline is written all over its face. Social Democracy for religious schools! Everybody is just waiting for a strong man to come along.

The *Nietzsche*: The publisher that wants the paperback rights is Harper & Row. Indeed an excellent house. I heard about this because the editor for philosophy there asked me which of your major works was still untranslated. I immediately recommended the three-volume *Philosophie*. He also told me that one of their representatives had visited Heidegger, who "in the course of the conversation urged upon us to publish a translation of Karl Jaspers' *Der philosophische Glaube angesichts der Offenbarung*, which he considers an extremely important work." I thought you should know that. Perhaps it will please you. That is, curiously enough, the book that will appear in the series edited by Nanda Anshen, which will also be published by Harper & Row. The man with whom I am corresponding is Fred Wieck. I assume he will be in touch with you about the rights.

I escaped from the insane heat of New York on Monday and came to our vacation spot. Heinrich is still working. He came from Bard for the weekend yesterday evening, completely exhausted and more or less dehydrated. It's cool here and a wonderful summer. We go for walks, and I swim. Unfortunately, Heinrich has to go back to the college for two weeks. At the moment, he has disappeared in the woods, and this letter has to go to the post office. Otherwise it won't leave here until Monday.

It is a relief to know that a planned course of therapy has been begun now.

All my very best
Your   Hannah

378 *Karl Jaspers to Hannah Arendt*

Basel, June 16, 1965

Dear Hannah!

Just a few quick lines in reply to your good letter of June 11.

I've read the Graetz, and I'm of your opinion. He has clearly grasped the central point. The major reason for the confusion and failure of these conspirators lay in the self-deception underlying their intentions. Graetz apparently feels, too, that the clarification of all that, of how things really were, is crucial today if the Federal Republic is to have a future. He did show Beck in the proper light after all. The article about Graetz had misled me on that. But despite all this I take no real pleasure in the play. It seems to me that the basic idea loses its force in the plethora of images. Almost all those images are present in quite authentic form in the literature. It becomes tedious sometimes to hear these details again. The important things are given hardly any weight—for example: the long discussion between Witzleben[1] and Beck, which has not been preserved in detail but in which they clashed and then parted ways. What emerged there in Beck had substance, not just because of his courage but also because of the calmness, clarity, loyalty, and simplicity of the soldier, the likes of which at that time hardly existed at all anymore. Also, the wonderful freedom with which Beck questioned his comrades and did not bellow at them, achieving something like a tragic stature after all and remaining in the end the only unsullied figure. Stauffenberg continued to lie to others when he certainly must have known that Hitler was still alive. Beck required that whenever a command was issued it also be stated that Hitler's death was not confirmed, but that his destruction remained the only essential task because he was morally dead. Beck did not want to lie, and he didn't lie, not even in the final crisis, when failure was absolutely certain. That has nothing to do with the basic idea and signifies only Beck's personal stature. I found the whole play in this series of scenes very well done as a montage. Perhaps it is going too far to say that I did not find passion and mood, everything that Hochhuth has. But Graetz's remarkably clear understanding of the facts of July 20 is extraordinary. Again I suspect this work is the product of a primarily rational process supported by psychological concepts. He has read your *Eichmann*. He found his key points there. That does not diminish his artistic achievement. It could also be that the reading of your book was a catalyst that set off a process already prepared in him. The issue here isn't priority but the motive behind the insight. I respect this work, but I don't really reverberate to it. It is exciting and yet, I think, not ultimately powerful. Shall I keep the manuscript here until you come? Or should Erna send it somewhere? May I perhaps pass it on to Hochhuth?

I'm happy about Heidegger's comment. He was here last winter with a group of theologians who were discussing my book. By chance I heard something of what went on there, but only this one thing: Heidegger did not understand my concept of the symbol. It seems to me that there is something appealing about Heidegger at the moment. I've experienced this and think back on it with nostalgia and horror. There is something in him, and something substantial, but you can't rely on anything with him. And awful things happen. You know how much I would like to write a short book about Heidegger.[2] At the center of it would be the room that is as good as empty today, that is, metaphysics, and in which one meets Heidegger. Then, at that level, the disparity between metaphysical positions and the emergence of forces that don't manifest themselves outright. And from there, on to the meaning of his polemic, the factual aspects of the polemic, the consequences of it for the conduct of his life right down to biographical detail. But I won't manage it. I would be happy if I could at least manage to finish my book about you and the independence of thought. At the moment, the prospects are not good, but one can't really know for sure.

I have to make another report: Exactly seven days ago I had another heavy hemorrhage, and I'm still very debilitated from it. But it took a different course this time, astonishingly. Bernstein came the minute it began and administered the necessary shots, which I didn't get last time until twelve hours after the onset of the bleeding. Then Krupp and Bernstein insisted on a transfusion right away, which was not done last time until the fourth day. The result was that the bleeding stopped completely nine hours after it began, and it has not recurred yet. That happens sometimes with blood transfusions. No one knows quite why or how. In any case, I've been lucky. On some days I feel as if I were shutting myself off from the business and concerns of public life. But then if I have a better day, a kind of spring seems to activate itself somewhat in me again. Erna's care and diligence are touching. She does everything, supervises the cleaning women, prepares our food, and creates the proper cheerful atmosphere. I feel a philosophical affinity with her even though I'm unable to put it into words. Of Gertrud I needn't speak. She is the joy of my days. Her own complaints are not insignificant. She fell on the steps here a week ago. She wasn't badly hurt, but the swollen knee has yet to heal completely.

You write about my *Nietzsche* and a paperback edition of it. I'm happy to have your confirmation of this fact. Have you received the translation itself? Wallraff wrote to me about it. If he should be a good translator, would he be a possibility for the *Kleine Schule* with Helen Wolff?

As for the book Nanda Anshen has: I haven't heard anything more since the contract was signed. Ashton was going to send me suggestions for cuts. So far, I have heard nothing from him. I'm afraid the whole thing is languishing with him, perhaps because he was given much too much time. Nanda Anshen, from whom I had a letter practically every week back then, is keeping complete silence now. Could you possibly call them both when you're in New York and prod them a bit?

Warmest greetings to you both, also from Gertrud

Your

Karl

---

379   *Karl Jaspers to Hannah Arendt*

Basel, July 5, 1965

Dear Hannah!

Your suggestions to Harper & Row were a great success. I've received a letter from Fred Wieck. He wants to publish the book *Der philosophische Glaube angesichts der Offenbarung*. But he doesn't know that Nanda Anshen secured a contract for it with his firm long since. I hope now that there will be some action taken on this apparently forgotten project. According to his contract, Ashton should have delivered the translation in October 1964. I'm enclosing a carbon copy of my reply to Mr. Wieck.

I won't report in detail about myself. Cortisone has afforded me considerable relief. The doctor is trying now to determine the smallest possible dose and a combination of medications that will provide long-term relief. I haven't been out of the house for months. Most of the time I spend lying on the chaise longue.

I'm looking forward to your visit so much that the pleasure of that prospect is brightening these weeks for me already. I'll catch you up then on everything there is to tell.

Warmest greetings to you both from Gertrud and

Your

Karl

---

380   *Hannah Arendt to Gertrud and Karl Jaspers*

July 6, 1965

Dearest Friends—

Your marvelous letter from out of your illness. Good cheer and equanimity shine through, the wonderful calm of all these years. I'm guessing that your hand is better and that the pain has responded to the medication after all. We talk about you every day here, and my thoughts wander to Basel and the Austrasse every hour.

We'll talk about Graetz when I'm there. Perhaps I'll bring another letter I've received in the meantime—always with the prison duly noted as the return address. —I don't know much about Beck. I liked the fact that Graetz made Helldorf the key figure, made him a "hero," as it were, because I see him the same way. As for the rest, I think we are pretty much in agreement. None of these things are works of art, but as reportage it is good and, in my view, well done. And it is a start at speaking the truth. And there is a freedom from ideology and lack of sentimentality I like. Graetz is a new type, better perhaps than people like Ossietzky, whom I always found rather intolerable despite all my admiration for his personal courage. What is blessedly absent in Graetz is that bombastic tone of conviction.

Heidegger's remark: I think it not unlikely that he had already made it in some form or another in Basel but that the only thing reported to you was the unpleasant remark. Nathalie Sarraute, a French writer of Russian-Jewish background, said to me here that only in America do people pass on compliments that are made behind one's back. In France, on the other hand, she said, every hostile remark gets back to you with amazing rapidity.

Helen Wolff already had a translator for the *Kleine Schule*. I suggested Wallraff to her months ago. I can't explain the business with Nanda Anshen, but I'll try to reach her by phone—I don't think she is in New York now. I'm just about to leave our paradise for two days in New York.

Send us a line to let us know how you are. A postcard is enough. And if there should be any changes in your plans. Otherwise, we'll continue to plan on just before mid-August.

With all best wishes from us both—

Your

Hannah

381   *Hannah Arendt to Gertrud and Karl Jaspers*

Palenville, July 25, 1965

Dearest Friends—

Thank your for your letters[1] that sounded so reassuring. I go back to New York tomorrow, and I'll hardly have a chance to write from there. In the meantime, Piper has persuaded me, through one of his so-called colleagues, to do a radio talk in Cologne with Carlo Schmid[2] about revolution. If they don't lock me up right away there, which isn't too likely, I want to fly directly from there to Italy for about three days to see Mary [McCarthy]. Heinrich doesn't want to join me. He prefers to go to Zurich. My only reason for writing today is to give you our dates:

We'll fly from New York to Cologne on July 31 or August 1 and will stay there until the 6th. Then I'll go to Italy and Heinrich, to Zurich, Waldhaus Dolder. I'll be in Zurich by about the 10th or 11th at the latest and will call right away. We've made reservations at the Krafft am Rhein; Heinrich only until the 23rd. Then he wants to get together with his friend Robert [Gilbert] for a week. I think I'll stay through the end of the month, if that is all right with you. Our ship leaves Rotterdam on September 7, and we want to spend a few days in Holland, which Heinrich has not seen yet.

Nothing has worked out right with Piper this time, so I'll have to read proofs for the revolution book while I'm in Europe. It won't really be so terrible.

Here, where I can always work so well, I've reworked two lectures into long essays. Unfortunately, they're in English, and I hesitate to impose them on you. One is about truth and politics,[3] actually a by-product of the Eichmann mess: Should one, may one simply speak the truth in politics? The second is about Brecht[4] and has to do with our long debate: a good poem is a good poem.

I'm glad to know that the Saner family is with you. Hochhuth and Saner—they are, I think, your "pupils," but not just pupils. Sometimes we don't have much luck with our sons and have to wait for our grandchildren. That, too, is quite wonderful. I really look forward to seeing Saner. I find his style and mode of thinking extraordinarily sympathetic. Please give him my best regards.

Now the question remains where you can reach me in case something or other shouldn't work out or should be changed. I assume that we'll be staying at the Hotel Bristol in Cologne. I asked Piper and Zilkens, a friend I met on a train, to make reservations for us. But I'm still not sure of this yet. The simplest thing would be for me to call you—but I don't want to disturb you. But with Saner there, he will probably answer the phone. I hate the idea of dragging you from your sofa or

desk. But I'll probably call anyhow—because that's just the way I am.
Until soon! With all best wishes and regards

Your
Hannah

P.S. As you have probably heard, Ashton has turned in the translation. Quite astonished to hear that it might be considered late. He overstepped the deadline by *only* a year.

382   Hannah Arendt to Karl Jaspers

New York, September 20, 1965

Lieber Verehrtester—

We've been home again for almost a week now, and tomorrow my semester begins.[1] Heinrich, who is taking this semester off, has just gone to Bard for a week anyway to see that things are in order. I'm finding settling back in here particularly difficult this time. I'm really still with you, and it's only my shadow sitting here at the typewriter. I'm thinking, hoping, one of you will send me a line soon to say how you are and how the pain is.

I should tell you about Cologne, which seems to me to be much farther back in time than Basel. It was a total disaster, but not because of the director of the scholarship foundation—even though he was somewhat hostile—but because of the students, who turned out in droves. Two years ago I suggested the idea of founding an association of former scholarship students. The director and the students were very enthusiastic, but then they talked about it for two years without doing anything. The first thing that became clear in Cologne was that they had all forgotten (the students, not the director) that it was supposed to be for *former* students and not a student organization. It was by no means clear to them that those are two completely different things. Second, no one, including the director, had understood that the whole thing could be meaningful only if the students or former scholarship students put it together, and not the bureaucracy of the foundation. The students, strongly on my side as far as their mood went, were extremely aggressive with the director, whom they accused of not being open to new ideas. He, with good reason, balked at the additional work this would mean. I said that all they needed from the foundation administration was addresses for a mailing. Certainly the administration won't refuse you that. Then you need a little money—either from the foundation or (much better) from private sources. (There were a few friends of Zilkens present at the meeting —a lawyer, a businessman, a doctor—and it was absolutely clear that they would have contributed immediately and would have attended to additional funding. The students took no notice of that at all.) Of course they could have the addresses. But the students remained aggressive toward the director, really for no cause. It never occurred to them that they could do something themselves that was not commanded or recommended to them from above. Not even after both Heinrich and I told them over and over again that they could. They were not stupid or ill intentioned, just totally helpless and vexed. Like children—although all of them were in their early or middle twenties. Then the following complaints were voiced: Scholarship students know each other only and at best if they study at the same university and if a university official involves himself with them. They complained justifiably that they didn't have the addresses of other universities and didn't have the faintest idea what was going on at them. For example, it turned out that the Cologne group was planning a trip to Poland and that Tübingen was, too—but neither group knew about the other's plans. Every scholarship student is, in principle, eligible to take part in the annual gatherings—except that no one in Munich knows what is going on in Cologne and vice versa. If a scholarship student visits another university, he has no way of finding other scholarship students there. Etc., etc. In short, the famous German talent for organization that never works unless it has to do with work or ideology. I was left with the feeling that they would never manage to get their house in order in this respect. The foundation is and remains a very good institution for encouraging individual talent. Politically, it will never amount to anything. Hopeless—

Holland was very beautiful, not just the magnificent museums but also the country and the people. Still no wild prosperity but a healthy financial stability in all classes of society. Model workers' settlements and amazing engineering feats around the Zuider Zee. People say there: God created the world, and the Dutch created Holland, which accurately reflects reality. They keep reclaiming new, fertile land and settling farmers on very handsome farms. All in Friesland. And wonder of wonders—there's a long waiting list of people who want to go and farm these lands, even though the work is still hard. Cows are still milked by hand in the fields. The hatred for Germans is still very strong, and it's easy to imagine in this peaceful, reasonable country how horrified and desperate the Dutch must have felt about the hordes that overran them. They all know German very well, better than English, but they try not to speak it if at all possible. I was at two very different parties with Dutch intellectuals. We spoke only English, and if they didn't understand something, I translated it into German, which they all understood almost as well as I. They were grateful for the help, spoke perhaps a sentence or two of German, and then went back to English. That was true in personal conversations, too. The waiters were often, not always, somewhat impudently ironic with German guests, sarcastic, with an undertone of impertinence that otherwise doesn't exist there.

The voyage home was very nice, with a very pleasant cabin. But there too everything was on the modest side. They economize there, too, and the food was downright bad, which is something that just doesn't happen elsewhere in first class. We didn't mind. Heinrich grumbled, and we found consolation in treating ourselves to the very best French red wines. And read novels—I, Virginia Woolf, whom you probably don't know. Very good, a great literary talent, in many respects odd, always very original.

The telephone has started ringing off the hook here, and I have to close this overly long chatterbox of a letter. Oh, yes, *Saner*. I still haven't gotten hold of Kenneth Thompson at the Rockefeller Foundation, and I have to put it off until next week. I'll send word right away then.[2]

All my very best
Your
Hannah

383   *Karl Jaspers to Hannah Arendt*

End of September 1965[1]

Dear Hannah!

It was nice to have your letter today. Yes, we are together in this lovely but also not very predictable world. The laws of nature are certain, more certain still is a human being, the most certain thing there is; but not at all or in any way objectively so, not by contract or by mutual agreement.

Your report about Cologne is dreadful. It was of course of great interest to me. And your impressions of wonderful Holland. That's just the way it is.

My condition changes a lot, as you saw when you were here. I've had times again when I couldn't work. My hand and arm wouldn't let me write. But the main problem is the weariness. It's too tedious to report. I have my ups and downs. Every once in a while I'm "given a break," and at those times I get *more* cortisone, as I did just recently, for example, in the form of injections in a finger joint and one wrist. The local pain disappears in those places for two days and remains mild for a longer period. At the same time, the cortisone is absorbed into the body, reducing all my pains and increasing my vitality. That's the case today. I can write unhindered, as you can see. From time to time the doctors give me these better days and hope they are not doing any damage. All the ups and downs are not worth reporting. On the whole, our spirits are good. And the possibilities for improvement remain. Gertrud is very well at the moment.

My essay,[2] which you are familiar with, I've had copied by Herr Feess,[3] and after looking through it once again, I've sent it to Augstein. Now I'm working on a last essay about trends and aspects of life in the Federal Republic. This will be my absolutely last political essay. But progress on it is painfully slow. Then comes your book, on the independence of thought, and then the great philosophers, with Hegel first. I'll see.

My sister is here, a familiar presence who conjures up the old atmosphere. We enjoy talking about the past and about how things are in Oldenburg now, and we find much that is good.

The volume of my little political writings of 1945–1965 is nearly ready.[4] I've read here and there in it, and was essentially pleased with it. Over twenty years, always the same. Unmistakable in intent, but expressed with moderation. Hardly a strident tone. But I do sense, alas!, fading confidence over the years. That is kept up by an act of will, now too. We can't allow ourselves to give up on *all* good possibilities. How different the mood was in 1945, 1946. We were mistaken. Some things strike me as naïve now. But that remains the same today; I am still "naïve."

Give my regards to Heinrich. I wish him, for his leave, that he will make good progress with his plan and retain his lively interest in it: to express the basic elements of philosophical truth in brief form. He can do that. That could be a wonderful thing. In contrast to our prolixity.

You are taken up entirely by work and are doing well by your students—as a "philosopher."

Warmest greetings, also from Gertrud

Your Karl

384 Karl Jaspers to Hannah Arendt

Basel, October 7, 1965

Dear Hannah!

You would like to have at least a brief word from time to time. Gertrud is well, and I'm in a better period again. These changes in my condition occur constantly. You know that firsthand. I'm now getting injections in particularly painful joints and with good results. I'm working, sometimes an hour both morning and afternoon. Then I'm tired. On the whole, I'm quite content.

Today I received Robinson's book[1] from Macmillan, with the compliments of the author. It is thicker than your Eichmann book and at first glance deadly boring, but I will have to read it through and study it closely. It presents itself like a huge boulder intent on crushing and destroying your book. It seems based on false premises. Corrects "mistakes." They are frequently similar to the claim in Grüber's hate-filled article[2] against you: A. was born in Königsberg. A "mistake" of this kind is of no significance whatever in this context. It conveys the important information, which is that you grew up in Königsberg. In some other context the mistake might be relevant, for instance, apropos of your acquiring American citizenship. The lack of understanding for what is important is what makes this book so wearisome and unfruitful. But there is nothing for it: I'll have to read it. What do you think of it?

I've had a book about Hitler's illness sent to you.[3] You, like me, want "to know everything." This book was written by a Swiss psychiatrist in the style in which psychiatrists write: endless repetitions, a lot of fussy detail. The upshot: *Not a trace of hysteria, not* a diagnosis of a "psychopathic personality," which has always been dubious anyhow. Instead: *Certainly* the parkinsonism of Hitler's last years, certainly the symptoms of Parkinson's disease decades earlier, which are recognized as a consequence of Encephalitis lethargica (from the flu).

This phenomenon was discovered (by Economo[4] in Vienna) at the end of World War I and described in such a way that Hitler's symptoms can be recognized as identical. This encephalitis itself is *not* proved. Hitler must have been affected by it when he was twelve years old. That is made to seem plausible. It is comparable to the paralysis: if that can be proved, then there *must* have been a syphilis infection, even if that cannot be proved.

If Hitler were subjected to a criminal trial, he would not be able to plead outright insanity, but he could claim "reduced mental competence." The author is clear about his point: It was not Hitler who was "guilty"; it was the German people who followed him.

The book is thorough and medically well thought out. I consider it medically definitive.

Warmest greetings to you both, also from Gertrud

Your Karl

Writing still does not go well. And so my handwriting is worse than usual. You'll be able to decipher some of this. Excuse me!

385   Hannah Arendt to Karl Jaspers

October 23, 1965

Lieber Verehrtester—

Thank you for your letter. I'm troubled by your tiredness. When I was there, I noticed it hardly at all. Does it come from not being able to sleep at night, from being worn down by pain? And do the cortisone injections help? They are used a lot here, often with very good results, which are, however, always only temporary. I was very relieved to know that Gertrud has recovered so fully. That was already very evident when I was in Basel.

First things first: Saner. The Rockefeller Foundation's response was very friendly. As I suspected, they do not actually have any money for Switzerland. Switzerland is neither underdeveloped nor has it ever declared war on America. A grievous error, as it turns out. But in general the foundation is giving money only to underdeveloped countries, Latin America, Asia, and Africa. But: perhaps they could make an exception, especially in view of the great weight that your recommendation[1] carries. They asked if Saner had been in touch yet with Jacques Freymond[2] in Geneva (whom I know) or the German

Volkswagen Foundation. In any case, they will contact Saner, and not only by letter but also in as personal a way as possible.

Robinson: I didn't even know the book had been published. It has been announced for two and a half years now. It was, of course, deliberately not sent to me. I have got hold of it now but haven't looked at it yet. I just spoke with *The New York Review of Books*, which asked me to write a long response to it. And I'll doubtless do that as soon as I have a little more time.

George Agree[3] was here yesterday. He tried to read to me your letter in German on the telephone, and that was (vastly) more difficult to understand than it is to read your handwriting. But he did have the letter very well translated immediately, and you will be hearing from him very soon. He is very happy about this "dialogue" and asked whether I thought it a good idea for him to go to Europe to speak with you. I would have said yes instantly if his German were better. Interpreters never work out quite right. His wife is German. Perhaps something can be worked out. He has a wealth of ideas. He just suggested to the Americans to let the Germans have a major role in the exploration of space. Other countries, too, but the Germans especially, so that Erhard[4] will have something to show for himself if he doesn't get in on atomic weapons. I told Agree about my experience with the scholarship students. He said a foundation should be formed that gives scholarships to people who work here as interns (like doctors training in a hospital) for voluntary associations, such as his own, which are as numerous here as grains of sand on the shore. There they would learn how to get things in motion without stepping on everyone else's toes, also without the polemic and aggressiveness that struck him in Germany, too, and that he considers the natural consequence of powerlessness.

And now for some sad news: Jarrell,[5] an American poet, a good friend of ours, committed suicide. He was a figure out of a fairy tale if I ever saw one, incredibly sensitive and very intelligent and witty as well. He just wasn't able to handle life any longer. I saw him last in February when I gave a lecture at the university where he was teaching, and he introduced me in an incredibly charming and witty way. Lowell, who is probably the best poet here at the moment, is coming tomorrow to give me a more detailed report. Whatever I understand of English poetry I owe to Jarrell, who years ago read aloud to me for hours at a time—not his work but the "classics." Lowell and Jarrell were close friends, both people of great generosity. I heard

Lowell's name for the first time twenty years ago from Jarrell, who was already very well known then. And he always said to me: Believe me, Lowell is America's real poet, not I.

The papers reported today that Tillich died of a heart attack. He was never really close to me, but now I'm sad that old Mutton Legs (as we called him) won't turn up anymore, drink vast quantities of red wine, and then stagger cheerfully home. He was fundamentally stupid, without any judgment, but in an odd way those very qualities were part of a genuine "Christianity." In all the years I knew him, I never heard him speak badly of anyone, not even of his enemies.

But there are other things, for which we have to be thankful. A colleague of Heinrich's, Ted Weiss, is a well-known poet here[6] and has just published another volume of poetry in which the two best poems[7] are not only dedicated to Heinrich but also describe him—the way he speaks, the way he is, the way he affects people, the way he deals with a foreign language. There is also a nice one about me—about my mode of thought.[8] The poems about Heinrich are amazingly insightful. Years ago Jarrell wrote a short, very funny novel about a college here,[9] in which he portrayed Heinrich and me for posterity, under different names of course. What strange animals we really are here, and with what openness and warmth we have been received—and with what great willingness to understand us and not let us feel our alienness!

Give my regards to Saner and Hochhuth and Erna—not necessarily in that order. Through Saner's and Hochhuth's presence, it's as if another lovely piece of land has grown up around the house in Basel.

And warmest greetings to you both from

Your
Hannah

386 Hannah Arendt to Karl Jaspers

New York, December 5, 1965

Lieber Verehrtester,

I haven't heard from you for so long that I am concerned. And I haven't written for so long myself because I've been buried under a mountain of work, obligations, and so forth. That is also why I'm dictating this letter today. Please don't take it amiss.

Piper sent your political writings. I'm familiar with some of them, and the ones I don't know I haven't been able to read yet. I have to put off everything until the Christmas vacation. But what has become of your analysis of the Bundestag debate on the statute of limitations? I thought it was going to appear in *Der Spiegel*, but I haven't seen it there.[1]

I'm sending you today my response to the Robinson book,[2] along with a review by a certain Laqueur that appeared here in *The New York Review of Books*.[3] Apart from that, the book has received practically no attention here. The only other review was one favorable to me in the *Herald Tribune*.[4]

My warmest greetings to you both—I'll write during the Christmas vacation.

Your
Hannah

387   *Karl Jaspers to Hannah Arendt*

Basel, December 10, 1965

Dear Hannah!

It is really unforgivable that I haven't written for so long. And there are no excuses for me. A few weeks ago I wrote a long letter[1] in response to your last one and at the same time an even longer one to Mr. Agree (who wrote to me with a care and attention to detail I found touching). I lost both letters along with a third. My age? Which also accounts for the clumsy ink splotches in these first few lines.

And so I'll write again what I had in my head before. The main thing: the two poems for Heinrich. I find it wonderful that a poet could see him and express what he saw. The way Heinrich has shaped his life, if one may make a comparison with the great figures, is in the mold of Socrates and Ammonios Sakkas (who was the teacher of Origen and Plotinus)[2]: a personal influence of which we would know nothing unless others had made it known. But *only* Socrates found his Plato, and nothing like that has ever happened again. Impulses have reached you from Heinrich; I haven't failed to see that. But it seems to me just as Plato's ideas could not have taken shape without Socrates, so yours could not have become what they are without Heinrich. It is a different kind of productivity that is able to translate those impulses. Heinrich made a deep impression on me, quite apart from the love I feel for him. Please send us the volume of poems and say on which pages the two poems appear. But not, of course, until you have some time.

The mood of your letter stayed with me a long time: an expression of your alien existence in a world where people have received you so warmly that you could feel at home there if it were not for this "something" in your background and nature. But how wonderful it is despite that! People like your poet friend and other friends seem to exist only in America. I thought again of the barely visible shadow of sadness on your being, which is otherwise so vital, so open to the world, so affirming of it, and so full of joy in life. Also of your insight into the way things work: basically so pessimistic—and yet illuminated by the greatness of humanity, which is your standard and whose reality through the millennia is your inspiration.

The suicide of one of your poet friends came as a profound shock to you. One never knows—one is really at a loss in the face of such a deed—and resists psychiatric explanations and attempts to make it understandable. The suicide deserves our greatest respect and our restraint from judgment. His act can be one of the greatest self-mastery. Only human beings and no other creatures are capable of it.

Muschg[3] died suddenly here, of a heart attack while he was at the post-office counter. His death affected me oddly. He was here two days before his death to bring me a new book of his.[4] We spoke as if we were close friends. We hadn't seen each other for years and had only exchanged letters occasionally. He spoke about the end of German literature and the end of German studies. In the twenties there were still the last great figures: Kafka, Brecht—he mentioned Hofmannsthal, Rilke, George, too! Today, nobody. This awareness of the self-destruction of the German spirit, to which he as a Swiss felt he fully belonged, was the impulse behind his *Tragische Literaturgeschichte*.[5] What he saw, he saw reflected in all the failures of our time, on a grand scale and not just in the horror of our political catastrophe. Muschg lacked moderation, could be odd and amazingly wrongheaded. —But he was a person whose basic experience of life guided and inspired his work. I realized this only at his passing.

You have inquired at the Rockefeller Foundation on Saner's behalf. I am afraid that, in keeping with the friendly American manner, the holding open of a chance is really only a polite way of saying no. But I join you in not giving up hope entirely. Saner and the whole family are a joy to us. Saner's mother died.[6] She had a dreadful cancer, and her death was long and difficult. She was a believer, a pious member of her denomination, and was close to her son. It was completely clear to her what her illness was and that she had to die now. She said to her son in her last days, in her concern for him: I can't understand how one can die with only philosophy to fall back on! But she never tried to convert her children and had not the slightest trace of missionary zeal or intolerance. When the pastor of her church wanted to come, she agreed to have him but said: He can read to me from the Bible (which she knew almost by heart anyhow) but not explain anything. Saner is very sad but inexhaustibly active. He still has time to care for his family down to the last minor detail.

Your response to Robinson arrived today. I've read only the beginning. It begins wonderfully. Blow for blow, exciting. You seem to be doing him in. At the end there won't be anything left for the reader but an impeccably autopsied corpse.

I am amazingly well. The pain is hardly perceptible any longer. Even more important, my basic health is good again; the fever is gone. I'm much better than I was during the weeks of your visit. I'm working again. But walks are still difficult. Too weak. Only a few steps every few days. Gertrud is well. The physical weakness of age makes itself felt and is sometimes quite bothersome. But her spirit is as lively as ever; she responds with great vitality.

From her, too, warmest greetings to you both

Your Karl

388 Karl and Gertrud Jaspers to Hannah Arendt

Basel, January 10, 1966

Dear Hannah!

No word from you for a very long time. Was my last letter too illegible? Are you so busy that you have no time to write unless there is something particularly urgent to attend to? I asked last time for the two poems your poet friend wrote about Heinrich—my handwriting was probably indecipherable. As you see, I'm working harder at it this time. It's going better because my condition is quite tolerable indeed.

I imagine you lecturing on the *Critique of Judgment* and Spinoza —and the students flocking to you, and you advising each one and listening to their questions. And on top of that you are presumably still giving outside lectures? Wonderful, all this activity!

618

The world situation is dreadful. Vietnam, India, Indonesia, and Rhodesia as well. All of it is so unreasonable, the people involved so pigheaded. It looks as if everything were leading toward a great explosion. It doesn't happen because America and Russia don't want to go to war with each other. The atom bomb is our salvation? If only Russia and the USA would form an alliance to keep the atom bomb away from all other countries!

I sent my manuscript[1] off to Piper today. It turned out to be very long. Completely unsuitable for *Der Spiegel*. I'm a little uneasy about it. I've never written so unequivocally and harshly about the Federal Republic. I don't want to precipitate a personal scandal. But my desire to write this my last word on German politics kept me from holding back. Now I'll turn to better things: more work on your book about the independence of thought.

Gertrud is not as well as I. She suffers from her great forgetfulness, her vertigo while walking, her awkwardness, and frequent fatigue. It's old age. But she can be lively and high-spirited, especially in the evening. Her powers of empathy are if anything heightened and become in themselves a source of suffering. Her judgment in crucial human matters remains unchanged. Her hearing continues to deteriorate. But all in all, we are happy together, and we are grateful for the kindness everyone shows us and for the way Möhrle cares for us so ably and thinks of all the essentials.

This is just a word of greeting, sent in hopes of coaxing a few lines out of you!

From both of us to both of you
Warmest greetings,
Your Karl

P.S. One more important thing that I almost forgot. Your revolution book[2] came from Piper. We were both delighted by your dedication. How wonderful that is! —I'm reading the book through again in one sitting now. It seems to me remarkable for its depth of insight, clarity of presentation, and, most important, for the element of human nobility it brings to politics.

My long essay on the parliamentary debate did not appear in *Der Spiegel*. Augstein praised it, but in its present form it can't be printed. "A few minor changes," he wrote, would be all it needs. Would I permit him to make those changes? He wants to print it in the spring. I gave him my permission. But Piper is going to publish the essay in March. My last essay about the Federal Republic[3] is almost done.

More than 150 typewritten pages. This essay is certainly not possible for *Der Spiegel* either. If I want to appear there, I have to acquire another style. I can't do that. I suggested to Augstein that after the book is published I could do an interview with him for *Der Spiegel*.

That is to be my final political statement. It's enough. I'm already back with Hegel. But before that I want to try to continue with the Hannah book. [. . .]

Mr. Agree will have to be patient a little while longer. I found what he had to say very instructive.

[Handwritten note from Gertrud J.]
Things are really not all that bad with me yet! It's true of course that my vision is getting worse. But in accordance with the law "presiding at my birth"[4] I keep plugging along.

I'm glad that I don't have to type German politics anymore. —And I'm still not reconciled to being "without a country." But it is so wonderful that the man who once said to me, "I can promise you a year"[5] is still beside me in old age, working and brightening my life with his good cheer. Incredible.

Did the external events in New York cause you any trouble? Lotte [Waltz] is building a house on Corfu as an investment. We expect her soon.

Good companionship with Saners, and the children are delightful.

Warmest greetings to you and Heinrich
Your Gertrud

389   *Hannah Arendt to Karl Jaspers*

January 16, 1966

Lieber Verehrtester!

Yes, I haven't written for so horribly long because of so much going on here and excessive demands on my time—I can't really call it overwork. This constant flying back and forth is more strenuous than you think, particularly in the winter, when you can never quite know whether the plane will fly at all and where it will put you down. But I've had good luck with the weather so far. I came home for the Christmas vacation pretty exhausted, and then came the Christmas ruckus on top of that. Then too, I thought, and hoped, that Saner had shown you my long letter to him about the Rockefeller people. Oddly enough, I haven't heard anything from him but can't imagine that he didn't get my letter. He also hasn't written me how his meeting with Freund[1] went, with whom I spoke on the phone before he left for Europe; and I won't hear anything from Freund until he is back in New York.

I'm very pleased about your "harshness" with the Federal Republic, though I can understand that it might cause you some real annoyance at the moment. I'm so convinced of the provisional nature of that structure and of the impossibility of ever redeeming Adenauer's mistakes that I'm relieved to see you taking such a clear position. Yes, the world situation seems mad, and my confidence in Johnson is not very great. What gives me solace here is the very strong opposition to this insane Vietnam policy. But that is the least of it. What is so frightful, precisely because it is in some sense correct, is the insistence that we are "the greatest power" in the world, for implicit in that is perhaps not a claim to world rule but at least to the Pax Americana that Kennedy warned so strongly against. We will not remain "the greatest power." Within the foreseeable future China will be a major power of the first order and of course have a decisive influence in Asia. Do the Americans really think they can have that kind of influence or even share that influence with China? China, and probably no one else, has a great interest in this crazy, filthy, and pointless war. And China, it seems to me, is a threat not to America but primarily to Russia because of Siberia. I don't think things will come to all-out war with atomic weapons. And we can't win a war with infantry, simply because we cannot occupy and hold territory we manage to conquer.

The book with the poems about Heinrich was sent to you long ago (his name, alas!, is horribly misspelled—Blücher always becomes Bleucher here). Perhaps it has arrived in the meantime. I had the book sent shortly before Christmas. And I have yet to thank you for the book about the murder of the mentally ill.[2] The more one learns, the more dreadful it all becomes.

The Robinson affair is going full steam ahead. What I first sent you was too long for the magazine. *The New Yorker* wanted to have it, but I wanted to print it in the magazine in which I was attacked, so I cut it. I sent you the published text.[3] If anything, it was sharpened by the cutting. So far, we haven't heard anything from the organizations attacked. What I have heard unofficially, in part from employees of those organizations and other representatives of the

Establishment, is extremely positive. I've also learned that Robinson's book was paid for entirely by the Claims Conference[4] (which receives money from German payments to Israel and uses them for cultural purposes). Not even the Jewish Publication Society[5] wanted to contribute to the printing costs. Four clumsy "researchers" worked full time for two whole years on this trash. The upshot was that probably no one person read the whole manuscript through, and so no one saw that the book was swarming with internal contradictions. My source, who works in the same place as Mr. Robinson, thought the whole job cost between $160,000 and $200,000. I almost have the feeling that the Establishment won't even bother to defend itself but will let the whole matter, and Robinson along with it, quietly fade out of sight. That would be the most intelligent thing to do, of course.

Apart from Cornell[6] and flying back and forth I'm doing something odd on the side—perhaps I told you already. I'm rewriting my *Augustine*,[7] in English, not Latin, and in a way that people who haven't learned philosophical stenography can understand it. It's strange—this work is so far in the past, on the one hand; but on the other, I can still recognize myself, as it were; I know exactly what I wanted to say, and I can still even read Latin fluently in the passages by Augustine. This job just came to me out of the blue. Years ago a mad publisher bought the rights from me for several thousand dollars, and I sold them because the whole thing seemed so pointless to me; that is, I was convinced that the publisher would go broke anyhow (which in fact happened) and I could profit a bit from the bankruptcy. (Very immoral? Go ahead and laugh!) At any rate, I've been punished for my sins. Because what I hadn't foreseen was that Macmillan would buy up certain rights from the bankrupt publisher's assets. So here I am. They sent me quite a decent translation (by Ashton), which really wasn't usable because the text itself needed to be rewritten. So I'm doing that now, and I'm even enjoying it a little.

Things are fine with us. And part of the reason for that is that you are feeling better. Gertrud wrote such a cheerful letter. I'm sending a few more snapshots I took this summer, two prints of the Saner children.

Everything seems to be moving ahead very well here with your translations. I've gotten to know Wieck, whom I had only spoken to on the phone before. *Der philosophische Glaube* should be printed by now. I had long talks with Ashton, talked him out of a few cuts, and persuaded him to consult you about the others. I assume he did that.

The *Philosophie* should be coming out, too, as quickly as that can be accomplished with such a long (and great) text. And Helen Wolff has told me to expect the *Kleine Schule* for my inspection this month. Unfortunately, the paperback editions of the *Great Philosophers* won't be out until fall or this spring. In any case, they're not available now, and I really could have used them at Cornell. I'm enjoying my teaching there, a lecture course: Political Theory from Machiavelli to Marx, and a seminar: Political Experience in the 20th Century. Things are going well. I have to go back to Chicago in April, but there will be a few months of real peace in between.

I'm writing even this letter in haste. I have to go to my plane in a few minutes. I'll be home for good after next week.

Warmest greetings
Your
Hannah

390 Karl Jaspers to Hannah Arendt

Basel, January 25, 1966

Dear Hannah!

Many thanks! Your letter reflects your important work and also the strain of travel, especially in the winter.

Saner told me about your letter a while ago but didn't show it to me. He said now that he wrote to you long ago and reported to you. I presume, however, without having pressed him on the matter, that he wrote to you too late. His mother died a few weeks ago. During her illness—cancer, operation, a slow death—he was under great psychic and physical duress. His work on his book has been slowed, and he has to finish it as quickly as possible. Salmony is doing what he can to help. Saner may well be his best student.

What you say about politics—Vietnam—is unfortunately right. Kennedy, as I recall, asked about Vietnam at a meeting of his advisers: Can I still pull out? The question now is how can the USA pull out. The situation is dreadful for them. I think we Europeans should keep our mouths shut. The opposition and the pressure for peace is strong enough in the USA. It behooves us to show respect for the state to which we all owe our existence and relative security. Only China stands in the way. Russia would probably prefer peace, too, seeing that it is already in a secret alliance with the USA but can't either say that or act on it yet. How would it be if Johnson suggested a vote under the supervision of the UN:

1. Whether North and South Vietnam want all foreign troops to leave.

2. Election of a parliament under UN supervision.

3. The USA agrees to honor the election results.

This would prevent the USA from losing face, it seems to me.

But how easy it is to think up such schemes and how difficult to realize them. I felt the same way about my suggestions for the Federal Republic, which are now in print. The simple and rational solution doesn't work where there are great commitments of prestige, power, and emotion. I've just been reading about how Bismarck suggested to Salisbury[1] in about 1888 that Germany form an alliance with England, have it publicly ratified by Parliament and announced to the world. Germany would not build a fleet. If this alliance were made known, Bismarck argued, world peace would be assured for a long time. While agreeing in principle, Salisbury refused the offer for the time being, saying the majority in Parliament would not accept the idea and would instead remove him from office. But he hoped for a more opportune moment. Shortly after 1890, I've forgotten the year, Salisbury agreed and said the idea could now be easily realized. Caprivi, Foreign Minister Bülow, and the kaiser turned him down.[2] The kaiser wanted his fleet. And that's how history goes. Bismarck's life is extremely interesting. He's a man I can't stand because he exploited all the evil forces in Germany and made the Germans even worse than they already were. But in foreign policy he was a tactical genius and saw clearly far into the future. And he was always, by the way, for the path of peace. Just as he was after 1870, when he continued to work constantly for peace in Europe and declared Germany's needs satisfied. He was really totally isolated in Germany. His great mistake was to consider himself invulnerable under any monarch and to rely on that invincibility. After he was thrown out, he publicly declared himself (in Jena) in favor of parliamentary democracy. How great a difference a single man can make! And yet how minor a one if he is not at the same time a parliamentary educator of his country and if he does not embody its best nature.

Thank you for the poems. I'm still just feeling my way with them. I have to use a dictionary to translate them. I'm getting the basic feel of the poem for you. Wonderful! I still haven't understood the ones for Heinrich. They will come.

Your answer to Laqueur and Robinson is, in its brevity, convincing and devastating. What will Laqueur be able to say in response? If it isn't too much trouble, please send us his reply.

Last week, with the help of the documents that you made available to me, I recounted this drama of organized persecution—with all the appropriate quotations, even more than you used. I could add even more now, especially Hausner's trip to the USA. A short while ago —just one year after I'd put it aside—I started working on the book again. This drama is only one short chapter. The whole thing is present to me in my mind's eye. In concrete form, I have it down in outlines and notes, but I don't know if I'll manage to finish it or not. It is to show the independence of thought both in your thinking and in general as a possibility. It will not be a book just about you. I am actually misusing you in the sense that you gave me the idea for this book and that the lines of thought I am pursuing in it emanate from you. At the moment, I'm very enthusiastic about it. —I've had pain again in my right hand these last few days. This evening I'll get an injection. They usually help. Otherwise I'm well.

The financing of Robinson's book is interesting. It's a pity that that can't be published. Your question of how it is possible for a serious publisher to print something like that remains unanswered.

I'm very pleased about your work on *Augustine*. It's good that after about forty years you can feel at one with yourself and can recognize what you're able to say better now and what you meant back then. The theologian van Oyen,[3] by the way, used your *Augustine* as the basis for a seminar here a few years ago.

Oddly enough Wieck has not returned to me the contract that I signed weeks ago but that the publisher still had not signed. I've jogged his memory. Ashton wrote to me. It seems to me I should give him a free hand. He translates so well that I have accepted the cuts he suggested to me. In the title, *angesichts* will be replaced by "and."[4] Apparently that is the only linguistically acceptable solution. It obscures a key point but will not, I hope, produce any real misunderstanding.

You are lecturing on political theory from Machiavelli to Marx, not on what I had thought you were. So it's political philosophy again and not philosophy. It will surely be excellent.

Warmest greetings
Your
Karl

New York, February 19, 1966

Dearest Friends,

This is my birthday letter to you: I hope that you will both remain in good health, that we will see each other again—what more can one say? Your Augstein interview was very well received here. You probably know that, because of a mistake by *Der Spiegel*, it appeared in the same month in both *Commentary*[1] and *Midstream* (the publication of the Zionist organization).[2] The only truly positive and rather hysterical review of Robinson's book appeared in the same issue of *Midstream*. I understand that the editor (Shlomo Katz, something of a rattlebrain) wants to print your analysis of the Bundestag debate, too. I had told an acquaintance of mine who is in close touch with the magazine about your article. If *Commentary* is also interested in it, I would rather give it to them, but if not, then of course to *Midstream*. Don't let it bother you that I'm on the outs with them.

Wieck called from Harper. All the arrangements for your *Philosophie* are in perfect order, and Ashton is to begin translating immediately. He asked for more money—and rightly so. Wieck has gotten in touch with Springer. Ashton is really very good. I assume he has sent you his foreword to *Philosophischer Glaube*.

Laqueur's response was so short and weak that it wasn't worth the trouble to send it. Some other people wrote. I'm writing an answer to them now, and I'll send you the whole exchange once it's printed. Probably in a week or so. Apropos of financing that one can't expose in print: I heard from a reliable source that Musmanno received extra payment from the United Jewish Appeal[3] for his review in the *New York Times*. Jolly, what? The Jews are really quite out of their minds. No decent person does that kind of thing here. After all, we're not living in France.

Vietnam: We remain greatly concerned. Perhaps you have read about the discussions in the Senate Foreign Relations Committee under Fulbright.[4] Rusk[5] was subjected to seven hours of outright interrogation yesterday. We watched it all day on television. It was incredibly exciting and conducted on a high level, very impressive. I can hardly imagine something like this taking place in any other country. The key point in Rusk's argument was this nonsensical idea of a world revolution that has to be stopped in Vietnam. Behind that is perhaps the honest fear of the Chinese, which may be justified in principle but is out of place here. Quite apart from the fact that, in my view, it is not the United States or South Asia (India, for instance) that is threatened, but primarily Russia and then Australia and New Zealand. But we can't really know that, and while Kennan's and General Gavin's[6] "containment" theories may sound very appealing they probably cannot be carried out in practice. The worst thing about the whole business is that we are in no way capable of conducting a land war in Asia, and yet that is precisely what we are about to do. I really don't expect World War III, but sometimes I get a bit nervous despite myself. Just one more point about yesterday's television broadcast: This technological device infuses meaning into democracy again in this mass age, a meaning that it really never had before: the whole population can participate in deliberations like these; it is invited to participate in the most direct way. That is having its very obvious effects everywhere here.

Heinrich will go back to Bard next week; I, to Chicago in about a month. I've become a real wandering scholar. My teaching at Cornell went very well. I just read a few of the students' papers, which I was not obliged to grade (I had two good assistants). They really learned something, and that made this old teacher happy. In Chicago I'll lecture on something like basic questions of ethics (I've expressed it a little more elegantly), and I'm already properly nervous about the prospect. Heinrich is doing a kind of advanced seminar on the "moral vacuum" and plans to use your atom-bomb book as a basic text. I'll be making major use of your *Nietzsche* this time. Thank God that it's available in English now. Otherwise, I've continued to work at helping my old *Augustine* text back onto its legs, and now I have to write a new introduction to the totalitarianism book. It's going to be reprinted (in hard cover), and I have to discuss the literature on this subject that has appeared in the meantime. It's making for a lot of reading. That doesn't do me any harm, but I have to complain now and then. I'm not at all able to indulge my natural inclination to laziness.

We're thinking already about coming to see you again. How are things looking for you? Is it too early for you to say? September would be best for us—it's too tedious to explain why. I could leave here about the 10th and would have to be back around October 1. What do you think?

All my very best wishes!

Your

Hannah

Liebe Gute—be careful; don't go out alone; don't be reckless. I was very happy to hear that you liked my *Revolution*.[7] It seems to be an old-fashioned book. There aren't many people who like it.

Still another P.S.: Lieber Verehrtester, what do you think about the *Spiegel* report about Heidegger?[8] I didn't like it at all. People ought to leave him in peace. And then I have the feeling that the whole thing was staged and organized by the Adorno camp.

392 *Hannah Arendt to Karl Jaspers*

March 2, 1966

Lieber Verehrtester—

Mr. Freund from the Rockefeller Foundation called again yesterday about Saner. I hadn't heard anything from him until then. Saner made a very favorable impression, talked about Kant, and everything looks fine. Mr. Freund said that the chances of his getting this aid approved are very good. He suggested that the fellowship be granted through the university. That's the way the foundation customarily operates, always awarding money to institutions and only indirectly to individuals. That means that the University of Basel would make a pro forma application to the foundation—Freund said, "Two sentences will do"—and that Saner would then get his money paid to him every month. The amount would be $5,000 per year for two years. Freund thought he could manage this because Saner told him that Salmony would be willing to write a recommendation. That would be for the university only, because your recommendation is all the Rockefeller people need. Saner will be getting a letter from Freund spelling all this out, if he hasn't received it already.

The only reason I'm writing today is to say that if this particular arrangement poses any problems, there are other possibilities, e.g., a fellowship paid directly to Saner from America. But the Rockefeller people don't like that approach, and it would be much harder for Freund to get it approved. Freund promised me on the phone that he would mention this other possibility in his letter to Saner, but I'm not altogether sure that he'll do that. He really had no pressing reason to call me except to report what he had done and how the matter stood. I had the feeling he wanted to let me know—and let Saner know through me—that there was an alternative to his suggestion but that he was uncomfortable with that alternative. In other words: Saner should, if at all possible, act on the university suggestion but also not assume that that is the only possible route to go.

Freund again made the very best of impressions on me. We spoke about another case in which I am tangentially involved. It concerns a talented but slightly mad writer who dressed the foundation down ferociously because it had not automatically extended his fellowship. He behaved so very badly that I didn't want to have anything further to do with the matter. Freund's reaction was touching: the important thing, he said, was that the man had to have the money, and so the foundation had to try to renew the fellowship for him regardless. He, Freund, was grateful to me for having made clear to this person that the Rockefeller Foundation does not provide people with pensions for life. It was just a misunderstanding, and that was that. Freund was completely matter-of-fact about it. Very pleasant.

I'm writing in haste. Warmest greetings to you both

Your
Hannah

393 Karl Jaspers to Hannah Arendt

Basel, March 9, 1966

Dear Hannah!

You ask about the article on Heidegger in *Der Spiegel*. It was in large part a review of a book[1] that it seemed to me asked a very legitimate question: Can the basis for Heidegger's political judgments and actions be found in his philosophy? I've ordered the book but not received it yet. In this case I don't think it desirable "to leave Heidegger in peace." He is a presence, and one that everyone who wants an excuse for his own Nazi past likes to fall back on. The significance of his behavior seems to me of no small consequence for current politics in the Federal Republic.

It's a different story where personal matters are concerned. *Der Spiegel* has not just reviewed the book, but has also passed on some ugly rumors. The claim that Heidegger didn't come to see us anymore because Gertrud was a Jew is pure fabrication.[2] At moments like that, *Der Spiegel* reverts to its old bad manners. In my book on the Federal Republic I took a very positive view of *Der Spiegel*, and I think I can still do so. But things like this are annoying.

That Gertrud was a Jew was surely not the reason for his acting as he did. But when he left after his last visit with us in May 1933, he

629

was extremely impolite to her and hardly said good-bye at all. The reason was that she, as is her way, had spoken her mind very openly and directly, whereas I had spoken cautiously and indirectly, with great mistrust. I have never forgotten his rudeness to Gertrud on that occasion. Oddly enough, Gertrud herself has forgotten it, probably because it seemed insignificant to her, given the dreadful overall situation. I consider the reason that he gave after 1945, namely, that he was ashamed,[3] an excuse. The fact is that Gertrud and I were simply of no further interest to him. Our friend Oehlkers,[4] professor of botany at Freiburg, said to him before my sixtieth birthday that my birthday was coming, and was he planning to send his good wishes. Heidegger spoke very emotionally about me and said yes, of course. He didn't do it.[5] No more than he said a word in 1937 when I was stripped of my university post. I don't think we should read any fundamental meaning into these personal things. They just happen. They have great significance in the private sphere, for me at least, and they have their consequences. But statements such as *Der Spiegel* has made are not just oversimplifications. I would say things were just the same after 1945 as they were after 1933. Heidegger did not plan to break with us. It just happened. I didn't decide never to see him again after 1945. It just happened that way, unintentionally. It's true the circumstances in the two situations are very different. But there is a parallel in the unintentional nature of what happened in both instances.

I take a different view of what he did objectively. Never an anti-Semite himself, he sometimes behaved very well toward Jews, as he did when he wanted to protect someone like Brock[6] (as, by the way, almost all the old Nazis did). And sometimes he behaved badly, as in the official letter to Göttingen about the Jew Fränkel,[7] when he wrote just as the Nazis did. His behavior toward Husserl was another case of obedience to the Nazis. That all falls under the rubric of a vanishing sense of right and wrong. He probably never possessed such a sense, or, if he did, only by chance, so to speak.

I've just read Heidegger's reply in *Der Spiegel*.[8] I found it irritating and without quality.

Der Spiegel did not print my analysis of the parliamentary debate in the form you know it in. Nor was the magazine able to adapt it as planned. *Der Spiegel*'s sense of its readers and what it can expect of them or what interests them accounts in part for its success, of course. The form of my "fluoroscopic examination," as Augstein called my essay, does not fit the mold that makes *Der Spiegel* effective. I have no objections to that and actually approve of it. Sometime in mid-April *Der Spiegel* will, however, print in two installments a long passage from the third chapter of my book about the Federal Republic. I'm pleased about that. It means some publicity for the book at the same time. In that text, my sentences are apparently simple and immediately understandable, and sensational as well: From parliamentary state to party oligarchy, from party oligarchy to dictatorship, the "legal" route by way of the planned emergency laws and of the "inner emergency" to the further enlargement of the army and the coming together of all those tendencies, which, without the majority planning it that way, will ultimately lead to war with the East. The Federal Republic's army is too large already. Paul Gottschalk read in an Italian newspaper a few months ago that a German general said in a speech to a small group: We will win back the eastern territories, whether by peaceful means or by war. Unfortunately, he didn't bring me the paper. I would have liked to include the passage in that chapter. There seems to me to be no doubt that the generals are turning ideas like that over in their minds. My chapter suggests that possibility.

I haven't been able to work for two weeks. I had another "attack" with fever and pain and general weakness. Now, after two injections, which I can have only once a month because of the dangers connected with them, I am feeling much better again. But after four days the effects wear off. I hope it will be a while before things get bad again. I am working well right now.

Up to this point I dictated this letter. In the meantime Freund's letter to Saner arrived. Wonderful in its tone and content. The university will write to Freund, over the rector's signature. No negotiations or resolution of the board of regents is required. I was afraid they might be. No one has seen the rector's letter yet. I hope everything is in order.

I am happy to think that you will visit us again in September. Perhaps we will manage it once more. You will find us both changed, but you will be patient with us in our old age.

My work has not been progressing well in recent weeks. But at least something gets done. I've been studying Golo Mann thoroughly and have read almost everything by him. That will not be of much interest to you, but it is important to me to achieve some clarity in this project. The book still has no shape. It can appear to be an odd assortment of various themes, assembled quite by chance. As I conceive of it, it is held together by the presentation of independent thought in all kinds

631

of representatives and of the opposing forces they faced. Contemporaries are considered because I have experienced this phenomenon through them. Among them, the ones who have perhaps been personally most important to me will remain anonymous.

I would like to be able to show you the manuscript in September. But that is doubtful. Things have gone poorly again in recent days. At the moment—in the afternoon—I'm feeling fine and can write, though with some pain in my hand. But I'll lie down again soon and will read Golo. I'm touched by him and his fate. It is not easy to do justice to it. It seems to me to have an objective significance beyond the personal. And the importance of a lifetime's experience with younger contemporaries cannot be overestimated.

Max Weber will be included, too.

Always the inquiry into the miracle of independence, which no one truly achieves.

Warmest greetings to you both from Gertrud and me. I hope that you are well.

Your Karl

I received yesterday from Helen Wolff the second volume of the *Great Philosophers*.[9] I have to thank you again first. Now you have completed this extremely demanding editing task. I'm glad that the book is available in America now in such a handsome form.

394   Hannah Arendt to Karl Jaspers

New York, March 26, 1966

Lieber Verehrtester,

I'm writing in haste because I'm just about to leave for my two-month teaching stint in Chicago. Just these few lines to thank you and Gertrud very much for your letters.

I'm enclosing the printed correspondence[1] about my Robinson article. I hope this will be the end of it. The funny thing is that having spoken my mind publicly I'm being flooded with invitations from all the Jewish organizations to speak, to appear at congresses, etc. And some of these invitations are coming from organizations that I singled out to attack and named by name. Also, the Hebrew edition of *Eichmann* is finally coming out in Israel. I think the war between me and the Jews is over.

632

I'm very unhappy to hear that you're having another "attack." I hope the effect of the injections won't wear off so quickly this time. We'll let the plans for September stand, the middle of the month or somewhat earlier. I'm thinking about it and looking forward to it.

And I'm not good for anything today, certainly not for writing letters or even for dictating them.

Warmest greetings
Your
Hannah

395 *Hannah Arendt to Gertrud and Karl Jaspers*

Chicago, April 18, 1966

Dearest Friends—

Thank you for your letters.[1] This damned pain! If you are allowed to ask only once a day how he is feeling, how often may I ask? I don't really know how that should be calculated. I had some news already because Helen Wolff called Heinrich in New York and he passed the news on to me by phone. The second volume of *The Great Philosophers* is in all the bookstores here, and you have doubtless received the review in the *New York Times*.[2] What I have not received—Piper is unreliable—is your new Germany book,[3] about which the Chicago Press has presumably written you already. Since they have published your other political books, it probably makes sense to give it to them. The translator is always the question. There is no doubt that Ashton is the best, but he should be translating the *Philosophie*, and it would be better not to disturb him.

Saner wrote me, very pleased; and I'm very proud that I turned out to be right in the face of your pessimism—just a friendly way of saying no. I knew already because Mr. Freund wrote to me right away *to thank me!* (Please tell that to Saner, on whom American manners made a great impression. In this case, rightly so.)

I haven't written for a long time because the first weeks in Chicago were too demanding. A lot had piled up because I haven't been here for a year. On top of that I have a huge lecture course all of a sudden, with a great many so-called credit students, not just auditors. The credit students are all required to write essays, and it makes me weary just to think about it. All the more so because they are so-called graduate students, who are often of the opinion that length is the crucial factor. (When I arrived here, I found on my desk a manuscript of—believe it or not—seven hundred pages, part of it single spaced. A talented con man, nothing more. But because he is one of "our" students, I had to read the thing.) I'm lecturing on Basic Moral Propositions from Socrates to Nietzsche and giving a seminar on Nietzsche with your book as the basic text. That has finally become a realistic option now that the book is available in English. The students in the lecture course (with discussion groups) and in the seminar are excellent, but that means I have to stay right on top of things, too. They are eager to read whatever is recommended to them, and they don't let you get away with anything. I like that. And then there are office hours and doctoral exams and other such chores. In short, I'm a "professor." And on top of that the constant social obligations that have left me with hardly an evening free to sit quietly in my club.

Apropos of *The Great Philosophers*: you'll have seen that those idiots at the publishing house put me on the title page and the dust jacket. I protested immediately. Helen herself seems innocent. The reason for it (I assume) is that they are bringing out a new edition of *The Origins of Totalitarianism*, for which I'm writing a new introduction. Perhaps they think they can win me back with this ploy. Or something stupid like that. It has really angered me, and just how much it has I can tell because I'm getting red in the face just writing about it.

I'll save Heidegger for another time. Have you read this book about him?[4] I don't know it. You said yourself that anti-Semitism was not an issue. But the attacks on him are coming only from that quarter and no other. No one has the slightest inkling about the things you have said. Then, too, I can't prove it, but I'm quite convinced that the real people behind the scenes are the Wiesengrund-Adorno[5] crowd in Frankfurt. And that is grotesque, all the more so because it has been revealed (students found this out) that Wiesengrund (a half-Jew and one of the most repulsive human beings I know) tried to go along with the Nazis. For years now he and Horkheimer[6] have accused or threatened to accuse anyone in Germany who was against them of being anti-Semitic. A really disgusting bunch, and yet Wiesengrund is not untalented. I told you about him once.

The Gruppe 47 has arrived here in the meantime. After thinking about it for a long time I've decided to decline all the invitations (the Germans as well as the Americans asked me to come). They will probably make quite a scene here about Vietnam. I can only wind up in an uncomfortable position because I am totally opposed to our government in this matter myself. But the German way of dealing with these things—I had a preview of what's coming: Helen Wolff told me that one of the group, Klaus Wagenbach,[7] had told her that there was 20% unemployment in this country! She responded by sending him a newspaper article with the actual figure (I think it's 3½%, in reality little more than the people who can no longer be integrated into the work force). Whereupon Wagenbach replied that he knew better, and those figures were all falsified.

And to come back to *Eichmann* once again: A few weeks ago I received the enclosed letter from a Rabbi Dr. Arthur Hertzberg,[8] who is a major figure in the "Establishment" here and who, as you can see, attacked me in compliance with his marching orders. This apology is unfortunately not as nice as it looks. I'm quite sure that the only reason he wrote this letter is that the official position has changed. They've dropped poor old Robinson like a hot potato after having pushed him into this lunatic enterprise. Well, in any case, I'm assuming that this marks an end to the comedy. At least as far as the Jewish organizations are concerned. Privately, it will probably never come to an end—they are, after all, "intellectuals," which is a far worse breed than representatives of interests.

And finally, Saner: he shouldn't save but should see to it that his wife[9] has things a bit easier. That is much more important. For the future as well.

Warmest greetings—
Your
Hannah

---

396 *Karl Jaspers to Hannah Arendt*

Basel, April 29, 1966

Dear Hannah!

Frau Salmony is again so kind as to take a letter to you. You write from Chicago. We were happy to hear your news. I become livelier myself when I see you at your "great task," working with philosophical subjects and with gifted students, seemingly indefatigable, as if you were incapable of aging. You spoke once about your plan for a lecture course on the fundamentals of ethics from Socrates to Nietzsche. You have made some initial soundings of this subject in your books. It is an important one.

I am of course pleased that you are using my book as a point of departure in your Nietzsche seminar. I looked into this book a while ago (I'm more given to memories now than I used to be) and thought that it must make the reader's head swim, especially in the chapter about truth. It may well be relevant, but it is still painful sometimes. Since I have in recent years come to understand Max Weber better and more profoundly, or so I think, I see Nietzsche and Kierkegaard with somewhat different eyes. Both of them furthered the cause of honesty, with completely similar formulations. Neither of them was able to bear what he saw (and was able to express poetically and verbally in a way far superior to Max Weber). Nietzsche, in spite of his original antimetaphysical intentions, clung to eternal recurrence, to the metaphysics of the will to power, to the idea of the superman; Kierkegaard, to a sophisticated conceptual structure for interpreting Christian faith as faith by virtue of the absurd, an "ingenious" conceptual structure from which dialectical theology lives and for which it has fallen, so to speak, while suppressing the fact that Kierkegaard once declared this whole conceptual structure a poetic one and that he launched an attack against the church from which it is hardly capable of recovering. And those who take Nietzsche's metaphysics seriously forget his sentence about eternal recurrence, which was: I may be mistaken. But the fact remains that both of them, despite their own doubting of themselves as a result of their honesty, found their firm ground in it. It was very different with Max Weber. He was truly serious about unlimited honesty. That is what made him the archetypical modern man who opens himself completely to absolute inner chaos, to the battle between warring powers, and who doesn't allow himself any secret cheating but lives passionately, struggles with himself, and has no goal. He felt that all of science and learning taken together was totally incapable of providing fulfillment in life. He grasped that aspect of the Old Testament that is usually overlooked, namely, that we experience God not only as an ally, as a merciful lawgiver, but also as an evil presence, as a devil. Whoever thinks, as Max Weber did, not just theoretically, but who also lives out this human existence may well reach amazing heights but only momentarily; everything is called into question. And so his lifelong penchant for death, his inclination to thoughts of suicide. Ricarda Huch[1] thought him an actor. A young man from the Mommsen family recently wrote an important book about Max Weber's politics[2] (important because of many new sources), attributing his political thinking to contradictions in his concrete judgments, characterizing him as a representative of imperialism and, by virtue of his mode of thought, as someone who prepared the way for Hitler. Last year, when Max Weber's hundredth birthday was celebrated, people busied themselves endlessly with insignificant details and showed no real awareness at all of this man. I think about him a lot in connection with "independent thinking," the meaning of which I would like to illuminate by discussing your work. But up to now I've let myself digress into a multitude of themes, or, as at the moment, I've stopped work altogether (because of fatigue and pain). I would like to finish the book and haven't given up all hope, even though I haven't made any progress for weeks, except for occasional notes. But back to Max Weber: Although he was no genius and inferior to both Nietzsche and Kierkegaard, he is nonetheless, in comparison with those eternal adolescents and dubious figures, plainly and simply a man. And that is physically the case, too. They were all three sick men, but Max Weber was different. He did not suffer from paralysis or schizophrenia but from something as yet undiagnosed. He experienced in his life those elemental phases that are somehow grounded in biology: peaks of energy and productivity and then total collapse in which he couldn't even read anymore. In the last year of his life—we saw him during a last visit in Heidelberg, two months before his death—he was in a "manic" but completely disciplined state. He said that never had the sentences and concepts flowed from his pen with such clarity, ceaseless continuity, and force (the famous 170 pages at the beginning of *Wirtschaft und Gesellschaft* show that). He was incredibly prolific; he gave lectures that no student could forget. He was constantly making political trips and giving speeches; he glowed and suffered at the same time; and that suffering seemed without limits. If he had remained alive, he probably would have had another collapse. And at the end, his conscious dying, completely calm and without a trace of regret and with the words: What is true is the truth. I can still see him standing in our living room in front of Gertrud, raising himself on his tiptoes and speaking passionately as he told about a strange deceitfulness in the family, because Gertrud had hit the nail on the head with a question about Alfred Weber. When he left after dark he spoke his last words to me, ones that have always been an encouragement to me, apropos of my *Psychologie der Weltanschauungen*,[3] which had just been published. I told you about that before. It was as if he forgot nothing, not even the smallest human courtesies, in those last months when his life exceeded all bounds. By the way, are you having your students read my first lecture in *Vernunft und Existenz*, on Kierkegaard and Nietzsche? Earle translated *Vernunft und Existenz*[4] in America (originally published by the Noonday Press and a book that is still selling very well).

It seems good to me that you will not go to the Gruppe 47 gathering. You would surely find yourself in an awkward situation. The whole group sometimes strikes me as a form of self-aggrandizement in which people who really don't yet amount to much individually are trying to attach some value to themselves collectively.

I read the rabbi's letter with great pleasure. It is fantastic. What a quiet victory for your cause and your person! Of course it cannot be a public one. I presume that I may reprint the letter, omitting the writer's name, of course.

On Adorno: You have spoken about him in the same vein in which you write now. If the students can prove that he tried to ingratiate himself with the Nazis, why don't they make it publicly known? They have done that with other professors (in Bonn, for example, when Benno von Wiese produced his inanely pathetic excuses). That would be of great value to the universities. It seems that Adorno is becoming an authority in the Federal Republic, highly respected. What a fraud. In what I have read of him, I find nothing worthy of serious consideration, not even in his brilliant, vastly knowledgeable writings that examine things from every possible angle and in which he assumes a vantage point of the greatest wisdom. And yet he is taken seriously. I quickly become bored with him. Such hodgepodges of anything and everything that comes to mind are intolerable.

As you can see, my health gives me no real reason to complain. I can still read and chatter and dictate. Though only for a while. The tiredness along with the slight temperature is probably more crippling to my work than is the pain, which the medications are still able to lessen. And not a day passes when Gertrud and I are not happy together. It really is nice to grow so old.

My new book was issued yesterday. I asked Piper to send you two copies by airmail. Because Piper had already sent the page proofs to a lot of newspapers and radio stations, comment started coming in before the book was published, and it has all been negative. I'm also getting responses by word of mouth. Everyone is against me, even the critical young journalists and writers, like Gaus, for example. I sense that my way of thinking doesn't suit them. It's like an already present and widespread antipathy. I'm eager to see what will come of it all. I don't know yet in any detail what the responses really are like. I find it all a little unsettling. I'm gathering my notes and thoughts so that I won't be obliged to just let these gentlemen go without a response from me.

Warmest greetings to you both from Gertrud and

Your
Karl

May 8

I've been feeling much better since I wrote this letter and have spent a few wonderful days. Now I'm reading all your books once again and think that I grasp the whole much better now. And I'm making notes and excerpts. We will talk with each other in my book, if I can manage to write it.

397   *Hannah Arendt to Karl Jaspers*

Chicago, May 21, 1966

Lieber Verehrtester—

Your book[1] arrived just before the students' sit-in began. I immediately read it straight through, so fascinated by it and engrossed in it that I stayed up late into the night. I wanted to write the next day— but because of the students I didn't get to anything at all. Heinrich says: This is the most courageous book that a German has ever written about Germany. In any case, it is a wonderful book, both bold and just at the same time. It will continue to be read, even though it is so very much rooted in the events of this period. That is the very thing that makes it so lively. It has something strangely final about it. Everything in it is of the same importance and the same weight (except for the appendix about the elections perhaps), but of immediate political importance is the section on the emergency legislation. I can imagine that this book will not be well received in Germany. You say your "way of thinking" doesn't suit them. Unfortunately, that is very true. And what doesn't suit them is that you think concretely. (I had what was actually a very pleasant evening with a certain Klaus Wagenbach, member of the Gruppe 47, who has written an excellent biography of Kafka[2] and is now a publisher. The stereotypical quality of his political judgment is incredible; still so young and already totally incapable of learning anything. Sees in everything only more support for his

639

prejudices, can't absorb anything concrete, factual, anymore.) And in that sense it is a very "un-German" book. Also typical of this blind rebellion against Bonn is the universal rejection of Augstein that prevails among these intellectuals. They mistrust him because he's not pushing any ideological agenda. The very thing that speaks in Augstein's favor. Gaus: I already knew that he favored the Great Coalition. And that is of course a major issue. Everything you say is wonderfully illuminating and completely true. Much of the antipathy toward your book grows out of a total lack of understanding of anything political and a helplessness in dealing with it. And hence the unpleasant aggressiveness these people instantly fall into the minute they take an opposing position. And the amazing lack of judgment. I'd be grateful if you could tell me where major reviews have appeared. Then I can have Piper send them to me. The issues involved are of great importance.

Perhaps we can talk about Nietzsche in the fall. Your book is of enormous help. When I belatedly recommended your lecture on Nietzsche and Kierkegaard[3] to the students in my seminar—I had simply forgotten it—it turned out that they all knew it already. I was tickled. As I've learned from colleagues teaching in the college here, the students are getting "a sizable dose of Jaspers," as someone put it. And they're getting it as early as their last college year, primarily —and this should give you particular pleasure—from the man who teaches the history and philosophy of science.

The student unrest here, about which you have no doubt read in the papers, was really very salutary. For reasons I can't determine, the administration, which discusses with the students at length everything that concerns them, kept its silence on the matter of what I see as a not incorrect university policy regarding obligatory military service and presented the students with a fait accompli. The students were really not asking for anything more than to have all these issues subjected to thoroughgoing discussion first, and when, despite several attempts, they were not able to persuade the university to take part in such a discussion, they decided to show their teeth and occupy the administration building. Because there is a very intelligent and good man in the administration—he is at the very top; not the president, because he is a Jew, but in truth he is the president and everyone knows it—it all ended well. The police were not called in, and the students were not threatened. After three days they left voluntarily, and they spent the whole time in discussion and adhered strictly to all parliamentary rules. Everyone who wanted to speak was given a chance; everyone was heard; no one was booed; all motions were made according to the rules. In short, at no point were the students a mob. The building itself, which all of a sudden was sheltering about 450 students day and night—they slept on the floor, ate oranges and sandwiches—was kept impeccably clean and in good order the whole time. Every few hours, the students picked up and cleaned up. And when they decided to leave the building again—mainly because they might otherwise have done the university, "our university," irreparable harm—they stayed there through half the night, exhausted and hungry, to see that everything was left just as they had found it. A significant number of the faculty—but hardly anyone in the administration—were calling for harsh measures. And when it looked for a moment as if the university actually would call in the police, have the students arrested, and then expel them from the university, there were several young teachers, prominent among them the dean of the college (that is, from the administration), who by no means approved the students' methods but seriously considered subjecting themselves to arrest with them. I was not officially involved, but I had to talk with my students all the time, and I visited the occupied building several times and spoke with individual students there. The students called me in the middle of the night to confer with me. Most of them appeared for class, most of mine more dead than alive, however. I kept telling them, of course, that they had to leave the building as soon as possible, that they would otherwise suffer a major defeat. At no point was contact lost, and the willingness to listen and debate was always there. The most remarkable thing: there were no leaders before, but then leaders emerged. Primarily responsible for the exemplary order was a very gifted, twenty-year-old Jewish girl who led the proceedings and had absolute authority. Since then, people here have been racking their brains trying to define what new institutions are needed to let the students have a voice in everything that directly affects them but without giving them decision-making powers. Only a small minority is demanding that, and it will not prevail. But an overwhelming majority of the truly able students are demanding the right to be heard. And that they will get —I hope.

I went into this in such detail because I thought it might interest you both. The semester will soon be over here. I'll fly home on the 31st. I'm quite tired. I had the flu with fever and for the first time I called off classes because of illness. I'm getting old! (I promptly received a lovely bouquet of flowers "from your students" and another from that intelligent man from the administration whom I mentioned above and who had heard by chance I was ill.) Heinrich had it worse. He got shingles in the middle of the semester, and it really got him down because he kept working in spite of it. He's better now.

I'm thinking about September! Warmly

Your
Hannah

398   Karl Jaspers to Hannah Arendt

Basel, June 27, 1966
July 8, I let this lie so long![1]

Dear Hannah!

I still haven't replied to your kind letter of May 21. I can't say I've been unwell at all in recent weeks, though I continue to be tired. And along with that so much came down on me in the way of politics that I couldn't cope with it and am now thoroughly sick of the whole business. I'm calling it quits for good with politics—Gertrud has been asking me to do that for a long time—but of course I'm not saying that publicly. This political scribbling is seductive; it's all so much easier than philosophy. It lowers the level of one's inner being. A politician acting in the world, that is another thing; but I've done quite enough of this writing.

Your description of the student unrest in Chicago left me much impressed. It is worthwhile for you to speak and take part in such a situation. Your wonderful political books are philosophy. They are not the kind of writing I had fallen into for a while, the kind that drags one into the mill. The chains don't break. One becomes a desirable property for the radio and the press. But even that was an interesting experience. I will soon do one more interview, which will be my last, this time with a Swiss (Allemann).[2] I was very disappointed with Thilo Koch[3] this time. I'll tell you about it later.

But despite all that, the praise both of you gave my book was very gratifying to me. The project was worthwhile after all.

My book has been number one on the bestseller list here and in the Federal Republic for a few weeks now. But the real interest in it is minimal.

So far (two months) a little under 30,000. By comparison, Peter Bamm's *Alexander*[4] (a likable, old-fashioned, not outright bad book) sold 100,000 copies in its first month (my book, 20,000). Augstein put it very accurately in a letter to me. We are like mice on a treadmill, he said, setting in motion a paddle wheel whose paddles don't reach into the water. You have no doubt heard that Ulbricht[5] tried to make a stir. It produced some publicity for my book, but I didn't let myself be drawn into an exchange at all. I'm enclosing my reply[6] to his twelve-page letter. I've just sent off to *Die Zeit* an essay that deals with the whole affair and also includes my final word regarding Ulbricht's initiative.[7]

Heinrich's case of shingles was, I am sure, very troublesome. I know from experience. Along with the pain, the feverishness and fatigue are debilitating. You stay home with the flu, which is only to be expected even for a young person, and you write: "I'm getting old." You will in fact be sixty this year; I can't recall the exact date. You don't want to celebrate the day or reflect on it. Or so it seemed to me when I wrote to you in Paris ten years ago for your fiftieth birthday. And so I'll keep my silence now, but I will say one thing: "old" is not a word that applies to you. Your vitality will never fade, except perhaps a little when you reach your 80s.

Gertrud is growing old too, the two of us together. She is forgetful. Her ability to register things (not her memory) is reduced. That is very inconvenient. And then she is increasingly unsteady on her feet, subject to vertigo and weakness. Her soul, however, is more receptive, more sensitive than ever to essential nuances. She is sometimes angry and defensive toward the world. We enjoy telling each other about our childhood lives. We have done that before, but only hastily; now we do it in detail and with reflection.

Nahum Goldmann wants a "message" from me for the Jewish world congress in Brussels. The subject: Germans and Jews.[8] I don't want to refuse, but I'm having trouble doing it. I feel uncomfortable about the whole business. If you were here, you could correct my manuscript. But now there isn't time.

In a separate envelope I'm sending you a few reviews picked out of a pile I haven't organized. It's hardly worth it. What I said about China is reported incorrectly everywhere. Even Augstein misunderstood me.

Thanks to your influence, the University of Chicago Press, the publishing house I like best after Helen Wolff, is offering me a contract for my *Bundesrepublik*. I'm pleased. Helen Wolff and three other publishers later inquired after this same book. Astonishing!

Warmest greetings from us both.

Your Karl

P.S. I'm enclosing the letter from Benno von Wiese,[9] too, and would appreciate it if you would return it to me.

I was a bit disappointed with the University of Chicago Press, by the way. They sent me a *printed* contract with *nothing struck out* (e.g., an option on all my future books and other impossible terms). Now I'll have to see if they'll accept my deletions.

399 Hannah Arendt to Karl Jaspers

New York, July 4, 1966

Lieber Verehrtester—

I've been wanting to write you for weeks but haven't gotten around to anything because I was having the apartment renovated, and it was quite a job. Then the heat descended on us. Heinrich, whom I had exiled during the renovating, moved back in, and once everything was restored to order, I restored myself.

Before I forget it: I still owe you an answer to your question about Adorno.[1] His unsuccessful attempt to align himself with the regime in 1933 was discovered by the Frankfurt student newspaper *Diskus*.[2] He responded with an indescribably pathetic letter,[3] which, however, impressed the Germans a great deal. The really repulsive aspect of the thing is that he, the only half-Jew among Jews, did this without informing his friends. He had hoped that being Italian on his mother's side (Adorno versus Wiesengrund) would help him through.

I'm writing today mainly about the Germany book. I've seen a very few reactions, and I must say I'm amazed, on the one hand, by the animosity of the public response and, on the other, by the fact that the book is on the top of the bestseller list. You will have seen that an extremely hostile and mean-spirited review appeared here in *The New York Review of Books*,[4] too, and by a Neal Ascherson, the Bonn correspondent for the London *Observer*. I don't want to write any more about this. We'll soon have a chance to talk about it.

You know that the Chicago Press has asked me to write an introduction to the book. If everything had not been so chaotic here, I would have written about it. I said of course I would if Jaspers agreed to it, and Maurice English[5] wrote me that you had agreed. Why they need it isn't entirely clear to me, unless it's because people here really are very poorly informed about Germany.

Ashton was here yesterday. He has, thank God, agreed to take on the translation and plans to have it done in the fall. I thought about abridging the appendices. But then we both felt that that would be a pity from every point of view, and Ashton made what to me seems a very good suggestion. He would like to see the first two sections published here as a separate book, together with *Die Schuldfrage*, which has appeared in Germany with a new foreword.[6] He is sure that he can "sell" this to Harper's. We were both of the opinion that the whole statute-of-limitations debate really belongs with *Die Schuldfrage*, or at any rate can just as well be published along with it. What do you think of the idea? We would, of course, need the consent of Chicago University Press, because it has the option for the whole book. It could be that it—that is, Chicago Press—would itself like to publish this new edition of *Die Schuldfrage*. I would see no objections to that, except that it would delay publication of *Die Schuldfrage* because they can't publish two books by Jaspers at the same time. What do you think? I assume that Ashton will write to you himself. He will also tell you that his work on *Philosophie* will not be delayed by his taking on this translation.

I won't write the foreword until Ashton's translation is done, because it will be easier for me if I have the English text. That also has the great advantage that we'll see each other before I write the foreword.

Do you know the report about the Auschwitz proceedings, a collection of the trial reports for the *Frankfurter Allgemeine*, which was published by Athenäum?[7] It is really dreadful, mainly because it documents atrocities that were not committed under orders at all. I mention it because I am supposed to write the foreword for the English edition.[8] One hardly knows what one should say.

Now for another question: you probably recall that you once gave me, in connection with my application for restitution, a letter about my prospects for habilitation [qualification] in Heidelberg.[9] At that time, all such applications were refused. Now some supplementary regulations have recently come out, on the basis of which, my lawyer[10] tells me, we should attempt a resubmission of the old application. The great advantage would be that I could receive a pension. The German consulate here recommended this lawyer to me as a real expert on this kind of restitution question. My own lawyer committed suicide four years ago.[11]

As things were explained to me, the situation is this: There is a possibility that those people for whom habilitation was practically assured can be brought in under these new regulations. The lawyer needs another letter from you to attempt this. He has drafted it, and I am sending it to you as he drafted it, which does not mean that you should sign it in its present form. He seemed to think it very important that you were familiar with the Rahel biography. You will recall that I had Annchen [Anne Weyl] bring it to you back then. Also important but more doubtful in my eyes would be your statement that the faculty usually approved the candidate if the professor responsible for the habilitation so requested. You will see that the lawyer has expressed this negatively, that is, that you never had the experience of having the faculty turn down a habilitation paper that you had approved. I told the lawyer that the colloquium was not really an exam. But that too may be a debatable point. I'm enclosing the letter in three copies, should you find that you can simply sign it.

It is still brutally hot here, but our apartment is pleasantly cool. Heinrich is correcting his papers, and when he is done, we'll go to Palenville until the end of August. Mail can be addressed to us either at Chestnut Lawn House, Palenville, New York, or simply at our New York address. I hope all is well with you. And, please, don't take it amiss that I've dictated this letter. I have to see to it that I wrap up everything in a few days here so that we can get away, and I'm a bit pressed for time.

In the meantime the thermometer has climbed well above 100, and even our apartment is unbearable. I'm fleeing; Heinrich will follow day after tomorrow in the morning.

How are you? How do things stand with Erna's leave? What arrangements will you make while she's gone?

One last note on the Germany book: We should probably omit the concluding remark about the election results. Hardly anyone here will understand it.

All warmest regards—
Your   Hannah

Basel, July 11, 1966

Dear Hannah!

I'm replying to your letter right away. The unsettled state of your life—the renovation of the apartment, the extreme weather conditions in New York—is very palpable in it. You need some real leisure in Palenville, and Heinrich, whom you spoil, with you.

First of all, the supplementary letter. It served me very well as a basis because it showed me what the legally important points were. I rewrote it nonetheless, for one thing, to bring a little of my style to it, but for another to show the situation in Heidelberg a little more clearly and in keeping with the reality there.

If it does not meet your needs, I'll be glad to rewrite it again. In that case, please send it back to me with your corrections. The matter is of such importance that it is worth doing with the greatest care. It would represent some major supplementary security for your old age. I hope it will come through.

I haven't seen *The New York Review of Books*. You can tell me about it.

I would assume that the publisher wants a foreword from you because you are such a well-known personality in the USA and so can help launch my book, as I did in the past for yours in Germany. It will make work for you. That is the only thing that speaks against it.

Ashton's suggestion (*Schuldfrage* and Augstein interview and the Bundestag debate in another book) strikes me as excellent. *Die Schuldfrage* appeared quite a while ago with Dial Press (in 1946, I believe) and is presumably long since out of print (otherwise I would have heard of a new printing). But we probably should check with them. I have Ashton's letter already. I will answer it soon—very pleased with *everything* suggested.

Having already read many of the reports in the *Frankfurter Allgemeine Zeitung*, I do not want to read the Auschwitz book again. It is unbearable and goes beyond anything one could imagine. One has to be aware of it. Gertrud read it all. It was almost impossible to free her from the mood it induced.

We are well. The complaints of age you know about are with us. I am still benefiting from the effects of my last injection and can write without difficulty.

Erna is on vacation. The Saners offered as early as last year to stay with us. Ursula and little Stefan are here.[1] The two older children are with grandparents and other relatives.[2] Renie[3] will come from Holland tomorrow for a week to help out. And then, cleaning women are here every day (except Sunday). The children are a real joy for Gertrud but also quite tiring. But the pleasure she takes in these youngsters is more important to her.

The *entire* beginning of the Germany book—the September elections—should of course be omitted.

Warmest greetings,
Your Karl

Another word about my book: There was a great to-do here because Ulbricht (GDR) wrote me a letter twelve pages long. I wrote an essay for *Die Zeit*[4] (with idiotic paragraph heads supplied by the editorial staff) to close the books on the issue. I'll tell you both all about it. For the last few weeks now every last provincial newspaper in Germany has carried my name in headlines. I can imagine that every German who reads newspapers knows my name at the moment. Well, now that's all over. A strange experience with all the trimmings.

401   *Hannah Arendt to Karl and Gertrud Jaspers*

Palenville, August 10, 1966

Lieber Verehrtester, liebe Gute—

This letter is so long overdue. We're having it much too good here, and it's so easy to fall into lazy ways. And then, I'm already picturing myself with you, and that makes all letter writing seem superfluous. Are the Saners still with you, or is Erna back yet? I'll soon be able to inspect everything for myself.

First of all: Heinrich will not come this time. After a winter of very heavy work he finally has some peace here—he is very well—and he wants to stick with his work. On top of that he has some dental work that he has been putting off for a long time and that finally has to be taken care of. So you'll have to make do with me. Exactly which day I'll come I can't say yet. There will be a meeting of the American Political Science Association in New York at which I am supposed to give a talk ("Truth and Politics"). The talk is on the 7th, but the meeting lasts longer, and it would be impolite to leave right away. So I will come sometime between September 12 and 15. I'll write from here to the Hotel Euler (I know, it's a bit grand for me, but I've sold two things to *The New Yorker*, "Brecht" and "Truth and Politics,"[1] so I'm very rich), because it, along with the Drei Könige, is the only hotel that doesn't have buses as overnight guests and doesn't keep kicking one out all the time. That really is annoying. (So you see: with sixty I'm turning over a new leaf. I'm going to play the "old lady" for all it's worth.) Now the question remains: How long? I thought for three weeks, but you have to say if that is too much. I wanted to have Annchen [Anne Weil] and possibly Mary [McCarthy] come to Basel, because I have no desire to travel around. I've also refused all lectures, radio talks, etc. in Germany. At the end of October I have to be back in Chicago, and I have a number of lectures to do in the winter—I find it hard to refuse any engagement for $1,000 or more —and in the meantime I prefer to keep my mouth shut. I want to see my family in Zurich, and I don't mind running over there. Let me know what you think. And please tell me, too, what I can bring for Erna. She hasn't gotten anything decent from me for a long time now.

Now to the letters. Thank you very much for dealing with the restitution certification so promptly. It was perfect, and the lawyer has already made a legally very impressive document of it. My feeling is that nothing will come of it, but we should give it a try.

I see with great pleasure that you are still at the top of the bestseller list. That speaks well for the reading public. It is a very great success, similar to *Die geistige Situation der Zeit*. I hope it doesn't end the same way.[2] The parallels make me a bit uneasy. At my request, Piper sent me a pile of reviews. I think it's best if I bring them along. We can discuss what we will tell the American reader. I had a letter from Chicago today from Maurice English, who was apparently very ill (had an operation). He can't give an answer yet about publishing both part of this book and *Die Schuldfrage*. Ashton and I both feel it would be better if Harper's published it, because that would speed things up, but we have to make the offer to Chicago first. As far as the contract is concerned, I would assume that there will be no problem. You can certainly cut out anything you want to cut.

You write about my 60 years and mention that I never replied to the wonderful letter you wrote at my fiftieth birthday. I was probably just never in the right mood. Then, too, there was a disaster connected with that birthday. I was in Paris, and the Weils (Annchen's husband and sister[3]) had invited me over. It was unforgettable because, after grand preparations had been made, with champagne, etc., he was so incredibly rude and insulting to me that I never entered his house again. We made peace quite a while ago—he came to visit us in New

York, etc. But the incident was somewhat symbolic: birthdays never come off just right. Unimportant. Growing old is another matter. There I've always had great ambitions. If I'm going to grow old, then please let me turn gray with dignity, not with this "bloom of youth" stuff à la Alfred Weber. I'll do my best with this but will have some difficulty because my horses still find it very easy to get out of hand on me. But otherwise—these decades I have shared with you two— all Heinrich and I need do is imitate you. It's just the way we want things to be; all it took was for you to show us how. One thing you haven't succeeded at, and that's because the gods have played you a dirty trick. And that is Goethe's gradual disappearance from view. One can afford that only if the world is in some kind of order. But now you are more in view than ever. And that's very, very nice.

And then there is coming closer to death. That troubles me, I think, very little. I have always enjoyed life, but then again not so much that I want it to go on forever. I've always found death a pleasant companion—not one to inspire melancholy. Illness I would find very unpleasant, burdensome, or worse. What I would like to have is a sure and decent way of committing suicide if need be. I'd like to have it in hand.

I read a short article in the paper about the Nahum Goldmann business[4] with you, Baron, Scholem, Gerstenmaier, etc. But I'd like to see what you had to say about it. You can show it to me later. There is so much to talk about—in politics, too. Johnson, whom I consider very dangerous; Mao, who I think is either dead or half dead—this report about his swimming[5] seemed to me a proof that he isn't there any longer. I'm going to start counting the days soon. I was happy to have Benno's letter,[6] which I'm enclosing.

Now I have to write the introduction for the Auschwitz book[7]— an odd occupation for one's vacation. I have just written a long review of a two-volume biography of Rosa Luxemburg,[8] a good book, English in the way the great English biographies of statesmen are, supplied with a whole critical apparatus and many previously unknown sources, letters in particular. So little was known about her because she was so incredibly reticent, though not secretive. And the man who wrote the book, Nettl,[9] completely unknown. Rumor has it that he's a businessman!—as if he were her last suitor. A very satisfactory job. In connection with this I read Eduard Bernstein,[10] a very intelligent man. But what a repulsive hypocrite Kautsky[11] was. As you can see, I'm starting to ramble.

Good-bye for now, and send me a brief word on whether the dates are all right.

Warmly
Your
Hannah

I'm glad that there seem to be a good many Germans who are happy to have you speak the undisguised truth to them. And we have to continue to hope that those people will eventually make themselves heard. I'll see you both next summer.

Your   Heinrich

402 *Karl Jaspers to Hannah Arendt*

Basel, August 17, 1966

Dear Hannah!

So you will come between September 12 and 15! Any day is of course fine with us. Do write and let us know exactly which one it will be. And three weeks and only in Basel! Wonderful! We are happy in anticipation of this time together. You should have everyone you like come to Basel. Piper, who was going to come see me now, has put off his visit because you will not be going to Munich. Gaus said to me weeks ago that he hoped to see you. I replied that you would certainly like to see him, but that I would not favor your making a trip because I am too selfish. His response: Then he would come to Basel. —Perhaps we will see Mary McCarthy, too. But that might be difficult because of the language. Your relatives: They will be those good people who were here last year with the problem of a daughter whose studies outside Israel you financed? Shouldn't they come to Basel, too, or, rather, do they and you want that?

It saddens us both that Heinrich will not come. I had feared that he might not come, given his aversion to travel. And I understand his feelings very well. He promises to make the trip next year. That is a long way off.

Erna is back again. We are well cared for. We had four good weeks with the Saners. The two youngest children, Ursula and Stefan, were with us. The two others stayed, quite happily, with their grandparents. But it was a great deal of trouble for Frau Saner, even though we made everything as simple as possible (meals from the Fröschenbollwerk,[1]

651

cleaning women every day except Sunday). But she was "not at home." She never let us feel that. A good atmosphere and good talk always prevailed. And she thanked us. But next year Herta[2] and my sister will stay with us. The only difference that will make is that we will have to move the time back a few months. We haven't discussed this with the Saners yet. Unfortunately, it has become completely impossible for me to go to a hotel. Mere physical existence demands so many little things, and because of her own physical frailties Trudelein can't tend to me the way she could in past years.

A "respectable means of committing suicide" has been a problem for us since the Nazi period and it remains one. It is vexing that in our technological age such a thing is not simply available. The drugs always have to be reasonably fresh; they spoil with time. The Nazis, always in the forefront in technical matters, used capsules containing cyanide along with some other ingredients that prevented the dreadful burning in the throat and esophagus and speeded up absorption through the stomach. When Himmler was recognized on the American front, he had one of these capsules under his tongue. A few seconds after he was recognized, he fell down dead in front of his captors. Nobody knows how Göring got hold of a capsule. As is done with all prisoners on incarceration, all his body cavities were examined, even his navel. Napoleon wanted to commit suicide after his first defeat in 1813. For decades he had had an opiate at hand for the eventuality that he found suicide advisable. It had long since lost its effectiveness. He took it, had severe abdominal pains, and was ill for a few days. In the Nazi years we obtained cyanide from a chemist, and the other ingredients as well. The preparation of the draught was somewhat complicated and required some skill. One couldn't know whether one would have time enough. And to work with laboratory precision while facing death is no small task. We had morphine, but not in heavy enough concentrations that one injection would have sufficed. I found at that time that even good physicians were theoreticians on the matter of suicide; they were, in any case, short on practical advice. —They had Veronal, which is relatively stable. You have to take a lot of it. But with tea that poses no great problem. Then you become unconscious, profoundly so, and you die of pneumonia in a few days if the stomach is not pumped out. With very large doses (several tubes) the process can be speeded up.[3] My brother[4] committed suicide with heroin, which, if you have the connections, you can acquire in the illegal drug trade. He lost consciousness after a few hours and noticed before

652

he did that he was no longer able to swallow. My mother, observant as she was, realized what was happening but put off calling a doctor and said nothing to my father. Then she called a friend of Enno's who was the director of the hospital in Oldenburg and said to him: "Gerhard, you mustn't pump out his stomach. This is what Enno wanted." And Gerhard proved himself a loyal friend. —And then, almost every doctor is cautious. Doctors are legally liable for their prescriptions and mustn't be the cause of suicides. The supervision of pharmacies is so strict and extensive that both pharmacists and doctors are under scrutiny. The "free world" is not free because it prohibits suicide. —In this instance it is democratic, not aristocratic, and to the advantage of the majority of suicides, who act for psychological reasons (that is, the suicides who are saved are mostly grateful afterward that they were saved), but to the disadvantage of the minority, who truly and freely desire their own death. How different the situation in the ancient world! —One more "case": Max Weber's sister—Lily Schaefer, a wonderful, sovereign personality, a friend of Gertrud's—committed suicide because of a complicated situation that would be too involved to recount here. She was visiting at Gruhle's,[5] and when he was away on a trip, she turned on a gas fixture in a small room. She covered the whole thing in a noncommittal letter she left behind, not really a letter of farewell at all. Max Weber spoke at the graveside. I don't think I ever saw him as shaken as on that occasion. He had loved his sister very much. He celebrated the freedom of man, who is able to take his own life. "It gave me what it could; now it's enough." The minister was relegated to just standing there.

What I sent to Brussels[6] I'll show you here. I hope there's nothing in it that will bother you. You are in it, although I don't mention you by name (your talk in Berlin in about 1949).

We have much to talk about. So I will stop for now. It all goes so much easier in person.

I'm writing a few lines to Heinrich on a separate sheet.

Warmest greetings
Your Karl

Basel, August 18, 1966

Dear Heinrich Blücher!

Gertrud and I regret very much that we will not be able to see you and speak with you. You want your peace and to continue with your work. No one can have any objections to that. So will it be next year? We'll hold you to your word. May the course of things permit you to carry out that intention.

I thank you for your response to my Germany book. I too have the sense that it is indeed being read and that some of my ideas are taking hold even with people who are my opponents. A few letters, especially from students, have been very gratifying. Such are the Germans! They are not intellectually down and out. But the dreadful danger exists that these few will be overwhelmed and lose courage. They have no real cohesion among themselves. And in the public arena the babblers are, unfortunately, still very much present. The Jewish Germans are sorely missed. Some of them were at least intelligent babblers; and others were the most insightful people. That they are no longer there accounts for this dreary decline in the level of discourse.

Warmest greetings

Your Karl

New York, September 2, 1966

Dearest Friends—

Just a quick note with my arrival date. I won't fly from here until the 15th—I couldn't manage it any sooner—and I'll be in Basel on the morning of the 16th. I'll call then. I've got a room in the Hotel Euler, thank God.

Just received word from Chicago, where the press is trying at the moment to acquire the rights for the *Schuldfrage*. We'll talk about this when I'm there.

Warmest greetings and until soon!

Your   Hannah

October 1966[1]

Dear, dearest Friends—

Thank you for everything. And see to it that we see each other again.

As always, Your Hannah

Basel, October 11, 1966

Dear Hannah!

You are still almost present for me here in Basel. Your flowers are in the hallway, this forest of dematerialized asters, an enchanting vision that gives us pleasure every day. There is no sign yet of their starting to wilt.

It was wonderful of you to make Basel your European headquarters for several weeks and to be with us. The luxury of having time was something new. Our talks were those of people who have grown older, you a little, I, much older. They were as delightful as ever; perhaps they sometimes reached a new depth, without being as boisterous as before. We reconfirmed for ourselves in all the many topics we discussed our common mode of thought, about which there is little that can be expressed in words. In it also is joy in the beauty of the world, horror at the evil, the attempt to reach the outer limits of thought, and calm.

My talks with you, and your patience with me—for you I am still the same person I have always been, and so I can reveal myself as I am now—were very encouraging for me. They are still making themselves strongly felt. I have been liberated not only from a book[1] (that is only an external consequence but a very important one), but also from many things that limit me, from politics above all, and from old ways. Now I'm out in the open air; I can return to philosophy as my subject, and I am already doing so. Gertrud is pleased about that. She has been rightly urging me to take that step for a long time.

When you left, you were more worried about us than on previous occasions. I can't object, of course, given how uncertain everything is in light of our advanced age and our many, though in themselves not yet threatening, symptoms. But I resist giving in to that thought as long as the end is not clearly in sight. For the time being Gertrud and I live in the hope that we will see you and Heinrich next year,

655

even though that hope is less strong than it was in earlier years. —
But finally, in a very different vein: we always and never take leave
of each other.[2]

On the subject of October 14[3] I will say nothing more. May your
life be happy and full and Heinrich continue to bring joy to you as
the philosopher immortalized in the three wonderful poems.

Warmest greetings to you both from Gertrud and

Your Karl

Have a wonderful celebration. Your life is still enjoyable and far from
the trials of old age. —We are happy every day in spite of the severe
pain that my beloved patient endures without complaint.

Again, best wishes and warmest greetings! How nice that you found
each other!

Your Gertrud

407   *Hannah Arendt to Gertrud and Karl Jaspers*

October 13, 1966

Dear, dearest Friends—

I still have one foot in Basel, and when I look out the window and
see the Hudson, I can't quite believe it. In my thoughts, I wander
through all the rooms in your house. I start downstairs, linger with
Gertrud in the living room, until I finally wind up in the study. When
I think about what you said, I hear the tone of your voice.

Things were as usual with Annchen [Anne Weil] in Brussels. Her
husband and sister came, and that was as usual. Except that her sister
has become grossly fat—though she is by nature slim—while Annchen
has become markedly thinner and holds her weight. Still, it's very
strange, as if the two of them had a certain combined weight and the
one takes on what the other doesn't have. Weil was as usual, too, alas!
I told some story or another (utterly unimportant), and he came back
with: I know a much better story and will now put you to shame,
whereupon he produced a dreadful, embarrassing yarn. It's hard to
believe, but there it is. And on top of it all the two sisters and he have
convinced themselves that he is something like the greatest philosopher
of the century. There is some truth to that in the sense that he is not
stupid, though he is rather boring.

A very good flight home; Heinrich at the airport, extremely happy to see me; and at home he'd laid in flowers, chocolates, and very good wine. The next morning at seven (literally) West German Radio called. I nearly died of fright at first—a long-distance call at 7 AM—and almost fell out of bed. Then a man I don't know and whose name I didn't understand asked if he couldn't drag me out of bed once again at seven tomorrow to wish me happy birthday officially and then to broadcast this right away on the radio. I'm afraid I wasn't even polite. Here nobody knows a thing, except for close friends. But tomorrow our friends—about 20 people—will get champagne and some good food here, though it will be cold. I've just come from putting in the order. It's fine with me because I still haven't settled down to work yet anyhow. And then I'll have a chance to wear your beautiful neck-lace.[1] Heinrich was very taken with it, and I look at it again every day.

I called Ashton yesterday. It would be good if you could send directly to him a copy of your reply to your critics,[2] particularly the pages about America and China, when you send them to Munich. Is that possible? The people in Chicago need that material urgently. I'll speak with them as soon as I get there, which will be at the end of next week.

I'm writing this claptrap letter out of pure longing!

All our very best wishes and regards to Erna

Your

Hannah

P.S. Just received a handwritten letter from Piper from the hospital. His handwriting doesn't look bad. The letter is particularly pleasant and cordial.

408 *Hannah Arendt to Karl Jaspers*

Chicago, November 3, 1966

Lieber Verehrtester—

Your letter and your telegram. I wanted to write right away, but then this birthday rolled over me—flowers, telegrams, etc. The Germans all knew, the consul general, the ambassador in Washington, etc., and, to my unending surprise, the executive committee of the SPD. We had a little party, but with champagne and only good friends. Then came Chicago, quite a lot to do and dreadful weather. In short, a bit of a whirl, and I mean that quite literally because the wind whirls around you here the minute you venture onto the street. By the way, I had an especially cordial letter from Klaus Piper. And several from his wife. But all that seems so far away again.

The things that stay with me are my weeks in Basel and your letter and your telegram. You have seen quite accurately. I have suddenly aged a lot this time. Not physically, it seems to me; but it is the beginning of old age, and I'm really quite content. I feel a little as I did as a child—wanting finally to be grown up. Now I feel I've achieved equanimity, that I'm closer to you both. And grateful that I can learn how to grow old under your tutelage. For you will of course always remain the same for me.

You no doubt overinterpreted my departure somewhat. What you saw was my fear, and I've had that for a long time. I just let it out all at once, like a cat out of the bag. For the rest, I think as you do—we'll see each other next year, and we shouldn't think too far into the future.

There's been a change in the mood here. The students still don't quite realize—but they do have an inkling—that the times of the civil rights movement are over, and I fear that all their interest in politics will collapse. The Vietnam War, which almost all the students oppose, can't take the place of the civil rights movement, because they can't do anything about the war, while they were able to do and did do a great deal for many years. If they were really serious about their antiwar games, they would all let themselves be drafted and then show the government their teeth. As long as the army is made up of the less gifted, it is easy to see what the consequences of that will be. Quite apart from the fact that those people like to go to war—it's a real change for them.

None of it looks good. I share Gertrud's pleasure that you are out of politics. There is nothing more to be said about German affairs now anyhow. Things operate there on automatic pilot, without interest—I hope! I heard from Augstein, by the way, pretty lame. No interest. *Der Spiegel* is getting worse (the new series about the SS is downright bad; low-grade); I have the feeling that Augstein has lost interest.

How far along are you with your *Antwort an die Kritiker*? I've spoken with the [University of Chicago] Press here, and both Ashton and you can have, of course, as much leeway as you need. Things stand differently with *Die Schuldfrage*. The book has been on the market as a paperback since 1961, and for the time being the publisher doesn't want to release it. I spoke with Shugg, the director of the Press.

Maurice English has left, alas and alack! I don't like Shugg much. He has a new executive editor, Philipson, with whom I'll have lunch next week. I hope he'll take some trouble.

Concerning China: I just read an article I found interesting. The present "cultural revolution" is China's preparation for war. China is firmly convinced, the author claims, that America will attack sooner or later. But China assumes that Russia (?) and public opinion in the U.S. will prevent America from using atomic weapons, in which case the Chinese think, quite rightly (?), that they can win the war. I find all this quite conceivable; and Johnson is truly capable of anything. He can land this country in the most dreadful mess. A war with China could call absolutely everything here into question. Unimaginable but very possible.

Now I've gone and pestered you with politics, and I'm so pleased to think of you firmly ensconced in philosophy again and (perhaps) writing your Hegel book.[1]

One last thing: A few days ago I had a visit from a student,[2] who made an excellent impression on me. He came because he is working on Max Weber, for the moment on *Wissenschaft als Beruf* with the intention of doing a doctoral dissertation on Weber later. He is presumably of German (Jewish) background. He was born in Switzerland but grew up here and speaks fluent German. He came to ask if you had ever had a part in the controversy over Weber that sprang up after the publication of *Wissenschaft als Beruf* (one that a number of people did enter into at the time). He also wanted to know where else, aside from your publications specifically about Weber, you had substantive things to say about him. I don't have any books here and couldn't give him a proper answer to the second question. And I couldn't answer the first one because I don't know the answer. I said that as far as I knew you had not taken a role in any controversy at that time. Could you let me know if that is right? And, if possible, while I'm still here in Chicago? This student is also a professional musician on the side; he directs the student orchestra here, which is said to be very good. He will probably go to Europe next year. If the impression he has made holds up, I would ask you to consider speaking with him. If my impression is correct, that could be very important—not only for the student but also for Max Weber.

I'll be here until November 22, then in New York again until spring.

With you in love—
Hannah

November 10, 1966

Dear Hannah!

Gertrud is writing this because I am in bed. I'm already much better, and there is nothing to worry about. But I won't, I'm sorry to say, be able to answer your important questions about Max Weber for another few days. When your letter arrived, I was in the midst of being filmed for television.[1] The upshot: ague and bronchiectasis. I guess I shouldn't be doing anything like that anymore either. But I have to ask you to have patience for a few days more.

With warmest greetings from us both to you both

Your
Karl[2]

Basel, November 16, 1966

Dear Hannah!

I'm sorry that your letter with the questions about Max Weber will not reach you in Chicago. I'll answer briefly:

1. I did not enter into the controversy over *Wissenschaft als Beruf* in 1919. It didn't seem worthwhile. The George people played a particularly prominent role, presenting their unpleasant points of view, as uncomprehending of scholarship as they were arrogant in their judgments. There was no real discussion.

2. I have no doubt told you before how, shortly after the publication of *Wissenschaft als Beruf*, Max Weber, Thoma (a jurist), and I sat talking together one Sunday afternoon in the garden of the lovely house on the Ziegelhäuser-Landstrasse. Weber's talk, which had caused a great stir at the time, was of course the main topic of conversation. This talk was tough, implacable, and moving.

I said something to this effect: You say nothing about the meaning of scholarship. If it is no more than what you say it is, then why do you bother with it? I spoke about Kant's "ideas" and said that every branch of science and scholarship acquires a meaning that goes beyond scholarship only by virtue of an idea. Max Weber knew next to nothing about Kantian ideas and did not respond. Finally, I said, turning to Thoma: "He doesn't know himself what meaning scholarship has and why he engages in it." Max Weber winced visibly: "Well, if you insist:

to see what one can endure, but it is better not to talk of such things."

3. The values discussion before 1914 stirred up the intellectual world (at first at the sociologists' congress) as hardly anything before it had. People sensed that something threatening was raising its head there. It seemed as if the humanities, as they were actually being carried on, were in danger of having to change themselves at their very roots. An element of uncertainty had undermined claims to a scientific objectivity that had been taken for granted and now was in part shown to be spurious.

It was characteristic of this discussion that a few people (among them Oncken, Spranger,[1] and others) decided to hold a "secret meeting" with Max Weber in hopes that the self-discipline of a small circle of mature scholars would enable them to reach their goal of better agreement among themselves. This meeting is reported in the history of the Association for Social Politics,[2] which appeared in the 1930s after the association was disbanded (I think the history was written by the association's last secretary, Boese).[2] The meeting ended with Max Weber saying sadly: "You don't understand me after all."

4. And indeed this goal could not be reached by means of objective and logical understanding. What was at issue was a demand that could not be met. The whole debate turned on whether one chooses to recognize that demand and consequently strikes out on a new path or whether one neither understands the demand nor wants it. It expresses perhaps the highest task of humanistic, sociological, psychological, and historical cognition. It has to do not just with methodology but with the scholar's whole orientation to life.

5. Whenever I spoke with Max Weber, I was always very shy, didn't really discuss but dared only to ask occasional unlikely, even impertinent questions (a few sentences I gleaned from him in conversation became my key to Max Weber). I said to him at that time something like this: "Understanding cannot be separated from valuation. What you are demanding is present in very simple form in Galilei: The circle is not nobler than the ellipse, and I can follow that without any difficulty. But you want to separate things that apparently have to be separated in a totally different way because they remain in fact constantly linked. The highest perception, you say, is to be reached by means of a 'suspension of valuation.' But how is that to be achieved?"

However I may have articulated that question, Max Weber didn't respond to it. In his language, the problem seemed simpler than it is. But in reality he experienced it on a profound level where its irresolvable nature always drove him on all the more, motivated by the tension in himself to come a little closer to the solution that took him further on the path toward the infinite. That quality changes the content, mood, and meaning of all his research. Once one is attuned to that, one senses it in almost all of Max Weber's work, which is fundamentally different from other works on the same subject.

6. I don't recall publishing anything on this, but I have written some things about it, which are now lying illegible and unpublishable among my masses of papers.

7. If your student comes to Basel, I will be glad to speak with him about this. On the basis of my past experience, this issue tends to get bogged down in the kind of endless methodological discussions that the Max Weber centennial in 1964 produced. I'm afraid that in the interpretation of Max Weber I would remain ununderstood myself.

You're back in New York now and have some peace until spring. That is wonderful. Perhaps you will have some good new ideas or will be able to work out some that you have come upon in the meantime.

I am feeling quite well again, or at least very tolerable. Gertrud is in almost top form. Paul Gottschalk is with us for two weeks. It is a great pleasure for Gertrud to revive in her conversations with him ever more memories, reaching back more than half a century, of the various branches of the family, and I share in her pleasure. Paul himself is admirably energetic despite his 85 years, continuing to make business trips all over Europe and to come up all the time with new ideas for his secondhand bookstore.[3]

As always, warmest greetings from Gertrud and me to you both

Your Karl

411 *Karl Jaspers to Hannah Arendt*

Basel, November 29, 1966

Dear Hannah!

I made a stupid mistake. I commissioned the bank by phone to send you a check (reason: payment from German Radio according to the enclosed postal slip). The written notice from the bank was such that I assume the check is invalid. Not even your name was spelled correctly. Please just send it back to the bank (Genossenschaftliche Zen-

tralbank, Basel, Aeschenplatz), giving your address and your name.
Excuse the mix-up!

Warmly
Your Karl

Gertrud sends warmest regards.

412 Hannah Arendt to Karl Jaspers

December 12, 1966

Lieber Verehrtester,

I'm dictating letters today because I'm still in a rather indescribable chaos. I had a number of lectures to give right after leaving Chicago. They were a success but at the same time rather strenuous. Usually there were seminars and lectures and discussions one on the heels of the other from three in the afternoon until eleven at night.

Thank you very much for the Max Weber letter. I had the key points copied and sent to Mr. Botstein.[1]

In the meantime you will have heard from Ashton, who wrote you that we have talked about the remaining questions. I think it would be of great help if you could add a few pages about the present state of affairs. How right you were! I have the feeling that the Germans have provisionally invented a new governmental form—the two-party dictatorship. What will happen now seems quite clear to me. The two parties will be at each other's throats behind closed doors. The Social Democrats, who in their great wisdom had decided to take over the government no matter what the cost if the country went into a crisis, will lose by a large margin in the next elections, and then one way or another we'll probably wind up with Mr. Strauss—the nation's savior in its hour of need!

I feel such a great need to talk with you, but what can we do? I don't think the gain in the NPD's[2] votes is important, but it probably is important that all the world and, above all, Mr. Strauss are now saying: "There you have it. We have to become nationalistic again."

I assume that Ashton wrote to you about the 5% clause. If it is true that they want to change the voting laws so that small parties are eliminated altogether—which Ashton couldn't have known about when he wrote to you—then it seems to me that you were right in that respect, too. The most this would require of you is perhaps to

663

change this passage somewhat to take at least the main point into account: the elimination of all opposition.

The mysterious check: I didn't cash it at first because I simply couldn't imagine what it was for. German Radio has somehow managed to create total confusion. They sent to your address an honorarium that was due me and that I had asked them to deposit directly into my account in Zurich (Schweizerische Kreditanstalt). I wound up cashing the check here after all so that you wouldn't have to be bothered with it anymore. It's really too stupid. It probably won't matter that my name is written wrong. If I should get the check back, I'll send it to the bank you named.

Warmest greetings to you both
Your
Hannah

413 Karl Jaspers to Hannah Arendt

Basel, January 3, 1967

Dear Hannah!

Many thanks for your letter. It is really wonderful how you carry on indefatigably with your work despite the excess demands placed on you. I would like to be along sometime on one of your glorious lecture tours and experience it all and know what you are speaking about. You can tell me when we get together in the summer.

I'm finishing my "Reply," the second book about the Federal Republic. It took much longer than I expected. It will go to the printer next week. I am thoroughly sick of politics.

We are tolerably well. Gertrud has gotten over an infection with which she was seriously ill. Now she seems recovered, is in good spirits but still physically tired. With me, the signs of age continue to come, none of which are dangerous in themselves but that do alter one's overall state. My head is still sometimes almost as alert as it used to be. But I do everything unhurriedly, without pushing, and I allow myself to read whatever I like. I no longer acknowledge a "duty" to work. I am increasingly inconsiderate toward "the world"—in that I have no choice. The pile of unanswered mail has grown so large that it is beyond dealing with.

I will write the afterword for Ashton's translation as soon as my book is on its way. I have to ask him to be patient with me a little while longer.

I've read, among other things, a lot of Polybius. I was interested but put off by it all the way through. To name him, after Herodotus and Thucydides, as the third great Greek historian seems ridiculous to me. He is one source of that flat, modern historiography, of facile judgments. The way he represents the Roman "constitution" as the source of Roman power and greatness may be essentially correct, but in terms of analysis it falls way below what we understand now. But then again, there are wonderful passages now and then, like the famous scene of Scipio in the Carthage he has destroyed.[1]

You see what odds and ends I occupy myself with and how I give myself up to intellectual whims.

This is no more than a greeting today for you both from us both

Your Karl

414 *Hannah Arendt to Karl Jaspers*

January 16, 1967

Lieber Verehrtester—

Your letter came a few days ago and day before yesterday, late in the evening, because the envelope had wandered around here in this large apartment house, the wonderful photos that Gertrud sent. I was grateful and happy to see her handwriting after you had told me about her illness, and it didn't even occur to me that she had probably sent the letter off before the infection hit her. When the photos arrived, we both said almost at the same time that what we really wanted to do was board the next plane and go back where we really belonged. What an amazing gift this friendship is! And how it has grown, which happens very rarely, since Heinrich has come into it. The photos are marvelous, couldn't be better. The photo of both of you is technically brilliant, too, because, without showing your eyes, it captures your look. I think I'll replace with this one an older photo, also very, very nice, that I have on my desk. And Gertrud still so beautiful, always a bit sad but now sad and wise. The portrait of you with a compelling seriousness about it. That people can look like this is, I think, ultimately the only *visible* thing that can be shown from a long life.

The month of December was, as usual, very unsettled for us. Everything comes together at once. The holidays and the conferences of the professional organizations—this year the historians and the modern languages. Everybody comes to New York. And then Mary [McCarthy] appeared suddenly for a week to attend to all sorts of business. Which was very nice. But then again people and "parties." Even Heinrich was drawn into the hubbub, but because he likes Mary a lot, he didn't mind. We gave a very nice party for her, to which she invited her friends, who are for the most part mine too (though not entirely). She arrived with a case of first-class red wine, which I am downing slowly but surely. Then came the New Year's Eve party, not too big this time, about thirty people. Esther and I managed it beautifully because, at two in the morning, we jointly threw everybody out. And after that I had two weeks of jury duty, not, unfortunately, for criminal cases but only for civil suits, every day from 9 to 5, which I enjoyed a lot and learned a great deal from. The whole business is really quite wonderful. You sit together with people from all classes, and the deliberations are very impressive, on the one hand because everyone takes the matter of justice very seriously and on the other because everyone is very happy to be there even though it means a significant loss of money and time for just about everyone. It is a duty of citizenship, and people are happy to assume it. And they perform it without any pretensions. Everyone speaks, but no one pushes himself on the others or tries to impress them. The lawyers try to impress the jury, of course, but they hardly ever succeed. For the most part, verdicts are reached solely on the basis of evidence. Even if the plaintiffs make obviously false statements under oath, people are not swayed by that and are not prejudiced against that part of the complaint that is justified. The objectivity and impartiality are quite astonishing, even in quite simple people. That the plaintiffs, as in one case, have been in this country for twenty years and can't speak a word of English (Puerto Ricans) makes no difference. The court makes do with an interpreter and that's that. If the lawyers have failed to sort out the facts and present them decently in petty cases that never should come before a court in the first place, the jury will sit for hours trying to get things straight. What ultimately matters is what the facts say and the law applicable to the case, which the judge explains to the jury. The judge says repeatedly: "If you don't like the law, there's nothing you can do about it as a juror. You still have to decide by it. You can change the law as a citizen but not now in your role as juror." The law is not regarded as fundamentally immutable. The possibility that it will have to be changed is always kept open.

But I'm starting to ramble. And in view of our mad Vietnam escapades, the scandal with the Manchester book,[1] the uncertainty about Kennedy's murder—it has turned out that a majority of the people don't believe the Warren Report—we're in need of something to raise our spirits a little. I'd also like to know very, very much what is really going on in China. If things go on as they are, Chiang Kai-shek may well march in one day, which wouldn't exactly please me either. But apart from all this, things are fine with us. Heinrich has to go back to the college next month, the last time before his retirement. The college wants to keep him, but he still isn't sure and wants to know precisely what the terms would be. Under no circumstances will he plague himself further with administrative chores. But on the other hand, it seems to me that he would enjoy continuing to lecture without any other duties. I'll have some peace now until the end of March. My first task is to write an introduction to an English edition of Walter Benjamin.[2] I've already looked through the translation. I'll have to do a detailed job because he is completely unknown here, and his work is quite complicated. And everything goes so slowly with me. I need such a long, slow start for the smallest project. I have to laugh when I read that you think you have slowed down. Compared with others—. But I see with great pleasure that *Bundesrepublik* is still on the bestseller list. It is a great success after all.

Just as I had gotten this far, Heinrich came with the mail. In it was a charming letter from Erna [Möhrle] that greatly eased my mind. She writes about a television interview[3] and the German reaction, which was in part very hostile. I have heard nothing of all this. I'm glad that your *Antwort* is finished. Yes, it is time to call a halt with politics, not just because you don't want to do anything more with it and shouldn't feel obliged to do any more, but also because there really won't be much more that needs to be said for some time to come. We are in agreement about Polybius. He was just the first, coming from the outside, to see certain things that the Romans didn't see because they took them for granted. In that respect, one can still learn from him. As for trivia, you should have seen me in recent days. I'm one of three judges here for the National Book Awards in the category Philosophy, Science, and Theology[4]—quite an important business here. And I've had to at least look at literally dozens of books. This is one of those "honors" that one can't refuse and that steal one's time. But to make a long story short: No really important, much less first-class, book has been published this year. And if I could have my way, which of course I can't, I would say: No prize.

All this just to give you some news of us and to give me a chance to take a bit of a breather with you. About the New Year I needn't say anything; you know what I wish for both of you and for us.

Warmest greetings, Your
Hannah

415 *Hannah Arendt to Gertrud and Karl Jaspers*

March 21, 1967

Dearest Friends—

Saner wrote to tell us you were not well. He said you were both improving, and I'm taking my comfort in that. But I'm finding it a bitter pill to swallow that I can't just run around the corner to look in and see how things are. Don't think that you have to write, nor Erna either. I've asked Saner to keep me informed, and I'm sure he will.

Things have changed here to the extent that I have decided, as I probably have not written to tell you yet, to take a very good post at the New School here, Graduate Faculty. Also for only one semester per year. It will be hard for me to leave Chicago and its really excellent students, but the traveling back and forth twice a year and my long absences from home were wearing on us both. Heinrich, who will officially retire this year, will still continue to teach. He has never, I don't think, had as great success with students and faculty as he is enjoying right now. But he will be home much more. He is well. We're making plans for the summer and want to come earlier this time, in August, if that is all right with you, because Heinrich will presumably teach in the fall this year and the college will start up again in early September.

The winter here was very harsh, very cold, and with constant snow-storms, the latest of them this morning. And on top of that the very depressing political situation. I just read again your *Bundesrepublik* along with your *Antwort*[1] to your critics, which is highly illuminating on many details. As far as America is concerned, I would not be so optimistic now. I don't know whether you have been following the exposés on the CIA,[2] which have shown that almost our entire intellectual life is riddled through with this nonsense, and the unions most

668

of all. And apart from the young people, no one is concerned about it. The Congress for Cultural Freedom is one of the organizations most heavily implicated by recent revelations; Lasky is surely a key figure, perhaps Bondy, too. I wish Mary [McCarthy] were here. Then I wouldn't feel so alone at least. She was in Vietnam and is writing a series of articles about it now.[3] I was very pleased by your comments on Günter Grass.[4] One can't say enough good things about him. I got to know Uwe Johnson here, too. When you're not working, read his *Zwei Ansichten*,[5] a fine book.

By the way, in your *Antwort*, on page 202, there's something curious. You write about the "American sentence" that says: "An extraordinary person is an ordinary person." That sentence isn't from any American; it's from you. You said that during a conversation last year, and I was so struck by it that I wrote it down right away upstairs. We were talking about our normalcy, and you said that as a closing word.

This is a pathetic letter that doesn't even say how worried I am. I'll go to Chicago next week for the last time. I dread it a little, because the students feel they're being left in the lurch. But I'm also somewhat worried about all the work—too boring to recount. I would so much like to have a year again for myself, without any obligations.

Please take care of yourselves and get healthy again!

With very warmest greetings
Your
Hannah

416   Karl Jaspers to Hannah Arendt

Basel, March 24, 1967

Dear Hannah!

Your last letter came a long while back. The glance that your generous and magnifying eye cast on us was very warming for us. I thank you for it.

Heinrich will continue with his teaching, free now, I hope, of all administrative chores. In teaching he can exercise one of his great talents: educating the young and opening their minds to great thinkers and issues. That teaching must not stop. He is irreplaceable. People understand that, too, as I have heard from you before. So I am hoping things will work out.

This is just a greeting for today so that you don't remain without any word at all from us. I am dictating this because my hands hurt from the polyarthritis and hurt even more when I write.

These rheumatic complications have become more troublesome, the pain and the muscular weakness. On top of that I had the flu and have so-called bronchiectasis now. I haven't worked anymore for weeks. The last thing I did was write my short political comments on the German situation. "Vom unabhängigen Denken" lies untouched. I hope my condition will improve again. But in old age one falls ill quickly and recovers only slowly. The possibility remains. Gertrud is relatively well for someone 88 years old. Her heart is weak, of course, but still adequate. She is, as she has always been, full of initiative and bright ideas, although she does complain of fatigue and vertigo. Well, this all sounds a little pathetic. Things are not so bad. But I feel I can't leave you completely without news. We are both enjoying life. I don't have to keep on writing and publishing. That's not so important anyhow. We are having as many visitors and engaging in as many activities as we like, within the limits of our condition.

Warmest greetings
Your Karl

I'm adding this postscript so that you can see I can still write. I'm feeling better today.

What are you doing? Working on anything new?

Ashton is, as always, quite superb. His suggestions are always right. I'm very grateful to him. He must be a man of real stature.

417   *Hannah Arendt to Karl Jaspers*

Chicago, April 13, 1967

Lieber Verehrtester—

Our letters crossed in the mail. I was so happy to have yours. Heinrich read it to me right away on the telephone before forwarding it to me.

I'm writing in haste today because I just received a letter from my lawyer about the restitution business (you remember, habilitation, etc.). The ministry denied the request at first, which we expected (an appeal to the federal court, or whatever it's called, has been entered anyhow). But in the letter denying the request the thing mentioned as particularly decisive was that the Rahel book had not been completed, because two chapters were missing from it at the time. Now my lawyer, who is in Germany at the moment, writes me that he thinks it possible a statement from you could help—though he is by no means certain. The essence of the statement should be that:

> "this comprehensive work on Rahel, even without the two chapters that were added when it was published as a book, represented a complete habilitation project."[1]

My lawyer would perhaps like to come to Basel to discuss this or a similar statement with you. I wrote him that in view of your health I was not at all sure that you could see him, and I suggested that he take care of everything by mail, etc. But in case he should call, his name is Dr. Randolph H. Newman (alias Neumann). At the moment he is staying in Berlin, Bristol Hotel Kempinski, 1 Berlin 15, Kurfürstendamm 27. Telephone: 8 81 06 91. He is legally very acute, very energetic, in other respects—you'll see if he should get in touch with you. The whole business has been delayed somewhat, unfortunately, because I just got his letter of April 6. It went by way of New York. As for the thing itself, I'm not altogether comfortable with it. A biography customarily ends with the death of the subject. All the statements in the world can't change that. But perhaps . . . If you don't want to make a statement in this regard, please just say no straight off. I really don't think it will help much anyway. But, as I said, this lawyer is very energetic and by no means stupid. And he is of the opinion that I am not taking sufficient interest in this "object" of which I would be the subject.

Forgive this stupid letter. I'm writing under double pressure—from Dr. (! very important) Newman and my so-called duties here. More on that another time. I was at Harvard for a very interesting historians' conference on the Russian Revolution. Only specialists in that field—from England, France, Germany, Holland, and America. Not more than twenty-eight people. I was the only one who was not a specialist, didn't know Russian, etc. Between Harvard and Chicago I flew to New York quickly to say good morning and good night to Heinrich, which he duly appreciated. He is very well. The doctor won't see him again for another three months.

Warmest greetings—I keep thinking of Gertrud's succinct sentence: "We wanted to grow old together. Now we'll have to put up with it."[2] This wonderful closeness.

All best wishes
Your
Hannah

Basel, April 24, 1967

Dear Hannah!

I wrote to Mr. Newman right away.[1] I hope with sufficient emphasis and precision. In my view, you are completely in the right in this matter, and it is worth the trouble.

We are glad that we will see you both and speak with you in August. There are quite a few changes from last year. My neuritis has gotten somewhat worse, with the result that the pain caused by movement cannot be completely eliminated (with cortisone) and that the muscular atrophy makes walking somewhat difficult. But none of it bad. Gertrud is in excellent form. It seems hardly possible that she should have so much initiative and so many ideas at 88.

> Warmest greetings to you and Heinrich
> Your Karl

June 10, 1967

Dearest Friends—

I came home from Chicago quite tired a week and a half ago, and since then we've spent most of our time glued to the radio. The Israelis did a wonderful job,[1] even though Nasser was a paper tiger. I like Dayan's proclamations a lot,[2] and I read yesterday—hidden away somewhere—a report from Jerusalem that said he has suggested to Jordan a federation or confederation. That would solve a lot of problems at one stroke. There's no question that Russia is behind the whole business and will continue to push for a peace conference at which Vietnam could be discussed at the same time. I just heard that the Soviet Union has broken off diplomatic relations and threatened Israel with sanctions. The worst could be yet to come—although I think that as far as Israel is concerned the worst will be significantly less bad than it would have been if Israel had not attacked. But the situation remains somewhat uncomfortable, and we're feeling a little uneasy as we get ready for our trip. I've just written to the Hotel Euler and reserved a room for us starting on August 1.

It seems such an eternity since I heard from you last. Thank you very much for the medical report, which was reassuring for me. Helen Wolff was here yesterday, and we indulged in the fondest of thoughts about you both. She takes great pleasure in the letters you send when you have received royalties. Also, I'm working on some publishing projects with her. She is going to publish a volume of Benjamin's essays here,[3] edited and introduced by me, and I have just signed a contract with Harcourt, Brace for an essay volume—*Men in Dark Times*—in which I will collect all my so-called portraits of recent years. Chicago Press will very soon be publishing the *Bundesrepublik*, with a short foreword by me.[4] It is a good sign that your *Antwort*, too, has been on the bestseller list ever since it was published.

After an unusually cold spring, summer broke out here a few days ago, and I think we will go to our beloved Palenville again at the end of next week. (Address: Chestnut Lawn House, Palenville, N.Y.; telephone: 518 Orange 8-3313. But mail will be promptly forwarded from New York.) At the end of July—I'm not sure exactly when—we'll fly to Zurich and will stay there a few days before we resettle in Basel. We've already booked our return passage by ship—August 30 from Genoa. We'd like to wander around a little more in northern Italy.

My restitution lawyer, with the help of your wonderful letter, seems to have gotten some results after all—which I did not think he would. A very energetic man! At any rate, the matter will be reopened. We'll just have to see.

That's all for today. Really just a sign of life.

Warmly
Your
Hannah

420   *Hannah Arendt to Gertrud and Karl Jaspers*

Jerusalem, August 26, 1967

Dearest Friends—

Just a word to say hello. I won't write until we reach New York. Very nice here, very interesting, very amicable with my family and old friends.

Thoughts of you are with me.

Warmest greetings—Hannah

October 1, 1967

Lieber Verehrtester—

How are you? I don't know where I should picture you to myself
—in your desk chair, newly elevated to a throne,[1] or on the sofa. How
are you managing with the pain?

After Israel we had a few lovely days in Genoa in a fantastic hotel
in which—God knows from what antediluvian times—not only the
halls and the stairway but also the bathrooms were in marble. Then a
good and restful sea voyage. Whereupon Heinrich topped it all off by
coming down with phlebitis. That's why I'm writing only now. There
was too much to do. It still isn't entirely better but almost as good as
new. With his leg propped up he looked just like one of the cartoons
one often sees: elderly gentleman with gout. The whole thing reminded
him of an old Chaplin film. As you can see, we have weathered this
episode with good humor. And I'm sitting contentedly at home now
because Heinrich's illness gave me a welcome excuse not to go to the
University of Michigan for an honorary doctorate and a huge ceremonial program. Just to be home is wonderful, to think about the
household, get some new linoleum for the kitchen, cook, and do just
almost all these domestic things, and if a human race gone mad had
not invented the telephone, it would all be that much better.

Israel: In many respects, in most actually, very encouraging. It's
really quite wonderful that an entire nation reacts to a victory like that
not by bellowing hurrah but with a real orgy of tourism—everybody
has to go have a look at the newly conquered territory. I was in all
the formerly Arab territories and never noticed any conqueror behavior
in the stream of Israeli tourists. The Arab population was more hostile
than I expected. In the market in Jerusalem (the Old City), the hawkers
who used to run after you turned their backs to the passersby. When
I was there—hardly any open sabotage had occurred yet—the Israelis
were remarkably indifferent to this, like the Germans in Holland. The
West Jordanian territory that was under Hussein,[2] very well admin-
istrated, nothing like what I remember it to have been thirty years
ago. Very good road system, good buildings, no desperate poverty,
the little cities very clean, etc. Just the opposite in the territories that
had been held by the Egyptians, the Gaza strip. Incredibly shabby
except for the big plantations that are cultivated with the most primitive
methods by absentee owners who pay their workers starvation wages.

Revolting. The refugees in the UNRWA camps[3] have it considerably better. They're housed in barracks at least and not in windowless clay huts that could come from the time of the troglodytes. Nasser should be hung instantly. Feudal rule in the worst sense of the term but under the guise of socialism. Things are apparently similar in Syria, but I didn't go there myself. In emplacements on the northern border, large stores of whips were found, which were to be used to encourage the soldiers. Similar things occurred on the Egyptian front in Sinai but not in Transjordan! There is no question that the Israeli military performed well, but also none that they were up against a most extraordinarily inferior opponent. The Israelis have no cause for worry as long as that does not change in any decisive, revolutionary way. But it can change, and it can change very quickly, as one can see from the example of oriental, Arabic-speaking Jews who come from these same backgrounds and who performed admirably in the war. I spent the whole week from early in the morning until late in the evening being driven all over the country. You will recall my family—the Fürsts. They have one son-in-law who, as an Egyptian Jew, speaks fluent Arabic;[4] the other is, as you know, a German,[5] and the two young couples took some time off to show me everything. And that too was quite wonderful. I mean this odd family, the parents half from Königsberg and half from Berlin; the two daughters with these two husbands, of all people. And they all get on famously. The brothers-in-law have the best of relationships. The German speaks fluent Hebrew. A little humanity and everything goes beautifully. I felt very much at ease. And as far as the country itself is concerned, one can see clearly from what great fear it has suddenly been freed. That contributes significantly to improving the national character.

I could say a lot more. I spoke with a great many people there and cleverly avoided all official contact. An old friend who has been in the country for over thirty years thought officialdom would not have been hostile toward me but would surely have sicced a dozen reporters on me to ask what I think about things now.

I still have seen hardly anyone here. Alcopley was here and told about his visit with you. Mary (McCarthy) is here and is hoping to go to Hanoi. She has just published an excellent attack on the Johnson administration.[6] Her husband[7] is in the foreign service, but this won't harm him in the least. There is still some real freedom here, and Johnson is really wiped out. Public opinion as expressed in the papers, the universities, and by writers still counts for something. When all the people concern themselves with what is happening to the country, then so-called historical necessity doesn't amount to much.

Dearest friends, I'm just rattling on because I don't know exactly how things are with you.

Warmest greetings, as always
Your
Hannah

---

422 *Hannah Arendt to Karl Jaspers*

November 25, 1967

Lieber Verehrtester—

I've just finished reading your autobiographical writings[1] (which, incidentally, have already lost their binding after only Heinrich and I have read them—our penny-pinching Piper!). They make a very nice little book. Much was familiar to me—home and youth.[2] The exact story of how you came to leave Heidelberg made exciting reading.[3] I had read it before in *Der Spiegel*.[4] (If you had asked me, I would have thought you shouldn't have mentioned me,[5] not for "private" reasons but because it was an unnecessary diversion and gave your decision another motive that really carried no weight at all.) It is a wonderful portrait of a state of mind that is unfortunately by no means a thing of the past. Very exciting too is the "history of an illness" in all its details, most of them unknown to me. Unique in medical literature, I would think.

I heard from Ashton and Casper that they had heard from you, and I gathered that you are feeling considerably better. Am I mistaken? I was very worried because I hadn't heard anything from you. Your letters to them[6] eased my mind a lot.

I was in Chicago and have just gotten back to New York. Heinrich is very well, but his leg still isn't completely back to normal. Otherwise, hardly anything new to report—except that the country and the universities in particular are in tumult. It's hard to predict what will come of it all. I was very pleased with the students in Chicago. Classes and lectures are going on there more or less undisturbed because the administration and the new president, Edward Levi, in particular are handling things so well. Practically speaking there is always only one key issue: If the students protest, the police must not under any circumstances be called in. As long as that doesn't happen, things don't get out of hand, and the direction student opinion takes hardly ever drifts toward extremes. They get really rebellious only if the administration treats them like criminals, which they clearly are not, and threatens to call in the police or take disciplinary action against them. Then they regard the university as their enemy and no longer see it as a place where controversies can be resolved. And then one might as well close up shop.

With all best wishes—

Warmly
Your
Hannah

Heinrich sends warmest greetings.

423 *Hannah Arendt to Karl and Gertrud Jaspers*

New York, February 20 1968

Lieber Verehrtester, dearest Friends—

The enclosed manuscript,[1] which is of course meant for you both, I wrote for Bavarian Radio, which will presumably be broadcasting it in the course of the day. For today I have nothing more or different to say. The sentence "Loyalty is the mark of truth" is from Heinrich, and everything else here is really written around that.

I'm sorry that I cannot be with you today, as I was five years ago. I could perhaps have come over the weekend for two days, three at the most, but that seemed to me pointless, particularly in the midst of birthday turmoil. I hope these days will bring you a little pleasure in spite of it all.

We sit here much worried. We have no great desire to watch another republic go to the dogs. But as we all know, so-called world history shows little regard for our desires.

All best wishes and warmest greetings

Your
Hannah

Basel, April 4, 1968

Dear Hannah, dear Heinrich,

Karl is on the way to recovery. He brought pneumonia and pleurisy down on himself through his own foolishness. He went about stark naked getting ready for bed and on the next day he was sick. He promises to be careful now. And I will provide him with gentle reminders because he will probably forget. —He is still weak but is eating well and so will get his strength back. He doesn't ask to get up; and, at the doctor's request, I'm not supposed to encourage him. But this morning he did take a few steps with the nurse and Mr. Saner.

Would you please read this bulletin to my friend and cousin? Address: Paul Gottschalk, 84 University Place, New York, N.Y. 10003. He should not worry. Karl is getting better.

Warmly
Your Gertrud

425   *Hannah Arendt to Gertrud and Karl Jaspers*

May 5, 1968

Dearest Friends—

We were much relieved to have Gertrud's medical bulletin, and I'm assuming, because I haven't heard anything further, that things are continuing to improve. I haven't written because I had too much to do. I've just gotten back from Chicago and am still very busy with work related to the New School job. And also with all the things that are going on here. McCarthy[1] is the only real ray of light, but the chances of his being elected are not very good. Still, he has changed the climate in the country decisively, a fact that will remain regardless of what happens in the fall.

I'm writing today to consult with you about possibilities for the summer. Heinrich was not very well this whole winter, and though he is better now, he does not want to go to Europe, and I don't want to leave him alone for a long time. So I will be able to come for only a short time and could fit the trip in best in the second half of June. It's highly unlikely that I could come any earlier. Heinrich will get an honorary doctorate from Bard in mid-June, and I have to be here for that. Before that, right after the semester is over, we want to go to the country for a few weeks, to a good hotel, where we can really rest up. I'm very tired—the semester and the household and politics. Then, when I come back from Europe (Heinrich will have already gone), we'll go as usual to Palenville. None of this is absolutely certain yet. Heinrich will go for another complete physical next week, but I'm almost certain the doctor will give him a clean bill of health.

Let me know how things look for you. I'm flexible after mid-June and can arrange things differently. And in any case—until soon.

As always, with concern and warmest wishes

Your
Hannah

426 Hannah Arendt to Gertrud and Karl Jaspers

June 13, 1968

Dearest Friends—

I'm writing in haste. I can't come. Heinrich had a heart attack, not an infarction. We don't know yet what course it will take. In any case, we have to wait it out. I'll be in touch.

As always
Your
Hannah

427 Karl and Gertrud Jaspers to Hannah Arendt and Heinrich Blücher

Basel, June 17, 1968

Dear Hannah, dear Heinrich!

We share your dismay over Heinrich's heart attack. That is of course still not a catastrophe. But it does introduce a distressing uncertainty, which will, I hope, in the coming weeks and months develop into something you will become accustomed to, one additional danger added to the natural dangers of life. But it will remain an element that alters one's sense of health and security.

Excuse this wretched handwriting. I can't improve on it because of the pain I constantly have to cope with due to this so-called arthritis.

We are sorry that your trip to Europe and to see us will have to be canceled for the time being because of Heinrich's illness. But there is nothing for it.

We are happy. One cannot live by hope alone.

If you feel like it, let us hear from you soon.

Your Karl

As you see, my hand can't write. I think we have reason to be content. It was a great pleasure for us to share in the Saners' good news: in early July he will receive the Hermann Hesse Prize, which carries an award of 10,000 marks.[1] The two of them are buying their festive clothes for the ceremony. And he is preparing his speech. At first I thought I would go along, but I'm too unsteady on my feet. We eagerly await good news from you.

Good-bye and warmest greetings
Your Gertrud

428 *Hannah Arendt to Karl and Gertrud Jaspers*

June 26, 1968

Lieber Verehrtester, dearest Friends—

Your handwritten letter gave us great pleasure. It just goes to show how much we cling to the concrete and visible.

I'm writing today only to let you know that Heinrich is doing astonishingly well. The doctor had him admitted to the hospital because he was worried that an infarction might be coming on. Instead, Heinrich recovered very rapidly there. His electrocardiogram is completely normal again, and everything else is in the best of order. He was discharged from the hospital last week and has been following a nearly normal routine at home since then—just living carefully and eating salt-free. But well supplied with schnapps, and he can smoke pipes and cigars (which are not inhaled) with moderation. Tomorrow, the college, which awarded him an honorary doctorate, will send a delegation, including the president, to make up for the ceremony he missed. I've already laid in the champagne, and the caviar, too, which Heinrich isn't allowed to eat. If everything continues as it is, the doctor will probably let us go to Palenville in early or mid-July. The doctor was really worried at first but isn't any longer. He thinks that with a little caution and no severe restrictions Heinrich can live comfortably and well with this thing. He wasn't really himself all winter, and now he is better than he has been for a long time. The fatigue is gone, too.

We were both very happy to hear about Saner's Hesse Prize. Early recognition is a really nice thing. Give him our regards and our congratulations. —The letter that Gertrud forwarded was from my niece, who is moving with her husband[1] to Regensburg, where he is taking on his first job. She still has some exam to complete at the university in Vienna herself. A very pleasant situation for them. She thought I was already in Basel. I had neglected to let her know in time about my change in plans.

I could say a lot about politics. It seems to me that children in the next century will learn about the year 1968 the way we learned about the year 1848. I also have a personal interest. "Danny the Red" Cohn-Bendit[2] is the son of very good friends of ours from our Paris days, both of them dead now.[3] I know the boy. He visited us here, and I've seen him in Germany, too. A thoroughly good sort. The major factor here is McCarthy, who has all the young people on his side. Things are in an extremely dangerous state here, too; but I sometimes think this is the only country where a republic at least still has a chance. And besides that, one has the feeling that one is among friends.

All our best. Warmly — Hannah

429 *Hannah Arendt to Gertrud and Karl Jaspers*

Palenville, July 27, 1968

Dearest Friends—

I wanted to wait a bit and see how things went with Heinrich. He is doing beautifully. It's always the same story. He becomes very ill; the doctors are pessimistic; he goes to the hospital—and suddenly the whole thing is over. When he was very young he suffered for six months from diarrhea that refused to yield to any treatment, and he was reduced to skin and bones. The doctors whispered TB and gave him up for dead. Whereupon his friend Robert said: If you're going to die anyhow, we ought to take a trip to Italy first. So they climbed into Robert's car, and after a week Heinrich was completely healthy, and they had a look at Italy together for the first time. These events don't faze him in the least. I was the one who had to recover from my fright. He takes things as they come. He wasn't at all upset even during his really awful heart attack.

If things continue to go well with him, I'll probably come for at least a short visit. But I want to keep an eye on things here for at least another month. The doctor is very optimistic now. Thank God we got out of New York just in time to avoid the real heat wave. The evenings are always cool here, and during the day it's pleasantly warm. Politically, things don't look very good. Wallace,[1] the racist candidate from Alabama, is gaining ground every day, and no one knows how the two big party conventions will end. I've been able to watch first-hand the student rebellion at Columbia (which is very near us). The university has a particularly dreadful administration, and much of what is happening is very understandable. What is not understandable is that the university called in the police. The students sent the president a lengthy memo last October to which he never responded. He didn't even acknowledge receiving it. That only embittered the students. And there is the Negro question. And the disintegration of the major cities, the collapse of public services, all of it very concrete: the failure of the schools, the police, the postal service, public transportation.

I'm working in peace here—mainly on an essay on power and violence.[2] I'm trying to understand to some degree the experiences of recent years here. But I don't know whether I'll succeed.

How are things with you now—and I mean by that: right now, this very minute? And as I ask that, I can grasp only with difficulty that it is the middle of the night and that you are (I hope) sleeping peacefully. For our part, we will have a glass of wine and play a game of chess before we go to bed. We haven't done that since Paris.

All our very best wishes
Your
Hannah

430 Gertrud Jaspers to Hannah Arendt

Basel, July 31, 1968

Beloved Hannah,

Your letter saying that Heinrich is on his way back to health arrived today. I am very happy for you. With us, the situation is such that Karl is very tired and sleeps a lot. I worry, but he is very patient and philosophical, very loving.

"I can promise you a year."

And we recently celebrated the sixty-first year since we first met[1] —He complains that his memory is fading. Mine left me so much in the lurch when I was still young that I gave up on it altogether. That made life very difficult for me, and it has always made it difficult for others to assess me. But my nature seems to have communicated itself to the people who were important to me. Eventually with you; and very quickly with Heinrich.

After a good night's sleep Karl is lying asleep again in the next room, the most recent *Spiegel* in front of him. Salin visited him yesterday. That's good for him. Rossmann comes, too. And today Hochhuth. That pulls him out of his tiredness. Saner will be back again soon. That will be nice for both of us.

A sad letter? But we laugh with Erna, whose cheerful nature is such a blessing.

And in the Jewish "Kaddish" prayer it says: "What is man that Thou shouldst think of him?" Legalistic religion destroyed so much. My mother's[2] religiosity was deep and filled our home with love.

Thinking fondly of you
Your Gertrud

---

431   *Hannah Arendt to Gertrud and Karl Jaspers*

Palenville, August 20, 1968

Dearest Friends—

Heinrich is doing so well that I've decided to make a quick trip after all—though I'll be able to stay only a week or so. If things work out as I expect them to, I'll be there on Sunday, September 1. I'll stay at the Euler again and will call. I still haven't booked my flight, and it's possible I won't get there until the 2nd.[1]

Everything else when I see you.

Warmest greetings
Your
Hannah

And thank you for Gertrud's good letter!

---

432   *Hannah Arendt to Gertrud and Karl Jaspers*

October 8, 1968

Dearest Friends—

Saner has written, and so now I know. And I am sitting here thinking about you both and about the parting that is before us, just when, we

683

cannot know. But what is going through my mind and what I feel is beyond the grasp of language—among other reasons, because I am overcome by gratitude for all you have given me.

With love
Your
Hannah

433 Telegram, Gertrud Jaspers to Hannah Arendt

Basel, February 26, 1969

Karl died 1:43 PM, Central European Time.[1]

Trude

Speech given by Hannah Arendt at the public memorial service for Karl Jaspers, University of Basel, March 4, 1969

We have come together, in the public arena that he loved and honored, to take leave of Karl Jaspers. We want to make clear to the world that when he left it—as a very old man and after an amazingly happy and blessed life—something vanished from it. As *he* spoke, no one else is speaking, has spoken, or probably will speak again for some time to come. That shows us what we have lost, but that is not the important thing here. For ultimately, Goethe's line applies: "For the earth will bring them forth again, as it has always brought them forth from time immemorial." The important thing is that those who hear and understand his language do not become fewer.

Earthly humans need bodily existence. Even those who knew only his works and not the man needed the assurance that there was someone behind the books—in Basel, on Austrasse—with a living voice and gestures. For only that guarantees that what is in the books was reality and that what was real in one person should also be possible for everyone else. He wanted to be and could be an example for others.

But by that I do not mean in writing books. The books are an expression of and symbol for a unique way of being in the world, of being a man among men. Every so often someone emerges among us who realizes human existence in an exemplary way and is the bodily incarnation of something that we would otherwise know only as a concept or ideal. In a singular way, Jaspers exemplified in himself, as it were, a fusion of freedom, reason, and communication. In his life he represented that fusion in exemplary form, so that, in reflecting on it, he could describe it in such a way that we from henceforth cannot think of these three things—reason, freedom, and communication—as separate but have to think of them as a trinity.

That Jaspers became a philosopher—and not a psychiatrist or politician—was not a given for him at birth. He often said that without the illness that did not determine his life but only the way he had to live he probably would never have become a professor of philosophy. Whenever he talked that way, I always thought about that passage in *The Republic* where Plato says half ironically that the fruitful soils for philosophy are either exile or a certain sickliness or a small, insignificant country where one cannot make one's mark in a life of action. (Would Plato have become a philosopher if things had stood better with Athens?)

Since Plato there have not been many philosophers for whom action and politics represented a serious temptation. But Jaspers? He could have said with Kant, "It is so sweet to think up constitutions." And if he had not been born in a country that ruins its great political talents in a mysterious way or doesn't let them come to full expression, and if he had not been ill, it would have been easy to imagine him as a statesman. And in a certain sense, this basic gift, just as strong as his philosophical one, did come into its own in him after 1945. For almost a quarter century he was the conscience of Germany, and that this conscience resided on Swiss soil, in a republic and in a city that is a kind of polis, is surely no mere coincidence. He was born for the ways of a democratic republic, and he took the greatest of pleasure in human exchange that was conducted in that spirit. Nothing, in any case, pleased him so much in recent years as the conferring on him of Swiss citizenship. He used to say that for the first time he could be in agreement with a state. That was no rejection of Germany. He knew that citizenship and nationality did not need to coincide—for he was and remained a German—but he knew too that citizenship was not merely a formality either.

We don't know what happens when a human being dies. All we know is that he has left us. We cling to the works, and yet we know that the works don't need us. They are what someone who dies leaves behind in the world that was there before he came and will go on when he leaves it. What becomes of them depends on the course the world

685

takes. But the simple fact that these books represent lived life—that fact does not become immediately apparent to the world and can be forgotten. What is at once the most fleeting and at the same time the greatest thing about him—the spoken word and the gesture unique to him—those things die with him, and they put a demand on us to remember him. That remembering takes place in communication with the dead person, and from that arises talk about him, which then resounds in the world again. Communication with the dead—that has to be learned, and we are beginning to learn it now in the communion of our mourning.

Notes

Special abbreviations used in these notes:

A.   Arendt   L.   letter

J.   Jaspers   n.   note

Letter 1

1. In the summer semester of 1926, J. gave a seminar titled "Schelling, besonders seine Philosophe der Mythologie und Offenbarung." L. 110 indicates that this letter was written in connection with the seminar.
2. Handwritten remark by J.: "not interpret but communicate."
3. It was J.'s practice to answer questions like these in the seminar sessions. Therefore, there is no reply from him in the form of a letter.

Letter 2

1. In a conversation, J. had pointed out flaws in A.'s dissertation, *Der Liebesbegriff bei Augustin. Versuch einer philosophischen Interpretation.* (For its publication, see L. 10, n.1.) She had not yet fully completed it, but, despite that, J. recommended that she receive her doctorate. The oral exam was held on November 26, 1928. J.'s assessment follows. He rec-ommended a grade no higher than II-I (cum laude).
    "A philosophical interpretation of Augustine demands the ability to perceive, in reading a text that is largely rhetorical and preacherly, the intellectual structures and the pearls in which the intellectual content is concentrated and which leap out at one here and there in their brilliance. A reader of this difficult text will catch only occasional glimpses of the text's real subject. The writer of this dissertation has the ability to spot the essentials. She has not simply gathered together everything that Augustine says about love. She has chosen to omit some important ideas— for example, that about love and cognition and all the edifying formula-tions. She set herself the task of delineating intellectual structures, laying them out clearly, and working them through. While studies like Maus-bach's (on Augustine's ethics) gather material together and so have a reductive and softening effect, this study draws distinct lines, and the positions that Augustine takes within them are let stand in all their sharpness.
    "The three sections deal with Augustine's understanding of love in terms of its three different sources: the idea of death, which makes the earthly *appetitus* pointless; the idea of true being; the idea of the community of the history of man since Adam. The first section, the simplest one, is in my opinion absolutely clear, in every point complete and flawless. The second part, more difficult and interesting in its subject matter, tends to wander in some passages; in others, ideas remain undeveloped. In the quotations some errors appear, some of which have been corrected, others of which require more work. The third section is not finished yet but clearly shows the path the study will follow.

"As a mode of objective understanding, the method does some violence to the text. The foreword and the execution of the whole make clear that no attention is given to the great transformations in Augustinian thought that came about in the course of his life. Neither historical nor philosophical interests are primary here. The impulse behind this work is ultimately something not explicitly stated: through philosophical work with ideas the author wants to justify her freedom from Christian possibilities, which also attract her. She does not try to assemble the didactic pieces of the whole into a system, but focuses instead on how they do not fit together, and so gains insight into the existential origins of these ideas.

"That she sometimes assigns too rigid meanings to words that Augustine used interchangeably in contrasting groups, such as *amor, caritas, delectio* on the one hand, *cupiditas, concupiscentia* on the other, is defensible, but she has not always escaped the danger of having Augustine say things that are not in the text. Some of these errors have been corrected as a result of our discussions. But in view of the real accomplishment here, which is one of objective philosophizing with historical material, this failing mars the work but does not invalidate it. I hope that it has been reduced to a minimum. But because of it, this otherwise impressive work, outstanding in its positive content, can unfortunately not be given the highest grade. Therefore: II-I."

Letter 3

1. Selma Stern-Täubler, 1890–1981, was a historian and wife of Eugen Täubler, professor of ancient history at Heidelberg University.
2. Akademie für die Wissenschaft des Judentums, in Berlin.
3. In 1929, A. began work on her book about Rahel Varnhagen, which was not published until after World War II, first in English translation: *Rahel Varnhagen: The Life of a Jewess* (London, 1958); then in German: *Rahel Varnhagen: Lebensgeschichte einer deutschen Jüdin aus der Romantik* (Munich, 1959). Rahel Varnhagen, 1771–1833, was a German-Jewish literary figure. Her salon in Berlin was for a long time a meeting place for the Romantics and later for the writers of the "Young Germany" school. Her correspondence and memoirs are among the most important documents of the late Romantic period.

Letter 4

1. Augustine, *De Genesi ad litteram libri duodecim.*

Letter 5

1. Benno von Wiese, 1903–1987, later a Germanist in Bonn, was a student of J.'s and a close friend of A. in their youth. His doctoral dissertation was *Friedrich Schlegel: Ein Beitrag zur Geschichte der romantischen Konversionen* (Berlin, 1927).

2. *Aurelii Augustini Opera omnia*, ed. J. P. Migne, *Patrologia latina 32–47*.
3. *Aurelii Augustini Opera omnia, Corpus Scriptorum Ecclesiasticorum Latinorum* (Vienna-Leipzig).
4. Notgemeinschaft der deutschen Wissenschaft, predecessor of the present Deutsche Forschungsgemeinschaft.
5. See L. 3, n. 3.
6. Günther Stern, b. 1902, became well known later as a writer under the name Günther Anders.

Letter 6
1. Martin Heidegger, 1889–1976, German philosopher, was at this time a friend of J.'s. A. had studied with him in 1924–25.
2. Martin Dibelius, 1883–1947, Protestant theologian, was, from 1915, professor for exegesis of the New Testament at the University of Heidelberg. A. studied theology with him.

Letter 10
1. The publishing house of Julius Springer in Berlin. From 1925, J. published the dissertations of his students in the series Philosophische Forschungen. The ninth and last dissertation in the series was Hannah Arendt's *Der Liebesbegriff bei Augustin. Versuch einer philosophischen Interpretation* (Berlin, 1929).

Letter 14
1. Probably a lecture on Rahel Varnhagen; not preserved in J.'s literary remains.

Letter 19
1. Karl Jaspers, *Die geistige Situation der Zeit*, Sammlung Göschen, vol. 1000 (Berlin, 1931).
2. Not in J.'s literary remains.
3. Paul J. Tillich, 1886–1965, a Protestant theologian, had been, since 1929, professor of philosophy at the University of Frankfurt. He emigrated in 1933, taught at Union Theological Seminary in New York, 1933–55; was University Professor at Harvard, 1955–62; then, John Nuveen Professor of Theology at the University of Chicago.
4. An essay of this description cannot be located.

Letter 20
1. See L. 19, n. 2.

Letter 21

1. Karl Jaspers, *Philosophie*, 3 vols. (Berlin, 1932).
2. Vol. 3 of *Philosophie*.

Letter 22

1. Karl Jaspers, *Max Weber: Deutsches Wesen im politischen Denken, im Forschen und Philosophieren* (Oldenburg in Oldenburg, 1932). For later editions, J. changed the title to *Max Weber: Politiker—Forscher—Philosoph*.
2. *Ibid.*, 7.
3. *Ibid.*, 21.
4. "Max Weber als Forscher."
5. Hannah Arendt-Stern, "Aufklärung und Judenfrage," in *Zeitschrift für die Geschichte der Juden in Deutschland* 4, no. 2/3 (1932): 65–77.
6. Afra Geiger, a Jewish friend of Gertrud J. and student of J. and Heidegger, died in the Ravensbrück concentration camp.

Letter 23

1. Jaspers, *Max Weber*, 65.
2. The work was published by Verlag Gerhard Stalling as a volume in the series Schriften an die Nation.

Letter 25

1. See L. 22, n. 5.
2. Karl Hillebrand, 1829–1884, was a historian and journalist. His essay was "Rahel, Varnhagen und ihre Zeit," in his *Zeiten, Völker und Menschen*, vol. 2, *Wälsches und Deutsches*, 2nd ed. (Strassburg, 1892): 417–58.

Letter 28

1. What these "belated thanks" refer to could not be determined. It is possible that J. responded to L. 27, in a letter that has not been preserved.

Letter 29

1. J. had been invited to the Rencontres at Schloss Colpach, where artists, scholars, and politicians met every year.
2. A., who was living in Paris as a stateless emigrant, wanted to meet J. at Colpach. The meeting did not take place because of the "infinitely complex red-tape existence of stateless persons"; see L. 34.
3. Pierre Viénot, 1897–1944, was undersecretary in the French Foreign Office in the government of Léon Blum. When France fell to the Germans, he fled to North Africa. After a period of imprisonment in France, he became

ambassador to England for De Gaulle's government-in-exile. He died shortly before France was liberated.

4. Aline Mayrisch de Saint-Hubert, 1874–1947, literary figure, patron, and friend of many well-known persons, mainly German and French, was hostess of the Rencontres at Colpach.

5. Hans Pollnow was a translator J. met at Colpach. Among his works is a translation into French of J.'s book on Descartes. On A.'s relationship with Pollnow, see L. 39.

Letter 30

1. Melvin J. Lasky, b. 1920, was a U.S. journalist; in 1943–45, an army historian in France and Germany. After the war, he visited J. frequently. Later he founded and coedited the periodical *Der Monat.*

2. A. published many essays in the United States from 1941 on. Which of them is meant here cannot be determined.

3. Hans Jonas, b. 1903, philosopher and historian of religion, emigrated to England in 1933, to Palestine in 1935. He went to Canada in 1949, and from 1955 was a professor at the New School for Social Research in New York, where A. started teaching in 1968. They had been friends since they studied together in Marburg in 1924. J. had known Jonas since the publication of the first part of his gnosis studies: Hans Jonas, *Die mythologische Gnosis,* pt. 1 (Göttingen, 1934).

4. In 1938, the Reich Publication Office started making it difficult for Jaspers to publish, and in 1943 it forbid all publication by him.

5. Karl Jaspers, "Erneuerung der Universität: Rede, gehalten zur Eröffnung der medizinischen Kurse an der Universität Heidelberg am 15.8.1945." First printed in *Die Wandlung* 1 (1945–46): 66–74.

6. The philosophy faculty began teaching again on January 8, 1946. In September 1945, J. had already been officially reinstated in his post, retroactive to April 1 of that year.

7. In the first semester after the resumption of classes, one of J.'s lecture courses was on the "intellectual situation in Germany." He developed his book *Die Schuldfrage* from this lecture series; see L. 38, n. 2.

8. Gertrud J. enclosed the following message: "Dear Hannah Arendt, I send you my warmest greetings. I was so pleased to read your essays. Unfortunately, I know little English, and my hardness of hearing is troublesome to me. Life is hectic now, visitors all day long! It would interest you. My husband is flourishing again after a dreadful winter and now that the regime has collapsed. He is happy and active. —I think you are an excellent housewife! Thank you very much! Your Gertrud Jaspers."

Letter 31

1. In 1933 and after, J. tried to arrange a teaching position in Zurich. In connection with this effort, he lectured there in March 1936 on "Das radikal Böse bei Kant" ("Radical Evil in Kant"). For reasons that cannot

be determined, he was not offered a post. Yet the rumor spread that he was teaching in Zurich.

2. See L. 30, n. 5.

3. *Partisan Review* was a literary magazine revived in New York in 1937 by William Phillips and Philip Rahv.

4. See L. 30, n. 7.

5. Sigrid Undset, 1882–1949, a Norwegian writer, published in October 1945, an essay, "The Reeducation of the Germans," to which J. responded on November 4, 1945, in *Die Neue Zeitung* ("An American newspaper for the German population"). The essay and J.'s response were reprinted in Karl Jaspers, *Die Antwort an Sigrid Undset . . .* (Constance, 1947).

6. *Die Wandlung: Eine Monatsschrift*, edited by Dolf Sternberger, with Karl Jaspers, Werner Krauss, and Alfred Weber on the editorial board, was published in Heidelberg, 1945–49.

7. Dolf Sternberger, 1907–1989, was a German journalist and political scientist; editor of the *Frankfurter Zeitung*, 1934–43; from 1945, editor of *Die Wandlung*; became a professor of political science at Heidelberg in 1960. He was a friend of A. and J.

8. Hannah Arendt, "Approaches to the German Problem," *Partisan Review* 12, no. 1 (Winter 1945): 93–106.

9. Beginning in 1941, A. worked for the Commission on European Jewish Cultural Reconstruction. From 1949 to 1952, she was executive director of Jewish Cultural Reconstruction, an organization established in 1948 to locate and reclaim Jewish books and religious objects.

10. From 1945 to 1947, A. taught European history in the Graduate Division of Brooklyn College.

11. Heinrich Blücher, 1899–1970, an autodidact and member, in 1919, of the Communist party of Germany, met A. in 1936, in Paris. They married in 1940. He started lecturing on the philosophy of art at the New School for Social Research in New York in 1950, and was professor of philosophy at Bard College, Annandale-on-Hudson, New York, from 1952 to 1968.

12. Edouard Daladier, 1884–1970, chairman of the Radical Socialist party, was premier of France in 1933–34.

13. Bertolt Brecht, *Gesammelte Werke* 8 (Frankfurt, 1967): 815.

Letter 32

1. Erna Dugend-Jaspers, 1885–1974, was two years younger than J. They remained closely attached all his life.

2. Hannah Arendt, "Race-Thinking before Racism," *The Review of Politics* 6, no. 1 (January 1944): 36–73; "Imperialism, Nationalism, Chauvinism," *The Review of Politics* 7, no. 4 (October 1945): 441–63.

3. Hannah Arendt, "German Guilt," *Jewish Frontier Anthology 1934–45* (New York, 1945): 470–81. Previously published as "Organized Guilt and Universal Responsibility," *Jewish Frontier* 12, no. 1 (January 1945): 19–23.

4. *Von der Wahrheit*, vol. 1 of *Philosophische Logik*, was written during the

war but could not be published until 1947, when it came out in Munich. See also L. 103, n. 3.

5. J. also wrote during the war the "completely revised" fourth edition of his 1913 *Allgemeine Psychopathologie* (Berlin/Heidelberg, 1946).

6. See L. 29.

7. The theological faculty of the University of Heidelberg, like the medical faculty, resumed teaching in November 1945, before the university as a whole reopened. J. gave a lecture course there, "Einführung in die Philosophie," for two hours each week.

8. In the context of his "Einführung in die Philosophie."

9. See L. 31, n. 8.

10. See n. 3.

11. Dwight Macdonald, 1906–1982, was editor of *Politics*. The article referred to is his "The Responsibility of Peoples," *Politics* (March 1945): 82–93.

12. J.'s relationship with Thomas Mann, 1875–1955, was one of cool distance, which was played down somewhat in this letter.

13. Thomas Mann, *Friedrich und die grosse Koalition* (Berlin, 1915).

14. This probably refers to Mann's speech "Deutschland und die Deutschen," which appeared in Stockholm, in *Neue Rundschau* (October 1945).

15. Thomas Mann, *Deutsche Hörer! Fünfundfünfzig Radiosendungen nach Deutschland*, 2nd, enlarged, ed. (Stockholm, 1945). J. had bought, in 1918, the *Betrachtungen eines Unpolitischen* (Berlin, 1918) and had probably read it then.

16. Golo Mann, b. 1909, studied for his doctorate under J. and received it in 1932 with a dissertation on Hegel: Gottfried Mann, *Zum Begriff des Einzelnen, des Ich, und des Individuellen bei Hegel* (Heidelberg, 1935). J. maintained a close friendship with him for many years—until their disagreement over A.'s Eichmann book.

17. Franz Werfel, 1890–1945, poet, dramatist, and novelist, died on August 28 in California.

Letter 33

1. Hasso von Seebach, b. 1909, was a friend of Adam von Trott (see L. 50 and L. 50, n. 3) during their university years.

Letter 34

1. See Ls. 29 and 32.

2. See L. 31, n. 5.

3. *New Yorker Staats-Zeitung und Herold* was a German-language newspaper in New York, founded in 1835.

4. Karl Jaspers, "Geleitwort," *Die Wandlung* 1: 3–6.

5. A. was hoping that Macdonald would publish in *Politics* the *Wandlung* introduction and the speech "Erneuerung der Universität"; see L. 30, n. 5.

6. Leo Baeck, 1873–1956, German-Jewish theologian, was, in 1933, presi-

dent of the Reich Committee of German Jews. He spent 1943–45 in Theresienstadt concentration camp; after the war, he became a highly respected representative of liberal Jewry and honorary president of the World Congress of Progressive Jewry.

7. Hans Delbrück, 1848–1929, was a historian who taught at the University of Berlin from 1896 to 1921.

8. Martha Arendt-Cohn, 1874–1948; see L. 55.

9. The organized persecution of the Jews on the night of November 9, 1938 ("Crystal Night"), which resulted in the burning of the synagogues in Germany, in the demolishing of thousands of Jewish shops, in innumerable murders, and in the abduction of more than 30,000 Jews.

10. Walter von Molo, 1880–1958, was an Austrian-German novelist and playwright.

11. See L. 32, n. 3.

12. Hannah Arendt, "Organisierte Schuld," *Die Wandlung* 1 (1945–46): 333–44.

13. Plan of U.S. Secretary of the Treasury Henry Morgenthau, Jr., 1891–1967, the essence of which was reduction of Germany to an agrarian country. It was presented at the 1944 Quebec Conference but rejected by President Roosevelt.

14. Karl Jaspers, *Nietzsche: Einführung in das Verständnis seines Philosophierens* (Berlin/Leipzig, 1936).

15. Paul Oskar Kristeller, b. 1905, historian of philosophy and specialist in the Renaissance, went to the United States in 1939.

16. Ernst Hoffmann, 1880–1952, historian of philosophy, was, from 1922, a professor at Heidelberg and a colleague of J.'s.

Letter 35

1. "Organisierte Schuld"; see L. 34, n. 12.

2. Karl Jaspers, "Vom lebendigen Geist der Universität," in Karl Jaspers and Fritz Ernst, *Vom lebendigen Geist und vom Studieren. Zwei Vorträge* (Heidelberg, 1946): 7–40.

3. Friedrich Gundolf, 1880–1931, literary historian, writer, and friend of J.'s, was, from 1920, professor of literary history at Heidelberg.

4. The inscription, on the university building, read: "Dem lebendigen Geist" ("To the living spirit").

5. In January 1946, J. gave a seminar on Kant's *Kritik der Urteilskraft*.

6. At the same time, he gave two lecture courses: "Einführung in die Philosophie" ("Introduction to Philosophy") and "Die geistige Situation in Deutschland" ("The Intellectual Situation in Germany").

Letter 36

1. Josef Maier, b. 1911 in Leipzig, went to the United States in 1933. At the time this letter was written, he was in the U.S. Army, in Germany,

and, as a friend of A.'s, he got in touch with the Jasperses. He later became professor of sociology at Rutgers University.

2. Not in the literary remains.
3. James D. Collins, "An Approach to Karl Jaspers," *Thought* 20 (1945): 657–691. A. may have meant by "the other" another by Collins: "Philosophy of Existence and Positive Religion," *The Modern Schoolman: A Quarterly Journal of Philosophy* 23, no. 2 (January 1946): 82–100.
4. Karl Löwith, 1897–1973, philosopher and friend of J.'s, emigrated in 1934 by way of Italy and Japan to the United States. In 1952, he became a professor at Heidelberg.
5. This 1946 book by American philosopher George A. N. Santayana, 1863–1952, appeared in German in 1951, as *Die Christusidee in den Evangelien*.
6. John Dewey, 1859–1952, the American philosopher and educator; his *Problems of Men* was published in 1946.
7. Bertrand Russell, 1872–1970, the British mathematician and philosopher, whose *Physics and Experience* was published in 1946; the German translation, *Physik und Erfahrung*, appeared in 1948.
8. Hannah Arendt, "What Is Existenz Philosophy?" *Partisan Review* 13, no. 1 (Winter 1946): 34–56.
9. Slight variation of a sentence from J. in L. 35.

Letter 37

1. It cannot be determined what letter is meant.
2. Marianne Weber, 1870–1954, was the wife of Max Weber and a close friend of J. and Gertrud J.
3. The packages of food that A. supplied right after the war to the Jaspers household and occasionally to friends such as Marianne Weber were often sent in care of Josef Maier and Melvin Lasky.
4. Karl Löwenstein, 1891–1973, went to the United States in 1934. In 1936, he became a professor of political science at Amherst College.
5. Karl Jaspers, "Culture in Ruins: 3 Documents from Germany," in *Politics* (February 1946): 51–56. This was a translation of his "Geleitwort" ("Introduction") to *Die Wandlung*; see L. 34, n. 4.

Letter 38

1. William Phillips; see L. 36.
2. Published as Karl Jaspers, *Die Schuldfrage* (Heidelberg, 1946).
3. See L. 34, n. 12.
4. Kurt Rossmann, 1909–1980, historian of philosophy, was, after the war, J.'s assistant until J. went to Basel. In 1957, he became a professor at Heidelberg, and, in 1964, J.'s successor at the University of Basel.
5. See L. 36, n. 8.
6. Hannah Arendt, "Zionism Reconsidered," *Menorah Journal* 33 (August 1945): 162–96; published in German as "Der Zionismus aus heutiger

Sicht," in Hannah Arendt, *Die verborgene Tradition: Acht Essays* (Frankfurt am Main, 1976): 127–68.

Letter 39

1. L. 37 is meant here, and the letter of April 17, 1946, from Gertrud J. to A. This letter contains a note from J.: "Dear Hannah! Just a word of greeting and thanks for today. I hope a letter sent by way of L. [Lasky] will have reached you by now. I'll write again soon. Our American friend [Lasky] wants to take this letter with him and is waiting for it, therefore my haste! Your Karl Jaspers."
2. Gertrud J. had reported this in her April 17 letter. For Pollnow, see L. 29, n. 5.
3. Walter Benjamin, 1892–1940, was a friend of A.'s during their exile years in Paris. She wanted to help him emigrate; see letter of April 8, 1939, from Benjamin to Gerhard Scholem in Walter Benjamin, *Briefe*, ed. G. Scholem and T. W. Adorno, 2 vols. (Frankfurt am Main, 1966): 810.
4. Gertrud J. wrote, in her letter of April 17: " 'Our' problem is never discussed here. It seems to me as if it were not a fit subject. The only people I can speak with are our American friends, especially the emigrants. The immeasurable want everywhere in Germany is surely an excuse, but for me, this lack of good will widens the breach."
5. In the same letter, Gertrud wrote: "My husband often said to me after '33: 'Trude, I am Germany.' I found that too glib."
6. Waldemar Gurian, 1902–1954, a German journalist, emigrated to the United States in 1937. He became a professor of political science at the University of Notre Dame and editor of *The Review of Politics*.
7. Hermann Broch, 1886–1951, lived in the United States after 1938 and was a friend of A. there. His book *Der Tod des Vergil* was published in New York in 1945.
8. The allusion is to the folk song "Wenn ich ein Vöglein wär' und auch zwei Flüglein hätt', flög ich zu dir . . ." ("If I were a little bird and had two wings, I would fly to you . . .").

Letter 40

1. See L. 36, n. 8.
2. The manuscript is meant. The German version, "Was ist Existenz-Philosophie?" appeared in Hannah Arendt, *Sechs Essays* (Heidelberg, 1948): 48–80.
3. A. wrote in a note to the English text (see L. 36, n. 8) that Heidegger had forbidden his "teacher and friend" Husserl to enter the building used by the philosophy faculty because he "was a Jew." She reported that it was rumored "he had offered his services to the French occupation government [to assist] in the reeducation of the German people."
4. Edmund Husserl, 1859–1938, German philosopher, was the founder of phenomenology.

5. Hannah Arendt, "Privileged Jews," *Jewish Social Studies* 8, no. 1 (January 1946): 3–30.
6. See L. 32, n. 2.
7. Friedrich Krause, ed., *Dokumente des Anderen Deutschland*, vol. 4, *Deutsche innere Emigration: Anti-nationalsozialistische Zeugnisse aus Deutschland* (New York, 1946).
8. Georg P. Fedotov, 1886–1951, was a Russian church historian. The essay referred to is probably G. P. Fedotov, "Russia and Freedom," *New Review*, no. 10 (1945): 189–213.
9. Karl Jaspers, *Die Idee der Universität* (Berlin/Heidelberg, 1946).

Letter 41

1. Hannah Arendt, "Uber den Imperialismus," *Die Wandlung* 1 (1945–46): 650–66.
2. This could refer to the German version of Hannah Arendt, "The Seeds of a Fascist International," *Jewish Frontier* (June 1945): 12–16. But there is no German text of this description in J.'s literary remains.
3. *The Protocols of the Elders of Zion* was a nineteenth-century forgery that describes purported aims and plans of the Jews to achieve world dominance. The authors are unknown. In persecutions of the Jews even before the Nazi period, this book played a prominent role.
4. *The Demons, also known as The Possessed*, appeared in 1871–72.
5. Benjamin Disraeli, 1804–1881, member of Great Britain's Conservative party, was prime minister from 1874 to 1880.
6. Eamon de Valera, 1882–1975, was prime minister of Ireland for many years, then president.
7. Antonio Oliveira Salazar, 1889–1970, was prime minister and virtual dictator of Portugal for many years.
8. See Ls. 22 and 23.
9. This project was never carried out.
10. Friedrich Rückert, *Ausgewählte Werke in sechs Bänden*, ed. Philipp Stein, 2 (Leipzig, n.d.): 338–39.

Letter 42

1. See L. 36, n. 8.
2. A. became acquainted with the existentialist philosopher Jean-Paul Sartre, 1905–1980, during her exile in Paris. It is uncertain whether the reference here is to a meeting after the war or to a letter.
3. Studienstiftung des deutschen Volkes (Scholarship Foundation of the German People) was established in 1925, disbanded in 1934; in 1948, it was reestablished as the Stiftung zur Förderung Hochbegabter (Foundation for the Advancement of the Highly Talented).
4. Ecole Normale Supérieure is the French institute for the education of the intellectual elite.
5. See L. 35, n. 2.

6. Karl Jaspers, "Vom lebendigen Geist der Universität," in Karl Jaspers and Fritz Ernst, *Vom lebendigen Geist und vom Studieren*, 26.
7. Otto Regenbogen, 1891–1966, a classical philologist, was a professor at Heidelberg until 1959.
8. Horst Wessel, 1907–1930, a student and member of the Nazi party, was author of "Die Fahne hoch . . ." (the Horst Wessel song). The National Socialist government gave it a place beside "Deutschland über alles" as a national anthem.
9. Gerhard Ritter, 1888–1967, was a professor of modern history at the University of Freiburg, 1925–56. A. is referring to his "Der deutsche Professor im 'Dritten Reich,' " *Die Gegenwart* 1, no. 1 (December 24, 1945): 23–26; published in English as "The German Professor in the Third Reich," *The Review of Politics* 8, no. 2 (April 1946): 242–54.
10. Salman Schocken, 1877–1959, prominent businessman and publisher, founded Schocken Verlag in Berlin in 1931. He emigrated to Palestine in 1933, and after the war built up his publishing house again in New York, under the name Schocken Books.

Letter 43

1. At first, the term "displaced persons" (DPs) meant the forced laborers and other expatriated, non-German foreigners the Allies found in Germany and in territories occupied by the Germans. Later, it was used in the broadest sense to mean all people driven from their homeland.
2. This was a British military camp at the foot of Mount Carmel in Palestine. It later served as a refugee camp.
3. Illegally immigrating Jews who were caught in Palestine by the British were transferred from the Atlit camp to camps on Cyprus, which was also under British control.
4. *Die Schuldfrage*, 10, 29ff. This book, published by Lambert Schneider (Heidelberg, 1946), was later published by Artemis in Zurich. Quotations are from the latter edition.
5. At the time this letter was written, the verdicts in the Nuremberg trials of Nazi leaders accused of war crimes had not been reached.
6. See *Die Schuldfrage*, 11, 48ff.
7. Karl Jaspers, "Thesen über politische Freiheit," *Die Wandlung* 1 (1945–46): 460–65.
8. See *Die Wandlung* 1 (1945–46): 172–75, 527–37.
9. Karl Jaspers, "Von der biblischen Religion," *Die Wandlung* 1 (1945–46): 406–13.
10. Paul Herzog, b. 1902, was a German journalist and publisher, and author of "Cholm-Schädelstätte," *Die Wandlung* 1 (1945–46): 431–48.
11. Alfred Dreyfus, 1859–1935, was an officer in the French army who was convicted and sentenced to deportation for life because of alleged treason. The resultant controversy spread throughout France during 1894–1906. Emile Zola fought prominently for his rehabilitation. He was ultimately freed and completely exonerated. He had been the first Jew on the French

general staff, and was the victim of strong anti-Semitic sentiment in France.

12. In September 1946, J. went to the Recontres Internationales in Geneva.
13. A. became acquainted with French writer Albert Camus, 1913–1960, during her exile in Paris.
14. Jean Wahl, 1888–1974, a French philosopher, became a professor at the Sorbonne in 1927. He wrote several articles about J. and was among the first to introduce J. and German existential philosophy to France.
15. Alphonse de Waelhens, b. 1911, was a Belgian philosopher and professor at the University of Louvain.
16. Alphonse de Waelhens, "Un véritable existentialisme: la philosophie de Karl Jaspers," *Orbe* 2, no. 5 (1946): 11–25.

Letter 44

1. Karl Jaspers, "Vom europäischen Geist," lecture given at the Rencontres Internationales, September 1946. This lecture, with those of the other participants and the records of discussions, is printed in *L'Esprit européen: Textes in-extenso des conférences et des entretiens organisés par les Rencontres Internationales de Genève 1946* (Neuchâtel, 1947): 291–323.
2. Ernst Mayer, 1883–1952, physician and philosopher brother of Gertrud J., worked intensively with J. on his *Philosophie* and was, in his own writings, perhaps J.'s most important "fellow philosopher." See Karl Jaspers, *Philosophische Autobiographie*, revised and enlarged ed. (Munich, 1977): 47–53, and Karl Jaspers, "Lebenslauf Ernst Mayers," *Arztliche Mitteilungen* 37, no. 24 (1952): 543–44.
3. Paul Gottschalk, 1880–1970, book dealer and cousin of Gertrud J., was close to Karl and Gertrud Jaspers all his life. See Paul Gottschalk, "Memoiren eines Antiquars," special reprint from *Börsenblatt für den Deutschen Buchhandel* (Frankfurt am Main, n.d.).
4. Stephen Spender, b. 1909, British poet and critic; for his lecture, see *L'Esprit européen*, 215–33.
5. This refers to Gundolf's affiliation with the George circle, a group of literary apostles who collected around German poet Stefan George.
6. Georges Bernanos, 1888–1948, French novelist and political writer; for his lecture, see *L'Esprit européen*, 263–90.
7. Abraham a Sancta Clara, 1644–1709, was one of the most eloquent preachers of the post-Reformation period.
8. Julien Benda, 1867–1956, French philosopher and writer; for his lecture, see *L'Esprit européen*, 9–36.
9. It is noteworthy that in this letter J. does not mention the presence of Georg Lukács (1885–1971). J. took part in the discussion of Lukács' lecture, just as Lukács did in the discussion of Jaspers'. The controversy between them was regarded as one of the high points of the entire event. J. and Gertrud J. were also present at a reception the Hungarian Library in Geneva gave in Lukács' honor.
10. See L. 36, n. 8.
11. Lambert Schneider, 1900–1970, was a publisher who had also headed

Schocken Verlag, 1931–38, and the Carl Winter Universitätsverlag, in Heidelberg. After the war, he established his own publishing house, Lambert Schneider, in Heidelberg.

12. See L. 41, n. 1.
13. Presumably not L. 41 (which is also about the Jewish problem), because A. discusses L. 41 in L. 43. A letter must have been lost, or J.'s memory failed him here.
14. In the winter semester 1946-47, J.'s lecture course was "Deutsche Gegenwart und Philosophie" ("Germany Today and Philosophy").
15. In the summer semester of 1946, J.'s lecture course was "Von der Wahrheit" ("On Truth").
16. In the summer semester of 1946 and in the following winter semester, J. conducted a seminar on problems in the philosophy of history.

Letter 45

1. Dodo Singer-Mayer, daughter of Gertrud J.'s brother Arthur Mayer.
2. *Time* 48, no. 13 (September 23, 1946): 28–29. See L. 44, n. 1.
3. Georges Bernanos, *Les grandes cimetières sous la lune* (Paris, 1938); in English, *A Diary of My Times* (1938).
4. Georges Bernanos, *Lettre aux Anglais* (Rio de Janeiro/Algiers, 1943); in English, *A Plea for Liberty* (1944).
5. Gertrud J. to A. on August 15, 1946.

Letter 46

1. This reference must be to L. 44, from Zurich.
2. Hannah Arendt, *Sechs Essays* (Heidelberg, 1948).
3. Karl Jaspers, *Allgemeine Psychopathologie*, 4th, completely revised ed. (Berlin/Heidelberg, 1946).
4. Johannes Hoops, 1865–1949, was professor of English at Heidelberg from 1901.
5. See L. 43.
6. This passage may have influenced the subtitle of A.'s *Eichmann in Jerusalem: A Report on the Banality of Evil.*
7. See L. 42.
8. See L. 42.
9. See L. 40.
10. Victor Gollancz, 1893–1967, was a British publisher, writer, and humanitarian.
11. Gustav Mayer, 1871–1948, Gertrud J.'s brother, was a historian of the German workers' movement.
12. See Hannah Arendt, "Die verborgene Tradition," in her *Sechs Essays*, 84ff.

Letter 47

1. This refers to a report in a letter of October 28, 1946, from Gertrud J.
2. From his youth, J. suffered from bronchiectasis, secondary cardiac insufficiency, and chronic hemorrhages. See his "Krankheitsgeschichte," in *Schicksal und Wille: Autobiographische Schriften*, ed. H. Saner (Munich, 1967): 109–42.
3. See the end of L. 44.
4. "Wir spüren noch, worauf es ankommt, aber wir haben es nicht mehr." Notes on the Rencontres de l'esprit européen in Geneva. *Die Weltwoche* (September 20, 1946).
5. See L. 45, n. 2.
6. See L. 42, no. 10.
7. From Nietzsche's poem "Vereinsamt." The first stanza ends with the line "Happy the man who still has—a homeland!" The last one ends: "Woe to him who has no homeland!"

Letter 48

1. Not in the literary remains.
2. Before the founding of the Federal Republic of Germany, the Information Control Division issued licenses for printed matter.

Letter 49

1. The following declaration accompanied this letter dated "Heidelberg, November 30, 1946": "Dear Hannah Arendt! Regarding the translation of my book *Die Schuldfrage* in America, I make the following declaration: 1. According to the terms of my contract with the publisher Lambert Schneider, I possess the translation rights. 2. I herewith give to you these translation rights to dispose of as you see fit. With warmest greetings   Karl Jaspers"
2. This was the "enclosed sheet of paper" mentioned in L. 46.
3. J. wrote "CID," which was the abbreviation for the Criminal Investigation Division; surely what he meant was the Information Control Division (ICD).
4. Not in the literary remains.
5. *Commentary* had asked for the translation rights to "Vom europäischen Geist."
6. De la Baconnière published the volumes of the Rencontres Internationales de Genève.
7. Karl Jaspers, *Vom europäischen Geist* (Munich, 1947).

Letter 50

1. Karl Jaspers, *Psychologie der Weltanschauungen* (Berlin, 1919).
2. See L. 46, n. 1.

3. Adam von Trott zu Solz, 1909–1944, a German diplomat, was sentenced to death and executed in connection with the July 20, 1944, attempt to assassinate Hitler.
4. See L. 31, n. 10.

Letter 52

1. Not in the literary remains.
2. The title of the lecture course in the summer semester of 1947 was "Geschichte der Philosophie im Altertum" ("History of Philosophy in the Ancient World").
3. Issue No. 12 of *Die Wandlung*.
4. A conference of foreign ministers took place in Moscow in March–April 1947 with the purpose of forming a unified German administration. No agreement was reached.
5. Victor Gollancz's book *In Darkest Germany*, widely read at the time, appeared in London in January 1947. It is uncertain whether J. is referring to this book or, possibly, to a talk Gollancz gave in Germany.
6. Presumably an allusion to *In Darkest Germany*, 118–19.

Letter 53

1. Not in the literary remains.
2. The U.S. military government's regulations on commercial dealing with enemy countries placed severe limitations on publication of German writers and specified, among other things, that income from translations made in the United States was to be paid to the U.S. Treasury.
3. Hermann Weyl, 1885–1955, a German mathematician and philosopher, went to the Institute for Advanced Study in Princeton in 1933.
4. To Hannah Arendt's *Sechs Essays*. Major sections of this copy of a draft are identical with those in the printed version, but the last page and a half was heavily reworked and considerably expanded. It was made available again in 1976 in Hannah Arendt, *Die verborgene Tradition: Acht Essays*, 7–11.

Letter 54

1. In the draft of the dedicatory preface was a passage that A. later revised: "I could hardly know at that time how difficult it would be someday to meet people without suspicion, and that a time would come when doing so, which reason and attentiveness to the individual so clearly demand of us, could appear to be an act of rash, profligate optimism. What, after all, has in the meantime become more natural and obvious than to ask every German we meet: Which of us did you murder?"
2. From a passage that is the same in both draft and printed versions: "None of the following essays was, I hope, written without awareness of the facts

of our time and without awareness of the Jewish fate in our century. But in none of them, I think and hope, have I taken this basis of fact as a given, in none have I accepted the world created by those facts as necessary and indestructible."

3. This refers to a passage in the draft, which appears in somewhat different form in the printed version: "First of all, the few who exist in all nations have to try to communicate with each other. If they are to do that, it is important that they not cling desperately to their own national pasts, pasts that can't explain anything anyhow (for Auschwitz cannot be explained by German history any more than it can by Jewish history); that they know that the Flood is upon us and that we are all like Noah in his ark; and that they are still able to summon up gratitude for the fact that there are still, relatively, so many Noahs who are floating about on the seas of the world and trying to steer their arks as close to one another as they can."

4. See L. 41 and L. 41, n. 9.

5. See L. 43.

Letter 55

1. This was the contract for the translation of *Die Schuldfrage*.

2. A letter of March 6, 1947, from the London publishing firm Secker & Warburg inquiring about the possibility of an edition of *Die Schuldfrage* for England.

3. Hermann Weyl wrote to A. March 19, 1947, about various writings by J.

4. The lecture was not enclosed with the letter (see L. 56), nor was it later included in the English translation.

5. Ernst Landsberg, 1860–1927, historian of German law, was a professor in Bonn from 1899.

6. Paul Ludwig Landsberg, 1901–1944, was a German philosopher.

7. Letter of February 23, 1947, from Gertrud J. to A. What follows is addressed to Gertrud J.

8. Hasso von Seebach; see L. 33, n. 1.

9. Ludwig B. Lefebre was at that time a member of the U.S. occupation army; he worked later as a psychotherapist in San Francisco.

10. Paul Arendt, 1873–1913, was an engineer.

11. Martin Beerwald, 1869–1942, was a businessman.

12. Clara Beerwald, 1900–1931, became a pharmacist.

13. Eva Beerwald, b. 1902, is a dental technician.

14. See L. 34, n. 9.

15. This was reported by Gertrud J. to A. in her letter of February 23, 1947.

16. The Jewish Agency for Palestine was established by League of Nations mandate to act as official representative of the Jews to the British mandatory government. It promoted the economic, social, and other interests of the Jewish population in Palestine.

Letter 56

1. As early as 1946, J. had received an invitation to give guest lectures in Basel. He declined at that time because he had already accepted the invitation to the Rencontres in Geneva. The Free Academic Foundation and the Faculty of Philosophy and History of the University of Basel extended the invitation again in 1947. This time J. accepted, and he gave the lectures in July 1947.
2. Fritz Ernst, 1905–1963, had been professor of medieval and modern history at Heidelberg since 1937. After the war, he was important in the revival of the university. J. was therefore in close contact with him.
3. Fritz Ernst, "Vom Studieren," in Karl Jaspers and Fritz Ernst, *Vom lebendigen Geist und vom Studieren*, 41–62.

Letter 57

1. See Ls. 53 and 54.
2. Ernst Wiechert, 1887–1950, was a German novelist whose anti-Nazi lectures led to his being sent to the concentration camp at Buchenwald. After release, he was under Gestapo surveillance and was not allowed to publish.
3. Werner von Trott zu Solz, 1902–1965, was the older brother of Adam von Trott zu Solz; see L. 50, no. 3.
4. Karl Mannheim, 1893–1947, sociologist, was professor in Frankfurt am Main 1930–33. He emigrated to England. In his *Geistige Situation der Zeit* (8th printing of 5th ed., 155ff.), J. portrayed Mannheim as the typical sophist.
5. What follows is addressed to Gertrud J.
6. Eugen Kogon, b. 1903, is a political scientist and journalist. A. is asking for his book *Der SS-Staat: Das System der deutschen Konzentrationslager* (Munich, 1946).
7. A. was working on her book *The Origins of Totalitarianism*; see Ls. 61 and 67, where it is referred to as the "imperialism book," a work-in-progress designation that is used throughout the correspondence.
8. Benno von Wiese and F. K. Scheid, "49 Thesen zur Neugestaltung deutscher Hochschulen," *Volk im Werden*, ed. Ernst Krieck, 1, no. 2 (1933): 13–21.
9. J.'s address in Heidelberg was Plöck 66. This refers to a visit Benno von Wiese made to J. on J.'s sixtieth birthday, in February 1943.

Letter 58

1. See Ls. 22–24 and 59.
2. Karl Freiherr vom Stein zum Altenstein, 1770–1840, was a Prussian statesman.
3. See L. 52, n. 2.
4. Mo Ti, c. 479–381 B.C., Chinese philosopher and social ethicist, is regarded by some as the founder of a religion whose teachings were widely known in ancient China.

5. Tsin (or Ch'in) Shi Huang Ti, Chinese emperor, 221–210/206 B.C., created the first unified, bureaucratically centralized state in China, the name of which derives from that of his dynasty.

6. What J. reports here is based on Marcel Granet, *La civilisation chinoise: La vie publique et la vie privée* (Paris, 1929): 55ff., 114ff.

7. In the summer semester of 1947, J. gave a seminar on Kant's *Kritik der reinen Vernunft*.

8. See L. 10, n. 1.

9. Albrecht Haushofer, 1903–1945, was a poet and dramatist, whose *Moabiter Sonette*, written in prison, appeared in 1946. Because of his ties to the resistance movement, he was arrested in 1945 and shot by the Gestapo.

10. Karl Haushofer, 1869–1946, Bavarian major general, was, from 1921 to 1939, professor of geography in Munich. He was the main advocate of geopolitics in Germany.

Letter 59

1. See L. 56, n. 1.

2. In Basel J. gave the lectures published in his *Der philosophische Glaube* (Munich, 1948). The fifth lecture, "Philosophie und Unphilosophie," was not given.

Letter 60

1. The vacation in Crans was an extra, added to the honorarium for the Basel lectures.

2. Heinrich Barth, 1890–1965, was a Swiss philosopher. J. later became his colleague at the University of Basel.

3. Karl Barth, 1886–1968, Protestant theologian, was the leading spokesman for dialectical theology. He held various professorships in Germany in 1921–35 and became professor of philosophy at Basel in 1935. He maintained a relationship of ironic distance with J.

4. Probably the philosopher and psychologist Hans Kunz, 1904–1982, whose *Die anthropologische Bedeutung der Phantasie*, 2 vols., appeared in Basel in 1946.

5. Vercors, pseudonym of Jean Bruller, b. 1902, a French writer and co-founder of the resistance publishing house Les Editions de Minuit, which published avant-garde work after the war.

Letter 61

1. Martha Mundt in the 1930s worked for the Bureau International du Travail of the League of Nations in Geneva.

2. See L. 32, n. 4.

3. Adolf Frise was coauthor of the work, *Denker und Deuter im heutigen Europa* (Oldenburg/Hamburg, 1954). Hermann Zeltner eventually did the article about J., pp. 102ff.

4. Abbreviation for Lefebre; see L. 55, n. 9.
5. See L. 10, n. 1.

Letter 62

1. In December 1947, J. was offered a post at the University of Basel. A. knew this from Gertrud J.'s letters. J. accepted the offer at the end of February 1948, and they moved to Basel in March 1948.
2. Karl Jaspers, "Unsere Zukunft und Goethe," *Die Wandlung* 2 (1947): 559–78.
3. Kurt Wolff, 1887–1963, a German publisher, cofounded Pantheon Books in New York in 1942. In 1961, he and his wife began publishing under the imprint "A Helen and Kurt Wolff Book" with Harcourt, Brace & World (later Harcourt Brace Jovanovich). A. was a friend of the couple, and an especially close friend of Helen Wolff after Kurt Wolff's death.
4. Berlin, 1913.
5. The birthdays in February of both Karl and Gertrud Jaspers.
6. Henriette Mendelssohn, 1774 or 1775–1831, was the youngest daughter of the German Jewish philosopher Moses Mendelssohn, 1729–1786 (see L. 135).

Letter 63

1. This was the row house at Austrasse 126, which was made available to Jaspers for life.
2. In January 1941, the board of the Free Academic Foundation in Basel had invited J. to give guest lectures at the university. A definite and immediate position with the university was not offered, but a year's salary was. J. accepted and requested permission from the Reich Ministry of Education to lecture in Basel for two years. In May, the rector of the University of Heidelberg wrote him: "In accordance with the wishes of the Foreign Office, I am not able to approve Prof. Dr. Jaspers' request to give guest lectures at the University of Basel." A year later, the board's desire was indirectly communicated to Ernst von Weizsäcker, undersecretary for foreign affairs. He let J. know that there was no longer any objection to the guest lectures. At the same time, the Foreign Office forbade Frau Jaspers to leave the country. J. therefore could not accept the invitation.
3. Gertrud J.'s brothers Fritz, Heinrich, and Otto Mayer had emigrated to Palestine.

Letter 64

1. Hannah Arendt, "Konzentrationsläger," *Die Wandlung* 3 (1948): 309–30.

Letter 65

1. Erna Baer, later Wiesner, b. 1921, ran the household on Austrasse until February 1952.
2. On the move to Basel, see Karl Jaspers, "Von Heidelberg nach Basel," in *Schicksal und Wille: Autobiographische Schriften*, 164–83; Paul Meyer-Gutzwiller, "Karl Jaspers und Basel," in *Basler Stadtbuch* (1970): 149–63.

Letter 66

1. Dated April 8, 1948, presumably regarding the move to Basel: "Felicitations, best wishes, good luck, bonne chance. Hannah."
2. See L. 64, n. 1.
3. In the summer semester 1948, J. lectured three hours a week on "Probleme einer Weltgeschichte der Philosophie" ("Problems of a World History of Philosophy"). In these lectures he seems to have outlined for the first time his idea of the axial age.
4. Anna Weyl; see L. 53.
5. *Von der Wahrheit*.

Letter 67

1. On March 24, 1948, J. published in *Rhein-Neckar-Zeitung* a public statement, which, in the situation at that time, may have appeared to be a mollifying justification for leaving. It said in part: "I reached my decision with an eye toward the cause for which I have worked my whole life. My task is philosophy. I want to do my work wherever I am in the service of a supranational task. My staying here would not amount to a confession any more than my leaving to go to Basel is a confession." This statement appeared, somewhat abridged, in *Aufbau* 19, no. 16 (April 16, 1948): 15.
2. *Aufbau; Reconstruction: An American Weekly Published in New York*, the weekly newspaper of the German-Jewish immigrants, published since 1934. It was originally printed in German; later, partially in English. In the years 1941–45, A. published in it more than forty articles in German.
3. Karl Jaspers, *The Question of German Guilt*, trans. E. B. Ashton (New York, 1947).
4. See L. 62, n. 3.

Letter 68

1. Because J. had lost almost all his money during the war, he did not have to pay to join the retirement plan.
2. Gertrud J. was able to remain in the house at Austrasse 126 after J.'s death.
3. J.'s beginning basic salary was 1,100 francs per month; the rent was 300 francs.

4. In the summer semester of 1948, J. gave a seminar on Hegel's philosophy of history.
5. The book, *Vom Ursprung und Ziel der Geschichte*, appeared in two editions (Zurich: Artemis; Munich: Piper) as early as 1949.
6. His successor at Heidelberg was Hans-Georg Gadamer, who started in 1949.
7. J. received the Goethe Prize of the city of Frankfurt am Main in 1947.
8. In 1947, the University of Lausanne awarded J. an honorary doctorate *ès lettres*.

Letter 69

1. Elliot Cohen, 1899–1959, editor of *Commentary* from its founding in 1945.
2. See L. 55.
3. Daniel F. Malan's National party won the elections of 1948 in the Union of South Africa. As prime minister, Malan, 1874–1959, introduced the policy of apartheid.
4. In 1929, Hitler became a member of the Reich Committee, founded that year. This brought the National Socialist German Workers' party out of political isolation and placed it at the head of nationalistic forces in the Weimar Republic. The Reichstag elections of September 14, 1930, then brought it the sensational gain from 12 seats to 107.
5. Judah Leon Magnes, 1877–1948, was chancellor and first president of Hebrew University in Jerusalem. He was a pioneer in the struggle for understanding between Jews and Arabs.
6. *Von der Wahrheit*, 936ff.
7. See L. 31, n. 13.

Letter 70

1. Karl Jaspers, "Die Achsenzeit der Weltgeschichte," *Der Monat* 1, no. 6 (1948–49): 3–9. *Commentary* published this essay in a translation by Ralph Manheim: "The Axial Age of Human History: A Base for the Unity of Mankind" 6, no. 5 (November 1948): 430–35.
2. Paul Häberlin, 1878–1960, J.'s predecessor, held a chair for philosophy, psychology, and pedagogy. J.'s teaching commitment was for philosophy, including psychology and sociology.

Letter 71

1. When the British left Palestine, on the expiration of their mandate, the Jewish National Council, on May 14, 1948, proclaimed the existence of the state of Israel, which took in three-fourths of Palestine. In response, neighboring Arab countries attacked Jewish settlements in the new state on May 17. Hostilities continued until June 1949.
2. This refers to J.'s "axial age," the period between 800 and 200 B.C., when

the intellectual foundations of humanity were established in China, India, Palestine, and Greece.

Letter 72

1. Walter von Reichenau, 1884–1942, German field marshal, fought on the Eastern Front. Earlier, as head of the Army Office in the Reich Ministry of Defense, he played a major role in integrating the army into the National Socialist state. He was a strong racist.
2. Flora Mayer, née Wolff, 1882–1967, wife of Gustav Mayer.
3. Abraham A. Fraenkel, 1891–1965, German mathematician, taught at Marburg and Kiel before going, in 1929, to Hebrew University in Jerusalem.

Letter 73

1. See L. 70, n. 1.
2. See L. 31, n. 9.

Letter 74

1. Henriette Jaspers-Tantzen, 1862–1941.
2. Dagobert Runes, 1902–1982, received a Ph.D. from the University of Vienna. In the United States, he was a lecturer, writer, and editor. He became editor-in-chief of the Philosophical Library in 1940.
3. Karl Jaspers, "Philosophie und Wissenschaft," *Die Wandlung* 3 (1948): 721–33.

Letter 75

1. Ben Halpern, "Guilty, but Not Answerable," *Jewish Frontier* (April 1948): 41–60.

Letter 76

1. This is an allusion to Goethe's *Faust*, Scene 5, line 1034: "Mein Vater war ein dunkler Ehrenmann."
2. Eugen Rosenstock-Huessy, 1888–1973, German legal historian and sociologist, emigrated to the United States in 1934 and taught at Harvard.
3. When J. left Heidelberg in March 1948, he published a mollifying justification in *Rhein-Neckar-Zeitung*; see L. 67, n. 1. The reaction in the German press was violent. He was accused of "treason" and "desertion." Among other reproaches, his critics said he had spoken as a representative of a better Germany, and now he was abandoning Germany in its misery for the sake of a better life for himself; he had appealed to his countrymen to bear their common fate together, and now he was escaping that fate himself; he had given young people a vision of the future, but now that

it was time to realize that vision he was leaving them in the lurch. J. never made a public response to any of these reproaches.

4. See L. 32, n. 3.

Letter 77

1. Karl Jaspers, *The Perennial Scope of Philosophy*, trans. Ralph Manheim (New York, 1949). This is the translation of *Der philosophische Glaube*.

Letter 78

1. Letter of December 4, 1948, from A. to the Philosophical Library, Attention: Mr. Runes.

Letter 79

1. Alfred L. Copley (known, as an artist, as Alcopley), b. 1910 in Dresden, went to New York in 1937, where he was a friend of A. and her husband.
2. This was a story from the *New York Times* of December 18, 1948, about the founding of the Judah L. Magnes Foundation. The caption to the picture reads: "Supreme Court Justice William C. Hecht, Jr., with the incorporation papers as Dr. Hannah Arendt and James Marshall, two of the directors, look on."
3. A contraction of *Weihnachten* (Christmas) and Hanukkah.

Letter 80

1. In a letter of January 6, 1949, Dial Press asked A. to send a copy of *Die Schuldfrage* to the Italian publishing house La Nuova Italia Editrice Firenze. A. typed her L. 80 directly on the Dial Press letter.
2. La Nuova Italia Editrice Firenze. On the Italian translation of *Die Schuldfrage*, see L. 81 and L. 81, n. 2.
3. This would mean the two German-language editions of *Die Schuldfrage*; see L. 43, n. 4.

Letter 81

1. The U.S. edition of *Die Schuldfrage (The Question of German Guilt)*; only 276 copies of it were sold in 1948.
2. Karl Jaspers, *La colpa della Germania: A cura di Renato de Rosa* (Naples, 1947).
3. Karl Jaspers, *Psicopatologia general*, trans. Roberto O. Saubidet and Diego A. Santillán, 2 vols. (Buenos Aires, 1950-).
4. After the Republic of Indonesia declared its independence in 1945, the Dutch government tried to regain control by a "police action" in December 1948.
5. Abdullah (or Abdallah) ibn Hussein, 1882–1951, since 1946 king of the

Hashemite kingdom of Jordan, was assassinated for advocating a peaceful settlement with Israel.

6. See L. 74, n. 3.

Letter 82

1. J. wrote L. 82 on the copy of his letter of January 25, 1949, to Mrs. Rose Morse of the Philosophical Library.
2. This refers to several copies of the contract for the U.S. edition of *Der philosophische Glaube*; see L. 77, n. 1.
3. The stipulations that the publisher will be "responsible for choosing a good translator" and that the translation rights will revert to the author if, after the printing is sold out, "a new printing is not undertaken forthwith."

Letter 83

1. Karl Jaspers, *Tragedy Is Not Enough*, trans. Harald A. T. Reiche, Harry T. Moore, and Karl W. Deutsch (Boston, 1952). The translation of the whole work was never done.

Letter 84

1. For the first edition, see L. 21, n. 1. The second edition, in one volume (Berlin/Heidelberg), appeared in 1948.
2. Wera Lewin, Ph.D., historian, was giving a series of lectures in Basel at the time. In a letter of January 15, 1949, Gertrud J. had asked A. whether a translation of a book by Lewin (which cannot be identified) could be published in America.
3. The Jewish Publication Society of America was founded in 1888 to promote publications on the religion, history, and literature of the Jewish people.
4. Eugen Täubler, 1879–1953, historian, was a professor at Heidelberg, 1924–33, then privatdocent at the Institute for the Study of Judaism in Berlin. From 1941, he was in exile in the United States.
5. Selma Stern-Täubler; see L. 3, n. 1.

Letter 85

1. Robert Warshow was at this time managing editor of *Commentary*.
2. Willy Andreas, 1884–1967, was a professor of modern history at Heidelberg, 1923–46.

Letter 86

1. Nietzsche, "An die Jünger Darwins," in *Gesammelte Werke* (Musarion), 23 vols. (München, 1920–29), 20: 130.

Letter 87

1. Karl Jaspers, "Solon," in *Synopsis: Festgabe fur Alfred Weber* . . . , ed. Edgar Salin (Heidelberg, 1948): 177–90.
2. Gerhard (Gershom) Scholem, 1897–1982, Jewish historian of religion and first to conduct research on Jewish mysticism, went to Jerusalem in 1923, and was a professor at Hebrew University, 1933–65. He advocated peaceful settlement with the Arabs. A friend of A., he became an acquaintance of J. in later years.
3. Karl Reinhardt, 1886–1958, was a classical philologist.
4. Karl Reinhardt, *Sophokles* (Frankfurt am Main, 1933).
5. Karl Reinhardt, *Von Werken und Formen: Vorträge und Aufsätze* (Godesberg, 1948).

Letter 88

1. In 1950, Routledge & Kegan Paul, in London, published the same translation as the U.S. edition of *Der philosophische Glaube*; see L. 77, n. 1.
2. This was the first national congress on philosophy in Argentina; it was held in Mendoza from March 30 to April 9, 1949.
3. Karl Jaspers, "Die Situation der Philosophie heute," in *Actas del I. Congreso Nacional de Filosofia: Actas 1–3* (Buenos Aires, 1950). German text: pt. 2, 922–26; Spanish text: 927–30.
4. Luigi Pareyson, b. 1918, had published a book about J.: *La filosofia dell' esistenza e Carlo Jaspers* (Naples, 1940).

Letter 89

1. Helmut Kuhn, b. 1899, was a philosopher; he was not a Jew. He taught in the United States, 1938–49, then in Erlangen and, from 1952, in Munich.
2. *Von der Wahrheit*, 475ff.

Letter 90

1. When he received the Goethe Prize in 1947, J. gave a talk, "Unsere Zukunft und Goethe"; see L. 62, n. 2. In the Goethe bicentennial year, 1949, it was published in Germany as a small book. On March 20, 1949, *Welt am Sonntag* called attention to this publication by printing a critical passage about Goethe from it, with the title "Auflehnung gegen Goethe?" and the subtitle "Eine kritische Untersuchung." The Bonn Romanist Ernst Robert Curtius, 1886–1956, apparently assumed that this was part of a new work and that J. was starting a campaign against Goethe. He published a vehement polemic, "Goethe oder Jaspers?" in *Tat* (April 2, 1949). He said, in part: "Jaspers has made clear since 1945 that he aspires to the hotly contested post of a *praeceptor Germaniae*. He has made our collective guilt so plain to us that we can continue to live only with a guilty conscience. A Wilhelm von Humboldt of our time, he laid out guidelines

for German universities, until he turned his back on them. A *praeceptor Helvetiae*-to-be. As a reformer, he then discovered a new faith, which he calls 'biblical religion' and the point of which is that Judaism and Christianity are just about the same. He is crowning these national pedagogical efforts with a 'campaign in Switzerland' that is directed against Goethe. *Habemus papam!*"

For J., who had known Curtius for many years, this attack came as a complete surprise. He drafted an open letter to Curtius, but never published it. In *Rhein-Neckar-Zeitung*, May 10, 1949, a group of Heidelberg professors took his side in a public declaration. "Concerned about the academic level of intellectual controversy," they distanced themselves from Curtius. He replied in the same newspaper, May 17, 1949, with an article, "Darf man Jaspers angreifen?" He followed that with a final word "on his own behalf" in *Die Zeit*, July 2, 1949: "Goethe, Jaspers, Curtius." For several months, there was a flood of newspaper articles about Jaspers and Curtius. Most writers did not agree with Curtius's aggressive polemic, but also did not support J.'s criticism of Goethe. For J., the incident seemed more and more to be a litmus test of the German public's mind, which, as he saw it, remained given to blind respect for authority and to the appeal to nationalistic instincts. It cannot be determined what material J. sent to A. and whether it was accompanied by a letter.

2. In July 1949, under the honorary presidency of Herbert Hoover, a two-week conference on Goethe was held in Aspen, Colorado. Among the participants, in addition to Curtius, were José Ortega y Gasset, Albert Schweitzer, Ernst Simon, Stephen Spender, and Thornton Wilder.

3. Robert M. Hutchins, 1899–1977, president, 1929–45, and then chancellor, 1945–51, of the University of Chicago, was chairman of the Goethe Bicentennial Foundation in 1949.

4. Walter P. Paepke, b. 1896 in Chicago, was president of the Container Corporation of America and president and director of the Aspen Corporation.

5. Arnold Bergsträsser, 1896–1964, cultural historian and sociologist, was a professor at Heidelberg, 1928–37. He went to the United States in 1937, and from 1954 taught political science at Freiburg.

6. Joseph R. McCarthy, 1909–1957, Republican senator from Wisconsin and chairman of the Permanent Subcommittee on Investigations of the Committee on Government Operations, was the moving force behind a wave of anti-Communist persecution in the early 1950s, based on defamation and intimidation and directed against civil servants, intellectuals, and the army, among others.

7. Sidney Hook, 1902–1989, was an American philosopher, teacher, and writer.

8. With Jewish Cultural Reconstruction; see L. 31, n. 9.

9. Hilde Fränkel, secretary after the war to Paul Tillich at Union Theological Seminary in New York, had been a friend of A.'s in Frankfurt in 1930–31. She died in 1950.

Letter 91

1. Karl and Gertrud J. spent their vacation, until August 14, in the Villa Nimet in St. Moritz.
2. After L. 90, at least one letter, referred to here, from A. to J. is missing; a letter from J. to A. may have preceded it.
3. In the summer of 1949, A. and her husband moved from their furnished rooms to the first apartment of their own in New York: 130 Morningside Drive.
4. Hannah Arendt, "Parteien und Bewegungen," *Die Wandlung* 4 (1949): 459–73.
5. Presumably the lecture "Goethes Menschlichkeit," which J. gave at the Goethe celebration at the University of Basel, June 17, 1949.
6. See "Goethes Menschlichkeit," in Karl Jaspers, *Rechenschaft und Ausblick: Reden und Aufsätze*, 2nd ed. (Munich, 1958): 72. The Goethe quote is from "Belagerung von Mainz": "It is just part of my nature; I would rather commit an injustice than put up with disorder," *Goethes Werke*, 14 vols. (Hamburg: 1948–60), 10: 391.
7. Jan de Witt, 1625–1672, Dutch statesman; from 1653 until shortly before he was killed, he was, for all practical purposes, the leader of the republic.
8. Georg Simmel, 1858–1918, was a German philosopher and sociologist.
9. This word cannot be read with certainty. It may be *hinreissend* (captivating, ravishing, enchanting), rather than *hinweisend*.
10. Presumably in the context of a lecture on the philosophy of the Middle Ages that extended over two semesters—winter 1935–36 and 1936–37.

Letter 92

1. Not in the literary remains.
2. See, among other passages, Hegel, *Vorlesungen über die Geschichte der Philosophie, Samtliche Werke*, ed. Glockner, 26 vols. (1927–40), 19: 373.
3. Ernest Renan, 1823–1892, was a French scholar of religion, a historian, and a philosopher.
4. See Karl Jaspers, *Notizen zu Martin Heidegger*, ed. H. Saner (Munich/Zurich, 1978). On the postwar correspondence, see Preface, 17–18.
5. J. was invited to the Rencontres Internationales in Geneva in September 1949. He spoke there on September 8 about conditions for and possibilities of a new humanism. The theme of the conference was "Pour un nouvel humanisme." Other speakers were René Grousset, Karl Barth, R. P. Maydieu, Paul Masson-Oursel, Maxime Leroy, Henri Lefebvre, J. B. S. Haldane, and John Middleton Murry.

Letter 93

1. Salo W. Baron, 1895–1989, historian, was professor of Jewish studies at Columbia University, 1930–63, his program becoming, in 1950, the Center for Israel and Jewish Studies. He was also president of Jewish Cultural Reconstruction and editor of the quarterly *Jewish Social Studies*.

2. Martin Heidegger, "Uber den 'Humanismus': Brief an Jean Beaufret," in his *Platons Lehre von der Wahrheit* . . . (Bern, 1947): 53–119.
3. Heidegger had already published several studies on Hölderlin, but his Nietzsche lectures had not appeared; A. probably had access to a private manuscript.
4. Heidegger's "hut" in the Black Forest.
5. Gertrud J. had added a note to L. 92, in which she said that Albrecht Mayer, b. 1916, the son of Ernst Mayer, had died.

Letter 94
1. This must refer to two letters (of November 1 and 16, 1949) from Gertrud J. to A. The literary remains contain no letters from J. to A. in this period.

Letter 95
1. J. is referring to his use of "Lieber Herr Blücher," when he felt he should have addressed a stranger as "Sehr geehrter Herr Blücher."
2. A. made a typewritten copy for her husband "to forestall all desperate attempts to read this." The copy contains a number of misreadings. Blücher did not reply directly to J., but wrote a letter to A. on January 29, 1950 (see L. 98, n. 1), and left it up to her to give J. whatever of it she thought appropriate.

Letter 96
1. Karl Jaspers, *Man in the Modern Age*, trans. Eden and Cedar Paul (London, 1933).

Letter 97
1. Anne Weil, née Mendelssohn, a friend of A.'s since their youth.
2. Erna Baer; see L. 65, n. 1.

Letter 98
1. See L. 95, n. 2. After her stay in Paris, A. visited J. once again in Basel. She presumably showed him the following passages, to which L. 98 is a reply:

"Many small works by Jaspers. During my illness I was able to read at least the lecture on Nietzsche and Christianity, which is as bright and warm as the light in Greece is said to be. How much a thinker's favorite words convey. Do you recall how I called your attention to Jünger's repeated use of the phrase 'high and dreadful pleasure'? Similarly, I somehow have to smile happily whenever the word 'erhellen' [to illuminate] slides off Jaspers' tongue. The more I immerse myself in his comprehensive work, the *Logik*, the more clearly I see how this 'noble soul'—excuse the old-fashioned and Romantic phrase—has managed to preserve in its purity the hidden and profound undercurrent of the Enlightenment, that genuine element of real freedom that breaks forth in Kant and Lessing and that is purged of all the hocus-pocus of both pantheism and its Christian reincarnations, and to bring that undercurrent up into the light of day. In this way, the Enlightenment is transformed into an illumination, a process of self-comprehension for man becoming man. The functionality of rational self-awareness is set in motion, makes a vital orientation *in* Being possible instead of a knowledge about Being, in loyal stewardship of Kant's will, truly creating room for faith, that is, showing faith the unending path through the Creation to the Creator, where man—by virtue of existence and of a rationality conceived of almost in the sense of Platonic eros, penetrating transcendentally through the modes of the 'encompassing'— soars, so to speak, through Being. It's as if the essence of Western thought had carved a spiral from Plato to Augustine, Cusanus, Kant, and the explosion of Nietzsche. This work is suddenly very close again to the essence of Platonic thought, and it is almost as if one should say: Western thought has progressed to this point. This work bears a strange and yet quite clear relationship to Hegel. It does not, of course, use the achievements of Western thought as milestones that lead to the truth embodied in Jaspers; nor does it place them in a new light. Kant did that, and Nietzsche brought them to an explosive, white-hot glow. Instead, it mobilizes these elements in a new way, unfolds them in this functionality (for it is *more* than a 'systematic') of rational self-awareness. And so this work stands directly in the tradition—in that Jaspers is right—but it would still have been justified not to bear the title *Logik*, which is a formal bow to the tradition, but, helping the tradition along, rather openly to bear the title mentioned in the text: 'Systematic of Rational Self-Awareness.' I could say much more on the delineation of the modes of the Encompassing. Today all I want to do is call attention to how here, too, he draws from the hidden, most profound tradition. The correspondences he sees were anticipated in the Goethe quote: In nature is everything that is in the spiritual, and something more. In the spiritual is everything that is in nature, and something more. Then, too, you will be delighted with the interpretation of *Nathan der Weise*. This is the first true discovery of the real content of Lessing's play.

"I can't write anymore; I really have to take it easy. Jaspers' letter was wonderful. As if he suddenly came into this stranger's room, softly but as if he belonged here, completely naturally. Like a symbolic act of his 'communication.' I'm glad he felt as if I was there with you in Basel. If he only knew how he has always been present with us all these years, asked for his judgment on everything and, in normal issues, often providing a standard to measure the course of events. I couldn't write all that to him. You know how directly and uninhibitedly I can express myself man to man, and how, perhaps for that very reason, I fall into indirection in the written word. So please convey to him from this what you like, and, above all, give him my thanks."

2. *Von der Wahrheit*, the first volume of *Logik*.
3. These planned volumes were on theories of category and method; one on the theory of science was also considered.

Letter 99

1. Not in the literary remains. Herbert Read, 1893–1968, was an English critic, poet, and editor.
2. Hans Paeschke, b. 1911, was secretary of the German-French Society in Paris, 1932–34, then studied philosophy and literature. In 1939–42, he was editor of *Neue Rundschau*, and from 1947 of *Merkur*.
3. The last issue of *Die Wandlung* appeared in December 1949.
4. Les entretiens de Pontigny were held in the abbey of Pontigny from 1905 to 1940 under the direction of Paul Desjardins, 1859–1940. The discussions dealt with philosophical, literary, and social problems, and had an expressly international character. After 1940, Desjardins' daughter, Madame Heurgon-Desjardins, conducted them in Royaumont, then in Cerisy-la-Salle.
5. Karl Jaspers, "Uber Bedingungen und Möglichkeiten eines neuen Humanismus," *Die Wandlung* 4 (1949): 710–34.
6. Presumably Rudolf Bultmann's book *Das Urchristentum im Rahmen der antiken Religionen* (Zurich, 1949). In 1924–25, A. studied Protestant theology with Bultmann (1884–1976) at Marburg; J. had known him since the 1920s.

Letter 100

1. From the second stanza of Ludwig Uhland's poem "Frühlingsglaube": "The world grows more beautiful each day, / One doesn't know what may yet come, / There is no end to the blossoming." Franz Schubert set this poem to music, but whether J. had Schubert's composition in mind is questionable.
2. Oswald Spengler, 1880–1936, was a philosopher and historian. The reference here is to the cultural morphology of his *Der Untergang des Abendlandes*, 2 vols. (Vienna/Leipzig, 1919–22). Arnold J. Toynbee, 1889–1975, was a British historian and cultural philosopher. In their studies of the morphology of cultures, Spengler and Toynbee begin with the assumption that different cultures (eight in Spengler, twenty-three in Toynbee) display similar structures and that as a consequence the rise and fall of cultures are structurally determined.
3. Hilde Fränkel; see Ls. 90, 91. J. seems to be referring to a letter from A., perhaps to Gertrud J., that has not been preserved.
4. Plato, *Phaedo*, 115a.
5. In the summer semester of 1950, J. lectured for three hours weekly on Plato.
6. V. Rose, *Aristotelis qui ferebantur librorum fragmenta* (Leipzig, 1886). Paul Wilpert, "Neue Fragmente aus Περὶ τἀγαθοῦ," *Hermes* 76 (1941).

Letter 101

1. The Student Council (Asta: Allgemeiner Studentenausschuss) at the University of Heidelberg had invited J. to give some guest lectures. He accepted the invitation in 1950.
2. For the British edition of *Vom Ursprung und Ziel der Geschichte*.
3. These quotations of Churchill on Hitler were enclosed:

   "1. In Great Contemporaries: 'Those who have met Hitler face to face in public business or on social terms, have found him a highly competent, cool, well-informed functionary with an agreeable manner and a disarming smile.'

   "2. In a Press Statement, London *Times*, November 7, 1938 (sic! two days before the pogroms), page 12, column 2: 'I have always said that if Great Britain were defeated in war, I hope that we shall find a Hitler to lead us back to our rightful position among the nations. ' "

Letter 102

1. Alexander Rüstow, *Ortsbestimmung der Gegenwart: Eine universalgeschichtliche Kulturkritik*, vol. 1, *Ursprung der Herrschaft* (Erlenbach/Zurich, 1950).
2. Alexander Rüstow, 1885–1963, was a sociologist and neoliberal economist.
3. Jakob Friedrich Fries, 1773–1843, was a mathematician, physicist, and philosopher. In opposition to Hegel, and using Kantian ideas, he developed a variation of positivism in which he interpreted the world and the history of man according to the laws of natural science and as an organism. His school of thought was revived in the twentieth century by Leonard Nelson, 1882–1927.
4. Alexander Rüstow, *Der Lügner: Theorie, Geschichte, und Auflösung* (Erlangen, 1910).
5. Alfred Weber, 1868–1958, sociologist, and friend of J.'s, had been a professor at Heidelberg since 1904.
6. The lectures were published in the same year, as *Vernunft und Widervernunft in unserer Zeit* (Munich, 1950).
7. The Heidelberg physician Dr. Wilhelm Waltz, 1891–1962, and his wife, Erika (known as Lotte), b. 1905. They were close friends.
8. Karl Jaspers, "Zu Nietzsches Bedeutung in der Geschichte der Philosophie," *Neue Rundschau* 61 (1950): 346–58.

Letter 103

1. East Prussian peninsula on the Baltic.
2. Alfred Kazin, b. 1915, became a literary critic and author widely known for, among other books, *On Native Grounds* (1942) and *Walker in the City* (1951).

3. Karl Jaspers, *Philosophische Logik*, vol. 1, *Von der Wahrheit*, 2nd ed. (Munich, 1958): 25.
4. Gertrud J. had added a note to L. 102 to say she had been in Holland to see her youngest brother Fritz Mayer, visiting from Palestine.
5. On June 25, 1950, North Korean troops crossed the border into South Korea, beginning a war that lasted until 1953 and involved Communist China on one side and the United Nations on the other.
6. The New School for Social Research in New York City: see, too, L. 31, n. 11.

Letter 104

1. Karl Heinrich Bauer, 1890–1978, a surgeon and close friend of J.'s, became a professor at Breslau in 1933 and at Heidelberg in 1943. He was rector of the University of Heidelberg after the war, and the most active figure in the reconstruction of the university.
2. Inge Bauer, née Fuchs.
3. Karl Schwarber, 1889–1950, had been director of the Basel University library since 1935.
4. The passage presumably meant is: "The crucial task before humanity today is not to become dragons ourselves in our battle with the dragon and yet not to lose the strength we need to subdue the dragon"; see *Rechenschaft und Ausblick*, 2nd ed., 324.

Letter 105

1. This refers to the graphic presentation of the mutual relations of the modes of the Encompassing.
2. *Von der Wahrheit*, 47.
3. Karl Jaspers, "Uber Gefahren und Chancen der Freiheit," *Der Monat* 2, no. 22–23 (1949–50): 396–406.
4. Gotthold Ephraim Lessing, 1729–1781, was a German dramatist and critic.
5. The Congress for Cultural Freedom that met in Berlin in June 1950. See L. 142, n. 7.
6. Ignazio Silone, 1900–1978, antifascist Italian writer.
7. Elliot E. Cohen, "What do the Germans propose to do? An Address to the German People," *Commentary* 10 (September 1950): 225–28. This was Cohen's talk at the Berlin Congress for Cultural Freedom.
8. Hannah Arendt, "The Aftermath of Nazi Rule: Report from Germany," *Commentary* 10 (October 1950): 342–53.
9. See L. 43, n. 1.
10. Theodor Heuss, 1884–1963, was president of the Federal Republic of Germany, 1949–1959.
11. Alexandre Koyré, 1892–1964, French philosopher, emigrated to the United States during the war and taught at the New School in New York. See also L. 353.

Letter 106

1. Ludwig Curtius, 1874–1954, classical archeologist, was, among other things, a professor at Heidelberg, 1920–28, and a close friend of J.'s since then. This refers probably to his *Deutsche und antike Welt: Lebenserinnerungen* (Stuttgart, 1950).
2. Ernst Mayer, *Dialektik des Nichtwissens*, with a forward by Karl Jaspers (Basel, 1950).
3. A.'s friend Waldemar Gurian taught at Notre Dame; see L. 39, n. 6.
4. Karl Jaspers, "Marx und Freud," *Der Monat* 3, no. 26 (1950–51): 141–50.

Letter 107

1. See L. 105, n. 8.
2. See L. 105, n. 7.
3. At the Congress for Cultural Freedom, Berlin, June 1950. See L. 142, n. 7.
4. This probably refers to a letter of March 7, 1950, from Heidegger to J., in which he says he had never set foot in Heidelberg and J.'s house again after 1933 "because I was simply ashamed."
5. See Ls. 75 and 77.
6. Hannah Arendt, "Der imperialistische Charakter: Eine psychologisch-soziologische Studie," *Der Monat* 2, no. 24 (September 1950): 509–22.
7. Sargon of Akkad, c. 2340–2305 B.C., was the founder of the first Semitic dynasty in Mesopotamia.
8. See L. 102, n. 6.
9. See L. 106, n. 4.
10. Joachim Bannes, *Hitlers Kampf und Platos Staat: Studie über den ideologischen Aufbau der nationalsozialistischen Freiheitsbewegung* (Berlin, 1933).
11. Dionysius the Younger, tyrant of Syracuse, 367–357 and 347–344, was tutored by Plato at his court in 366 and 361; see Plato, Letter 7.
12. For J.'s view of the prophet Ezekiel, see Karl Jaspers, "Der Prophet Ezekiel: Eine pathographische Studie" (1947), in his *Aneignung und Polemik: Gesammelte Reden und Aufsätze zur Geschichte der Philosophie*, ed. H. Saner (Munich, 1968), 13–21.
13. Wilhelm Weitling, 1808–1871, was the first German theoretician of communism.
14. Ferdinand Lassalle, 1825–1864, was a German follower of Marx and founder of the Social Democratic party in Germany.
15. J. is no doubt drawing here on Gustav Mayer's *Friedrich Engels: Eine Biographie in zwei Bänden*, 2nd ed., 1 (Berlin, 1933): 245ff., especially 284ff.
16. Dean Acheson, 1893–1971, was U.S. secretary of state, 1949–53.
17. George C. Marshall, 1880–1959, was U.S. army chief of staff during World War II, secretary of state, 1947–49, and at this time secretary of

defense. He originated the Marshall Plan, which gave U.S. support to European recovery efforts.

18. The Sicilian expedition against Syracuse, 415–413 B.C., brought catastrophic defeat to the Athenians.

Letter 108

1. Hannah Arendt, *The Origins of Totalitarianism* (New York, 1951). All previous comments about A.'s "imperialism book" refer to this work.
2. See L. 103 and L. 103, n. 3.

Letter 109

1. These are the first two lines of the poem "Der Schnupfen" (The Cold) by Christian Morgenstern.
2. Karl Marx, "Debatten über das Holzdiebstahlsgesetz" (1842), *Marx Engels Werke*, vols. 1–7 (Moscow, 1927–35), 1: 109–47.
3. A. had visited Heidegger in Freiburg in February 1950.
4. Kurt Blumenfeld, 1884–1963, was a leading Zionist and a close friend of A.'s.
5. Probably Karl Barth's *Die Kirche zwischen Ost und West* (Zollikon-Zurich, 1949).

Letter 110

1. See L. 1, n. 1.

Letter 111

1. Gertrud J. mentioned a visit by Ernst and Ella Mayer in her letter of May 6, 1951.
2. See L. 106, n. 2.
3. Walter A. Kaufmann, b. 1921, German philosopher and literary historian, came to the United States in 1939, and became a professor of philosophy at Princeton in 1947.
4. For its issue of March 24, 1951, *The Saturday Review of Literature* had on its cover a drawing of A. made from a photograph. It contained a review of her book *The Origins of Totalitarianism*, by Hans Kohn, 10–11.

Letter 112

1. A short letter from Heinrich Blücher was enclosed with L. 111.
2. Nietzsche stayed in the Oberengadin from 1879.
3. Hannah Arendt, "Totalitäre Propaganda: Ein Kapitel aus *Ursprünge des Totalitarismus*," *Der Monat* 3, no. 33 (June 1951): 241–58.

4. Klaus Piper, b. 1911, was a German publisher. In the postwar years, he published most of J.'s books, and a friendship gradually developed.

Letter 113

1. A. became a United States citizen on December 11, 1951.
2. Paul A. Schilpp, b. 1897 in Dillenburg, Germany, went to the United States in 1913. At the time of this letter he was professor of philosophy at Northwestern University. He was editor of the Library of Living Philosophers, 1939–1981.
3. Hannah Arendt, "Karl Jaspers: Citizen of the World," in *The Philosophy of Karl Jaspers*, ed. Paul A. Schilpp, Library of Living Philosophers, vol. 9 (New York, 1957): 539–49.

Letter 114

1. J. wanted to write the whole history of thought in the form of a "World History of Philosophy." He had three aspects in mind; later, six. Among them, the personal assumed priority for him, and in the following years he worked on *Die grossen Philosophen* from this perspective. He completed only volume 1 of this project; the rest remained fragmentary. On his early overall concept, see Karl Jaspers, *Weltgeschichte der Philosophie: Einleitung*, edited from the literary remains by H. Saner (Munich / Zurich, 1982).
2. Golo Mann, "Vom Totalen Staat," *Die Neue Zeitung* (October 20 (?), 1951): 14.
3. James Burnham, b. 1905, was an American sociologist and journalist. See Golo Mann, "James Burnham, der Philosoph und der Politiker," *Neue Schweizer Rundschau* 18 (April 1951): 719–30.
4. Arthur Koestler, 1905–1983, born in Austro-Hungary, was an editor, writer, and independent thinker. See Golo Mann, "Was uns nicht helfen kann: Bemerkungen zu einem neuen Roman von Arthur Koestler," *Neue Schweizer Rundschau* 19 (July 1951): 183–87.

Letter 115

1. Yaddo is an artists' and writers' colony in Saratoga Springs, New York, where, on Alfred Kazin's recommendation, A. was a guest for the week of January 20–27, 1952.
2. This was the officially required sworn statement that one will sponsor a visitor or immigrant, including certain financial obligations he or she may incur.
3. F. W. J. von Schelling, *Philosophische Untersuchungen über das Wesen der menschlichen Freiheit und die damit zusammenhängenden Gegenstände* (Stuttgart, 1809).
4. See L. 1, L. 1, n. 1, and L. 110.

Letter 116

1. See L. 114, n. 2.

Letter 117

1. In a letter of January 30, 1952, Gertrud J. told A. that Erna Baer, the Jasperses' housekeeper, wanted to emigrate to America.
2. Jewish Cultural Reconstruction; see L. 31, n. 9.

Letter 119

1. This was A.'s cousin Ernst Fürst, b. 1910, and his wife, Kate, née Levin, b. 1911.

Letter 120

1. This refers to two letters Gertrud J. sent to A. in March.

Letter 121

1. A. was a Guggenheim Fellow for 1952–53.
2. Anne Weil; see L. 97, n. 1.
3. Schmuel Mayer, son of Fritz Mayer and nephew of Gertrud J.
4. On February 21, 1952, Gertrud J. wrote to A.: "The change in maids will not bother you. Our new 'Erna' is a dear creature who is easy to get along with." This was Erna Möhrle, b. 1920, who from this time until Gertrud J.'s death (May 1974) ran the Jaspers household. A close bond developed between her and both Karl and Gertrud Jaspers.

Letter 122

1. A. later dropped this project.
2. Refers to the "Zueignung an Karl Jaspers" that formed the preface of A.'s *Sechs Essays*, 10.
3. Jeanne Hersch, b. 1910, a student of J.'s, was a friend of both Karl and Gertrud Jaspers. In 1956, she became professor of systematic philosophy at the University of Geneva.

Letter 123

1. Czeslaw Milosz, b. 1911, Polish writer, was living in Paris then. He later emigrated to the United States. In 1953, J. wrote a foreword for his *Verführtes Denken*; it was not included in the U.S. edition, *The Captive Mind* (1953).
2. François Bondy, b. 1915, was a Swiss journalist and essayist.

3. Karl Jaspers, "Uber meine Philosophie," in *Rechenschaft und Ausblick*, 1st ed. (Munich, 1951): 333–65.
4. See L. 113, n. 3.

Letter 124
1. In the summer semester of 1952, J. lectured three hours weekly on "Die Grundfragen der Philosophie" ("Basic Questions of Philosophy").

Letter 125
1. Karl Jaspers, *Vernunft und Existenz* (Groningen, 1935).
2. In connection with publication of Hermann Broch's *Gesammelte Werke*, A. edited the two posthumous volumes, *Dichten und Erkennen* (Essays, vol. I) and *Erkennen und Handeln* (Essays, vol. 2) (Zurich, 1955). She also wrote an introduction to the first volume, 5–42.

Letter 126
1. J.'s nephew and his wife: Enno E. Dugend, 1915–1980, musician; and Herta M. Dugend-Münch, b. 1913.
2. Erna Dugend-Jaspers; see L. 32, n. 1.

Letter 127
1. The treaty to establish a European Defense Community (EDC) was signed on May 27, 1952, in Paris, by France, Italy, Belgium, Holland, Luxembourg, and the Federal Republic of Germany. It was never ratified.

Letter 129
1. A.'s visit in Basel at the end of May.

Letter 130
1. André Malraux, *Psychologie der Kunst: Das imaginäre Museum* (Baden-Baden, 1949).
2. A.'s lecture, "Ideologie und Terror," was later published in *Festschrift für Karl Jaspers*; see L. 141, n. 1.

Letter 131
1. Ernst Mayer had to undergo an operation.

Letter 132

1. This refers to A.'s August visit to Karl and Gertrud J. in St. Moritz.
2. See L. 112, n. 2.
3. See L. 87, n. 1.
4. Karl Jaspers, *Einführung in die Philosophie: Zwölf Radiovorträge* (Zurich, 1950).
5. The theory of category, which was to be the second volume of *Logik*; see L. 98, n. 3.
6. J.'s idea of an axial period (c. 800–200 B.C.) during which the first great religions, philosophies, and literatures emerged in Asia and in the West at the same time and with the same originality.
7. Bard College, in Annandale-on-Hudson, New York.

Letter 133

1. L. 129 is probably meant; there is a reply to it from Heinrich Blücher, August 5, 1952; see L. 132. It could refer, however, to a letter that has not been preserved, if Blücher's response was delayed.
2. Village in the Catskill Mountains, north of New York City, where A. and her husband frequently spent their summer vacations.
3. Probably the two versions of *Die Idee der Universität* (Berlin, 1923; Berlin/Heidelberg, 1946).
4. On her departure from St. Moritz, A. had apparently packed books or manuscripts of J.'s by mistake.
5. *Lebensrückblick* (Zurich/Wiesbaden, 1951). Lou Andreas-Salomé, 1861–1937, was a writer and friend of Nietzsche, Rilke, and Freud.
6. Paul Rée, 1849–1901, physician and psychologist, was a friend of Nietzsche and Lou Andreas-Salomé.
7. This passage apparently goes back to conversations held in St. Moritz.

Letter 134

1. The manuscript of A.'s book on Rahel Varnhagen; see L. 3, n. 3.
2. Christian Wilhelm Dohm, 1751–1820, political writer and Prussian government official, was a pioneer in Jewish emancipation.
3. David Friedländer, 1750–1834, businessman and writer, was another pioneer in Jewish emancipation.
4. Karl August Varnhagen von Ense, 1785–1858, diplomat and writer, was Rahel Varnhagen's husband.
5. Friedrich von Gentz, 1764–1832, Prussian government official and journalist, was a close associate of Metternich.
6. Pauline Wiesel, née Cesar, 1777–1848, was a friend of Rahel Varnhagen.
7. Alexander von der Marwitz, 1787–1814, was a friend of Rahel Varnhagen.
8. Karl Count von Finckenstein, 1772–1811, was a Prussian diplomat and fiancé of Rahel Varnhagen.

9. Achim, 1781–1831, and Bettina, 1785–1859, von Arnim.
10. Presumably "Die Klosterbeere: Zum Andenken an die Frankfurter Judengasse," in Bettina von Arnim, *Werke und Briefe*, ed. Gustav Konrad, 3 (Darmstadt, 1963): 263ff.
11. Wilhelm von Humboldt, 1767–1835, was a scholar and Prussian statesman; see L. 246.
12. Wilhelm Dilthey, 1833–1911. As a psychologist, he was the creator of a theory of understanding based on "historical processes of the psyche"; as a philosopher, the founder of an epistemology of the humanities.
13. Wilhelm Dilthey, *Leben Schleiermachers*, 2nd ed., ed. Hermann Mulert, 1 (Berlin/Leipzig, 1922): 228.
14. Georg Misch, 1878–1965, was a philosopher and advocate of Dilthey's school.
15. Lujo Brentano, 1844–1931, was an economist.
16. In the winter semester 1952–53, J. lectured three hours weekly on "Die grossen Philosophen" ("The Great Philosophers").

Letter 135

1. Walther Rathenau, 1867–1922, German industrialist, journalist, and politician, was minister of reconstruction, 1921, and Reich foreign minister, 1922. He was assassinated.
2. The Varnhagen Archives, almost fully intact and catalogued, are in the Jagiellonian Library in Cracow, Poland. See Deborah Hertz, "The Varnhagen Collection Is in Krakau," *The American Archivist* 44, no. 3 (Summer 1981).
3. *Correspondence between Varnhagen and Rahel*, ed. Ludmilla Assing-Grimelli, 6 vols. (Leipzig, 1874–75).
4. *Rahel: Ein Buch des Andenkens für ihre Freunde*, 3 vols. (Berlin, 1834).
5. Rebekka Friedländer, b. 1782, wife of Moses Friedländer, was a successful novelist under the name Regina Frohberg.
6. Caroline von Humboldt, 1766–1829, was the wife of Wilhelm von Humboldt; see L. 134, n. 11.
7. Comte de Mirabeau, 1749–1791, French revolutionary leader and orator, was a member of the States-General, 1789, and president of the National Assembly, 1791.
8. Shabbatai Zevi, 1626–1676, was a messianic Jewish heretic who later converted to Islam. He proclaimed himself the Messiah and had many followers among Eastern European Jews. His influence was felt into the eighteenth century.
9. Karl Jaspers, "Von den Grenzen pädagogischen Planens," *Basler Schulblatt* 13, no. 4 (1952): 72–77.
10. The reference is not to something J. wrote. It may mean a book borrowed from him, perhaps Marcus Tullius Cicero, *Vom Gemeinwesen*, Latin and German, introduced and newly translated by Karl Büchner (Zurich, 1952).
11. Kurt Blumenfeld, "Walther Rathenau," typescript.
12. This letter, probably from Michael Bullock, is not in the literary remains.

Letter 136

1. According to both tributes in *Arztliche Mitteilungen* (issue 24, December 20, 1952), Ernst Mayer died on October 9.
2. Ella Mayer, 1887–1965.
3. Recontres Internationales, in Geneva in 1946; see L. 44.

Letter 137

1. Hans (Hanno) Waltz, 1930–1983, son of Lotte and Wilhelm Waltz (see L. 102, n. 7), was a physician.
2. Stefan Andres, 1906–1970, was a German writer. For Kristeller, see L. 34, n. 15.
3. "Leni" is an endearing nickname for Helene.
4. Mary McCarthy, 1912–1989, who also wrote nonfiction, became a close friend of A.'s.
5. Adlai E. Stevenson, 1900–1965, the Democratic party's candidate, lost to Dwight D. Eisenhower in this election and in 1956.
6. Robert A. Taft, 1889–1953, senator from Ohio, tried, unsuccessfully, in 1948 and 1952 to become the presidential candidate of the Republican party. Alfred Hugenberg, 1865–1951, German industrialist, press and film tycoon, and conservative Reichstag deputy, did not belong to the Nazi party, but took part, as Reich minister of economics and agriculture, in forming Hitler's government.
7. Paul von Hindenburg, 1847–1934, German field marshal, was president of the Reich, 1925–34. He made Hitler chancellor in 1933.
8. Eric Voegelin, b. 1901, German political scientist, philosopher of history, and scholar of religion, taught, from 1938, at various U.S. universities.
9. Eric Voegelin, *The New Science of Politics* (Chicago, 1952).

Letter 138

1. Letter of November 16, 1952, from Heinrich Blücher to J.

Letter 139

1. After A.'s visit with Heidegger in Freiburg in early February 1950, correspondence, broken off in 1933, was resumed. The letter from Heidegger mentioned here is dated December 15, 1952.
2. Letter of July 24, 1952, from J. to Heidegger.

Letter 140

1. *Cézanne: 10 Water Colors* (New York, 1947).

Letter 141

1. Hannah Arendt, "Ideologie und Terror," in *Offener Horizont: Festschrift für Karl Jaspers* (Munich, 1953): 229–54.
2. "Ideologie und Terror," 231.
3. Max Weber, "Die protestantische Ethik und der Geist des Kapitalismus," in his *Gesammelte Aufsätze zur Religionssoziologie* 1 (Tübingen, 1920): 17ff. For the methodological reflection J. refers to, see 82–83.

Letter 142

1. J. had written a foreword for Milosz's book; see L. 123, n. 1.
2. Alfred A. Knopf, New York publisher of Milosz's *The Captive Mind.*
3. Moses Hadas, 1900–1966, was professor of Latin and Greek at Columbia University, 1944–66.
4. On the occasion of his seventieth birthday, J. was awarded an honorary doctorate by the University of Heidelberg, an honorary membership in the Society of German Neurologists and Psychiatrists, and an honorary membership in the General Medical Society for Psychotherapy of Vienna.
5. The Permanent Subcommittee on Investigations, of which Joseph McCarthy had become chairman in early 1953 (see L. 90, n. 6); the Senate Internal Security Subcommittee; and the House Un-American Activities Committee.
6. Whittaker Chambers, *Witness* (New York, 1952). See A.'s discussion of this book: "The Ex-Communists," *Commonweal* 57 (March 20, 1953): 595–99.
7. In June 1950, 118 scholars, artists, and writers from twenty-one countries had founded, in Berlin, the Congress for Cultural Freedom. They discussed pertinent problems and unanimously accepted a manifesto that proclaimed in Article 1, the "axiomatic truth that freedom of the mind is one of the inalienable human rights." An international general secretariat, to be located in Paris, was established, and committees were formed in various countries. The president of the American Committee for Cultural Freedom was George S. Counts, an educator. Among the vice presidents were the geneticist Hermann J. Muller and historian Arthur Schlesinger, Jr. Irving Kristol was executive director; James Burnham and Sidney Hook were members of the executive committee.
8. Huey P. Long, 1893–1935, was governor of Louisiana, 1928–31, and U.S. senator, 1931–35.
9. Mary McCarthy, with A., Nicola Chiaromonte, Dwight Macdonald, Richard Rovere, Arthur Schlesinger, Jr., and others, tried to found a magazine to be called *Critic.* The project had to be abandoned for lack of funding.
10. Irving Kristol, b. 1920, social scientist, was managing editor of *Commentary,* 1947–52, coeditor of *Encounter,* 1953–58. The magazines sponsored by the Congress for Cultural Freedom were the English *Encounter,* the German *Der Monat,* and the French *Preuves.*

11. See L. 148, n. 9.
12. See L. 145, n. 2.
13. Nietzsche, *Der Wille zur Macht*, no. 608.
14. Hannah Arendt, "Understanding and Politics," *Partisan Review* 20, no. 4 (July / August 1953): 377–92.
15. Heinrich Braun, 1854–1927, was a Social Democratic politician and writer.
16. *Aus nachgelassenen Schriften eines Frühvollendeten* (Stuttgart, 1919). Otto Braun, 1897–1918, was the son of Heinrich and Lily Braun. Julie Braun-Vogelstein was Heinrich Braun's third wife.

Letter 143

1. John Peter Zenger, 1697–1746, went to New York from the Palatinate in 1710 and founded an opposition newspaper, the *New York Weekly Journal*, in 1733. He was acquitted in a trial for libel with intent to incite. This decision is regarded as the first victory for freedom of the press in the United States.

2. Other members of the honorary presidium were Benedetto Croce, John Dewey (both deceased at this time), Salvador de Madariaga, Jacques Maritain, Reinhold Niebuhr, and Bertrand Russell. J. never took part in any of the Congress's events, but he did occasionally send messages to its gatherings, including the founding congress in Berlin and the 1951 meeting in Bombay. He was not a member of the German committee, to which, among others, Willy Brandt, Alexander Mitscherlich (see L. 365, n. 1), and Carlo Schmid (see L. 381, n.2) belonged. For the congress of 1953 in Hamburg he let himself be elected to the honorary committee but, in a letter of June 12, refused this time to send opening remarks: "I have found it a serious lack for a long time that the Congress is not openly and energetically opposing McCarthy's actions in America. . . . Unfriendly observers could say that the Congress is fighting for the West against Russia, not for freedom and against every form of totalitarian threat." Because he too was of this opinion, he eventually severed his connections with the Congress entirely.

3. Reinhold Niebuhr, 1892–1971, American Protestant theologian, was a professor at Union Theological Seminary, in New York.

4. Karl Jaspers, "Wahrheit und Unheil der Bultmannschen Entmythologisierung," lecture given on Swiss Theologians' Day, 1953, in *Schweizerische theologische Umschau* 23, no. 3–4 (1953): 74–106.

5. Karl Jaspers, *Lionardo als Philosoph*, lecture given for the Department of Art History, University of Basel (Bern, 1953).

6. Karl Jaspers, "Die Idee des Arztes," lecture given for the celebration of Swiss Physicians' Day, 1953, in *Schweizerische Arztezeitung* 34, no. 27 (1953): 253–57.

7. *National-Zeitung* (Basel), May 21 and 22.

8. James A. Wechsler, at that time editor-in-chief of the *New York Post*, had belonged to the Young Communist League at Columbia University

twenty years earlier. Senator McCarthy summoned him before his committee and accused him of operating the *New York Post* in a Communistic spirit. He supported his case by citing a book, allegedly written by Wechsler, that was supposedly in the libraries of the United States Information Agency in Europe. But the title of the book was never named in the hearings. Wechsler was one of the most courageous fighters against McCarthy.

9. In this passage, J. draws on an article by Manfred Geroge, "McCarthy bedroht Amerikas Pressefreiheit," *National-Zeitung*, no. 227 (May 22). The article mentioned several criticisms that New York newspapers had made of McCarthy, but the only journalist named was Wechsler.

Letter 145

1. See L. 143, n. 4. The quotes that follow are from Karl Jaspers and Rudolf Bultmann, *Die Frage der Entmythologisierung* (Munich, 1954).
2. Hannah Arendt, "Religion and Politics," *Confluence* (September 1953): 105–26.
3. Jaspers and Bultmann, *Die Frage*, 20.
4. *Ibid.*, 41.
5. *Ibid.*, 40.
6. Roy M. Cohn, 1927–1986, was chief counsel for Senator Joseph McCarthy's Permanent Subcommittee on Investigations. G. David Schine, b. 1927, was chief consultant to the subcommittee. In June 1953, they were sent to Europe to check for Communist subversion in U.S. overseas libraries.
7. George S. Counts, 1889–1974, was professor of education at Teachers College of Columbia University, 1927–1956. See also L. 142, n. 7.
8. On June 12, 1953, the *New York Times* published an article, " 'Refuse to Testify' Einstein Advises Intellectuals Called in by Congress," in which a letter of May 16, 1953, from Albert Einstein to William Frauenglass is quoted. After Frauenglass, a Brooklyn teacher, had been interrogated by the Committee on Un-American Activities, he asked Einstein to make a public statement that would "strengthen the will of American teachers and the public at large to resist the new attack of the obscurantists." Einstein replied, in the letter cited above, "that every intellectual called before a Congressional Investigation Committee should refuse to testify, and must be prepared for jail and economic ruin, in short, for the sacrifice of his personal welfare in the interest of the welfare of his country." The publication of this letter drew worldwide attention.
9. The attack on Einstein was distributed as a statement of the American Committee for Cultural Freedom. It was also sent out as undated news from the committee, printed on official letterhead paper containing not only the names of the members of the U.S. committee, but also those of the international committee, thus creating the possible misunderstanding that the European members were in agreement with this statement.

Letter 146

1. See L. 113, n. 3. In German translation: Hannah Arendt, "Karl Jaspers: Bürger der Welt," in *Karl Jaspers*, ed. P. A. Schlipp (Stuttgart, 1957): 532–43.
2. At the end of the Schilpp volume, J. responded to all twenty-four of the essays it contained.
3. "Philosophische Autobiographie," which forms the first section of the Schilpp book.
4. Heinrich Rickert, 1863–1936, philosopher, was the main spokesman of the Southwest German school, and J.'s colleague and antipode at Heidelberg.
5. The proposed chapter on Heidegger never appeared in a printed version of the "Philosophische Autobiographie" during J.'s lifetime. It was first published in the revised and enlarged second edition of *Philosophische Autobiographie*, 92–111.
6. Letter of November 16, 1952.

Letter 147

1. Fritz Kaufmann, 1891–1958, a Jewish privatdocent in philosophy at Freiburg im Breisgau, was relieved of his post in 1933. He became a professor at the University of Buffalo, and moved to Zurich after his retirement.

Letter 148

1. L. 146.
2. The undated news from the American Committee for Cultural Freedom cited in L. 145, n. 9.
3. See L. 145, n. 8.
4. Renato de Rosa, b. 1921, studied history and philosophy in Naples and Heidelberg, and, after 1945, medicine in Heidelberg; he qualified in surgery. He was a close friend of Gertrud and Karl Jaspers from the winter of 1940–41.
5. Rose Feitelson, b. 1914, became a friend of A. and Heinrich Blücher on their arrival in New York in 1941. From 1965, she was writer and editor for the American Jewish Committee. See L. 226.
6. After de Rosa had completed his medical studies (J. had moved to Basel in the meantime), he wanted to return to Naples to study, as he told A., "comprehension psychology" in its most real form, in the streets of the city. But because his German certification was not recognized in Italy, he stayed in Germany.
7. It cannot be determined which essays A. sent. Apart from the essay named in n. 8, "Religion and Politics" (see L. 145, n. 2) was certainly among them.
8. Hannah Arendt, "Ideology and Terror: A Novel Form of Government," *The Review of Politics* 15, no. 3 (July 1953): 303–27. For the shorter German version, see L. 141, n. 1.

9. A. gave these lectures, "Karl Marx and the Tradition of Political Thought," for the Christian Gauss Seminar in Criticism at Princeton University. They, and those given at New York University, were incorporated into her *The Human Condition* (1958); see L. 169, n. 3.

Letter 149

1. *Albert Einstein als Philosoph und Naturforscher*, ed. Paul A. Schilpp, Philosophen des 20. Jahrhunderts series (Stuttgart, n.d.).
2. The names of Paul Ricoeur and Jean Wahl are missing from this list.
3. See L. 145, n. 9.
4. Gerhard Huber, b. 1923, was assistant to J. 1952–56, and professor of philosophy and pedagogy at the Eidgenössische Technische Hochschule in Zurich from 1956.

Letter 150

1. See L. 111, n. 3.
2. Kurt Hoffman, b. 1922 in Vienna, served in the U.S. State Department, 1949–53. He was then a journalist and lecturer in American literature and history at the University of Munich, and, later, department chief for Bavarian Television there. J. had known him since 1945.

Letter 151

1. See L. 148, nn. 7 and 8.
2. In the winter semester of 1953–54, J. lectured three hours weekly on "Die grossen Philosophen 2. Teil" ("The Great Philosophers, Part 2").
3. Walter Kaufmann, *Nietzsche: Philosopher, Psychologist, Antichrist* (Princeton, NJ, 1950).
4. Walter Kaufmann, "Jaspers' Beziehung zu Nietzsche," in *Karl Jaspers*, 400–29.
5. Eduard Baumgarten, b. 1898, philosopher and sociologist, taught sociology at Stuttgart, Mannheim, and Freiburg after the war. He had an argumentative friendship with J. from the early 1920s.
6. See Ls. 111, 112.

Letter 152

1. See L. 83, n. 1.
2. Benno von Wiese; see L. 5, n. 1.

Letter 153

1. At seventy-one, J. was already past retirement age.
2. A conference of the United States, Great Britain, France, and the Soviet Union on German reunification. No solution was reached.
3. See L. 127, n. 1.

Letter 154

1. See L. 31, n. 9.

Letter 155

1. See L. 143.
2. A. received an Arts and Letters Award in Literature for *The Origins of Totalitarianism*. In 1964, she was elected a regular member of the National Institute of Arts and Letters, founded in 1898, which has 250 members.

Louis Hartz?

Letter 156

1. Leo Strauss, 1899–1973, German-Jewish historian and philosopher, emigrated to the United States in 1938, taught at the New School for Social Research, in New York, 1938–49, then at the University of Chicago and at Claremont Men's College, in California. J. is referring to his *Die Religionskritik Spinozas als Grundlage seiner Bibelwissenschaft* (Leipzig, 1930).

Letter 157

1. On the hundredth anniversary of Friedrich Schelling's death (August 20, 1854), a conference was held in Bad Ragaz, Switzerland, September 22–25, 1954.
2. Karl Jaspers, "Schellings Grösse und sein Verhängnis." It later appeared in *Studia Philosophica* 14 (Basel, 1954): 12–38.
3. See L. 1, n. 1.
4. See L. 114, n. 1.

Letter 158

1. This lecture was not published.
2. "The victorious cause pleased the gods, but the defeated one pleases Cato." From Lucan, *Pharsalia (Bellum civile)*, I, line 128. A., who came across this quote in early readings of Gentz, was particularly fond of it and used it several times in important contexts: in her *Rahel Varnhagen*, written in the 1930s (1957, p. 68); in her philosophical lectures; as the final sentence of *The Life of the Mind: Thinking* (1978, p. 216); and, finally, on a sheet of paper found in her typewriter at the time of her death that bore the heading: "The Life of the Mind. Part III. Judging." She probably meant it as an epigraph.

In *Thinking*, A. ascribes the quote to "Old Cato," but it belongs to

Cato the Younger, Cato Uticensis. In his epic describing the civil war between Caesar and Pompey, in ten books, Lucan glorifies Cato Uticensis as an anti-Caesarean republican and the model of genuine Roman character. On A.'s page for *Judging*, after the Lucan quote, is a quote from Goethe's *Faust*, II, lines 11,404–407: "If I could rid my path of magic, / could totally unlearn its incantations, / confront you, Nature, simply as a man, / to be a human being would then be worth the effort." The connection is probably that Lucan had removed the gods (the "magic," the "incantations") from his understanding of history. His Cato was entirely on his own, "simply as a man," true to nothing but his own republican principles, with his freedom-loving outlook in contrast to the spirit of the times, and judging without regard for success or failure.

3. Leo Strauss, *The Political Philosophy of Hobbes: Its Basis and Its Genesis*, trans. from German ms. by Elsa M. Sinclair (Oxford, 1936).
4. Leo Strauss, *Natural Right and History* (Chicago, 1953).
5. Gerhard Krüger, 1902–1972, was a German philosopher.

Letter 160

1. Karl Jaspers and Rudolf Bultmann, *Die Frage der Entmythologisierung*.
2. This refers to a letter of August 29, 1954, from Gertrud J. to A.
3. *Du: Schweizerische Monatsschrift*, no. 9 (September 1954). Special Issue: *Die Philosophie im Bilde*.
4. Claire Roessiger's photo of J., p. 42.
5. Karl Jaspers, "The Political Vacuum in Germany," *Foreign Affairs* 32 (1953–54): 595–607. This did not appear in German.
6. Karl Jaspers, "The Fight Against Totalitarianism," *Confluence* 3, no. 3 (1954): 251–66. In German: "Im Kampf mit dem Totalitarismus," in Karl Jaspers, *Philosophie und Welt*, 76–96; see L. 226, n. 2.

Letter 161

1. The critical passage in the *Confluence* article reads: "In view of my general approval, my disagreements as to the method of investigation and as to certain evaluations of the data are negligible" (p. 256). J. used this remark in the German version: *Philosophie und Welt*, 83.
2. Peter Waltz, b. 1931, son of Lotte and Wilhelm Waltz (see L. 102, n. 7), was a chemist.
3. Eidgenössische Technische Hochschule.

Letter 162

1. Goethe, "Wiederfinden," in *West-Ostlicher Divan*, fourth stanza.
2. Questionnaires of this sort were used by many universities to determine the students' judgment of the instructors' teaching qualifications.
3. See L. 19, n. 1.
4. See L. 125, n. 2.

Letter 163

1. Leonardo Olschki, 1885–1961, was a Romanist who taught at the University of Heidelberg, 1908–32.
2. See L. Olschki, *Geschichte der neusprachlichen wissenschaftlichen Literatur*, 3 vols. (Heidelberg, 1919–); on Leonardo, see, in particular, 1: 252–413; on Galileo, vol. 3.
3. Leonardo Olschki, *Dante "Poeta Veltro"* (Florence, 1953).
4. This information probably derived from a verbal communication. Olschki's book *L'Asia di Marco Polo* did not appear until 1957.
5. During the war and immediately after it, but particularly during the McCarthy Committee years, the majority of states passed laws requiring from teachers sworn declarations of loyalty. In 1949, the University of California added to the existing state requirement the explicit declaration that the teacher did not belong to the Communist party. Thirty-one professors who refused to sign the oath were fired.
6. Olschki became E. R. Curtius's successor at the University of Heidelberg when Curtius, German historian of literature, went to Bonn in 1929.
7. Erich Auerbach, 1892–1955.
8. Manfred Bukofzer, 1910–1955.
9. Golo Mann, *Vom Geist Amerikas: Eine Einführung in amerikanisches Denken und Handeln im zwanzigsten Jahrhundert* (Stuttgart, 1954).

Letter 164

1. Under this greeting, written on a picture postcard, the following lines were added: "In time Frau Arendt will find still more camels of this breed in this particular desert. With warmest regards to you, Your Leonardo and Kate Olschki."

Letter 165

1. L. 163 and a letter of February 15, 1955, from Gertrud J.
2. This international conference, sponsored by the Congress for Cultural Freedom, on "The Future of Freedom," took place September 12–17, 1955 in Milan. A. spoke on "The Rise and Development of Totalitarianism and Authoritarian Forms of Government in the Twentieth Century." Her talk was published by the Congress as a typescript, then in *The Future of Freedom*, a compilation of papers submitted to the conference (Bombay, 1955), 180–206.
3. Gertrud J. had written to A. that Dr. Waltz had suffered a heart attack.
4. Johannes N. Theodorakopoulos, who had studied philosophy with J. at Heidelberg.
5. Eric Hoffer, 1902–1983, as a social philosopher later lectured at the University of California, Berkeley. His first book was *The True Believer* (1951). In February 1983, he received the Presidential Medal of Freedom, the highest civilian award in the United States. In an interview, he re-

sponded to the remark "You are an intellectual" by saying, "No, I'm a longshoreman."
6. Beverly Woodward; see L. 224.

Letter 167

1. British term for a society formed by secret alliances among the Kikuyu and some other tribes of Kenya, who in 1949–50 rebelled against British colonial rule and white domination.
2. J. G. Herder, *Sämtliche Werke*, ed. Bernhard Suphan, 33 vols. (Berlin, 1877–1914): 15, 137.
3. Wilhelm Starliner, *Grenzen der Sowjetmacht* (Würzburg, 1955).
4. See L. 157, n. 2; the reprinted lecture was in *Merkur* 9 (1955): 11–34.
5. See L. 160, n. 6.

Letter 168

1. Gertrud J. to A., July 11, 1955.

Letter 169

1. Karl Jaspers, *Schelling: Grösse und Verhängnis* (Munich, 1955).
2. Hannah Arendt, "The Personality of Waldemar Gurian," *The Review of Politics* 17, no. 1 (January 1955): 33–42; reprinted in Hannah Arendt, *Men in Dark Times* (New York, 1968): 251–62.
3. The book appeared as *The Human Condition* (Chicago, 1958); in German: *Vita Activa oder Vom tätigen Leben* (Stuttgart, 1960).
4. See L. 165, n. 2.

Letter 172

1. To Hannah Arendt, *Elemente und Ursprünge totaler Herrschaft* (Frankfurt am Main, 1955).

Letter 173

1. A letter of September 16, 1955, from Gertrud J. to A. indicates A. had enclosed a handkerchief.
2. Johannes N. Theodorakopoulos.

Letter 175

1. See L. 165, n. 2.
2. Among the participants in the conference were Raymond Aron, Sidney Hook, John Kenneth Galbraith, Arthur Schlesinger, Jr., Friedrich von

Hayek, Manes Sperber, Bertrand de Jouvenel, and Theodor Litt. See the book mentioned in L. 165, n. 2.
3. See L. 172, n. 1.

Letter 176

1. Not in the literary remains. It must have been a reproduction of the gravestone relief of father and son ("Ilissos relief") from the 4th century B.C.

Letter 179

1. This project, also called "the little politics book" and "introduction to politics" (see Ls. 187, 204, 209, and 222), was not completed. See L. 233.
2. This refers to a letter of December 19, 1955, from Gertrud J. to A. The student was Beverly Woodward.

Letter 180

1. Probably André Grabar, *La Peinture Byzantine* (Geneva, 1953).
2. The epigraph in A.'s *The Origins of Totalitarianism*. See L. 103 and L. 103, n. 3.
3. Between J.'s letters 177 and 180 there is only one from A. in the literary remains. The phrase "sending me the passages and their interpretation" must refer to the lost letter.
4. This has not been identified.
5. Gerhard Knauss, b. 1928, professor of philosophy at Saabrücken University in 1971.
6. Knauss's doctoral dissertation was *Gegenstand und Umgreifendes*, vol. 3 of Philosophische Forschungen, Neue Folge, edited by J. (Basel, 1954).
7. Hans-Georg Gadamer, b. 1900, a philosopher akin to Heidegger, had known J. earlier.

Letter 181

1. The four-volume Artemis edition of Goethe's letters, which appeared from 1949 to 1951.
2. Erich Frank, *Wissen, Wollen, Glauben: Gesammelte Aufsätze zur Philosophiegeschichte und Existentialphilosophie* (Zurich/Stuttgart, 1955).
3. *India: Paintings from Ajanta Caves*, introduction by M. Singh (New York, 1954).
4. See the preface to J.'s *Schelling*.
5. See Edgar Allan Poe's story "Descent into the Maelstrom."
6. Franz Grillparzer, *Sämtliche Werke*, 10 vols., 9 (Stuttgart, 1872): 34.

Letter 182

1. See L. 113, n. 3, and L. 146, n. 1.
2. The fourth, unrevised, edition (Berlin/Göttingen/Heidelberg, 1954).
3. Max Weber, "Agrarverhältnisse im Altertum," in his *Gesammelte Aufsätze zur Sozial- und Wirtschaftsgeschichte* (Tübingen, 1924): 1–288.
4. Max Weber, "Die protestantische Ethik und der Geist des Kapitalismus," in his *Gesammelte Aufsätze zur Religionssoziologie* (Tübingen, 1920): 1–206.

Letter 183

1. J.'s "Philosophische Autobiographie" and "Antwort" in *The Philosophy of Karl Jaspers*, ed. P. A. Schilpp; see L. 113, n. 3, and L. 146, n. 1.

Letter 184

1. Hannah Arendt, "Was ist Autorität?" *Der Monat* 8, no. 89 (February 1956): 29–44.
2. Hannah Arendt, "Was ist Autorität?" "In this connection, I would like to mention Heidegger's superb interpretation of the simile of the cave in his 'Platons Lehre von der Wahrheit.' in which he demonstrates that Aletheia is transformed into Orthotes, truth into correctness," p. 36.
3. Timaeus's speech about the beginnings of the world.
4. Book 6 of *Republic*.
5. Martin Heidegger, "Platons Lehre von der Wahrheit," in *Geistige Uberlieferung 2* (1942): 96–124.
6. J.'s marginalia read: "H. treats Plato as if he were a man with 'doctrines.' —just like Zeller—totally un-Platonic mode. No dialectic—no genuine following of the movement of thought—some kind of phantasm—nihil —takes the place of existence-transcendence—Plato incorrectly characterized. Overall claims are somewhat ridiculous."
7. See Plato's seventh letter.
8. *Politikos*, 293cff.
9. J.'s "Philosophische Autobiographie" and "Antwort."
10. In the summer semester of 1956, J. lectured three hours weekly on "Philosophie in der Lebenspraxis" ("Philosophy in Everyday Life").
11. On Kierkegaard.
12. Hannsjörg A. Salmony, b. 1920, was an assistant in the department of philosophy at Basel, 1956–60. In 1961, he became Barth's successor as professor of philosophy there.
13. Henri Frédéric Amiel, 1821–1881, was a Swiss writer and philosopher. The selections mentioned here were never published.

Letter 185

1. See J.'s "Antwort" to Walter Kaufmann in *The Philosophy of Karl Jaspers*, ed. P. A. Schilpp, 842ff. See L. 113, nn. 2, 3.

2. See J.'s "Antwort" to Eduard Baumgarten in *ibid.*, 825, 834–35, 847ff.
3. See L. 186.
4. See J.'s "Antwort" in *The Philosophy of Karl Jaspers*, 753.
5. This news was from a letter of April 19, 1956, from Gertrud J. to A.

Letter 189

1. Niouta Ghosh, née Wilbouchevich.

Letter 190

1. Karl Jaspers, *Die Atombombe und die Zukunft des Menschen: Ein Radiovortrag* (Munich, 1957).
2. Karl Jaspers, "Unsterblichkeit," in N. M. Luyten et al., *Unsterblichkeit* (Basel, 1957): 31–41.
3. Not published.
4. Not published.
5. Eirene and Andrée Mayer, grandchildren of Ernst and Ella Mayer; Paul Gottschalk, a cousin of Gertrud J.
6. Karl Jaspers, *Philosophie*, 3 vols. (Berlin/Göttingen/Heidelberg, 1956).

Letter 191

1. Edna Fürst, b. 1943, daughter of A.'s cousin Ernst Fürst.

Letter 192

1. Carl Joachim Friedrich, b. 1901, who went to the United States in 1922, was professor of government at Harvard University.

Letter 194

1. See L. 72, n. 2.
2. Philip Mayer, at that time professor of social anthropology at Rhodes University, in Grahamstown.

Letter 199

1. Elisabeth ("Elke") Gilbert. She was the wife of writer and composer Robert Gilbert, 1899–1978, who had been a close friend of Heinrich Blücher since 1917.

Letter 200

1. This refers to the invasion of Hungary by Soviet troops to put down an anti-Communist uprising.

Letter 201

1. For A.'s next visit, which could not be planned for earlier than 1958.
2. The four-power conference held in Geneva July 18–23, 1955, on the reunification of Germany. The Soviet Union seemed agreeable to reunifying Germany at that time, but on condition that NATO and the Warsaw Pact be disbanded.
3. Sir Bernard L. Montgomery, Viscount Montgomery of Alamein, 1887–1976, British field marshal, was at that time chief of the imperial general staff and representative to the North Atlantic Treaty Organization.
4. Kant, *Der Streit der Fakultäten*, 2. Abschnitt, 7.
5. Moshe Dayan, 1915–1981, Israeli general and politician, was Israeli chief of staff during the Sinai Campaign of 1956.
6. After the proclamation of the independent state of Israel in May 1948, more than 800,000 Palestinians left; most of them were expelled.
7. When Egypt's president Nasser nationalized the Suez Canal in 1956, Britain and France invaded Egypt, but withdrew, under pressure from the Soviet Union and the United States, and were replaced by a United Nations force.

Letter 202

1. John Foster Dulles, 1888–1959, was at that time U.S. secretary of state.
2. Jawaharlal Nehru, 1889–1964, was then prime minister, India's first.
3. *Die grossen Philosophen.*

Letter 203

1. Nikita Khrushchev, 1894–1971, was, from 1953, first secretary of the Central Committee of the Communist party and, from 1958, premier of the Soviet Union.
2. On the atom bomb and the future of man. See L. 190, n. 1. Using it as a point of departure, J. developed his book of the same title; see L. 206, n. 1.

Letter 204

1. The German edition of *Karl Jaspers*, edited by P. A. Schilpp; see L. 146, n. 1.
2. Adalbert Stifter, 1805–1868, was an Austrian novelist.
3. Sa'ud Sa'ud ibn 'Abd al-Asis, 1903–1969, was king of Saudi Arabia, 1953–65.
4. *The Tao of Painting: A Study of the Ritual Disposition of Chinese Painting*, with a translation of the *Chieh Tzu Yuan Hua Chuan* or *Mustard Seed Garden Manual of Painting 1679–1701*, by Mai-Mai Sze, 2 vols. (New York, 1956).

Letter 205

1. This refers to the Sinai Campaign of late October–early November 1956 and Israel's policies thereafter.
2. The "Suggestion of the USSR for a Draft Resolution of the UN" of October 18, 1954, attempted to work out a comprehensive list of the characteristics of an aggressor.
3. General Paul von Hindenburg was elected Reich president in 1925 and reelected in 1932.
4. *The Chinese on the Art of Painting*, translations with comments by Osvald Sirén (Peking, 1936).
5. This refers to a book planned for "Weltgeschichte der Philosophie" (see L. 114, n. 1) that was to present the interaction between philosophy, myth, language, and art.
6. Mai-Mai Sze; see L. 204, n. 4.
7. Lin Yutang, 1895–1976, Chinese writer and philologist, edited *Laotse* (Frankfurt am Main/Hamburg, 1955). Lao Tzu, c. 604–531 B.C., was a legendary Chinese philosopher and a founder of Taoism.
8. Tschuang-tse (Chuang-tzu), 369–286 B.C.?, was a Chinese Taoist philosopher.
9. *Lao-tse's Tao te King*, trans., introduced, and commentary by Victor von Strauss (Leipzig, 1870).

Letter 206

1. The Göttingen Declaration of April 1957, signed by eighteen German physicists, in which they recommended that Germany not be equipped with nuclear arms. They stated: "In any case, none of the signatories would be willing to take part in any manner in the development, testing, or deployment of nuclear weapons." See Karl Jaspers, *Die Atombombe und die Zukunft des Menschen: Politisches Bewusstsein in unserer Zeit* (Munich, 1958), 268–77.
2. Alfred North Whitehead, 1861–1947; his book *The Concept of Nature* was published in 1920.
3. Walter Kaufmann, "German Thought Today," *The Kenyon Review* 19, no. 1 (Winter 1957): 15–30.

Letter 207

1. Walther Bothe, 1891–1957, German physicist, received the Nobel Prize, with Max Born, in 1954.
2. This criticism is due in part to incomplete knowledge of the facts. A subsequent elaboration of this point can be found on pages 268–77 of *Atombombe*; see L. 190, n. 1; L. 206, n. 1. On the history of the German atom bomb, see Robert Jungk, *Brighter than a Thousand Suns: A Personal History of the Atomic Scientists*, trans. James Cleugh (New York, 1958).

743

Letter 208

1. Not dated by J. The letter is a handwritten postscript to a letter written by Gertrud J. to A.
2. On June 9, 1957, the musician Robert Oboussier (b. 1920) was murdered in Zurich. Bob, as he was called by J. and Gertrud J., was a close friend who also had strong ties to Ernst and Ella Mayer.
3. Johann Joachim Winckelmann, 1717–1768, was the founder of scientific archeology.
4. This presumably refers to a letter from A. to J. that is lost.
5. Karl Jaspers, *Die grossen Philosophen*, vol. 1 (Munich, 1957).

Letter 209

1. See L. 208, n. 5.
2. *The Human Condition*; see L. 169, n. 3.
3. See L. 179, n. 1.
4. This presumably refers to *Die grossen Philosophen*, 74ff.
5. See *Die grossen Philosophen*, 387–90.
6. Plato's epigrams are meant.
7. Karl Jaspers, *Descartes und die Philosophie* (Berlin/Leipzig, 1937).
8. This is the concluding sentence of the preface to J.'s radio lecture "Die Atombombe und die Zukunft des Menschen."
9. Georgi M. Malenkov, 1902–1988, was deputy premier of the U.S.S.R., 1946–53, and premier, 1953–55. When this letter was written, he had been replaced as premier and expelled from the party's Central Committee.
10. Hannah Arendt, "Totalitarian Imperialism: Reflections on the Hungarian Revolution," *The Journal of Politics* 20, no. 1 (February 1958): 5–43.
11. Gertrud J.'s letter of June 26, 1957.

Letter 210

1. Georgi Zhukov, 1896–1974, Soviet marshal and minister of defense, 1955–57, was named to the party presidium in 1957, but was stripped of his party and government functions the same year.

Letter 211

1. Kant, *Kritik der Urteilskraft*, paragraph 56.

Letter 212

1. Nagarjuna was an Indian Buddhist philosopher of the second century B.C. J. described his philosophy in his *Die grossen Philosophen*.
2. T. S. Eliot, 1888–1965, American-born English poet, critic, and dramatist.

Letter 213

1. Richard Reich, "Vom Wesen totaler Herrschaft. Zur deutschen Ausgabe von Hannah Arendt's *The Origins of Totalitarianism,*" *Neue Zürcher Zeitung* (September 28, 1957): 6.

Letter 214

1. Sputniks 1 and 2, which were put into orbit by the U.S.S.R. on October 4 and November 3, 1957.
2. Jeanne Hersch, *Die Ideologien und die Wirklichkeit: Versuch einer politischen Orientierung* (Munich, 1957).
3. Hannah Arendt, *Fragwürdige Traditionsbestände im politischen Denken der Gegenwart: Vier Essays* (Frankfurt am Main, n.d.).
4. *Ibid.*, 144.
5. *The Human Condition* (*Vita Activa* in German edition) was published in 1958; see L. 169, n. 3.
6. The First International Congress of Cultural Critics took place, June 30–July 5, 1958, in Munich in connection with the 800th anniversary of the city's founding. A. was a participant. See Hannah Arendt, "Kultur und Politik," in *Untergang oder Übergang: Erster Kulturkritikerkongress in München* (Munich, 1959): 35–66.
7. This article, orginally planned for *Commentary* and written at the end of 1957, did not appear until 1959: "Reflections on Little Rock," *Dissent* (Winter 1959): 45–56.

Letter 215

1. The essay "Totalitarian Imperialism: Reflections on the Hungarian Revolution"; see L. 209, n. 10.
2. Marie Luise Gothein was the wife of historian Eberhard Gothein (1853–1923). J. knew her through the Max Weber circle.
3. Rabindranath Tagore, 1861–1941, Indian poet and writer.

Letter 217

1. See L. 209, n. 10.
2. Karl Jaspers, foreword to Melvin Lasky, *Die ungarische Revolution: Die Geschichte des Oktober-Aufstandes nach Dokumenten, Meldungen, Augenzeugenberichten und dem Echo der Weltöffentlichkeit: Ein Weissbuch* (Berlin, 1958).
3. The day Claus von Stauffenberg attempted to assassinate Hitler. See L. 366, n. 3.
4. Milovan Djilas, b. 1911, was vice president of Yugoslavia. He was stripped of his Communist party functions in 1954 and later sentenced to prison several times because of his critical writings, especially *The New Class* (1957). J. had in his library the German edition (*Die neue Klasse: Eine Analyse des kommunistischen Systems*), published in Munich in 1960. At

the time of this letter, his knowledge of the book was presumably based on reports and on A.'s essay.

5. See L. 167, n. 3.
6. Mao Tse-tung (Zedong), 1893–1976, Chinese Communist leader, was chairman of the People's Republic of China, 1949–59. When he gave up his position as head of state, he retained leadership of the party. In 1957, a collection of his poems had not yet been published in German. The source of J.'s knowledge of them cannot be determined.

Letter 218

1. Rainer Maria Rilke, "Briefwechesel in Gedichten mit Erika Mitterer, Dreizehnte Antwort," in his *Sämtliche Werke* 2 (Frankfurt, 1955–): 318.

Letter 219

1. See L. 209, n. 10.
2. In 1918–19.
3. J. is presumably alluding to the *Carta del lavoro* approved by the fascist-controlled national council of corporations in 1927. His source was *Benito Mussolini: Der Geist des Faschismus: Ein Quellenwerk*, ed. H. Wagenführ (Munich, 1940): especially 53.

Letter 220

1. Fritz Mayer, 1890–1976, and his wife, Frieda, née Jacobson, 1892–1971.
2. *Die Atombombe und die Zukunft des Menschen*; see L. 206, n. 1.
3. See L. 209.
4. *Fragwürdige Traditionsbestände*; see L. 214, n. 3.

Letter 221

1. On May 13, 1958, in Bremen, A. gave a lecture, "Die Krise in der Erziehung," later published in *Bildungskritik und Bildungsreform in den USA* (Heidelberg, 1968): 11–30.
2. Elke Gilbert. See also L. 226, n. 1.
3. See L. 206, L. 206, n. 1; and L. 207.
4. Paul Ricoeur, b. 1913, was a French philosopher.

Letter 222

1. See L. 179, n. 1, and L. 233, n. 2.

Letter 223

1. The recommendation for Beverly Woodward; see L. 221.
2. Psalm 90:10.

3. See L. 214, n. 3.
4. The lines that were struck out deal with the irrationality of all limits in communication.
5. Karl Jaspers, *Reason and Existenz: Five Lectures*, trans. and introduction by William Earle (New York, 1955).
6. Heinrich Blücher had added a note to L. 222.

Letter 224

1. Suggestions for cuts follow at this point:

"That would look something like this:

"Beginning of p. 29: only the first paragraphs about greatness and history.

"Then, p. 92: purpose of the presentation, again with some cuts.

"And on p. 98: insert pp. 46–49.

" 'Paradigmatic Individuals': a few large cuts in Socrates: pp. 122–124; the small print. The same: pp. 125–126. Buddha and Confucius: the small print at the beginning of the section as a note. Cuts in Confucius: pp. 159–60, 184–5. Mostly the small print.

"Discussions of the 'Paradigmatic Individuals': pp. 214ff. No major cuts but a number of small ones, mostly just one sentence. But a suggestion: take out the two paragraphs 'Warum die vier?' 218–19 and make the first paragraph 'Es gibt andere—nicht zu vergleichen' the introductory paragraph of the section on p. 214. Then put the second paragraph 'Die vier zusammen' after p. 105 [*sic*], after the first introductory paragraph before Socrates. Then, too: p. 215: strike the small print.

"It's hard for me to indicate which individual sentences I've struck. We can talk them over with the help of my copy, which I'll bring along to Basel. These are the only large cuts so far (that is, up to and including Plato. A large cut in Plato: 239–40—the discussion of Schleiermacher and Hermann, but retaining p. 239, line 15: Schon die frühesten Dialoge—Neuerungen nicht vor). I'll try to finish the Augustine before I come. The main problem is the translation of the quotes, which one can't very well leave to the translator. A question apropos of that: Where in Plato does the 'Zugkraft zum Sein' (p. 282) come from? And if there are several passages, please give them to me. Some of the dialogues—Republic, Parmenides, Timaeus—have been translated by Cornford, who is superb. The others mostly only by Jowett, who is almost unusable."

Letter 225

1. See L. 224, n. 1.

Letter 226

1. See L. 148, n. 5. The travel dates follow here:

"On May 21, I'll be in Zurich and will call if that's all right with you. You can reach me:

"May 5–11, with Anne Weil, Luxembourg, 28 Rue A. Fischer
"May 16–20, Cologne, Hotel Bristol.
"I'll have a little apartment in Zurich—a friend who is visiting in America at the moment: % Britschgi, Minervastr. 26. On May 26 I'll be in Geneva for the Institut des Etudes Internationales, 132, rue de Lausanne. On June 3 I'll be in Heidelberg and for a few days after that in Frankfurt. After that, until the end of June: Zurich. From June 29 to July 6 in Munich. After that, before I come to see you, probably in Geneva again for a few days, where Blumenfeld [see L. 109, n. 4] will be."

2. Karl Jaspers, *Philosophie und Welt: Reden und Aufsätze* (Munich, 1958).

Letter 227

1. This letter was sent to Anne Weil's address in Luxembourg. The "friend" could mean her or Rose Feitelson.

Letter 228

1. In addition to L. 227, a letter of May 3, 1958, from Gertrud J.
2. The European Coal and Steel Community was founded in 1951 for the regulation of a common market in coal and steel. It is now part of the Common Market.

Letter 229

1. In 1958, J. received the Peace Prize of the Deutschen Buchhandel. At the award ceremony, on September 28, in St. Paul's Church, in Frankfurt, A. gave the eulogy.
2. Johannes Zilkens was a Cologne physician and friend of A.
3. Arthur Cohen was at this time owner of Meridian Books, which published the second edition of *The Origins of Totalitarianism* (New York, 1958).
4. Alex Morin conducted the negotiations for the U.S. edition of *Die Atombombe* on behalf of the University of Chicago Press. See L. 274, n. 7.
5. Chaim (Viktor) Arlosoroff, 1899–1933, was a Zionist labor leader in the foreign-affairs division of the Zionist executive committee from 1931. He was murdered in Tel Aviv.
6. Chaim Weizmann, 1874–1952, Jewish scholar and president of the World Zionist Organization, served as provisional president of Israel, 1948–49, and first president, 1949–52.
7. J. wanted to give A. a silk velvet dress for the prize ceremony in Frankfurt; see L. 230.
8. The philosopher Alexandre Koyré (see L. 105, n. 11) and his wife.

Letter 230

1. J. had spent his summer vacation this year in Locarno.
2. "Der Arzt im technischen Zeitalter" and "Wahrheit, Freiheit und Friede."

3. The following handwritten postscript was added to the letter:

"I finally wrote to Praeger from Locarno to say 'No' because he was so indecisive. My letter of refusal crossed in the mail with a letter from him, in which he sent me a clear and quite good contract. But it was too late; in the meantime I had mailed my assent to Morin.

"I am somewhat disappointed by Morin's offer because of its incompleteness and lack of clarity:

"Generous royalties: 9% for the first 5,000, 10½% up to 10,000, and 12½% for copies sold beyond that. *But, I* am supposed to pay for the translation, the cost of which is undetermined and should be borne by the publisher. That is why I made *a counteroffer*: 7% for the first 5,000, 10% up to 10,000, and 11% for anything beyond that, but the publisher has to pay for the translation. I also suggested that I get an advance of 400 dollars, half to be paid at the signing of the contract and the other half when the book is published.

"Marjorie Grene has agreed to undertake the translation under two conditions: She wants my approval of her as the translator (I answered that I'd be glad to approve—in spite of things that I told you about and that I am ignoring at this point), and she wants you to look the translation over (I answered that you are busy with important work and would be able at most to spot-check the translation to get an impression of its quality but would under no circumstances read over the entire translation, let alone make corrections).

"I heard nothing for a while; then came a letter saying Mr. Morin was out of town and would write as soon as he got back (just the same story as with Praeger). —

"Praeger's contract provides for:

5%   up to 3,000
7½%   up to 6,000
10%   for anything above.

The publisher assumes the cost of translation.
An advance of $500.

"Well, I can't play one against the other. I am writing this just for your information.

"I have sent two copies of the book to Marjorie Grene upon Morin's request.

"I would, of course, like to see the matter settled quickly—how prompt and frequent and enthusiastic Morin's first letters were! Marjorie Grene says she will have the translation finished by January 1st. That sounds good. Now there is this indecision!"

Letter 231

1. She was supposed to translate *Die Atombombe*. The translation was eventually done by G. B. Ashton.
2. Ernst Mayer, *Kritik des Nihilismus* (Munich, 1958).

Letter 232

1. See L. 229, n. 1. Published as Hannah Arendt, "Humanitas," in *Karl Jaspers, Vier Ansprachen anlässlich der Verleihung des Friedenspreises des Deutschen Buchhandels"* (Frankfurt am Main, 1958): 17–28. Also printed under the title "Karl Jaspers"; see n. 4.
2. See the penultimate paragraph of the eulogy.
3. See Thucydides, *History of the Peloponnesian War.*
4. Karl Jaspers, "Wahrheit, Freiheit und Friede"; Hannah Arendt, "Karl Jaspers," *Reden zur Verleihung des Friedenspreises des Deutschen Buchhandels 1958* (Munich, 1958).

Letter 233

1. The U.S. edition of *Vita Activa: The Human Condition*; see L. 169, n. 3.
2. The Princeton lectures on the concept of revolution were later reworked into a book, *On Revolution* (New York, 1963); *Uber die Revolution* (Munich, n.d. [1965]). On the book for Piper, see L. 179, n. 1.
3. Circular of the Main Rabbinate of Israel, dated July 2, 1957.
4. The massacre at Deir Jassim took place on April 8, 1948.
5. The town in Czechoslovakia that was destroyed in June 1942 by the SS in revenge for the assassination of Reinhard Heydrich, architect of the Nazis' "Final Solution" and then governor of Czechoslovakia.
6. On the same piece of paper as L. 233.
7. Arthur Mayer, 1874–1958, was a businessman.
8. Isak Dinesen was the pen name of Karen Blixen, 1885–1962. The U.S. edition of *Schicksalsanekdoten* appeared in 1958; the book was published in Germany in 1960.
9. Theodor Heuss; see L. 105, n. 10.

Letter 234

1. Hannah Arendt, *Die Ungarische Revolution und der totalitäre Imperialismus* (Munich, 1958); "Totalitarian Imperialism: Reflections on the Hungarian Revolution," *Journal of Politics* 20, no. 1, (1958): 5–43.
2. Presumably Balfour Brickner, *As Driven Sand: The Arab Refugees* (New York, 1958).
3. See L. 190, n. 5.
4. Mies Mayer, née Jörg.

Letter 235

1. A telegram of January 29, 1959: "We have just read with great pleasure, dear Hannah, of the awarding of the Lessing Prize to you. Warmest greetings. Gertrud, Karl Jaspers."
2. A. was awarded the Lessing Prize of the city of Hamburg in 1959.

3. In the winter semester of 1958–59, J. lectured for two hours weekly on "Erweckende Philosophen" (Lessing, Kierkegaard, Nietzsche).
4. This refers to the Peace Prize awarded to J. in St. Paul's Church in Frankfurt; see L. 229, n. 1.
5. Gertrud J. had written to A. on January 6, 1959.

Letter 236
1. Gertrud J. had her eightieth birthday on February 26, 1959.
2. The novel *Doctor Zhivago* by Boris Pasternak, 1890–1960, was published in the United States by Pantheon. It appeared in almost every Western country in 1957–58.

Letter 237
1. *On Revolution*; see L. 233, n. 2.

Letter 238
1. In September 1959, the Colloques de Reinfelden were held near Basel. Under the title "Tradition et Evolution," twenty-one scholars discussed current philosophical-political problems. Raymond Aron and Eric Voegelin gave the keynote papers. See Raymond Aron, George Kennan, Robert Oppenheimer et autres, *Colloques de Reinfelden* (Paris, 1960).
2. Raymond Aron, 1905–1983, was a French sociologist and journalist. The essay A. read was "La société industrielle et les dialogues politiques de l'occident."
3. In a letter of March 1, 1959, Gertrud J. made up the word *überfreut* to express great happiness.

Letter 240
1. Max Born, 1882–1970, was a German physicist, who taught in Great Britain, 1933–54, and then retired to Bad Pyrmont, Germany. He was awarded the Nobel Prize in 1954.
2. In *Die Welt*, March 28, 1959, Heinz Liepmann published an essay in which he argues against overvaluing the natural sciences. On April 11 Max Born responded with a letter to the editor, which contained this passage: "I agree with you that a 'blind respect for science' should be combatted. But I would think it much more important for you to come out against the mindless perpetuation of traditional attitudes held by the bearers of our culture, the poets and philosophers and so forth. As an example, I cite the brilliant but in reality dreadful book by Jaspers, who in fact describes the changed status of physics clearly but then remains totally bogged down in outdated political and moral concepts that cannot help us deal with our present difficulties." J. was probably surprised and wounded by this attack, because Born had occasionally sent him signed

copies of his writings and because only a short while before, in his New Year's address of 1958–59, broadcast by South German Radio, he had spoken of J. as "a great German philosopher, for whom I feel great respect," a comment he had made expressly in connection with *Die Atombombe und die Zukunft des Menschen.*

3. Karl Jaspers, "The UN Is Undependable," *The New Republic* (May 18, 1959): 12–13.

4. Walter Lippmann, 1889–1974, American journalist and author. The article mentioned in n. 3 appeared in connection with "Lippmann's Berlin Proposals."

Letter 241

1. E. B. Ashton emigrated from Vienna to the United States in the 1930s. He later translated into English various works by J., among them, *Philosophie.*

Letter 242

1. Karl Jaspers, *Existentialism and Humanism: Three Essays*, ed. Hanns E. Fischer, trans. E. B. Ashton (New York, 1952). The translations are of "Solon," "Unsere Zukunft und Goethe," and "Uber Bedingungen und Möglichkeiten eines neuen Humanismus."

2. From Sartre's *L'existentialisme est un humanisme* (Paris, 1946).

Letter 243

1. A. wrote "Huber," but she no doubt meant Stanley Hubbard; see L. 244, n. 1.

2. Roger W. Shugg, b. 1905, historian and publisher, was director of the University of Chicago Press, 1954–67.

3. A. is presumably referring to the debate over a peace treaty with Germany and the question of German reunification. In January 1959 the Soviet Union sent a draft treaty to the three Western powers and the governments of East and West Germany. "The right of the German people to reestablish the unity of Germany" was to be recognized, but any use of force to achieve this goal renounced. Reunification was to be primarily a task for the two German states. That presumed a recognition of the division between them. The Western powers were willing to take a more flexible position than previously, but West Germany, led by Chancellor Konrad Adenauer, insisted that there could be only one route to reunification: free elections in all of Germany. This stand effectively blocked the way to a peace treaty, which led to the development that A. feared in this letter, namely, that East Germany would become a satellite of the Soviet Union. This letter and the next one no doubt provided J. with his point of departure for *Freiheit und Wiedervereinigung*; see L. 266, n. 1.

Letter 244

1. Stanley Hubbard, b. 1924, studied and took his doctorate with J. His dissertation on Nietzsche and Emerson was published in the series Philosophische Forschungen, Neue Folge 8 (Basel, 1958).
2. For this revised version, see L. 288, n. 3.
3. Handwritten addition.
4. Berthold Martin, b. 1913, doctor of medicine, was, since 1957, a member of the Bundesrat, and at this time chairman of the committee for cultural affairs and public relations.
5. *Deutsche Universitätszeitung. Monatsschrift für die Universitäten und Hochschulen* had been published since 1946.
6. Manfred Thiel, b. 1917, was a journalist and editor of the magazine *Studium generale.*
7. *Studium generale. Zeitschrift für die Einheit der Wissenschaften im Zusammenhang ihrer Begriffsbildungen und Forschungsmethoden* had existed since 1947. J. was on its editorial board until 1967.
8. Ludwig Raiser, b. 1904.
9. Heinrich Popitz, b. 1925, sociologist, had been a student of J. He was a professor at Basel, 1959, and at Freiburg, from 1964.
10. Franz Büchner, b. 1895, a pathologist, was a professor at Freiburg, 1936–63.
11. J. was on the editorial board from 1960 to 1966.
12. Raiser and Popitz did not become members of the board; Ludwig Dehio (Marburg) and Peter R. Hofstätter (Wilhelmshaven) took their places.

Letter 245

1. Hannah Arendt, *Von der Menschlichkeit in finsteren Zeiten* (Munich, 1960).
2. *Lessing und Aristoteles* (Frankfurt am Main, 1940). Max Kommerell, 1902–1944, literary historian, was a member of the George circle.

Letter 246

1. Wilhelm von Humboldt, "Uber den Entwurf zu einer neuen Konstitution für die Juden" (July 17, 1809), in *Gesammelte Schriften,* ed. Berliner Akademie der Wissenschaften, 17 vols. (Berlin, 1903–36), 10, 97ff.
2. Berthold Martin; see L. 244, n. 4.
3. See "Zur Gründung der Universität Berlin," in *Gesammelte Schriften* (see n. 1 above), 139–60.
4. See "Antrag für Fichte," in *Gesammelte Schriften* (see n. 1 above), 72–73.
5. See Goethe's letter to Christian Gottlob von Voigt of February 27, 1816, in *Goethes Briefe,* 50 vols. (Weimar, 1887–1912) (*Goethes Werke,* Sophien-Ausgabe, 4. Abteilung).

Letter 247

1. Not dated by J. This is a handwritten note added to a letter of this date from Gertrud J. to A.
2. This refers to a letter from A. not preserved in the literary remains.

Letter 248

1. Not dated by A. It is clear from the context that the letter belongs here.
2. Manheim's translation of *Die grossen Philosophen*.
3. The illness of Erna Möhrle, the J.s' housekeeper.

Letter 249

1. Not in the literary remains.
2. On November 9, 1955, when A. was staying in Basel, she and J. drafted the following letter, dated November 9, 1955, which they hoped would entitle her to receive restitution payments, which were pensions paid by the German government to refugees from Nazi Germany. As L. 399 makes clear, the appeal was refused, contrary to the expectations A. expresses in this letter. See L. 399, n. 9. A positive settlement was not reached until 1971.
   "Signed by J., the letter read:
   "In 1928, Dr. Hannah Arendt-Blücher wrote an excellent thesis for me on Augustine (degree awarded in 1929). The work was published by Springer Verlag in 1929 as part of a series entitled 'Philosophische Forschungen' and edited by me. After finishing her degree, Hannah Arendt, on the suggestion of Heidegger, Dibelius, and myself, was awarded a research fellowship by the Deutsche Notgemeinschaft to enable her to finish a book on Rahel Varnhagen. This work, I hoped, would lead to her habilitation [qualification], which, in view of her outstanding intellectual abilities, should have been conferred on her as a matter of course. I have no doubt that the faculty of my department would have concurred. The year 1933 put an end to all such plans. The book on Rahel Varnhagen was finished except for the last two chapters.
   "I am quite convinced that under the conditions prevailing before 1933 she would have succeeded in an academic career in spite of being a woman. Later publications that have received international acclaim have since confirmed her intellectual stature."
3. J. received an honorary doctorate from the University of Paris in 1959.

Letter 250

1. This last sentence was handwritten by Gertrud J.

Letter 251

1. See L. 249, n. 2.
2. Marianne Wendt, 1907–1959, studied classics and German literature from 1925 to 1929 at Heidelberg and had been a friend of A.'s since that time.

Letter 253

1. See L. 262, n. 2.
2. See L. 256, n. 4.
3. Handwritten note by J.

Letter 254

1. Letters from Gertrud J. dated December 24 and 26, 1959.
2. A. and her husband had moved to 370 Riverside Drive, in New York City.
3. A. had received an offer to teach at the University of Würzburg.
4. The prize was awarded by the Longview Foundation for "Reflections on Little Rock"; see L. 214, n. 7.
5. Wolfgang Sauerländer was an editor for Pantheon Books.
6. Karl Jaspers, "Epikur," in *Weltbewohner und Weimaraner: Ernst Beutler zugedacht*, ed. by Benno Reifenberg and Emil Staiger (Zurich/Stuttgart, 1960): 111–33.

Letter 255

1. The introduction to the U.S. edition of *Die grossen Philosophen*.
2. *Lektor* corresponds to editor in U.S. publishing.

Letter 256

1. Hannah Arendt, *Von der Menschlichkeit in finsteren Zeiten*, 32–33.
2. Gerhard Schröder, b. 1910, was minister of the interior of the Federal Republic of Germany at this time.
3. *Deutscher Bundestag*: 103rd session, Bonn, February 18, 1960, 5579.
4. Karl Jaspers, "Der philosophische Glaube angesichts der christlichen Offenbarung," in *Philosophie und christliche Existenz: Festschrift für Heinrich Barth zum 70. Geburtstag am 3. 2. 1960*, ed. Gerhard Huber (Basel/Stuttgart, 1960), 1–92. Nanda Anshen, a free-lance editor, published J.'s essay as part of the series Religious Perspectives (New York, 1967).

Letter 257

1. On the rearrangement of material, see the editor's introduction in Karl Jaspers, *Die grossen Philosophen: Nachlass 1. Darstellungen und Fragmente*, ed. H. Saner (Munich/Zurich, 1981), vi–vii. See also L. 259.
2. J.'s talk "Wahrheit und Wissenschaft" was given at the celebration of

the five hundredth anniversary of the University of Basel, June 30, 1960.
3. To appoint a successor to philosopher Heinrich Barth.
4. Paul Wilpert, 1906–1967, was a historian of philosophy and teacher.
5. See L. 184, n. 12.

Letter 258

1. See L. 45, n. 1.
2. See L. 262, n. 2.
3. See L. 254.
4. Robert Gilbert; see L. 199, n. 1.

Letter 259

1. Carl Wilhelm Jaspers, 1850–1940, became chief administrator in Butjadingen in 1879 and director of the Savings and Loan Bank in Oldenburg in 1896.

Letter 260

1. Jules Keller, b. 1923 in Germany but a resident of the United States since 1952, was at this time pastor of St. John's Church in Lincoln, Nebraska. Later he was pastor of Prospect Church, Cambridge, Massachusetts, and then professor of linguistics at Hellenic College, Greek Orthodox Theological Seminary, in Boston.
2. Hannah Arendt, "Der Mensch, ein gesellschaftliches oder ein politisches Lebewesen," *Die deutsche Universitätszeitung* 15 (October 1960): 38–47.

Letter 261

1. Karl Jaspers, "Das Doppelgesicht der Universitätsreform," *Die Deutsche Universitätszeitung* 15, no. 3 (1960): 3–8.
2. John F. Kennedy and Richard Nixon. See also L. 263.
3. Presumably an allusion to the Geneva conference of foreign ministers in 1959, called to solve the Berlin crisis; no agreement was reached.
4. A leftist faction in Japan was opposing ratification of a security agreement with the United States. It was ratified on June 22, 1960.

Letter 262

1. *Der philosophische Glaube angesichts der Offenbarung*; see L. 313, n. 1.
2. Karl Jaspers, "Der philosophische Glaube angesichts der christlichen Offenbarung," in *Philosophie und christliche Existenz: Festschrift für Heinrich Barth zum 70*; see L. 256, n. 4.

Letter 263

1. A village in the Catskill Mountains, north of New York, where A. and her husband spent their summer vacations in 1960 and 1961.
2. On August 10, 1960, North German Radio had broadcast a discussion between Thilo Koch, a journalist, and J. on German reunification. J. advanced the thesis, frequently repeated later, that reunification should not take precedence over freedom; that freedom was more important. He formulated his position in the provocative phrase "Nur die Freiheit— allein darauf kommt es an" ("Only freedom—that is all that matters"), which was used as the title of the printed version of the discussion in the *Frankfurter Allgemeine Zeitung*, August 17, 1960. There was much comment, both in Germany and internationally.
3. The translation of Jaspers' *Philosophie*.
4. The manuscript for the U.S. edition of *Die grossen Philosophen*.
5. For the translation of *Der philosophische Glaube angesichts der Offenbarung*.

Letter 264

1. Dag Hammarskjöld, 1905–1961, was the Swedish secretary-general of the United Nations, 1953–61. The Congo had won its independence on June 30, 1960; a few days later mutiny broke out in the army, and Patrice Lumumba, the prime minister, asked the United Nations to send troops. Hammerskjöld, against strong opposition from the Soviet Union, moved more and more toward the position of Lumumba's enemies, fearing Lumumba's radicalization might cost the Congo its independence.
2. J. had published five articles in *Die Zeit* during August and September 1960. They were reprinted in *Freiheit und Wiedervereinigung: Uber Aufgaben deutscher Politik* (Munich, 1960), 16–75.
3. This was the uprising of East Berlin workers on June 17, 1953.
4. The Federal Republic of Germany and the German Democratic Republic became members in 1973.
5. In 1807–08, during the Napoleonic Wars, Johann Gottlieb Fichte, 1762–1814, gave fourteen famous lectures, called "Reden an die deutsche Nation."
6. In the fall semester of 1960 A. gave a Kant seminar at Columbia University.

Letter 265

1. Not dated by A.; added to L. 264.
2. Adolf Eichmann, 1906–1962, was Gestapo chief of the Jewish Office during World War II and implemented the Nazis' "Final Solution." Presentation of evidence against him lasted from April 11 to August 14, 1961. He was sentenced to death for crimes against the Jewish people and against humanity in December and executed on May 31, 1962.

Letter 266

1. All the essays referred to were collected in Karl Jaspers, *Freiheit und Wiedervereinigung*; see L. 264, n. 2.

Letter 269

1. Gertrud J.'s letter to A. of November 14, 1960.
2. J. gave a lecture course, "Philosophie der Gegenwart" ("Philosophy of the Present"), during the winter semester of 1960–61.
3. *Freiheit und Wiedervereinigung*; see L. 264, n. 2.
4. Max Weber's dedication in *Gesammelte Aufsätze zur Religionssoziologie*.
5. For the U.S. edition of *Der philosophische Glaube angesichts der Offenbarung*.

Letter 270

1. Hannah Arendt, *Vita Activa oder Vom tätigen Leben*; see L. 169, n. 3.
2. Max Weber's study "Die protestantische Ethik und der Geist des Kapitalismus"; see L. 141, n. 3.
3. *Vita Activa*, 366, n. 30.
4. Presumably Max Scheler's essay "Der Bourgeois und die religiösen Mächte," which contains a discussion of Weber's study in n. 2 above. See Max Scheler, *Gesammelte Werke* 3 (Bern, 1955): 362ff., 378ff., and elsewhere.
5. R. H. Tawney, 1880–1962, was a British economic historian. J. alludes to his *Religion and the Rise of Capitalism* (1926); published in German as *Religion und Frühkapitalismus* (1946).
6. "The mountains will be in labor, and a ridiculous mouse will be brought forth."
7. Richard Thoma, 1874–1957, was a professor of constitutional law at Heidelberg, 1911–28.
8. Since the title of the essay in the festschrift for Heinrich Barth was "Der *philosophische* Glaube angesichts der christlichen Offenbarung" and the later book was *Der philosophische Glaube angesichts der Offenbarung*, this word is probably an error of dictation or of transcription.

Letter 272

1. In May 1960 the Israeli secret service abducted Eichmann from Argentina and took him to Israel for trial.
2. Nahum Goldmann, 1894–1982, scholar and writer, served as president of the World Zionist Organization and of the World Jewish Congress.
3. David Ben Gurion, 1886–1973, proclaimed Israel's independence as head of the provisional government, 1948–49; prime minister of Israel, 1949–53, 1955–63.
4. In connection with the lecture course "Philosophie der Gegenwart"; see L. 269, n. 2.

Letter 273

1. After incorporating in the Treaty of Versailles the thesis that Germany alone was responsible for World War I, the victorious powers wanted to bring some Germans whom they regarded as war criminals before an Allied military tribunal. To prevent this, the German government put the accused on trial before the German Supreme Court.

Letter 274

1. An enemy of the human race.
2. Samuel Schwarzbard, 1886–1938, Jewish writer, shot his parents' murderer in Paris in 1926. A. probably wrote "Shalom" by mistake, instead of "Shmuel."
3. Pogroms had taken place in more than 370 towns in 1918–20 and claimed about 30,000 victims.
4. Ernest Bevin, 1881–1951, British labor leader, was foreign secretary at that time.
5. Martin Bormann, 1900–1945, Nazi leader, had perhaps the most pervasive influence on Hitler during the war. He committed suicide.
6. *Freiheit und Wiedervereinigung*; see L. 264, n. 2.
7. Karl Jaspers, *The Future of Mankind*, translation by E. B. Ashton of *Die Atombombe und die Zukunft des Menschen* (Chicago, 1961).

Letter 275

1. Hatred of the human race; Tacitus, *Annals XV*, 44, 5.

Letter 276

1. Dolf Sternberger, "Sehnsucht nach der Unsterblichkeit," *Frankfurter Allgemeine Zeitung* (Dec. 31, 1960), review of A.'s *Vita Activa*.

Letter 277

1. The review appeared under the title "Fate Is Not Blind," *Time 77* (January 27, 1961): 77–78.
2. *New York Times Book Review* (January 29, 1961), 6.
3. Hans J. Morgenthau, 1904–1980, was a professor of political science at the University of Chicago at this time.
4. *Saturday Review* (February 18, 1961), 18.
5. Robert Lowell, 1917–1977, was one of the most distinguished poets in the United States at this time.
6. Paul A. Schilpp; see L. 113, n. 2.
7. King John, of England, 1167–1216, king from 1199 to 1216, was called John Lackland because, through a series of unsuccessful campaigns and as a result of a quarrel with Pope Innocent III, he lost most of his territories.

8. Pinchas Lavon, 1904–1976, Israeli politician, held various ministerial posts from 1950 to 1955. Actions by the secret police, the reasons for which have never been disclosed, led to his downfall in 1955.
9. See L. 43, n. 11.
10. William Shawn, editor-in-chief of *The New Yorker*.

Letter 278

1. Dated January 14, 1961, by J., obviously incorrectly, because this letter is a response to L. 277.
2. Dr. Robert Servatius (d. 1983) was Eichmann's defense attorney.
3. Israel's workers' union, of which Lavon was the general secretary.
4. J. gave a lecture course on "Die Chiffren der Transzendenz" ("The Secret Codes of Transcendence") during the summer semester of 1961.

Letter 279

1. This letter was preceded by a postcard dated Evanston, February 15, 1961: "As you can see, I have found Havannah once more—and as a sign that we're thinking of you—with warmest greetings your Hannah." Added below was: "It is wonderful to see the past come alive again. Best wishes—Ulrike Brüsauer."

Letter 280

1. The New York publishing house Harcourt, Brace & World.

Letter 281

1. Letter of March 27, 1961, from A. to Kurt and Helen Wolff.
2. William Jovanovich, b. 1920, was president of the publishing house Harcourt, Brace, which in 1960 was renamed Harcourt, Brace & World and in 1970 Harcourt Brace Jovanovich.
3. Kyrill Schabert, 1909–1979, was, with Kurt and Helen Wolff, a founder of Pantheon Books. He became president after the firm was sold to Random House in 1961.

Letter 282

1. The interview with François Bondy, "Karl Jaspers zum Eichmann-Prozess," was broadcast on April 9, 1961, by Radio Studio Basel.
2. Martin Buber, 1878–1965, Zionist theologian and social philosopher, emigrated to Palestine in 1938. His *Ich und Du* (*I and Thou*) influenced both Christian and Jewish thinkers.
3. Benjamin Halevi, one of the three judges for the Eichmann trial.

760

Letter 283

1. Not found in the literary remains.
2. Letter of March 27, 1961, from Kurt Wolff to A.; the literary remains contain no such draft.
3. Irene Klenbort, 1943–1991, was, it turned out, afflicted with multiple sclerosis.

Letter 285

1. See L. 282, n. 1.
2. Mosche Landau, b. 1912, member of the Supreme Court of Israel, presided over the Eichmann trial.
3. In addition to Landau, they were Benjamin Halevi and Yitzhak Raveh.
4. Gideon Hausner, 1915–1990, was attorney general of Israel, 1960–63, and as such, the main prosecutor.
5. Alfried Krupp von Bohlen und Halbach, 1907–1967, was the sole owner, after 1943, of the Krupp Works, makers of arms, ordnance, and heavy machinery.
6. A.'s cousin Ernst Fürst and his wife, Kate, née Levin.
7. Peies: Orthodox Jews with long locks of hair; caftan Jews: Orthodox Jews wearing long coats.

Letter 286

1. The three judges—Landau, Halevi, and Raveh.
2. The unsuccessful attempt of exiled Cubans, trained by the CIA, to land at the Bay of Pigs in April 1961 to spearhead an anti-Castro uprising. President Kennedy assumed responsibility.
3. Charles de Gaulle, 1890–1970, French general and head of the Free French in England during World War II, was president of the Fifth Republic, 1959–69. In April 1961, French generals in Algeria attempted an unsuccessful coup d'état, leading to official negotiations with the rebel provisional government established in Algeria in 1958.
4. Raoul Salan, 1899–1984, was a French general and politician who openly supported the coup d'état in Algeria and later headed the Organisation de l'Armée Secrete (OAS) in Algeria. Maurice Challe, 1905–1975, was another French general who supported the coup d'état in Algeria.
5. This alludes to the victory of Francisco Franco, 1892–1975, as chief of the rebel Falange, over the republican government during the Spanish Civil War.
6. J. wrote "subordination" instead of "insubordination."

Letter 287

1. Golda Meir, 1898–1978, was a founder of Israel, foreign minister, 1956–65, and prime minister, 1969–74.
2. Pinhas F. Rosen, 1887–1979, was Israeli minister of justice, 1948–61.

Letter 288

1. Konrad Adenauer, 1876–1967, was chancellor of the Federal Republic of Germany, 1949–63.
2. Heinrich Grüber, 1891–1975, Protestant theologian, after 1945 provost of the Church of Mary in Berlin, testified as a witness during the Eichmann trial.
3. *Die Idee der Universität: Für die gegenwärtige Situation entworfen von Karl Jaspers und Kurt Rossman*, 2nd revised ed. (Berlin/Göttingen/Heidelberg, 1961).

Letter 289

1. James Harrington, 1611–1677, was an English political philosopher and author.
2. Elisabeth Piper-Holthaus, b. 1924.
3. Mary McCarthy, who was suffering from a slipped disk.
4. Winfried Martini, b. 1905, was a German journalist.

Letter 290

1. Letter of June 16, 1961, from A. to K. Schabert.

Letter 292

1. This letter is lost.
2. Charlotte Beradt, née Aron, 1901–1986, was active as a journalist in Berlin, and in New York after 1940. She was a friend, from her youth, of Heinrich Blücher, and later of A. as well.

Letter 293

1. Susanne Rossmann, née Sommerfeld, 1920–1976.
2. Apparently the possibility of Rossmann's (see L. 38, n. 4) being offered a position in Basel had been discussed during A.'s stay there.
3. Fritz Bauer, 1903–1968, district attorney of Hessen. He had petitioned the federal government in Bonn to initiate extradition proceedings; his request was denied.
4. Joseph H. Kaiser, b. 1921, an expert on international law, was, from 1955, a professor at the University of Freiburg.
5. André Gide, 1869–1951, prolific French writer and editor, wrote about his homosexuality in several more or less autobiographical novels.
6. Eugen Fink, 1905–1975, was a philosopher and teacher whose thinking was close to that of Husserl and Heidegger.
7. Stefan George, 1868–1933, esoteric German poet, was the center of an exclusive literary group, the "George circle." He had considerable influence on the art and thought of his time.
8. Gerald Gross, b. 1921, was vice president and managing editor of Pantheon

Books at this time. He had previously been production manager and editor at Harcourt, Brace, and later was vice president of Boston University.

9. Haines Falls, New York. See L. 263, n. 1.
10. The political situation in France after the unsuccessful coup d'état of the French generals in April 1961 was very unstable.
11. In July 1961, Tunisian forces laid siege to the French air and naval base in Bizerte; the French broke the siege, and both sides agreed to a UN cease-fire. Habib Bourguiba, the Tunisian president, who had previously declared himself to be a friend of the Jewish state, now turned against Israel. See *American Jewish Yearbook* (1962): 432–37.

Letter 294

1. Not in the literary remains.
2. *Die grossen Philosophen.*
3. Stanley Unwin, 1884–1968, was co-owner of the publishing house George Allen and Unwin, London.
4. Construction of the Berlin Wall had begun on August 13. It was put up to keep East Germans from defecting to the West.
5. A. and her husband went to Haines Falls on August 11; see L. 263, n. 1. A. was in New York from August 18 to 20.

Letter 295

1. Presumably a coinage combining "Bolshevist" and "Khrushchev."

Letter 296

1. Elfriede Heidegger-Petri, b. 1893.
2. A. had written this in 1958, when J. received the Peace Prize awarded by the Deutschen Buchhandel; see L. 229, n. 1.
3. See J.'s later vehement opposition to the great coalition in his *Wohin treibt die Bundersrepublik? Tatsachen. Gefahren. Chancen* (Munich, 1966): 261ff.
4. The Munich Pact of September 1938, by which Great Britain and France agreed to German annexation of the Sudetenland in Czechoslovakia.
5. The radio station in the U.S. sector.
6. *Der philosophische Glaube angesichts der Offenbarung*; see L. 313, n. 1.
7. Not in the literary remains.

Letter 297

1. See L. 261.
2. Hans Egon Holthusen, b. 1913, was a writer and literary critic.

Letter 298

1. Nehru was at this time the moral leader of the unaligned nations.
2. See L. 294, n. 4.

Letter 299

1. J.'s last letter included one of November 6, 1961, from Gertrud J. to A.
2. Isaiah 40:6.

Letter 300

1. This was the "Deutschland Plan" of the SPD of March 18, 1959, a three-phase program for reunification: a conference of the two Germanies; establishment of a parliamentary council made up of both Germanies; laws passed applying to both Germanies.
2. The chapter "Adenauer" in *Freiheit und Wiedervereinigung*, 85–95, was published separately in *Die Zeit*, November 25, 1960, under the title "Der Staatsmann Konrad Adenauer: Eine kritische Würdigung aus der Feder eines Philosophen."
3. *Letters*, 7th letter, 350ff.
4. "Was ist Aufklärung?" in Immanuel Kant, *Gesammelte Schriften*, ed. Preussische Akademie der Wissenschaften, 22 vols. (Berlin, 1900–42): 8, 40. Kant there calls the Age of Enlightenment *"Frederick's* century."
5. This program, established by President Kennedy in 1961, sent volunteers to other countries to help with human and economic development programs.
6. When the pro-Western province of Katanga seceded from the recently independent Congo, the United States refused the more neutralist Congo government's request for help.
7. Kurt Schumacher, 1895–1952, Social Democratic politician, was a founder of the new SPD and one of the "fathers of the German constitution."

Letter 301

1. Ernst Reuter, 1889–1953, German Social Democratic politician, became mayor of Berlin in 1951.
2. Handwritten remark by Heinrich Blücher.
3. Fred Stein and Will Grohmann, *Deutsche Portraits* (New York/Stuttgart, 1961).
4. Franz Joseph Strauss, 1915–1988, was West Germany's minister of defense at this time.
5. Glenn Gray, 1913–1977, author and professor of philosophy at Colorado College.
6. Karl Jaspers, "Heidelberger Erinnerungen," *Heidelberger Jahrbücher* 5 (1961): 1–10.

Letter 302

1. A. dedicated her book *On Revolution* "For Gertrud and Karl Jaspers— with admiration, friendship, and love."
2. Otto Mayer, 1887–1961, was a businessman.
3. Fritz (see L. 220, n. 1) and Heinrich (1885–1973) Mayer; Erna Mayer-David, b. 1904.
4. Hydrogen bombs, it was believed, if detonated at high altitudes, release less radioactive material to the surface of the earth, and are therefore "cleaner" than atomic bombs.
5. "Karl Jaspers zum Eichmann-Prozess: Ein Gespräch mit François Bondy," *Der Monat*, no. 152 (May 1961): 15–19. See L. 282.

Letter 303

1. L. 302 included a letter from Gertrud J.
2. Ella Mayer, who was at that time being treated successfully for pernicious anemia.
3. Henry H. Zolki, d. 1962.
4. There was controversy over the efficacy of bomb shelters in a nuclear attack.

Letter 304

1. Karl Jaspers, *The Great Philosophers*, ed. Hannah Arendt, trans. Ralph Manheim, 1 (New York, 1962).
2. Ernst Moritz Manasse, professor of philosophy at North Carolina College.
3. *Der philosophische Glaube angesichts der Offenbarung*; see L. 313, n. 1.
4. See L. 262, n. 2.
5. L. 295.

Letter 305

1. See L. 306.
2. This letter was preceded by a telegram sent on the same day: "After great initial fright relieved to hear no danger to life. Gertrud, Karl."

Letter 306

1. Letters of March 26 and 27, 1962, from Gertrud J. to A., reported: Erna Möhrle is doing well after a minor operation and will go home for a week to recuperate.

Letter 307

1. "Makers, Shapers, and Agents Provocateurs in the World of Thought," Charles Frankel's review of J.'s *The Great Philosophers*, *The New York Times Book Review*, April 1, 1962.

2. Letter of January 27, 1962, from Gertrud J. to A.
3. See L. 306, n. 1.

Letter 308

1. The city where Gertrud J.'s parents lived.
2. *Die grossen Philosophen.*
3. Hans Saner, b. 1934, was J.'s assistant from this time until the latter's death.
4. Of April 1, 1962.

Letter 310

1. *Der philosophische Glaube angesichts der Offenbarung.*
2. Town in the Black Forest where Erna Möhrle's parents lived.
3. J. gave a speech, "Freiheit und Schicksal in der Wirtschaft," on this occasion, October 6, 1962.
4. In the elections for the Bundestag of September 1961, the Christian Democratic Union and Christian Social Union parties did not obtain an absolute majority, but thanks to a coalition with the FDP (Free Democratic party), Adenauer was reelected chancellor.

Letter 311

1. Undated letter.
2. The Femegericht were medieval secret courts in Germany. During the early years of the Weimar Republic, the name was used for political murderers of the extreme right, some of whom were not punished, owing to the rightist judicial system.
3. A drop in the Dow-Jones index that was alarming at the time, but turned out to be temporary.

Letter 312

1. Letter of August 12, 1962, in which Gertrud J. reports on J.'s health.
2. For J.'s eightieth birthday, February 23, 1963.
3. "Karl Jaspers zum Eichmann-Prozess"; see L. 282, n. 1, and L. 302, n. 5.
4. In July 1962, De Gaulle and Adenauer reviewed a large parade of French and German troops near Reims. In September 1962, De Gaulle paid his first state visit to the Federal Republic of Germany, during which he was given an enthusiastic reception by the German people. Later, in January 1963, a friendship treaty was signed.

Letter 313

1. Karl Jaspers, *Der philosophische Glaube angesichts der Offenbarung* (Munich, 1962).
2. De Gaulle's concept of a Europe "from the Atlantic to the Urals."
3. On October 22, 1962, President Kennedy officially requested that Soviet ballistic missles in Cuba be removed and launching sites be destroyed. He also imposed a naval quarantine of Cuba and called on the Organization of American States and the UN Security Council for backing. Nuclear confrontation between the two superpowers seemed imminent. On October 28, Khrushchev agreed to withdraw the missiles; the United States agreed not to invade Cuba. The crisis was officially ended in January 1963.
4. Bruno Dechamps, "Der Mut muss ernst genommen werden," *Frankfurter Allgemeine Zeitung* (October 24, 1962): 1.
5. Indonesia had been trying to take over Netherlands New Guinea since the beginning of 1962. Through the mediating efforts of the United Nations and the United States, agreement was reached that in October 1962 the United Nations, and in May 1963 Indonesia, would assume its administration.
6. During the Suez Crisis of 1956, Gamal Abdel Nasser, 1918–1970, Egypt's president, nationalized the canal. When Israel attacked Egypt, Britain and France entered the fighting, to retake the canal. The United States favored their withdrawal, and the U.S.S.R. threatened intervention. UN forces replaced them.

Letter 314

1. Fidel Castro, b. 1927, Cuban revolutionary, led the successful fight against dictator Fulgencio Batista. He has been premier of Cuba since 1959.
2. Walter Ulbricht, 1893–1973, a founder of the German Communist party, was chairman of the council of state of the German Democratic Republic from 1960. He ordered the building of the Berlin Wall.
3. Gerhard Casper, b. 1937, became a professor at the University of Chicago Law School in 1966, and, in 1979, its dean. The letter was addressed to Charlotte Beradt (see L. 292, n. 2), a close friend.
4. Erich Schellhaus, b. 1901, was a member of the presidium of the Bund der Vertriebenen (Union of Refugees) and minister in Lower Saxony.
5. Karl Jaspers, "Freiheit und Schicksal in der Wirtschaft," *Basler Nachrichten* (October 8, 1962): 13–14.

Letter 315

1. Cuba refused to cooperate with the planned international inspections.
2. Hugo Stinnes, 1870–1924, had, in 1924, control over 1,500 legally independent firms and nearly 2,900 other businesses. His powerful position as head of the Stinnes Combine was built on vertical integration and extreme diversification of his holdings.

3. *Ahnung und Gegenwart* (1815), by Joseph von Eichendorff; *Nachsommer* (1857), by Adalbert Stifter.

Letter 316

1. "Wie Erinnerung an das Erlebte zur Auffassung der Gegenwart führt." It was included in Karl Jaspers, *Provokationen: Gespräche und Interviews*, ed. H. Saner (Munich, 1969): 147–68.
2. See L. 269.
3. Apparently the draft of the contract, which has not been preserved, contained a clause disclaiming any intent on the author's part to offend religious feelings.
4. On October 10, 1962, *Der Spiegel* published an article, "Bedingt abwehrbereit" ("Only partially prepared for defense"), on the fall NATO troop maneuvers, which sparked controversy throughout the country. On October 27, executives of the magazine were arrested and editorial offices searched. The action, ordered by Franz Josef Strauss, minister of defense, was based on suspicion of treason and suspected bribery of officials. The suspicion turned out to be unfounded, and Strauss was forced to resign.
5. The Bonn Convention, May 26, 1952, was signed by the three Western occupying powers. It superceded the occupation statute of 1949.

Letter 317

1. Gertrud J. and A. had been exchanging occasional letters since the early postwar years. This correspondence became much more active in the early 1960s.
2. A. had written to Gertrud J. on November 28, 1962, and about this appointment in Chicago said: "Did I tell you that I have accepted a 'position' at the University of Chicago? Only one quarter (10 weeks including an eight-week lecture *or* seminar course) per year and perhaps a few weeks of residence to work with the students. Very good pay and absolute freedom: if I don't want to, I don't even have to give lectures or seminars; I just have to be there. So I've become a professor after all."
3. The suggestion sent on December 5, 1962, to Anshen for emendation of the contract.
4. To E. B. Ashton, December 5, 1962, on possible abridgments for the English translation of *Der philosophische Glaube angesichts der Offenbarung*.

Letter 318

1. Klemens von Klemperer, b. 1916, was professor of modern history at Smith College.
2. "Freiheit und Schicksal in der Wirtschaft"; see L. 314, n. 5.
3. The *Der Spiegel* executives arrested on October 27, 1962. Rudolf Augstein, b. 1923, had been publisher of *Der Spiegel* since 1946. Conrad Ahlers,

1922–1980, was a *Spiegel* editor; in 1968 he became spokesman for the German government.

4. Gerhard Casper; see L. 314, n. 3.
5. Carl von Ossietzky, 1889–1938, editor in chief of *Die Weltbühne*, was accused in 1931 of passing military secrets to enemy powers and sentenced to eighteen months in prison. After the burning of the Reichstag, in 1933, he was again arrested, and sent to concentration camps at Sonnenburg and later at Papenburg-Esterwegen. He died in a Berlin hospital as a result.
6. Franz Reinholz, b. 1904, was a journalist, and at this time director at North German Radio.

Letter 319
1. See L. 318, n. 3.
2. *Elemente und Ursprünge totaler Herrschaft*; see L. 172, n. 1.

Letter 320
1. Talks with François Bondy taped in 1962: "Der Philosoph in der Zeit" was aired on February 22, 1963, by North German Radio; "Der Philosoph in der Politik" appeared in *Der Monat*, no. 175 (April 1963): 22–29.
2. Heinz F. B. Zahrnt, b. 1915, was a writer on theology. His talk with J. was aired in February 1963 and printed in the same year: Karl Jaspers / Heinz Zahrnt, *Philosophie und Offenbarungsglaube: Ein Zwiegesprach* (Hamburg, 1963).
3. Hannah Arendt, "Eichmann in Jerusalem," appeared as a five-part series, *The New Yorker* (February and March 1963); as a book (New York, 1963).

Letter 321
1. Paul Meyer-Gutzwiller, b. 1909, was at that time director of Radio Studio Basel. He and J. were friends during the entire postwar period.
2. J.'s eightieth birthday, on February 23, 1963.

Letter 322
1. A. read the first chapter of her Eichmann book on the radio in Cologne. The reading was followed, on the next day, by a debate, also broadcast.

Letter 323
1. Matthias Grünewald, c. 1500–1530, was a German Gothic painter. His renowned altarpiece is in the Museum Unterlinden, in Colmar, France.
2. Martin Schongauer, 1445?–1491, was a German engraver and painter who established a school of painting in Colmar. His most famous painting is "Madonna of the Rosehedge," in Colmar's Church of Saint-Martin.

Letter 324

1. The letter, of April 6, 1963, reports, among other things, that J., who had been ill, was recovering.
2. A.'s book *On Revolution* was reviewed by Harrison E. Salisbury in the *New York Times*, April 1, 1963.
3. The review by William O. Douglas, "The Guts of Freedom," appeared in the *Washington Post*, March 17, 1963.

Letter 325

1. Letter of April 19, 1963, from Gertrud J. to A.
2. Wilhelm Weischedel, 1905–1975, philosopher, was then professor at the Free University of Berlin.

Letter 326

1. Adolf Bernstein, b. 1918, was J.'s family doctor from 1963 to 1969.

Letter 327

1. *Die Ungarische Revolution und der totalitäre Imperialismus*; see L. 234, n. 1.
2. See L. 234.

Letter 328

1. See L. 37, n. 4.

Letter 329

1. Studienstiftung des deutschen Volkes.

Letter 331

1. In 1961, J. was invited to join the search committee of the international Balzan Foundation. Prizes comparable in amount to the Nobel prizes were to be awarded in 1963 for furthering peace and humanitarian causes and for major contributions in the fields of biology, history, mathematics, and music. J. thought that only people of world renown should be considered for these new prizes, and it seemed especially important to him that an outstanding individual be nominated for the peace prize. J. and A. probably discussed this in Basel in February and March. A. may have suggested that an individual who had worked for racial integration (in South Africa, if possible) be honored. By the time J. received materials she sent him on possible candidates (see n. 4), he had made up his mind: he wanted to propose John F. and Robert Kennedy for their efforts to bring about racial integration. He acted on A.'s suggestion to the extent

of naming Trevor Huddleston as a "second possibility." The peace prize was eventually awarded to Pope John XXIII. In a letter dated September 17, 1963, J. proposed awarding a prize in political science to A.

2. Dan Jacobson, b. 1929, is a South African novelist and short-story writer who has lived in England since 1954.

3. Brief recommendations of Trevor Huddleston, Alan Paton, and Nelson Mandela.

4. President John F. Kennedy and his brother Robert, who was then U.S. attorney general.

5. The Civil Rights Act was passed in 1964; the Voting Rights Act, in 1965.

6. Trevor Huddleston, b. 1913, was an Anglican clergyman who, after World War II, did missionary work in the black slums of South Africa.

7. James West, b. 1914, was at this time director of information for the Organization for Economic Co-operation in Paris.

8. During the Third Reich, Nazi officials set up Jewish councils of elders to act as administrators of Jewish communities.

9. Rudolf Kastner, 1906–1957, was one of the leaders of the Hungarian Jews during the Nazi period. An Israeli court cleared his name after his murder.

10. See L. 55, n. 16.

Letter 332

1. Emil Henk, 1893–1969, an industrialist, was part of the Social Democratic resistance against Hitler. During the period when Gertrud J. was in danger, she spent some time hiding at his home. Henk took an active part in rebuilding the University of Heidelberg, and was a close friend of the Jasperses.

2. Theodor Haubach, 1896–1945, a leading Social Democrat and, until 1933, press chief of the Berlin police department, was a student, and friend, of J.'s. A member of the Kreisau Circle, an intellectual group opposed to Hitler, he was executed in connection with the unsuccessful July 20 attempt to assassinate the Führer.

3. Carlo Mierendorff, 1897–1943, a leading Social Democrat and general secretary of the union of transportation workers, had been in a concentration camp, 1933–38. He was killed in an air raid.

4. See L. 72.

5. Eugen Gerstenmaier, b. 1906, a theologian and politician, was a member of the "Confessing Church" during the Nazi period, and president of the West German Bundestag, 1954–69.

6. See L. 57, n. 3.

7. Theodor Haubach, *Versuch einer Phänomenologie des ästhetischen Bewusstseins im Grundriss* (Heidelberg, 1923).

8. Carl Friedrich Goerdeler, 1884–1945, leading thinker of the resistance movement, was scheduled to become Reich chancellor after Hitler's death. He was executed in connection with the July 20 assassination plot.

9. Henning von Tresckow, 1901–1944, German army staff officer, led his

officers on the Eastern Front in a conspiracy against Hitler. When his and others' plans failed, he committed suicide at the front on July 21.

10. Ludwig Beck, 1880–1944, chief of the German army general staff, 1935–38, was one of the major leaders in planning Hitler's overthrow. He committed suicide when the July 20 plot failed.

11. Karoline Möhrle-Zeufle, 1887–1963, died on July 25, 1963. J. must have written this letter over several days.

12. Marie Bonadurer, b. 1905, Erna Möhrle's and Gertrud J.'s physician.

13. Medi Geitel, cousin of J. (youngest daughter of Theodor Tantzen; see L. 334, n. 2), was studying in Freiburg and temporarily helped keep house at Austrasse.

14. Gotthilf Möhrle, 1882–1963, was a master cabinetmaker.

15. Irma Möhrle, b. 1924, Erna's sister.

16. Willi Möhrle, b. 1930, cabinetmaker; Irene Möhrle-Schmelzle, his wife, b. 1931.

17. J.'s remark seems to be based on inaccurate information. At the conference in Miami the state governors, unable to reach agreement on the question of civil rights, voted 38 to 3, on July 23, 1963, to refer the question to a special committee, which was to give it top priority. See also L. 331, n. 5.

Letter 333

1. Maria Löwe, 1897–1963, studied library science in Berlin and worked as a librarian for the British Information Services in New York after emigrating to the United States.

2. Albert H. Friedländer, b. 1927 in Berlin, had been in the United States since 1940.

3. The talk and discussion took place on July 23, 1963.

4. This women's Zionist organization was founded in 1912 to provide medical care in Palestine and to advance Zionist ideas in the United States.

5. This was a letter of July 24, 1963, from Gunther Lawrence, director of public information of the Union of American Hebrew Congregations.

6. Heinrich Himmler, 1900–1945, was appointed head of the SS (Hitler's bodyguard) in 1929, and by 1936 controlled both the political and criminal police for the entire country. He was the principal organizer of the "final solution." In 1945, he tried to negotiate the release of Jews from German-controlled territories and Germany's surrender to the Allies. For this, Hitler stripped him of all offices and expelled him from the party. He committed suicide in a British prisoner-of-war camp.

7. A. wrote "Graf Hellbach"; she clearly meant Helldorf, as a passage (page 135) in the German edition of her Eichmann book shows. See also L. 380. Wolf Heinrich Graf von Helldorf, 1896–1944, was chief of police in Potsdam, 1933–35, and after 1935 police president of Berlin. He was a major figure in the July 20 conspiracy against Hitler, and was hanged.

8. Nelson R. Mandela, b. 1918, South African lawyer, politician, and fighter

against apartheid, was sentenced to life imprisonment in 1964. He was released in 1990 and continued the fight on a world stage.

9. See L. 331, n. 1.

Letter 334

1. Georg Ferdinand Springer, b. 1924, physician and publisher, studied after the war in Heidelberg and in Basel. His acquaintanceship with J. probably dates from then.
2. Theodor J. Tantzen, 1877–1947, brother of J.'s mother, was prime minister of Oldenburg, 1919–23 and 1945–46, then minister and deputy prime minister in the first cabinet of Lower Saxony.
3. Alfred Seiffert, 1883–1960, was director of the Heidelberg University nose, ear, and throat clinic, 1942–54.
4. Fabian von Schlabrendorff, b. 1907, jurist, was author of *Offiziere gegen Hitler* (Frankfurt am Main/Hamburg, 1959). He worked with Tresckow in the unsuccessful attempt to kill Hitler by planting a bomb in his airplane. He was sentenced to death in connection with the July 20 plot, but escaped execution.
5. Eberhard Zeller, *Geist der Freiheit: Der zwanzigste Juli* (Munich, 1954).
6. Anselm Radbruch, who was killed in the Battle of Stalingrad. His father, Gustav Radbruch, 1878–1949, was a legal philosopher and politician, and a close friend of J.'s.
7. See Theodor Heuss, *Hitlers Weg: Eine historisch-politische Studie über den Nationalsozialismus* (Stuttgart/Berlin/Leipzig, 1932).

Letter 335

1. The materials mentioned in L. 331, n. 3; not found among the literary remains.
2. Trevor Huddleston, *Naught for Your Comfort* (London, 1956).

Letter 336

1. See L. 317, n. 2.
2. Maurice Joly, *Gespräche in der Unterwelt zwischen Machiavelli und Montesquieu oder Der Machiavellismus im XIX. Jahrhundert* (1864) (Hamburg, 1948).
3. See L. 41, n. 3.
4. Ernst A. Simon, 1899–1988, had been professor of education at Hebrew University in Jerusalem since 1928.
5. For A.'s criticism of Michael A. Musmanno, see *Eichmann in Jerusalem*, 192–94. Musmanno in turn published several essays attacking A.; see *Die Kontroverse: Hannah Arendt, Eichmann und die Juden* (Munich, 1964): 85ff., 114ff.
6. For Scholem, see L. 87, n. 2. The exchange of letters was first published in Tel Aviv in the *Mitteilungsblatt*, no. 33 (August 16, 1963), and reprinted

in *Neue Zürcher Zeitung* (October 20, 1963) and in *Encounter* (January 1964). It is also included in *Die Kontroverse*, 207ff (see n. 5 above).

7. See L. 331 and L. 331, n. 9.

8. Kurt Becher, Obersturmbannführer and later Standartenführer of the SS, was involved in the deportation of Hungarian Jews in ways not altogether clear. He testified, in Germany, as a witness for the defense during the Eichmann trial.

9. Brigitte Granzow, b. 1926, was an editor for West German Radio in Cologne. The translation was eventually approved by A.

Letter 337

1. See L. 336, n. 6.

2. In the next to last paragraph of A.'s letter to Scholem, she writes: "I am now in fact convinced that evil is always merely extreme but never radical; it has no depth and no demonic dimension. It is able to devastate the entire world precisely because it spreads over the surface like a fungus. But only goodness is deep and radical."

3. In the first section of *Religion innerhalb der Grenzen der blossen Vernunft*, Kant defines "radical evil" as a turning upside down of the relationship between duty and inclination.

4. This is the title of a poem by Schiller. J.'s use here probably refers to A.'s description of herself during her visit. She frequently referred to herself as "the girl from a foreign land," both in conversation and in letters: for example, in a letter, February 9, 1950, to Heidegger: "I feel like what I really am, namely a girl from a foreign land."

Letter 338

1. John Gross, "Arendt on Eichmann," *Encounter* (November 1963): 65–74.

2. Hermann Cohen, 1842–1918, was a German-Jewish philosopher and founder of the Marburg school.

3. Franz Rosenzweig, 1886–1929, a German-Jewish philosopher, was a proponent of religious existentialism. J. alludes to the following essays: Rosenzweig, "Einleitung in die Akademieausgabe der jüdischen Schriften Hermann Cohens" and "Uber den Vortrag Hermann Cohens 'Das Verhältnis Spinozas zum Judentum,'" in Rosenzweig, *Kleinere Schriften* (Berlin, 1937): 299–350, 351–53.

4. Rolf Hochhuth, b. 1931, a playwright, was acquainted with J. and Gertrud J. On September 24, 1963, Hochhuth's *Der Stellvertreter* was performed at Basel's Stadttheater. It was an indictment of the role Pope Pius XII and the Catholic church played in the persecution of the Jews during World War II. In October, Radio Studio Basel taped the interdenominational discussion mentioned in this letter, and aired it on October 11. On this discussion and J.'s contribution to it, see *Basler Stadtbuch* (1965): 212–16.

5. Arnold Künzli, a political scientist then living in Basel, was moderator.
6. Rudolf Morsey, b. 1927, professor of modern history since 1970.

Letter 339

1. Paul Arnsberg, "Aus der Perspektive der Geborgenheit: Rezension von Ben Hechts Buch *Perfidy* (New York, 1963)," *Frankfurter Allgemeine Zeitung* (October 28, 1963). Ben Hecht, 1894–1964, was an American journalist, playwright, and novelist.
2. Hecht harshly criticized the Jewish Councils and the Jewish Agency, as well as the legal proceedings, in Kastner's case. Arnsberg, in his review, said Hecht had exaggerated many things in a perfidious way and had thereby rendered ill service to any attempt, which Arnsberg considered necessary, to rewrite the history of the founding of the state of Israel.
3. Samuel Krupp, 1892–1974, gynecologist, was J.'s family doctor until 1963 and remained a friend until J.'s death.

Letter 341

1. The sociologist Karl Mannheim; see L. 57, n. 4.
2. Tubja Rübner, a poet who wrote in Hebrew and in German.
3. See L. 338, n. 1.
4. Konrad Kellen, "Reflections on *Eichmann in Jerusalem*," *Midstream* (September 1963): 25–35.
5. Eva Michaelis-Stern, "Tragt ihn mit Stolz, den gelben Fleck," *Das Neue Israel* (September 1963): 151–54; Meier Teich, "Ein Diskussionsbeitrag zu Hannah Arendts *Eichmann in Jerusalem*, *Das Neue Israel*, 154–59.
6. Ernst Simon, "Hannah Arendt—eine Analyse," in *Nach dem Eichmann-Prozess: Zu einer Kontroverse über die Haltung der Juden* (London/Jerusalem/New York, 1963): 51–97.
7. In the U.S. edition of *Eichmann in Jerusalem*: ". . . Dr. Leo Baeck, former Chief Rabbi of Berlin, who in the eyes of both Jews and Gentiles was the 'Jewish Führer.' " The name "Jewish Führer" was criticized because it had been used as an ironic epithet by Eichmann's subordinates. See Adolf Leschnitzer, "So war Rabbiner Leo Baeck," in *Nach dem Eichmann-Prozess*, 25–30. A. omitted it in the German edition.
8. Meier Teich's article, cited in n. 5 above, attributes a number of errors to A.'s description of the persecution of Rumanian Jews: 156–59.
9. Jon Antonescu, 1882–1946, Rumanian general and politician, was, during World War II, leader of both state and army. He was executed as a war criminal in 1946. A.'s thesis was that the Rumanian government under him initiated pogroms before the Nazis expressed such intentions. Teich's article (n. 5 above) demonstrates that "as early as May 29, 1940, the German-Rumanian Treaty defined persecution of Jews as one of the Rumanian government's most important obligations" (157). J. presumably interpreted this to mean that the initiative for the persecution of the

Rumanian Jews was more likely to have come from Hitler than from Antonescu.

10. Bavarian Television showed this series in the fall of 1964.
11. A one-time honorarium for all television rights.

Letter 342

1. Kennedy was shot and died on November 22, 1963.
2. President Abraham Lincoln was assassinated five days after General Robert E. Lee's surrender of his Confederate forces.
3. Ernst Levy, 1881–1968, jurist and professor of Roman law at Heidelberg, 1928–35, was a colleague of J.'s there. He emigrated to the United States, but upon retirement lived in Basel for a number of years.

Letter 343

1. Lee Harvey Oswald, who had been apprehended for shooting Kennedy, was shot to death in Dallas on November 24, 1963, by Jack Ruby, a nightclub owner.
2. Sabina Lietzmann, "Amerikas Blaustrumpf Nr. 1," *Frankfurter Allgemeine Zeitung* (September 16, 1963).
3. Jacob L. Talmon, b. 1916, Jewish historian of Polish background, was, since 1960, a professor at Hebrew University in Jerusalem.
4. Isaiah Berlin, b. 1909, English political scientist and philosopher, in 1957 became professor of social and political sciences at Oxford University.
5. Tubja Rübner; see L. 341.
6. This organization was founded in 1948 to represent destitute Jews who had a claim to German restitution payments. Its headquarters was in Frankfurt.
7. Kurt May was head of the United Restitution Organization. See also L. 359, n. 10.
8. Jacob and Nehemiah Robinson wrote articles against A.'s Eichmann book; see *Die Kontroverse: Hannah Arendt, Eichmann und die Juden* (L. 336, n. 5), 150–51, 223–32.

Letter 344

1. An ultraconservative secret society founded in 1958 by Robert H. Welch and named after John M. Birch, 1918–1945. Under the pretext of fighting Communism, it engaged in slanderous campaigns against individuals and organizations it disapproved of.
2. Rolf Hochhuth, *Der Stellvertreter* (Hamburg, 1963). See L. 338, n. 4.
3. The Germanophobe and anti-Semitic ideology of this movement, formed in 1898 by French royalists, called for "integral nationalism," and its members fought parliamentary democracy, hoping to reinstate the monarchy.
4. "Sons of the Covenant." This was an independent organization devoted

to ethical and charitable purposes, founded in 1843 by German-Jewish immigrants to the United States.

Letter 345

1. Golo Mann, "Hannah Arendt und der Eichmann-Prozess," *Neue Rund-schau* 74, no. 4 (1963): 626–33.
2. See L. 337, n. 2.

Letter 347

1. Not in the literary remains.
2. See L. 336.
3. *The New York Times Book Review* (June 23, 1963): 4–6.
4. J. eventually settled on the title "Von der Unabhängigkeit des Denkens." He worked on the book—never finished—in the last years of his life.
5. Friedrich Reck-Malleczewen, 1884–1945, physician and writer, was killed in Dachau. For A.'s assessment of him, see *Eichmann in Jerusalem*, 91, 97 (U.S. ed.); 138 (German ed.). In the former, Reck-Malleczewen and J. were mentioned as two of the few exceptional individuals who never had anything to do with the National Socialist movement; in the latter, this passage is toned down.
6. Theodor Haecker, 1879–1945, was a philosopher in the fields of culture and religion.
7. Golo Mann, "Hannah Arendt und der Eichmann-Prozess," *Neue Rund-schau*, 630.
8. Gerhard Ritter, *Carl Goerdeler und die deutsche Widerstandsbewegung* (Stuttgart, 1954).
9. Friedrich Meinecke, *Weltbürgertum und Nationalstaat: Studien zur Genesis des deutschen Nationalstaates* (Munich/Berlin, 1907).
10. August Neidhardt von Gneisenau, 1760–1831, was a Prussian general. J. is presumably referring to chapter 8 in Meinecke's book.

Letter 348

1. Not among the literary remains.
2. Emil Henk, *Die Tragödie des 20. Juli 1944* (Heidelberg, 1946).
3. Friedrich Percyval Reck-Malleczewen, *Tagebuch eines Verzweifelten* (Lorch, 1947).
4. Hannah Arendt, "The Deputy: Guilt by Silence?" *New York Herald Tribune Magazine* (February 23, 1964): 6–9. In German: "Der Stellvertreter in USA," *Neue deutsche Hefte*, no. 101 (September/October 1964): 111–23.
5. Followers of Francis Joseph Cardinal Spellman, 1889–1967, who was at the time the spokesman for conservative Catholicism in America.
6. See L. 155, n. 2.
7. Karl Jaspers, *Nikolaus Cusanus* (Munich, 1964).

8. Karl Jaspers, *Three Essays: Leonardo, Descartes, Max Weber*, trans. by Ralph Manheim (New York, 1964).
9. Karl Jaspers, *Max Weber: Politiker—Forscher—Philosoph* (Munich, 1958); see L. 22, n. 1.
10. *Max Weber*, 7.
11. Angelo Giuseppe Roncalli, 1881–1963, Pope John XXIII. A. wrote the afterword for the book *Johannes XXIII: Geistliches Tagebuch* (Freiburg, 1968): 361–72. The piece had previously been published as "Der christliche Papst," *Merkur* 20, no. 4 (April 1966): 362–72. It also is in Hannah Arendt, *Men in Dark Times*.

Letter 349
1. Dietrich Bonhoeffer, 1906–1945, Protestant pastor and theologian and resistance leader, was executed in Flossenbürg concentration camp.
2. Golo Mann, "Hannah Arendt und der Eichmann-Prozess," 630.

Letter 350
1. Karl Jaspers, "Bemerkungen zu Max Webers politischen Denken," in *Antidoron: Edgar Salin zum 70. Geburtstag*, ed. E. von Beckerath *et al.* (Tübingen, 1962): 200–14. Edgar Salin, 1892–1974, an economist and sociologist, was professor at Heidelberg, 1924–27, then at Basel. J. had known him at Heidelberg, and Salin was instrumental in J.'s appointment at Basel.
2. The Alldeutscher Verband was a political organization founded in 1891 to stimulate German national consciousness, enhance the awareness of German culture abroad, and create a dynamic foreign and colonial policy for Germany.
3. Friedrich Naumann, 1860–1919, founded the National Socialist Union to achieve democratic and social reforms in both the state and the economy, so that workers would support the state, the nation, and a "social monarchy."
4. See L. 351, n. 5.

Letter 351
1. Letter of April 19, 1964, from A. to Emil Henk. .
2. Axel Freiherr von dem Bussche, b. 1919, an army officer, was a member of the German resistance. The plan mentioned was for him to present a new style of officer's coat to Hitler. Explosives would be hidden in the coat's pockets and be set off when he embraced the Führer. The opportunity never came. He was later severely wounded in battle.
3. Ernst Schnabel, b. 1913, a writer, was then editor in charge of the third radio program of North German Radio and of the station Free Berlin.
4. On June 13, 1964, Eastern Michigan University awarded A. an honorary doctorate of laws.

5. Raul Hilberg, *The Destruction of the European Jews* (Chicago, 1961).
6. Kurt Rossmann was one of the candidates to succeed J.

Letter 352

1. See L. 332 and L. 332, nn. 1 and 2.
2. The interview was called "Nur die Freiheit—allein darauf kommt es an."
3. Hans Herzfeld, 1892–1982, was a historian and professor at the Free University of Berlin, 1950–60. The phrase "rightist institution" presumably refers to Radio Free Europe.
4. See L. 319, in which J. tells a similar story about Piper's wanting him to do an interview after the publication of *Die Atombombe.*
5. Peter Zschokke, b. 1898, was head of the education department of the canton Basel-Stadt.
6. Rudolf W. Meyer, b. 1907, was a professor of philosophy at the University of Zurich.
7. Rudolf W. Meyer, *Leibniz und die Europäische Ordnungskrise* (Hamburg, 1948).

Letter 353

1. Albert Wohlstetter, b. 1913, was professor of political science at the University of Chicago, 1965–80.
2. Nathalie Sarraute, b. 1902, was a Russian-born French writer. See Hannah Arendt, "Nathalie Sarraute," *The New York Review of Books* (March 5, 1964); in German: *Merkur* 17, no. 8 (August 1964).
3. See L. 165, especially n. 5.

Letter 354

1. Barry M. Goldwater, b. 1909, U.S. senator from Arizona, 1953–64, 1968–87, was the Republican presidential candidate in 1964. An ultra-conservative, he lost the election to Lyndon Johnson.
2. The report of a presidential commission headed by Chief Justice Earl Warren, 1891–1974, which found Oswald solely responsible for the assassination of President Kennedy.

Letter 355

1. This is a misunderstanding on J.'s part. It is the innkeeper, not Heinrich Blücher, who keeps an eye on village morality.
2. Gertrud J.'s note reads: "Beloved Hannah, that you exist! Beginning of September suits us beautifully—by then all the visitors will be gone and Erna is not taking her vacation until mid-September! We're still managing

the housework easily. A lot of work with deadlines—but I hope for the last time. Regards to you both!"

3. Karl Jaspers, "Nikolaus Cusanus: Vortrag zum 500. Todestag," broadcast by Radio Studio Basel, August 10, 1964.
4. *Von der Wahrheit*, 936–43.
5. Not in the literary remains.
6. Stefan Moses was visiting German writers at that time to take photographs for the *Jahresheft 1964* of the magazine *Magnum*.

Letter 357

1. See L. 38, n. 6.
2. *The New York Times Book Review* of May 19 and June 23, 1963.
3. Michael A. Musmanno, "Man with an Unspotted Conscience: Adolf Eichmann's Role in the Nazi Mania Is Weighed in Hannah Arendt's New Book," *The New York Times Book Review* (May 19, 1963).

Letter 358

1. L. 357 was accompanied by a letter from Gertrud J. to A. with the same date.

Letter 359

1. Two internal memos of the Anti-Defamation League, March 11 and 27, 1963; they contained guidelines and materials for discrediting A.'s *Eichmann in Jerusalem*.
2. Dated April 10, 1963.
3. Siegfried Moses, 1887–1974, was a German Zionist who moved to Palestine in 1936 and was comptroller of the state of Israel, 1949–61. The enclosed letters to A., dated March 7 and 24, 1963, tell about the outrage of the Jews over A.'s Eichmann articles in *The New Yorker*.
4. This is the page in the German edition of *Eichmann in Jerusalem*.
5. Dated May 24, 1963.
6. *Aufbau*, July 26, 1963.
7. Open letter by A. of July 29, 1963, addressed to Kurt May.
8. For example, a letter written by Ernoe Landau, which confirmed A.'s statement that no deportations of Jews took place in Bulgaria.
9. Kurt May's article in *Aufbau* of July 26, 1963; see L. 343 and L. 343, n. 7.
10. Israeli Attorney General Gideon Hausner; see L. 285, n. 4.
11. *Die Kontroverse: Hannah Arendt, Eichmann und die Juden.*

Letter 360

1. Transcript of an interview with Günter Gaus, broadcast October 28, 1963, by ZDF, a German TV station, as part of the series Zur Person and entitled "Was bleibt? Es bleibt die Muttersprache"; later published in Günter Gaus, *Zur Person: Porträts in Frage und Antwort* (Munich, 1964): 13–32.
2. It is unclear whether J. had a specific work by Ernst Mayer in mind here or the fact that all of Mayer's philosophical writings could be taken as a subtle homage.
3. Ludwig Curtius, *Deutsche und antike Welt: Lebenserinnerungen* (Stuttgart, 1950): 365ff. Also, his *Torso: Verstreute und nachgelassene Schriften* (Stuttgart, 1957): 289–301, which refers to a letter Curtius wrote, February 21, 1933, on the occasion of J.'s fiftieth birthday. Presumably J. had that in mind here.
4. Robert M. W. Kempner, b. 1899, German-born U.S. lawyer and political scientist, was a U.S. staff prosecutor at the international military tribunal in Nuremberg, 1945–46, that tried high Nazi officials.
5. *Die Zeit* (September 25, 1964): 18.
6. Friedrich Karl Fromme, "Die Banalitat des Bösen: Zur deutschen Ausgabe von Hannah Arendts umstrittenem Buch *Eichmann in Jerusalem*," *Frankfurter Allgemeine Zeitung* (September 29, 1964).
7. "Was ist deutsch?" was broadcast in July 1965. See L. 377, n. 2.

Letter 361

1. In October 1964, Nikita Khrushchev was stripped of his position as premier and first secretary of the Communist party.
2. Khrushchev's removal from power was, from China's point of view, a necessary condition for improving relations with the Soviet Union.

Letter 362

1. A press conference A. gave with Piper at the 1964 Frankfurt Book Fair.
2. Joseph Wulf, b. 1912, German-Jewish historian, became director of the International Center of Documents for Research on National Socialism in 1967. The review was written by Alexander Mitscherlich; *Der Spiegel* 19, no. 5 (January 27, 1965): 78–79.
3. See L. 360, n. 4.
4. The Committee on Social Thought, at the University of Chicago, to which A. had belonged since the fall of 1963.
5. Mikhail A. Suslov, 1902–1982, was a chief Communist ideologist in the Soviet Union. He held government posts under Stalin, Khrushchev, and Brezhnev.
6. Leon Trotsky, 1879–1940, Russian revolutionary, served in various government positions under Lenin. After Stalin succeeded Lenin, he was

removed from power, and in 1929 ordered to leave the Soviet Union. He was murdered in exile in Mexico in 1940, presumably by a Soviet agent.
7. In early September 1964, 36-year-old Horst Schwirkmann, a counter-espionage agent responsible for protecting the West German Embassy in Moscow against wiretapping, was attacked and seriously poisoned by mustard gas.
8. Three young men—Michael Schwerner, Andrew Goodman, and James Chaney—who had been working for civil rights in Mississippi were found murdered on August 4, 1964. After extended court proceedings, seven men who had taken part in the attack were convicted of the crime and given prison sentences of up to ten years.

Letter 363

1. Fernande Weill-Blum, b. 1908, was an old friend of the J. household. Her brother, André Blum, b. 1909, was a dealer in livestock.
2. At the beginning of the interview with Gaus, A. said she had "bid philosophy a final farewell" and now considered "political theory" her field.
3. After lengthy debate in the Reichstag in 1914, the Social Democratic party, which had been pacifist in outlook, voted to approve the war credits proposed by bourgeois interests, an action that triggered a crisis within the party.
4. The *Berliner Tageblatt* (1872–1939) and the *Vossische Zeitung*, also a Berlin daily (since 1911, but under another name 1917–34), were traditional, liberal papers that, like the rest of the bourgeois German press, practiced and advocated the withhholding of news during World War I.
5. After Khrushchev's fall from power in 1964, Leonid Brezhnev, 1906–1982, was named first secretary of the Communist party Central Committee. Aleksey Kosygin, 1904–1980, became premier.
6. Sophie, 1921–1943, and Hans, 1918–1943, Scholl were leaders of the Munich University student resistance group Weisse Rose. Both were tortured and hung by the Gestapo.

Letter 364

1. Dr. Hans Rössner, b. 1910, was at that time editor in chief of Piper Verlag.

Letter 365

1. Alexander Mitscherlich, 1908–1982, a psychoanalyst and writer, was director of the Sigmund Freud Institute in Frankfurt am Main, 1960–76. On the review, see L. 362 and L. 362, n. 2.
2. A.'s letter, of November 27, 1964, was addressed to Professor Landmann, at Berlin's Free University: "A few days ago I received a report of a

debate, organized by the Friends of Hebrew University and chaired by you at the Free University of Berlin, which had as its subject my book *Eichmann in Jerusalem.* According to this report a certain Shlomo Aronson made the following remarks about me:

"That he knew me personally; that I did not know until age twenty that I was Jewish; that I had said that 'I belonged to no people'; and that 'I had not come to terms to this day' with the fact of being Jewish.

"In response to this I want to state: Mr. Aronson does not know me; I have never to my knowledge set eyes on him. I took part in Jewish religious instruction at school from my seventh year on, stayed out of school on high holidays and went to the synagogue. In addition, my grandfather, Max Arendt, was president of the Jewish congregation in Königsberg, my hometown. I never said that 'I belong to no people' or that 'I have not come to terms to this day with the fact of being Jewish.' On the contrary, I have always and long before 1933 stressed that I belong to the Jewish people.

"Apparently Mr. Aronson also discussed my views on the state of Israel; according to the report I received, his statements on this subject contain as much truth as those concerning my person. They are pure fabrications.

"Further, Dr. Scheffler apparently claimed that I had 'raised an across-the-board accusation against the Jewish Councils' because they had decided in 1933 (?) to face the realities. This is not only nonsense, because there were no Jewish Councils in 1933, but also untrue. Here is what I said: 'Of course these negotiations during the early stages of the regime were entirely different from the Jewish Councils' later collaboration.'

"Since these are not errors of fact or differences of opinion but outright lies, I ask you to take effective action to set the record straight."

3. Chou En-lai, 1898–1976, a founder of the Chinese Communist party, was premier of China from 1949.
4. Richard Lowenthal, *World Communism: The Disintegration of a Secular Faith* (New York, 1964). Born in 1908, he was a German political scientist who became a British citizen in 1947. Since 1961, he had taught at the Otto-Suhr Institute of the Free University in Berlin.
5. See L. 308, n. 3.

Letter 366

1. Julius Leber, 1891–1945, Social Democratic politician and early opponent of National Socialism, was a leader in the resistance movement against Hitler. He was hung for high treason.
2. *Ein Mann geht seinen Weg: Schriften, Reden und Briefe von Julius Leber,* published by his friends (Berlin, 1952).
3. Claus Schenk Graf von Stauffenberg, 1907–1944, chief of staff to the head

of the Reserve Army, was a leading organizer of the assassination plot of July 20, 1944. He was executed in connection with that attempt.

4. Max Weber, *Gesammelte Aufsätze zur Religionssoziologie* 1 (Tübingen, 1920): 563.

5. William Penn, 1644–1718, politically and religiously influential Quaker, who founded the colony of Pennsylvania.

Letter 367

1. Karl Jaspers, *Three Essays: Leonardo, Descartes, Max Weber* (New York, 1964).

2. See L. 314, n. 3.

Letter 368

1. Madeleine Salmony-Huber, b. 1926, wife of H. A. Salmony (see L. 184, n. 12), worked as J.'s secretary for several years and was a good friend of the Jasperses.

Letter 369

1. See L. 321, n. 1.

2. "Eichmann in Jerusalem: Ein Gespräch über das gleichnamige Buch von Hannah Arendt mit Peter Wyss," broadcast February 14, 1965, by Radio Studio Basel.

3. "Für Völkermord gibt es keine Verjährung," interview with Rudolf Augstein, *Der Spiegel* (March 10, 1965): 49–71.

4. Richard Jäger. For his statements during the debate on the statute of limitations, see *Protokolle des Deutschen Bundestages*, 170th session, March 3, 1965, and 175th session, March 25, 1965.

5. Benno von Wiese, "Bemerkungen zur 'unbewältigten Vergangenheit,' " *Die Zeit* 19, no. 52 (January 1, 1965): 9–10.

6. Manfred Müller, "Von der Banalität des Bösen," *Diskus: Frankfurter Studentenzeitung* (December 1946): 4.

7. *Politikon: Göttinger Studentenzeitschrift für Niedersachsen*, n. 9 (January 1965), published essays and documents on this topic under the heading "Universität im Dritten Reich."

8. Erwin Panofsky, 1892–1968, German-American art historian, had taught at Princeton since 1935.

9. A resistance group founded in 1942 and named for the place of their meetings, an estate in Silesia. Among its members were Theodor Haubach and Carlo Mierendorff.

10. Letter from Edwin T. Mason, dated January 27, 1965.

11. See L. 307, n. 1.

12. In 1964, students at the University of California, Berkeley, demonstrated

for the right to be politically active on campus, to have a voice in university decisions, and to end discrimination against minority students.

13. "As for the rest, I am for . . . ."

Letter 371

1. See L. 369, n. 3.

2. Augstein said during the interview that "to my knowledge not a single judge and not a single public prosecutor from the Nazi period has yet faced a criminal court" and that therefore "the legitimacy of punishment for crime [is] simply dubious" (p. 53).

3. Augstein expressed the opinion that even Jewish organizations, Israel, and other states that condoned the continuation in office of people like Globke and Vialon (see n. 5 below) had placed themselves "in a questionable light" (p. 53).

4. In March 1960, a meeting took place in New York between Adenauer and Ben Gurion. Later allegations that a deal involving arms had been made then were denied by Ben Gurion (see the *Spiegel* interview of March 31, 1965). No public documents on this subject exist. Eichmann was not apprehended until May 11, 1960. It is unclear what newspaper notice A. is referring to here.

5. Hans Globke, 1898–1973, a government lawyer and expert on citizenship matters, drafted the commentary on the Nuremberg racial laws of 1935 and provided a basis for more anti-Jewish laws. Under Adenauer he was appointed state secretary of the Chancellery and served from 1953 to 1963. Friedrich-Karl Vialon, b. 1905, a lawyer, was, under Hitler, director of the finance department of the Reichskommissariat of Ostland, the department that organized confiscation of Jewish property. Under Adenauer, he became undersecretary in the federal ministry for economic cooperation.

6. Heinrich Lübke, 1894–1972, agronomist and politician, was federal minister of food, agriculture, and forestry, 1953–59, and from then until 1969, president of the Federal Republic of Germany. Under Chancellor Ludwig Erhard, the Senate counsel for justice, Carl Creifels, b. 1907, was to be appointed a federal judge. Lübke refused to sign the appointment because Creifels had served in the Nazi ministry of justice.

7. An informal association of writers and critics that was formed in 1947 and included some of the best-known German writers of the postwar period.

8. Under Israeli criminal law, capital punishment is abolished in Israel, but continues to be enforced for crimes against the people of Israel and can in that situation be applied retroactively.

9. In view of Eichmann's crime against humanity, J. felt that Israel's invoking of a purely national judicial competence was too limited. He went on to say: "A new frame of mind is taking shape all over the world, one based on more than mere opinion. It represents an attitude that is so serious that I have to judge it by fresh criteria if I am to apprehend it in its full meaning."

10. The debate on the statute of limitations began on March 10, 1965. On March 25, the Bundestag passed a law that changed the beginning date of the twenty-year limitation for Nazi crimes punishable with life imprisonment from May 8, 1945, to December 31, 1949.
11. In a letter dated February 28, 1965, Gertrud J. had told A. that Ella Mayer's death was imminent.

Letter 372

1. Karl Jaspers, *Kleine Schule des philosophischen Denkens* (Munich, 1965).

Letter 373

1. Penciled note by J. on the undated letter.
2. Of March 24, 1965.
3. Goethe, *Faust II*, verses 11404–405. A.'s recollection of the line differs slightly from Goethe's words.
4. Karl Kraus, 1874–1936, was an Austrian writer and a great satirist.
5. Karl Kraus, *Die Dritte Walpurgisnacht*, in *Werke* (H. Fischer edition), vol. 1, 3d ed. (Munich, 1965): 9. A.'s quote differs slightly from Kraus's word order.
6. Theodor W(iesengrund) Adorno, 1903–1969, was a philosopher and sociologist, and a major representative of the Frankfurt school. See also L. 399 and L. 399, nn. 2, 3.
7. Michael Landmann, 1913–1984, philosopher at the Free University in Berlin since 1950, was J.'s first assistant during the Basel period. On the controversy between A. and Landmann, see L. 365, n. 2. Documents on it can be found in the Library of Congress in Washington, D.C.
8. Richard Schmid, "Avantgarde im Biedermeierstil: *The New Yorker*: Porträt einer ungewöhnlichen Zeitschrift," *Die Zeit*, numbers 12, 13 (March 26, April 2, 1965).
9. Schmid writes that *The New Yorker* published a literary profile of Thomas Mann in December 1941, and as several letters show, Golo Mann was annoyed by its style and tone. He "calmed down" only when a number of Americans assured him that the article was considered a tribute. In letters to Agnes E. Meyer about this, he referred to *The New Yorker* as a "satirical magazine," and then used the term in his criticism of A.'s Eichmann articles.
10. Wolfgang Graetz, b. 1926, was a German writer. The play mentioned is his *Die Verschwörer* (Munich, 1965).

Letter 374

1. Werner Kaegi, 1901–1979, was a Swiss historian and professor at the University of Basel from 1935.

2. Apparently J. is quoting this phrase from a letter that has not been pre-served in the literary remains.
3. The third lecture in *Kleine Schule des philosophischen Denkens*.
4. During the winter semester of 1931–32, J. lectured four hours a week on logic. That was apparently the first time he presented his theory of the modes of the Encompassing and the modes of truth, which later, as peri-echontology, became the heart of his *Philosophische Logik*. This theory was the "key to the key cabinet" J. mentions in this letter.
5. Christiane Zimmer, b. 1902, daughter of Hugo von Hofmannsthal, had been a friend of the Jasperses since her marriage to the Indologian Heinrich Zimmer.

Letter 375

1. Natalie Jefroikyn was Heinrich Blücher's second wife; A. was his third wife.
2. Günter Grass, b. 1927, was a German writer, artist, and member of Gruppe 47. Uwe Johnson, 1934–1984, was a German novelist who later became a friend of A.
3. Hans Magnus Enzensberger, b. 1929, German writer, was another mem-ber of Gruppe 47.

Letter 376

1. "Graetz: Bombe aus Butzbach," *Der Spiegel* 19, no. 18 (April 28, 1965): 142–47.
2. Karl Jaspers, "Sommes-nous sûrs que la guerre soit impossible? Un en-tretien avec le Socrate de notre temps par Guy Valaire," *Réalités*, no. 236 (September 1965): 70ff.
3. J. was awarded the Prix littéraire international de la Paix in Liège in 1965.
4. Karl Jaspers, *Nietzsche: An Introduction to the Understanding of His Philosophical Activity*, trans. Charles F. Wallraff and Frederick J. Schmitz (Tucson, 1965).

Letter 377

1. Neither Graetz's play nor the letter is preserved in the literary remains.
2. "Was ist deutsch?" was broadcast in July 1965 by German Radio in Cologne. It was reprinted in Karl Jaspers, *Hoffnung und Sorge* (see L. 383, n. 4), 346–65.
3. Rolf Hochhuth, "Der Klassenkampf ist nicht zu Ende," *Der Spiegel* 19, no. 22 (May 26, 1965); later in *Krieg und Klassenkrieg* rororo 1455 (Ham-burg, 1971), 28–44. On the concept of property, see 33–34.
4. Rudolf Augstein, "Die Ziege des Herrn Seguin: Charles de Gaulle und sein Gaullismus," *Der Spiegel* 19, no. 24 (June 9, 1965): 40–63.

Letter 378

1. Erich von Witzleben, 1881–1944, retired German field marshal, was executed as a conspirator in the July 20, 1944, plot against Hitler.
2. Notes for such a work were published posthumously: Karl Jaspers, *Notizen zu Martin Heidegger*; see L. 92, n. 4.

Letter 381

1. In addition to L. 379, there were two letters from Gertrud J., July 2 and 9, 1965.
2. Carlo Schmid, 1896–1979, was a professor of international law and vice president of the Bundestag 1967–72.
3. Hannah Arendt, "Truth and Politics," *The New Yorker* (February 25, 1967): 49–88; reprinted in Hannah Arendt, *Between Past and Future* (New York, 1968): 227–64. In German: "Wahrheit und Politik," in *Philosophische Perspektiven: Ein Jahrbuch*, ed. R. Berlinger and E. Fink, 1 (1969): 9–51; reprinted in Hannah Arendt, *Wahrheit und Lüge in der Politik* (Munich, 1972): 44–92.
4. Hannah Arendt, "What Is Permitted to Jove," *The New Yorker* (November 5, 1966): 68–122; reprinted in Hannah Arendt, *Men in Dark Times*, 207–49. In German: "Quod licet Jovi . . . Reflexionen über den Dichter Bertolt Brecht und sein Verhältnis zur Politik," *Merkur* 23, no. 6 (June 1969): 527–42, and no. 7 (July 1969): 625–42; reprinted in Hannah Arendt, *Walter Benjamin, Bertolt Brecht: Zwei Essays* (Munich, 1971), 63–107.

Letter 382

1. A. taught at Cornell University during the fall semester 1965–66.
2. A. was going to help Hans Saner get a Rockefeller grant.

Letter 383

1. Date handwritten by A. on the undated letter.
2. "Die Bundestagsdebatten über die Verjährung von Morden des NS-Staates."
3. Willy Feess, b. 1927, was studying philosophy and was J.'s "technical assistant" for several years; he later became a physician.
4. Karl Jaspers, *Hoffnung und Sorge: Schriften zur deutschen Politik 1945–1965* (Munich, 1965).

Letter 384

1. Jacob Robinson, *And the Crooked Shall Be Made Straight: The Eichmann Trial, the Jewish Catastrophe, and Hannah Arendt's Narrative* (New York, 1965).
2. Heinrich Grüber, "Hannah Arendt: Report in Jerusalem," in *Die Kon-*

troverse: Hannah Arendt, Eichmann und die Juden, 235–39. J.'s phrase may be based on incorrect memory. In some writing in the literary remains, J. did subject the piece to criticism, but the criticism is objective and reflects some respect for Grüber. There is no mention of a "hate-filled article," and the phrase hardly describes the tone and content of Grüber's essay.

3. Johann Reckenwald, *Woran hat Adolf Hitler gelitten? Eine neuropsychiatrische Deutung* (Munich/Basel, 1963).

4. Konstantin Alexander Freiherr von Economo, 1876–1931, was an Austrian neurologist.

Letter 385

1. J.'s evaluation of Saner's dissertation, "Kants Weg vom Krieg zum Frieden."

2. Jacques Freymond, b. 1911, Swiss political scientist, was director of the Ecole des Hautes Etudes Internationales in Geneva, 1955–78, and professor of the history of international relations at the University of Geneva, 1958–77.

3. George Agree, b. 1921, was, at the time, executive director of the National Committee for an Effective Congress.

4. Ludwig Erhard, 1897–1977, chancellor of the Federal Republic of Germany, 1963–66.

5. Randall Jarrell, 1914–1965, was a poet, novelist, and critic.

6. Theodore R. Weiss, b. 1916, a poet, was professor of English literature at Bard College, 1964–69.

7. "Two for Heinrich Bluecher" and "A Satyr's Hide," in *The Medium* (New York, 1965): 50–54.

8. "The Web, for Hannah Arendt," *The Medium*, 40–41.

9. Randall Jarrell, *Pictures from an Institution: A Comedy* (New York, 1954).

Letter 386

1. The piece did not appear in *Der Spiegel*, but was published, as "Zweites Stück," in *Wohin treibt die Bundesrepublik?*

2. The manuscript for "The Formidable Mr. Robinson," which was published in *The New York Review of Books* (January 28, 1966), under the title "The Formidable Dr. Robinson: A Reply."

3. Walter Laqueur, "And the Crooked Shall Be Made Straight," *The New York Review of Books* (November 11, 1965).

4. This must be an error. No review of Robinson's book was published in the *Herald Tribune*, but one did appear in the *New York Times* (December 20, 1965).

Letter 387

1. There is a letter to A. dated November 22, 1965, among J.'s literary remains with a penciled note: "Not sent because lost." Since all the topics

in this "lost" letter are raised and covered in greater detail in L. 387, the earlier version is not given here.

2. Ammonius Saccas, c. 175–242, Alexandrian philosopher and founder of Neoplatonism.

3. Walter Muschg, 1898–1965, was a Swiss literary critic, and, from 1936, a professor at the University of Basel.

4. Walter Muschg, *Studien Zur tragischen Literaturgeschichte* (Bern/Munich, 1965).

5. Walter Muschg, *Tragische Literaturgeschichte* (Bern, 1948).

6. Frieda Saner, née Gerber, 1898–1965.

Letter 388

1. Parts one and two of *Wohin treibt die Bundesrepublik?*
2. Hannah Arendt, *Uber die Revolution* (München, 1965).
3. Part three of *Wohin treibt die Bundesrepublik?*
4. Quote from Goethe's *Urworte Orphisch.*
5. Because J. suffered from chronic inoperable bronchiectasis, he thought he would not live long.

Letter 389

1. Gerald Freund, b. 1930, was associate director of the Rockefeller Foundation.

2. Gerhard Schmidt, *Selektion in der Heilanstalt 1939–1945*, with a foreword by Karl Jaspers (Stuttgart, 1965).

3. See L. 386, n. 2.

4. Conference on Jewish Material Claims against Germany. At negotiations conducted in The Hague, this association of thirteen Jewish organizations represented the interests of Jews not living in Israel. The negotiations led to the Luxembourg Agreement on Restitution of September 10, 1952.

5. An organization founded in 1888 in the United States to disseminate books on Jewish religion, history, and literature.

6. See L. 382, n. 1.

7. A.'s dissertation on the concept of love in Augustine. See L. 10, n. 1.

Letter 390

1. Robert Arthur Talbot Gascoyne-Cecil, 3rd marquess of Salisbury, 1830–1903, was then British foreign secretary and prime minister.

2. Leo Graf von Caprivi, 1831–1899, German officer and politician, succeeded Bismarck as chancellor. Bernhard Fürst von Bülow, 1849–1929, German politician and diplomat, was secretary of state for foreign affairs, 1897–1900, and imperial chancellor, 1900–09. Wilhelm II, 1859–1941, was German emperor and king of Prussia, 1888–1918.

3. Hendrik van Oyen, 1898–1980, was, from 1948, professor for systematic theology at the University of Basel.
4. The German title *Der philosophische Glaube angesichts der Offenbarung* was translated as *Philosophical Faith and Revelation* (San Francisco, 1967).

Letter 391

1. Karl Jaspers, "The Criminal State and German Responsibility: A Dialogue," trans. W. J. Dannhauser, *Commentary* 41, no. 2. (February, 1966): 33–39. This is an abbreviated version.
2. Karl Jaspers, "No Statute of Limitations for Genocide: A Conversation with Karl Jaspers," trans. H. Zohn, *Midstream* 12, no. 2 (1966): 3–18. Complete version.
3. This ia an organization founded in New York in 1939 to collect money for Jewish American charitable institutions.
4. J. William Fulbright, b. 1905, five-term U.S. senator, was, at this time, chairman of the Senate Foreign Relations Committee. One of the first senators to oppose the Vietnam War, he used these televised hearings to widen the national debate.
5. Dean Rusk, b. 1909, was secretary of state, 1961–69.
6. George F. Kennan, b. 1904, was a U.S. diplomat and historian. James M. Gavin, b. 1907, was a U.S. general and diplomat.
7. This is in response to a lengthy note Gertrud J. had added to L. 390: "Unfortunately my English is not good enough for me to read the book of poetry, but *Revolution* is a magnificent book that I have read with pleasure."
8. "Mitternacht einer Weltmacht," *Der Spiegel*, no. 7 (February 7, 1966): 110–13.

Letter 393

1. Alexander Schwan, *Politische Philosophie im Denken Heideggers* (Köln/Opladen, 1965).
2. The *Spiegel* article on Heidegger, cited in L. 391, n. 8, does not claim this explicitly, but suggests that this may have been the case.
3. In a letter to J. in 1950, Heidegger states that the reason he stopped visiting J. was not "because a Jew lived there but simply because I was ashamed."
4. Friedrich Oehlkers, 1890–1971, German botanist, taught at Tübingen and Darmstadt, before becoming a professor at Freiburg in 1932.
5. In December 1943, Heidegger sent J. a copy of his *Vom Wesen der Wahrheit* with a handwritten inscription: "A belated gift for your sixtieth birthday, with best wishes. Martin Heidegger."
6. Werner G. Brock, 1901–1974, German-Jewish philosopher and privat-docent at the University of Freiburg, 1931–33, emigrated to England (Cambridge). He resumed teaching at Freiburg after the war.
7. Eduard Fränkel, 1888–1970, a classical philologist, taught at Kiel and Göttingen before becoming professor at Freiburg in 1931. He emigrated

to England and was professor of Latin philology at Oxford. The reference here is to an assessment of Eduard Baumgarten that Heidegger wrote, December 16, 1933, for the faculty of Göttingen, in which he is said to have written: "After Baumgarten failed with me, he associated quite a bit with the Jew Fränkel who used to teach at Göttingen but has since been let go here." See Karl Jaspers, *Notizen zu Martin Heidegger*, 14ff.

8. *Der Spiegel* 20, no. 11 (1966): 12.
9. Karl Jaspers, *The Great Philosophers*, ed. Hannah Arendt, trans. Ralph Manheim, 2 (New York, 1966).

Letter 394

1. *The New York Review of Books* (March 17, 1966).

Letter 395

1. Not preserved in the literary remains.
2. The review was by J. Collins, *The New York Times Book Review* (April 10, 1966).
3. Karl Jaspers, *Wohin treibt die Bundesrepublik?*
4. See L. 393, n. 1.
5. See L. 373, n. 6.
6. Max Horkheimer, 1895–1973, a philosopher, was one of the founders of the Frankfurt school.
7. Klaus Wagenbach, b. 1930, was a writer and a publisher.
8. Rabbi Arthur Hertzberg, b. 1921 in Poland, had come to the United States in 1924; he was at this time professor of history at Columbia University. His letter was dated March 31, 1966.
9. Elisabeth Saner-Schwammberger, b. 1933.

Letter 396

1. Ricarda Huch, 1864–1947, was a German writer of verse, novels, and criticism.
2. Wolfgang J. Mommsen, *Max Weber und die deutsche Politik: 1890–1920* (Tübingen, 1959).
3. In J.'s interleaved copy of the first edition of *Psychologie der Weltanschauungen*, there is a handwritten note: "When, in April 1920, Max Weber left our house for the last time, he said to me in the semidark as he took leave at the door: 'Your book tempts one to dip into it here and there; I haven't read all of it yet.' (Of course!) 'It's very worthwhile.' (Really?) 'It's *very* worthwhile. —Thank you for the book, *thank* you.' Pause. 'I hope you will continue to be productive. —I shall comment on your book on another occasion.' (Earlier, when we were talking together, he told me that he had mentioned my name twice in his last works and why)."
4. Karl Jaspers, *Reason and Existenz: Five Lectures*; see L. 223, n. 5.

Letter 397

1. *Wohin treibt die Bundesrepublik?*
2. Klaus Wagenbach, *Franz Kafka: Eine Biographie seiner Jugend, 1883–1912* (Bern, 1958); *Franz Kafka in Selbstzeugnissen und Bilddokumenten*, rororo Bildmonographien, no. 91 (Reinbek b. Hamburg, 1964).
3. First lecture in *Vernunft und Existenz.*

Letter 398

1. Handwritten note.
2. "Wohin treibt die Bundesrepublik? Ein Gespräch mit Fritz René Allemann," broadcast July 24, 1966, by Radio Studio Basel; published in Karl Jaspers, *Provokationen*, 197–213; see L. 316, n. 1.
3. Thilo Koch, b. 1920, was a journalist, who, after publication of *Wohin treibt die Bundesrepublik?*, interviewed J. on the radio and distanced himself from J.'s attacks on all "those ill-informed people" who favored compromise during the debate on the emergency law. "I take it that among these people you include members of the German Bundestag, and, with all due respect, I have to say that this thundering accusation from Basel goes too far for me, Professor." J. regarded these words as self-serving and probably an attempt to curry favor with the politicians attacked by name. See Karl Jaspers, *Antwort: Zur Kritik meiner Schrift "Wohin treibt die Bundesrepublik?"* (Munich, 1967): 115–16.
4. Peter Bamm, *Alexander oder Die Verwandlung der Welt* (Zurich, 1965).
5. In East Germany's council of state, Ulbricht had quoted from prepublication excerpts of *Wohin treibt die Bundesrepublik?* in *Der Spiegel*, and then banned the book in the German Democratic Republic. In early June 1966, he wrote a long letter to J., referring to J.'s article "Eine Chance wird vertan" in *Welt am Sonntag* (May 8, 1966), in which J. advocated a discussion between the West and East German Socialist parties. J. responded only to acknowledge receipt of the letter. He feared that an exchange of letters might be misused for propaganda purposes. He replied publicly in his *Antwort: Zur Kritik meiner Schrift "Wohin treibt die Bundesrepublik?"* 151–67.
6. Handwritten note added: "(Sorry, can't find it right now.)"
7. Karl Jaspers, "Kein deutscher Dialog," *Die Zeit* 21 (July 1, 1966).
8. "Grussbotschaft von Karl Jaspers zur Fünften Plenartagung des Jüdischen Weltkongresses," in *Deutsche und Juden*, Edition Suhrkamp 196 (Frankfurt, 1967): 109–21.
9. It is impossible to determine what letter J. is referring to here.

Letter 399

1. See Ls. 373, 395, 396.
2. *Diskus: Frankfurter Studentenzeitung* 13, no. 1 (January 1964): 6: an open letter to Theodor Adorno (see L. 373, n. 6) by a student, Claus Chr. Schroeder, who asked if he was the author of a review in the monthly

Die Musik, June 1934, "Amtliche Mitteilungsblatt der Reichsjugend-führung." Theodor Wiesengrund-Adorno had reviewed several new works for male chorus in that issue, and had praised a song cycle by Herbert Müntzel, "Die Fahne der Verfolgten," with words from Baldur von Schirach's book of poetry with the same title, a volume that the "poet" had dedicated to "Adolf Hitler, the Führer." The review is matter-of-fact, but contains some phrases that even today can be regarded only as obsequious gestures to the Nazis. Adorno apparently was not bothered by the fact that some of the poems advocated mass murder. Schroeder asks Adorno to explain how he can reconcile his statement in "Minima moralia" that after Auschwitz it was impossible to write poems in German anymore with the fact that "before Auschwitz you had [approved of] such monstrous songs"; how he can claim the moral authority to "enlighten German youth about the inhuman pogroms of Nazi anti-Semitism." After the war, Schroeder wrote, Adorno "condemned all those who were guilty by association for what had taken place in Germany in 1934 and thereafter. (I refer, for instance, to your remarks on Heidegger.)" And all this time, Adorno had kept secret his authorship of this review.

3. Adorno's reply followed Schroeder's letter in the same issue of *Diskus*: "I deeply regret having written that review," especially because "it deals with poems by Schirach" and made use of a "phrase of Goebbels'." Then come his excuses; after which he says he "would like to leave it up to the reader's sense of justice to decide whether those incriminating sentences should be given any weight in assessing my work and my life. . . . No one who is aware of the continuity in my work could possibly compare me to Heidegger, whose philosophy is fascistic at the very core." What presumably angered A. was Adorno's tactic of insincerity: choosing to ingratiate himself with the Nazis in parenthetical phrases and then asserting in full sentences that his words had not been meant that way; and pointing to someone guiltier to make himself look better. Throughout his letter he uses a logic of evasion that makes it an "indescribably pathetic" document indeed.

4. *The New York Review of Books* (July 7, 1966).

5. Maurice English was then senior editor of the University of Chicago Press.

6. In 1962 J. wrote a new afterword for *Die Schuldfrage*, used when the work was reissued in the collections *Lebensfragen der deutschen Politik* and *Hoffnung und Sorge*.

7. Bernd Naumann, *Auschwitz: Bericht über die Strafsache gegen Mulka und andere vor dem Schwurgericht Frankfurt* (Frankfurt am Main, 1965).

8. Bernd Naumann, *Auschwitz: A Report on the Proceedings Against Robert Karl Ludwig Mulka and Others Before the Court at Frankfurt*, trans. Jean Steinberg, introduction by Hannah Arendt (New York, 1966).

9. See L. 249, n. 2. In July 1966 J. once more wrote a short recommendation, in which he stressed emphatically that the probability of A. being habilitated bordered on certainty. The letter reads:

"Dr. Hannah Arendt-Blücher has asked me to elaborate on my statements of November 9, 1955, by commenting on the general practice of granting habilitations in 1933 and, in particular, on what her own prospects for habilitation were at that time.

"The basic requirement for being habilitated was that the habilitation thesis be accepted by a professor assigned to the candidate. In the case of Dr. Arendt I was that professor, because I had also supervised her doctoral dissertation. I read her habilitation thesis—a biography of Rahel Vernhagen—at that time, before she left Germany. The thesis was completely finished except for the conclusion, and Dr. Arendt knew that it met with my full acceptance.

"Approval by the entire faculty was the second step. No habilitation thesis I had passed had ever been rejected by the faculty.

"For all practical purposes, habilitation was assured at this point. The colloquium that followed was not really an examination, but, rather, as the name suggests, a discussion between the candidate and members of the faculty. In all the decades during which I have participated in such colloquia not a single candidate ever 'failed' at this point."

10. Randolph H. Newman, 1904–1975.
11. See L. 303, n. 3.

Letter 400

1. Ursula Saner, b. 1963; Stefan Saner, b. 1965.
2. Clara Saner, b. 1957, and Johanna Saner, b. 1960.
3. Eirene Mayer; see L. 190, n. 5.
4. See L. 398, nn. 5 and 7.

Letter 401

1. See L. 381, nn. 4 and 3.
2. J.'s book had been published shortly before Hitler's assumption of power; see L. 19, n. 1.
3. Eric Weil and Katherine Mendelssohn.
4. See L. 398. The symposium, "Deutsche und Juden—ein ungelöstes Problem," had taken place on August 4, 1966, in Brussels, during the fifth plenary meeting of the Jewish World Congress. J.'s message of greeting was read in public on that occasion.
5. In the summer of 1966, it was reported all over the world that Mao had swum across the Yangtze River.
6. Benno von Wiese; see L. 398.
7. See L. 399, n. 8.
8. Rosa Luxemburg, 1870–1919, Polish-German revolutionary and writer. A.'s review, "A Heroine of the Revolution," of Peter Nettl's *Rosa Luxemburg*, 2 vols. (1966), was in *The New York Review of Books* (October 6, 1966), 21–27; reprinted in Hannah Arendt, *Men in Dark Times*: 33–56.
9. Peter Nettl, b. 1926, an executive director of an international export

organization for twelve years, has, since 1963, taught political science and sociology at Nuffield College, Oxford, and at Leeds University.

10. Eduard Bernstein, 1850–1932, was a German socialist politician and writer, and associate of Engels.
11. Karl Kautsky, 1854–1938, Austrian Socialist politician and editor, had been Engels's private secretary in 1881. He opposed Bernstein's revisionist policy to reform Marxism.

Letter 402

1. A restaurant near where J. lived.
2. Herta Dugend, daughter-in-law of Erna Dugend, J.'s sister.
3. After the death of J. and Gertrud J., six capsules of potassium cyanide, large amounts of morphine, and several packages of Veronal were found in their house.
4. Enno E. Jaspers, 1889–1931, was a jurist, and later a member of the board of directors of the Oldenburg savings and loan institution.
5. Hans W. Gruhle, 1880–1958, a psychiatrist, was, from 1919, a professor at Heidelberg University.
6. The message of greeting to the Jewish World Congress.

Letter 405

1. Small, undated card. "October 1966" is on the back in J.'s handwriting. A. presumably left it behind in Basel.

Letter 406

1. A. convinced J. during her visit to give up work on the project "Von der Unabhängigkeit des Denkens."
2. Alludes to lines J. quotes in the second volume of his *Philosophie*, page 71 in the German edition.
3. A.'s sixtieth birthday. The J.s sent a telegram that day: "With you in love and gratitude—Gertrud and Karl."

Letter 407

1. J. had given A. a pearl necklace.
2. The manuscript of J.'s new book, *Antwort: Zur Kritik meiner Schrift "Wohin treibt die Bundesrepublik?"*

Letter 408

1. The planned essay on Hegel to be included in *Die grossen Philosophen*.
2. Leon Botstein, b. 1946, became president of Bard College in 1970.

Letter 409

1. The shooting of Hannes Reinhardt's television film "Karl Jaspers—Ein Selbstporträt" had just begun.
2. The entire letter is in Gertrud J.'s handwriting.

Letter 410

1. Hermann Oncken, 1869–1945, was a historian and professor at Heidelberg, 1907–23. Eduard Spranger, 1882–1963, was a psychologist and teacher.
2. Franz Boese, *Geschichte des Vereins für Sozialpolitik 1872–1932* (Berlin, 1939).
3. Paul Gottschalk had a secondhand bookshop in New York that specialized in scholarly periodicals.

Letter 412

1. See L. 408, n. 2
2. Nationaldemokratische Partei Deutschlands, a right-wing German party.

Letter 413

1. J. was reading the two-volume Artemis edition of Polybius (Zurich/Stuttgart, 1961).

Letter 414

1. William Manchester, *The Death of a President* (New York, 1967). The book contains a detailed report of Kennedy's assassination and related events. Prepublication excerpts in *Look* magazine sparked the "scandal" A. mentions, namely, a public debate on Manchester's presentation. The Kennedy family, which had originally cooperated in the project, withdrew its approval of it.
2. Walter Benjamin, *Illuminations*, ed. and introduction by Hannah Arendt (New York, 1968).
3. Interview with Peter Merseburger, January 1967, in which J. strongly criticized Chancellor Kurt Georg Kiesinger and his Great Coalition of Christian Socialists and Social Democrats.
4. The National Book Awards, financed in part by the American Book Publishers Council, were prizes for the best books published in various categories.

Letter 415

1. See L. 296, n. 3, and L. 398, n. 3.
2. Early in 1967, articles appeared in newspapers revealing the financial and ideological dependence of many public institutions on the Central

Intelligence Agency. One was an article in *Ramparts* 5, no. 9 (March 1967), which exposed the close link between the U.S. National Student Association (NSA) and the CIA. Even highly esteemed publications outside the United States, like *Encounter*, *Preuves*, and *Der Monat*, received such financial support, although many of their top personnel were unaware of this fact.

3. Mary McCarthy, "Report from Vietnam," *The New York Review of Books* (April 29, May 5, 18, 1967); "Vietnam Solution" (November 9, 1967); all four articles were reprinted in *Vietnam* (New York, 1967).
4. See *Antwort*, 230–31.
5. Uwe Johnson, *Zwei Ansichten* (Frankfurt am Main, 1965).

Letter 417

1. See L. 418, n. 1.
2. In a remark added to L. 416.

Letter 418

1. The letter was dated "Basel, April 18, 1967," and read:
   "I have to answer your question of 4/17/67 with a formal reply and a description of the actual facts.
   "Mrs. Hannah Arendt-Blücher never submitted a request for habilitation. Anyone who is familiar with the situation of that time knows that the dean would not have accepted such a request.
   "In actual fact there was not the slightest doubt of her qualifications for habilitation. I had read her Rahel study in the version that was later published. The work is rightly considered a masterpiece. All that was lacking were two short final chapters. Even without this brief conclusion the study was in my opinion—both at the time and now—more than adequate as a habilitation thesis. Through this work Mrs. Arendt demonstrated that she was not someone who merely harbored the desire to habilitate at some point but was somone who had actually fulfilled all the requirements."

Letter 419

1. In the Six-Day War, June 5–10, 1967, Israel was victorious against Egypt, Jordan, and Syria, and took the West Bank, the Golan Heights, and the Sinai.
2. Moshe Dayan became Israel's minister of defense at the end of May 1967.
3. See L. 414, n. 2.
4. Karl Jaspers, *The Future of Germany*, trans. E. B. Ashton (Chicago/London, 1967).

Letter 421

1. J. had had his desk and chair raised so that he could sit down and get up with less pain.
2. Hussein Ibn Talal, b. 1935, became king of Jordan in 1953.
3. United Nations Relief and Works Agency for Palestine Refugees in the Near East, an agency formed in 1949.
4. Shmu'el Pinto, b. 1932.
5. Michael Brocke, b. 1940.
6. See L. 415, n. 3.
7. James West; see L. 331, n. 7.

Letter 422

1. Karl Jaspers, *Schicksal und Wille: Autobiographische Schriften.*
2. *Ibid.*, "Elternhaus und Kindheit."
3. *Ibid.*, "Von Heidelberg nach Basel."
4. "Erfahrung des Ausgestossenseins: Karl Jaspers über seinen Weggang aus Deutschland," *Der Spiegel* (October 2, 1967).
5. *Schicksal und Wille*, 180.
6. J. was at this time still dictating some business letters, but his personal correspondence (usually handwritten) had ceased almost completely.

Letter 423

1. A.'s speech "Karl Jaspers zum 85. Geburtstag," broadcast by Bavarian Radio, February 23, 1968. Printed in *Erinnerungen an Karl Jaspers*, ed. by K. Piper and H. Saner (Munich/Zurich, 1974): 311–15.

Letter 425

1. Eugene J. McCarthy, b. 1916, Democratic senator from Wisconsin, 1958–70, ran, unsuccessfully, for the Democratic presidential nomination in 1967. He was a strong opponent of the Vietnam War.

Letter 427

1. For his dissertation, *Kants Weg vom Krieg zum Frieden*, Hans Saner was awarded the Hermann Hesse Prize of the city of Karlsruhe in 1968.

Letter 428

1. Edna Brocke, née Fürst, and Michael Brocke.
2. Daniel Cohn-Bendit, b. 1945, was a leader of the student rebellion of 1968 in Paris, later in Frankfurt, Germany.
3. Erich and Herta Cohn-Bendit.

Letter 429

1. George C. Wallace, b. 1919, governor of Alabama, was the candidate of the American Independent party in the 1968 presidential election.
2. Hannah Arendt, "Reflections on Violence," *Journal of International Affairs* (Winter 1969): 1–35; expanded version in Hannah Arendt, *On Violence* (New York, 1970).

Letter 430

1. Karl and Gertrud J. had met on July 14, 1907, and celebrated the anniversary of this day every year. The words quoted by Gertrud were spoken by J. at their engagement, because he did not expect to live long.
2. Clara Mayer, née Gottschalk, 1845–1912.

Letter 431

1. H. A. flew to Zurich on August 31 and stayed in Basel for a week.

Letter 433

1. J. died on Gertrud J.'s ninetieth birthday. A. flew to Basel to be present at the private funeral on March 3 and to take part in the official memorial service of the University of Basel on March 4. At that service she gave a speech that was her last public pronouncement on J. In the years that followed, she wrote to Gertrud J. at irregular intervals. The speech was printed in *Basler Universitätsreden* No. 60 (Basel, 1969): 18–20.

Index of Works
by Hannah Arendt

This list includes only those works mentioned in this volume. Page numbers in boldface type refer to bibliographical information.

801

Index of Works
by Karl Jaspers

This list includes only those works mentioned in this volume. Page numbers in boldface type refer to bibliographical information.

Index

Page numbers in boldface type refer to biographical information.

Baeck, Leo, 28, 533, **695–96**, 775
Baeck Institute, 564
Bamm, Peter, 643
Bard College, 190, 191, 201, 207, 216,
219, 223, 225, 239, 249, 264, 270, 281,
375, 384, 470, 535, 582, 602, 608, 627,
678, 680, 694, 727
Baron, Salo W., 141, 143, 240, 650, **716**
Barrett, William, 32, 34
Barth, Heinrich, 93, 168, 397, 472, **707**,
740, 756, 758
Barth, Karl, 341, 479, **707**, 716
Basel, University of, 91, 92, 100, 101,
103–5, 109, 120, 128, 132, 154, 390,
394, 426, 628, 706
Bauer, Fritz, 446, **762**
Bauer, Inge, 155, **721**
Bauer, Karl Heinrich, **721**
Baumgarten, Eduard, 228, 232, 286, 287,
734, 792
Bay of Pigs invasion, 436, 438, 464, 761
Beacon Press, 106, 110–13, 128, 131
Becher, Kurt, 524, **774**
Beck, Ludwig, 514, 578, 580, 599, 602,
603, 606, **772**
Benda, Julien, 57, 65, **701**
Ben Gurion, David, 417, 419, 423, 425,
434, 435, 522, 528, 586, **758**, 785
Benjamin, Walter, xix, 41, 197, 667,
673, **698**
Bentley, Eric, 48
Beradt, Charlotte, 445, 472–74, 501,
502, 524, 579, **762**, 767
Bergsträsser, Arnold, 136, **715**
Berlin, Isaiah, 535, **776**
Berlin crisis, 396, 443–45, 448, 450,
454–55, 458, 460–61, 465, 467, 485,
487, 756
Berliner Tageblatt, 574
Berlin University, 377, 593
Bermann-Fischer (publisher), 86
Bernanos, Georges, 57, 59, 65, 701
Bernstein, Adolf, 503, 580, 601, 604,
770
Bernstein, Eduard, 650, **796**
Bevin, Ernest, 415, **759**
Bismarck, Otto Fürst von, 51, 99, 448,
544, 624, 790
Blixen, Karen, *see* Dinesen, Isak
Blücher, Heinrich (Monsieur), vii, viii,
xi, xvii, xxi, xxiv, 29, 52, 55, 66, 69,

73, 74, 76, 85, 91, 100, 101, 107, 113,
118, 119, 122, 132, 134, 153–54, 163,
167, 168, 178, 181, 195, 197, 198, 200,
204, 238, 241, 253, 259, 261, 263, 272,
275, 282, 290, 294, 302, 309, 317, 319,
321, 335, 340–42, 356, 361, 363, 374,
377, 385, 386, 388, 392, 395, 414, 427,
432, 433, 440, 449, 473–75, 478, 484,
486, 489, 504, 507, 511, 518, 520, 525,
534, 539, 542, 547, 550, 555, 557–59,
561, 571, 575–76, 591, 592, 594, 609,
611, 633, 639, 644, 646–48, 650, 651,
655–57, 665, 670, 671, **694**, 741, 762,
787; academic career of, 154, 158, 169,
190, 191, 201, 203, 206, 207, 216, 223,
225, 227, 232, 235, 239, 243, 249, 264,
270, 281, 289, 295, 297, 310, 354, 375,
384, 387, 396, 455, 470, 480, 521, 535,
582, 602, 608, 627, 667–69, 678, 680,
694, 727; birthday celebration for,
362; correspondence with Jaspers,
143–44, 146–47, 185–86, 189–91,
276–80, 283, 284, 287, 353, 382–84,
399–403, 442–45, 450–53, 463–67,
472, 476, 498, 543, 653, 654, 717; in
Europe, 424, 439, 446, 499, 501–3,
577, 596, 609; illnesses of, 351,
456–57, 459, 462, 468, 521, 526, 529,
530, 533, 537, 540, 543, 544, 546, 548,
642, 674, 679–83; photographs of,
124, 126, 133, 159, 418, 421, 426;
poems about, 615, 616, 618, 621, 624
Blumenfeld, Jenny, 246, 248, 268, 269
Blumenfeld, Kurt, 168, 197, 201, 204,
217, 219, 241, 244–50, 267–70, 314,
315, 351, 352, 437, 439, **723**
B'nai B'rith, 539
Boese, Franz, 661
Bondy, François, 181, 431, 432, 434,
496, 550, 554–56, 560, 669, **725**, 760
Bonhoeffer, Dietrich, 547, **778**
Bormann, Martin, 415, **759**
Born, Max, 367, 743, **751–52**
Boethe, Walther, 315, **743**
Botstein, Leon, 663, **796**
Brandeis University, 252
Braun, Heinrich, 217, **731**
Braun, Otto, 217, **731**
Braun-Vogelstein, Julie, 85, 217, 219,
731
Brecht, Bertolt, 24, 607, 617

808

Federal Bureau of Investigation (FBI), 137
Fedotov, Georg P., 43, **699**
Feess, Willy, 611, **788**
Feitelson, Rose, 349, **733**, 748
Femegericht, 479, 766
Fichte, Johann Gottlieb, 93, 186, 191, 277, 377, **757**
Finckenstein, Karl Count von, 194, **727**
Fink, Eugen, 447, 453, **762**
Finkelstein, Louis, 583
First World War, 279, 400, 531, 578, 613
Fischer, Hanns E., 369
Ford Foundation, 214, 215
Foreign Affairs, 249, 492
Forschungsgemeinschaft, 276
Foundation for the Advancement of the Highly Talented, 699
Fraenkel, Abraham, A., 116, **711**
Franc, S., 150
France, 279, 280, 309, 406, 436, 448, 449, 569; Algeria and, 454, 472; anti-Semitism in, 55; Germany and, 482; May 1968 uprising in, 681; and Munich Pact, 455; postwar, 37, 48; Resistance in, 64, 66; and Suez crisis, 306
Franco, Francisco, 436, 519, **761**
Frank, Erich, 276, 739
Frank, Joe, 183
Frankel, Charles, 475, 765
Fränkel, Eduard, 630, **791–92**
Fränkel, Hilde, **715**
Frankfurter Allgemeine Zeitung, 453, 528, 534, 566, 582, 645, 657
Frauenglass, William, **732**
Frederick the Great, 27, 464
French Revolution, 278, 362
Freud, Sigmund, 160, 727
Freund, Gerald, 621, 628, 629, 631, 633, **790**
Freund, Michael, 564
Freymond, Jacques, 613, **789**
Friedländer, Albert H., **772**
Friedländer, David, 192, **727**
Friedländer, Moses, 199
Friedländer, Rebekka, 198, 199, **728**
Friedrich, Carl Joachim, 296, 349, **741**
Fries, Jakob Friedrich, 151, **720**

Frise, Adolf, 97, 707
Frohberg, Regina, *see* Friedländer, Rebekka
Fulbright, J. William, 626, **791**

Gadamer, Hans-Georg, 276, 554, 710, **739**
Galileo, 254
Gandhi, Mohandas K., 308, 325
Gascoyne-Cecil, Robert Arthur Talbot, Marquess of Salisbury, 624, **790**
Gaus, Günter, xxii, xxiii, 565, 572, 575, 593, 638, 651, 782
Gavin, James M., 627, **791**
Gegenwart, Die, 51
Geiger, Afra, 17, **692**
Geneva conference, 1959, 396, 756
Gentz, Friedrich von, 193, 198, 244, **727**, 735
George, Manfred, 732
George, Stefan, 447, 617, 701, **762**
German Book Guild, 310
German character, 17–19, 87–88, 94, 128, 245–46
Germany, 41, 58, 72, 190, 199, 207, 212, 218, 237, 245–46, 271, 279, 311, 313, 314, 356, 374, 384–85, 389, 400–1, 406, 412, 440, 452, 483, 520, 544, 585, 598–99, 601, 609–10, 621, 622, 631, 639–40, 670; and atomic weapons, 315; and Berlin crisis, 444, 450, 458, 460, 465–66, 485; and Eichmann trial, 414, 433, 435, 446, 467, 478–79, 530, 535, 586; elections in, 438, 454; after First World War, 413; France and, 482; Hochhuth affair in, 527–28, 547; Nazi, *see* Nazism; nineteenth-century, 624; postwar, 31–32, 34, 37, 46, 48, 51, 53, 54, 56, 62–63, 81, 83–85, 90–91, 93, 99, 114–15, 128, 157–58, 161; resistance in, 516–17, 519, 545, 547, 549–52, 566, 577, 578, 580, 582, 595, 599, 602–3, 606; reunification of, 397–98, 44–49, 455, 464, 587; *Spiegel* affair in, 490, 492, 494–95; statute of limitations in, 581, 586–88; university reform in, 49–50, 78, 88, 293, 383; workers' and soldiers' councils in, 338

Gerstenmaier, Eugen, 650, **771**
Gestapo, 115, 545
Ghosh, Niouta, 299, 449
Gide, André, 447, **762**
Gilbert, Elisabeth (Elke), 741
Gilbert, Robert, 441, 446, 462, 502, 507,
596, 607, **741**
Globke, Hans, 586, **785**
Gneisenau, August Neidhardt von, 544,
777
Goebbels, Joseph P., 89, **794**
Goerdeler, Carl Friedrich, xi, 513, 517,
520, 544, 545, 578, 580, 582, **771**
Goethe, Johann Wolfgang von, 100,
102, 139, 193, 194, 198, 248, 276, 279,
282, 375, 377, 507, 525, 593, 650, 684,
711, 714–16, 718, 736, 739, 753,
786
Goldmann, Nahum, 410, 643, 650, **758**
Goldwater, Barry M., xvi, 558, 560,
568, 571, **779**
Gollancz, Victor, 63, 72, **702**, 704
Göring, Hermann, 54, 62, 652
Gothein, Eberhard, **745**
Gothein, Marie Luise, 328, **745**
Göttingen Declaration, 341, **743**
Gottschalk, Paul, 56, 152, 159, 293, 631,
662, 678, **701**, 741, 797
Graetz, Wolfgang, 593, 595, 597,
599–603, 606, **786**
Granzow, Brigitte, 524, 543, **774**
Grass, Günter, 597, 669, **787**
Gray, Glenn, 468, **764**
Greece, ancient, 72, 164, 189, 505
Greenberg, Clement, 52, 123
Grene, Marjorie, 354, 366–68, 373, 749
Groeben, Alexandra von der, 114–15
Groeben, Jobst von der, 114–15, 512,
513
Gross, Gerald, 448, **762–63**
Grüber, Heinrich, 438, 527, 612, **762**,
788–89
Gruhle, Hans W., 653, **796**
Gruner, Bertha, 448
Grünewald, Matthias, 499, **769**
Gruppe 47, 587, 634–35, 638, 639
Guggenheim Foundation, 180–82, 201
Gundolf, Friedrich, 33, 57, 128, **696**,
701
Gurian, Waldemar, 41, 135, 159, 164,
264, 265, 410, 698, **722**

Häberlin, Paul, **710**
Hadas, Moses, 209, **730**
Haecker, Theodor, 544, **777**
Halevi, Benjamin, 432, 510, 760, 761
Halpern, Ben, 121–23, 162
Hamilton, Alexander, 357, 360
Hammarskjöld, Dag, 399, 400, **757**
Harcourt, Brace, 153, 167, 370, 427–32,
440, 449–50, 471, 673, 708, 760
Harper & Row, 406, 484, 494, 497–98,
602, 605, 626, 645
Harpprecht, Klaus, 489
Harrington, James, 440, **762**
Harvard University, 176, 216, 221, 230,
235, 249, 296, 349, 405, 671
Haubach, Theodor, 512, 513, 551, 552,
771, 784
Haushofer, Albrecht, 89, 90, **707**
Haushofer, Karl, 89, **707**
Hausner, Gideon, 510, 564, 625, **761**
Hebrew University in Jerusalem, 116,
117, 524, 535, 576; Society of Friends
of, 593
Hecht, Ben, 528, **775**
Hecht, William C., Jr., 712
Hegel, Georg Wilhelm Friedrich, 59,
140, 149, 160, 170, 258, 277, 315, 317,
350, 448, 611, 620, 659, 695, 710, 718,
720, 796
Heidegger, Martin, vii, xvii, xix, 6–8,
63, 142, 225, 226, 229, 314, 327, 345,
447, 448, 453, 457, 459, 602–4, 606,
634, **691**, 717, 723, 733, 739, 774, 791,
792; correspondence with Jaspers,
140–41, 161–62, 167–68, 206, 722,
729; during Nazi period, 43, 47, 48,
628–30, 698, 794; on Plato, 284, 288,
740
Heidelberg University, 58, 63, 81–83,
92, 100, 102, 109, 122, 128, 132, 139,
151, 152, 154, 158, 162, 184, 187, 188,
255, 296, 645, 647
Heidelberg Workers and Soldiers'
Council, 338
Heine, Heinrich, 63, 70, 199, 245, 279
Helldorf, Wolf Heinrich Graf von, 517,
606, **772**
Henk, Emil, 512, 513, 545, 549, 551,
771
Hennig, John, 228
Herder, Johann Gottfried, 14, 260

Herodotus, 665
Hersch, Jeanne, 63, 181–84, 202, 219, 228, 236, 286, 302, 327, 342, 475, 477, 554, **725**
Hertzberg, Arthur, 635, **792**
Herzfeld, Hans, 554, **779**
Herzog, Paul, 55, **700**
Hessische Nachrichten, 56
Heurgon-Desjardins, Madame, 719
Heuss, Theodor, 158, 359, 520, **721**
Heydrich, Reinhard, **750**
Hilberg, Raul, 549, 550
Hillebrand, Karl, 20, **692**
Hillel societies, 522
Himmler, Heinrich, 517, 524, 545, 642, **772**
Hindenburg, Paul von, 203, 311, **729**, **743**
Hitler, Adolf, vii, xi–xiii, 46, 62, 79, 84, 89, 155, 166, 174, 202, 279, 303, 386, 448, 520, 533, 544, 637, 710, 720, 729, 759, 776, 778, 783, 785, 788, 794, 795; assassination attempt on, 518, 545, 549, 603, 704, 745, 772, 773; and atomic bomb, 315; illness of, 612–13; Jews and, 45, 90, 255, 304, 308, 358, 536, 539, 592; resistance against, 512, 513, 771
Hobbes, Thomas, 140, 166, 244, 325, 349
Hochhuth, Rolf, 527–28, 539, 545–47, 561, 577, 593, 599, 601, 603, 607, 615, 683, **774**
Hochland, 170
Hoffer, Eric, 258, 557, **737–38**
Hoffman, Ernst, 33, 34, **696**
Hoffman, Kurt, 228, 231, **734**
Hofmannsthal, Hugo von, 14, 617, 787
Hölderlin, Friedrich, 142, 278, 717
Holland, 127, 483; German occupation of, 609–10
Holm, Søren, 228
Holthusen, Hans Egon, 458, 461, **763**
Hook, Sidney, 137, 213, 223, 225, **715**, 730
Hoops, Johannes, 61, **702**
Hoover, Herbert, 715
Horkheimer, Max, 634, **792**
Houghton Mifflin, 68
Hubbard, Stanley, 370, 371, 374, 752, **753**

Huber, Gerhard, 285, **734**
Huch, Ricarda, 636, **792**
Huddleston, Trevor, 509, 518, 521, **771**
Hugenberg, Alfred, 203, **729**
Humboldt, Caroline von, 199, **728**
Humboldt, Wilhelm von, 194, 314, 376, 377, 714, **728**
Hungarian Revolution, 304–6, 333, 401, 403, 741
Hunter College, 212
Hussein, Ibn Talal, 674, **799**
Husserl, Edmund, 43, 47, 48, 630, **698**, 762
Hutchins, Robert M., 136, **715**

Idealism, German, 277
Imperialism, 54, 55, 98, 122, 151, 401
India, 449, 619, 626; ancient, 72, 74, 276
Indonesia, 438, 619
Innocent III, Pope, 759
International Court of Justice, 416, 418, 424
Isaiah, 411
Israel, 126–27, 182, 279, 280, 304–5, 308, 309–11, 360–61, 419, 449, 503, 522, 622, 674–75; Eichmann trial in, 402, 409–11, 413–18, 420, 423–25, 427, 430–37, 439, 467, 469–70, 510, 524, 527, 586; massacre of Arabs in, 358; in Six-Day War, 672; *see also* Palestine
Italy, 37; elections in, 454

Jacobson, Dan, 508, 509, 514, 518, 520, 521, **771**
Jäger, Richard, 581, 784
Japanese-Americans, internment of, 30
Jarrell, Randall, 614, 615, **789**
Jaspers, Carl Wilhelm (J.'s father), 393, **756**
Jaspers, Enno E., 653, **796**
Jaspers, Gertrud, vii, xxiii, xxiv, 181, 293, 316, 329, 355, 356, 361, 380, 463, 472, 475, 482, 488, 512, 526, 527, 532, 533, 541, 546, 551, 566–67, 573, 589, 590, 600, 604, 611, 618, 637, 638, 647, 648, 654, 655, 658, 662, 665, 671, 672; birthday gifts to, 364, 427, 429; CARE packages sent by Arendt to, 24,

37–38, 41, 51, 59; correspondence
with Arendt, 37–38, 40–42, 51,
59–60, 202–3, 338–39, 362,
384–86, 404—6, 475, 480, 501–2, 560,
591, 620, 622, 678–80, 682–83, 693,
698, 779–80; death of brother of,
468–69; illnesses of, 236–37, 503–5,
515, 580, 583–84, 594–95, 619, 643,
664; and J.'s death, 684; during Nazi
period, 519–20, 552, 629–30; and
Palestine, 51, 106; Renato de Rosa
and, 229, 231, 233, 236
Jefferson, Thomas, 357, 360, 362, 583,
587
Jefroikyn, Natalie (Natascha), 596, **787**
Jensch, Klaus, 440
Jeremiah, 140, 411
Jesus of Nazareth, 186, 189, 221, 512
Jewish Academy (Berlin), 4, 5, 7
Jewish Agency for Palestine, 80, 705
Jewish Frontier, 121, 123
Jewish Publication Society, 130, 622,
713
Jewish Theological Seminary, 583
Jews, 10, 11, 41, 44, 65, 78, 86, 95,
98–99, 128, 132, 157, 161, 304–5,
313, 513, 517–19, 544, 550, 585,
592–93, 622, 643; American, 31, 135,
247, 249, 250, 258, 471; discrimination
against, *see* Anti-Semitism; and
Eichmann case, 410–11, 415–17, 420,
423, 425, 435–37, 446, 510–12, 516,
522–27, 530–32, 535–36, 546,
563–64, 566, 568, 586–87, 632, 635;
Germanness and, 17–19, 24, 87,
90–91, 94, 245–46, 248; history of,
55, 98, 199–200; Hochhuth and, 539,
545–46; in Israel, 116–18, 126–27,
182, 280, 358, 419, 435; in postwar
Europe, 31–32, 53–54, 77, 82–84;
and Rahel Varnhagen, 192–95,
197–200, 204, 312; self-identification
of, 29, 35, 63, 70
John XXIII, Pope (Angelo Roncalli),
547, 771, 774, **778**
John Birch Society, 538, 776
Johnson, Lyndon B., xv, 534, 571, 621,
624, 659, 675, 779
Johnson, Uwe, 597, 669, **787**
Joly, Maurice, 521
Jonas, Hans, 22, 24, 133, **693**

Jordan, 305, 503, 675
Jovanovich, William, 429, 432, 450, **760**
Jugendalijah, 314
Jünger, Ernst, 717
Justice Department, U.S., 536

Kaegi, Werner, 594, **786**
Kafka, Franz, 42, 617, 639
Kaiser, Joseph H., 447, **762**
Kant, Immanuel, 89, 129, 160, 171, 176,
233, 234, 238, 258, 273–77, 287, 304,
308, 314, 316–18, 320–22, 325, 331,
335, 342, 346, 348, 349, 371, 375, 451,
464, 524, 556, 559, 562, 565, 569, 572,
577, 582, 595, 628, 660, 685, 718, 757,
764, 774
Kastner, Rudolf, 510, 524, **771**, 775
Katz, Shlomo, 626
Kaufmann, Fritz, 226, **733**
Kaufmann, Walter A., 170, 172, 230,
232–35, 286, 314, 344, **723**
Kautsky, Karl, 650, **796**
Kazin, Alfred, 153, 156, 180, **720**, 724
Keller, Jules, 394, 396–98, **756**
Kempner, Robert M. W., 565, 568, **781**
Kennan, George F., 627, 751, **791**
Kennedy, John F., xvi, xx, 426, 438–40,
443, 444, 449, 451, 452, 455, 458, 460,
461, 465, 469, 471, 482, 483, 485–87,
508, 509, 621, 623, 761, 764, 767, 770,
771; assassination of, 533, 534, 538,
547, 558, 667, 776, 797; election of,
399, 405, 421
Kennedy, Robert, 508, 509, 534, 536,
770, 771
Kenyon Review, The, 48, 314
Khrushchev, Nikita, xvi, 307, 318, 320,
334, 436, 438, 444, 445, 448, 449, 454,
483, 485, 567, 569–71, 573, 576, **742**,
767, 781, 782
Kiepenheuer (publisher), 326, 498
Kierkegaard, Søren, 222, 228, 301, 512,
549, 636–38, 640
Kiesinger, Kurt Georg, 797
Klemperer, Klemens von, 468, 492
Knauss, Gerhard, 228, 276, 281, 282,
739
Knopf, Alfred A., 209, **730**
Koch, Thilo, 642, 757, **793**
Koestler, Arthur, 174, 219, **724**

814

Manheim, Ralph, 129, 133, 134, 137, 256, 342, 348, 349, 363, 364, 368, 379, 380, 386, 391, 397, 457, 462, 463, 480, 497, 499, 532, 537, 546, 556, 579, 710, 712, 754, 765, 778, 792

Mann, Golo, 27, 36, 174–78, 180, 228, 255, 258, 372, 541, 544, 548, 550, 553, 554, 593, 631, 632, **695**, 786

Mann, Thomas, 27, 32, 34, 36, 39, 110, 590, 593, 695, 786

Mannheim, Karl, 86, 135, 348, 349, 531, **706**

Mao Tse-tung, 335, 401, 576, 650, **746**

Marshall, George C., 163, **722–23**

Marshall, James, 712

Martin, Berthold, 372, 373, 395, **753**

Martini, Winfried, 440, **762**

Marwitz, Alexander von der, 193, **727**

Marx, Karl, xix, 137, 149, 160, 162–63, 170, 186, 187, 205, 216, 243, 448, 623, 625, 722

Mau Mau movement, 260, 738

May, Kurt, 536, 564, **776**

Mayer, Arthur, **750**

Mayer, Ella, 293, 297, 344, 361, 723, **729**, 744, 765, 786

Mayer, Ernst, 56, 88, 115, 142, 184, 196, 202, 204, 205, 225, 245, 246, 293, 297, 541, **701**, 717, 722, 723, 726, 729, 744, 781

Mayer, Frieda, **746**

Mayer, Fritz, 410, 469, **708**, 721, 725, **746**, 765

Mayer, Gustav, 63, **702**, 711, 722

Mayer, Heinrich, 708, **765**

Mayer, Otto, 468–69, 708, **765**

Mayer, Philip, 741

Mayrisch de Saint-Hubert, Aline, 21, **693**

Meinecke, Friedrich, 544

Meir, Golda, 437, **761**

Mendelssohn, Henriette, 101, **708**

Mendelssohn, Moses, 193, 199, **708**

Menorah Journal, 40, 563, 697

Menuhin, Yehudi, 114, 120

Meridian Books, 352

Merkur, 147, 150, 152, 153, 155, 170, 261

Meyer, Rudolf W., 555, **779**

Meyer-Gutzwiller, Paul, 497, 581, **769**

Michelangelo, 276

Midstream, 532, 626

Mierendorff, Carlo, 512, 513, 517, 520, **771**, 784

Milosz, Czeslaw, 181, 209, 219, 267, **725**, 730

Mirabeau, Comte de, 199, **728**

Misch, Georg, 195, **728**

Mitscherlich, Alexander, 576, 731, **782**

Molo, Walter von, 32, **696**

Mommsen, Wolfgang J., 636

Monat, Der, 157, 160, 162, 170, 171, 260, 480, 693

Montesquieu, Charles de Secondat, 175, 208

Montgomery, Sir Bernard L., 304, **742**

Moore, Russel F. (publisher), 369

Morgenstern, Christian, 723

Morgenthau, Hans J., 421, **759**

Morgenthau, Plan, 32, 696

Morin, Alex, 352, 354, 367, 370, 371, 373, **748**, 749

Morse, Rose, 123, 127, 713

Morsey, Rudolf, 527, **775**

Moses, 186, 189

Moses, Siegfried, 564, **780**

Moses, Stefan, 561, **780**

Mo Ti, 89, **706**

Muller, Herman J., 730

Mundt, Martha, **707**

Munich Pact, 455

Muschg, Walter, 617, **790**

Musmanno, Michael A., 523, 563, 564, 626, 773

Mussolini, Benito, 338

Nagarjuna, 324, **744**

Napoleon, 652

Nasser, Gamal Abdel, 483, 503, 672, 675, 742, 767

Nationaldemokratische Partei Deutschlands (NPD), 663, 797

National Institute of Arts and Letters, 240, 546

Nationalism, 17, 88, 279–80, 398, 400–1

National Socialist Union, 548, 778

NATO, 398, 448

Naumann, Friedrich, 548, **778**

Nazism, 27, 46, 58, 62, 69, 72, 76, 88, 93, 111, 114–15, 131, 134, 155, 310, 404, 558–59, 588, 652; academics

818

Socrates, 149, 186, 189, 288, 289, 317, 324, 512, 530, 616, 634, 635
Solon, 189
Sorbonne, 48, 379, 380
South Africa, 111, 521
Soviet Union, *see* Russia
Spain, 59, 436
Spanish Civil War, 219, 519
Spellman, Francis Joseph, Cardinal, 545, 777
Spender, Stephen, 57, 64, 215, 701, 715
Spengler, Oswald, 149, **719**
Spiegel, Der, 490, 492, 494–96, 550, 554–56, 568, 574, 576, 581, 582, 584–90, 597, 599, 601, 616, 619, 620, 626, 628–31, 658, 676, 683, 768–69
Spinoza, Baruch de, 87, 139–42, 194, 199, 241, 244, 274, 527, 569, 572, 594, 618
Spranger, Eduard, 661, **797**
Springer, Georg Ferdinand, 126, 518, 626, **773**
Springer, Julius, 8, 9, 691
SS (Schutzstaffel), 84, 517, 539, 658
Stalin, Josef, 24, 137, 150, 163, 174, 205, 307, 320, 570, 571, 781
Starliner, Wilhelm, 261, 335
State Department, U.S., 52, 60, 65, 137, 568
Stauffenberg, Claus Schenk Graf von, 578, 580, 603, 745, **783–84**
Stein zum Altenstein, Karl Freiherr vom, **706**
Stern, Günther, xv, 6, **691**
Sternberger, Dolf, 31, 33, 38, 39, 41, 44, 58, 62, 74, 75, 104, 105, 107, 114–16, 131, 158, 345, 421, 453, 566, 569, 573, 576, 581, 584, **694**
Stern-Täubler, Selma, 4, 130, **690**
Stevenson, Adlai E., 203, 231, 233, 234, 338, **729**
Stifter, Adalbert, 309, **742**
Stinnes, Hugo, 487, **767**
Strauss, Franz Josef, 468, **764**, 768
Strauss, Leo, 241, 244, 247, 535, **735**
Strauss, Victor von, 312, 743
Studium generale, 372, 753
Suez crisis, 305, 306, 483, 742
Suslov, Mikhail A., 570, 573, **781**
Syria, 675

Tacitus, 419
Taft, Robert A., 203, **729**
Tagore, Rabindranath, 328, 331, **745**
Talmon, Jacob L., 535, **776**
Tantzen, Theodor J., 519, **773**
Täubler, Eugen, 4, 130, 690, **713**
Tawney, Richard Henry, 407, **758**
Teich, Meier, 775
Theodorakopoulos, Johannes N., 268, 269, **737**
Thiel, Manfred, 372, **753**
Thirty Years' War, 115
Thoma, Richard, 408, 660, **758**
Thomas à Kempis, 35, 315
Thompson, Kenneth, 610
Thought, 36
Thucydides, 355
Thyssen, Johannes, 228
Tillich, Paul J., 13, 14, 32, 116, 119, 170, 213, 615, **691**, 715
Time magazine, 59, 65, 421
Tocqueville, Alexis de, 263, 279
Toynbee, Arnold J., 149, 158, **719**
Treasury Department, U.S., 52
Tresckow, Henning von, 513, 517, 519, 547, 580, **771–72**
Trotsky, Leon, 571, **781–82**
Trott zu Solz, Adam von, 69, 695, **704**
Trott zu Solz, Werner von, 85, **706**
Truman, Harry S, 118, 216, 307
Tschuang-tse, 312, **743**
Tsin Shi Huang Ti, 89, **707**

Uhland, Ludwig, 719
Ulbricht, Walter, 485, 643, 648, **767**, 793
Ulm Academy for Visual Arts, 383
Undset, Sigrid, 28, **694**
United Jewish Appeal, 626
United Nations, 311, 365, 399–401, 413, 414, 416, 418, 419, 424, 425, 455, 458, 483, 624; Relief and Works Agency, 675, 799
United Restitution Organization, 536, 776
United States, 30, 168, 263–64, 279, 443–44, 451–52, 595, 668, 675–76; anti-Communism in, 137, 210–15, 217, 223, 235–36, 249; anti-Semitism

United States (*cont.*)
in, 90, 249; atomic weapons of, 304,
309, 315, 374, 619, 659; and Berlin
crisis, 365, 396, 444, 454, 458,
460–61; and Cuba, 436, 438, 482–87;
educational system in, 374–75;
elections in, 203, 210, 231, 233–34,
311, 396, 405, 558, 560–61, 568, 571,
678, 682; foreign policy of, 352, 464;
Germany and, 490; Israel and, 127,
503; and Kennedy assassination,
533–34, 536, 538, 558; and
Khrushchev's fall, 569; in Korean
War, 160, 163–64; racism in, 386,
508–9, 538, 558, 571, 682; in Second
World War, 552; student unrest in,
471, 583, 658, 676–77, 682; and Suez
crisis, 306; in Vietnam War, 594, 621,
623–24, 626–27, 667
Unwin, Stanley, 450, **763**
USSR, *see* Russia

Varnhagen von Ense, Karl August, 193,
727
Varnhagen von Ense, Rahel A. F., xii,
xvii, 5, 10, 11, 14–16, 19, 20, 192–96,
198–200, 241, 295, 646, 670, 671, **690**,
691
Vatican, 539
Vercors, 95, 96, **707**
Verlagsgesellschaft (publisher), 152, 153
Vialon, Friedrich-Karl, 586, **785**
Viénot, Pierre, 21, **692**
Vietnam War, 594, 619, 621, 623–24,
626–27, 634, 658, 667
Voegelin, Eric, 203, **729**, 751
Volkswagen Foundation, 614
Voltaire, François Marie, 589, 590, 592
Vossische Zeitung, 574

Waelhens, Alphonse de, 56, **701**
Wagenach, Klaus, 635, 639, **792**
Wahl, Jean, 56, 57, 147, 149, **701**, 734
Wallace, George C., 682, **800**
Wallraff, Charles F., 600, 604
Waltz, Erika (Lotte), 188, 205, 224, 254,
257, 259, 274, 289, 319, 366, 380–81,
399, 620, **720**
Waltz, Hans (Hanno), 203, **729**

Waltz, Peter, 251, 252, **736**
Waltz, Wilhelm, **720**, 737
Wandlung, Die, 23, 26, 28, 31–35, 41,
42, 54, 55, 57, 60–62, 72, 101, 104,
105, 114, 115, 127, 139, 147, 520, 694
Warren, Earl, 561, **779**
Warren Report, 558, 667, 779
Warshow, Robert, 131, 132, **713**
Wars of Liberation, 45, 55
Washington Post, 500
Weber, Alfred, 151, 225, 552, 637, 650,
694, **720**
Weber, Marianne, 37, 38, 41, 59, 67,
697
Weber, Max, ix, xx, 88, 148, 150, 203,
208–9, 225, 228, 282, 287, 328, 406,
412, 453, 541, 546, 550–52, 554, 556,
567, 578, 632, 636–37, 653, 659–63,
697, 758, 792; Calvinism of, 209, 407,
408; on Heidelberg Workers and
Soldiers' Council, 338; Kurt Wolff
and, 328; nationalism of, 16, 87,
548–49
Wechsler, James A., 220, **731–32**
Weil, Anne (Annchen), 179, 340, 352,
381, 440, 446, 474, 499, 502, 531, 537,
557, 562, 649, 656, **717**, 748
Weischedel, Wilhelm, 501, **770**
Weiss, Theodore R. (Ted), 615, **789**
Weitling, Wilhelm, 163, **722**
Weizmann, Chaim, 352, **748**
Weizsäcker, Ernst Freiherr von, 708
Welch, Robert H., 776
Welt, Die, 485
Weltwoche, Die, 65
Wendt, Marianne, 381, 384, **755**
Werfel, Franz, 27, **695**
Wesleyan University, 395–96, 468, 479,
480
Wessel, Horst, **700**
West, James, 509, **771**
Weyl, Anna, 73, 106, 108, 110, 646
Weyl, Hermann, 73, 78, 80, 83, 88, **704**,
705
Whitehead, Alfred North, 314, **743**
Weichert, Ernst, 84, **706**
Wieck, Fred D., 602, 605, 622, 625, 626
Wieruszowski, Helen (Leni), 78, 81–83,
91, 116–17, 156, 158, 249
Wiese, Benno von, 5, 6, 86, 236, 244,
581, 638, 644, 650, **690**, 706

Wiesel, Pauline, 193, 198, **727**
Wilhelm II, Kaiser, 790
William of Orange, 465
Wilpert, Paul, 390, 719, **756**
Winckelmann, Johann Joachim, 316, **744**
Winston, Richard, 368
Witt, Jan de, 139, 465, **716**
Witzleben, Erich von, 603, **788**
Wohlstetter, Albert, 557, **779**
Wolff, Helen, 100, 102, 429, 437, 462,
    475, 477, 497, 499, 546, 550, 552, 556,
    557, 579, 592, 595, 600, 604, 606, 623,
    632–35, 644, 672, **708**, 760
Wolff, Kurt, 100, 107, 108, 111, 113,
    117, 124, 321, 322, 326–28, 330–33,
    335–37, 340, 342, 348, 349, 363, 397,
    422, 423, 425, 427–32, 435–37, 440,
    441, 450, 453, 457, 462, 471, 472, 476,
    481, 484, 488, 490, 497, 528, 537, **708**,
    760
Woodward, Beverly, 341, 343, 346, 739
Woolf, Virginia, 610
Wulf, Joseph, 568, 574, **781**
Würzburg, University of, 386, 391, 755
Wyss, Peter, 581

Xenophanes, 392

Yale University, 170, 183, 492, 547,
    555

Zahrnt, Heinz F. B., 496, **769**
Zeit, Dei, 403, 494, 565, 581, 585, 593,
    595, 643, 648
Zeller, Eberhard, 519
Zeltner, Hermann, 707
Zenger, John Peter, 218, **731**
Zevi, Shabbatai, 200, **728**
Zhukov, Georgi, 320, **744**
Zilkens, Johannes, 351, 607, 609, **748**
Zimmer, Christiane, 596, **787**
Zimmer, Heinrich, 787
Zionism, 19, 65, 98, 99, 106, 197–98,
    200, 244, 248, 304, 417, 419, 516, 527,
    531, 550, 626
Zola, Emile, 700
Zschokke, Peter, 555, **779**

Berlin on Arendt
Jaspers reputation

Why didn't she describe to Jaspers?
her visit to Heidegger
BAD faith?

royalty statements!
advances